Students
Get Learning that Fits You

Effective tools for efficient studying

Connect is designed to help you be more productive with simple, flexible, intuitive tools that maximize your study time and meet your individual learning needs. Get learning that works for you with Connect.

Study anytime, anywhere

Download the free ReadAnywhere® app and access your online eBook, SmartBook® 2.0, or Adaptive Learning Assignments when it's convenient, even if you're offline. And since the app automatically syncs with your Connect account, all of your work is available every time you open it. Find out more at **mheducation.com/readanywhere**

"I really liked this app—it made it easy to study when you don't have your textbook in front of you."

- Jordan Cunningham, Eastern Washington University

iPhone: Getty Images

Everything you need in one place

Your Connect course has everything you need—whether reading your digital eBook or completing assignments for class, Connect makes it easy to get your work done.

Learning for everyone

McGraw Hill works directly with Accessibility Services Departments and faculty to meet the learning needs of all students. Please contact your Accessibility Services Office and ask them to email accessibility@mheducation.com, or visit **mheducation.com/about/accessibility** for more information.

Peak Performance

Twelfth edition   **SUCCESS IN COLLEGE AND BEYOND**

Sharon K. Ferrett, Ph.D.
Cal Poly, Humboldt

Dedication

To the memory of my parents, Albert Lawrence Ferrett and Velma Mary Hollenbeck Ferrett, for setting the highest standards and their seamless expression of love.

To my husband, Sam, and our daughters, Jennifer and Sarah; all teachers, they've tried out exercises and offered valuable suggestions. With thanks and love.

—Sharon K. Ferrett

PEAK PERFORMANCE: SUCCESS IN COLLEGE AND BEYOND, TWELFTH EDITION

Published by McGraw Hill LLC, 1325 Avenue of the Americas, New York, NY 10019. Copyright ©2024 by McGraw Hill LLC. All rights reserved. Printed in the United States of America. Previous editions ©2021, 2018, and 2015. No part of this publication may be reproduced or distributed in any form or by any means, or stored in a database or retrieval system, without the prior written consent of McGraw Hill LLC, including, but not limited to, in any network or other electronic storage or transmission, or broadcast for distance learning.

Some ancillaries, including electronic and print components, may not be available to customers outside the United States.

This book is printed on acid-free paper.

1 2 3 4 5 6 7 8 9 LWI 28 27 26 25 24 23

ISBN 978-1-266-60255-9 (bound edition)
MHID 1-266-60255-0 (bound edition)

ISBN 978-1-266-85731-7 (loose-leaf edition)
MHID 1-266-85731-1 (loose-leaf edition)

Associate Portfolio Manager: *Angela Petit Lichter*
Product Developer: *David Ploskonka*
Marketing Manager: *Natalie King*
Senior Content Project Managers: *Melissa M. Leick; Katie Reuter*

Manufacturing Project Manager: *Sandy Ludovissy*
Content Licensing Specialist: *Gina Oberbroeckling*
Cover Image: *Crazymedia007/Shutterstock*
Compositor: *Straive*

All credits appearing on page or at the end of the book are considered to be an extension of the copyright page.

Library of Congress Cataloging-in-Publication Data

Names: Ferrett, Sharon K., author.
Title: Peak performance : success in college and beyond / Sharon K.
    Ferrett, Ph.D., Cal Poly, Humboldt.
Description: Twelfth Edition. | New York : McGraw Hill LLC, [2023] |
    "Previous editions ©2021, 2018, and 2015"--Copyright page.
Identifiers: LCCN 2022039316 | ISBN 9781266602559 (Bound Edition :
    acid-free paper) | ISBN 9781266857317 (Loose-leaf Edition)
Subjects: LCSH: Academic achievement. | Performance. | Career development.
    | Success.
Classification: LCC LB1062.6 .F47 2023 | DDC 371.26/4--dc23/eng/20220912
LC record available at https://lccn.loc.gov/2022039316

The Internet addresses listed in the text were accurate at the time of publication. The inclusion of a website does not indicate an endorsement by the authors or McGraw Hill LLC, and McGraw Hill LLC does not guarantee the accuracy of the information presented at these sites.

mheducation.com/highered

Brief Table of Contents

Table of Contents

PART ONE

Building Foundation Skills

1 Be a Lifelong Learner 1

2 Build Peak Habits 45

3 Expand Your Emotional Intelligence 71

Emotional Intelligence and Maturity 72

A Positive Attitude and Personal Motivation 79

Overcome Obstacles with Positive Habits and Mental Shifts 88

4 Manage Your Time 105

Use Time Effectively 106

Setting Priorities 109

Time-Management Strategies 114

Time Management and Your Learning Style 118

Overcome Obstacles with Better Time-Management Habits 120

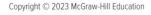

5 Maximize Your Resources 143

PART TWO
Basic Skills and Strategies

6 Listen and Take Effective Notes 177

7 Actively Read 207

8 Improve Your Memory Skills 243

9 Excel at Taking Tests   271

10 Express Yourself in Writing and Speech   303

PART THREE
Application

11 Become a Critical Thinker and Creative Problem Solver 337

12 Create a Healthy Mind, Body, and Spirit 377

The 12th Edition Major Revision Themes

The 12th edition of Peak Performance *continues to provide students with common-sense strategies for excelling in school, career, and life.* Peak Performance *delivers the essential tools for managing time and resources by showing students how to*

- Empower themselves to feel that they belong in college through the power of grit, perseverance, and resiliency.
- Learn to acknowledge, name, and manage emotions in a positive way.
- Practice a positive, open mindset that focuses on growth, learning, and effort.
- Learn how habits work and how to replace counter-productive habits with positive habits that will help them in college and beyond.
- Learn to integrate all learning styles and critical and creativity for maximum success.
- Learn how to seek out mutual support and resources on campus for challenges new students face, and remain persistent in pursuit of their goals.
- Focus sustained effort to cultivate essential qualities for school, job, and life success.

Diversity Inclusivity and Equity Updates

Considerable thought went into revising both the textual material and images in the 12th Edition of Peak Performance to support the values of diversity, equity, and inclusion. The following provides a sampling of changes that were made to ensure that Peak Performance, 12e, speaks to every student:

- using gender neutral pronouns
- incorporating more representation of neurodiversity
- provide examples that are inclusive for students with a range of physical abilities
- created a wider range of options for students with learning disabilities
- framed conversations around health and nutrition with body positive language
- destigmatizes mental health issues in order to serve students more effectively
- increased diversity in photo content
- updated famous quotes throughout to reflect a gender balance

Chapter Breakdown

CHAPTER 1

- Reframed language around stress to account for systemic racism and prejudices
- Removed terms that could be viewed as non-inclusive to the LGBTQ+ community
- Streamlined activities to be inclusive to those with neurodiverse conditions
- Updated images for better representation and diversity
- Revised to be inclusive for on and off campus learners

CHAPTER 2

- Rewritten with more inclusive examples of how to build healthy habits
- Deleted idioms to remove barriers for ELL students

CHAPTER 3

- Included more examples beyond just activities for able-bodied students
- Rewritten sections with people-first language
- Shifted focus off personal appearance

CHAPTER 4

- Updated images for better representation and diversity
- Deleted idioms to remove barriers for ELL students
- Updated content to apply to online and in-class learners

CHAPTER 5

- Revised text to address students of various financial backgrounds
- Incorporated digital resources for greater access
- Removed language that assumes a student has sight (i.e., "look at," "see")

CHAPTER 6

- Incorporated the use of gender-neutral pronouns
- Expanded content to be inclusive of those with mobility issues
- Included strategies for students with neurodiverse conditions

CHAPTER 7

- Revised instruction to be inclusive of those with physical mobility issues
- Included instruction around various accessible resources

CHAPTER 8

- Edited content to accommodate learners with disabilities
- Revised to include a more balanced representation of gender and ethnicities

CHAPTER 9

- Updated content to reflect online and in-person learners
- Updated images for better representation and diversity

- Edited content to accommodate learners with disabilities

CHAPTER 10

- Updated with digital resources for great accessibility including audio books, screen readers, etc.
- Revised language to remove barriers for ELL students
- Updated images for better representation and diversity

CHAPTER 11

- Revised language to remove barriers for ELL students
- Increased gender balance with new examples

CHAPTER 12

- Provided more positive language around body image and nutrition
- Increased supportive language around mental health awareness
- Revised content around eating disorders to be more inclusive and sensitive
- Reframed approach to discussing addiction

CHAPTER 13

- Incorporated the use of gender-neutral pronouns
- Increased gender balance with new examples
- Revised to prioritize mental health and wellness
- Updated images for better representation and diversity

CHAPTER 14

- Updated images for better representation and diversity
- Revised instruction to be inclusive of those with physical mobility issues
- Revised to be inclusive for on and off campus learners

Major Connect Updates

APPLICATION-BASED ACTIVITIES

These are self-graded assignments that measure students' ability to apply what they have learned using their critical thinking skills. In each of the 20 scenarios, the student helps a "friend" who is struggling with an issue related to the topic. By asking questions and making recommendations, the student helps their friend solve the problem. A virtual instructor provides assistance to the student as needed. Commonly assigned topics include Time Management, Goal Setting, Note Taking, Test Anxiety, and many others.

Animated Videos Covering Core Topics

Twenty animated videos address key topics from time management, goal setting, to note taking. These animations are two to four minutes in length and include assignable review questions.

Global Updates and New Features

- **Open Mindset:** Instructors stress the importance of a positive attitude as a foundation for all learning. Woven throughout the book is the concept that talent and abilities are not as important as *effort, grit,* and the *willingness to learn and grow.* An *open, positive mindset* is focused on growth and resiliency while a negative, *closed mindset is fixed* on being right and resisting change and growth. A positive mindset helps students overcome obstacles.
- **Habits:** From the last edition, instructors told us students want to succeed in college and beyond, but sometimes they need help implementing the skills taught in class. Therefore, **Building Better Habits** was a major focus. This feature will help students implement the skills and concepts they learn in class. The Habit Cycle will teach students how to identify triggers for their habits and how to create a productive behavior routine and a reward that leads to a cycle of success. This feature is based on actual brain science and is threaded throughout the book, with a new habit introduced in every chapter. These topics include health, time management, test taking, and so on. This content supports the strengthening of this editions' theme of resiliency and a positive, open mindset.
- **Personal Evaluation Notebook Activities:** Instructors told us they love these activities because students can easily apply what they learn.
- **Expanded and Updated Research:** We have updated the latest brain research throughout the book to help students see the "why" behind concepts and strategies.
- Based on instructor feedback, we revamped some of our feature boxes to make the book more accessible and less potentially distracting to

students. **Get Involved** and **Leverage Your Success** have been moved to the instructor manual.
- Our **Connect** product includes a chapter-specific video series highlighting time management, goal setting, reading, note taking, and other critical topics as well as assessments based on critical thinking and decision making.
- Instructors told us they liked the **ABC's of Self-Management** so we've expanded and clarified this feature with a focus on mindfulness. A scene opens each chapter and is followed by a journal entry which provides the opportunity to apply the method by completing a worksheet. Learning to acknowledge and manage emotions is critical for school and life success. With practice, students will have: 1. Increased *self-awareness,* 2. Increased *self-acceptance,* and 3. *Improved relationships* that focus on empathy.

Peak Performance Features

Every chapter includes the following features. These features were written and designed to help students apply, practice, and better understand the core concepts explored in each chapter.

Chapter Features

HABIT CYCLES

Building Better Habits is a major focus in the 11th edition and is included in every chapter. The Habit Cycle will teach students how to identify the things that trigger their bad (and good) habits, how to create a positive routine behavior, and how to identify a reward that leads to a cycle of success.

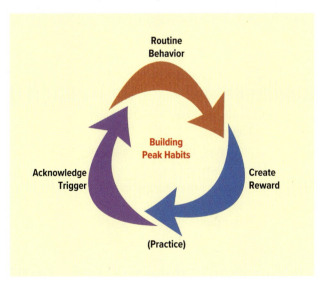

Personal Evaluation Notebook 2.2

Overcome Obstacles with Habits

Write out possible obstacles that you might face and think of creative ways to overcome them using the Habit Cycle.

State a concrete, simple goal:

1. Write out one to two specific obstacles to that goal.

   _____

   _____

   _____

2. Write out one to two specific ways to overcome those obstacles.

   _____

Personal Evaluation Notebooks

The PEN exercises are a chance for students to evaluate what they have learned in the chapter up to that point, and apply it so that they are better prepared to move on to the next topic in the chapter. To save space, many of these exercises will be on the Web.

Peak Progress

The Peak Progress exercises in every chapter help students create the results they want by encouraging them to consider and practice key concepts. They will learn new strategies, helpful tips, and how to apply the **Adult Learning Cycle** *and the* **ABC Method of Self-Management.**

Peak Progress 3.3

Differences between High School and College

Entering college brings a new level of responsibility and expectations as compared to your previous educational experiences, mimicking what is expected on the job as well as managing your personal life. For example, in college, you are expected to

- Have more responsibilities and budget your time and money.
- Express your opinions logically, not just give facts.
- Motivate yourself.
- Handle more freedom and independence.
- Attend larger classes that meet for longer periods but less often.
- Be responsible for knowing procedures and graduation requirements.

- Write and read more than you have before.
- Think critically and logically.
- Receive less feedback and be tested less often but more comprehensively.
- Use several textbooks and supplemental readings.
- Complete more work and turn in higher-quality work.
- Interact with people of different values, cultures, interests, and religions.
- Learn to be tolerant and respectful of diversity.
- Encounter new ideas and critique those ideas in a thoughtful way.
- Get involved in the community, school clubs, volunteer work, and internships related to your major.

Think Creatively and Critically

These features provide situations to help students think in creative ways and apply critical thinking skills. Each feature also includes scientific research pertaining to the example.

Research shows that people who routinely practice mindfulness and meditation activated neurons in the part of the brain (prefrontal cortex) that controls attention and focus.[1]

Chloe is always late because she does several things at once and is scattered. Her family, friends—everyone—continually tell her how frustrating it is that she keeps them waiting. She finally got the message when her best friend texted her that she was tired of her inconsideration and the group was leaving for a party without her. The rush she always felt from doing many things at once and keeping up with texts and e-mails was replaced with the realization that she had let others down.

- What negative characteristics are being demonstrated by someone who is habitually late?
- What problems does this create—in school, on the job, in personal situations?
- Do you think that practicing meditation or mindfulness would help her to be more attentive and focused? What are specific strategies that you would suggest to help her become more focused, attentive, and dependable.

End-of-Chapter Features

Taking Charge

The Taking Charge feature is an opportunity for students to review what they've learned and prepare for assessments.

Career in Focus

In each chapter, these workplace case studies help students understand the practical applications of the chapter by applying what they've learned to a career situation.

Peak Performer Profile

Each Peak Performer Profile highlights people who have demonstrated the qualities, attitudes, and skills of a Peak Performer. Students are asked critical thinking questions that pertain to the Peak Performer and his or her success.

Review and Applications

Practice is a core concept in this book. It is not enough to read about successful strategies. This feature will help students choose one strategy to change. This reinforces the power of taking small changes.

Case Studies

Throughout this book we have tried to highlight the connection between college success and career success. This feature provides a college-based case study and then connects the same strategies to a career-based case study. Students will see that the strategies that make them successful in college will make them successful in their careers.

Applying the ABC Method of Self-Management Worksheets

These worksheets provide the opportunity to apply the opening chapter concepts which involves acknowledging, naming, and managing emotion and making positive choices. Mindfulness helps students take the next step from theoretical concepts to practical application and change self-destructive behaviors to positive, constructive actions that are consistent with goals.

Career Development Portfolio

These activities help the student to connect what they've learned in a chapter to what they may want from a career or what they will need to do as they are building a career.

Ancillaries

Lassi: Learning and Study Strategies Inventory

The LASSI is a 10-scale, 60-item assessment of students' awareness about and use of learning and study strategies related to skill, will, and self-regulation components of strategic learning. The focus is on both covert and overt thoughts, behaviors, attitudes, and beliefs that relate to successful learning and that can be altered through educational interventions. Research has repeatedly demonstrated that these factors contribute significantly to success in college and that they can be learned or enhanced through educational interventions such as learning and study skills courses.

The LASSI is available in print or online at www. hhpublishing.com. Ask your McGraw-Hill Education sales representative for more details.

Instructor Resources

Located in Connect, these extensive resources include chapter goals and outlines, teaching tips, additional activities, and essay exercises. Also included are unique resource guides that give instructors and administrators the tools to retain students and maximize the success of the course, using topics and principles that last a lifetime. Resources include:

- Instructor Manual
- Retention Kit, containing:
  - Facilitator's Guide
  - Tools for Time Management
  - Establishing Peer Support Groups
  - Developing a Career Portfolio
  - Involving the Faculty Strategy
  - Capitalizing on Your School's Graduates
- Course Planning Guide
- Sample Syllabi
- PowerPoints
- Test Bank—includes matching, multiple choice, true/false, and short answer questions

Customize Your Text

Peak Performance can be customized to suit your needs. The text can be abbreviated for shorter courses and can be expanded to include school schedules, campus maps, additional essays, activities, or exercises, along with other materials specific to your curriculum. However you want to customize, we can make it happen, easily. McGraw-Hill Education can deliver a book that perfectly meets your needs. Contact your McGraw-Hill Education sales representative for more information:

United States: 1-800-338-3987
Canada: 1-866-270-5118
E-mail: student.success@mheducation.com

Acknowledgments

We would like to thank the many instructors whose insightful comments and suggestions provided us with inspiration and the ideas that were incorporated into this new edition:

Reviews

Barbara Blackstone	University of Maine at Presque Isle
Dudley Chancey	Oklahoma Christian University
Norman Crumpacker	Mount Olive College
Laura Ringer	Newberry College
Carol Decker	Tennessee Wesleyan College
Kina Lara	San Jacinto College South
Tanya Stanley	San Jacinto College
Belinda Manard	Kent State University at Stark
Sherri Singer	Alamance Community College
Deborah Olson-Dean	North Central Michigan College
Gina Garber	Austin Peay State University
Richard Fabri	Husson University
Becky Samberg	Housatonic Community College
Curtis Sandberg	Berea College
Nicole Griffith-Green	Ashland Community & Technical College
Dr. Kristi Snuggs	Edgecombe Community College
Carolyn Camfield	Oklahoma Panhandle State University
Tara Cosco	Glenville State College
Carol Martinson	Polk State
Charity Ikerd Travis	Somerset Community College
Ruth Hoffman	University of Illinois
Richard Garnett	Marshall University
Miriam Moore	Lord Fairfax Community College
Denise Baldwin	University of Jamestown
Julie Hunt	Belmont University
Amy Hassenpflug	Liberty University
Dean Bortz	Columbus State Community College
Car Kenner	St. Cloud State University
Tora Johnson	University of Maine at Machias
Jeff Rankinen	Pennsylvania College of Technology
Julie Bennety	Central Methodist University
Melanie Deffendall	Delgado Community College
Kelly Moore	Idaho State University
Mike Wood	Missouri State
Mark Daddona	Clayton State University

Valerie Merriwether	Oakland Community College
Paula Hood	Coastal Carolina Community College
Sandra Lancaster	Grand Rapids Community College
Oliver Brook	Sierra College
Ericka Haynes	University of Louisiana

Acknowledgements

Patricia White	Danville Community College
Nikita Anderson	University of Baltimore
Skip Carey	Monmouth University
Michael Dixon	Angelo State
Elizabeth S. Kennedy	Florida Atlantic University
Christopher Thompson	Loyola University Maryland
Linda Kardos	Georgian Court University
Dianne Aitken	Schoolcraft College
Amanda Mosley	York Technical College
Laura J. Helbig	Mineral Area College
Jane Johnson	Central Michigan University
Cora Dzubak, Ph.D.	Penn State York
Andrew Webster	Belmont University
Darin LaMar Baskin	Houston Community College
Linda B. Wright	Western Piedmont Community College
Shelly Ratliff	Glenville State College
Ann C. Hall	Ohio Dominican University
Kaye Young	Jamestown Community College
Joseph Hayes	Southern Union State Community College
Yvonne M. Mitkos	Southern Illinois University Edwardsville
Linda Girouard	Brescia University
Teresa Houston	East Central Community College
Debra Starcher Johnson	Glenville State College
Sandra Soto-Caban	Muskingum University
Liz Moseley	Cleveland State Community College
Christopher Tripler	Endicott College
Rachel Hoover	Frostburg State University
Kay Cobb	University of Arkansas at Cossatot
Jeff Bolles	University of North Carolina at Pembroke
Amanda Bond	Georgia Military College
Catherine Heath	Victoria College
Patrick Peyer	Rock Valley College
Andrea Conway	Houstonic Community College
Alisa Agozzino	Ohio Northern University
Joseph Kornoski	Montgomery County Community College
Claudia Bryan	Wallace Community College
Virginia Watkins	Texas A&M International University
Kim Childress	Eastern New Mexico University-Roswell
Mark Smith	Temple College
Eva Menefee	Lansing Community College
Ross Bandics	Northampton Community College
Chad Brooks	Austin Peay State University
Conchita C. Hickey	Texas A&M International University
Billie Anderson	Tyler Junior College
Kay Adkins	Ozarka College
Becky Osborne	Parkland College
Kathie L. Wentworth, M.Ed.	Trine University
Shawndus Gregory	Phillips Community College
Susan Underwood	Arkansas Tech University
Jalika Rivera Waugh, Ph.D.	Saint Leo University
Ryck Hale	Iowa Lakes Community College
Melanie Marine	University of Wisconsin-Oshkosh
Leah Lidbury	University of Wisconsin-Oshkosh
Mike Wood	Missouri State University
Carla Garrett	San Jacinto College
Nancy Sleger	Middlesex Community College
Tonya Greene	Wake Technical Community College
Dr. Elisah B. Lewis	University of Miami School of Business
Robyn Linde	Rhode Island College
Diane Taylor	Tarleton State University
Cheyanne Lewis	Blue Ridge Community and Technical College
Megan Osterbur	Xavier University of Louisiana
James Wallace	Indiana University Northwest
Maria LeBaron	Randolph Community College
Keith Ramsdell	Lourdes University
Kelly Moor	Idaho State University
Kathryn Jarvis	Auburn University
Joel Krochalk	Lake Superior College
Karen Smith	East Carolina University
Chandra Massner	University of Pikeville
Mike Hoffshire	University of New Orleans
Billy Wesson	Jackson State Community College
Liza Brenner	Glenville State College
Dr. Priscilla T. Robinson	Hinds Community College-UT
Kristi Concannon	King's College
Jodi P. Coffman	Santa Ana College
Judith Lynch	Kansas State University
Daniel Rodriguez	Palo Alto College
Liese A. Hull	University of Michigan
Kim Thomas	Polk State College
Virginia B. Sparks	Edgecombe Community College
Terry Bridger	Prince George's Community College
Dewayne Dickens	Tulsa Community College

Michelle Yager	Western Illinois University
Shane Y. Williamson	Lindenwood University
Michael Starkey	University of Rhode Island
J. Lesko-Bishop	Rose State College
Jon Meeuwenberg	Muskegon Community College
Melissa Johnson	Hazard Community & Technical College
C. Miskovich	Randolph Community College
Mary Carstens	Wayne State College
Grace Palculict	South Arkansas Community College
Bev Greenfeig	University of Maryland
Nancy Michael	Columbia College Chicago
Erika Deiters	Moraine Valley Community College
Ileka Leaks	Limestone College
Christopher Fields	Franklin University
Brandi Baros	Pennsylvania State University–Shenango
Ken Weese	El Paso Community College
Linda Wheeler	Jackson State University
Sharon C. Melton	Hinds Community College
Chris Kazanjian	El Paso Community College
Kim Wagemester	Kirkwood Community College
Nari Kovalski	Atlantic Cape Community College
Gretchen Starks-Martin	College of St. Benedict & St. Cloud State University
Stephen Coates-White	South Seattle Community College
Cathy Hall	Indiana University Northwest
Susam Epps	East Tennessee State University
F. Janelle Hannah-Jefferson	Jackson State University
Cecile Arquette	Bradley University
Nancy Lilly	Central Alabama Community College
David Roos	Dixie State University
William McCormick	University of Central Oklahoma
Sue Maxam	Pace University
Tracy Ethridge	Tri-County Technical College
Dr. Reyes Ortega	Sierra College
Susan Sies	Carroll Community College
Leigh Smith	Lamar Institute of Technology
Mary Silva	Modesto Junior College
Donna Wood	Holmes Community College
Gretchen Haskett	Newberry College
Debbi Farrelly	El Paso Community College
Miriam Foll	Florida State College at Jacksonville
Paul DeLaLuz	Lee University
Mirjana Brockett	Georgia Institute of Technology
Mari Miller Burns	Iowa Lakes Community College
David Hall	Clarendon College
Kimberly Britt	Horry Georgetown Technical College

Buck Tilton	Central Wyoming College
Dr. Roxie A. James	Kean University
Ashleigh Lewis	Tyler Junior College
Kathleen Hoffman	Anoka Ramsey Community College–Cambridge Campus
J. Andrew Monahan	Suffolk County Community College
Shane Armstrong	Marymount California University
LuAnn Walton	San Juan College
Katrina Daytner	Western Illinois University
Adrian Rodriguez	Portland Community College
Kirsten Miller	Columbia College
Geneva Baxter	Spelman College
Sheer Ash	San Jacinto College
Sara Henson	Central Oregon Community College
Darla Rocha	San Jacinto College
Debra Ellerbrook	Concordia University Wisconsin
Adolfo Nava	El Paso Community College
Anthony Westphal	Shasta College
Barbara J. Masten	Lourdes University
Shannon Maude	Blue Mountain Community College
Barbara J. Masten	Lourdes University
Mary Ann Ray	Temple College
Kimberly Dasch-Yee	Holy Family University
David Trimble	El Paso Community College
Susan Selman	Patrick Henry Community College
Nicki Michalski	Lamar University
Donna Hanley	Kentucky Wesleyan College
Stephen Van Horn	Muskingum University
Beverly Hixon	Houston Community College
Bruce A. Wehler	Pennsylvania College of Technology
Hilary Billman	Northern Michigan University
Jonathan Villers	Alderson Broaddus University
Lynn M. Fowler	Cosumnes River College
Rico Gazal	Glenville State College
Marcia Laskey	Cardinal Stritch University
Cheryl Spector	California State University, Northridge
Christopher Lau	Hutchinson Community College
Gail Malone	South Plains College
Elias Dominguez	Fullerton College
Vincent Fitzgerald	Notre Dame de Namur University
Jayne Nightingale	Rhode Island College
Annette Sisson	Belmont University
Kathie Erdman Becker	South Dakota State University
Kendra Hill	South Dakota State University
Jennifer Parrack-Rogers	Blue Ridge Community College
Virginia Wade, Ed.D.	Marymount California University
Dixie Elise Hickman	American InterContinental University
Gail Tudor	Husson University

Wayne Smith	Community Colleges of Spokane	David Housel	Houston Community College
R. Lee Carter	William Peace University	Sandra Sego	American International College
Pam Nussbaumer	Anne Arundel Community College	Joseph Selvaggio	Three Rivers Community College
Eric Belokon	Miami-Dade College	Michael Abernethy	Indiana University Southeast
Karen O'Donnell	Finger Lakes Community College	Jean Buckley-Lockhart	LaGuardia Community College
Jean Raniseski, Ph.D.	Alvin Community College	Jane M. McGinn, Ph.D.	Southern Connecticut State University
Sandra Berryhill	Triton College	Christine M. ViPond	Lord Fairfax Community College
John Paul Manriquez	El Paso Community College	Ami Massengill	Nashville State Community College-Cookeville Campus
Pamela Bilton Beard	Houston Community College-Southwest	Kevin Ploeger	University of Cincinnati
Janet Florez	Cuesta College	Keith Bunting	Randolph Community College
Holly Seirup	Hofstra University	Laura Skinner	Wayne Community College
Susan Wilson	Portland Community College	Mary Lee Vance	Purdue University Calumet
James K. Goode	Austin Peay State University	Dr. Hanadi Saleh	Miami-Dade College
Walter Tucker	Miami Dade College–North Campus	Judith Shultz	Fond du Lac Tribal and Community College
Andrea Smith	Florida Gateway College	Bertha Barraza	Mt. San Jacinto Community College
Aubrey Moncrieffe Jr.	Housatonic Community College	Patricia Twaddle, M.Ed.	Moberly Area Community College
Susan Bossa	Quincy College		
Kathy Daily	Tulsa Community College Southeast Campus	Misty Engelbrecht	Rose State College
Anita Leibowitz	Suffolk County Community College	Scott Empric	Housatonic Community College
		Tim Littell	Wright State University
Dr. Steve Holcombe	North Greenville University	Kerry Fitts	Delgado Community College
Stephanie Huskey	Tennessee Wesleyan College	Judith Isonhood	Hinds Community College
Sarah Sherrill	West Kentucky Community & Technical College	Michael Kuryla	State University of New York–Broome
Carol Billing	College of Western Idaho	Bryan Barker	Western Illinois University
Heather Mayernik	Macomb Community College	Jerry Riehl	University of Tennessee
Joanna Reed	Sussex County Community College	Eunice Walker	Southern Arkansas University
		Therese M. Crary	Highland Community College
Robert Melendez	Irvine Valley College	Pauline Clark	West Valley College
Jennifer Garcia	Saint Leo University	Christopher Old	Sierra College
Jennifer Treadway	Blue Ridge Community College	Lisa Marie Kerr	Auburn University at Montgomery
Marian Teachey	South Piedmont Community College	Remona Hammonds	Miami-Dade College–West Campus
Cindy Sledge	San Jacinto College–South	Sarah Strout	Dominican College
Lourdes Rassi, Ph.D.	Miami-Dade College		
Dr. Arlene Trolman	Adelphi University		
Keri Keckley	Crowder College		
Desiree Fields-Jobling	Brookline College		
Agostine Trevino	Temple College		
MaryJo Slater	Community College of Beaver County		
Beth Shanholtzer	Lord Fairfax Community College		
Cheryl Ziehl	Cuesta College		

Also, I would like to gratefully acknowledge the contributions of the McGraw Hill editorial staff—specifically, David Ploskonka, for his considerable effort, suggestions, ideas, and insights.

—Sharon K. Ferrett

SCANS: Secretary's Commission on Achieving Necessary Skills

Competency Chart

Competencies and Foundations	Peak Performance Chapters That Address SCANS Competencies
	Chapters 6, 7
• Monitors and Corrects Performance systems	Chapters 4, 6, 7, 12
• Improves or Designs Systems	Chapters 4, 5, 6, 11
Interpersonal Skills: Works with Others	
• Participates as Member of a Team-contributes to group effort	Chapters 2, 3, 13
• Teaches Others New Skills	Chapters 2, 3, 13
• Serves Clients/Customers-works to satisfy customers' expectations	Chapters 1, 3, 43
• Exercises Leadership-communicates ideas to justify position, persuade and convinces others, responsibly challenges existing procedures and policies	Chapters 2, 3, 13
• Negotiates-works toward agreements involving exchange of resources, resolves divergent interests	Chapters 2, 3, 13
• Values diversity and works inclusively and welcomes input and collaboration from people with diverse backgrounds.	Chapter 12
Technology: Works with a Variety of Technologies	
• Selecting technology	Chapters 10, 14, Tech for Success
• Applying technology	Chapters 5, 10, 14, Tech for Success
• Maintaining technology	Chapters 10, 14
• Solving problems	Chapters 10, 11
• Staying current in technology	Chapters 5, 10, 14
Personal Qualities	
• Responsibility, character, integrity, positive habits, self-management, self-esteem, sociability	Chapters 2, 3, 13
Basic Skills	
• Reading—locates, understands, and interprets written information in prose and in documents, such as manuals, graphs, and schedules	Chapters 7, 10
• Writing—communicates thoughts, ideas, information, and messages in writing and creates documents, such as letters, directions, manuals, reports, graphs, and flowcharts	Chapter 10

Source: United States Department of Labor, 2018.   *(continued)*

SCANS: Secretary's Commission on Achieving Necessary Skills *(concluded)*

Competencies and Foundations	Peak Performance Chapters That Address SCANS Competencies
• Arithmetic/mathematics—performs basic computations and approaches practical problems by choosing appropriately from a variety of mathematical techniques	Chapter 11
• Listening—receives, attends to, interprets, and responds to verbal messages and other cues	Chapters 6, 13

Thinking Skills

• Creative thinking—generates new ideas	Chapter 11, Personal Evaluation Notebooks, Think Creatively and Critically
• Decision making—specifies goals and constraints, generates alternatives, considers risks, and evaluates and chooses best alternative	Chapter 11, Case Study, Personal Evaluation Notebooks, Think Creatively and Critically
• Listening—receives, attends to, interprets, and responds to verbal messages and other cues	Chapters 6, 13
• Seeing things in the mind's eye—organizes and processes symbols, pictures, graphs, objects, and other information	All chapters, with a strong emphasis in Chapter 11
• Knowing how to learn—uses efficient learning techniques to acquire and apply new knowledge and skills	Chapter 1
• Reasoning—discovers a rule or principle underlying the relationship between two or more objects and applies it when solving a problem	Chapter 11

Do I Belong in College?

Many of my students have told me I'm like a cheerleader, rooting them on to success. I know they all have what it takes to succeed, even when they have their own doubts. Why? Because I've been there, too. As I stepped onto the beautiful University of Michigan campus, I questioned whether I belonged. My small farming community seemed far away, and I felt out of place. Many students had come from fancy prep schools and wealthy families. I had gone to a one-room schoolhouse and then to a tiny high school in the thumb of Michigan. I was putting myself through college with part-time jobs and baby-sitting in exchange for room and board.

I was asking myself questions you might be asking no matter your background or family history. *Would I be able to make it here? Did I belong?* I thought back to a time in high school when I also questioned whether I belonged. I learned to overcome an intense fear of public speaking by sticking with it, practicing, and developing grit and perseverance. I ended up on the debate team and winning a state speaking contest. How had I made this transformation from shy and fearful to feeling confident in front of people? *The secret was shifting to a positive, open mindset where change is a given.* I knew that I could accept and love myself at the present moment and with effort grow and learn and achieve my goals.

I felt that same fear when I entered a Ph.D. program at Michigan State University. I was surrounded by smart, confident scholars who had graduated from excellent schools. *Did I belong here?* I looked at my habits and personal qualities and realized that my experiences as a farm kid made me a hard worker and persistent, I knew that no amount of effort was too great to achieve the goal of graduating. I was incredibly grateful for the opportunity to be admitted to a competitive graduate program. I wanted to make my parents proud because they never had the choices that I had. *I chose a positive, open mindset that focused on effort and growth. I worked hard, developed grit and determination, and bounced back after setbacks—qualities I learned growing up on a farm.* I visualized myself as a successful college graduate and held that image firmly in my mind whenever I was discouraged.

I returned to our farming community and taught for a year in the same one-room schoolhouse that I (and my father) had attended. It was my mission to encourage the students to develop their full potential and set high goals. I believed in them and told them that they could succeed in college. "*You belong,*" I said often. They all had the same work ethic that I had and that discipline would serve them well. From there I went on to teach in college. Over the years, I have had many students who wondered if they belonged in college. I assured them that they did indeed belong and cheered them on to graduate.

I would have never dreamed of being a college professor and an administrator when I was in high school, but, at only 24 years old, I accepted a dean position at Delta College, a large community college in Michigan. A few years later, I moved to California as Dean of Continuing Education at Humboldt State University (now Cal Poly, Humboldt). I developed a new program in student success. That project launched this book and became my life's work. Over the years, I have had several students who wondered if they belonged in college. I helped them replace negative thoughts and behavior with positive habits. I watched them become confident and engaged students. I felt I was on the brink of something important. I was. Over the years I have seen the power of habits and how they change lives. *With awareness and practice, students can learn to manage their emotions and choose positive behaviors.*

Throughout this book, we talk about the attributes of a "peak performer" and attempt to define success—in school, career, and life. However, in the end, *you* have to define success for yourself. Only you can determine what drives you, what makes you happy, and what will become your own life's work. What I know for sure is that an open, positive mindset that focuses on growth, grit, and resiliency will support your goals.

If I could give you only three pieces of advice as you journey to find your passion in life, they would be

1. **Develop perseverance, resilience, GRIT.** How do you respond to setbacks? Do you throw up your hands, get angry, blame others, and quit when the going gets rough? Do you believe that your intelligence and qualities are fixed and that you can't change? Or do you take a deep breath, acknowledge the situation, name your emotions, and make choices that help you learn, stretch, and bounce back. *A positive mindset focuses on growth and effort. You can cultivate resiliency, grit, and perseverance through effort, learning, and practice. Learning to manage your emotions is key to success!*

2. **Create positive HABITS.** *Positive habits flow out of a positive, open mindset. They support your goals and use the whole of your intelligence to help you stretch and grow.* Keep it simple and focus on one change at a time. For example, exercise every day and you will find that this one habit spills over into other areas of your life. You will be healthier and more positive when you learn to identify and manage your emotions. Be your own best friend!

3. **ENGAGE and connect with people.** You will feel that you belong in school and at work when you relate well and build connections with other students, faculty, and staff. Join clubs, music, theater, athletics, and other events and connect with others who are positive and supportive. Getting involved and making connections helps create a sense of belonging and well-being and often results in life-long friendships. We are a community of beings. *Everything and everyone are interconnected and interdependent.* Everyone belongs!

And when you need a little help developing your own "cheer" along the way, please drop me an e-mail at **sharonferrett@gmail.com**. *I believe in you!*

—**Sharon K. Ferrett**

Getting Started

Congratulations! You are about to start, or restart, an amazing journey of opportunity, growth, and adventure. You may be at this point in your life for a number of reasons: You may be going to college right after high school; you may be focusing on a specific career or trade and want to acquire the appropriate skills or certification; or you may be returning to school after years in the workforce, needing additional skills or just looking for a change.

Whatever your reasons, this is an opportunity for you to learn new things, meet new people, acquire new skills, and better equip yourself both professionally and personally for the years ahead. This book is designed to get you started on that journey by helping you (1) learn how you learn best—and incorporate new ways to learn; (2) maximize available resources and seek out new opportunities; (3) relate what you are exploring now to future success on the job; and (4) learn how to accept and manage your emotions, love yourself and strive to become the best version of yourself.

Now that you have your book in hand, you are ready to get started. Or are you really ready? What else should you be aware of at this point? You may have already attended a basic orientation session where you learned about school and community resources and program requirements. Going through orientation, meeting with your advisor, and reviewing your catalog will help you get oriented. Additionally, this quick review is designed to outline the essentials that you will want to know, so that you not only survive but also make your first year a success. Peak Progress 1 provides a handy checklist for the essential tasks you need to consider and accomplish the first week of school. Add to this list any tasks that are unique to your situation or school.

Why Are You Here?

College success begins with determining your goals and mapping out a plan. A good place to start is to reflect on why you are in college and what is expected of you. You will be more motivated if you clarify your interests and values concerning college. You will read in Chapter 3 the reasons students don't graduate from college, including juggling multiple responsibilities, having poor study skills and habits, and lacking preparation, motivation, and effort. College is a commitment of many precious resources you can't afford to waste—time, money, and mental energies. Consider the following statements and your reasons for being in college, and share this in your study team or with students you meet the first few weeks of class:

- I value education and want to be a well-educated person.
- I want to get a good job that leads to a well-paying career.
- I want to learn new ideas and skills and grow personally and professionally.
- I want to get away from home and be independent.
- I want to make new friends and have new experiences.

Peak Progress

Tasks to Accomplish the First Week of School

- Attend orientation and meet with an advisor. Ask questions and determine available resources. (See Peak Progress 2 for questions to ask.)
- Register and pay fees on time.
- Set up an e-mail account and check it daily.
- Check deadlines and procedures. Never just quit going to class.
- Buy books and keep receipts. Establish a record-keeping system.
- Find out the location of classrooms, parking, and school resources.

- Know expectations and requirements. Get a syllabus for each class.
- Create an organized study area. Post instructors' names, e-mails, office locations, and hours, as well as important deadlines.
- Form study teams and exchange e-mails and phone numbers. Get to know instructors and other students.
- Explore resources, such as the library, learning skills center, health center, and advising center.
- Go to all classes on time and sit in the front row and get to know others.

- I want to learn to manage my emotions, grow and become the best version of myself.
- I want to fulfill my goal of being a college-educated person.

Jot down what you want from college and why you're motivated to get it.

_____
_____
_____
_____

List four values that are most important to you and how college will help you achieve them.

1. _____
_____
2. _____
_____
3. _____
_____
4. _____
_____

What You Need to Know and Should Not Be Afraid to Ask

You don't want to learn the hard way that you need one more class to graduate, only to find it's offered only once a year (and you just missed it). Make your time with your advisor productive by getting answers to important questions that will help you map out your coursework. Peak Progress 2 provides a handy checklist of common questions to get you started.

What Do You Need to Do to Graduate?

You will be more motivated and confident if you understand graduation requirements. Requirements vary among schools. Don't rely on the advice of friends. Go to orientation and meet with your advisor early and often. Check out the catalog and make certain you know what is required to graduate. Fill in the following:

GRADUATION REQUIREMENTS

- Number of units required:
- General education requirements:
- Curriculum requirements:
- Residency at the school:
- Departmental major requirements:
- Cumulative GPA required:
- Other requirements, such as special writing tests and classes:

How to Register for Classes

Find out if you have an access code and the earliest date you can register. Meet with your advisor, carefully select classes, and review general education and major requirements. Add electives that keep you active and interested. Make certain that you understand why you

1. What classes do I need to take for general education?
2. Can a course satisfy both a general education and a major requirement?
3. Can I take general elective (GE) courses for Credit/No Credit if I also want to count them for my major?
4. How can I remove an F grade from my record?
5. What is the deadline for dropping courses?
6. Can I drop a course after the deadline?
7. What is an "educational leave"?
8. What is the difference between a withdrawal and a drop?
9. Do I need to take any placement tests?
10. Are there other graduation requirements, such as a writing exam?
11. Where do I find out about financial aid?
12. Is there a particular order in which I should take certain courses?
13. Are there courses in which I must earn a C- or better?
14. How do I change my major?
15. Which of my transfer courses will count?
16. What is the minimum residency requirement for a bachelor's degree?
17. Is there a GPA requirement for the major?
18. Is there a tutoring program available?
19. If I go on exchange, how do I make sure that courses I take at another university will apply toward my degree here?
20. What is a major contract, and when should I get one?
21. When do I need to apply for graduation?
22. How do I apply for graduation?
23. What is a degree check?
24. What is the policy for incomplete grades?
25. Can I take major courses at another school and transfer them here?
26. As a nonresident, how can I establish residency in this state?
27. How do I petition to substitute a class?
28. Once I complete my major, are there other graduation requirements?
29. What is academic probation?
30. Is there any employment assistance available?
31. Is there a mentor program available in my major department?
32. Are there any internships or community service opportunities related to my major?

are taking each class, and check with your advisor that it is meeting certain requirements.

Many colleges have a purge date and, if you miss the deadline to pay your fees, your class schedule is canceled. You may not be able to get into classes and may have to pay a late fee.

Know the Grading System

Learn the minimum grade point average (GPA) that you need to maintain good standing. If your GPA falls below 2.0, you may be placed on academic probation. The GPA is calculated according to the number of credit hours each course represents and your grade in the course. In the traditional system, A = 4 points, B = 3 points, C = 2 points, D = 1 point, and F = 0 points (your school may have a different system, so ask to be sure). To calculate your GPA, first determine your total number of points. Following is an example:

Course	Grade Achieved	Number of Credit Hours	Points
Political Science	C	2	$2 \times 2 = 4$
Psychology	B	3	$3 \times 3 = 9$
English	A	3	$4 \times 3 = 12$
Personal Finance	A	1	$4 \times 1 = 4$
TOTAL		9	29

Then, to arrive at your GPA, you must divide your total points by your total number of credit hours:

GPA = total points divided by total number of credit hours

Thus, in this example,

GPA = 29 divided by 9 = 3.22

Monitor your progress and meet with your instructors often, but especially at midterm and before final exams. Ask what you can do to improve your grade.

Adding or Dropping Classes

Ask about the deadlines for adding and dropping classes. This is generally done in the first few weeks of classes. A withdrawal after the deadline could result in a failing grade. Also, make certain before you drop the class that

- You will not fall below the required units for financial aid.
- You will not fall below the required units for playing sports.
- If required, the class is offered again before you plan to graduate.
- You don't need the class or units to meet graduation requirements.
- You are meeting important deadlines.
- You talk with the instructor first.
- You talk with your advisor.

Never simply walk away from your classes. The instructor will not drop you, nor will you be dropped automatically if you stop going to class at any time during the semester. It is your responsibility to follow up and complete required forms.

An Incomplete Grade

If you miss class due to illness or an emergency, you may be able to take an incomplete if you can't finish a project or you missed a test. Check out this option with your instructor before you drop a class. Sign a written agreement to finish the work at a specific time and stay in touch with the instructor through e-mail and by phone.

Withdrawing or Taking a Leave of Absence

Some students withdraw because they don't have the money, they can't take time off from work, they lack child care, or they are having difficulty in classes. Before you drop out of college, talk with your advisor and see if you can get the support and motivation to succeed. If you want to take a leave to travel, want to explore other schools, are ill, or just need to take a break, make certain that you take a leave of absence for a semester, a year, or longer. Taking a leave means that you do not have to reapply for admission, and generally you fall under the same category as when you entered school.

Transferring

Before you transfer to another school, know the requirements, which courses are transferable, and if there is a residency requirement. If you plan to transfer from a two-year school to a four-year school, your advisor will help you clarify the requirements.

Expectations of Professors

Most professors will hand out a syllabus that outlines their expectations for the class. Understand and clarify those expectations and the course requirements right from the first day of class. Worksheet 1 is a convenient guide to complete when checking your progress with your instructor. Complete a similar form for each class. You'll want to have contact information about your professor, office hours, location of office, and so on. Every week or so reflect on how you're doing in every class and develop a relationship with your professors so that you are known as a serious student who wants to excel. Continually assess how you're doing and make adjustments as necessary. Reflect, assess, and adjust. This takes just a small amount of time and effort, but can result in big returns such as a meaningful relationship, clarification, and a better grade. It is also an excellent habit to get into for job success. Knowing your supervisor's expectations and checking deadlines, goals, progress, and ways to improve job performance are vital for peak performance.

The Best Strategies for Success in School

In this text, we will focus on a number of strategies that will help you determine and achieve your goals. The Best Strategies for Success in School provides a comprehensive list of the proven strategies you will find woven throughout this text. Apply these to your efforts in school now and through your course of study. You will find that not only are they key to your progress in school, but also they will help you develop skills, behaviors, and habits that are directly related to success on the job and in life in general.

Commitment

The best strategies in the world can't help you if you're not committed to acquiring new skills and creating positive long-lasting habits. Reflect on how committed you are to succeeding in college and in life. Are you just going to skim through this book or are you going to dig out key points, reflect on concepts, practice creating positive habits, and do the exercises? Take the challenge: go to class; read; reflect; write; experiment; and engage and connect with professors, other students, and campus activities. If you're committed and willing to learn new ideas and change your habits, you're on your way to being a peak performer.

The Best Strategies for Success in School

1. **Choose an open and positive mindset.** Believe that you can enhance your intelligence and positive qualities through effort, perseverance, and grit. These beliefs will help you grow, create a sense of curiosity, a passion for learning, and the ability to bounce back. Love and accept who you are at this moment and focus on becoming the best version of yourself. You are your best resource.

2. **Attend every class and be an active and prepared participant.** Show that you are engaged and interested by being on time, sitting in front, participating, asking questions, and being alert. School is your job. Show up and be prepared!

3. **Pretest yourself.** THIS IS THE NUMBER ONE PROVEN TIP. Make up tests and take samples. Even better, do this with your study team. Pretesting reduces anxiety and gives you practice. You will see where you need to put in more effort.

4. **Write a summary.** After you preview the chapter, close the book and write a short summary. Go back and fill in with more details. Do this after each reading. Summarize out loud and share with your study team. This enhances learning.

5. **Know your instructors.** Choose the best instructors, call them by their preferred names and titles, e-mail them, and visit them during office hours. Arrive early for class and get to know them better. Get to know at least one instructor each term and stay in touch. This person may become your mentor and friend.

6. **Know expectations.** Read the syllabus for each course and clarify the expectations and requirements, such as tests, papers, extra credit, and attendance. Ask questions. What can I do to improve my grade?

7. **Join a study team.** You will learn more by studying with others than by reading alone. Make up tests, give summaries, ask questions and teach others. TEST YOURSELF. This is a proven technique for getting good grades.

8. **Organize your study space.** Create a quiet space, with a place for school documents, books, catalogs, a dictionary, a computer, notes, pens, and a calendar. Eliminate distractions by closing the door, and focus on the task at hand. Study first and then socialize. Do first things first.

9. **Map out your day, week, and semester.** Write down all assignments, upcoming tests, meetings, daily goals, and priorities on your calendar. Review your calendar and goals each day. Do not socialize until your top priorities are completed.

10. **Get help early.** Know and use all available campus resources. Go to the learning center, counseling center, and health center; get a tutor; and talk with your advisor and instructors about concerns. Get help at the first sign of trouble.

11. **Give school your best effort.** Commit yourself to being extra disciplined the first three weeks—buy your textbooks early; take them to class; get to class early; keep up on your reading; start your projects, papers, and speeches early; and make school a top priority. The first month is critical for making positive habits.

12. **Use note cards.** Jot down formulas and key words. Carry them with you and review them during waiting time and right before class. This works!

(continued)

The Best Strategies for Success in School (concluded)

13. **Review often.** Review and fill in notes immediately after class and again within 24 hours. Active reading, note taking, and reviewing are the steps that improve recall. Review over time to increase your recall. Use small chunks of time.

14. **Study everywhere.** Review your note cards before class, while you wait for class to begin, while waiting in line, before bed, and so on. Studying for short periods over a period of time is more effective than cramming late at night.

15. **Identify your strengths and weaknesses.** Be open to grow and change and believe that you are capable of increasing your intelligence and positive qualities. They are not fixed. Put more emphasis on effort and less on talent.

16. **Organize material.** You cannot remember information if it isn't organized. Logical notes help you understand and remember. Use a mind map for outlining key facts and supporting material. Develop a system that works for you.

17. **Dig out information.** Focus on main ideas, key words, and overall understanding. Make questions out of chapter headings, review chapter questions, and always read summaries. Ask questions as you read and listen to lectures.

18. **Look for associations.** Improve memory by connecting patterns and by linking concepts and relationships. Define, describe, compare, classify, and contrast concepts. Use creative ways to increase your memory by using all your senses.

19. **Ask questions.** What is the obvious? What needs to be determined? How can you illustrate the concept? What information is the same and what is different? How does the lecture relate to the textbook? Make questions out of chapter headings.

20. **Bounce back.** The most successful students learn that failure is just an indicator. Learning involves setbacks and making mistakes. Effort is the key. Keep going.

21. **Study when you are most alert.** Know your energy level and learning preference. Maximize reviewing during daytime hours. Block out mornings or afternoons.

22. **Turn in all assignments on time.** Give yourself an extra few days to review papers and practice speeches. Sometimes 20 percent more effort results in 80 percent improvement. Talk with your professors if you're having difficulties.

23. **Make learning physical.** Read difficult textbooks out loud and standing up. Draw pictures, write on a chalkboard, and use visuals. Tape lectures, go on field trips, and study with others. Integrate all learning styles. Read out loud.

24. **Review first drafts with your instructor.** Ask for suggestions and follow them to the letter. Share your first drafts with your study team or learning center.

25. **Pay attention to neatness.** Focus on details and turn in all assignments on time. Use your study team to read and exchange term papers. Proofread several times.

26. **Practice! Nothing beats effort.** Practice speeches until you are comfortable and confident. Give your speech to your study team or in your classroom.

27. **Recite and explain.** Pretend that you are the instructor and recite main concepts. What questions would you put on a test? Give a summary to others in your study group. Make up sample test questions in your group. This really works!

(continued)

The Best Strategies for Success in School *(concluded)*

28. **Take responsibility.** Don't make excuses about missing class or assignments or about earning failing grades. Accept reality, be honest and take responsibility for your choices and mistakes and learn from them. Breathe and move on.

29. **Ask for feedback.** When you receive a grade, be reflective and ask questions: "What have I learned from this?" "How did I prepare for this?" "How can I improve this grade?" "Did I put in enough effort?" Based on what you learn, what new goals will you set for yourself? Information helps you grow and learn.

30. **Negotiate for a better grade before grades are sent in.** Find out how you are doing at midterm and ask what you can do to raise your grade. Offer to do extra projects or retake tests. Be sincere and show you want to improve.

31. **Always do extra credit.** Raise your grade by doing more than is required or *expected.* Immerse yourself in the subject, and find meaning and understanding.

32. **Take responsibility for your education.** You can do well in a class even if your instructor is boring or insensitive. Ask yourself what you can do to make the class more effective (study team, tutoring, active participation). Be flexible and adapt to your instructor's teaching style. You are creative and your best resource!

33. **Develop a positive, open mindset.** Attitude is key! Focus on what brings you joy and look for the good in life. Be grateful for all that you have even the small pleasures and blessings. Focus on the positive actions that you need to overcome obstacles, and consistently take steps to meet your goals.

34. **Stay healthy.** You cannot do well in school or in life if you are ill or have low energy. Invest time in exercising regularly, eating healthy, getting enough sleep, and avoid alcohol, cigarettes, and drugs. Binge drinking not only destroys brain cells, but can be deadly. Reduce stress by deep breathing, meditating and being mindful, allowing negative emotions to float away and focusing on making positive choices that align with your goals.

35. **Dispute negative thinking.** Pay attention to your thoughts and emotions. Practice being able to tolerate distress and learn to breathe and be in the present moment. Dispute irrational thoughts and replace with positive, realistic and helpful self-talk. You are not your feelings. Allow these thoughts and emotions to float away.

36. **Organize your life.** Hang up your keys in the same place, file important material, and establish routines that make your life less stressful. Pick up every day.

37. **Break down projects.** Overcome procrastination by breaking overwhelming projects into manageable chunks. Choose a topic, do a rough draft, write a summary, preview a chapter, do a mind map, and organize the tools you need (notes, books, outline).

38. **Make school your top priority.** Working too many hours can cut into study time. Learn to balance school, your social life, and work so that you're effective.

39. **Meet with your advisor to review goals and progress.** Ask questions about requirements, and don't drop and add classes without checking on the consequences. Develop a good relationship with your advisor and your instructors. Take advantage of all the resources available to help you.

(continued)

The Best Strategies for Success in School *(concluded)*

40. **Be persistent.** Whenever you get discouraged, just keep following positive habits and strategies and you will succeed. Success comes in small, consistent steps. Be patient and keep plugging away. *Effort* is key to success.

41. **Spend less than you make.** Don't go into debt for new clothes, a car, CDs, gifts, travel, or other things you can do without. Education is the best investment you can make in future happiness and job success. Keep your life simple.

42. **Use critical thinking, and think about the consequences of your decisions.** Don't be impulsive about money, sex, smoking, or drugs. Don't start a family until you are emotionally and financially secure. Practice impulse control by imagining how you would feel after making certain choices. Be creative by exploring many options and being flexible. Consider the long-term consequences to your choices.

43. **Don't get addicted.** Addictions are a tragic waste of time. Ask yourself if you've ever known anyone whose life was better for being addicted. Do you know anyone whose life has been destroyed by alcohol and other drugs? This one decision will affect your life forever. Don't start smoking or taking drugs. Replace quick fixes with meditation, mindfulness, nature and healthy relationships.

44. **Know who you are and what you want.** Visit the career center and talk with a career counselor about your interests, values, goals, strengths, personality, learning style, and career possibilities. Play to your strengths and interests. Try out internships and part-time jobs. What brings you joy?

45. **Use creative problem solving.** Think about what went right and what went wrong this semester. What could you have done that would have helped you be more successful? What are new goals you want to set for next semester? What are some creative ways to overcome obstacles? How can you solve problems instead of letting them persist? Use critical thinking to make sound decisions.

46. **Contribute.** Look for opportunities to contribute your time and talents. What could you do outside of class that would complement your education and serve others? Check out internships, volunteer, and service learning opportunities.

47. **Take advantage of your texts' resources.** Many textbooks have accompanying websites, DVDs, and study materials designed to help you succeed in class.

48. **Respect yourself and others.** Be supportive, tolerant, and respectful. Look for ways to learn about other cultures and different views and ways to expand your friendships. Surround yourself with people who are positive and successful, who value learning, and who support and respect you and your goals.

49. **Focus on gratitude.** Look at the abundance in your life—your health, family, friends, and opportunities. You have so much going for you to help you succeed.

50. **Just do it.** Newton's first law of motion says that things in motion tend to stay in motion, so get started and keep working on your goals! *Create positive habits* that support your goals and practice, practice, practice. *Once again, effort is key.*

Progress Assessment

Course: _____

Instructor: _____

Office: _____ Office hours: _____

Phone: _____ E-mail: _____

1. How am I doing in this class?

_____

_____

_____

2. What grades have you recorded for me thus far?

_____

_____

_____

3. Are there any adjustments that I should make?

_____

_____

_____

4. Am I missing any assignments?

_____

_____

_____

5. Do you have any suggestions as to how I can improve my performance or excel in your class?

_____

_____

_____

Complete a similar form for each class. You'll want to have contact information about your professor, office hours, location of office, and so on. Every week or so reflect on how you're doing in every class and develop a relationship with your professors so that you are known as a serious student who wants to excel.

Be a Lifelong Learner

LEARNING OUTCOMES

In this chapter, you will learn to

1-1 Demonstrate how a positive, open mindset creates perseverance

1-2 Identify self-management techniques for success

1-3 Create a personal mission statement

1-4 Identify skills and competencies for school and job success

1-5 Identify your learning style

1-6 Identify your personality type

1-7 Explain how to integrate learning styles and personality types

1-8 Apply the Adult Learning Cycle and integrate the VARK system

1-9 Describe how to overcome obstacles with positive habits and better focus

SELF-MANAGEMENT

> *It's the first week of classes and I'm already overwhelmed. How will I manage all this? Do I even belong here? I'm feeling anxious and worried.*

Wayne0216/Shutterstock

Are you feeling like this? Are you afraid you will never achieve your goals? Instead of focusing on negative feelings, channel your energies into positive results and envision yourself being successful. A positive, open mindset focuses on growth and learning. Perseverance and grit flow from these beliefs. You can fulfill your potential with effort and positive habits. In this chapter, you will learn about self-management and how to use self-assessment, critical thinking, visualization, and reflection to become a success in all facets of life. Relax; you do belong. You have grit. Accept all your feelings and breathe deeply to relax and become clear about your goals. You have the ability to make good choices to meet these goals.

JOURNAL ENTRY The transition to college is a major change. Describe your emotions and how you're coping with all the changes of college. **Worksheet 1.1** will help you apply the steps to regulate emotions. Think about the transitions and obstacles you may have faced to get to this point and what you did to overcome them.

F or a long time, I've asked the question, What makes the difference? Why is it that some people succeed in spite of obstacles, hardships, and setbacks and others fail even though they have ability, talent, and a high IQ? *The answer is that people who are successful— peak performers—have a positive, open mindset. They understand the power of perseverance and grit. A positive mindset is focused on growth and flows from the belief that skills and essential qualities can be cultivated and enhanced through effort, practice, and perseverance.* Peak performers know they can motivate themselves to improve in school, reach their goals, and create a love of learning. This isn't about picking up a few tips, but involves a new way of seeing. It involves a core belief that their intelligence is not fixed, but can be developed through effort and resilience. They are able to bounce back from setbacks by turning obstacles into opportunities for growth. They know that learning is lifelong and are curious and passionate about learning and growing through effort. In short, peak performers have grit.

Lately, you may have been asking yourself, "Who am I?" "Why am I in school?" "What course of study should I take?" "What kind of job do I want?" or "What should I do with my life?" These are all important questions. Some you may have already answered—and some of those answers may change by tomorrow, next week, or next year. And that's OK. This is all part of a continual process—of learning about yourself and what you want out of life. *Whatever your goals are in life, a college degree will help you to succeed both personally and professionally.*

As you journey on the road to becoming a peak performer, this book will show you methods that will help you master self-management, learn critical skills, set goals, and achieve success. One of the first steps is self-assessment. Self-assessment requires seeing yourself objectively. This helps you determine where you are now and where you want to go. Then, by assessing how you learn—including your learning and personality styles—you will discover how to maximize your learning potential.

The many exercises, journal entries, and worksheets throughout this text support one of its major themes—that success in school and success in your career are definitely connected! The skills, qualities, and habits you learn and practice today will guide you throughout your life. Perseverance and grit all flow from an open, positive mindset that focuses on growth.

What Is a "Peak Performer"?

Peak performers come from different locations, ages, cultures, and genders. *They have one common factor: they have an open, positive mindset that focuses on growth and effort.* This growth mindset is based on the belief that they can develop their full potential by cultivating essential personal qualities and enhancing their intelligence. This belief leads to curiosity, a love of learning, joy, and positive choices. Anyone can become a peak performer by setting goals, putting in the effort to achieve them, and by being resilient in the face of setbacks. Peak performers excel by focusing on results. They know how to change their fixed, negative thoughts into positive, open, and realistic beliefs. They break down long-term goals into daily action steps and positive habits. They realize that taking small, consistent steps can produce big changes over the long haul. They are persistent and realize

Peak Performers

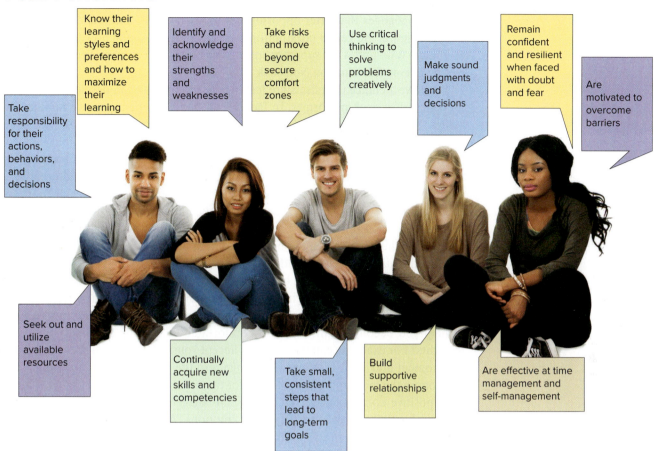

Andrey_Popov/Shutterstock

the value of completing their degree. They bounce back by seeing mistakes and set-backs as challenges and opportunities to grow. They are curious and awake to the wonder of life. They know they belong. Peak performers have growth mindsets and know that growth takes effort, persistence, and sheer determination. They practice the power of breath and mindfulness to stay calm and in the present moment.

Peak performers accept reality and are clear about the situations that they face. They practice deep breathing and mindfulness to identify and manage their emotions. They know that they are not their emotions and can allow them to float away. In spite of challenges, they resist the urge to overreact or give up and instead choose healthy behaviors that help them succeed. In short, they are their own best friend.

Self-Management: The Key to Reaching Your Peak

What is a primary strength of every peak performer? A positive, open attitude that focuses on healthy ways to manage emotions! Peak performers **acknowledge** and accept reality and with mindfulness, pay attention to their thoughts and emotions. They **breathe deeply** to calm down and create clarity about the situation. They are able to hold these two seemingly opposite thoughts at the same time: *they love and accept who they are at the present moment and commit themselves to growing, learning, and being the best version of themselves.* They **consciously choose** the most appropriate actions for the situation that will result in positive long-term consequences. They see that life is interconnected and interdependent and a series of inevitable changes that offer opportunities to learn, grow, and manage emotions. This life view is the key to peak performers. Does this describe how you approach each day? Who and what supports and sustains you? Check your attitude by completing **Personal Evaluation Notebook 1.1**.

You have a choice. Mindsets are just beliefs and anyone can develop the powerful beliefs of a peak performer. In fact, we all had this open, positive mindset as babies. We took on the most difficult tasks of learning to walk and talk with zest. We never decided that the tasks were too hard or not worth the effort, but jumped in with enthusiasm and resiliency. We can recapture that exuberant learning by focusing on growth. Instead of dwelling on problems, create options, alternatives, and behaviors to keep you on track. With practice, you can retrain your brain to create a positive mindset. The more you practice allowing your negative thoughts to float away, you rewire your brain to actively develop a positive mindset. Being mindful can help you live in the present moment and tasks seem more meaningful and less daunting. Develop grit through focus!

A positive, open attitude is one of the many components of **self-management**. Are you aware of your thoughts and emotions? Do you have the ability to tolerate distress? Are you aware of the power of breathing deeply and mindfulness to help you become calm? Are you comfortable at holding seemingly opposite thoughts? For example, can you love and accept yourself just as you are at this present moment and want to grow and change into the best version of yourself? Can you choose the most appropriate action for the situation and one that leads to long-term positive consequences? Think of self-management as a toolkit to help you discover healthier ways to manage your emotions. Along with a positive attitude, important techniques in this toolkit include awareness, mindfulness, visualization, and critical thinking. Transform your relationships with self-management.

Self-Assessment

One of the first steps in becoming a peak performer is awareness and **self-assessment**. Out of self-assessment comes recognition of the need to learn new tasks, skills, relate well with others, set goals, manage time and stress, and create a balanced, productive life. Self-assessment requires facing the truth and seeing yourself objectively. It isn't easy to admit you procrastinate or lack certain skills. Honest self-assessment is the foundation for making positive changes. An open, positive mindset wants honest feedback so growth can flourish.

Self-assessment can help you

- Focus on growth and where you want to improve
- Acknowledge, accept, and manage emotions with mindfulness and awareness
- Be resilient and bounce back from setbacks
- Use critical thinking and reasoning to make sound decisions
- Determine your interests and what you value and clarify goals
- Change negative patterns of thinking and behaving
- Create a positive, open, and motivated state of mind
- Work more effectively with diverse groups of people for mutual support
- Thrive when stretching yourself and redirect stress into energy
- View setbacks as challenges and opportunities for growth and learning
- Determine and capitalize on your strengths

Personal Evaluation Notebook

Am I a Positive Person?

Having a positive, open attitude is key to effective self-management. Most people believe they are generally positive but often are not truly aware of their negative, unkind self-talk or behavior. Answer the following questions to determine your overall outlook. After you have answered the questions, ask a friend, co-worker, or family member to answer the questions about you. Were your answers the same?

	Mostly True	Sometimes True	Rarely True
I believe that I can learn new things and enhance my intelligence.	_____	_____	_____
I look for the positive in each situation.	_____	_____	_____
I do not take offense easily.	_____	_____	_____
I welcome constructive criticism and use it to improve & grow.	_____	_____	_____
I am resilient, kind to myself, and not easily discouraged.	_____	_____	_____
I love & accept myself at this present moment & want to grow and change.	_____	_____	_____
I do not take everything personally.	_____	_____	_____
I take responsibility and face problems, even when it is not comfortable so that I can grow.	_____	_____	_____
I am capable of coping with change.	_____	_____	_____
I don't look for perfection in myself.	_____	_____	_____
I don't look for perfection in others.	_____	_____	_____
I have healthy, supportive, interconnected relationships.	_____	_____	_____
I can forgive myself & others and move on. I don't dwell on mistakes.	_____	_____	_____
I do not become overly involved or disturbed by others' problems.	_____	_____	_____
I am open & do not make snap judgments about people.	_____	_____	_____
I praise others for their accomplishments.	_____	_____	_____
I don't start conversations with something negative.	_____	_____	_____
I view mistakes as opportunities to grow, stretch, and learn.	_____	_____	_____
I know if Plan A doesn't work, then Plan B will. I am flexible & accept change.	_____	_____	_____
I know how to tolerate and manage difficult emotions & situations.	_____	_____	_____

Add up the check marks in each column. If your "Mostly True" column scores are the highest, you are already a very positive and open person. If you have several check marks in the "Rarely True" column, you may want to reflect on how you can become a more positive person who is open to growth and learning.

- Recognize irrational and negative thoughts and behavior
- Create positive habits that support your goals
- Utilize resources that maximize your energies and efforts

The world is full of people who believe that, if only the other person would change, everything would be fine. This book is not for them. Change is possible if you take responsibility for your thoughts and behaviors and are willing to practice new ways of thinking and behaving. With consistent effort, growth and change will happen.

Self-assessment is very important for growth at school and for job success. Keep a portfolio or digital archive of your awards, performance reviews, training program certificates, and projects. Assess the results achieved and set goals for improvement. At the end of each chapter, you will find a Career Development Portfolio worksheet, which will help you relate your current activities to future job success. This portfolio will provide you with a lifelong assessment tool for learning where you are and where you want to go and is a place for documenting your results. This portfolio of skills and competencies will become your guide for developing marketable skills throughout your career. Chapter 14 further explores how to develop an effective portfolio and prepare for your future career.

Creativity and Critical Thinking Skills

Throughout this book, you will be asked to apply creative and critical thinking skills to college and life. **Critical thinking** is a logical, rational, systematic thought process that is necessary in understanding, analyzing, and evaluating information in order to solve a problem or situation. Creativity is experiencing the world with wonder and curiosity and using new approaches to solve problems. It's being flexible and imaginative. Self-management involves using your creativity and critical thinking skills to make the best decisions and solve problems.

Using critical thinking helps you

- Suspend judgment until you have gathered facts and considered source
- Search for evidence that supports or contradicts your initial assumptions, opinions, and beliefs
- Ask, "Is this true? How can I be certain?"
- Adjust your opinions as new information and facts are known
- Ask questions, research and examine the problem closely
- Reject incorrect and ignore irrelevant information
- Reflect on how you act
- Recognize and dispute irrational thinking
- Consider likely consequences to your actions
- Develop creativity in problem solving

Because critical thinking determines the quality of the decisions you make, it is an important theme throughout this book. You use your critical thinking and creativity skills every day—from analyzing and determining your learning styles to communicating effectively with family members, classmates, and co-workers.

Make sure to complete the exercises and activities throughout this book. **Think Creatively** case studies throughout the text highlight that we are constantly making decisions that often have many repercussions—both positive and not-so-positive. Work through these to enhance your creative and critical thinking skills.

Visualization and Affirmations

Visualization and affirmations are powerful self-management tools that help you focus on positive actions and outcomes. **Visualization** is the use of imagination to see goals clearly and envision engaging successfully in new, positive behavior. For example, "I see myself engaged in college, doing well, and graduating. I can see myself walking across the stage and my friends and family applauding. I feel such a sense of accomplishment. I did It!" **Affirmations** are positive self-talk and thoughts that counter self-defeating patterns of thought with more positive, hopeful, and realistic thoughts and feelings. For example, "I am friendly, kind, respectful, and fun to be around. I have many friends because I'm a good friend. I am open and positive and know that I can grow through experience and effort."

Using visualization and affirmations can help you create positive thoughts, relax, boost your confidence, change your habits, and perform better on exams, in speeches, or in sports. You can use them to rehearse for an upcoming event and practice coping with obstacles.

Through self-management, you demonstrate that you are not a passive spectator in your life; you are responsible for your self-talk, images, thoughts, and behaviors. When you observe and dispute negative thoughts and replace them with positive and realistic thoughts, images, and behaviors, you are practicing critical thinking and creativity. You are taking charge of your life, focusing on what you can change, and working toward your goals. In short, a positive, open mindset helps you focus on growth and learning.

You can practice visualization anytime and anywhere. For example, between classes, find a quiet place and close your eyes. It helps to use relaxation techniques, such as taking several deep breaths and seeing yourself calm, centered, and focused on your goals. This is especially effective when your mind starts to chatter and you feel overwhelmed, discouraged, or stressed. See yourself achieving your goals. Say to yourself, "I feel calm and centered. I am taking action to meet my goals. I will use all available resources to be successful. My intelligence and personal qualities are not fixed. I can grow, change, and stretch daily."

Reflection

Another important self-management tool is **reflection**. To reflect is to think about something in a purposeful way, with the intention of gaining a deeper understanding. When you are aware and attentive to your thoughts and feelings, you gain insight into who you are now, who you've been in the past, and who you'd like to be in the future. Sometimes the process causes us to reconsider our previous beliefs and behavior and explore new alternatives and ideas. Reflection can activate the prefrontal circuits in the brain and help strengthen your mind and make your brain more flexible and resilient. Research shows that when you focus attention on the mind, circuits in your brain can be changed and you can improve your health and relationships. Learn breathing techniques to calm your mind and you'll be able to respond calmly in creative ways.

Don't confuse reflection with daydreaming. Reflection is conscious, focused, and purposeful—not simply letting your mind wander. When you reflect, you acknowledge your thoughts and feelings and then either let them go or direct your thoughts and actions in more positive ways. Reflection helps you develop empathy, kindness, and compassion as you develop the ability to understand yourself and others. *As you practice reflection, the connections among your neurons fire and grow and you create a more integrated and balanced brain.* You feel flexible and freer.

Reflection helps you to clarify your feelings and thoughts and consciously choose the most appropriate action. For example, let's say you are feeling angry with a friend. With reflection you are able to feel your anger and choose not to act upon it. With reflection you can accept your feelings and love and accept yourself. You may choose to talk calmly with your friend. Your thoughts and feelings do not have to control you or your actions. With practice you can learn to be more positive, balanced, calm, and integrated and less prone to becoming angry and lashing out. Be still and tune in.

A convenient way to reflect is to meditate or spend a few minutes each day sitting quietly and simply recording your thoughts, such as in a journal. This text provides an opportunity to practice reflection and critical thinking, including a **Journal Entry** exercise at the beginning of each chapter and a follow-up **Worksheet** at the end of each chapter.

Throughout the text, we'll explore additional self-management techniques that focus on certain aspects of your schoolwork, employment, and personal life. **Peak Progress 1.1** explores the ABC Method of Self-Management, a unique process to help you work through difficult situations and achieve positive results. It uses skills such as acceptance, awareness, mindfulness, and critical thinking to find positive outcomes.

Peak Progress   1.1
The ABC Method of Self-Management

Earlier in this chapter, you answered some questions to determine if you approach everyday life with a positive attitude. Researchers believe that positive, optimistic thinking improves your skills for coping with challenges, which may also benefit your overall health and minimize the effects of stress.

What does "negative thinking" mean? If you are thinking negatively, you may tend to

- Filter out and eliminate all the good things that happen and focus only on bad things
- Blame yourself (or someone else) automatically when something bad happens
- Anticipate the very worst that could happen and dwell in fear
- Feel like a failure and give up easily
- Believe that effort is not worth it
- Criticize yourself—either aloud or internally—in a way you would never do to someone else
- Determine that you can't change or grow
- Waste time complaining, criticizing, reliving, making up excuses, rather than creating solutions and moving on.

The good news is that anyone can learn and grow with a positive mindset. Be aware of patterns of defeating thoughts that are obstacles in achieving your goals.

Dispute these negative and irrational thoughts with a positive mindset focused on growth.

Clear thinking will lead to positive emotions. Let's say you have to give a speech in a class and speaking in public has caused you anxiety in the past. Your anxious mind might say, "I am terrified, sick to my stomach, have shaky hands, increased heartrate, my breathing is shallow I and am sweating. What if I get sick in front of everyone? What if I lose my notes or forget my main points? What if everyone laughs at me?" Try this affirmation: "Public speaking is a skill that can be learned with practice and effort. I will not crumble from criticism and, even if I don't do well, I can learn with practice and grow from constructive feedback. I will explore all the resources available to me, I will practice, and I'll do well in this class." Then visualize yourself calm, confident, and relaxed as you give my presentation in front of the class. You are focused and attentive to the audience, and making your key points. The audience is engaged and responding with warmth and acceptance. You feel accomplished and connected.

Self-management can be as simple as ABC. These steps help you manage your thoughts, feelings, and behaviors so that you can create the results you want.

A = Acknowledge reality: Accept the situation that triggered your emotions and fully acknowledge your emotions.

(continued)

The ABC Method of Self-Management *(concluded)*

B = Breathe: Breathe deeply so that you create space for reflection and become calm and focused. Accept and feel beloved just as you are at this present moment and commit to learning and growing into the best version of yourself.

C = Choose: Consciously choose the most appropriate response for this situation and that will result in positive long-term consequences.

Let's use another example. When you read the quote at the beginning of this chapter, you might have felt the same way—overwhelmed. You are in a new situation, with many new expectations. Let's apply the ABC Method to focus your energies on developing a positive outcome. For example, you might say,

A = Acknowledge: "It's the first week of class and I have a mountain of reading and lecture notes to go over. I feel overwhelmed and fearful. What if I fail? What if I can't keep it all straight—learning styles, personalities, and temperaments? These other people are probably a lot smarter than me. Maybe I should drop out."

B = Breath: "Wow. I need to slow down and refocus my chattering mind. I will breathe deeply until I'm calm and focused. I belong here. I love and accept myself and want to grow become the best version of me."

C = Choose: "I choose to put this situation in perspective instead of overreacting. Going to college is a big change, but I have handled new and stressful situations before. I welcome this new challenge to grow and stretch. I choose to put a lot of effort into my classes and break big jobs into small tasks. I choose to use proven strategies like testing myself and joining a study team. There are lots of resources available to help even if I face setbacks. I am persistent. I can do this!"

Dispute negative thoughts and replace them with open, positive thinking, you feel energized, and your thoughts spiral upward: "I accept that I'm feeling overwhelmed and can tolerate these feelings because they are normal in new situations. I know with deep breathing and mindfulness, I can calm down and sooth myself. I will choose healthy ways to manage these overwhelming emotions. I choose to eat healthy, exercise regularly, spend time in nature and meditate. So many resources are available to me—my instructor, my classmates, my advisor, and the book's resources. I will get to know at least one person in each of my classes, and I will take a few minutes to explore at least one resource at school that can provide support. I will go to classes, test myself, and study in teams. I see myself confident and energized and achieving my goals. I will persist. I belong here! I am growing and learning daily."

In the end-of-chapter **Worksheets** throughout this text, you will find opportunities to practice the ABC Method of Self-Management for any stressful situation.

Tools to Help You Reach Your Peak

This product is full of strategies and tools to help you reach your peak performance. The **ABC Method of Self-Management** will help you challenge and dispute negative and irrational thinking, it will help you reflect upon your beliefs and determine if they are helpful and supportive or limiting. When you become discouraged, go through the steps and replace negative thoughts and feelings with optimistic, realistic, and hopeful thoughts. This is where creativity and critical thinking come in. Your emotions and thoughts are not you and do not have to control you or your behavior.

A feature called **Think Creatively and Critically** will help you practice using both creativity and critical thinking. This feature will also weave in brain research that shows you that the brain continues to grow and change. Brain research has shown that the brain takes the shape the mind rests upon.[1] If you continually rest your mind on self-criticism, doubt, worry, and anxiety, your neurons will fire together and you will have low self-esteem, become discouraged, and be quick to anger. However, *when you practice mindfulness, see the good in yourself and life, let go of negative thoughts, and focus on your goals, your brain will grow in self-confidence, calm strength, and resiliency.* Be positive and open to growth.

The Habit Cycle feature will show you how to consciously plan and change your behaviors so that better behaviors become automatic habits and part of your everyday life.

Other features in this book will help you learn new skills, become more focused, and get the most out of staying in college. Let's get started!

Be Persistent and Resilient to Succeed in College and Beyond

At the beginning of the book, I wrote a letter to you to share my experiences of doubt and confusion. There will be times in college and in a new job when you might feel that you don't belong. This is a normal and common feeling and shouldn't result in you quitting college or a job. As we will stress throughout the book, resiliency and persistence are important qualities for college and job success. You have to overcome setbacks, and you must be willing to make positive changes by building better habits. All the exercises and examples are designed to engage you in college; connect you with new friends, faculty, staff, and co-workers; and, in short, keep you in college. These same strategies and habits will allow you to successfully transfer into the world of work. The key to creating a sense of belonging is to engage and connect. All of these features are designed to help you feel as if you belong in college and help you overcome obstacles. With an open, positive mindset, you will focus on growth and resiliency. You belong!

Discover Your Purpose: A Personal Mission Statement

At the beginning of the chapter, you were asked to write about why you're in school and how it relates to your life plan. In the **Getting Started** section, you also explored many reasons you are attending college, such as to learn new skills, get a well-paying job, and make new friends. Thinking about the answers to these and related questions gets you started on writing your mission statement. As the poet Mary Oliver asked, "What do you plan on doing with your one wild and precious life?" "How will you use this gift?"

A **mission statement** is a written statement focusing on desired values, philosophies, and principles. It looks at the big picture of your life, from which your goals and priorities will flow. *When you have a sense of purpose and direction, you will be more focused and your life will have more meaning.* Don't be concerned if you don't feel that you have enough experience or direction to write a complete mission statement. It does not have to be lengthy and detailed, but simply a reflection of your values and interests at this point in your life. You can revise your mission statement as you grow and change. Your draft might say, "I want a job that is flexible and challenging. I know I like working with people. I value service and I want to make a difference in the world. I like to work with children. I may want to study child development and ways to use play to engage children and help them learn. I'd like to travel, so having a month or so off would be great. *When my life is over, I want to be known as a person who was well-traveled, well-spoken, well-educated, and that I changed lives for the better. I was kind and my life made a difference.*"

In one sense, you are looking at the end result of your life. What do you want to be remembered for? What legacy do you want to leave? What—and who—do you think will be most important to you? Think about your values or what you consider to be very important and regard highly. What is desirable and worthy of your time and effort? For example, if you value your health above all else, you will make it a top priority and make time to exercise, eat well, and get enough sleep. This value will become a habit that will help shape your life.

Here is another example of a mission statement: "I want to thrive in a health care career that allows me to use my creativity, grow in knowledge from mentors and colleagues, and advance into leadership positions. I value relationships and flexibility. I want to work closely with patients and make a positive impact in my profession. I want to provide an effective balance with personal interests, including having a family, traveling, and participating in my community." Your mission statement will change as you grow.

Think about how a college education will help you fulfill your mission in life. If you have chosen a profession (e.g., physical therapist or teaching), you may want to include the aspects of the career that interested you (such as helping others achieve healthy lifestyles or educating and nurturing young children). Your mission statement (**Personal Evaluation Notebook 1.2**) will help you overcome obstacles.

Skills for School and Job Success

What does it take to succeed in a job? Based on feedback from employers, the Secretary's Commission on Achieving Necessary Skills (SCANS; **Figure 1.1**) lists the skills and competencies that are necessary for job, as well as academic, success. Rate your skills by using honesty and critical thinking to complete **Personal Evaluation Notebook 1.3**.

Discover How to Enhance Your Learning

For decades, the idea that students have individual learning styles—which have often been divided into visual, auditory, and kinesthetic or tactile categories—was generally well-accepted. Clearly, everyone processes information differently and students differ in ability and preferences. Some students learn best in a structured lecture and others prefer a more hands-on approach. Researchers caution, however, that these divisions are too blunt to capture the complexity of the human mind or to appreciate the unique variations that exist in people. Some students may not even try to learn certain skills. take particular classes or professors because they think the teaching style doesn't match their preferred learning style. Keep in mind that although you may have a preference, you do not have a fixed style that fits neatly into a distinct category. By having an open mindset you can integrate various styles and combine words, visuals, and tactile methods. This approach will help you enhance creativity and imagination. In addition there are evidence-backed strategies that enhance learning for all students. *There is solid evidence that quizzing can aid memory and help virtually everyone retrieve information.*

Integrate All Learning Styles

Some people are more comfortable with sequential, logical, and factual thinking. They may favor facts and order, and they may think in a logical, detailed thought process. Other people may be more inclined to use an intuitive and insightful approach to solving problems and processing new information. They are more

Personal Evaluation Notebook

Writing Your Personal Mission Statement

To write your mission statement, begin by answering these (or similar) questions:

1. What do I value most in life? What gives my life meaning?

   _____

   _____

2. What nouns and/or adjectives best describe me? (designer, creative, builder)

   _____

   _____

3. Which verbs best describe what I like to do? (create, explore, write, draw)

   _____

   _____

4. What is my life's purpose? List one change in this world I'd like to make.

   _____

   _____

5. What legacy do I want to leave? What do I want my life to mean?

   _____

   _____

6. How will completing college help get me there?

   _____

   _____

7. Draft a personal mission statement.

   _____

   _____

   _____

   _____

   _____

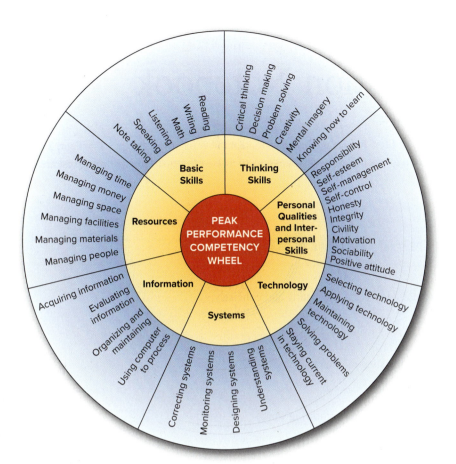

Figure 1.1

Peak Performance Competency Wheel

SCANS recommends these skills and competencies for job success. *Which of these skills have you been acquiring?*

Shutterstock/elenabsl

Personal Evaluation Notebook 1.3

Peak Performance Self-Assessment Test

Assess your skills and behaviors on a scale of 1 to 5 by placing the appropriate number for you in the line. **1 = Poor, 2 and 3 = OK, and 4 and 5 = Excellent** Examples are given for each. Review your answers to discover your strongest and weakest areas.

Area

1. Reading _____

    (e.g., comprehending; summarizing key points; reading for pleasure)

2. Writing _____

    (e.g., using correct grammar; presenting information clearly and concisely; documenting accurately)

3. Speaking _____

    (e.g., expressing main points in an interesting manner)

4. Mathematics _____

    (e.g., understanding basic principles and formulas; showing work)

5. Listening and note taking _____

    (e.g., staying focused and attentive; recording key points)

6. Critical thinking and reasoning _____

    (e.g., assessing facts; making decisions; linking material)

7. Creative problem solving _____

    (e.g., developing options; weighing alternatives)

8. Positive visualization _____

    (e.g., creating mental images to support goals)

9. Knowing how you learn _____

    (e.g., recognizing preferred learning style; integrating all styles)

10. Honesty and integrity _____

    (e.g., doing the right thing; telling the truth; presenting original work)

11. Positive attitude and motivation _____

    (e.g., being optimistic; identifying personal motivators; establishing goals)

12. Responsibility _____

    (e.g., keeping commitments; not blaming others)

13. Flexibility/ability to adapt to change _____

    (e.g., being open to new ideas; seeing the big picture)

(continued)

Personal Evaluation Notebook 1.3

Peak Performance Self-Assessment Test (*concluded*)

Area

14. Self-management and emotional control _____

   (e.g., taking ownership of thoughts and behaviors)

15. Self-esteem and confidence _____

   (e.g., focusing on strengths; maintaining a positive self-image)

16. Time management _____

   (e.g., setting priorities; planning; accomplishing tasks)

17. Money management _____

   (e.g., budgeting; minimizing debt; saving)

18. Management and leadership of people _____

   (e.g., inspiring; communicating; delegating; training)

19. Interpersonal and communication skills _____

   (e.g., building rapport; listening; being an effective team member)

20. Ability to work well with culturally diverse groups _____

   (e.g., respecting and celebrating differences)

21. Organization and evaluation of information _____

   (e.g., identifying key points and ideas; summarizing; documenting)

22. Understanding technology _____

   (e.g., using essential programs; troubleshooting basic problems)

23. Commitment and effort _____

   (e.g., being persistent; working consistently toward goals)

comfortable with using their intuition, like to think abstractly, intuitively, and synthesize the big picture. You can integrate all learning styles. *A specific style may come more naturally to you, but you should try to develop and integrate them all.* They will benefit you in different aspects and courses in your life.

It's important to note that current research suggests that the left and right brain difference is more of a metaphor than a completely accurate representation of the brain. Harvard neuroscientist, Stephen Kosslyn explains that the right and left hemispheres do specialize in different mental functions. However, the idea that people rely more heavily on one side of the brain simplifies the complexity of the brain. Neuroimaging research shows that language is distributed across the hemispheres and perception also involves both sides of the brain. Instead of labeling yourself in an artificial category, realize that brain structure and function vary between people and the brain is complex. An open, positive mindset will help you to focus on growth, curiosity, and effort. *The key to success is to integrate a variety of learning styles and stretch yourself to learn and grow.*

Are You a Reader, Listener, or Doer?

Your brain allows you to experience the world through your senses. One simple way to explore how you learn best is to ask yourself if you are a reader, listener, or doer. Do you get more information from *reading and seeing, talking and listening,* or *doing*? Of course, you do all these things, but you may have a preferred style. For example, you may organize information visually and prefer using illustrations. A person who prefers studying a concept by observing, visualizing, or reading prefers a **visual** learning style. Someone who prefers a verbal lesson by listening is considered an **auditory** learner. A **kinesthetic** learner prefers doing a physical activity. **Reading** and writing were also separated out as important ways that some people learn information. As you'll see, the **VARK** system stands for *Visual, Auditory, Reading, and Kinesthetic. We will use the VARK system to integrate learning and help you think through the Adult Learning Cycle in different and creative ways.*

Personal Evaluation Notebook 1.4 has a Learning Style Inventory or guide that will help you discover your preferred learning style. It is not meant for a distinct category.

VISUAL LEARNERS

Visual learners prefer to see information and read the material. They learn most effectively with pictures, graphs, illustrations, diagrams, timelines, photos, and pie charts. They like to perceive in three-dimensional space and re-create through visualization. They might use arrows, pictures, and bullets to highlight points. Visual learners are often holistic in that they see pictures in their minds that create feelings and emotion. They often use visual descriptions in their speech, such as "It is clear . . .," "Picture this . . .," or "See what I mean?" Visual learners tend to

- Remember what they see better than what they hear
- Prefer to have written directions they can read
- Learn better when someone shows them rather than tells them
- Like to draw, sketch, and visualize information
- Like graphs, pictures, and diagrams
- Keep a list of things to do when planning the week
- Gesture frequently while talking and watch facial expressions
- Like to read for pleasure and to learn

AUDITORY LEARNERS

Auditory learners prefer to rely on their hearing sense. They may like music and prefer to listen to information, as in lectures. They like to talk, recite, and summarize information aloud. Auditory learners may create rhymes out of words and play

Personal Evaluation Notebook 1.4

Learning Style Inventory

Determine your learning preference. Complete each sentence by checking a, b, or c. No answer is correct or better than another.

1. I learn best when I

_____ a. have a visual presentation of the information.

_____ b. hear information.

_____ c. have hands-on experience.

2. I like

_____ a. pictures and illustrations.

_____ b. listening to recordings and audio books.

_____ c. working with people and going on field trips.

3. For pleasure and relaxation, I love to

_____ a. read.

_____ b. listen to music.

_____ c. garden or play sports.

4. I tend to be

_____ a. contemplative.

_____ b. talkative.

_____ c. a doer.

5. To remember my student ID, I need to

_____ a. look at my ID card over and over.

_____ b. say it out loud several times.

_____ c. write it down several times.

6. In a classroom, I learn best when

_____ a. I have a good textbook, visual aids, and written information.

_____ b. the instructor is interesting and clear.

_____ c. I am involved in doing activities.

7. When I study for a test, I

_____ a. read my notes and write a summary.

_____ b. review my notes aloud and talk to others.

_____ c. like to study in a group and use models and charts.

8. I have

_____ a. pay attention to visual details.

_____ b. fun telling stories and jokes.

_____ c. a great time building things and being active.

9. I often

_____ a. remember faces but not names.

_____ b. remember names but not faces.

_____ c. remember events but not names or faces.

10. I remember best

_____ a. when I read instructions and use visual images to remember.

_____ b. when I listen to instructions and use rhyming words to remember.

_____ c. with hands-on activities and trial and error.

11. When I give directions, I might say,

_____ a. "Turn right at the yellow house and left when you see the large tree."

_____ b. "Turn right. Go three blocks. Turn left onto Buttermilk Lane."

_____ c. "Follow me," after giving directions by using gestures.

12. When navigating in a new city, I prefer to

_____ a. use a map and find my own way.

_____ b. stop and get directions from someone.

_____ c. drive around and figure it out by myself.

Score: Count the number of check marks for all your choices:

Total a choices _____ (visual learning style)

Total b choices _____ (auditory learning style)

Total c choices _____ (kinesthetic learning style)

The highest total indicates your dominant learning style. If you are a combination, that's good. It means you are integrating styles already.

• Know How You Learn
Everyone has their own way of learning. *What type of learning style do you think best suits this person?*

music that helps them concentrate. When they take study breaks, they listen to music or chat with a friend. They are usually good listeners but are easily distracted by noise. They also tend to listen to their feelings and thoughts and intuition. They not only have self-understanding, but also tend to have empathy for others. They are people smart. They often use auditory descriptions when communicating, such as "This rings true . . .," "It's clear as a bell . . .," "Do you hear what you're saying?" or "My intuition says.. . ."

Auditory learners tend to

- Remember what they hear better than what they see
- Prefer to listen to instructions
- Like lectures and relate information to their own experiences
- Like to listen to music and talk on the telephone
- Plan the week by talking it through with someone
- Use rhyming words to remember
- Learn best when they hear an assignment as well as see it

Auditory learners may enjoy being on radio, trial lawyer, counselor, or musician.

READER/WRITER LEARNERS

Reader/writer learners prefer to learn information through words on a printed page. They like to write information and teach with words. They like to write out summaries, rewrite their notes, write letters, and read for understanding. They learn best when they read, talk, and write information. They tend to

- Write and rewrite notes
- Write questions and summaries
- Be logical, have the ability to reason, and solve problems
- Respond in writing

Reader/writers may enjoy being authors, lawyers, journalists, or scientists.

KINESTHETIC LEARNERS

Kinesthetic learners are usually well-coordinated, like to touch things, and learn best by doing. They like to collect samples, build models, and use note cards, and often like to spend time in nature. They like to connect abstract material to something concrete and make it practical. They are good at hands-on tasks. They often like field trips and working with their hands. They often use phrases such as "I am getting a handle on . . .," "Let's see how this works . . .," and "Let's put these samples in classifications that.. . ."

Kinesthetic learners tend to

- Create an experience
- Use hands-on activities

- Build things and put things together
- Use models and physical activity
- Write down information
- Apply information to real-life situations
- Draw, doodle, use games and puzzles, and play computer games
- Take field trips, observe nature, and collect samples
- Relate abstract information to something concrete

Kinesthetic learners may enjoy being a chef, a surgeon, a medical technician, a nurse, an automobile mechanic, an electrician, an engineer, a forest ranger, a police officer, or a dancer.

Intelligence: What Factors Are Involved?

Because each of us has a unique set of abilities, perceptions, needs, and ways of processing information, learning styles vary widely. We all have more than one learning style. *The key is not to try to fit yourself in a box, but to see what styles tend to describe you and then integrate all styles for success. Styles are not fixed, but fluid. This is simply a guide.*

General intelligence, which IQ tests assess reliably, has proven a solid predictor of life outcomes and a good estimate of abstract reasoning ability. The hard sciences have shown that there is a strong association between mental abilities and the concept and well-established constructs of general intelligence. Humans are difficult to measure and quantify, however, and in the 1980s the theory of multiple intelligences challenged the construct of general intelligence. Howard Gardner, who wrote *Frames of Mind: The Theory of Multiple Intelligences,* describes relatively independent intelligences. He said his theory was not based on experimental evidence which is harder to prove or disprove. He maintained that there are different cognitive abilities on which the same student can score high or low. Clearly intelligence is not the only factor that predicts how a person will do in college or in life. As we will discuss later, EQ or emotional intelligences looks at a number of traits, such as conscientiousness, honesty, empathy, effort, persistency, and resiliency as important for school and life success. People with an open mindset can

• **Learning Styles**
There is no one best way to learn. *How do you think you can develop and integrate different learning styles?*

Huntstock/Getty Images

acknowledge scientific facts about the mind and IQ tests and also explore the concept of different cognitive abilities or intelligences.

1. **Verbal/linguistic.** Some people are **word smart**. They have verbal/linguistic intelligence and like to read, talk, and write information. They have the ability to argue, persuade, entertain, and teach with words. Many become journalists, writers, or lawyers. **To learn best:** Talk, read, or write about it.

2. **Logical/mathematical.** Some people are **logic smart**. They have logical/mathematical intelligence and like numbers, puzzles, and logic. They have the ability to reason, solve problems, create hypotheses, think in terms of cause and effect, and explore patterns and relationships. Many become scientists, accountants, or computer programmers. **To learn best:** Conceptualize, quantify, or think critically about it.

3. **Spatial.** Some people are **picture smart**. They have spatial intelligence and like to draw, sketch, and visualize information. They have the ability to perceive in three-dimensional space and re-create various aspects of the visual world. Many become architects, photographers, artists, or engineers. **To learn best:** Draw, sketch, or visualize it.

4. **Musical.** Some people are **music smart**. They have rhythm and melody intelligence. They have the ability to appreciate, perceive, and produce rhythms and to keep time to music. Many become composers, singers, or instrumentalists. **To learn best:** Sing, record, mix, rap, or play music.

5. **Bodily/kinesthetic.** Some people are **body smart**. They have physical and kinesthetic intelligence. They have the ability to understand and control their bodies; they have tactile sensitivity, like movement, and handle objects skillfully. Many become dancers, carpenters, physical education teachers, or coaches and enjoy physical activities and sports. **To learn best:** Build a model, dance, use note cards, or do hands-on activities.

6. **Environmental.** Some people are **outdoor smart**. They have environmental intelligence. They are good at measuring, charting, and observing plants and animals. They like to keep journals, collect and classify, and participate in outdoor activities. Many become park and forest rangers, surveyors, gardeners, landscape architects, outdoor guides, wildlife experts, or environmentalists. **To learn best:** Go on field trips, collect samples, go for walks, and apply what you are learning to real life.

7. **Intrapersonal.** Some people are **self-smart**. They have intrapersonal (inner) intelligence. They have the ability to be contemplative, self-disciplined, and introspective. They like to work alone and pursue their own interests. Many become writers, counselors, theologians, or self-employed entrepreneurs. **To learn best:** Relate information to your feelings or personal experiences or find inner expression.

8. **Interpersonal.** Some people are **people smart**. They have interpersonal intelligence. They like to talk and work with people, join groups, and solve problems as part of a team. They have the ability to work with and understand people, as well as to perceive and be responsive to the moods, intentions, and desires of other people. Many become mediators, negotiators, social directors, social workers, motivational speakers, or teachers. **To learn best:** Join a group, get a study partner, or follow or start a blog. These two terms (intrapersonal and interpersonal) can be hard to remember. When you think *interpersonal,* think *international*– across people, across nations.

Discover Your Personality Type

Your learning style is often associated with your personality type—your "temperament." The concepts of personality and temperament are not new. Early writings from ancient Greece, India, the Middle East, and China addressed various temperaments and personality types. The ancient Greek founder of modern medicine, Hippocrates, identified four basic body types and a personality type associated with each body type. Several personality typing systems grew out of this ancient view of body/mind typing. The *Enneagram* is an ancient system with roots in the Middle East in the fourth century. It was first introduced to America by the spiritual teacher and mystic G.I. Gurdjieff around 1920. It has nine types that are defined by how you handle the basic fears and insecurities developed in early childhood with the goal of self-revelation and integration. The Enneagram is increasing in popularity because it focuses on growth and becoming whole. This system highlights core strengths and specific areas of attachment and fears and helps observe non-judgmentally without over reacting. There are many books available such as The Wisdom of the Enneagram by Don Richard Riso and Russ Hudson and you can complete a questionnaire by going to the website, www.EnneagramInstitue.com.

• Understanding Personality Types
Psychologists have developed a variety of categories to identify how people function best. *What personality type or types might apply to this person?*

Dragon_Fly/Shutterstock

Carl Jung's Typology System

In 1921, psychologist Carl Jung proposed in his book *Psychological Types* that people are fundamentally different but also fundamentally alike. He identified three main attitudes/psychological functions, each with two types of personalities:

1. *How people relate to the external or internal world.* **Extroverts** are energized and recharged by people, tending to be outgoing, impulsive, energetic, confident, social, and competitive. They tend to be optimistic, fun, and talkative and are often uncomfortable with being alone. They are often risk-takers, dominant, and comfortable in the spotlight. **Introverts** enjoy solitude and reflection, preferring the world of ideas and thoughts. They are energized by time alone. They tend to have a small but close set of friends and are more prone to self-doubt and shyness and may feel awkward in social situations. They tend to be kind, thoughtful, focused, creative, cooperative, and loyal; ask questions; and are good listeners. Introvert–extrovert relationships often result in creative collaboration.

2. *How people perceive and gather information.* **Sensors** learn best from their senses and feel comfortable with facts and concrete data. They like to organize information systematically, set goals, and meet deadlines. They are decisive and pay attention to specifics. They are pragmatic, sensible, practical, and realistic. They are focused on the present and what is actual, and value common sense and experience. **Intuitives** feel more comfortable with theories, insights, abstraction, imagination, and speculation. They respond to their intuition and rely on hunches and nonverbal perceptions. They focus on innovation, the big picture, and the future and are interested in what is possible. They tend to be curious, flexible, and open-minded.

3. *How people prefer to make decisions.* **Thinkers** like to plan ahead and analyze problems with facts, rational logic, and analysis. They tend to be direct and use a systematic evaluation of data and facts for problem solving. They value justice, competence, and objectivity. They usually don't take things

personally. **Feelers** are gentle, sensitive to the concerns and feelings of others, tactful, and appreciative; value harmony; and dislike conflict. They focus on relationships and are subjective.

Jung suggested that differences and similarities among people can be understood by combining these types. Although people are not exclusively one of these types, he maintained that they have basic preferences or tendencies.

The Myers-Briggs Type Indicator

Jung's work inspired Katherine Briggs and her daughter, Isabel Briggs Myers, to design a personality test, called the Myers-Briggs Type Indicator (MBTI), which has become the most widely used typological instrument. They added a fourth attitude/psychological function (judgment/perception), which they felt was implied in Jung's writings, focusing on *how people live.* Many other books and interpretations followed, including *Please Understand Me,* by David Keirsey and Marilyn Bates, and *What Type Am I?* by Renee Baron. Most are some variation of Jung's original work. **Judgers** prefer orderly, planned, structured learning and working environments. They like control and closure. **Perceivers** prefer flexibility and spontaneity and like to allow life to unfold. Thus, with the four attitudes/psychological functions (extroverts vs. introverts, sensors vs. intuitives, thinkers vs. feelers, and judgers vs. perceivers), the MBTI provides sixteen possible personality combinations. Although we may have all eight preferences, one in each pair tends to be more developed.

If you're interested in taking the Myers-Briggs Type Indicator, The Enneagram, or other personality inventories, visit the career center or online sites. They will not only give you the tests, but also help interpret them and offer help for choosing a major and career based on your strengths and interests. In the next section, we will present a simple way to discover your personality types and how each type relates to majors and careers. Any inventory is simply a guide and not meant to label, but it may help give you insight into your preference. Keep in mind that one of the most important aspects of personality is the introvert–extrovert trait. Although these traits tend to stay throughout adulthood, an introverted child can learn to be an excellent public speaker and enjoy socializing and an extrovert can learn to be mindful, focused, and calm and enjoy quiet time alone. *In short, we can stretch and grow and expand beyond our inborn temperaments. Be open to growth and learning. Self-awareness and observation can help us become healthy and whole.*

Connect Learning Styles and Personality Types: The Four-Temperament Profile

You now are aware of your preferred learning styles and have a sense of your personality type. How are these connected? How can you use this information to improve your learning skills and participate in productive group and team situations?

The Four-Temperament Profile demonstrates how learning styles and personality types are interrelated. **Personal Evaluation Notebook 1.5.** includes questions that will help you determine your dominant temperament. Remember, this guide is not fixed, but fluid.

Personal Evaluation Notebook

The Four-Temperament Profile

The following statements indicate your preferences in working with others, making decisions, and learning new information. Read each statement, with its four possible choices. Mark 4 next to the choice MOST like you, 3 next to the choice ALMOST ALWAYS like you, 2 next to the choice SOMEWHAT like you, and 1 next to the choice LEAST like you.

1. I learn best when I
   _____ a. rely on logical thinking and facts.
   _____ b. am personally involved.
   _____ c. can look for new patterns through trial and error.
   _____ d. use hands-on activities and practical applications.

2. When I'm at my best, I'm described as
   _____ a. dependable, accurate, logical, and objective.
   _____ b. understanding, loyal, cooperative, and harmonious.
   _____ c. imaginative, flexible, open-minded, and creative.
   _____ d. confident, assertive, practical, and results-oriented.

3. I respond best to instructors and bosses who
   _____ a. are factual and to the point.
   _____ b. show appreciation and are friendly.
   _____ c. encourage creativity and flexibility.
   _____ d. expect me to be involved, be active, and get results.

4. When working in a group, I tend to value
   _____ a. objectivity and correctness.
   _____ b. consensus and harmony.
   _____ c. originality and risk-taking.
   _____ d. efficiency and results.

5. I am most comfortable with people who are
   _____ a. informed, serious, and accurate.
   _____ b. supportive, appreciative, and friendly.
   _____ c. creative, unique, and idealistic.
   _____ d. productive, realistic, and dependable.

6. Generally, I am
   _____ a. methodical, efficient, trustworthy, and accurate.
   _____ b. cooperative, genuine, gentle, and modest.
   _____ c. high-spirited, spontaneous, easily bored, and dramatic.
   _____ d. straightforward, conservative, responsible, and decisive.

7. When making a decision, I'm generally concerned with
   _____ a. collecting information and facts to determine the right solution.
   _____ b. finding the solution that pleases others and myself.
   _____ c. brainstorming creative solutions that feel right.
   _____ d. quickly choosing the most practical and realistic solution.

(continued)

Personal Evaluation Notebook

The Four-Temperament Profile (*concluded*)

8. You could describe me as

_____ a. analytical.

_____ b. caring.

_____ c. innovative.

_____ d. productive.

9. I excel at

_____ a. reaching accurate and logical conclusions.

_____ b. being cooperative and respecting people's feelings.

_____ c. finding hidden connections and creative outcomes.

_____ d. making realistic, practical, and timely decisions.

10. When learning at school or on the job, I enjoy

_____ a. gathering facts and technical information and being objective.

_____ b. making personal connections, being supportive, working in groups.

_____ c. exploring new possibilities, tackling creative tasks, and being flexible.

_____ d. producing results, solving problems, and making decisions.

Score: To determine your style, mark the choices you made in each column below. Then add the column totals. Highest number in

- Column a, you are an analyzer
- Column b, you are a supporter
- Column c, you are a creator
- Column d, you are a director

	Choice a	Choice b	Choice c	Choice d
1.	_____	_____	_____	_____
2.	_____	_____	_____	_____
3.	_____	_____	_____	_____
4.	_____	_____	_____	_____
5.	_____	_____	_____	_____
6.	_____	_____	_____	_____
7.	_____	_____	_____	_____
8.	_____	_____	_____	_____
9.	_____	_____	_____	_____
10.	_____	_____	_____	_____
Total	_____	_____	_____	_____
	Analyzer	**Supporter**	**Creator**	**Director**

Add up your totals to determine what type of learner you are and read further.

The following descriptions elaborate on the four temperaments in **Personal Evaluation Notebook 1.5.** Which is your dominant temperament: analyzer, creator, supporter, or director? Keep in mind that inventories provide only clues. People change over time and react differently in different situations. Various careers include people of all temperaments. Use this knowledge to discover your strengths and become a well-rounded, balanced learner and team contributor. Peak performers know not only their dominant or preferred style but also the way to integrate other styles when appropriate.

Analyzers

Analyzers tend to be logical, thoughtful, loyal, exact, dedicated, steady, and organized. They like following direction and work at a steady pace. The key word for analyzers is *thinking.* (See **Figure 1.2.**)

Strengths: Creating concepts and models and thinking things through.

Goal: To gain intellectual recognition; analyzers are knowledge seekers.

Classroom style: Analyzers relate to instructors who are organized, know their facts, and present information logically and precisely. They dislike the ambiguity of subjects that lack right or wrong answers. They tend to seem more concerned with facts, abstract ideas, and concepts than with people.

Learning style: Analyzers often perceive information abstractly and process it reflectively. They learn best by observing and thinking through ideas. They like models, lectures, textbooks, and solitary work. They like to examine how things work. They evaluate and come to a precise conclusion.

Supporters

People who are supporters tend to be cooperative, honest, sensitive, warm, and understanding. They relate well to others. They value harmony and are informal, approachable, and tactful. In business, they are concerned with the feelings and values of others. The key word for supporters is *feeling.* (See **Figure 1.3.**)

Strengths: Clarifying values, creating harmony, and being a loyal team player.

Goal: To create harmony, meaning, and cooperation; they are identity seekers.

Classroom style: Supporters tend to learn best when they like an instructor and feel accepted and respected. They are easily hurt by criticism. They like to integrate course concepts with their own experiences. They relate to instructors who are warm and sociable, tell interesting stories, use visuals, and are approachable. They learn best by listening, sharing ideas and feelings, and working in teams.

Effective Traits	Ineffective Traits	Possible Majors	Possible Careers	How to Relate to Analyzers
Objective	Too cautious	Accounting	Computer programmer	Be factual
Logical	Abrupt	Bookkeeping	Accountant	Be logical
Thorough	Unemotional	Mathematics	Drafter	Be formal and thorough
Precise	Aloof	Computer science	Electrician	Be organized, detached, and calm
Detail-oriented	Indecisive	Drafting	Engineer	Be accurate and use critical thinking
Disciplined	Unimaginative	Electronics	Auto mechanic	State facts briefly and concisely
		Automotive	Librarian	

Figure **1.2**

Profile of an Analyzer

Put a check mark next to the descriptions that apply to you. *Do you recognize any analyzer traits in yourself?*

Figure 1.3

Profile of a Supporter

Supporters want things done harmoniously and want to be personally involved. Their favorite question is "Why?" *Do you recognize any supporter traits in yourself?*

Effective Traits	Ineffective Traits	Possible Majors	Possible Careers	How to Relate to Supporters
Understanding	Overly compliant	Counseling or therapy	Elementary teacher	Be positive
Gentle	Passive	Social work	Physical therapist	Be sincere and build trust
Loyal	Slow to act	Family and consumer science	Social worker	Listen actively
Cooperative	Naive	Nursing	Psychologist	Focus on people
Diplomatic	Unprofessional	Medical assisting	Counselor	Focus on personal values
Appreciative	Can be overly sensitive	Physical therapy	Nurse	Create a comfortable, relaxed climate
		Education	Medical assistant	Create an experience they can relate to

Learning style: Supporters perceive information through intuition and process it reflectively. They like to deal with their feelings. They prefer learning information that has personal meaning, and they are patient and likable. They are insightful; they are imaginative thinkers and need to be personally involved.

Creators

Creators are innovative, flexible, spontaneous, creative, and idealistic. They are risk takers; they love drama, style, and imaginative design. They like fresh ideas and are passionate about their work. The key word for creators is *experience.* (See **Figure 1.4.**)

Strengths: Creating visions that inspire people.

Goal: To make things happen by turning ideas into action; they are experience seekers.

Classroom style: Creators learn best in innovative and active classrooms. They relate to instructors who have a passion for their work; who are challenging, imaginative, and flexible; and who present interesting ideas and make the topic exciting.

Learning style: Creators learn by doing and being involved in active experiments. They perceive information concretely and process it actively. They like games,

Figure 1.4

Profile of a Creator

Creators want things done with a sense of drama and style. Their favorite question is "What if?" *Do you recognize any creator traits in yourself?*

Effective Traits	Ineffective Traits	Possible Majors	Possible Careers	How to Relate to Creators
Imaginative	Unrealistic	Art	Writer	Be enthusiastic
Creative	Unreliable	English	Event planner	Be involved
Visionary	Inconsistent	Music	Travel agent	Be flexible
Idealistic	Hasty	Design	Hotel manager	Be accepting of change
Enthusiastic	Impulsive	Hospitality	Graphic artist	Focus on creative ideas
Innovative	Impatient	Marketing/Advertising	Musician	Talk about dreams and possibilities
	Fragmented	Theater	Composer	
		Communications	Journalist	
			Drama teacher	
			Florist	
			Costume designer	

role-playing, stories, plays, music, illustrations, drawings, and other visual stimuli. They ask questions and enjoy acting on ideas. They are usually good public speakers. They are future-oriented and good at seeing whole systems.

Directors

Directors are dependable, self-directed, conscientious, efficient, decisive, and results-oriented. They like to be the leader of groups and respond to other people's ideas when they are logical and reasonable. Their strength is in the practical application of ideas. Because of this ability, they can excel in a variety of careers, such as law enforcement, banking, and legal professions. The key word for directors is *results.* (See Figure 1.5.)

Strengths: Integrating theory with practical solutions.

Goal: To find practical solutions to problems; they are security seekers.

Classroom style: Directors relate to instructors who are organized, clear, to the point, punctual, and results-oriented. They prefer field trips and hands-on activities.

Learning style: Directors learn by hands-on, direct experience. They learn best by practical application. They work hard to get things done.

Integrate Styles to Maximize Learning

Just as there is no best way to learn, there is no one instrument, assessment, or inventory that can categorize how you learn best. Any learning style assessment or theory is, at best, a guide and not meant to be a fixed determination of abilities or to put you into a fixed category. Instead of focusing on what differentiates, focus on what boosts learning for all students. For example, there is solid research that testing yourself helps with memory and recall. How can you integrate all styles and use all your senses to enhances learning?

Effective Traits	Ineffective Traits	Possible Majors	Possible Careers	How to Relate to Directors
Confident	Aggressive	Law enforcement	Lawyer	Set deadlines
Assertive	Pushy	Construction	Police officer	Be responsible for your actions
Active	Insistent	Engineering	Detective	Focus on results and achievements
Decisive	Overpowering	Carpentry	Consultant	Do not try to take control
Forceful	Dominating	Business/ Management	Banker	Do not make excuses
Effective leader		Forestry	Park ranger	Communicate schedule changes
Results-oriented			Sales representative	
			Administrator for outdoor recreation	

Figure 1.5

Profile of a Director

Directors want to produce results in a practical manner. Their favorite question is "How?" *Do you recognize any director traits in yourself?*

We have discussed several inventories that offer guidance for determining how you learn, process information, and relate to others. They also provide clues for possible college majors and careers that fit your personality. Use these inventories as a guide, not a fixed determination. All learning styles are connected, and we use all of them, depending on the situation, task, and people involved. You will grow and change over time. *Tune into your natural talents and abilities, and expand your effectiveness by integrating all learning styles and adapting innovative approaches.* For example, learning to play an instrument, laugh, dance, sing, write stories, and draw can help you develop a sense of design, synthesis, empathy, and effective communication skills and be a more imaginative and creative person. Experiment, risk, think critically and creatively. Consume experiences, not things. You are free to make mistakes, to learn, wonder, experiment, stretch, and grow.

Psychologist William James believed that thoughts can change the structure and function of our brains. *Breakthroughs in neuroscience have shown that the brain is capable of growth and change. The power of an open and positive mindset finally gains scientific credibility.* Think of what you can accomplish if you have a positive, open attitude, work in alignment with your natural preferences and strengths, integrate various learning styles, and create positive habits. The Peak Performance Learning Pyramid in **Figure 1.6** illustrates how you can maximize your effectiveness by integrating learning styles and moving up from passive to active, engaged learning. Now that you have assessed how you learn best—as well as new ways to learn—let's explore how learning is a never-ending cycle.

Adjust Your Learning Style to Your Instructor's Teaching Style

Just as we all have different learning styles, your instructors will have a variety of teaching styles. Rather than resisting, find ways to adapt. For example, if you prefer a highly structured lecture, focusing on facts, and taking notes, you may feel

Figure **1.6**

Peak Performance Learning Pyramid

Maximize your effectiveness by integrating various learning styles and skills as you move up the pyramid. *What additional skills and learning styles would enhance your learning ability?*

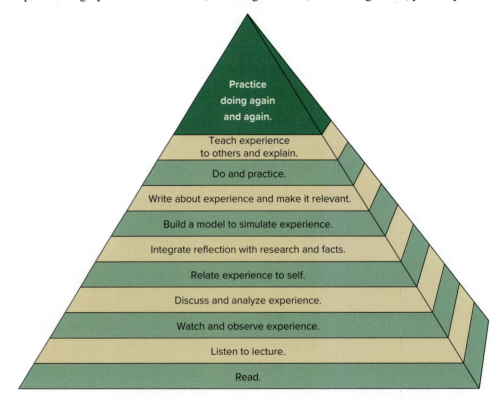

uncomfortable in a student-centered course where ideas and class discussion are key, and you work in small groups with little structure. The following strategies may help you succeed:

- Ask questions and clarify expectations.
- Be open, flexible, and try new approaches.
- Be an active participant in class and go to every class.
- Get to know other students and form study teams.
- Seek out other points of view.
- See exercises and class discussions as learning opportunities.
- Visit your instructor during office hours and ask what you can do to improve.
- Do any extra-credit projects that are offered.
- Try looking at the whole of a concept before breaking it into parts.
- If the instructor jumps around a lot in a lecture or digresses, ask for main points.
- Write out possible obstacles and creative ideas for overcoming setbacks.
- *Make up tests, pretest yourself, and share with your study team. This really works!*

Let's say you prefer warm relationships and a nonstructured class. You find yourself in a traditional, content-centered, straight lecture class with few visuals or class discussion. Here are a few suggestions for adapting:

- Read the syllabus and know expectations.
- Listen attentively and take detailed notes.
- Clarify the weight of each test, paper, or project.
- Make certain you know and meet each deadline.
- Focus on the lecture and avoid talking to others during class.
- Work in a study team, discuss lecture concepts, and predict test questions.
- Ask for examples from the instructor and study team.
- Take advantage of the logical sequence of material and take notes accordingly.
- Add color, supporting examples, and drawings to your notes.
- Connect lectures to drawings, photographs, and diagrams in the textbook.
- Ask the instructor for visuals that help illustrate the points made in class.
- Have your questions ready when talking to your instructor during office hours.
- Focus on facts, logic, definitions, and descriptions.
- *Make up tests, pretest yourself and share with your study teams. This works!*

You could drop the class and sign up for a class with another instructor. However, in the workplace you will interact with people who have a variety of personality types and learning styles, so it's important for you to learn coping and adapting skills now. Why not view this as an opportunity to grow, learn, and adapt?

The Adult Learning Cycle

David Kolb, a professor at Case Western Reserve University, developed an inventory that categorizes learners based on how they process information:

1. Concrete experience: learn by feeling, listening, and talking
2. Reflective observation: learn by observing, visualizing, and intuition
3. Abstract conceptualization: learn by thinking, writing, and reading
4. Active experimentation: learn by doing and hands-on activities

We Learn

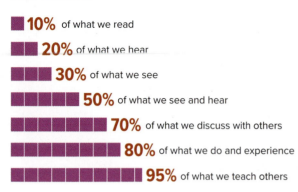

- **10%** of what we read
- **20%** of what we hear
- **30%** of what we see
- **50%** of what we see and hear
- **70%** of what we discuss with others
- **80%** of what we do and experience
- **95%** of what we teach others

Kolb's theory about learning styles is similar to Carl Jung's four attitudes/psychological functions (feeling, intuition, thinking, and sensation). The crux of Kolb's theory is that you learn by practice and repetition. Thus, do it and do it again.

The Adult Learning Cycle is an adaptation of both Kolb's and Jung's theories. It includes a fifth stage (teach) and illustrates how the stages are complementary to one another. (See **Figure 1.7**.)

1. **FEEL and LISTEN.** *Why do I want to learn this?* What personal meaning and interest does this have for me? I learn by feeling, listening, having personal experiences, and talking with others. I listen to my thoughts and feelings and share them with others.

2. **OBSERVE and VISUALIZE.** *How does this work?* I learn by watching, observing, imagining, intuition, and reflecting on past experiences.

3. **THINK and WRITE.** *What does this mean?* I learn by thinking, reading, gathering information, and writing. I like words, ideas, and logic.

4. **DO and PRACTICE.** *What can I do with this?* I learn by doing, applying ideas, and hands-on activities. How can I synthesize this information?

5. **TEACH and PRACTICE AGAIN.** *How can I relay this information to others?* I learn by demonstrating and explaining, as well as by acknowledging and rewarding positive outcomes. What can I add to this information to make it fresh and creative?

Depending on your preferred learning style, the information to be learned, and the situation, you may find yourself starting the cycle at different stages. *The key to learning is practice and repetition.* As you repeat the stages, meaning and recall are strengthened. To make learning long-lasting, you need to find ways to use all your

Figure **1.7**
The Adult Learning Cycle

The key to learning is practice and repetition. *Why is "Teach" an essential, unique step?*

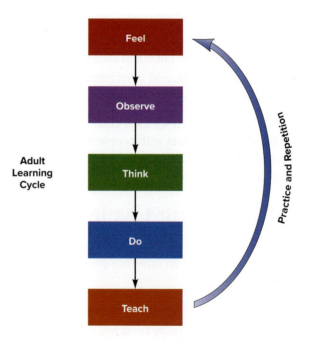

senses and to make it meaningful. VARK is integrated throughout the cycle. For example, let's say you are taking a web design class:

1. **FEEL and RELATE.** What personal meaning, interests, and relevance does this subject have for me? Why do I want to take this class? What are the benefits to my coursework and career? How does this relate to what I already know, such as other areas of programming and design? Which new skills will translate well to other courses and interests, such as setting up a website for a new club I have joined? I'll *listen* to your feelings and listen to others. I'll use *auditory* cues by finding music to illustrate ideas or use background music as I learn.

2. **OBSERVE and IMAGINE.** I'll observe my instructor and other students. How does this computer work? What is new and different? I'll *visualize* information and use color, models, and pictures and draw or sketch possible layouts. I'll watch how other students learn. I'll reflect on what I'm learning by re-creating it visually.

3. **THINK and WRITE.** I'll think about problems logically and sequentially. Which tasks are difficult to learn or remember? I'll analyze things and break them down into their parts. I'll evaluate new ideas and gather information. I'll *read* the manual and jot down instructions. I'll *write out* obstacles and reread instructions when I'm stumped. I'll write a summary and read it.

4. **DO and PRACTICE.** I learn by trial and error. I'll jump in and try new tasks. Learning web design is a great example of hands-on learning. I'll find new applications and test new ways of doing things by using my body and *kinesthetic* methods. I'll experience doing a task as my instructor or a friend helps me. I'll monitor the results I'm getting.

5. **TEACH and PRACTICE AGAIN.** I will demonstrate to someone else what I've learned. I'll answer questions and ask for feedback. I'll practice again and again.

Then return to Stage 1 and reaffirm the benefits of learning this valuable new skill.

You will be most effective if you integrate all the learning styles and use all your senses. In each chapter, we will explore practical examples of the Adult Learning Cycle integrated with the VARK learning styles. Using the VARK system will help you think through and apply the Adult Learning Cycle in different ways. This will help you think of ways you can integrate visual, auditory, reading and writing, and kinesthetic learning styles in everything you are learning. For example, use pictures, maps, diagrams, charts, illustrations, visualization, fantasy, metaphors, stories, and mind maps to make connections and enhance your learning through *visual* thinking. Use lectures, tapes, reading out loud, and music to enhance your *auditory* thinking. *Read and write* and summarize to enhance words. Use direct experience, field trips, role playing, simulation, laboratory experimentation, and manipulation of information to activate your *kinesthetic* thinking.

Overcome Obstacles

On your journey to success, you will run into stumbling blocks. One of the best ways to overcome obstacles is to anticipate likely setbacks and develop a written plan to overcome them. For example, you have looked forward to college and moving into the dorms. So you're surprised during the first semester that you are homesick and miss your old friends, home, and surroundings. You want to go home often, might question your decision to come to this college, or even whether you belong in college at all. You are not alone. *Most students experience homesickness.* What you need is a plan. *Instead of feeling lonely, get busy and become more engaged with your classes, clubs, and activities.* Make a habit of being open and willing to grow and change. This is an opportunity to stretch yourself.

Focus

The "M" word: **multitasking**. In our high-speed world of fast food, multimedia, and instant gratification, it's no wonder that we think we can do it all at once. We don't really multitask; rather, we have several projects going on at once, but we attend to only one at a time.

Enhanced productivity? On the contrary. Have you ever seen someone walk off the curb while on the phone? Many would argue that *multitasking* really means you aren't doing anything very well because you're trying to do too many things at the same time. Layering task upon task only complicates our hectic lives even more. However, we have demands on our time and have to figure out the best way to accomplish as much as possible.

Mindfulness is the key. Rather than multitasking, focus on one thing at a time for a short period of time. For example, take a few minutes right now and review what you've just read about learning styles and your instructors' teaching styles. Jot down each one's name and how you would characterize their teaching. Put an asterisk by those whose teaching style is a little more challenging for you. Write down three specific strategies you want to try during the next class. Choose just one item and focus. Make it simple by trying just a few techniques now to find out what works for you. You might decide that when you are having a conversation with friends or your family that your phone is put out of sight. *Being fully present for another person is one of the best gifts you can give. In one word: FOCUS.*

Keep it simple and do just one thing each day that will help you to engage in college and your job and connect to students, faculty, and co-workers. Let's say it's the first week of classes and you're still getting to know your way around, feeling a little homesick, and wondering if you really belong here. So you want to become more engaged and connected. Choose one or two clubs or activities to explore and attend. *Choose one or two students in every class to get to know better.* Maybe ask if they'd like to study at the library with you or take a walk and explore the campus. Let's say you have a part-time job and feel excluded by your co-workers. Show up on time, focus on your job, be pleasant and respectful, and connect with customers or other co-workers. It's easy to complain; make it a habit to stay calm, focused, and professional. Start small and keep it simple. You will have difficult days at college and on your job; hang in there and focus on the positive. *When you're engaged in activities and connected with others, you will feel as if you belong and enjoy college, work, and life in general.* Use this experience to grow and learn, get connected, and find meaning.

In Chapter 4, we'll tackle time management in more detail, but focusing your time and efforts and finding what works for you are essential to every topic in this book and everything you do, in both school and life. This book provides a litany of proven strategies, but it's up to you to find out what works—and to stick with it until it's a habit!

TAKING CHARGE

Summary

In this chapter, I learned to

- **Create a positive, open mindset.** Peak performers have an open, positive mindset that focuses on growth, effort, and love of learning rather than a fixed, negative mindset.

- **Practice self-management.** I know I am responsible for my own success, and I will learn and practice self-management techniques and behaviors that will make me successful.

- **Self-assess.** Objectively seeing myself will help me recognize my need to learn new skills, relate more effectively with others, set goals, manage time and stress, and create a balanced and productive life. I welcome feedback so I can grow and learn.

- **Use my critical thinking skills.** I use a logical, systematic thought process and creativity to make sound choices and good decisions. I am open to exploring many options.

- **Visualize success.** Visualization is a self-management tool I can use to see myself being successful. I will also use affirmations (positive self-talk) to focus on what's important.

- **Reflect on information.** I reflect on how experiences are related and what I can learn from them, including drawing and keeping a journal to record my thoughts.

- **Create a personal mission statement.** Reflecting on my values, interests, and goals gives my life purpose and meaning. I want my life to make a difference.

- **Make connections between skills for school and job success.** The Secretary's Commission on Achieving Necessary Skills (SCANS) outlines skills and competencies that are critical to success in school as well as in the job market.

- **Determine my learning style.** Knowing my preferred learning style, such as visual, auditory, reading and writing, or kinesthetic, tells me how I learn best.

- **Explore various personality types.** Personality typing has been around for centuries and can help me understand myself and others better. I will use this information for growth.

- **Create teams by using the Four-Temperament Profile.** Knowing how to work with others' traits and strengths helps to build an effective team, and helps me learn to work well with others.

- **Integrate learning styles and personality types.** I incorporate features of other styles to maximize my learning and use all my brain power to learn new skills and information.

- **Apply the Adult Learning Cycle.** This five-step process demonstrates that learning comes from repetition, practice, and recall. Integrate VARK into the cycle.

- **Adjust to my instructor's teaching style.** I will use creative strategies to maximize my learning in every class. I have the ability to adapt and grow and make each class work.

- **Make it simple by focusing my time.** I can accomplish much more by focusing my efforts on the task at hand instead of being distracted.

- **Create lasting change through the power of habits.** I learned that by making just one key change, I can create positive habits in several areas of my life.

Performance Strategies

Following are the top 10 strategies for becoming a lifelong learner.

- A positive, open mindset creates growth and sees challenges as opportunities.
- Practice self-management and emotional control to create the results you want.
- Use critical thinking, creativity, reflection, and honesty in self-assessment.
- Practice visualization and state affirmations that focus on positive outcomes.
- Create a personal mission statement to give you direction, purpose, and meaning.
- Make the connection between school and job success.
- Discover your learning and personality styles and integrate all learning styles.
- Apply the Adult Learning Cycle to maximize your learning.
- Make it simple by focusing on one task or strategy at a time.
- It's not that complicated. You will have more success in school, work, and life if you have a positive and open mindset that embraces change and views challenges as opportunities to learn and grow. You will be able to bounce back from setbacks knowing that with effort you can learn new strategies to achieve your goals.

Tech for Success

- **Blog or digital journal.** Enhance critical thinking and creativity by keeping a journal of reflection and self-assessment. This allows for easy updating and gathering of information, which can be pulled into your career portfolio later.
- **Mission statement note cards.** To keep yourself motivated and focused, write your goals and mission statement on note cards and share them with family and friends.
- **Online self-assessments.** Check with the career center to explore careers that fit your personality, such as the Learning and Study Strategies Inventory (LASSI).

Endnotes

[1] J. A. Dusek, H. H. Out, A. L. Wohlhueter, M. Bhasin, L. F. Żerbini, M. G. Joseph, H. Benson, and T. A. Libermann, "Genomic Counter-Stress Changes Induced by the Relaxation Response," *PLOS ONE* 3, no. 7 (2008), p. e2576.

[2] Paul Bach-y-Rita, *Brain Mechanisms and Sensory Substitution* (New York: Academic Press, 1972).

Study Team Notes

Career *in* Focus

michaeljung/Shutterstock

Louis Parker
ACCOUNTANT AND FINANCIAL PLANNER

Related Majors: Accounting, Business Administration, Economics, Finance

Setting Business Goals

Louis Parker is a certified public accountant (CPA) and financial planner. In 2004, he started his own business, Parker Inc., by offering accounting services. Louis prepares taxes, financial reports, and payroll, and he does bookkeeping for individuals and small businesses. He employs three full-time and one part-time assistant but needs five full-time workers to help during peak tax season (January–April).

To get feedback on his services, Louis occasionally does a survey of his clients. The survey shows whether his clients are getting the services they want at prices they believe are reasonable. Louis uses the results of the survey to set goals and plan for the future.

One of Louis's goals is to continually increase business, as Louis believes that, without marketing and growth, his business will decline. Louis has used telemarketing services and social media to help him initiate contact with prospective clients.

A few years ago, Louis decided to add financial planning because his clients were continually asking for his advice in financial areas. Financial planners help clients attain financial goals, such as retirement or a college education for their children. Louis was able to get certified in financial planning. Because he is affiliated with a financial services organization, he sometimes helps clients invest in the stock market, mainly in mutual funds. Currently, financial planning is only 10 percent of his business, but Louis's goal is to eventually increase that amount to 30 percent.

CRITICAL THINKING How might a survey of his clients help Louis assess his personal strengths and weaknesses? What strategies should he put in place to follow up on client feedback? How can he incorporate the feedback into his long-term goals?

Peak Performer Profile

Blake Mycoskie

In just his thirties, Blake Mycoskie has already had an "amazing race" of a life. He started his first business (a campus laundry service) while attending college at Southern Methodist University. The business was successful and, after selling it, Blake continued to create successful businesses—five altogether. It was after competing on the CBS primetime show *The Amazing Race,* however, that Mycoskie realized his true passion. He returned to all of the countries he had raced through on the show and was struck by the extreme poverty of Argentina. He decided then that he needed to do something to help.

In May 2006, Mycoskie used the skills and experiences he had acquired creating and owning a company and took a risk by doing something he had no knowledge of: making shoes. TOMS: Shoes for Tomorrow was created, a shoe company that promised that for every pair of shoes purchased, TOMS would give a pair to a child in need. His initial pledge of 250 shoes to children in Argentina quickly outpaced his expectations, and on that first Shoe Drop, TOMS gave 10,000 pairs of new shoes to children Mycoskie had met on previous visits. By 2010, TOMS had given more than 600,000 pairs of new shoes to children in need around the world. In 2011, TOMS branched into eyewear and pledged the same kind of support to improve vision throughout the world.

In 2011, Mycoskie authored *Start Something That Matters,* a best-seller that highlights the importance of social entrepreneurship. Mycoskie has said that his favorite quote is by Gandhi: "Be the change you wish to see in the world." By thinking critically about his different areas of knowledge and passions, Mycoskie was truly able to understand how he could effect the change he wanted to see in the world.

PERFORMANCE THINKING How did Blake Mycoskie use the principles discussed in this chapter to create TOMS? Would the company have been as successful if Mycoskie had been unable to make the initial connection between his skills and his developing passion and new mission in life?

CHECK IT OUT TOMS's "One Day Without Shoes" movement asks people from all over the world to do one thing together: walk barefoot for a day. You can find out more about this, World Sight Day, and other company events that support their "One for One" mission at www.toms.com/our-movement. Read some of the "Notes from the Field" stories posted on the website. Which one most affected you? How are online movements such as this capable of making people better understand the difficulties faced by other people in the world?

Starting Today

Choose one strategy you learned in this chapter and apply it.

_____

_____

_____

What obstacles will you likely face? Write out a plan for overcoming them.

_____

_____

_____

Review Questions

Based on what you have learned in this chapter, write your answers to the following questions:

1. What is a peak performer? List at least three characteristics.

_____

_____

2. How can visualization help you overcome obstacles?

_____

_____

3. Explain how you can integrate VARK when dealing with feeling overwhelmed or homesick (visual, auditory, reading and writing, and kinesthetic).

_____

_____

4. How can knowing your learning style and personality type help you at work?

_____

_____

5. Why is it important to determine your instructor's teaching style as well as your own learning style?

_____

_____

Making a Commitment

In the Classroom

Eric Silver is a freshman in college. He doesn't know what major to choose and isn't even sure if he wants to continue going to college. At times, he feels like he's just doing this for his parents. In high school, he never settled on a favorite subject, though he did briefly consider becoming a private investigator after reading a detective novel. His peers seem more committed to college and have better study habits. Eric prefers a hands-on approach to learning, and he finds it difficult to concentrate while studying or listening to a lecture. However, he enjoys the outdoors and is creative. Once he gets involved in a project he finds interesting, he is very committed.

1. What strategies from this chapter would be most useful to help Eric understand himself better and gain a sense of commitment?

   _____

   _____

2. What would you suggest to Eric to help him find direction?

   _____

   _____

In the Workplace

Eric has taken a job as a law enforcement officer. He feels more comfortable in this job than he did in school because he knows he performs best when actively learning. He enjoys teamwork and the exchange of ideas with his co-workers. Eric also realizes that, in order to advance in his work, he needs to continue his education. He is concerned about balancing his work, school, and family life. He does admit that he did not excel in subjects he was less interested in. Eric never learned effective study habits but realizes that he must be disciplined when returning to college.

3. What suggestions would you give Eric to help him do better in school?

   _____

   _____

4. Under what category of learning style does Eric fall, and what are the ineffective traits of this style that he needs to work on most?

   _____

   _____

Applying the ABC Method of Self-Management

In the Journal Entry, you were asked to think about a time when you felt overwhelmed. How will a positive, open mindset help you make positive choices?

_____

_____

_____

Think about the obstacles you may have faced to get to this point and what you did to overcome them. How does having a positive mindset help you focus on growth?

_____

_____

_____

Now apply the ABC Method to the Self-Management section which opens Chapter 1:

A = Accept Reality: Acknowledge and accept the situation and your emotions.

_____

B = Breathe: Take a deep breath to calm, increase clarity, and feel beloved.

_____

C = Choose: Choose the most appropriate behavior for the most positive consequences.

_____

Write out a script. For example: Even though I'm feeling overwhelmed and anxious, I still love and accept myself at this present moment and continue to grow. I breathe deeply, calm down, and put this in perspective. I know that I can tolerate these feelings of distress. They will pass as I become more confident, aware of what is expected of me and become better at managing my time. I choose to talk with my instructors, look for resources that can help me, and form study groups. I will focus on being positive and healthy. With consistent practice, good study habits, and working with my professors, I'll be successful. I am so grateful for the opportunity to learn, grow, and stretch myself.

CHAPTER 1 | REVIEW AND APPLICATIONS

My Learning Style, Personality Types, and Temperament

LEARNING STYLES (VARK)

I am a(n) (circle one):

Visual learner   Auditory learner   Reader/writer learner   Kinesthetic learner

The following learning habits make me most like this learning style:

What features of the three other learning styles should I incorporate to make me a well-rounded learner? How can adding the reading/writing component help me be more effective (VARK).

PERSONALITY TYPES

I am a(n) (circle one from each pair):

Extrovert or introvert   Sensor or intuitive   Thinker or feeler   Judger or perceiver

The following characteristics make me most like these personality types:

How can I incorporate positive features of the opposite personality types?

TEMPERAMENTS

I am a(n) (circle one):

Analyzer   Supporter   Creator   Director

The following characteristics make me most like this temperament:

What positive behaviors/traits can I incorporate from the other three temperaments?

Applying the Four-Temperament Profile

You've explored your temperament and discovered your preferred learning style and personality type. Apply this knowledge by associating with people who have various styles and find ways to relate to and work more effectively with different people.

For example, let's say that you are assigned to a five-person team that will present a serious public health issue to your personal health class. You are a supporter type, and you find yourself having a conflict with Joe, a director type. You are in your first meeting, and Joe is ready to choose a topic for the group project, even though one team member is absent.

Apply the ABC Method of Self-Management to focus your energies on building rapport and understanding:

A = Actual event: "Joe wants to choose a topic for the group project, even though one person isn't here to voice her opinion."

B = Beliefs: "I think we are not taking the time to be sensitive to the needs of all the team members. Everyone should be present before we make a decision. Joe is trying to take control of the group and is just impatient. I'm worried that the absent group member will not like the decision or may be hurt that she wasn't involved. I resent being rushed and worry that conflict will result. Maybe this person will even quit the group."

C = Challenge: "What is the worst thing that could happen if we choose a topic today? We can always refocus later if we find this topic doesn't fit our goals. Chances are, the absent member would agree with the topic in question, anyhow. Joe is probably not impatient—he just wants to make a decision and get us moving. I'm glad our group is made up of different strengths and personalities. Our team members have complementary strengths and respect and work well with one another. I know that Joe will keep us moving forward and will be sensitive to my concerns that we listen to one another and respect one another's feelings."

Are you experiencing a similar situation or conflict in your school, work, or personal life? If so, use the ABC Method to visualize a positive solution:

A = Actual event:

_____

_____

B = Beliefs:

_____

_____

C = Challenge:

_____

_____

Autobiography

The purpose of this exercise is to look back and assess how you learned skills and competencies. Write down the turning points, major events, and significant experiences of your life. This autobiography, or chronological record, will note events that helped you make decisions, set goals, or discover something about yourself. Record both negative and positive experiences and what you learned from them. You may want to review SCANS and the qualities of peak performers to help you think of essential qualities and skills for college and job success. Reflect on how you learned essential qualities and skills. Add this page to your Career Development Portfolio—for example,

Year/Event	Learned Experience
2001 Moved to Michigan.	Learned to make new friends and be flexible.
2003 First job baby-sitting.	Learned responsibility and critical thinking.
2005 Grandmother became ill.	Helped care. Learned dependability, compassion.

Year/Event	Learned Experience

Build Peak Habits

LEARNING OUTCOMES

In this chapter, you will learn to

2-1 Describe an open, positive mindset and how it creates success

2-2 Describe the top 10 qualities of peak performers

2-3 Adapt and change by developing positive habits

2-4 Overcome obstacles with positive habits

SELF-MANAGEMENT

I would really like to get healthier and get into shape. I set up a really ambitious schedule of eating healthy and jogging and I joined a gym, but after a week I became discouraged. Running at 6 in the morning was too hard and I find myself grabbing snacks. I just couldn't make it to the gym every night, so now I feel like a failure. How do I create healthy habits when I'm so busy and clearly lack will power?

Stacy Able/Getty Images

Have you ever had a similar experience? Do you vow to start an exercise program and get in better shape only to find that you quit in a few days or weeks. In this chapter, you'll learn the power of habits and how they can create discipline and willpower. You will learn to focus on the patterns that shape college, job, and life success. The simple habit cycle illustrates simple steps for planning and creating lasting habits. You can leverage your success by taking little steps and creating daily practices that build positive habits. These habits change the way your brain works and make college, your job, and life more enjoyable. Little success accumulates into big changes.

JOURNAL ENTRY In **Worksheet 2.2**, think of a time when you knew what to do but kept repeating negative habits. How would positive visualization have helped you?

Throughout this text, we will discuss many strategies for doing well in school, your career, and your personal life. You will have a sense of your strengths and areas where you'd like to improve. You will learn how to manage your time, succeed at tests, become healthier, and develop healthy relationships. Acquiring knowledge and skills is one thing, but actually making these strategies part of your life is another. *That is where the power of a positive, open, growth mindset comes in.* There has been an explosion of brain research and books about the power of habits in the last decade, including *The Power of Habit* by Charles Duhigg and *Brainstorm* by Daniel J. Siegel, M.D. This important research has shown that people can take control and succeed by creating a growth mindset and positive habits.

Build Better Habits

Habits are powerful and shape your life. They include personal *qualities* like being honest, proactive, or resilient. **Habits** are consistent attitudes, behaviors, and activities that you create for success. The good news is you can take control and change your habits by deliberately choosing new positive attitudes and behaviors and consciously repeating them until they are part of your everyday life. Habits help you stretch and grow.

Take the simple act of walking. For most of us, walking and talking are routine and automatic. A person who is in a wheelchair, however, must navigate with thought and planning. A person who has a stroke must relearn to walk and talk and will tell you that they are complex activities that require intense concentration, focus, and hours of practice. A baby is undaunted by this obstacle and meets each day with enthusiasm and resolve. This complex series of tasks and movements becomes automatic. Habits can also be deliberately designed. *Each chapter in this book will feature a model (called the* **Habit Cycle***) that shows you how to change your negative habits into positive habits that support your goals.* Let's take another look at the Self-Management scene, which illustrates why it's so hard to create exercise habits.

Three Parts of a Habit

Starting a new exercise program can be daunting and requires motivation and effort. It helps if you start with a positive and open mindset that focuses on growth and resiliency rather than a negative attitude that gives up at the first setback. Sticking to it is the mark of a growth mindset. Habits can help you develop perseverance. There are three main parts to building a new habit: the *trigger,* the *behavior,* and the *reward.*

TRIGGERS

If you really want to start jogging every morning or doing yoga in a chair, it is important that you choose a simple **trigger** (like putting your running shoes or yoga pants right next to your bed the night before). This will help set the behavior in motion. *The shoes or yoga mat are the triggers* and once they are on, you're more likely to go for that run or do yoga.

Triggers can be anything. Some are *visual* such as a television commercial or picture of a hamburger, some are *auditory* such as a song or sound of a voice, some are *tactile* such as the feel of sand, and some activate the sense of smell such as flowers or passing a Cinnabon store. Some triggers relate to a *certain place and time of day,* like being in a classroom, or a specific study time. The library can be a powerful trigger for studying.

ROUTINES

A **routine behavior** is the behavior you usually perform when you see the trigger. A food commercial triggers the behavior of going to the fridge. The running shoes or yoga mat triggers the behavior of going for a run. When you are actively cultivating new habits, you'll need to think about what routine behavior you want to do each time. But soon, after repeating the habit a number of times, that behavior will become automatic. Routine creates growth.

REWARDS

Rewards keep you motivated! A **reward** can range from socializing, to food, or to feelings of belonging, pride, and accomplishment. In our jogging example, you could choose a reward such as jogging with a friend and having a healthy snack afterward. Once you have jogged for a week or so, the endorphins and other neurochemicals that a good workout releases will be an internal reward. Your brain will start to expect and crave the endorphins, socializing, and the sense of accomplishment and pride that you are sticking with a goal.

Building the Habit: The Habit Cycle

Eventually this will become an unconscious behavior, or habit! Building a habit involves four main steps:

Step 1   Acknowledge a trigger. (running shoes)
Step 2   Develop a routine behavior. (Put on your running shoes and go for your run)
Step 3   Create a reward. (good food and socializing)
Step 4   *Practice! Practice! Practice!*

You can learn new habits, but you must consciously apply and practice them. In a sense, you must "freeze" new patterns through consistent repetition. This doesn't

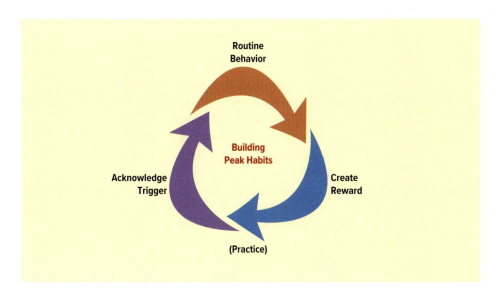

mean that you won't have a setback now and then, but you will be able to bounce back and get on track.

Applying the Habit Cycle: Homesickness

The Habit Cycle can be applied to anything. Homesickness is a big obstacle for many new students. Some students don't feel as if they belong and feel so lonely that they decide to drop out of college even if graduating is a strong goal. So how can they create habits that enhance their sense of belonging and help them become engaged and involved? The content will vary, but the process remains the same for all habits. Let's break it down.

First, let's determine when the *trigger* is most likely to occur. When I was in college, Sunday was the day that triggered homesickness. I knew my family would be having a nice dinner and be enjoying each other. So I created a *routine* that distracted me from feeling lonely and created a positive habit. I focused on exercise. I went for a hike or jog in the morning with a friend, had brunch with friends, and set up an intense study time in the afternoon at the library, followed by dinner at night with friends. I always called home every Sunday night to talk about the week and my fun-filled day—even though I was still homesick. My *rewards* were the endorphins after exercising, the socializing with friends, the good food, and the feelings of accomplishment after studying. It worked.

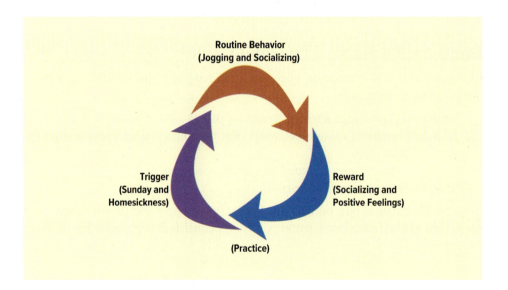

Over time, my routine was established and became automatic. I craved the endorphin rush so I started to exercise three or four times a week. Soon I was meeting more friends and becoming engaged in college activities. I felt I belonged. Exercise was my key habit, but it affected every aspect of my day. I ate better, slept better, became more involved and made many friends, and got better grades—all because of one **key habit**. *Key habits are habits that impact multiple aspects of your life: exercising, sleeping better, eating better.* What started out as a way to cope with homesickness has become a lifetime positive habit of exercise.

Knowing how to develop a positive, open mindset that focuses on growth will give you the confidence to take risks, grow, contribute, and overcome setbacks when you feel frustrated and discouraged. Let's look at how to turn strategies from this text into lasting habits.

The 10 Qualities of Peak Performers

In Chapter 3, we will discuss the importance of emotional maturity for school, job, and life success. You may have a high IQ, talent, skills, and experience, but, if you lack emotional maturity and such important qualities as responsibility, effort, commitment, a positive attitude, interpersonal skills, and especially character and integrity, you will have difficulty in all areas of life. However, it is not enough to review essential traits and qualities of emotional maturity. You must commit to making them part of your mindset and daily habits. Be willing to learn, grow, develop resilience, and confront challenges. Which of the ten qualities in **Figure 2.1** do you think is most important? How do you demonstrate this quality?

1. **Be honest.** As we will stress throughout this book, if you lack integrity, all your positive qualities—from skill and experience to intelligence and productivity—are meaningless. Practice the quality of honesty by being truthful, fair, kind, compassionate, and respectful. Doing the right thing is a decision and with practice it will become a habit.

2. **Be positive and open.** Greet each day and every event as opportunities to grow and learn. Neuroscience research has shown that people are more successful in college and at work when they are happier and more positive.[1] *A positive mindset is not wishful, magical thinking, it is based on the belief that essential qualities are not fixed but can be cultivated through effort and positive habits.* It is rational, resourceful thinking that confronts challenges and views them as opportunities for growth and learning. The ABC Method of Self-Management shows you how your thoughts create your feelings, which can affect how you interpret events. Learn to dispel negative thoughts and replace them with realistic, optimistic, and empowering thoughts and behaviors. Make a habit of creating a positive mindset that keeps you centered, rational, productive, and calm even in the midst of confusion and turmoil at college or in your job.

THE 10 QUALITIES OF PEAK PERFORMERS

1 Be honest.
2 Be positive.
3 Be responsible.
4 Be resilient.
5 Be engaged.
6 Be willing to learn.
7 Be supportive.
8 Be a creative problem solver.
9 Be disciplined.
10 Be grateful.

Figure 2.1

Peak Qualities

Peak performers translate positive qualities into action. *Do you demonstrate these qualities consistently?*

Image Source/Getty Images

3. **Be responsible.** You may not always feel like keeping your commitments to yourself or your instructors, friends, co-workers, or supervisors, but meeting obligations is the mark of a mature, responsible person. For example, a major obligation for many students is the timely repayment of student loans. Develop the quality of responsibility by doing what you say you're going to do, showing up on time, and keeping your agreements. Too many students want to bail when they feel overwhelmed or quit their job when they feel overworked and underappreciated. Stick with it!

4. **Be resilient.** Adversity happens to everyone. Even good students sometimes forget assignments, miss deadlines, and score low on tests. Even hard-working people receive critical feedback or get laid off or fired. A positive, open mindset does not look at failure as being fixed, but as an opportunity to learn and grow. The key is to develop resiliency and focus on effort and perseverance. Learn to reframe your setbacks as stepping-stones to your final goal and energize yourself to take positive action.

5. **Be engaged.** Peak performers do not sit back and wait for life to happen. They are engaged and active and want to contribute. This means shifting a self-centered "what's in it for me?" attitude to a "how can I be more involved and useful?" attitude. One way to sabotage your classes or career is to expect your instructors or supervisor to make your life interesting. Many careers can be boring or monotonous at times, and some classes are less than spellbinding. Develop the quality of being engaged and using your imagination and creativity to make any situation challenging and fun. Being engaged is the key factor in staying in college and keeping a job.

6. **Be willing to learn.** You may find yourself needing to take a remedial course, get tutoring, or brush up on basics. People with a positive, open mindset are willing to do, grow, and learn. They are flexible and constantly stretching themselves. Many employees can wind up in a job without growth potential if they refuse to learn new skills. The quality of being curious, willing to learn, and eager for growth will be a lifelong habit with practice.

7. **Be supportive and connect.** School provides an excellent opportunity to develop empathy and to support, cooperate, and collaborate with people from different backgrounds. Every day, look for opportunities for learning and growth for yourself and people around you. Mutual support and kindness are qualities worth developing into lasting habits. Healthy, supportive relationships require effort and care.

8. **Be a creative problem solver.** Creativity and critical thinking are not just skills, but a mindset that you can develop into habits. Challenge your beliefs and try new approaches to problem solving. Critical thinking also helps you distinguish between an inconvenience and a real problem. Some people spend a great deal of time and energy getting angry at minor annoyances or events they cannot change—such as bad weather, a delayed flight, or a friend who doesn't meet some expectation. Critical thinking helps you put events in perspective and "wakes up" your

• Be Willing to Learn
Many are finding it necessary to further their education after a number of years in the workforce. *What percentage of your fellow students are returning students? What are some of the reasons they are taking classes or pursuing a degree?*

Hemera Technologies/Getty Images

creative mind. Instead of postponing, ignoring, or complaining, you actively engage in exploring solutions and being focused.

9. **Be disciplined and use self-control.** Peak performers do what needs to be done, not simply what they want to do. They keep up on assignments, set goals, and carve out time throughout the day to focus on priorities. Discipline demands mental and physical conditioning, planning, and effort and being able to manage stress and anger. As Benjamin Franklin said, "Anger always has its reasons, but seldom good ones." Getting angry rarely solves problems, but it can create big ones. Through discipline and awareness, you can overcome impulsive reactions and learn to pause and breathe before reacting in haste. This key habit will serve you well in college, your job, and life.

10. **Be grateful.** Gratitude works. It is a key component of happiness and enhances well-being and creates a sense of meaning. Focus on what you have, not on what you don't have and don't compare your life with others. Learn to listen to, appreciate, and renew your body, mind, and spirit. Take time to rest, exercise, and eat healthy foods. Spend time reading, visualizing, creatively solving problems, writing, and challenging yourself to learn and be open to new ideas. Create quiet time for reflection and renewal. Write a letter to someone who has been kind or generous to you and read it to them. *Gratitude is a mindset that looks for the good and gives thanks every day for the opportunity to serve and grow.* Gratitude changes your life in so many positive ways.

> **"Wear gratitude like a cloak and it will feed every corner of your life."**
> **RUMI**
> *Poet*

The Importance of a Positive Attitude

A positive, open mindset that focuses on growth and learning is the most important factor in school and life success.[2] It allows you to transform your life through effort and the willingness to grow instead of looking at your intelligence and qualities as being fixed. It focuses on overcoming shortcomings instead of hiding them. It gives you the persistence to stick with it and stretch yourself in challenging times. It creates grit.

In Chapter 11, you will learn about the tendency to see what you already believe. People have mindsets that filter information. Each of us has attitudes or beliefs about people and events, and these attitudes influence what parts of our perception we allow our brain to interpret and what parts we filter out. Your attitude shapes the way you relate to others and to the world and even how you see yourself. You can create positive, open beliefs that help you succeed.

Most people resist change. Even when you are aware of a bad habit, it can be difficult to change it. However, the ability to adapt to new situations is not only important in school but also crucial in the workplace. Accountemps, a temporary staffing service for accounting professionals, asked 1,400 executives to rank the characteristics essential for an employee to succeed. From the list, "adapts easily to change" and "motivated to learn new skills" ranked #1 and #2.

Strategies for Creating Positive Change

Habits are learned and can be unlearned. Adopting new habits requires a desire to change, as well as consistent effort, time, and commitment. Try the following strategies for eliminating ineffective habits and acquiring lasting, positive new ones.

Brian Hagiwara/Getty Images

Is the glass half empty or half full?

1. **Be willing to change.** As with all learning, you must see the value of developing positive habits. It's easy to make excuses, but you must be willing to find reasons to change. Identify your goals: "I want to be more positive and get along with people." "I am determined to see problems as challenges and find creative alternatives." "I will take charge of my life. I have control over my thoughts and behavior."

2. **Focus on the positive.** Are you a glass-half-empty or glass-half-full type of person? Practice the ability to see the good qualities in yourself and others and the positive side of situations. Dispute negative thoughts with critical thinking, and use creative problem solving to explore the best alternatives—for example, "I missed my study group meeting. I'll e-mail my test questions to the group and offer to do extra summaries."

3. **Develop specific goals.** Statements such as "I wish I could get better grades" and "I hope I can study more" are too general and only help you continue bad habits. Goals such as "I will study for 40 minutes, two times a day, in my study area or library" are specific enough to help you measure your achievement.

4. **Start small.** You will become discouraged if you try too many changes, too fast. Instead of training for a marathon, set a goal of walking 30 minutes a day. Block out morning or afternoon to focus on studying and consistently do this until it becomes a habit. When completing **Personal Evaluation Notebook 2.1,** assess your habits and put a star by the areas you most want to work on. Keep it simple and just get started.

5. **Start small.** *Realize that consistently making positive changes each day will produce major results.* Sometimes the smallest changes make the biggest difference. For example, don't put off starting an exercise program because you don't have time for a long workout. Instead, get outdoors whenever possible. Similarly, being just a little more organized, finding small ways to be kind and supportive, and doing just a little more than what is expected of you are simple steps that can lead to positive change. That's the 80/20 rule (20 percent more effort for 80 percent more results) and it works.

6. **Use visualization and affirmations to imagine success.** Imagine yourself progressing through all the steps toward your desired goal. For example, see yourself concentrating in your quiet study area. Affirm, "I am calm and able to concentrate. I enjoy studying and feel good about completing projects." Before you get up in the morning, imagine your day unfolding effortlessly: "I am positive, organized, and focused."

7. **Observe and model others.** How do successful people think, act, and relate to others? Do students who get good grades have certain habits that contribute to their success? Research indicates that successful students study consistently in a quiet area, regularly attend classes, are punctual, and concentrate on the lecture. Model this behavior and form study groups with students who are motivated and have effective study habits.

8. **Be aware of your thoughts and behaviors.** For example, you may notice that the schoolwork you complete late at night is not as thorough as the work you complete earlier in the day. Awareness of this pattern may prompt you to change your schedule for schoolwork. You may encounter less stress in the morning when you take 10 minutes the night before to decide what to wear and check the next day's events.

Personal Evaluation Notebook

Make a Commitment to Learn and Apply Positive Habits

Read the following questions and answer each question by circling either Yes or No as each statement applies to you. Discuss with your study group.

Yes/No	1.	Have you created a study area that helps you concentrate?
Yes/No	2.	Do you make learning physical (field trips, using all your senses, being out in nature)? How?
Yes/No	3.	Do you preview each chapter before you read it? Describe.
Yes/No	4.	Do you create a positive, growth-oriented mindset each day?
Yes/No	5.	Do you write summaries of chapters?
Yes/No	6.	Do you outline your papers? Which method works best for you?
Yes/No	7.	Do you proofread your papers several times?
Yes/No	8.	Do you rehearse your speeches until you are confident?
Yes/No	9.	Do you attend every class?
Yes/No	10.	Am I attentive during class?
Yes/No	11.	Do you listen attentively and take good notes?
Yes/No	12.	Do you review your notes within 24 hours?
Yes/No	13.	Do you get help early? What resources have you used?
Yes/No	14.	Do you participate in class and ask questions?
Yes/No	15.	Have you developed rapport with each of your instructors?
Yes/No	16.	Have you joined a study team? For which classes?
Yes/No	17.	Do you study and review regularly each day?
Yes/No	18.	Do you complete tasks and assignments first and then socialize?
Yes/No	19.	Do you recite and restate to enhance your memory skills?
Yes/No	20.	Do you take advantage of campus and community activities?
Yes/No	21.	Can you create a motivated, resourceful state of mind?
Yes/No	22.	Do you know how to solve problems creatively? Explain.
Yes/No	23.	Do you use critical thinking in making decisions?
Yes/No	24.	Do you exercise daily? Describe your fitness routine.
Yes/No	25.	Do you maintain your ideal weight?
Yes/No	26.	Do you keep your body free of harmful substances and addictions?
Yes/No	27.	Do you support your body by eating healthy foods?
Yes/No	28.	Do you practice techniques for managing your stress? Explain.
Yes/No	29.	Have you developed an effective budget?
Yes/No	30.	Do you take the time for career planning?

If you answered No to many of these questions, don't be alarmed. We will be discussing strategies for many of these questions in the coming chapters. Select one of the habits you answered No to and turn it into a positive habit.

9. **Reward yourself.** Increase your motivation with specific payoffs for making a positive change in your behavior. "After I outline this chapter, I'll watch my favorite television show." Do this routine consistently until it becomes a habit. The reward should always come after achieving the results and be limited in duration. As your routine becomes automatic, your reward will shift to the internal feeling of accomplishment and pride.

10. **Be persistent.** Lasting change requires a pattern of consistent effort. Don't become discouraged and give up if you haven't seen a complete change in your behavior in a short time. Focus on growth and improvement. If you fall short one day, get back on track. Lasting change requires time and effort. Keep repeating your routine, reward yourself, and you'll soon see results, and you'll feel a sense of well-being.

Overcome Obstacles with Positive Habits

You can overcome obstacles by building better habits (**Personal Evaluation Notebook 2.2**). For example, let's say you just got home from class. It's the end of your day and you want to unwind, but you have a big paper due at the end of the week. You should sit down at your desk and begin writing, but you hear your roommates starting a movie and instead find yourself on the couch joining them. This becomes an obstacle for your study plan. The trigger is wanting to socialize, the routine is to join in, and the reward is fun with friends.

Acknowledge the *trigger* is hearing friends socializing outside your door. You create a *routine* of going to the library every afternoon so you can focus. You repeat this behavior until the place of the library and late afternoon trigger study time. Then come back and socialize for a half hour or so before or during dinner. Your *reward* is socializing and the pleasure of completing your work undistracted and getting better grades.

Overcome Obstacles to Change

The following are some obstacles that everyone, even peak performers, may encounter. (See Figure 2.2.) The key to overcoming obstacles is to anticipate and recognize them, and confront these resistors to change.

Personal Evaluation Notebook 2.2

Overcome Obstacles with Habits

Write out possible obstacles that you might face and think of creative ways to overcome them using the Habit Cycle.

State a concrete, simple goal:

1. Write out one to two specific obstacles to that goal.

   _____

   _____

   _____

2. Write out one to two specific ways to overcome those obstacles.

   _____

   _____

   _____

- **Lack of awareness.** Due to daily pressures, you may not recognize the need to make changes until there is a crisis. This concept is best demonstrated by the boiled-frog syndrome. Neurobiologist Robert Ornstein explained that, if you put a frog in a pot of water and heat the water very slowly, the frog remains

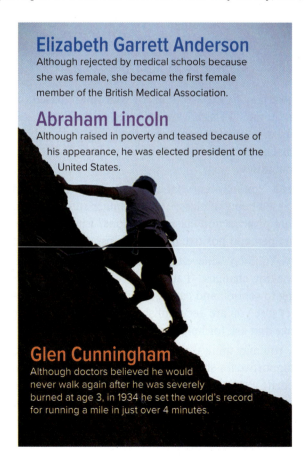

Elizabeth Garrett Anderson
Although rejected by medical schools because she was female, she became the first female member of the British Medical Association.

Abraham Lincoln
Although raised in poverty and teased because of his appearance, he was elected president of the United States.

Glen Cunningham
Although doctors believed he would never walk again after he was severely burned at age 3, in 1934 he set the world's record for running a mile in just over 4 minutes.

Figure **2.2**
Courage to Overcome

These peak performers demonstrated discipline, dedication, and a positive attitude to reach their goals despite obstacles. *What stands in your way of realizing your goals? What steps could you take to overcome obstacles?*

Javier Perini CM/Image Source

in the pot. The frog does not detect the gradual change in temperature until it boils to death. Sometimes you may be so preoccupied by daily pressures that you are unaware of the signals your body is giving you. In a sense, you become desensitized to the "pain." Take time each day to reflect about the state of your mind, body, and spirit, and look for signs of gradual pain, such as deterioration in grades or morale. This inner reflection develops self-awareness and helps you create positive, resourceful steps for getting back on track.

- **Fear of the unknown.** Change creates uncertainty. Some people even choose the certainty of misery over the uncertainty of pleasure. Fear blocks creativity, causes the imagination to run wild, and makes everyday frustrations look catastrophic: "I don't like my living situation and it's affecting my grades, but who knows what kind of roommate I would get if I asked for a change," or "I'd like to take a computer class, but I don't know if I could do the work." When you face a new and fearful situation, create a positive, open mindset that focuses on growth and opportunity to stretch yourself.

- **Familiarity and comfort.** Old habits become comfortable, familiar parts of your life, and giving them up leaves you feeling uneasy. For example, you want to get better grades and know you study best in a quiet area. However, you have always read your assignments while watching television and it's comfortable. Be open to trying strategies that have been proven to help students succeed.

- **Independence.** Making changes does not mean you are losing your independence or uniqueness. Instead of seeing your temperament or personality as fixed, realize that you can grow, stretch, and enhance your qualities. For example, let's say you are shy and awkward around others. You will not be inauthentic or selling out if you push your comfort zone and take the initiative to be more outgoing.

- **Security.** You may feel new ideas and beliefs may challenge your security. The old saying "knowledge is power" is definitely true and helps you overcome insecurities.

- **Tradition.** There may be expectations for your future based on your experiences at home: "I was always expected to stay home, raise my family, and take a job only to help supplement the family income. My sister says I'm selfish to go back to school at this time in my life." Don't let others define your goals or abilities.

- **Embarrassment.** You may fear that a new situation will embarrass you: "Will I feel embarrassed being in classes with younger students? Can I hold up my end of the team projects and class discussions? I haven't had a math course in 20 years." An open and positive mindset helps you focus on growth.

- **Responsibility.** You may believe the demands on your time are too great to allow for making changes: "I am overwhelmed by the responsibility of working, going to school, and caring for my family." Use time-management strategies to ensure you are accomplishing what you need to and identifying areas to change and ask for help.

- **Environment.** You may think your physical environment is too constricting: "My place is not supportive for studying. Our home is noisy, and there is no place where I can create a study area." It's important to negotiate when and where you can get your work done, such as at established quiet times or in the library.

- **Cost.** Your personal finances may be a concern: "It's too expensive to go to college. Tuition, textbooks, day care, and supplies all add up. Is it worth it?"

Look at your earning power with a college degree and focus on investing in education and learning.

- **Difficulty.** People can and do change with a positive, open mindset. It may seem difficult to change from a student on probation to an honor student, but it happens. People addicted to nicotine do manage to quit. People who are problem drinkers learn to drink in moderation. Alcoholics get and stay sober. Compulsive gamblers quit. Angry people learn to be patient and calm. People get out of debt and learn to save money. With effort and persistency, you can grow, be resilient, and create powerful positive habits.

See **Peak Progress 2.1** on applying the Adult Learning Cycle to developing positive habits.

Brain research has shown that college students often have increased emotional intensity, seek novelty, and like to create new friendships. All of these can enhance vitality and connectedness, but they also can lead to impulsivity and moodiness.[3]

Tracy and Cameron have been best friends since first grade and are now roommates. Tracy is fun and loyal but is scattered and unproductive and engages in risk taking. Cameron is organized, attends her classes, and studies for hours, while Tracy is focusing on going out drinking, meeting new people, or the drama in the residence hall. She says she wants to get better grades, develop more positive habits, and has asked Cameron for help.

- How can Cameron be accepting of Tracy's good qualities and allow a connection to stay strong while staying focused and productive?
- If you were Cameron, what would you say or do to help Tracy create and focus on important goals and drink in moderation?
- What resources are available on campus that might help Tracy?

THINK
CREATIVELY AND CRITICALLY

Peak Progress

2.1

Applying the Adult Learning Cycle to Develop Positive Habits

The Adult Learning Cycle can help you change your behavior and adopt long-lasting positive habits.

1. **FEEL and LISTEN.** *Why do I want to learn this?* I know that practicing positive habits and creating long-lasting changes will help me succeed in school, work, and life. What are some of my positive habits, and which ones do I need to change or improve? Do I display the 10 qualities of a peak performer? How can they increase job success? I will talk to others about my goals and listen to their response.

2. **OBSERVE and VISUALIZE.** *How does this work?* I can learn a lot about positive habits by watching others and trying new things. I will observe positive, motivated people who know how to manage their lives. What do they do? Are their positive habits obvious? I will visualize myself in this new positive habit.

3. **THINK and WRITE.** *What does this mean?* I will gather information by going to workshops and taking special classes. I will write out a plan and read it out loud. I will think about and test new ways of breaking out of old patterns, negative self-talk, and self-defeating behaviors. I will look for connections and associations with time management, stress and health issues, and addictive behaviors.

4. **DO and PRACTICE.** *What can I do with this?* I will focus on and practice one habit for a month.

I will reward myself when I make progress. I will focus on my successes and find simple, practical applications for using my new skills. Each day, I will take small steps. For example, I will spend more of my social time with my friends who like to hike or exercise, study together, and do other positive things that I enjoy, instead of hanging out with friends who just like to drink.

5. **TEACH and PRACTICE AGAIN.** *With whom can I share this?* I will share my progress with family and friends and review with them how I made changes.

Just like habits, the Adult Learning Cycle is more effective the more times you go through it. VARK helps you think through and apply the Adult Learning Cycle by integrating visual, auditory, reading and writing, and kinesthetic learning styles.

Visualize yourself in your new positive habit, and find ways to make them meaningful. *Write* out a plan to confront obstacles, and read it aloud. Now do it every day. Use your trigger to cue you to take steps. Then practice over and over again to create a routine and enjoy your reward. Write out your commitment and read it aloud:

_____

_____

_____

Personal Evaluation Notebook

2.3

Commitment Contract

Complete the following statements in your own words.

1. I most want to change _____

_____

_____

_____

_____

2. My biggest barrier is _____

_____

_____

_____

_____

3. The resources I will use to be successful are _____

_____

_____

_____

_____

4. I will reward myself by _____

_____

_____

_____

_____

5. The consequences for not achieving the results I want will be _____

_____

_____

_____

_____

Date _____

Signature _____

Contract for Change

Most people talk about changing, wishing they could be more positive or organized, but few put their commitment in writing. Many find it useful to take stock of what common resistors, or barriers, keep them from meeting their goals. Write a contract with yourself for overcoming your barriers. State the payoffs of meeting your goals. Use **Personal Evaluation Notebook 2.3** to begin drafting a personal commitment contract to achieve the "habit" of success.

TAKING CHARGE

Summary

In this chapter, I learned to

- **Practice the Habit Cycle**. I know that success comes from acknowledging triggers, creating behaviors that create a routine, creating a reward, and practicing.

- **Strive to become a peak performer**. Peak performers are successful because they develop positive qualities and practice good habits. They are positive, honest, responsible, resilient, engaged, willing to learn, supportive, disciplined, and grateful.

- **Develop a positive attitude**. I have an open mindset that focuses on growth and learning. I approach tasks with a can-do attitude and know I can change with effort. I focus on my strengths and create the thoughts and behaviors that produce the results I want.

- **Embrace change and develop positive habits**. I create habits by setting specific goals, focusing, taking small steps, and remaining positive and persistent.

- **Avoid and overcome obstacles and fears**. I overcome obstacles by sticking to it even when it's not going well. I can overcome fear and focus on positive outcomes.

- **Make a commitment**. I make a commitment to challenge myself, to be open to learning, growing, and creating positive habits. I know I can grow and change.

Performance Strategies

Following are the top 10 tips for developing good habits:

- Commit to changing self-defeating behaviors.
- Set realistic goals and specify behaviors you want to change.
- Be flexible and open to new things.
- Dispute irrational thoughts and describe events objectively.
- Work on one habit at a time, focusing on success.
- Be resilient and get back on track after setbacks.
- Use affirmations and visualization to stay focused.
- Reward yourself for making improvements.
- Observe your progress and make appropriate changes until you achieve the results you want.
- Surround yourself with support and positive influences.

Tech for Success

- **Inspiration.** In this text, you have read about many peak performers who have overcome major obstacles to get where they are today. Who truly represents a peak performer to you? If the person is even relatively well known, chances are you will find their story online. Spend at least a few minutes searching and reading about what makes this person stand out. Do you recognize any of the 10 qualities?
- **A log of positive qualities.** Record every time you demonstrate one of the 10 qualities of peak performers.

Eventually, this will create an ideal list of personal examples, which you can relay to a future employer. Keep a copy in your Career Development Portfolio. For example, "I demonstrated that I am a responsible person by taking on a second job in the summer so that I could pay off my student loans on time." "I demonstrated that I am resilient by bouncing back after my grandmother died. I took time to go home for a few days to support my parents, but I came back to school and did well."

Endnotes

[1] S. Lyubomirsky, L. King, and E. Diener, "The Benefits of Frequent Positive Affect: Does Happiness Lead to Success?" *Psychological Bulletin* 131 (2005), pp. 803–855.

[2] Carol D. Dweck, *Mindset: The New Psychology of Success* (New York: Ballantine Books, 2006).

[3] Daniel J. Siegel, *Brainstorm: The Power and Purpose of the Teenage Brain* (New York: Penguin Random House, 2015).

Study Team Notes

Career *in* Focus

Rick Torres
CARPENTER

Related Majors: Carpentry, Construction Management, Business, Computer Drafting and Design

Good Habits in the Workplace

Rick Torres is a carpenter who, like one-third of the carpenters in the United States, works as an independent contractor. This means Rick is self-employed and does a variety of carpentry jobs for homeowners, from building decks to completing remodeling jobs.

Rick starts by figuring out how to accomplish each task. Then he gives the customer a written time and cost estimate, purchases materials, completes the work, and hauls away construction debris. He needs basic math skills to provide an accurate estimate and to calculate the amount of materials required for the job. Book-keeping skills also help Rick keep track of his earnings and prepare to pay quarterly taxes. Carpentry work is often strenuous and requires expertise with large tools, such as power saws and sanders; the handling of heavy materials; and prolonged standing, climbing, bending, and kneeling. Rick often works outdoors and enjoys the flexibility and physical activity of his work. He has created the positive habits of hard work, showing up, and giving quality service to his customers.

Through the years, Rick has learned that good habits are essential to his future. Rick gains new customers through word of mouth. Customers pass his name on to others because he is reliable and has excellent skills. Rick's business has been successful because he cultivates positive attitudes and is committed to providing quality service. He shows up on time for appointments, is courteous, and follows through with his commitments. Occasionally, Rick works on neighborhood low-income projects. He sometimes hires younger carpenters to work with him and enjoys teaching them new methods of construction and positive habits.

CRITICAL THINKING What might be the result of poor work habits for a carpenter working as an independent contractor?

Peak Performer Profile

Fred Rogers

Fred Roger's life is a testament to having a positive open attitude, empathy, humility, and kindness. In addition to the very popular show, *Mr. Rogers' Neighborhood,* he was a composer of more than 200 songs, and an author of several books for children and adults. His children's books include the *Let's Talk About It* series. He also wrote the *Mister Rogers Playtime Book, You Are Special, The Giving Box, Mister Rogers Talks with Parents,* and *Dear Mister Rogers: Does It Ever Rain In Your Neighborhood?*

He earned his bachelor's degree in music composition at Rollins College in Winter Park, Florida in 1951. He went on to work in television as a floor director and assistant producer.

> "You rarely have time for everything you want in this life, so you need to make choices. And hopefully your choices can come from a deep sense of who you are."
>
> **FRED ROGERS**

PictureLux/The Hollywood Archive/Alamy Stock Photo

Fred Rogers was born in 1928 near Pittsburgh. He was a quiet child who was teased because of his weight and gentle demeanor. Because of the pain he endured from bullying, he decided that kindness was one of the most important attributes a person could develop. He focused on his love of music and becoming healthy. This sustained effort paid off. He became an accomplished musician, and established healthy habits including a daily swim. He maintained the same weight and healthy eating habits throughout his life. He developed healthy attitudes as well. *He knew that intelligence and abilities are not fixed, but with practice can be enhanced.* He focused on learning new skills and practicing kindness, compassion, and empathy. These attributes would define his life's work.

In 1953, Fred Rogers discovered educational television and knew he had found his passion. He moved back to Pittsburgh and created one of the first programs for children, *The Children's Corner.* It was revolutionary and cutting edge. Rogers served as puppeteer, composer, and organist in addition to producer. It won the Sylvania Award for the best locally produced children's program in the country. In addition to his work and being a husband and father, Fred Rogers earned an advanced degree from the University of Pittsburgh's Graduate School of Child Development. He also graduated from the Pittsburgh Theological Seminary and was ordained as a Presbyterian minister. His focus was to continue his work with children and families through television and mass media. *Mister Rogers' Neighborhood* grew in popularity and was available for national distribution through the National Educational Television and Public Broadcasting Service. Millions of children have grown up with the values of empathy and compassion.

Mr. Rogers said there were three ways to ultimate success:

1. To be kind.

2. To be kind

3. To be kind.

PERFORMANCE THINKING Explain how a positive, open, and resourceful attitude played a part in Fred Roger's success. What are some of the habits he established in his childhood and throughout life that contributed to his future achievements?

Starting Today

At least one strategy I learned in this chapter that I plan to try right away is

_____

_____

_____

What changes must I make in order for this strategy to be most effective?

_____

_____

_____

Review Questions

Based on what you have learned in this chapter, write your answers to the following questions:

1. Describe one or two qualities of peak performers that you'd like to foster.

_____

_____

2. Explain why a positive attitude is important in changing habits.

_____

_____

3. What are two or three resistors and obstacles to change?

_____

_____

4. Why are creating a routine and practicing so important to changing a habit?

_____

_____

Spreading Good Habits

In the Classroom

Carly is a welding student. She never liked high school, but her mechanical ability helped her get into a trade school. She wants to be successful and knows this is a chance for her to get a good job. Both of Carly's parents worked, so she and her brother had to get themselves off to school and prepare many of their own meals. Money has always been tight, and she hardly ever receives encouragement for positive behavior. She has never learned positive study or work habits, but is motivated to succeed.

Adam Crowley/Getty Images

1. What kind of study plan can you suggest to Carly to build her confidence and help her succeed?

   _____

   _____

2. What strategies in this chapter can help her develop positive, lasting habits?

   _____

   _____

In the Workplace

Carly is now working in a large farm equipment manufacturing plant. She has just been promoted to general supervisor in charge of welding and plumbing. She is a valued employee and has worked hard for several years for this promotion. Carly wants to ensure her success in her new job by getting training in motivation, team building, quality customer service, and communication skills.

3. What suggestions do you have for Carly to help her train her staff in good habits?

   _____

   _____

4. What strategies in this chapter can help her be more successful?

   _____

   _____

Building Better Habits

A 1960s study concerning willpower has become a classic study on how to increase delayed gratification and its long-term effects. Scientists at Stanford wanted to test the willpower of a group of four-year-olds. The tots were brought into a room and offered a deal: They could eat one marshmallow as soon as the adult left the room; or if they could wait a few minutes until someone returned, they could then have two marshmallows. About 30 percent distracted themselves by drawing or playing until the researcher came back. These kids showed self-regulatory skills and were rewarded with two treats. Many years later, the study was found and researchers tracked down many of the study's participants, who were now in high school. The tots who waited continued to demonstrate self-control years later. They earned better grades, had higher scores on the SAT, did fewer drugs, and had warm, supportive friendships. The ability to delay gratification for a greater reward had given them an advantage in many areas of their lives.

Let's say you crave academic success. Below is a Habit Cycle. Fill in the blanks to illustrate the *trigger,* the *routine,* and the *reward* to build a habit to achieve academic success.

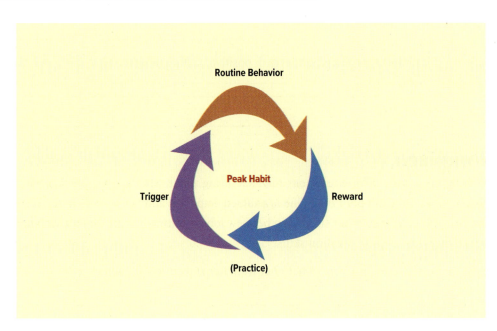

Applying the ABC Method of Self-Management

In the Journal Entry, you were asked to think of a time when you knew what to do to be healthier, but kept repeating negative habits. How would having a positive, open mindset which focuses on growth have helped you?

_____

_____

_____

Now apply the ABC Method of Self-Management and write out a script.

A = Acknowledge: Accept reality and pay attention to your emotions.

_____

_____

_____

B = Breathe: Take a deep breath, calm down, and feel beloved.

_____

_____

_____

C = Choose: Consciously choose the most appropriate action that will result in positive consequences.

Sample script: Even though I'm feeling discouraged, I love and accept myself and want to grow. I breathe deeply, calm down, and feel a deep spaciousness. I rest in this space and know that I can tolerate these feelings of discouragement. They will pass. I choose to focus on my health and energy. I'll get a full night's sleep, avoid drugs and alcohol, eat healthy, and exercise every day. I will practice mindfulness and meditate to calm my mind and create clarity. I have the ability and persistency to create healthy habits and the resiliency to overcome setbacks. Healthy habits will help me in my future career and in all areas of my life.

Overcoming Resistance to Change

Complete the following statements in your own words.

1. I resist _____

2. I resist _____

3. I resist _____

4. I resist _____

For each item you listed, write a strategy for overcoming your resistance to change.

1. _____

2. _____

3. _____

4. _____

Planning Your Career

Developing good planning habits will benefit your career. Use the following form to create a career action plan. Add multiple companies and contacts, or develop a page for each company. Add this page to your Career Development Portfolio.

Career objective:

_____

_____

What type of job?

_____

_____

When do you plan to apply?

_____

_____

Company:

_____

_____

City/State:

_____

_____

Whom should you contact?

How should you contact? Letter, e-mail, phone, or walk-in?

• Phone number:

_____

_____

• E-mail:

_____

_____

• Address:

_____

_____

Why do you want this job?

_____

_____

_____

PART ONE

Skills applicable to this job:

_____

_____

_____

Education:

_____

_____

• Internship/co-op:

_____

_____

• Courses taken:

_____

_____

• Grade point average:

_____

_____

References:

_____

_____

1. _____

2. _____

3. _____

Expand Your Emotional Intelligence

3

LEARNING OUTCOMES

In this chapter, you will learn to

3-1 Describe emotional intelligence and the key personal qualities

3-2 Describe a positive attitude and motivation

3-3 List the benefits of a higher education

3-4 Describe how to overcome obstacles with positive habits

SELF-MANAGEMENT

My roommate doesn't help with shared chores. I came home after a long day of classes to find the sink full of her dirty dishes and the garbage overflowing even though she said she'd take it out. I left a pointed note before I left for my part-time job. She texted me that the note was really rude and uncalled for. I was upset and distracted during the rest of my work shift and later I blew up at a co-worker. How can I handle my angry feelings in a more constructive way and not take my anger out on others?

Caiaimage/Sam Edwards/Getty Images

Have you ever had a similar experience? Are you easily offended by what others do or say? Have you said things in anger that have caused a rift in a relationship? Self-control is an important quality to learn for college, work, and life in general. In this chapter, you will learn how to control your emotions and create a positive and resourceful state of mind that focuses on growth.

JOURNAL ENTRY In **Worksheet 3.1**, describe a time when you were angry and lost control of your emotions. How did you feel? How did others react to your outburst? Visualize yourself calm and in control, and realize you have a choice in how you interpret events.

There is a tendency to define intelligence as a fixed score on an IQ test or the SAT or as school grades. While there are individual differences in intelligence and aptitudes, researchers are now learning that people have more capacity for lifelong learning and brain development than was previously thought. Effort, experience, cultivating personal qualities, and having an open, curious, and positive mindset that focuses on growth can make a huge difference in school and life success. In fact, research has indicated that persistence and perseverance are major predictors of college success. A landmark study by the American College Test (ACT) indicated that the primary reasons for first-year students dropping out of college were not academic but, rather, emotional difficulties, a negative attitude, and lack of motivation or purpose. In short, they didn't feel that they belonged. In the workplace, employees are often fired, not because they lack technical skills or intelligence, but because they had a negative attitude, were unwilling to learn, and could not connect or get along with others.

Employers list a positive attitude, motivation, honesty, the ability to get along with others, and a willingness to learn and grow as more important to job success than a college degree. *People who have an open and positive attitude know that through effort they can cultivate important qualities that are essential for building and maintaining strong, healthy relationships throughout life.* Essential personal qualities should be viewed as a foundation on which to build skills and knowledge.

In this chapter, you will learn the importance of emotional intelligence and why character is so important for school and job success. You will also develop personal strategies for maintaining a positive attitude and becoming self-motivated. You may realize that you are smarter than you think. You are smarter than your test scores or grades. Success in your personal life, school, and career depends more on a positive attitude, motivation, responsibility, self-control, and effort than on inborn abilities or a high IQ. Peak performers use the whole of their intelligence.

Emotional Intelligence and Maturity

Emotional intelligence is the ability to understand and manage oneself and relate effectively to others. **Maturity** is the ability to control impulses, think beyond the moment, and consider how words and actions affect others. People who have developed a set of traits that add to their maturity level increase their sense of well-being, get along better with others, are able to delay gratification, and enhance their school, job, and life success.

Emotional maturity contributes to competent behavior, problem-solving ability, socially appropriate behavior, and good communication. Being unaware of or unable to control emotions often accompanies restlessness, a short attention span, negativism, impatience, impulsiveness, and distractibility. Clearly, having emotional intelligence distinguishes peak performers from mediocre ones. Becoming more emotionally mature involves three stages:

1. **Self-awareness**—tuning in to yourself and accepting your emotions
2. **Empathy**—tuning in to others and forming healthy relationships
3. **Change**—tuning in to reality, accepting change, and creating the results you want

In Chapter 1, you explored strategies to increase your self-awareness and tune in to yourself. You assessed your skills and personal qualities in **Personal Evaluation Notebook 1.3**, Peak Performance Self-Assessment Test. By learning personality types, you also began to tune in to others as well. The central theme of this book is that you can use self-management to begin changing your thoughts, images, and behaviors to produce the results you want in every aspect of your life. Enhancing your emotional intelligence and focusing on positive personal qualities are key to success.

Character First: Integrity, Civility, and Ethics

Good character is an essential personal quality for true success. A person of good character has a core set of principles that most of us accept as constant and relatively non-controversial. These principles include fairness, honesty, respect, responsibility, caring, trustworthiness, and citizenship. Surveys of business leaders indicate that dishonesty is a top reason for on-the-job difficulties. If an employer believes an employee lacks integrity, all of that person's positive qualities—from skill and experience to productivity and intelligence—are meaningless. Employers usually list honesty or good character as an essential personal quality, followed by the ability to relate to and get along with others.

Following The Golden Rule (treating others as we want to be treated) is a simple way to weave integrity and civility into our everyday lives. The word *integrity* comes from the Latin word *integre,* meaning "wholeness." Integrity is the integration of your principles and actions. In a sense, people who have integrity "walk the talk" by consistently living up to their highest principles. Integrity is not adherence to a rigid code but, rather, a commitment to doing what is right—and the courage to do it even when it is difficult.

Civility is a set of tools for treating others with respect, kindness, and good manners, or etiquette. It also includes the sacrifices we make each day so that we live together peacefully. Civility (like integrity) requires **empathy**—understanding and having compassion for others. You can practice civility in your classes by being on time, turning off your cell phone, staying for the entire class, and listening to the instructor and other students when they speak. Civility is an important quality to learn for job and life success. Practice being aware of others' feelings and treating them with respect.

Ethics are the principles of conduct that govern a group or society. Because a company's reputation is its most important asset, most organizations have a written code of ethics that describes how people are expected to behave. It is your responsibility to know and understand the code of ethics at your place of employment and at school. Look on your school's website for statements regarding academic integrity, honesty, cheating, and plagiarism. **Cheating** is using or providing unauthorized help in test taking or on projects. One form of cheating is **plagiarism**, which means presenting someone else's ideas as if they were your own.

• **Be a "Class Act"**
These may seem like harmless acts, but they are clear examples of disrespect—for your instructor, your classmates, and your education. *How would an employer respond to this behavior on the job?*

Roy McMahon/Corbis

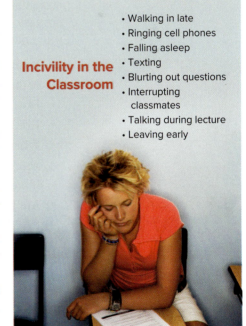

Incivility in the Classroom
- Walking in late
- Ringing cell phones
- Falling asleep
- Texting
- Blurting out questions
- Interrupting classmates
- Talking during lecture
- Leaving early

Research suggests poor sleep negatively affects every part of your life: including slowing of problem-solving skills, emotional management, poor judgment, and even increased criminal behavior.[1]

Devon's midterm exam will determine 50 percent of his final grade. He's missed several classes because of work and is afraid of failing the exam. He's tempted to buy a copy of the test. Help Devon think about the consequences if he cheats.

- If he buys it, what are the repercussions if he gets caught?
- What are potential repercussions if he *doesn't* get caught?
- How can he do better by getting more sleep? What would you advise Devon to do so that he stays on top of his studies and gets more sleep?

THINK
CREATIVELY AND CRITICALLY

The consequences of unethical behavior could result in an F grade, suspension, expulsion, or firing from a job. You always have the choice of telling the truth and being responsible for your own work.

Every day, you run into situations that test your character. **Personal Evaluation Notebook 3.1** includes questions and situations to get you thinking about your experiences. While completing this exercise, consider the personal qualities that make you smarter than you think you are, such as positive attitude, motivation, dependability, and honesty—for example, "I was raised on a farm in Michigan where hard work is valued and expected. Not only did I have farm chores, but I also worked in the garden, helped cook, and clean the house. What personal quality makes me smarter than my IQ or test scores?" If you answer "hard work," you're right. *That one personal quality—putting in extra effort—is key to success.*

Personal qualities, especially honesty, are very important when you are thinking of hiring someone to work for a business you own. A candidate sends in an outstanding résumé. She has a college degree, experience, and a great personality, and she is positive and motivated; but you find out she stole from her last employer. No matter how bright or talented someone is, you don't want a dishonest person working for you. Complete **Personal Evaluation Notebook 3.2** to see what qualities you would look for in a potential employee and which of those qualities you possess.

There is no universal code of ethics, and many questions about ethical issues do not have clear-cut answers. For example, taking money out of a cash drawer is clearly dishonest, but what about coming in late to work, padding your expense account, or using someone else's words without giving credit? You will be faced with situations in your personal, school, and business lives that will force you to make decisions that will be viewed as either ethical or unethical. Sometimes it is not easy. You will have to call on your own personal code of ethics. When defining your code and subsequent actions, ask yourself:

- Is this action against the law?
- Is this action against company policy or code of behavior?
- How would this situation read if reported on the front page of the newspaper?
- How would you explain this to your mother? To your child?
- What might be the negative consequences?
- Are you causing unnecessary harm to someone?
- If unsure, have you asked a trusted associate outside of the situation?
- Are you treating others as you would want to be treated?

Remember, unethical behavior rarely goes unnoticed!

Responsibility

Peak performers take responsibility for their thoughts, state of mind, and behavior. They don't blame others for their problems but, rather, use their energy to solve them. They are persistent and exert a consistently high effort to achieve their goals. When they say they are going to do something, they keep their commitment. People can depend on them.

Personal Evaluation Notebook 3.1

Character and Ethics

Integrity and honesty are essential qualities. It is important for you to assess and develop them as you would any skill. Use critical thinking to answer these questions.

1. What is the most difficult ethical dilemma you have faced in your life?

   _____

   _____

2. Do you have a code of ethics that helps guide you when making decisions? How did you develop it? Who or what was your guiding force?

   _____

   _____

3. Who have you known that is a role model for displaying integrity and honesty?

   _____

   _____

4. Do you have a code of ethics at your college? Where did you find it? (Hint: Check your school's website or ask the dean of students.)

   _____

   _____

Examples of being responsible include showing up on time and prepared for class, work, meetings, study teams, and so on. Responsible people own up to their mistakes and do what they can to correct them. The model in **Figure 3.1** illustrates many important, interrelated personal responsibilities. Other personal qualities related to responsibility include perseverance, punctuality, concentration, attention to details, follow-through, and respect for others. Responsibility is a key quality for college and job success.

Peak performers realize they are responsible for their attitudes and actions and know they have the power to change. They have an **internal locus of control**, which is the belief that control over life is due to attitude, behavior, choices, or character. People with an **external locus of control** have the belief that success or failure is due to outside influences, such as fate, luck, or other people. They are impulsive about immediate pleasures and easily swayed by the influences of others, and they often have a negative attitude and an inability to cope effectively with change, conflict, and frustration.

Learning to adjust to frustration and discouragement can take many forms. Some people withdraw or become critical, cynical, shy, sarcastic, or unmotivated. Blame, excuses, justification, and criticism of others are devices for those who cannot accept personal responsibility. Acknowledge your feelings, attitudes, and habits. Do they support your goal of graduating from college? If not, create a positive mindset.

Personal Evaluation Notebook 3.2

Skills and Personal Qualities

1. Jot down the skills, personal qualities, and habits you are learning and demonstrating in each of your classes.

Skills	Personal Qualities	Habits
_____	_____	_____
_____	_____	_____
_____	_____	_____

2. Pretend you own a business. List the skills and personal qualities you would want in your employees. *Which answers also appear in your lists above?*

Type of business:_____

Employees' Skills	Employees' Personal Qualities
_____	_____
_____	_____
_____	_____

Figure 3.1
Personal Responsibilities

What you do or don't do in one area of life can affect other areas of your life and other people. *What one area of personal responsibility would you improve?*

Photodisc/Getty Images

I am responsible for: Forming positive habits; Managing time and stress; My feelings and actions; Setting goals; Learning study and job skills; Knowing what resources are available; My decisions and choices; Asking for help; Assessing my skills; Personal and professional relationships; Paying back student loans; Major and career planning; Managing money; Keeping my agreements; My health and energy.

Being responsible creates a sense of integrity and a feeling of self-worth. For example, if you owe someone money or have a student loan, take responsibility for repaying the debt on schedule or make new arrangements with the lender.

Self-Control

If anger were a disease, there would be an epidemic in this country. Road rage, spousal and child abuse, and a lack of civility are just a few examples. *Emotionally mature people know how to control their thoughts and behaviors and how to resolve conflict without anger.* Conflict is an inevitable part of school and work, but it can be resolved in a positive way. Try to:

1. **Calm down.** Step back from the situation and take a deep breath. Take the drama out of the situation and observe what is happening, what behavior is triggering angry emotions, and what options you have in responding appropriately and positively. If you lash out verbally, you may cause serious harm to your relationship. Breathe.

2. **Clarify and define.** Determine exactly with whom or at what you are angry and why. What specific behavior in the other person is causing your anger or frustration? Determine whose problem it is. For example, your instructor may have an annoying tone and style of lecturing. Put it in perspective and learn to adapt and be tolerant.

3. **Listen with empathy and respect.** Empathy includes the ability to listen, understand, and respond to the feelings and needs of others. Take the tension out of the conflict by really listening and understanding the other person's point of view. Communicate that you have heard and understood by restating the other person's position.

4. **Use "I" statements.** Take ownership of your feelings. Using "I" statements— direct messages you deliver in a calm tone with supportive body language— can diffuse anger. Instead of blaming another person, express how a situation affects you. For example, you can say, "Carlos, when I hear you clicking your pen and tapping it on the desk, I'm distracted from studying." This is usually received better than saying, "Carlos, you're so rude and inconsiderate. You're driving me nuts with that pen!"

5. **Focus on one problem.** Don't rattle off every annoying behavior you can think of. Let's continue with the previous example: "In addition to clicking your pen, Carlos, I don't like how you leave your dishes in the sink, drop your towels in the bathroom, and make that annoying little sound when you eat." Work to resolve only one behavior at a time.

6. **Focus on win–win solutions.** How can you both win? Restate the problem and jot down as many different creative solutions as you can both agree on.

Don't let anger and conflict create more stress in your life and take a physical and emotional toll. You can learn to step back automatically from explosive situations and control them, rather than let your emotions control you. **Peak Progress 3.1** explores how you can use the Adult Learning Cycle to manage your emotions.

Self-Esteem and Confidence

Self-esteem is how you feel about yourself; your sense of self-worth. People with positive self-esteem have the confidence that allows them to be more open to new experiences and accepting of different people. They tend to be positive and open

Peak Progress

Applying the Adult Learning Cycle to Self-Control

The Adult Learning Cycle can help you increase your emotional intelligence. For example, you may have felt the same anger and frustration mentioned in the **Self-Management** exercise at the beginning of this chapter. Maybe it happened when you had an argument with your roommate, lost your keys, had a paper due, got cut off in traffic, or felt so overwhelmed with responsibilities that you reacted in anger.

1. **FEEL and LISTEN.** *Why do I want to learn this?* What personal meaning and interest does controlling my anger have for me? Has it been a challenge? Has it hurt important relationships in my personal life or at school or work? How will controlling my anger help me in those situations? I will acknowledge my feelings and get help. I will be mindful, listen to calming music, and getting fresh air and enjoying nature.

2. **OBSERVE and VISUALIZE.** *How does this work?* I can learn a lot about anger management by watching, listening, and engaging in trial and error. Whom do I consider an emotionally mature person? Whom do I respect because of his or her patience, understanding, and ability to deal with stressful events? When I observe the problems other people have, how do they express their anger? I'll relate to times I've been calm and patient and visualize myself in that same focused state.

3. **THINK and WRITE.** *What does this mean?* I will think about stressful situations and how I can act calmly. I will write out a script for how I'll react to likely stressful situations. I'll read it out loud. I'll

test new ways of behaving and break old patterns. I'll explore creative ways to solve problems instead of getting angry.

4. **DO and PRACTICE.** *What can I do with this?* I'll learn by doing and finding practical applications for anger management. I'll look into anger management strategies and reflect on what works and doesn't work. I'll practice being calm and centered every day. I'll count to 10, take a walk, and become more mindful.

5. **TEACH and PRACTICE AGAIN.** *Whom can I share this with?* I'll talk with others and share experiences. I'll model by example. I'll inquire about volunteering for Big Brothers/Big Sisters and mentoring so I can teach my skills to others.

Use the VARK system by integrating visual, auditory, reading and writing, and kinesthetic thinking. *Visualize* being calm and centered and in control of your emotions. Look at pictures of a calm, relaxing scene. Draw or sketch what happens to your body when you're angry and when you're calm and peaceful. *Observe* and *listen* to how peaceful people respond and how angry people react. *Listen* to calm and relaxing music and spend time in nature as you listen to the sounds. *Write out* a response to potential situations where you may become angry. *Read* your response out loud. Now just do it! Use *practical application.* Dance, sing, swim, stretch, or do yoga to reduce stress and anger. *Use your body* to calm yourself. Now return to Stage 1 and repeat. *Practice* again and again. Taking steps to control your anger pays off in all areas of your life.

to grow and learn. Because they have a sense of self-worth, they do not feel a need to put down or discriminate against others.

Confidence can develop from

- Focusing on your strengths and positive qualities and finding ways to cultivate them with others. Don't compare yourself with others.
- Learning to be resilient and move forward after disappointments and setbacks. Don't dwell on mistakes or limitations, but learn, grow, and move on.
- Using affirmations and visualizations to replace negative thoughts and images.
- Taking responsibility for your life instead of blaming others. You cannot control other people's behavior, but you have control over your own thoughts and behaviors.

- Learning skills that give you opportunities and confidence in your abilities.
- Focusing on gratitude. Look for the good in life and tell others that you appreciate them.
- Surrounding yourself with kind supportive people who feel good about themselves and make you feel good about yourself. Mutual support is key.

A Positive Attitude and Personal Motivation

There is an old story about three men working on a project in a large city in France. A curious tourist asks them, "What are you three working on?" The first man says, "I'm hauling rocks." The second man says, "I'm laying a wall." The third man says with pride, "I'm building a cathedral." The third man has a vision of the whole system. When college and work seem as tedious as hauling rocks, focus on the big picture. Your attitude, more than any other factor, influences your life. *A positive mindset creates a willingness to grow, learn, and act.* **Motivation** is the inner drive that moves you to action. Even when you are discouraged or face setbacks, motivation can help you keep on track. You may have skills, experience, intelligence, and talent, but you will accomplish little if you are not motivated to direct your energies and sustained efforts toward specific goals. Develop perseverance.

A positive open mindset attitude creates enthusiasm, vitality, optimism, and a zest for living. When you have a positive attitude, you are more likely to be on time, alert in meetings and class, and able to work well even on an unpleasant assignment. A negative, closed attitude can drain you of enthusiasm and energy and cause you to give up.

A Positive Attitude Encourages:

- Higher productivity and satisfaction
- An openness to learn and grow
- Persistent effort and hard work
- Creativity in solving problems and finding solutions
- The ability to work with diverse groups of people
- Enthusiasm and a "can do" outlook
- Confidence and higher self-esteem
- The ability to channel stress and increase energy
- A sense of purpose and direction

A Negative Attitude Makes You:

- Feel like a victim and helpless to make a change
- Focus on the worst that can happen in a situation
- Blame external circumstances for your attitude
- Focus on the negative in people and situations
- Believe adversity will last forever
- Be angry and blame other people

As discussed in Chapter 1, peak performers display a positive attitude even when faced with adversity. Having a positive attitude is more than simply seeing the glass as half full—it's a way of life.

How Needs and Desires Influence Attitudes and Motivation

One of the deepest needs in life is to become all that you can be by using all of your intelligence and potential. Abraham Maslow, a well-known psychologist, developed the theory of a hierarchy of needs in 1943. According to his theory, there are five levels of universal needs. **Figure 3.2** illustrates these levels, moving from the lower-order needs—physiological and safety and security needs—to the higher-order needs—the needs for self-esteem and self-actualization. Your lower-order needs must be met first before you can satisfy your higher-order needs. For example, participating in hobbies that foster your self-respect is difficult if you don't have enough money for food and rent. For some people, the lower-order needs include a sense of order, power, or independence. The higher levels, which address social and self-esteem factors, include the need for companionship, respect, and a sense of belonging. Self-actualization is the desire to matter, to live life as a peak performer, and to be all that we are capable of being. Living at your "peak" is using your full potential and giving it all you've got right now. The pyramid of motivational needs in **Figure 3.2** shows the relationship to student-related and job-related satisfiers.

As your lower-order needs are satisfied and cease to motivate you, you begin to direct your attention to the higher-order needs for motivation. As you go up the ladder of higher-order needs, you'll find that you're learning for the joy of new ideas and the confidence that comes from growing. You have more energy and focus for defining and pursuing your dreams and goals. You want to discover and develop your full potential. You not only love learning but also cultivate emotional maturity, character, and integrity. You are well on the path to self-actualization. According to Maslow, self-actualizing people embrace the realities of the world rather than deny or avoid them. They are creative problem solvers who make the most of their unique abilities to strive to be the best they can be. They are peak performers! Complete **Personal Evaluation Notebook 3.3** to assess what motivates you.

The Motivation Cycle

The motivation cycle in **Figure 3.3** amplifies what you learned in Chapter 1 about the power of visualization. It illustrates how your beliefs influence what you say to yourself, which in turn influences your physical reactions—breathing, muscular tension, and posture. These physical reactions influence your behavior—both your

Figure 3.2

The Basic Hierarchy of Needs

This pyramid illustrates motivational needs and how they relate to student- and job-related satisfiers.

Source: "Hierarchy of Needs" from *Motivation and Personality,* 3rd ed., by Abraham H. Maslow. Revised by Robert Frager, James Fadiman, Cynthia McReynolds, and Ruth Cox. 1987.

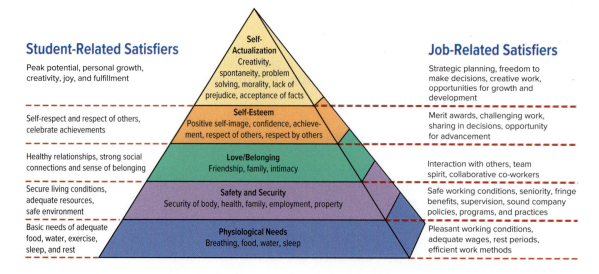

Personal Evaluation Notebook

Needs, Motivation, and Commitment

1. What needs motivate you at this time?

   _____

   _____

2. What do you think will motivate you in 20 years?

   _____

   _____

3. Complete this sentence: "For me to be more motivated, I need . . ."

   _____

   _____

4. Describe a time in your life when you were committed to something—such as a goal, a project, an event, or a relationship—that was important to you.

   _____

   _____

5. What habits helped you to be disciplined and maintain your motivation?

   _____

   _____

6. Let's say you are a 101-year-old wise elder. What advice would you give yourself at 18 and at 30 when you are a career professional?

   _____

   _____

verbal and nonverbal responses. Your emotions, body, and mind are interrelated—if you change one part, you change the whole system. Everything flows from a positive, open mindset.

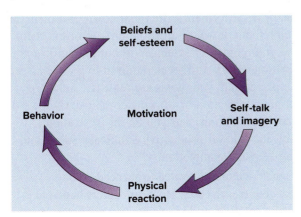

Figure 3.3
The Motivation Cycle

Your emotions, body, and mind respond to what you say to yourself. *What positive message can you send to yourself?*

Motivational Strategies

Keeping yourself motivated isn't always easy when you're feeling pressures from school, work, and family. However, you can use these motivational strategies:

1. **Act as if you are motivated.** Your attitude influences your behavior, and behavior influences attitude. The key is to first make a personal commitment to remaining positive and motivated. For example, pretend you are performing in a movie. Your character is a positive, motivated student. How do you enter the room? Are you smiling? What are your breathing, posture, and muscle tension like? What kinds of gestures and facial expressions do you use to create this character? When you act motivated, you become motivated. Study even when you don't feel like it and it will become a habit and part of your mindset.

2. **Use affirmations.** Any discussion of motivation must include your self-talk, what you say to yourself throughout the day. Once you start paying attention to your self-talk, you may be amazed at how much of it is negative. Countless thoughts, images, and phrases go through your brain daily almost unnoticed, but they have a tremendous influence on your mood and attitude. The first step, then, is to replace negative self-talk with affirmations (positive self-talk). For example, don't say, "I won't waste my time today." Instead, affirm, "I am setting goals and priorities and achieving the results I want. I have plenty of energy to accomplish all that I choose to do, and I feel good when I'm organized and centered." Complete **Personal Evaluation Notebook 3.4** to determine if your self-talk needs to become more positive.

3. **Use visualization.** If you imagine yourself behaving in certain ways, that behavior will become real. For example, businessman Calvin Payne knows the power of visualization. Before he graduated from college, he bought his graduation cap and gown and kept them in his room. He visualized himself crossing the stage in his gown to accept his diploma. This visual goal helped him when he suffered setbacks, frustration, and disappointments. He graduated with honors and now incorporates visualization techniques in his career. Visualization is a creative way to create success.

   Use visualization and imagery when you are working on a project. See scenes in detail as you sketch, draw, or write about these images.

4. **Use goals as motivational tools.** Just as an athlete visualizes crossing the finish line, you can visualize your final goal. Writing out your goal can be a great motivator and **Peak Progress 3.2** helps you distinguish long-term goals from short-term goals. For example, "I'm going to study in the library for two hours every day." "I'm going to graduate from college with a business degree in four years."

   Besides visualizing goals, peak performers write them down. Put them on your phone or computer or tape them on your bathroom mirror, or put them on yellow sticky notes around your computer screen. Without a specific goal, it's not easy to find the motivation, effort, and focus required to go to classes and complete assignments. Make certain your goals are realistic. Achieving excellence doesn't mean attaining perfection or working compulsively toward impossible goals. Trying to be a perfectionist sets you up for frustration, which can decrease your motivation, lower productivity, increase stress, and lead to failure. Take small steps toward completion.

5. **Understand expectations.** You will be more motivated to succeed if you understand what is expected of you in each class. Most instructors hand out a syllabus on the first day. Read it carefully and keep a copy in your class

Personal Evaluation Notebook 3.4

Self-Talk and Affirmations

Listen to your self-talk for a few days. Jot down the negative thoughts you say to yourself. For example, when you first wake up, do you say, "I don't want to go to class today"?

Do your thoughts and self-talk focus on lack of time, lack of money, or other problems? Observe when you are positive. How does this change your state of mind and your physical sense of well-being? List examples of your negative self-talk and positive affirmations. Writing out affirmations fires up your neurons and helps create lasting habits.

Negative Self-Talk	Positive Affirmations
1. _____	1. _____
2. _____	2. _____
3. _____	3. _____

Peak Progress 3.2

Setting Goals

As the Cheshire cat said to Alice: "If you don't know where you are going, any road will take you there." The key, then, is to figure out where you are going, and then you can determine the best way to get there. Goal setting will help you do that. But goals provide more than direction and a clear vision for the future. When appropriately understood and applied, they are very effective motivators.

It is helpful first to distinguish between goals and desires. Identifying what you want out of life (your mission statement, as discussed in Chapter 1) is an important step, but the goals themselves are not mere desires; rather, they are specific, measurable prescriptions for action. For example, if you want to be financially secure, you should start by identifying the actions that will help you fulfill that desire. Knowing that financial security is tied to education, you might make college graduation your first long-term goal. However, be careful how you construct this goal. "My goal is to have a college degree" is passive and vague. "I will earn my Bachelor of Science degree in computer technology from State University by June 2023" prescribes a clear course of action that you can break down into sequences of short-term goals, which then can be broken down into manageable daily tasks.

Your long-term goal always comes first. Sometimes when people are uncomfortable with long-term commitment, they try to address short-term goals first. Do not fall into this trap. Short-term goals are merely steps toward achieving the long-term goal, so they cannot even exist by themselves. To understand this better, imagine driving to an unfamiliar city and then trying to use GPS without having first determined where you are going. You must know where you are going before you can plan your route (as illustrated in the accompanying figure).

When defining your goals, remember:

- Desires and wishes are not goals.
- Goals prescribe action.
- Effective goals are specific and written.
- Goal setting always begins with a long-term goal.
- Short-term goals are the steps in achieving the long-term goal.
- Daily tasks are the many specific actions that fulfill short-term goals. In Chapter 4, we will explore using your goals to plan how to use your time best.

(continued)

Setting Goals *(concluded)*

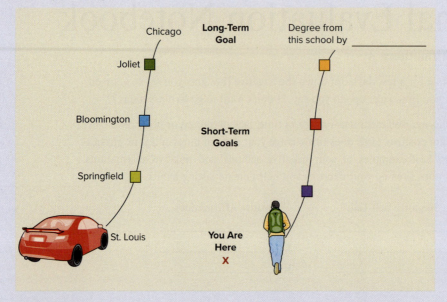

• Goal Setting

Setting goals is like planning a trip—first you need to know your destination (long-term goal). Then you determine the best route to get there, including the milestones along the way (short-term goals). *If your long-term goal is to obtain your college degree, write in some of the short-term goals you need to accomplish (such as completing coursework, consulting with advisors and instructors, obtaining financial resources, and internships).*

notebook. Review the syllabus with a study partner and clarify expectations with your instructor. Meet with your academic advisor to review general college and graduation requirements. You will find that what is expected of you in college—from personal responsibility to independent thinking—is likely to be much more intense than your previous educational experiences. (See **Peak Progress 3.3.**)

6. **Study in teams.** Success in the business world relies on teamwork—the sharing of skills, knowledge, confidence, and decision-making abilities. Teamwork aims for *synergy,* meaning the whole (the team's output) is greater than the sum of the parts (each member's abilities). When working as a team in school, you can

   - Teach each other material and outline main points.
   - Read and edit each other's reports.
   - Develop sample quizzes and test each other.
   - Learn to get along with and value different people. (We will explore healthy relationships in more detail in Chapter 13.)

7. **Stay physically and mentally healthy.** It can be difficult to motivate yourself if you are an online learner, if you are depressed, or if you don't feel well physically or emotionally. Illness can cause you to miss classes, fall behind in studying, and cause you to feel even more stressed. Eat well, get plenty of exercise and rest, and create a balance of work and play. If your depression or lack of well-being continues, seek professional help. Go to the health center or counseling center if you are depressed, anxious, or not feeling well in general. Don't wait. There are professionals who can help.

8. **Learn to reframe.** You don't have control over many situations or the actions of others, but you do have control over your responses. Reframing is choosing to see a situation in a new way. For example, to pay for school,

Peak Progress

Differences between High School and College

Entering college brings a new level of responsibility and expectations as compared to your previous educational experiences, mimicking what is expected on the job as well as managing your personal life. For example, in college, you are expected to

- Have more responsibilities and budget your time and money.
- Express your opinions logically, not just give facts.
- Motivate yourself.
- Handle more freedom and independence.
- Attend larger classes that meet for longer periods but less often.
- Be responsible for knowing procedures and graduation requirements.

- Write and read more than you have before.
- Think critically and logically.
- Receive less feedback and be tested less often but more comprehensively.
- Use several textbooks and supplemental readings.
- Complete more work and turn in higher-quality work.
- Interact with people of different values, cultures, interests, and religions.
- Learn to be tolerant and respectful of diversity.
- Encounter new ideas and critique those ideas in a thoughtful way.
- Get involved in the community, school clubs, volunteer work, and internships related to your major.

Joan works at a fast-food restaurant. She could have chosen to see this negatively. Instead, she has reframed the situation to focus on learning essential job skills. She is learning to be positive, dependable, hardworking, service-oriented, flexible, and tolerant. Joan has a new perspective on life.

9. **Reward yourself.** The simplest tasks can become discouraging without rewards for progress and completion. Set up a system of rewards for finishing projects. For an easier task, the reward might be a snack or a phone call to a friend. For a larger project, the reward might be going out to dinner or a movie. What rewards would motivate you?

10. **Make learning relevant.** Your coursework will be more motivating if you understand how the knowledge you gain and new skills you learn will relate to your career performance. You may be attending college just because you love to learn and meet new people. However, it's more likely that you are enrolled to acquire or enhance your knowledge and skills, increasing your marketability in the workforce.

The Benefits of Higher Education

You will be more motivated in your school—and more likely to graduate and excel—if you understand how attending college benefits you today and in the future.

HIGHER EDUCATION ENCOURAGES CRITICAL THINKING

Many years ago, being an educated person meant having a liberal arts education. *Liberal* comes from the Latin root word *liber,* which means "to free." A broad education is designed to free people to think and understand themselves and the world around them. The liberal arts include such areas as the arts, humanities, social sciences, mathematics, and natural sciences. Classes in philosophy, history, language, art, and sociology focus on how people think, behave, and express themselves. The liberal arts integrate many disciplines and provide a foundation for professional programs, such as criminal justice, journalism, computer systems, business, medicine, and law.

Technology is no longer a separate field of study from liberal arts but is an important tool for everyone. Employers want professionals who are creative problem solvers, have good critical thinking skills, can communicate and work well with others, can adapt to change, and understand our complex technical and social world. Liberal arts classes can help make a skilled professional a truly educated professional who integrates and understands history, culture, self, and the world. Be curious and committed to learn and grow new skills.

HIGHER EDUCATION IS A SMART FINANCIAL INVESTMENT

You will be more motivated to put in long hours of studying when you feel the goal is worth it. With rising costs and fluctuating job opportunities, some wonder if college is worth the investment. Statistics show it is. College graduates earn an average of well over $800,000 more in a lifetime than do high school graduates. (See **Figure 3.4.**) Although graduating from college or a career school won't guarantee you a job in your chosen field, it can pay off with more career opportunities, better salaries, more benefits, more job promotions, increased workplace flexibility, better workplace conditions, and greater job satisfaction. Many college career centers are committed to helping their students find employment. In addition, a college degree helps you to be a more creative person, enhances your critical thinking skills, improves relationships, opens up opportunities, exposes you to diverse people and situations, creates a knowledge base, and engages you in your community. People with college degrees tend to be healthier, exercise more, vote more often, and travel more.

Also, various reports from the U.S. Department of Labor indicate that people who attend at least two years of college tend to be more disciplined, have more self-confidence, make better decisions, and be more willing to adapt to change and learn new skills. They often have more hobbies and leisure activities, are more involved in their communities, and live longer, healthier lives.

Figure **3.4**

Annual Earnings and Employment Opportunities Based on Education

Statistically, the level of your education is directly related to your potential employment and income. *What other advantages, besides a good job and income, do you think education offers?*

Source: Bureau of Labor Statistics, Current Population Survey. April 2020.

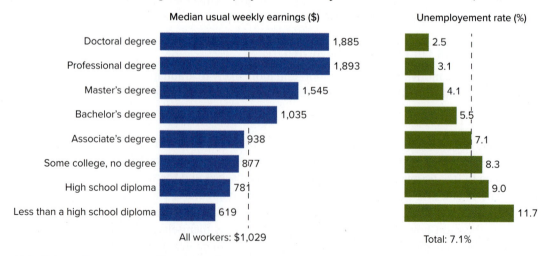

Earnings and unemployment rates by educational attainment, 2020

Note: Data are for persons age 25 and over. Earnings are for full-time wage and salary workers.

HIGHER EDUCATION PREPARES YOU FOR LIFE ON THE JOB

What you learn in school today correlates directly with finding and keeping a job, as well as succeeding in a chosen career. As you go through school, think about how the skills, personal qualities, and habits you are learning and demonstrating in class are related to job and life success. **Peak Progress 3.4** lists skills and qualities you are learning, practicing, and enhancing in your coursework and how they apply to job success.

As you develop your time- and stress-management skills, which we will explore in more detail later in this text, your habits in school and on the job will improve. Time management helps you show up for class on time and be prepared every day, leading to better grades. Punctuality in school will carry over to punctuality for work. Stress management may help you get along better with your roommates, instructors, or co-workers. Learning how to succeed in the school or college system can serve as a model for working effectively in organizational systems. Do you think you are maximizing your strengths, skills, and personal qualities? See **Peak Progress 3.5** to determine what kind of a worker/student you are and what you need to do to improve.

Peak Progress 3.4

Skills for School and Career

Skills	School Application	Career Application
Motivation	Attending class, being prepared and participating, submitting quality work on time	Performing exceptional work, striving to become proficient at necessary skills
Critical thinking	Solving case studies, equations, essays	Solving work problems, improving employee relations, responding to market changes
Creativity	Conducting experiments, developing term papers	Creating work solutions, developing products, launching sales campaigns
Time management	Scheduling studying, prepping for exams, completing papers and projects	Prioritizing workflow, hitting deadlines, product launches
Financial management	Paying fees and expenses, personal budgeting and saving, repaying student loans	Developing and managing departmental budgets, projecting growth and profits
Writing	Writing papers, speeches, essay exams, e-mails, blogs	Writing reports, e-mails, product descriptions, promotional material
Public speaking	Giving classroom speeches, presenting research, participating in class discussions	Delivering product presentations, leading and participating in meetings
Test taking	Taking quizzes and exams, applying for advanced degrees	Receiving performance reviews, certification, and licensure exams
Research	Finding, evaluating, and citing information	Linking processes to results, testing new products
Learning	Learning new content to fulfill major, maximizing learning styles	Learning new job skills, adapting to changes in technology
Systems	Understanding college rules, procedures, deadlines, expectations, resources	Understanding company rules, policies, reporting procedures
Technology	Using technology for papers, team projects, research, testing, course management	Using technology for developing reports, communicating, managing systems

Peak Progress

What Kind of Worker/Student Are You?

A peak performer or an *A* student

- Is alert, actively involved, and curious
- Consistently does more than required and shows initiative
- Consistently shows enthusiasm and resiliency
- Is positive and engaged and eager to learn
- Can solve problems and make sound decisions
- Is dependable, prompt, neat, accurate, and thorough
- Attends work/class every day and is on time and prepared

A good worker or a *B* student

- Frequently does more than is required
- Is usually attentive, positive, and enthusiastic
- Completes most work accurately, neatly, and thoroughly
- Often uses critical thinking to solve problems and make decisions
- Attends work/class almost every day and is usually on time and prepared

An average worker or a *C* student

- Completes the tasks that are required
- Shows a willingness to follow instructions and learn
- Is generally involved, dependable, enthusiastic, and positive
- Provides work that is mostly thorough, accurate, and prompt
- Misses some work/classes

A problem worker or a *D* student

- Usually does the minimum of what is required
- Has irregular attendance, is often late, or is distracted
- Lacks a positive attitude or the ability to work well with others

- Often misunderstands assignments and deadlines
- Lacks thoroughness
- Misses many days of work/classes

An unacceptable worker or an *F* student

- Does not do the work that is required
- Is inattentive, bored, negative, and uninvolved
- Is not dependable and turns in work that is incorrect and incomplete
- Misses a significant amount of work/class time

Worker

Stockbyte/Getty Images

Stockbyte/PunchStock

Student

Overcome Obstacles with Positive Habits and Mental Shifts

Positive Habits: Control Your Reactions

Even peak performers sometimes feel discouraged and need help climbing out of life's valleys. You will get discouraged at college even if you feel as if you belong and are doing well. You will get discouraged at work even if it is a great job. *The key is to create and maintain a positive mindset and learn to bounce back.* Seek out experiences that stretch you and embrace growth and change. Stick to positive habits and practice them every day until they become automatic. This is the hallmark of a positive, growth mindset.

HABIT

Let's take the incident presented in **Self-Management** at the beginning of the chapter. This common scene involves being angry when your roommate leaves dirty dishes in the sink and doesn't do the agreed-upon share of housework. The *trigger* is the dirty dishes (overflowing garbage, etc.). The *routine* is becoming angry, yelling, or leaving a nasty note. The *reward* is feeling self-righteous, put-upon, and a justification for rage.

BUILDING A NEW HABIT

To stop this self-destructive habit and gain self-control, you have to change the routine until it becomes automatic. For example, knowing you have an anger problem, you might want to choose a certain behavior ahead of time and follow the routine when the trigger occurs. Change the craving for anger and excitement to the craving for peace and well-being. Your *routine* will include an arranged time to meet with your roommate to discuss your arrangement. Present your case in a calm tone and then listen. Express your willingness to work things out so that you both can enjoy a tidy home to invite friends over to entertain.

The *trigger* is the dirty dishes. You decide to change your behavior from writing an angry note to talking calmly to your roommate, maybe over dinner. Your new *routine* is to breathe deeply, concentrate on your message, feel gratitude that you have a roommate you enjoy in many ways, and express your concerns and confidence that you can work this out. Continue to breathe deeply until you are calm and focused and are listening attentively. You will acknowledge her views and concerns and come up with an agreement. The *reward* is the feeling that you have self-control; you have faced a problem squarely and dealt with it in a calm, assertive, and productive way. You have satisfied the craving for peace and a healthy relationship. You have created a mindset.

Staying in College: Resiliency and Grit

The power of resiliency and grit can help you bounce back. Everyone gets off course now and then, but the key is to realize that setbacks are part of life.

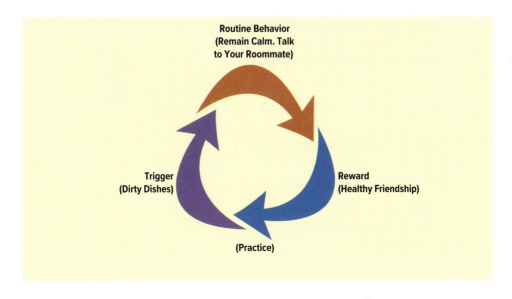

You have to become **resilient**—adapt to difficult or challenging life experiences, overcome adversity, bounce back, and thrive under pressure. **Grit** is a combination of passion, perseverance, and **hardiness** (a combination of commitment and control). These traits will give you the courage and motivation to turn rough patches into opportunities for personal growth. *In short, you can cultivate resilience and grit through effort and perseverance.* Persist!

Figure 3.5 shows reasons students have given for dropping out of college. Many of these reasons are excuses for not finding a creative way to persevere. For example, not all classes will be exhilarating, some may be boring or not relevant—but is that a reason to give up? If you think, "I'll be more motivated as soon as I graduate and get a real job," you may never develop the necessary qualities and skills to achieve that. Starting today, you should

- Commit to creating a positive, open mindset that focuses on growth.
- Surround yourself with positive, supportive, and encouraging friends.
- Tell yourself, "This is a setback, not a failure."
- Learn self-control and time-management strategies.
- Make certain you are physically and mentally renewed; get more rest, exercise more.
- Replace negative and limiting thoughts and self-talk with affirmations and positive visualization. Reaffirm that you belong in college.
- Reaffirm that college is worth the effort and pays off personally and professionally.

Create Positive Mental Shifts

For example, Steve comes from a long line of lumber mill workers. Although they have lived for generations in a college town, his family has never had anything to do with the college. Steve was expected to go to work at the mill right after high

Figure **3.5**

Reasons Students Do Not Graduate

Juggling the demands of work and school is a major reason why students drop out of college. Besides the reasons cited in this survey, students also struggle with poor study habits, managing their social time, and taking responsibility for their education—including asking for help. *Which "reasons" in the survey are you facing and how are you coping in order to achieve your goals?*

Source: Jean Johnson and Jon Rochkind with Amber N. Ott and Samantha DuPont, "With Their Whole Lives Ahead of Them: Myths and Realities About Why So Many Students Fail to Finish College." A Public Agenda Report for The Bill & Melinda Gates Foundation, December 20, 2009 and educationdata.org/collegeo-dropout.rate Melanie Hanson Sept 2021.

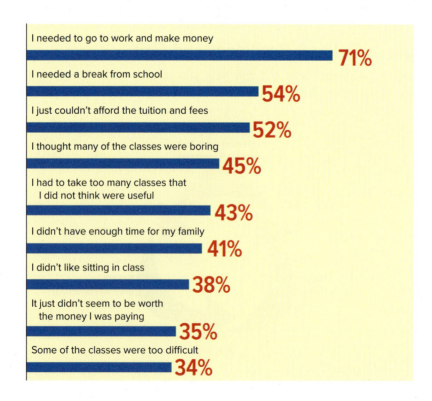

Reason	Percentage
I needed to go to work and make money	71%
I needed a break from school	54%
I just couldn't afford the tuition and fees	52%
I thought many of the classes were boring	45%
I had to take too many classes that I did not think were useful	43%
I didn't have enough time for my family	41%
I didn't like sitting in class	38%
It just didn't seem to be worth the money I was paying	35%
Some of the classes were too difficult	34%

school. He never thought about other options. However, during his senior year in high school, he attended Career Day. He met instructors and students from the local college who were friendly and encouraging. His world opened up, and he saw opportunities he had never considered. Steve experienced a major mental shift. Although he had to overcome a lack of support at home, he is now a successful college student with a bright future.

College is an ideal time to develop curiosity, your natural creativity, and explore new ways of thinking. Try the following:

1. **Create a support system.** Without support and role models, you may question whether you can succeed. First-generation college students, women in technical, welding, and computer programs, and men in nursing, childcare, elementary teaching programs may find support groups helpful. Cultural minorities, veterans, and students with physical disabilities or returning students may feel out of place. Some students may be told that they are not college material. You can find encouragement with a support system of positive, accepting people. Join a variety of clubs. Make friends with diverse groups of students and instructors.

2. **Reprogram your mind.** Affirmations and visualization can create a self-fulfilling prophecy. If you think of yourself as a success and are willing to put in the effort, you will succeed. Focus on your successes and accomplishments, and overcome limitations. For example, if you need to take a remedial math class, take it and don't label yourself as "dumb" or "math-impaired." Instead, focus on how improved your math skills will be. With effort and support you can grow and learn and achieve great success.

3. **Use critical and creative thinking.** Question limiting labels and beliefs. Where did they come from and are they accurate? Ask yourself, "What if?" Explore and stretch.

4. **Develop mutually supportive relationships.** Look for friends and professors who support you, but who also challenge and help you grow and learn and become your best.

5. **Take responsibility.** You are responsible for your thoughts, beliefs, and actions. You can question, think, and explore. You can achieve almost anything you dream.

6. **Learn new skills.** Be willing to learn new skills and competencies. Cultivate essential qualities and keep growing and learning. Develop grit and perseverance.

7. **Use the whole of your intelligence.** You definitely are smarter than you think you are. Use all your experiences and personal qualities to achieve your goals. Develop responsibility, self-control, dependability, sociability, character, manners, and all the other qualities necessary for school, job, and life success.

8. **Use the VARK system of integrating learning styles.** Visualize yourself feeling confident; use affirmations, "I'm a positive, motivated, and confident person." Write out affirmations and read them out loud. Stand relaxed and use your body to show confidence. Stand up straight, smile, put your shoulders back, and practice.

TAKING CHARGE

Summary

In this chapter, I learned to

- **Use the whole of my intelligence.** Developing emotional maturity and strong personal qualities is just as important to my future success as learning new skills and information. Essential personal qualities include character, responsibility, self-management and self-control, self-esteem, confidence, attitude, and motivation.

- **Focus on character first.** Strong leaders have an equally strong set of values. Having personal integrity gives me the courage to do the right thing, even when it is difficult. I display civility and empathy by interacting with family, friends, and colleagues with respect, kindness, good manners, empathy, and compassion. It's important for me to have a personal code of ethics that I follow in all facets of my life.

- **Take responsibility for my thoughts and behaviors.** I don't blame others for my setbacks, but focus my energy on positive solutions. I keep my commitments.

- **Manage and control my emotions, anger, and negative thoughts.** Conflict is an inevitable part of life, but it can be resolved in a positive way. I can redirect my negative thoughts and anger: (1) calm down, (2) clarify and define, (3) listen with empathy and respect, (4) use "I" statements, (5) focus on one problem, and (6) focus on win–win solutions.

- **Develop self-esteem and confidence.** Through self-assessment, I understand my strengths and will continue to learn new skills and competencies that will build my confidence.

- **Maintain a positive mindset.** A positive attitude influences the outcome of a task more than any other factor and increases motivation. Maslow's hierarchy of needs shows that I can fulfill my higher needs for self-esteem and self-actualization only when I have fulfilled my more basic needs first. The motivation cycle further demonstrates how affirmations, visualization, and self-talk affect my physical responses and behavior.

- **Realize the benefits of higher education.** A broad education in the liberal arts can help make me a truly educated professional by providing an integration and understanding of history, culture, ourselves, and our world. My college degree will pay off with more career opportunities, a higher salary, more benefits, more job promotions, increased workplace flexibility, better workplace conditions, and greater job satisfaction.

- **Bounce back.** Discouragement is the number one barrier to motivation. Setbacks will occur, but I have grit and resiliency. I focus on effort, positive actions, surround myself with supportive people, stay healthy, and focus on a positive mindset.

- **Create positive mental shifts.** I will dispute irrational, negative beliefs and replace them with positive beliefs that focus on growth. I know I can cultivate positive qualities.

- **Create positive habits.** I will illustrate a habit I want to create using the Habit Cycle.

Performance Strategies

Following are the top 10 strategies for expanding your emotional intelligence and personal qualities:

- Cultivate character and integrity.
- Create a personal code of ethics.
- Take responsibility for your thoughts, actions, and behaviors.
- Practice self-control.
- Develop positive self-esteem and confidence.
- Determine personal motivators.
- Use goals as motivational tools.
- Reward yourself for making progress, and strive for excellence, not perfection.
- Become resilient to bounce back from setbacks. Develop grit and perseverance.
- Create positive mental shifts.

Tech for Success

- **Ethics information online.** Search for articles on ethics, business etiquette, and codes of ethics. Check out different businesses, the military, government agencies, and colleges to find out if each has a code of ethics. Locate samples and bring them to class. What do the codes of ethics have in common?

- **Online discussion groups.** When you are interested in a topic or goal, it's very motivating to interact with others who share your interests. Join a discussion group and share your knowledge, wisdom, and setbacks with others. You will learn their stories.

- **Goal-setting examples.** Sharing your goals with others may inspire you. Use critical and creative thinking, stretch yourself, and reflect on what you want out of life.

Endnote

[1] M. Beckman, "Crime, Culpability, and the Adolescent Brain," *Science* 305, no. 5684 (July 30, 2004).

Study Team Notes

Career *in* Focus

Dragon Images/Shutterstock

Jacqui Williams
SALES REPRESENTATIVE

Related Majors: Business, Marketing, Public Relations

Positive Attitudes at Work

As a sales representative for a large medical company, Jacqui Williams sells equipment, such as X-ray and electrocardiograph (EKG) machines, to hospitals nationwide. Her job requires travel to prospective clients, where she meets with buyers to show her products and demonstrate their installation and use. Because Jacqui cannot take the large machines with her, she relies on printed materials and her iPad, from which she can point out new aspects of the machines she sells. The sales process usually takes several months and requires more than one trip to the prospective client.

Jacqui works on commission, being paid only when she makes a sale. Because she travels frequently, Jacqui must be able to work independently without a lot of supervision. For this reason, being personally motivated is a strong requirement for her position. Jacqui has found that what motivates her most is believing in the products she sells. Jacqui keeps up on the latest in her field by reading technical information and keeping track of the competition. She sets sales goals and then rewards herself with a short vacation.

Because personal relations with buyers are so important, Jacqui is careful about her health and well-being. While traveling, she keeps a positive mindset through affirmations, and she gets up early to eat a healthy breakfast and exercise in the hotel gym. She uses integrity by presenting accurate information and giving her best advice, even if it means not making a sale. Her clients describe Jacqui as positive and helpful, someone whom they look forward to seeing, and whose advice they trust.

CRITICAL THINKING In what way does having integrity, good character, and a code of ethics enhance a sales representative's business? Now that you know more about all it takes to be a successful sales rep, what appeals to you about this career? What would be most challenging?

Peak Performer Profile

Christiane Amanpour

"Amanpour is coming. Is something bad going to happen to us?"* That's how *CNN*'s Chief International Correspondent, Christiane Amanpour, says she's often greeted. Whether she appreciates the grim humor or not, Amanpour knows that her name and face have become linked in people's minds with war, famine, and death. But she has earned the respect of journalists and viewers around the world with her astute reporting from war-ravaged regions, such as Afghanistan, Iran, Israel, Pakistan, Somalia, Rwanda, and the Balkans.

Amanpour launched her career at *CNN* as an assistant on the international assignment desk in 1983, when some observers mockingly referred to the fledgling network as "Chicken Noodle News." "I arrived at *CNN* with a suitcase, my bicycle, and about 100 dollars,"* she recalls. Less than a decade later, Amanpour was covering Iraq's invasion of Kuwait, the U.S. combat operation in Somalia, and the breakup of the Soviet Union as these events unfolded.

Amanpour's globe-trotting began early. Born in London, Amanpour soon moved with her family to Tehran, where her father was an Iranian airline executive. Her family fled the country and returned to England during the Islamic Revolution of 1979. After high school, Amanpour studied journalism at the University of Rhode Island. She took a job after college as an electronics graphic designer at a radio station in Providence. She worked at a second radio station as a reporter, an anchor, and a producer before joining CNN.[†]

"I thought that CNN would be my ticket to see the world and be at the center of history—on someone

Albert H. Teich/Shutterstock

else's dime,"* she says, noting that she's logged more time at the front than most military units. Fear, she admits, is as much a part of her daily life as it is for the soldiers whose activities she chronicles: "I have spent almost every working day [since becoming a war correspondent] living in a state of repressed fear."*

Amanpour worries about the changes that have transformed the television news industry in recent years, as competition for ratings and profits has heated up.

But Amanpour remains optimistic. "If we the storytellers give up, then the bad guys certainly will win," she says. "Remember the movie *Field of Dreams* when the voice said, 'Build it and they will come'? Well, somehow that dumb statement has always stuck in my mind. And I always say, 'If you tell a compelling story, they will watch'."*

PERFORMANCE THINKING Christiane Amanpour demonstrates courage, integrity, and commitment. In what ways do you speak out for freedom, justice, and equality? Would you want a job that involves a lot of travel? How about a job where you are dealing with fear or risks much of the time? Would you like to work for a start-up or an established company? Answering these and similar questions will help you clarify your values, interests, and strengths and help you find a satisfying career.

CHECK IT OUT Visit www.cpj.org to see what's being done to safeguard the lives of journalists in the world's hotspots. Use the search field to find the manual "Journalist Security Guide" to see what precautions journalists themselves must take in high-risk situations.

---

* Christiane Amanpour, 2000 Murrow Awards Ceremony Speech, September 13, 2000. http://gos.sbc.edu/a/amanpour.html.
† CNN Anchors and Reporters: Christiane Amanpour. www.cnn.com/CNN/anchors_reporters/amanpour.Christiane.html.

Starting Today

At least one strategy I learned in this chapter that I plan to try right away is

_____

_____

_____

What changes must I make in order for this strategy to be most effective?

_____

_____

_____

Review Questions

Based on what you have learned in this chapter, write your answers to the following questions:

1. What personal qualities are essential to success in school and work?

_____

_____

2. Give an example of a short-term goal versus a long-term goal.

_____

_____

3. List at least two or three motivational strategies.

_____

_____

4. Explain how affirmations and visualization affect the motivational cycle.

_____

_____

5. Explain what a mental shift is and why it's important.

_____

_____

Getting Motivated

In the Classroom

Carol Rubino is a drafting and design major at a community college. To pay her expenses, she needs to work several hours a week. She is very organized and responsible with her school and work obligations. Most of her peers would describe Carol as motivated because she attends every class, is punctual, and works hard in school and at work. Throughout high school, Carol participated in extracurricular activities but never really enjoyed them. She likes college but questions if she'll be able to find a job in her field when she graduates. As a result, Carol sometimes feels as if she is just wasting time and money.

Martin Barraud/OJO Images/Getty Images

1. What strategies in this chapter can help Carol find a strong sense of purpose and motivation?

   _____

   _____

2. What would you recommend to Carol for creating a more resourceful and positive attitude?

   _____

   _____

In the Workplace

Carol is now a draftsperson for a small industrial equipment company. She has been with the company for 10 years. Carol is a valuable employee because she is competent and well liked. Carol has a supportive family, is healthy, and travels frequently. Although she enjoys her job, Carol feels bored with the mundane routine. She wants to feel more motivated and excited on the job, as well as in her personal life.

3. What strategies in this chapter can help Carol become more enthusiastic about work or find new interest in her personal life?

   _____

   _____

4. What would you suggest to Carol to help her get motivated?

   _____

   _____

Applying the ABC Method of Self-Management

In the **Journal Entry** at the beginning of the chapter, you were asked to describe a time when you were angry and lost control of your emotions. How would having a positive, open mindset that focuses on growth have helped you?

Now apply the ABC method to the situation and write out a script.

_____

_____

A = Acknowledge: Accept reality and pay attention to your emotions.

_____

_____

B = Breathe: Take a deep breath, calm down, and feel beloved.

_____

_____

C = Choose: With many options, choose the most appropriate action which will result in the most positive long-term consequences.

_____

_____

Sample script: Even though I'm feeling angry and resentful, I love and accept myself and want to grow. I breathe deeply, calm down, and know that I can tolerate these feelings. Acknowledging my anger will help me move to more positive feelings. Underneath my anger is sadness that my roommate is not respectful of my needs. I will allow these feelings to be felt and float away as I explore ways to communicate my needs and viewpoints. I choose to apologize for over overreacting and lashing out. I choose to sit down with my roommate and talk about sharing chores. I will practice acknowledging small irritations and directly and calmly discuss them instead of letting my anger build. I will focus on the good qualities and wonderful times that I have with my roommate and other friends.

REVIEW AND APPLICATIONS | CHAPTER 3

My Reinforcement Contract

Use this example as a guide; then fill in the following contract for one or all of the courses you are taking this term.

Name *Sara Jones*

Course *General Accounting*   Date *September 2021*

If I *study for 6 hours each week in this class and attend all lectures and labs.*

Then I will *be better prepared for the midterm and final exams.*

I agree to *learn new skills, choose positive thoughts and attitudes, and try out new behaviors.*

I most want to accomplish *a "B" in this course as a sound basis for advanced accounting courses.*

The barriers to overcome are *my poor math skills and becoming discouraged.*

The resources I can use are *my study group and the Tutoring Center.*

I will reward myself for meeting my goals by *going out to dinner with some friends and socializing.*

The consequences for not achieving the results I want will be *to reevaluate my major and reduce time socializing.*

REINFORCEMENT CONTRACT

Name _____

Course _____ Date _____

If I _____

Then I will _____

I agree to _____

I most want to accoumplish _____

The barriers to overcome are _____

The resources I can use are _____

I will reward myself for meeting my goals by _____

The consequences for not achieving the results I want will be _____

Self-Esteem Inventory

Do this simple inventory to assess your self-esteem. Circle the number that reflects your true feelings.

4 = all the time

3 = most of the time

2 = some of the time

1 = none of the time

1. I like myself and I am a worthwhile person.	4	3	2	1
2. I have many positive qualities.	4	3	2	1
3. Other people generally like me and I have a sense of belonging.	4	3	2	1
4. I feel confident and know I can handle most situations.	4	3	2	1
5. I am competent and good at many things.	4	3	2	1
6. I have emotional control and I am respectful of others.	4	3	2	1
7. I am a person of integrity and character.	4	3	2	1
8. I respect the kind of person I am.	4	3	2	1
9. I am capable and willing to learn new skills.	4	3	2	1
10. Although I want to improve and grow, I am happy with myself.	4	3	2	1
11. I take responsibility for my thoughts, beliefs, and behavior.	4	3	2	1
12. I am empathetic and interested in others and the world around me.	4	3	2	1
Total points	____	____	____	____

Add up your points. A high score (36 and above) indicates high self-esteem. If you have a high sense of self-esteem, you see yourself in a positive light. If your self-esteem is low (below 24), you may have less confidence to deal with problems in college or on the job. If you scored at the lower end, list some strategies you can implement that may help boost your self-esteem:

_____

_____

_____

CHAPTER 3 | REVIEW AND APPLICATIONS

Learning Styles and Motivation

You will feel more motivated and positive when you align your efforts with your learning and personality styles. Review your preference and style and think of the factors that help motivate you.

For example, *auditory learners* may be more motivated when they listen to their favorite inspirational music and say affirmations. *Visual learners* may be more motivated when they surround themselves with pictures and practice visualizing themselves as motivated and positive. *Kinesthetic learners* may be more motivated when they work on activities, dance, hike, jog, and work with others. It also helps to *write out your goals and read them out loud.* Now you've integrated VARK into your routine. (See "Are You a Reader, Listener, or Doer?" in Chapter 1 for the complete discussion.)

Analyzers may be more motivated when they think, reflect, write, and organize information into sequential steps. *Supporters* may be more motivated when they work in a group and make information meaningful. *Creators* may be more motivated when they observe, make active experiments, and build models. *Directors* may be more motivated when they clearly define procedures and make practical applications. (See "Connect Learning Styles and Personality Types: The Four-Temperament Profile" in Chapter 1 for the complete discussion.)

List the ways you can motivate yourself that are compatible with your learning style and personality type:

1. _____
   _____
   _____

2. _____
   _____
   _____

3. _____
   _____
   _____

4. _____
   _____
   _____

5. _____
   _____
   _____

Practice Self-Control

Self-control is one of the most important qualities for success in college, career, and life. Let's use a common example of road rage. You're driving along when someone cuts you off and causes you to brake quickly. Your heart is pounding and you feel the anger exploding within you. You feel like racing after the car and cutting him off or following him to his destination and confronting him. The reward would be feeling self-righteous and teaching the other driver a lesson. Fortunately, you have been practicing self-control and see this incident as another chance to practice mindfulness and behave in a calm, rational manner. The *trigger* is the car cutting you off. Your *routine* is to breathe deeply until your heart stops racing and you've calmed down. You slow down a bit and become more mindful of the importance of being alert. You give thanks that you're safe and remind yourself that your goal is to get safely home. The *reward* is feeling safe and in control. You feel a sense of well-being and gratitude that you are driving responsibly and that you've practiced self-control so often that it is now automatic.

Practice

Take an incident where you lost your temper or would have liked to use more self-control.

Overcoming Obstacles

List potential triggers for that habit. How will you remind yourself to do this?

Sketch your own Habit Cycle to illustrate trigger, routine, and reward.

List a few likely obstacles:

My plan for overcoming these obstacles:

Assessment of Personal Qualities

Category	Assessment	Y/N	Example
Emotional intelligence	Do I value and practice essential personal qualities?		
Character	Do I value and practice being a person of character and integrity?		
Civility	Do I treat others with respect and courtesy?		
Ethics	Do I have a code of ethics?		
Responsibility	Do I take responsibility for my thoughts and behavior?		
Self-control	Do I have self-control and know how to manage anger?		
Self-esteem	Do I have a realistic and positive sense of myself?		
Positive attitude	Do I strive to be positive and upbeat?		
Motivation	Do I create the inner drive and determination to achieve my goals?		
Self-actualization	Am I committed to growing and realizing my full potential?		
Visualization	Do I use visualization as a powerful tool for change and growth?		
Affirmation	Do I dispute and replace negative self-talk with affirmations?		
Critical thinking	Do I use critical thinking to challenge my beliefs and see new possibilities?		

The area I most want to improve is:

Strategies I will use to improve are:

Manage Your Time

LEARNING OUTCOMES

In this chapter, you will learn to

4-1   Determine how you use your time and how you *should* use your time

4-2   Use personal goals to identify priorities

4-3   List time-management strategies

4-4   Demonstrate the power of a positive, open attitude

4-5   Overcome obstacles with better time-management habits

4-6   Identify strategies to juggle family, school, and job commitments

SELF-MANAGEMENT

It's 7:30 a.m., I'm late for class, and I can't find my keys. It always seems like there's too little time and too much to do. I feel as if I have no control over my life. How can I manage my time and get organized?

Gorodenkoff/Shutterstock

Have you ever had a similar experience? Do you find yourself spending hours looking for things? Do you get angry at yourself and others because you feel frustrated and unorganized? In this chapter, you will learn how to take control of your time and your life and focus on priorities. Visualize yourself going through the day organized and centered. You have a clear vision of your goals and priorities, and you work steadily until tasks are finished. You feel the sense of accomplishment and completion. You are in charge of your time and your life.

JOURNAL ENTRY   In **Worksheet 4.1**, describe a time or situation when you felt overwhelmed by too much to do and too little time. What were the consequences?

> 66 We need time to dream, time to remember, and time to reach the infinite. Time to be. 99

GLADYS TABER
American writer (1899–1980)

I n this chapter, we look at time management with a positive, open attitude. Instead of controlling, suppressing, or constricting your freedom, time management enables you to achieve the things you really want and frees up time to enjoy life. Peak performers use a systematic approach that allows them to

- Organize projects and achieve results
- Accomplish goals and priorities by doing first things first
- Be effective, not just efficient by looking at the big picture
- Avoid crises and reduce stress through planning
- Remain calm and productive in the midst of turmoil
- Feel a sense of accomplishment through effort and perseverance
- Create positive habits with an open, optimistic mindset that focuses on growth

Everyone has the same amount of time: 24 hours a day; 168 hours in a week. You can't save or steal time. When it's gone, it's gone. However, you can learn to invest it wisely. This chapter will help you learn how to get control of your life by managing your time wisely and choosing to spend it on your main goals. You will discover that there is always time to do what you really want to do. Too many people waste time doing things that should be done quickly (if at all) and ignoring their long-term goals. Students are often overwhelmed with social media.

As you go through this chapter, think about what you want to achieve and how you can use your time skillfully to perform at your peak level. This chapter will help you become effective, not just efficient. You are efficient when you do things faster. You are effective when you do the right things in the right way. As a wise time manager, you can avoid feeling overwhelmed and falling behind in school, at work, or in your personal life. Whether you are an 18-year-old living on campus or a 45-year-old juggling school, family, and work, the principles in this chapter can help you manage your time and your life.

Use Time Effectively

Time management is much more than managing minutes, hours, and days. *Your attitude, energy level, and ability to concentrate have a major impact on how well you manage time.* Evaluate situations that may have spun out of control because you had a negative fixed attitude that caused you to give up easily, procrastinate, or fail to plan and how these situations may have affected other people. *Think of what you could accomplish with an open, positive attitude that is focused on effort, growth, and learning. How would being resilient and persistent help you manage your time and achieve your goals?*

Let's look at three important questions:

1. Where does your time go? (Where are you spending your time and energy?)
2. Where should your time go? (What are your priorities?)
3. What habits will help? (What mindset and strategies create success?)

Where Does Your Time Go?

You can divide time into three types: committed time, maintenance time, and discretionary time.

- **Committed time.** Committed time is devoted to school, labs, studying, work, commuting, family, and other activities involving the immediate and long-term goals you have committed to accomplishing. Your committed time reflects what is important to your career, health, relationships, and personal growth—what you value most.

- **Maintenance time.** Maintenance time is the time you spend "maintaining" yourself and your environment. Activities such as eating, sleeping, grooming (showering, styling your hair, cleaning your contact lenses, getting dressed, etc.), cooking, cleaning/laundry, gardening, shopping, caring for others, and bill paying use up your maintenance time.

- **Discretionary time.** The time that is yours to use as you please is discretionary time and should spend it on the most important things in your life, such as relationships with family and friends; service to the community; intellectual development; and activities that give you joy and relaxation and that contribute to your physical, mental, and spiritual well-being. These should tie in with your long-term goals of being healthy, feeling centered, joyful, and peaceful, and having loving relationships.

As you consider where your time goes, notice whether you are using most of the day for commitments. A good place to start is with an assessment of how you spend your time and energy. Complete **Personal Evaluation Notebook 4.1** (or use the weekly planner in **Worksheet 4.7** at the end of the chapter) to track how you use your time. The far right column asks you to indicate your energy level during the day: Do you feel focused and alert, or are you distracted or tired? Many people have certain hours during the day when they are most productive. Leverage your success by working smarter.

Fuse/Corbis/Getty Images

After you have recorded your activities, review your Time Log to determine how much time you are devoting to daily tasks, such as studying, commuting, and socializing. Complete **Personal Evaluation Notebook 4.2** and tally how much time you currently spend on various activities (and add others from your Time Log). Determining where you are currently spending your time will help you figure out the best way to use your time. Even if you are juggling school, work, and family, reflection will help you maximize what discretionary time you do have to be most effective.

Where Should Your Time Go?

The first rule of time management is to make a commitment to what you want to accomplish—in other words, to set goals. Goals are not vague wishes or far-away dreams. They are specific, measurable, observable, and realistic. A goal is a target that motivates you and directs your efforts. Daily goals should reflect long-term goals and values.

It's important to have a realistic picture of what your goals are and to observe and reflect constantly on how your daily activities are leading to larger goals. Written goals help

Personal Evaluation Notebook

4.1

Time Log

Fill in this Time Log to chart your activities throughout the day. Identify activities as committed (C), maintenance (M), or discretionary (D). Also determine your energy level throughout the day as high (H), medium (M), or low (L). Use **Worksheet 4.7** at the end of the chapter to chart your activities for more than one day to see patterns in how you spend your time.

Time	Activity	Type C/M/D	Energy H/M/L
12:00–1:00 a.m.			
1:00–2:00			
2:00–3:00			
3:00–4:00			
4:00–5:00			
5:00–6:00			
6:00–7:00			
7:00–8:00			
8:00–9:00			
9:00–10:00			
10:00–11:00			
11:00–12:00 (noon)			
12:00–1:00 p.m.			
1:00–2:00			
2:00–3:00			
3:00–4:00			
4:00–5:00			
5:00–6:00			
6:00–7:00			
7:00–8:00			
8:00–9:00			
9:00–10:00			
10:00–11:00			
11:00–12:00 (midnight)			

Personal Evaluation Notebook 4.2

How Much Time Do You Spend?

Fill in this chart to determine how much time you spend on certain activities. Use the information you compiled in **Personal Evaluation Notebook 4.1**. Change or add activities to the list as needed. If you recorded your activities for a week, include all the minutes as well as a daily average. Analyze and then make positive changes.

Activity	Time Spent	Activity	Time Spent
Attending class		Eating	
Working at a job		Sleeping	
Commuting		Cooking	
Studying		Shopping	
Working on class projects		Surfing the Internet	
Grooming		Socializing	
Exercising		Doing hobbies	
Doing household chores		Talking on the telephone	
Waiting in line		Watching television	
E-mailing/texting		Recreation (including video games)	
Study group		Other	
Social media		Other	

clarify what you want and can give you energy, direction, and focus to put them into action. Goals can be short term, intermediate, or long term and are easier to identify when they flow out of a mission statement that defines what is most important to you. Placing goals within time frames can help you reach them. Complete **Personal Evaluation Notebook 4.3** to map out your goals. Revisit your goals often and update as necessary.

Setting Priorities

Peak performers know how to schedule their time and know that there is always time for what is most important. Prioritizing helps you focus your effort and time on activities that are most important. This prevents your days from being not just a treadmill of activities, crises, and endless tasks, but a consistent effort on what is important.

   Urgent priorities *are tasks or activities that must be accomplished by a specific date or time to avoid negative consequences of time and money.* These tasks can include

Personal Evaluation Notebook 4.3

Looking Ahead: Your Goals

Complete this activity to help you create major targets in your life—or long-term goals. From these goals, you can write intermediate goals (two to five years), short-term goals (one year), and then immediate (or semester) goals. Use **Worksheets 4.5** and **4.8** to help you map out your goals. Save this in your Career Development Portfolio.

A. Mission Statement

You'll recall from Chapter 1 that your personal mission statement summarizes the life you want to have and reflects your philosophy based on your deepest values and principles. In the blanks, repeat (or revise) your thoughts from Chapter 1.

- What do I value most in life? What is important to me?

  _____

- Which verbs best describe what I like to do? What is my passion?

  _____

- What is my life's purpose? What do I want do to make a difference?

  _____

- What legacy do I want to leave? How do I want to be remembered?

  _____

Mission Statement:

_____

_____

B. Long-Term Goals (Accomplish in 10 Years or So)

Brainstorm all the specific goals you want to accomplish during your lifetime. Include goals for all areas of your life, such as education, career, travel, financial security, relationships, spiritual life, community, and personal growth. This list will be long, and you will want to add to it and revise it every year if your goals change. Following are a few incomplete statements that might help you brainstorm:

- My dreams include

  _____

  _____

- I most want to accomplish

  _____

  _____

- The places I most want to visit are

  _____

  _____

(continued)

Personal Evaluation Notebook 4.3

B.   Long-Term Goals (Accomplish in 10 Years or So)   (*concluded*)

- One thing I've always wanted to do is

_____

_____

C.   Intermediate Goals (Accomplish in the Next Five Years)
Then, list the goals you want to accomplish in the next five years, such as

- I will complete my degree.
- I will get a good paying job in my field.
- I will travel.

D.   Short-Term Goals (Accomplish this Year)
List goals you want to accomplish in the next year. Consider your answers to these questions:

- What is the major goal for which I am striving this year?
- How does this goal relate to my life's mission or purpose?
- Is this goal in conflict with any other goal?
- What hurdles must I overcome to reach my goal?
- What resources, help, and support will I need to overcome these hurdles?
- What specific actions are necessary to complete my goal?

E.   Semester Goals
List goals you want to accomplish this semester—for example,

- I will get to know one professor well this term and make new friends.
- I will go to all of my classes on time, prepared, and pretest myself.
- I will exercise for 30 minutes each day, with a friend if possible.

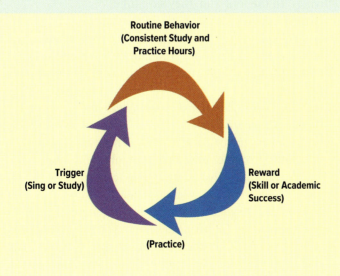

(continued)

Personal Evaluation Notebook 4.3

E. Semester Goals (*concluded*)

Be sure to include these goals in your daily and monthly planners. Consistently accomplishing these goals is the key to achieving your bigger goals. For example, let's do a Habit Cycle to illustrate your craving for academic success by setting daily goals: The *trigger* can be different cues for different people. You could use an organized desk, sharpened pencils, or your notebook. Lila has a sign hanging from her calendar near her computer that says "*Slow, but sure.*" Her aunt made it for her when she was taking singing lessons. It triggers within Lila a commitment to practice her routine. The reward in high school was singing well in band and at concerts. Now the routine is to study consistently for two hours each afternoon from 4 to 6 p.m. and again in the evening from 7 to 9 p.m. The reward is feeling organized, academic success, and breaks to eat, walk, and socialize with friends.

dropping a class, paying your fees, paying taxes, and turning in papers. For example, if you don't meet the deadline for adding or dropping classes, you have to pay more fees, may not get into the class, receive an F grade, or all your classes may be dropped.

Important priorities *are essential tasks or activities that support a person's goals and that can be scheduled with some flexibility.* Important activities support long-term goals and create the results you want—not just for today but also for future success. These activities and commitments include attending every class, creating study teams, completing homework, forming healthy relationships, planning, and exercising regularly. *People who spend time daily on important items prevent crises.* For example, if you build a personal fitness routine into every day, you will increase your energy, health, and overall sense of well-being and prevent medical problems that result from inactivity and weight gain. Long-term priorities must be built into your daily activities. In the long run, they save time.

Ongoing activities *are necessary "maintenance" tasks that should be managed carefully so they don't take up too much time.* As you go through your e-mail, mails, and phone calls, respond as necessary. You may be tempted to get a pet, but know this will be high maintenance. Ask yourself which activities meet your highest priority at this time.

Trivial activities *are nonessential tasks or activities that are completely discretionary and do not directly support a person's goals.* These tasks make up all the daily "stuff" of life that can be major time wasters. These unimportant activities can be fun, such as chatting online, checking your phone, looking up information, texting, checking Facebook or Instagram, going to parties, shopping, and watching TV. They can also be annoying, such as dealing with junk mail—both real and virtual. *The key is to stay focused on your important, top-priority items and schedule a certain amount of time for trivial activities.* For example, because checking Facebook, TikTok, Instagram, Twitter, e-mail, or texting friends can quickly eat up your discretionary time, limit these activities to just a few times each day. Get together in person and combine tasks such as walking, eating, exercising, and studying with friends.

Peak Progress

Investing Your Time in High-Priority Items: The 80/20 Rule

Whether you are a student or an executive your effectiveness will increase if you put in extra effort. This fun example will help you increase your awareness and you'll find examples all around you. According to the 80/20 rule (the Pareto Principle), 80 percent of the results flow out of 20 percent of the activities—for example,

- Eighty percent of the interruptions come from twenty percent of the people.
- Eighty percent of the clothes you wear come from twenty percent of your wardrobe.
- Eighty percent of your phone calls come from twenty percent of the people you know.

A look at your time wasters may reveal that you are spending too much time on low-priority activities and shortchanging your top priorities. Wasting time on low-priority activities is a major reason for not accomplishing major tasks.

Reverse the principle and create small changes that produce big results.

- Twenty percent more effort can result in an eighty percent better paper or speech.
- Twenty percent more time being involved and prepared in classes could produce eighty percent better results.

- Twenty percent more time developing positive relationships could reduce conflicts by eighty percent.
- Twenty percent more time taking care of yourself—getting enough sleep, eating healthy, exercising, and controlling stress—can result in eighty percent more effectiveness.

The 80/20 rule is a rule of thumb that reminds you to spend your time on the activities that are really important and achieve the results you want. Create a simple habit that can save you a lot of time. For example, get into the habit of always hanging up your keys and putting your phone in the same place and you could save hours of frustrating time looking for things. Changing a **key habit** can affect and spill over into all areas of your life. For example, people who exercise and start eating healthier also sleep better, have less stress, smoke less or quit, and are more patient with co-workers and friends. Families who eat together regularly have children who do better in school, have more confidence, and have better self-control. *What are small things you could do that would create significant results? Think of keystone habits that spill over and help you in various areas at college and at work. What role does a positive, open mindset play in creating habits?*

The small step of setting priorities every morning helps you focus on immediate goals. Your awareness of where your time goes becomes a continual habit of assessing, planning, and choosing tasks in the order of their importance. Now you can focus your efforts.

Questions to ask: Do I have a sense of purpose and direction? Are my goals clearly defined? Are any in conflict with each other? Are they flexible enough to be modified as needed? Do I invest time in high-priority tasks? Do I attend to small details that pay off in a big way? Refer to **Peak Progress 4.1** to see if the 80/20 rule applies to you.

Build a Prioritization Habit

Take time each morning to prioritize all the things you need to do for the week? Make prioritization a habit. Let's say that the *trigger* is a reminder on your smartphone. The *routine* is to spend 10 minutes prioritizing your tasks and to-do list in one place. Your *reward* is the wonderful feeling of being organized and motivated. Plus you'll have more time since you can check your phone and know where you need to be and what is due.

Time-Management Strategies

Use the following strategies to improve your time-management skills and help you achieve your goals in a balanced and effective way.

1. **Keep a calendar.** Jot down appointments, priorities, and deadlines on your phone or an inexpensive, pocket-size calendar that is easy to carry. *Keep it up-to-date by scheduling commitments, such as classes, labs, and work for the entire semester.* This helps you see the big picture. Review your calendar, each morning or each week, and list top priorities; due dates; and important school, work, and family activities. You can then determine tasks that must be done by a deadline, such as paying fees, dropping a class, or paying taxes. Schedule important activities that support your goals, such as classes, exercise, study teams, and deadlines for choosing a topic. Jot down people to see or call, such as your instructor or advisor, or activities, such as meetings or social events. *Remember, the shortest pencil is better than the longest memory.* For example, if your advisor gives you a code for registration, put it in your phone or on your calendar at the date and time for your registration. Don't just write your code on your binder or toss it into your backpack. Look for end of chapter worksheets which include handy calendars to help you plan your week, month, and semester. Write it down!

2. **Create a daily to-do list.** Some people like to write a to-do list for the next day, taking some time at the end of a day to review briefly what they want to focus on for the next day. Others like to write their list in the morning at breakfast or when they first get to school or work. *List the tasks you need to accomplish during the day and map them out on a daily calendar. Circle or place a number 1 by the most important priority to make sure it gets accomplished.* Make certain you build in time for family and friends. If you have children, plan special events. Bear in mind that the schedule should be flexible; you will want to allow for free time and unexpected events. Follow this schedule for 2 weeks and see how accurate it is. You can follow the format of the Time Log in **Personal Evaluation Notebook 4.1,** or see Worksheet 4.6, which includes a planner for mapping out your daily to-do list. (See **Figure 4.1** for tips on using a daily planner and to-do list and **Figure 4.2** on using your cell phone to help manage your time.) Check out downloading apps that can assist you with errands and checklists.

    Once you have written your list, do your urgent, top-priority items. Keep your commitments, such as attending every class, and study first and then socialize. When you see important items checked off, you'll be inspired. It's OK if you don't get to everything on your list. If tasks are left over, add them to your next to-do list if they are still important. Ask yourself, "What is the best use of my time right now?"

3. **Do the tough tasks first.** Start with your most difficult subjects, while you're fresh and alert. For instance, if you are avoiding your statistics homework because it is difficult, get up early and do it before your classes begin. Start projects when they're assigned. If you're at work, start with a project you've been putting off or that is difficult.

4. **Break projects down into smaller tasks.** Begin by seeing the whole project and then break it into manageable chunks. You may get discouraged if you face a large task, whether it's writing a major term paper or reading several chapters. Getting started is half the battle so take a few minutes to preview

Figure **4.1**

How to Use a Planner

The best way to use a planner to manage your time is to make it an essential part of your day. Check it in the morning and again before bed. Set out items needed for the next day. Some time-management experts even recommend giving your planner a name and finding it a "home" (a place in plain sight where it should always be put at the end of the day). *What name would you give your planner and where would its "home" be?*

Determine which works better for you:

A weekly planner (shown here) or a daily planner that has slots for each hour of the day (see *Worksheet 3.6*).

Size matters:

- It should be a convenient size for carrying.
- Spaces should be big enough to write in legibly.

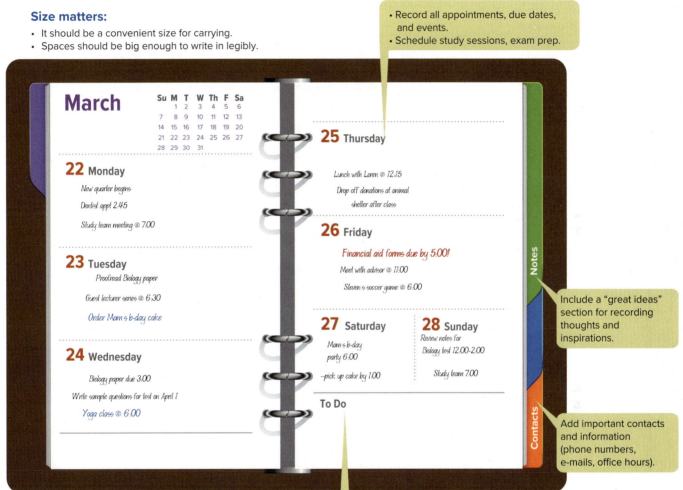

- Record all appointments, due dates, and events.
- Schedule study sessions, exam prep.

Include a "great ideas" section for recording thoughts and inspirations.

Add important contacts and information (phone numbers, e-mails, office hours).

Write down priorities and tasks for the week.

March

Su	M	T	W	Th	F	Sa
	1	2	3	4	5	6
7	8	9	10	11	12	13
14	15	16	17	18	19	20
21	22	23	24	25	26	27
28	29	30	31			

22 Monday
New quarter begins
Dentist appt 2:45
Study team meeting @ 7:00

23 Tuesday
Proofread Biology paper
Guest lecturer series @ 6:30
Order Mom's b-day cake

24 Wednesday
Biology paper due 3:00
Write sample questions for test on April 1
Yoga class @ 6:00

25 Thursday
Lunch with Loren @ 12:15
Drop off donations at animal shelter after class

26 Friday
Financial aid forms due by 5:00!
Meet with advisor @ 11:00
Steven's soccer game @ 6:00

27 Saturday
Mom's b-day party 6:00
-pick up cake by 1:00

28 Sunday
Review notes for Biology test 12:00-2:00
Study team 7:00

To Do

Notes

Contacts

Tips:

- Use only 1 planner for work, school, and personal.
- Record everything in it as soon as possible.
- Carry it all the time.
- Check it 3 times a day (such as breakfast, lunch, bedtime).

a chapter, outline the main ideas for your term paper, or write a summary at the end of a chapter. You will find inspiration in completing smaller tasks, and you will feel more in control.

Some students find a project board helpful for long-term projects, as shown in **Figure 4.3.** Separate the "board" into two columns: "Key Activities" and "Date Completed." In the date column, put today's date at the top and the project's due date at the bottom. With these two dates set, begin in the

Figure 4.2

Smartphone 101

Use the features on your phone to help you manage your time. Almost every cell phone has these basic features. Many also include video conferencing and three-way calling so you can communicate on projects. And a voice recorder allows you to summarize lectures, notes, and ideas. *Which ones do you already use?*

> ▶ **Alarm:** Set it for deadlines, appointments, meetings.
>
> ▶ **Calendar:** Record due dates for projects, exams, personal events.
>
> ▶ **Tasks:** Include a to-do list, errands, priorities.
>
> ▶ **Notes:** Type in reminders, instructions, and interesting thoughts.
>
> ▶ **Timer:** Limit (watching TV, texting), manage (exercising, studying), and remind (cooking, prescriptions).
>
> ▶ **Stopwatch:** Time tasks for future planning (reading a chapter, answering sample questions).
>
> ▶ **Internet access:** Download podcasts, read e-books, get directions.

activities column by listing in order the project-related tasks that need to be accomplished between the start and end dates. Go back to the date column and start plugging in optimal dates next to the tasks, working from beginning to end. Revise as necessary and allow time for proofreading and potential setbacks, such as computer problems.

5. **Consolidate similar tasks.** Grouping similar tasks can maximize your efforts. For example, if you need to make several calls, make them all at a specific time and reduce interruptions. Set aside a block of time to shop, pay bills, run errands, and return messages. Write a list of questions for your advisor, instructor, or study team. Make certain you know expectations, so that you don't have to repeat tasks.

6. **Study at your high-energy time.** Know your body rhythms and study your hardest subjects during your high-energy time. Review the Time Log to determine the time of day when you have the most energy, and complete **Personal Evaluation Notebook 4.4**. Guard against interruptions, and don't do mindless tasks or socialize during your peak energy period. For example, if your peak time is in the morning, don't waste time answering mail, cleaning, or doing other routine work. Use your high-energy time to do serious studying and work that requires thinking, writing, and completing projects. Use your low-energy time to do more physical work or easy reading or previewing of chapters. All of these tips can help you in college and job success.

Personal Evaluation Notebook

4.4

Your Daily Energy Levels

Keep track of your energy levels every day for a week or more. Revisit your Time Log in **Personal Evaluation Notebook 4.1** to determine your daily energy levels so that you can become more aware of your patterns.

1. What time(s) of the day are your energy levels at their peak?

_____

2. What time(s) of the day are your energy levels at their lowest?

_____

3. What tasks do you want to focus on during your high-energy time?

_____

4. What can you do to increase your energy at your low-energy time?

_____

7. Study everywhere and anywhere. Ideally, you should choose a regular study location with few distractions, such as the library. However, you should be prepared to study anywhere, and use unexpected downtime. Use flash cards to review formulas, dates, definitions, facts, and important data. Take class notes or a book with you to review during the five or 10 minutes of waiting between classes, for the bus, in line at the grocery store, or for appointments. Digitally record important material and lectures and listen to them while commuting, exercising, dressing, walking, or waiting for class to begin.

Project: Term Paper for Business Class 110	
Today's date: January 23, 2022	Due date: April 23, 2022
Key Activities	**Date Completed**
Explore topics	January 23
Finalize topic	January 28
Mind map outline	February 4
Initial library research	February 8
General outline	February 22
Library research	March 5
Detailed library research	March 10
Detailed outline	March 15
First draft	March 27
Do additional research and spell-check	April 5
Proof second draft; revise	April 10
Prepare final draft and proof	April 15
Paper finished and turned in	April 23

Figure 4.3

Sample Project Board

Making a project board is an effective time-management strategy. You can plan your tasks from start to end, or some people prefer to work backward—starting with the end date. *How can you incorporate your project board into your daily planner?*

8. **Block out a half day.** You will be more effective if you devote your morning or afternoon for serious study. Supplement these longer sessions with short sessions. Spread out your studying so that you review every few weeks. Don't cram in a marathon sessions.

9. **Get organized.** Think of the time you waste looking for items (and the unnecessary stress it causes). Choose your clothes and pack your lunch the night before, put your keys on the same hook, place your backpack by the door, put your mail and assignments in the same space, and keep records of bills and important information in your file. Keep an academic file that includes your grades and transcripts, tests, papers, and projects. If you need to negotiate a grade, you will have the background support you will need. Make sure you save and back up any important work.

10. **Be flexible, patient, and persistent.** Strive for excellence, not perfection. Stretch yourself and try new approaches. Give yourself at least 30 days to develop new habits. It often feels strange to do any new task. For example, pretesting is a proven strategy. Do it consistently in all your classes until your brain accepts this as a comfortable habit.

11. **Realize that you can't do it all (at least right now).** You may feel overwhelmed by too many demands and determine that some tasks are better done by others. You may want to exchange chores or combine activities such as social activities with studying.

12. **Create a habit.** Let's say you are constantly looking for your keys (see Self-Management feature at the beginning of the chapter). Your *trigger* is the key hook. You create a *routine* of always hanging up your keys when you walk in the door. If you forget, you repeat the routine again and again. Your *reward* is the wonderful feeling of being in control, disciplined, and organized. Practice every time you walk in the door.

Time Management and Your Learning Style

Many time-management strategies are designed for people who like routine, structure, and deadlines. They tend to be *convergent* thinkers because they are good at looking at several unrelated items and bringing order to them. By contrast, creative people like variety, flexibility, creativity, and innovation. They are usually *divergent* thinkers because they branch out from one idea to many. They are good at brainstorming because one idea leads to another and they are able to focus on the whole picture. Break the global view of the whole project into steps, break each of these steps into activities, and schedule and organize activities around the big goal. For maximum success, integrate the whole brain:

- **Focus on a few tasks.** Focus your efforts on one or two top-priority items instead of being scattered and distracted by busywork. Imagine putting on blinders and focusing on one step until it is completed, and then move on to the next step. This creates discipline. Set up a routine, be persistent, and reward yourself for completing tasks.

- **Write it down.** A daily calendar is vital to making certain that your activities support your short- and long-term goals. Write down phone numbers, e-mail addresses, and office hours of instructors and study team members. Highlight in color any deadlines or top-priority activities. Besides a daily calendar, use a master calendar in your study area and allow for variety and change. Check your calendars every day.

- **Use visuals.** One creative way to brainstorm, plan, and put your vision into action is to use a mind map (see **Figure 6.2** in Chapter 6). Use visual cues and sticky notes. When you think of an activity that will help you meet your goal, write it down. Sketch, draw, and use pictures and visualize yourself completing tasks.

- **Integrate learning styles.** *Visualize* yourself completing a project and create a vision board of your goals and dreams. Use *auditory* cues by recording yourself talking through ideas and project plans and read aloud. Make your project *physical* by adapting a hands-on approach and working with others to complete your project. Ask yourself, "Is there a way to simplify this task?" Planning, flexibility, and perseverance are important. **Peak Progress 4.2** explores the process of learning to take control of your time.

> **❝**Not knowing when the dawn will come, I open every door.**❞**
> **EMILY DICKINSON,** *poet*

Peak Progress

4.2

Applying the Adult Learning Cycle to Taking Control of Your Time and Life

Applying the Adult Learning Cycle will help you establish goals and create a plan to meet them. Let's say you decide you want to stop procrastinating and tackle a research paper that is due in two weeks.

1. **FEEL and LISTEN.** *Why do I want to learn this?* Planning my time better and getting organized are essential for juggling the demands of school, work, and life. I need to stop procrastinating. I'll listen to my favorite music while I break down the steps and do a project board. I'll review the steps out loud and with my study team and listen to suggestions. I will listen as I read my drafts out loud.

2. **OBSERVE and VISUALIZE.** *How does this work?* I can learn a lot about my writing assignment by looking at other research projects in this area. I will observe my professor as they talk about papers and show examples in class. I will visualize the final paper and see it all coming together as I work every day. I will do a mind map outline so I can see how all the components fit together. I will observe my study team as they review their projects and share ideas.

3. **THINK and WRITE.** *What does this mean?* I will think through how each point is written and how major points tie together and support my thesis. I will write out each main point and polish the theme. I will read directions for the paper again and make certain I've met all requirements. I will

complete my next draft and read it out loud. I will write a summary and read it out loud. I will review this with my study team and my professor and make corrections and follow suggestions.

4. **DO and PRACTICE.** *What can I do with this?* Each day, I'll work on one area of my paper and stay on schedule. I will print out a revised draft and manipulate information to see how it all fits together to create smooth transitions. I'll go to the Writing Center and ask for assistance and apply this feedback to my paper. Finally, I'll share my paper with my professor or teaching assistant and ask for advice. I will revise and revise until the paper is excellent.

5. **TEACH and PRACTICE AGAIN.** *Whom can I share this with?* I'll share and explain my draft with my study group and apply suggestions to my paper. As we exchange papers for review, I will share my ideas and suggestions with fellow students. I will save all papers so I can see my progress and share my suggestions with others. I will continue to reward myself with a break after I complete each task. I will feel pride for making positive changes and completing this major assignment.

Apply the VARK system by integrating visual, auditory, reading and writing, and kinesthetic learning styles. Use all your senses to leverage your success. Use pictures, maps, diagrams, charts, illustrations,

(continued)

visualization, fantasy, metaphors, and mind maps to make connections and enhance your learning through *visual* thinking. Use lectures, tapes, reading out loud, and music to enhance your *auditory* thinking. *Read and write* and summarize to enhance words. Draw, use direct experience, field trips, role playing, simulation, laboratory experiments, and manipulation of information to activate your *kinesthetic* thinking and learning. Be focused and persevere.

Overcome Obstacles with Better Time-Management Habits

Stop Procrastinating

Procrastination is a continual pattern of delaying and avoiding what is important. Let's use the power of persistence and positive habits to tackle this major obstacle. You've finally decided that you want to stop procrastinating and complete tasks and not gain weight by getting up and snacking. You may not know why you're procrastinating. Maybe you're a perfectionist and don't want to complete a project unless it's perfect.

Let's say that you find yourself getting up and grabbing a snack when you're not really hungry. The *trigger* is craving a break. You get up to stretch and walk by the candy bowl or refrigerator. Then you chat with your roommate. Create a *routine* where you sit for an hour or so and complete a set goal. Then get up and stretch and maybe take a 10-minute break to chat with your roommate and drink a glass of water or a cup of tea. Your *reward* is socializing by taking a brief break and that wonderful feeling of accomplishment. Create a new routine that provides a break and socializing without unhealthy snacking or drinking.

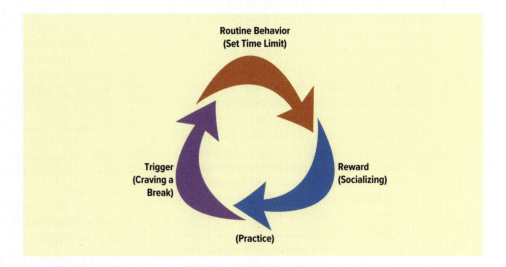

Complete **Personal Evaluation Notebook 4.5** to determine if you procrastinate too much and, if so, why.

Self-assessment is often the key to understanding why you procrastinate and to developing strategies to help you control your life and create the results you want.

Personal Evaluation Notebook 4.5

Procrastination

1. What is something I should have accomplished by now but haven't?

2. Why did I procrastinate? What are the consequences?

3. What kind of mindset would help me be more persistent and disciplined?

4. What kind of tasks do I put off?

5. When do I usually procrastinate?

6. Where do I procrastinate? Am I more effective in the library or at home?

7. What are small steps I could take to be more disciplined?

8. Who supports, or enables, my procrastination?

Once you have identified what is holding you back, you can create solutions and apply them consistently until they are habits. To avoid procrastination, try the following strategies.

1. **Set daily priorities.** Be clear about your goals and the results you want to achieve and allow enough time to complete them. Use your to-do list to check off tasks as you complete them. This will give you a feeling of accomplishment.

2. **Break the project into small tasks.** A large project that seems overwhelming can encourage procrastination. Do something each day that brings you closer to your goal. Use a project board or write down steps and deadlines that are necessary to achieve success. For example, as soon as a paper is assigned, start that day to choose a topic, the next day do research, and so on until each step leads to an excellent paper.

3. **Get organized.** Don't waste time looking for paper, pens, or your notes. Cut down on time-wasting searches by keep everything organized in your study area. Keep two folders—one for the day's assignment and another for papers completed and graded—or keep a file for

Am I a Procrastinator?
- I do what I enjoy rather than what should be done.
- I'm a perfectionist and worry about details or making mistakes.
- I'm concerned that I'll be judged.
- I get overwhelmed and give up easily.
- I may not be as smart as others. Maybe I don't have what it takes.
- I'm embarrassed because I put it off for so long—so I'll just write it off.
- I get easily distracted. It's not my fault things come up.
- I have talent so I shouldn't have to put this much effort in doing well.
- I'm a certain kind of person and I can't change.
- I work better under pressure and it's a great excuse when I don't finish.
- I lack the discipline or perseverance to complete a task.

Research shows that people who routinely practice mindfulness and meditation activated neurons in the part of the brain (prefrontal cortex) that controls attention and focus.[1]

Chloe is always late because she does several things at once and is scattered. Her family, friends—everyone—continually tell her how frustrating it is that she keeps them waiting. She finally got the message when her best friend texted her that she was tired of her inconsideration and the group was leaving for a party without her. The rush she always felt from doing many things at once and keeping up with texts and e-mails was replaced with the realization that she had let others down.

- What negative characteristics are being demonstrated by someone who is habitually late?
- What problems does this create—in school, on the job, in personal situations?
- Do you think that practicing meditation or mindfulness would help her to be more attentive and focused? What are specific strategies that you would suggest to help her become more focused, attentive, and dependable?

THINK
CREATIVELY AND CRITICALLY

each subject so you can review often before tests. Take a minute each night to get ready for tomorrow's task. This creates a positive mindset that is ready to start.

4. **Be consistent with study times.** Study anywhere and everywhere. Memorize vocabulary words while working out or preview a chapter right before class or post key words on your medicine cabinet so you can review while brushing your teeth. *It's also important to block out morning or afternoon blocks of two or three hours.* Some students blocked out time when classes were over while the material was fresh in their minds. Whatever you choose, maintain a slot every day for studying.

5. **Surround yourself with supportive people.** Ask for help from motivated friends, instructors, or your advisor, or visit the Learning Center for support. Sometimes talking out loud can help you clarify why you are avoiding a project. Study buddies or a study team also can help you stay on track. Just knowing that someone is counting on you to deliver may be enough to keep you from procrastinating.

6. **Tackle difficult tasks during your high-energy time.** Do what is important first, while you are at your peak energy level and concentration is easiest. Once you get a difficult task done, you will feel more energy. When your energy dips and you need a more physical, less mentally demanding task, return messages or tidy up your desk.

7. **Develop a positive attitude.** Negative emotions, such as anger, jealousy, worry, and resentment, can eat up hours of time and sap your energy. Instead, resolve to have a positive attitude and use affirmations. Think, "I get to work on my project today," instead of "I have to work on this project." Feel grateful that you have the opportunity to be in college. Resourceful and positive attitudes don't just happen; they are created.

8. **Reward yourself.** Focus on the sense of accomplishment you feel when you make small, steady steps and meet your deadlines. Reward yourself with a small treat or break when you complete activities and a bigger reward (such as a nice dinner or movie) when you complete a goal. Work first and play later. Be persistent and disciplined.

9. **Don't expect perfection.** You learn any new task by making mistakes. For example, you become a better writer or speaker with practice. Don't wait or delay because you want perfection. Your paper is not the great American novel. It is better to do your best than to do nothing. You can polish later, but avoiding writing altogether is a major trap. Do what you can today to get started on the task at hand. Stick with it!

Control Interruptions

Interruptions steal time. They cause you to stop projects, disrupt your thought pattern, divert your attention, and make it difficult to rebuild momentum. *To avoid time wasters, take control by setting priorities every day that will help you meet goals and reduce interruptions.* Don't let endless activities, e-mail, texting, and other

Personal Evaluation Notebook 4.6

Interruptions!

Keep a log of interruptions for a few days. List all the interruptions you experience such as social media, group texts, notifications, phone calls, etc. Also be aware of internally caused interruptions, such as procrastination, daydreaming, worry, negative thoughts, anger, and lack of concentration. Then think of possible solutions for handling the interruption the next time.

Interrupted by	Incident	Possible Solutions

people control you. For instance, if a friend calls, set a timer for 10 minutes or postpone the call until later, after you have previewed an assigned chapter or outlined a speech. Let calls go to voicemail if you are studying, or tell the caller that you will call back in an hour. Combine socializing with exercising or eating lunch. If you watch a favorite program, turn the television off right after that show. Take charge of your life by not allowing interruptions to control you. Complete **Personal Evaluation Notebook 4.6** to determine the sources of your interruptions. (Also see **Worksheet 4.3** to identify your time wasters.)

Peak performers know how to effectively live and work with other people. Try these tips to help you reduce interruptions:

1. **Create an organized place to study.** A supportive, organized study space can help you reduce interruptions and keep you focused. Have all your study tools—pencils, pens, books, papers, files, notes, a calendar, a semester schedule, and study team and instructor names and phone numbers—in one place so that you won't waste time looking for items you need. Keep only one project on your desk at a time, and file everything else away or put it on a shelf. If you have children, include a study area for them, close to yours, where they can work quietly with puzzles, crayons, or books. This will allow study time together and create a lifelong study pattern for them.

2. **Determine your optimal time to study.** When you are focused, you can study anywhere, anytime. However, to increase your effectiveness, do your serious studying when your energy level is at its peak.

3. **Create quiet time.** Discuss study needs and expectations with your roommates or family. You might establish certain study hours or agree on a signal, such as closing your door or hanging a "Quiet" sign, to let each other know when you need quiet time.

4. **Study in the library.** If it is difficult to study at home, study in the library. Once you enter, your brain can turn to a serious study mode. Sitting in a quiet

place and facing the wall can reduce interruptions and distractions. You can accomplish far more in less time, and then you can enjoy your friends and family.

5. **Do first things first.** You will feel more in control if you have a list of priorities every day. Knowing what you want and need to do makes it easier to say no to distractions. Make certain that these important goals include taking care of your health, taking time to exercise, eating right, and relaxing.

6. **Just say no.** Tell your roommates or family when an important test or project is due. If someone wants to talk or socialize when you need to study, say no. Set aside time each day to spend with your family or roommates, such as dinner, a walk, or a movie. They will understand your priorities when you include them in your plans.

Juggling Family, School, and Job

Many college students are juggling more than coursework and school activities. Many are spouses, partners, parents, caregivers (for both children and elderly relatives), and co-workers. Making the decision to attend college—or return to college—may have been difficult because of these commitments and responsibilities.

Having a family involves endless physical demands, including cleaning, cooking, chauffeuring to activities, helping with homework, and nonstop picking up. Anyone who lives with children knows how much time and energy they require. Children get sick, need attention, and just want you there sometimes for them.

The following strategies can help you succeed in school while juggling many roles:

1. **Be flexible.** Around children, certain kinds of studying are realistic, and other kinds are hopeless. Carry flash cards to use as you cook dinner or while supervising children's homework or playtime. Quiz yourself, preview chapters, skim summaries, review definitions, do a set number of problems, brainstorm ideas for a paper, outline a speech, review equations, sketch a drawing, or explain a chapter out loud. Save the work that requires deeper concentration for time alone. Study in the library when possible.

2. **Communicate with your family.** Let family members know that earning a college degree is an important goal and you need their support and understanding. Use every bit of time to study before you go home. Once home, let them know when you need to study and set up a specific time. Studies show that taking your family on a tour of your campus and classrooms helps to build support and understanding. Take your children to the library and special events on campus. Make your time with them fun.

3. **Delegate and develop.** Clarify expectations so that everyone contributes to the family. Even young children can learn to be important contributors to the family unit. Preschool children can help put away toys, set the table, and feel part of the team. Preteens can be responsible for cooking a simple meal one night a week and for doing their own laundry. When your children go to college, they will know how to cook, clean, do laundry, get up on time, and take responsibility for their lives. An important goal of being a good parent is to raise independent, capable, responsible adults.

4. **Find good day care.** Explore public and private day-care centers, preschools, family day-care homes, parent cooperatives, baby-sitting pools, other family members, and nannies. Line up at least two backup sources of day care. Ask for help.

5. **Prepare the night before.** Avoid the morning rush of getting everyone out the door. The night before, do tasks such as showering, packing lunches, and

checking backpacks for keys, books, notes, and supplies. Organization reduces stressful mornings.

6. **Use your school's resources.** Check out resources on campus through the reentry center. Set up study teams for all your classes. Make friends with other students who have children. (See **Chapter 5** for more resources for returning students.)

7. **Communicate with your employer.** Communicate your goals to your employer, and point out how learning additional skills will make you a more valuable employee. Some companies offer tuition reimbursement programs or even allow time off to take a class.

8. **Look into online options.** See if any of your classes are offered online or at alternate times, including evenings and weekends. An online class may fit better with your schedule, but it requires just as much commitment as any other class—maybe even more. See **Peak Progress 4.3** for tips on taking online courses.

9. **Increase your physical and emotional energy.** Focus on activities that relax you and help you recharge. Schedule time to meditate, walk, and read for pleasure. Exercise, dance, do yoga, get enough rest, and eat healthy foods. Keep a gratitude journal and remind yourself that you are blessed with a full and rewarding life. *Take good care of yourself. Exercise, eat healthy, and get as much sleep as you can.*

10. **Create positive time.** Unplug when you first come home and give your children your undecided time for 15 minutes or so. Don't buy your children toys to replace spending time with them. You can enjoy each other as you study together, garden, take walks, read, play games, or watch a favorite television show. The activity is secondary to your uninterrupted presence so make it quality time. At bedtime, share your day, talk about dreams, read a story, and express your love and appreciation. *Your children will remember and cherish these warm and special times forever, and so will you. Laugh often.*

• Balancing Your Life

Balancing family with work sometimes requires making trade-offs to have a more fulfilling life. *What can you do to create a more balanced life?*
Hero/Corbis/Glow Images

Peak Progress   4.3

Online Learning

Taking classes online became part of the college experience due to COVID. Some students liked the experience and others found it difficult. Even without the pandemic, some courses are offered only online. Most strategies that apply to taking traditional, face-to-face courses apply to online courses; however, your time-management skills may be even more critical for success. If you are taking an online course, ask yourself the following questions:

- Do I like to work independently? Am I a self-starter?
- Am I persistent and self-motivated?
- Am I comfortable e-mailing or phoning my instructor if I need help? Do I have a high-speed, reliable Internet connection?

- Am I comfortable asking questions and following up if I need more clarification? Do I like to read?
- Am I comfortable working online, including using basic software programs, submitting projects, testing, and collaborating via Skype or other services?
- Am I a procrastinator?

If you answered yes to most of these questions, an online course may be a good option for you. The following strategies will help you navigate online courses:

1. **Keep up on the coursework.** Think of it this way: What if you crammed a semester-long, face-to-face course, including all the reading, into one week? Many people try taking online courses that

(continued)

Online Learning *(concluded)*

way, waiting until the last minute to do the work. Instead, you must treat your online course as you would any other class by building it into your schedule. List due dates for assignments, tests, and projects. Build in time to read (the textbook as well as online materials) and study.

2. **Know the technology required for the course.** Make certain you have all the necessary equipment and software, and work out any bugs. Verify passwords and access to course websites, chat rooms, and so on. Ask for help if necessary.

3. **Communicate with the instructor.** In an online environment, you miss the nonverbal cues often given in a traditional course, so effective communication is even more important. Clarify the expectations for the class, including reading assignments, exams, projects, and papers, as well as how to deliver finished work to the instructor. How will you know if items are received? Where will your grade be posted? Is there a set time for the class or a chat room? Learn your instructor's office hours and the best time to respond by e-mail and phone. Ask for feedback from your instructor often and keep track of your progress. Verify your grade with your instructor before grades are submitted. (See Chapter 13 for tips on communicating online with instructors.)

4. **Communicate with other students.** Create online study teams to share notes, ask questions, and study for tests. If this is your first online course, knowing there are other students out there to work with can make it less daunting. You may find that

others have had the same questions about content and key points, technology problems, and so on that you do, and they may have answers.

5. **Check the school's tips.** Read any tips and frequently asked questions your school has posted about how to succeed in online courses. Many of them may be specific to the needs of the institution and its instructors. Explore resources.

6. **Watch for announcements.** Know how the instructor or school will alert you to any changes in assignments, tests, and upcoming events and check for them each week.

7. **Print out essential information.** If possible, print the syllabus, project assignments, and key content information so that you can quickly refer to it, especially when you do not have access to your computer. Annotate the material with questions you need to follow up on, possible test questions, and key points to remember.

8. **Sign in early.** If your course offers or requires participation in a chat room or message board, sign in early to make sure you are involved and can keep up on the discussion. Active participation may be a percentage of your total grade.

9. **Have a "Plan B."** To prepare for emergencies, locate computer labs on campus and in the community. If possible, ask a friend, roommate, or family member if you can use his or her computer if yours crashes. Create organized folders, and back up important material, such as assignments and papers.

10. **Don't cheat.** All rules of ethics and academic honesty apply to online courses just as they do to traditional courses. Your work and responses must be your own.

11. **Model successful behavior.** *Returning to school sends an important message that learning, growing, and being able to juggle family, a job, and school are worthwhile and rewarding.* It is important for children to see their parents setting personal and professional goals while knowing that the family is the center of their lives. You are modeling the importance of getting an education, setting goals, and achieving them.

12. **Balance your life.** *Reflect on all areas of your life and the time you are investing in them.* Decide if you are investing too much or too little in each area. Also, look at the roles you play in each area of your life. In the family area, you may be a wife, mother, daughter, and so on. In the work area, you may be a manager, a part-time worker, or an assistant. Accompanying each role in your life are certain goals. Some goals demand greater time than others, requiring trade-offs. For instance, you may have a big term paper due, so you trade off a family outing to accomplish this goal. Complete **Personal Evaluation Notebook 4.7** to determine how you can achieve balance.

Personal Evaluation Notebook

Keeping Your Life Goals in Balance

Several life areas are listed on this chart. Write one goal you have for each major area. Explain how you can commit a certain amount of time to meeting that goal and still maintain overall balance.

Life Areas	Goals	Expected Date of Completion
1. Career (job, earning a living)	_____	
	_____	
	_____	
2. Education	_____	
	_____	
	_____	
3. Spirituality (your inner being, peace of mind)	_____	
	_____	
	_____	
4. Relationships (your family, friends, associates)	_____	
	_____	
	_____	
5. Health (weight, exercise, food, stress, personal care)	_____	
	_____	
	_____	
6. Recreation (hobbies, sports, interests)	_____	
	_____	
	_____	
7. Finance	_____	
	_____	
	_____	
8. Home	_____	
	_____	
	_____	
9. Community involvement and service	_____	
	_____	
	_____	
10. Personal growth and renewal	_____	
	_____	
	_____	
11. Other	_____	
	_____	
	_____	
	_____	

TAKING CHARGE

Summary

In this chapter, I learned to

- **Assess where my time goes.** Knowing where I am already spending my time is essential for time management. I assess how much time I (1) commit to school, work, and other activities; (2) spend maintaining myself and home; and (3) devote to discretionary time.

- **Determine where my time should go.** I set goals to determine what I want to accomplish. I identify my values and priorities and use them to write a mission statement. I break down my tasks and goals by short term, intermediate, and long term.

- **Set priorities.** I know what I'd like to accomplish, what I should accomplish, and what is urgent and must be accomplished. I focus on urgent and important priorities, manage ongoing activities, and minimize my time on trivial activities.

- **Assess my energy level.** I know when my energy level is high and work on top-priority goals when I am alert and focused.

- **Break down projects.** I break a large project into manageable chunks. I make a project board, with deadlines for each assignment, and divide the assignment into realistic steps I can do each day. I consolidate similar tasks to maximize my efforts.

- **Study everywhere and anywhere.** I make the most of waiting time, commuting time, and time between classes. I know it is more effective to study in short segments throughout the day than to study late at night in a marathon session.

- **Get organized.** I will develop a habit of putting everything in its place and getting organized. Spending a few extra minutes organizing my space pays off later.

- **Integrate learning styles.** Focus on top-priority tasks, writing down upcoming events, using visual cues, and integrate learning styles and studying with others.

- **Overcome procrastination and interruptions.** By setting daily priorities, breaking large projects into manageable tasks, being positive, creating an organized place to study, and being disciplined, I can accomplish what needs to be done. I've learned to say no when necessary, and I reward myself after completing projects and finishing priorities.

- **Juggle family, school, and job responsibilities.** I communicate my educational goals to others in my life in order to establish expectations and create balance. I am flexible and creative with my time, focusing on schoolwork and involving others in the process.

- **Create positive habits.** My mindset focuses on growth and learning. I am persistent and resilient. Using the Habit Cycle, I'll create a routine that becomes automatic.

Performance Strategies

Following are the top 10 strategies for attentive listening and effective note-taking:

- Focus on goals and priorities.
- Keep a calendar and create a to-do list.
- Break down projects and consolidate similar tasks.
- Study at the right time, in the right space, and in blocks of time. Review often.
- Study everywhere and anywhere.
- Get organized.
- Be flexible, patient, and persistent.
- Don't procrastinate.
- Manage interruptions.
- Create balance.

Tech for Success

- **Semester calendar.** It's unavoidable—most of your tests and class papers will occur around the same time. Start planning your semester now by mapping out the major events and daily tasks you'll need to accomplish. A number of planning options are available with this text (worksheets and downloadable forms), or access planners online at a variety of websites, such as **www.timeanddate.com**.

- **Management gurus.** Best-selling authors and popular writers and speakers—such as David Allen ("getting things done"), Merlin Mann ("43 folders"), and the late Stephen Covey ("habits of highly effective people")—have developed strategies, methods, and even humorous takes on overcoming obstacles to effective time management. Visit their websites for advice on becoming more productive: **http://gettingthingsdone.com/**; **www.43folders.com**; **www.stephencovey.com**.

- **A personal time-out.** It's easy to waste hours shopping online, watching YouTube videos, and perusing the latest "find" on auction sites, such as eBay. You may need to give yourself a time-out or, rather, a "time's up." Set a timer as you get online and commit to turning off the computer when the timer goes off. Use your discretionary time wisely.

Endnote

[1] J. A. Dusek, H. H. Out, A. L. Wohlhueter, M. Bhasin, L. F. Zerbini, M. G. Joseph, H. Benson, and T. A. Libermann, "Genomic Counter-Stress Changes Induced by the Relaxation Response," *PLoS ONE* 3, no. 7 (2008), p. e2576.

Study Team Notes

Career *in* Focus

Ryan McVay/Getty Images

Deborah Page
FOOD SCIENTIST

Related Majors: Agricultural Science, Chemistry, Microbiology, Nutrition

Focus on Tasks

Deborah Page is a food scientist for a large company in the food-processing industry. Her job is to develop new food products and ways to preserve or store foods. To do this, she engages in research and conducts tests and experiments, keeping in mind consumer demand for safety and convenience. Occasionally, she analyzes foods to determine levels of sugar, protein, vitamins, or fat.

Because her job is task-oriented, Deborah has a great deal of freedom in structuring her day. Her company allows flexible scheduling, so Deborah arrives at work at 9:30 a.m., after her children have left for school. She can work until 6:30 p.m. because her children are involved in after-school activities and her husband picks them up by 5 p.m.

Deborah finds that she does her best work in late mornings and early afternoons. She plans research and testing during those times. She schedules most calls during the first hour at work and uses the latter part of her day to organize tasks for the next day. Good planning helps her manage her time well and focus on her tasks at hand.

Deborah's job includes a fair amount of reading, which she often tackles at home in the evening. That allows her to leave work early if needed to take her children to appointments or attend their sports activities. Giving attention to her family and personal interests helps Deborah create a balanced life.

CRITICAL THINKING Why is it important for Deborah to organize her time wisely? What are some of the prioritization strategies she uses daily to manage her time? What are some strategies to help her balance her personal and career commitments with a healthy, fulfilling lifestyle? Explore ways for Deborah to find time for herself for personal renewal.

Peak Performer Profile

Malcolm Gladwell

Referred to as a "pop sociologist," international best-selling author Malcolm Gladwell constantly analyzes the way we look at everyday events and concepts of time. By studying what we often think of as "ordinary," Gladwell looks at how these issues of time shape future success.

Gladwell's background is as varied as his way of thinking. His mother was born in Jamaica as a descendant of slaves and worked as a psychotherapist. His British father was a civil engineering professor at the University of Waterloo in Ontario, Canada. Gladwell was born in England and grew up in rural Ontario, graduating with a degree in history from the University of Toronto. In his distinguished career, he has been named one of *Time Magazine*'s 100 Most Influential People. He has worked as a staff writer for *The New Yorker* magazine since 1996.

In his book *Outliers: The Story of Success,* one of the major questions Gladwell explores is why some people, such as Bill Gates and the members of the Beatles, have become outrageously successful in their professions, whereas others have not. Gladwell formulates the hypothesis of the "10,000 Hour Rule." In this rule, he states that the key to success in any field or profession is largely due to practicing a task for a total of 10,000 hours (20 hours a week for 10 years). By making this long, extended time commitment (along with other factors), individuals can fully develop their innate abilities and succeed in their chosen field. (Recall how practice and repetition are key components of the Adult Learning Cycle discussed throughout this text.)

In *The Tipping Point: How Little Things Can Make a Big Difference,* Gladwell explores, among other things, how small actions can have a ripple effect and "spread like viruses do." He explores many historical and cultural situations in which actions by just a few rapidly lead to what he calls a "tipping point" of major change. (Similarly, the *Leverage Your Success* activities throughout this text reinforce how small, focused steps can accomplish more in the end.)

In *Blink: The Power of Thinking Without Thinking,* Gladwell studies our abilities to make snap decisions. In looking at short fragments of time, Gladwell reveals the benefits of expert judgment by citing examples of how certain experts have relied on their intuition rather than studied data. (Likewise, *Think Creatively and Critically* activities throughout the text exercise your critical thinking abilities to quickly solve everyday issues.)

Gladwell's writings have been considered insightful as well as controversial. However, his perceptions of time and critical thinking and the connections he finds to success and other social phenomena have spurred lively debates on the best ways to utilize time and focus efforts.

PERFORMANCE THINKING Do you think it's true that it takes 10,000 hours to become proficient in a profession? How does this idea relate to your success in a class? Have you ever relied on your intuition to solve a problem? Did you arrive at the right answer for you?

CHECK IT OUT Experts explore different approaches to thinking in the popular TED video series (**www.ted.com/**). Named for an alliance among the areas of technology, entertainment, and design (though including many more disciplines today), these brief talks challenge the world's most inspired thinkers to give the "talk of their lives." More than 1,400 TED Talks are available for free viewing online, including speakers such as Malcolm Gladwell, Al Gore, and Jane Goodall. How can watching these speeches affect the way you think?

Starting Today

At least one strategy I learned in this chapter that I plan to try right away is

_____

_____

_____

What changes must I make in order for this strategy to be most effective?

_____

_____

_____

Review Questions

Based on what you have learned in this chapter, write your answers to the following questions:

1. How does time management help you achieve your goals?

_____

_____

2. Explain the 80/20 rule. Give an example of when you've used a small amount of time to create a big change.

_____

_____

3. Name at least two or three time-management strategies.

_____

_____

4. What can you do to avoid procrastination?

_____

_____

5. Why is it important to control interruptions?

_____

_____

Juggling Family and School

In the Classroom

Laura Chen is a returning part-time student. She also works full time and takes care of her family. Her husband says he supports her goal to become a dental hygienist but does little to help with taking care of the children or housework. Their children are 12 and 14 and have always depended on Laura to help them with their homework and drive them to their activities. Laura prides herself on being efficient at home, as well as being a loving mother and wife. She has taken on a lot and doesn't have much help.

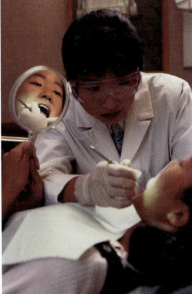

Keith Brofsky/Getty Images

1. What can Laura do to focus and create more balance in her life?

_____

_____

2. What strategies in the chapter would be most helpful to Laura?

_____

_____

In the Workplace

Laura is now a dental hygienist. She has always had a busy schedule, but she expected to have more free time after she graduated. Instead, she is even busier than before. Her children are active in school, and she feels it is important to be involved in their activities and schoolwork. Laura also belongs to two community organizations, volunteers at the local hospital, and is active in her church. Recently, she has been late for meetings and has been rushing through her day. Because she knows her health is important, Laura has resumed her regular exercise program. Since graduation, she has had difficulty finding time for herself.

3. What strategies can help Laura gain more balance in her life?

_____

_____

4. If you were Laura and based on your values, what priorities would you set?

_____

_____

Applying the ABC Method of Self-Management

In the Journal Entry at the beginning of this chapter, you were asked to describe a situation when you were overwhelmed by too much to do and too little time. How would having a positive, open mindset that focuses on growth help you to cope?

Now apply the ABC Method and write a script.

_____

_____

A = Acknowledge: Accept reality and pay attention to your emotions.

_____

_____

B = Breathe: Breathe deeply and feel beloved and calm.

_____

_____

C = Choose: Knowing you have many options, consciously choose the most appropriate action which will result in the most positive long-term consequences.

_____

_____

Sample Script: Even though I'm feeling anxious, worried, and frustrated, I still love and accept myself. I breathe deeply, calm down, and feel a vast spaciousness. I can tolerate these feelings of frustration and anger at myself for not getting more done. I am not my thoughts or my feelings. I allow them to float away and choose to focus on all I've accomplished. I choose to take simple steps to get more organized such as laying out my clothes, packing my backpack, and tidying up each night. I practice mindfulness and mediation to create quiet time to become centered and focused. I practice being kind to myself and rewarding myself when I've accomplished tasks. I know that learning time management skills will help me in my career and in all areas of my life.

My Time-Management Habits

Complete the following statements with a Yes or No response.

	Yes	No

1. I do the easiest and most enjoyable task first.
2. I do my top-priority task at the time of day when my energy is the highest and I know I will perform best.
3. I use my time wisely by doing high-return activities—previewing chapters, proofreading papers.
4. Even though I find interruptions distracting, I put up with them.
5. I save trivial and mindless tasks for the time of day when my energy is low.
6. I don't worry about making lists. I don't like planning and prefer to be spontaneous and respond as events occur.
7. My work space is organized, and I have only one project on my desk at a time.
8. I set goals and review them each semester and each year.
9. My workspace is open, and I like to have people wander in and out.
10. My study team socializes first, and then we work.
11. I have a lot of wasted waiting time, but you can't study in small blocks of time.
12. I block out a certain amount of time each week for my top-priority and hardest classes.

SCORING

1. Add the number of Yes responses to questions 2, 3, 5, 7, 8, 12.
2. Add the number of No responses to questions 1, 4, 6, 9, 10, 11.
3. Add the two scores together.

The maximum score is 12. The higher the score, the more likely you are to be practicing good time management. Which areas do you need to improve? Pick one of the "No" answers above that you will work on starting today and create a habit using the Habit Cycle for illustration.

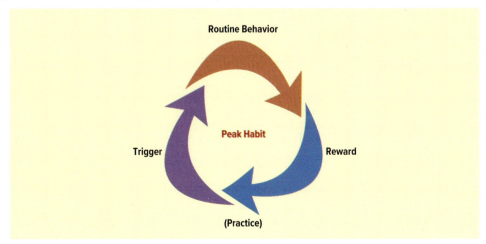

Time Wasters

Getting control of your time and life involves identifying time wasters and determining your peak energy level. It also involves identifying goals, setting priorities, and creating an action plan. Use critical thinking to answer the following questions.

1. What are the major activities and tasks that take up much of your time?

_____

_____

2. What activities cause you to waste time? Some common time wasters are
- Socializing
- Losing things and not organizing
- Doing what you like to do first
- Watching television
- Complaining and whining
- Being overly involved with other people's problems
- Not writing down deadlines

_____

_____

3. What activities can you eliminate or reduce?

_____

_____

4. When is your high-energy time?

_____

_____

5. When do you study?

_____

_____

6. Look at your committed time. Does this block of time reflect your values and goals? Explain your answer.

_____

_____

7. Do you complete top-priority tasks first? If not, which tasks do you usually tackle first?

_____

_____

Practice Goal Setting

Determine a personal desire or want and plan out a strategy of long-term, short-term, and daily goals that help you achieve it.

Goal-Setting Steps	Examples	Your Turn . . .
Step 1 **Plainly state your *desire* or *want*.**	"I want to be financially secure."	
Step 2 **Develop a long-term goal that will help you fulfill your stated *desire* or *want*.**	"I will earn a Bachelor of Science degree in computer technology from State University by June 2018."	
Step 3 **Develop short-term goals that will help you achieve the long-term goal.**	"I will enroll in all the classes recommended by my academic advisor."	
	"I will earn at least a 3.5 GPA in all my classes."	
	"I will join a small study group."	
Step 4 **Develop daily objectives that focus on achieving your short-term goals.**	"I will set aside 2 hours of study for every 1 hour in class."	
	"I will make note cards to carry with me and review them when I'm waiting for class."	
	"I will review the day's lecture notes with my study team to make sure I didn't miss any important points."	

Map Out Your Goals

Use this illustration as a visual guide for mapping out your goals. To get started, plug in your responses from **Personal Evaluation Notebook 4.3**.

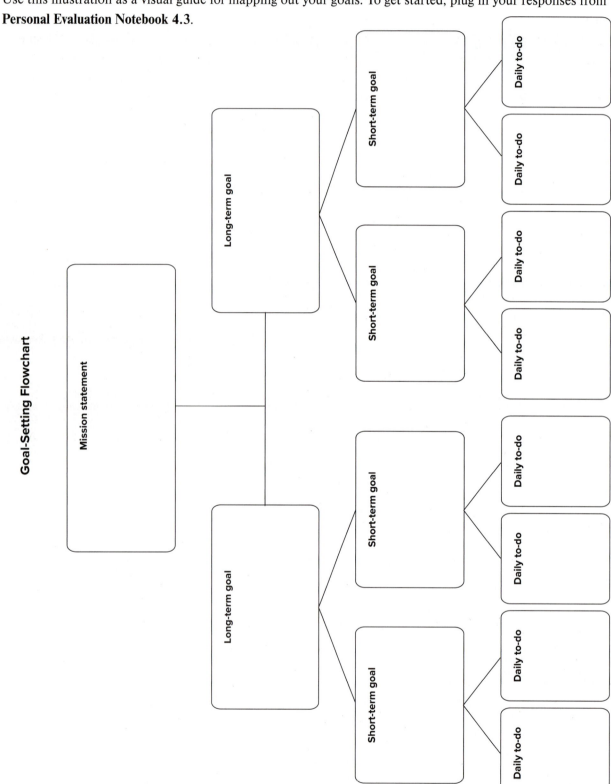

Goal-Setting Flowchart

- Mission statement
- Long-term goal
  - Short-term goal
    - Daily to-do
    - Daily to-do
  - Short-term goal
    - Daily to-do
    - Daily to-do
- Long-term goal
  - Short-term goal
    - Daily to-do
    - Daily to-do
  - Short-term goal
    - Daily to-do
    - Daily to-do

Daily Prioritizer and Planner: Your To-Do List

Consider the 80/20 rule discussed in **Peak Progress 4.1** as you use this form to prioritize your tasks and schedule your daily activities. On the left side, write down the tasks you want to accomplish during the day. Then enter those tasks in the "Activity" column, focusing on urgent and important tasks first. Also make sure you include your maintenance and committed activities. Check off your tasks on the left side once they are completed. At the end of the day, see what tasks did not get accomplished and, if need be, include them on tomorrow's to-do list.

	Time	Activity
Urgent	12:00–1:00 a.m.	
	1:00–2:00	
	2:00–3:00	
	3:00–4:00	
	4:00–5:00	
Important	5:00–6:00	
	6:00–7:00	
	7:00–8:00	
	8:00–9:00	
	9:00–10:00	
	10:00–11:00	
	11:00–12:00 p.m.	
Ongoing	12:00–1:00	
	1:00–2:00	
	2:00–3:00	
	3:00–4:00	
	4:00–5:00	
	5:00–6:00	
Trivial	6:00–7:00	
	7:00–8:00	
	8:00–9:00	
	9:00–10:00	
	10:00–11:00	
	11:00–12:00	

REVIEW AND APPLICATIONS | CHAPTER 4

Weekly Planner

Week of _____ / _____ / _____

Time	Sunday Activity	Monday Activity	Tuesday Activity	Wednesday Activity	Thursday Activity	Friday Activity	Saturday Activity
12:00–1:00 a.m.							
1:00–2:00							
2:00–3:00							
3:00–4:00							
4:00–5:00							
5:00–6:00							
6:00–7:00							
7:00–8:00							
8:00–9:00							
9:00–10:00							
10:00–11:00							
11:00–12:00 p.m.							
12:00–1:00							
1:00–2:00							
2:00–3:00							
3:00–4:00							
4:00–5:00							
5:00–6:00							
6:00–7:00							
7:00–8:00							
8:00–9:00							
9:00–10:00							
10:00–11:00							
11:00–12:00							

Urgent	Important	Ongoing

Month/Semester Calendar

Plan your projects and activities for the school term.

Month of _____					

Appointment   Date

Test   Date

Project   Due Date

Demonstrating Your Time-Management Skills

List all the factors involved in time management. Indicate how you would demonstrate them to employers. Add this page to your Career Development Portfolio.

Areas	Your Demonstration
Dependability	*Haven't missed a day of work in my job*
Reliability	
Effectiveness	
Efficiency	
Responsibility	
Positive attitude	
Persistence	
Ability to plan and set goals and priorities	
Visionary	
Ability to follow through	
High energy	
Ability to handle stress	
Ability to focus	
Respect for others' time	
Ability to overcome procrastination	
Reputation as a doer and self-starter	

Maximize Your Resources

LEARNING OUTCOMES

In this chapter, you will learn to

5-1 Identify your school's resources such as the library and technology

5-2 Manage your financial resources and save for the future

5-3 Demonstrate how you are your greatest resource

SELF-MANAGEMENT

Using a credit card is easy—in fact, much too easy. Before I knew it, I rang up thousands of dollars, and I can barely handle the minimum monthly payments. In addition to credit card debt, I have student loans to pay back. I feel like I'll be in debt forever.

© Hero Images/Getty Images

Are you struggling with your finances or finding it hard to make ends meet? Have you ever bought things that you didn't need or spent too much on a luxury item that you really couldn't afford? In this chapter, you will learn how to find and use your school and local resources to help you succeed in every area of your life, including financial. You will learn how to manage money, get on a debt-free track, and find ways to participate in your school and community using free activities.

JOURNAL ENTRY In **Worksheet 5.1**, write about a time when you set a financial goal, such as buying a new car. How difficult was it to achieve? What sacrifices did you have to make?

G oing to college is a big change. The strategies and information you learn throughout this book will help you cope with major life transitions, including the transition from college to career. In this chapter, we will look at ways of finding and using the resources available to you, including your inner resources, to adjust to change and meet your goals. A great deal of success in life depends on solving problems through decision making. This requires knowing what resources are available and having the good sense to use them.

When you enter college or a job, you are entering a new system and culture. It is your responsibility to understand how the system and culture work. This understanding includes knowing the system's rules, regulations, deadlines, procedures, requirements, and language. The culture is all the written and unwritten rules of any organization. It includes the work atmosphere and the way people treat each other. In a sense, you are learning how things are done and who best can solve specific problems. Knowing the system and culture reduces stress and anxiety. *Many advisors say the top advice they give students is to address problems as they occur and seek help when they need it.* Really, ASK FOR HELP!

Explore and Engage in Your School's Resources

Many college graduates say they regret not having been more involved and engaged in college and community activities and not using the amazing resources available. Your college experience will be much more rewarding and successful if you invest in making friends and getting to know professors and know where to go for help.

You may have attended an orientation program, gone on a campus tour, and visited the bookstore and student center when you applied to or arrived at school. You may have picked up a student newspaper or map or looked at the schedule of classes. This is a good place to start. Walking around campus, finding your classrooms before classes begin, and locating your advisor's and instructors' offices can help you feel more comfortable and reduce the anxiety of the unknown. You will be amazed at the support services and resources available at most schools. The resources we'll explore in this chapter include

- People resources: advisors, faculty, classmates, and counselors
- Program resources: offices for disabilities, areas of study, groups, clubs, and activities
- Online and information resources: catalogs, guides, and local news and events
- Financial resources: financial aid, credit agencies, financial planning services, scholarships, part-time jobs, and personal budgeting

- **Check Out What's Available**
Your school probably offers many resources to help you adjust, learn, and enjoy your college experience. *What are some resources you have already tapped into?*

Hero/Corbis/Glow Images

People Resources

The most important resources at school are the people with whom you work, study, and relate. Faculty, advisors, counselors, study team members, club members, sports teammates, guest speakers, administrators, and all the students with whom you connect and form relationships make up your campus community. These people will provide information, emotional support, and friendship—and they may even help you find a job! They want to see you succeed as much as you do.

ACADEMIC ADVISOR AND ADVISING CENTER

One of your most important contacts at school will be your academic advisor. This is a faculty member who is also an academic advisor and will help you prepare your major contract. Visit your academic department to find out your advisor's name, office number, and posted office hours. Check the catalog or go online and review requirements for your major and for graduation. It is best to make an appointment early in the semester and develop a good relationship. Once you declare your major, it is important to create a major contract. Do your part to be prepared, show up on time, ask questions, and follow through on suggestions to build a mutual supportive relationship. It is important to have an advisor who is accessible, takes time to listen, and will work closely with you to meet your academic goals. The *advising center* is also an important resource to help all students navigate academic life. Visit during your first semester. If you are *undeclared,* you will want to go to the advising center for general advising, for help in exploring majors and for help in navigating academic life. This center often includes career counselors. Advisors will also help clarify procedures, answer other academic concerns or questions, and refer you to offices on campus that can best meet your needs. Don't wait until your last year to review graduation requirements. (Review Peak Progress 2 in the Getting Started section for questions to ask your advisor. Also see Chapter 13 for more tips on communicating with advisors and instructors.)

INSTRUCTORS

Most instructors enjoy teaching and getting to know their students. At most universities and many colleges, faculty are also very involved in research, professional organizations, campus committees, community projects, and academic advising. It is important that you get to know your instructors and view them as a tremendous resource. Attend class regularly, show responsibility, and be prepared and engaged in class. As you get to know your instructors, ask what their research or teaching interests are and if you could be of help. Many students find internships

Ask your advisor

- Helpful suggestions concerning your academic program
- General education and other requirements
- If certain instructors are better suited to your learning style
- Potential career opportunities within the major
- The best sequence of classes and when certain courses are offered
- Service learning and volunteer programs
- Internships, co-ops, work study, and job placement programs
- Requirements for your major and substitutions available

Ingram Publishing/SuperStock

or part-time work through their instructors. Make it a goal to get to know at least one instructor well each term. You could have 10 important professional contacts when you graduate. Stay in touch.

MENTORS

A **mentor** is a role model who takes a special interest in another's goals and personal and professional development. This person may be a coach, an instructor, an employer, an advisor, or a colleague at work and can open doors for you. Check to see if your college has a formal mentoring program that connects students to faculty, staff, or more experienced students. Your instructor may be willing to serve as a mentor to help you make connections in your career. The point is to be engaged with people on campus.

PEERS

Your fellow students may be very involved in the learning community. They are active in orientation, campus tours, information and advising centers, clubs, and almost every service area on campus. Take the initiative to organize a study team or partner for each class; get to know your lab assistant, tutor, and other peers. This is a great way to improve learning, get help, and build a network of relationships. See **Peak Progress 5.1** for tips on setting up an effective study group. Unplug, look up, smile, and engage with other students and you will feel a sense of belonging. These connections may be lifelong.

Peak Progress   5.1
How to Form a Study Group

The old saying "Two heads are better than one" is never more true than when participating in a study group:

- Working in a study group gives you practice speaking in front of others and being an active part of a productive unit—skills that will be essential on the job.

- If someone is depending on your involvement, you are more likely to show up and come prepared. You may also become more organized, as others will get frustrated if you spend the time shuffling notes into order.

- When comparing notes, you will discover if you missed or misunderstood key points discussed in class or presented in the course materials.

- You are encouraged to explain things aloud to others (as in the "Teach and Practice Again" step in the Adult Learning Cycle). Speaking and listening to others can improve your ability to remember the information later, especially at test time.

Whether your instructor requires it or not, take advantage of the opportunity to buddy up with classmates who are focused on excelling. First, notice which classmates arrive on time, stay focused, and ask

thoughtful questions. Ask these individuals if they are interested in forming a study team, and exchange contact information. This can give you a tremendous advantage and help you feel engaged and connected.

Look for students whose learning styles complement each other (see Chapter 1 for learning styles). For example, one person may be great at taking notes, another at synopsizing the instructor's lecture, another at locating key information in the text, and another at formulating possible test questions. When you get to know each other better, you'll realize each person's strength.

You may want to meet online or choose a neutral place to meet and a consistent day and time to start and end. An ideal study group should have no more than six members. Otherwise, maintaining focus and attendance will be a challenge. Commit to doing your part. Online groups can be very effective.

The number one tip for getting good grades is pretesting yourself. Make up sample tests, take them, and then discuss. You can also talk through reading assignments, compare notes, review main points of lectures, write summaries, and work on major projects.

(continued)

Keep socializing to a minimum and focus on understanding the material. Ask questions, summarize, and review test results. In the last few minutes of each meeting, develop a tentative agenda for the next get-together.

If you see that another classmate is getting a group together, politely ask to join and let that person know your strengths and what you will bring to the group.

Participating in a study group can benefit anyone, especially older students who may feel out of place returning to school after an extended period. Many returning students bring practical, professional experience that offers a different perspective on the course material. This is a chance to connect more with the school and fellow classmates.

Networking is exchanging information or services for the purpose of enriching individuals, groups, or institutions. Not only is networking one of the best strategies for overcoming isolation and developing long-lasting relationships, but it will likely help you land a job and further your career. More than 60 percent of all jobs are found by networking—through friends, family, neighbors, co-workers, and acquaintances. At college, you have ample opportunity to build a diverse network of "who you know," including instructors, advisors, staff, alumni, and peers. Stretch your comfort zone by getting to know people with backgrounds different from yours. (See **Worksheet 5.2** for a handy guide.) Build a wide and diverse network at college and in the community by using these tips:

- **Get to know other students in class.** Unplug and introduce yourself to students around you. Jot down their names and commit them to memory. See who is interested in joining a study team or going to the library to study together and then for pizza or a jog.

- **Get to know students out of class.** Smile and say "hi" when you see them out of class, and take time to discuss lectures and assignments. Go to the student union, the library, and events at the multicultural and career center, and be friendly.

- **Get to know your instructors.** Throughout this book, you'll find tips for building supportive relationships with instructors. Make a commitment to be engaged.

- **Join clubs.** Almost every academic department has a club, and there are clubs where you can meet students who have similar interests, such as chess, skiing, religion, or music. Does your school offer any intramural sports you enjoy? If you can't find a club that interests you, consider starting one with other classmates.

- **Work on campus.** A great way to meet people and earn extra money is to work on campus. Check out the career center for work study and student assistant jobs.

- **Perform.** Join the band, choir, jazz group, or chamber readers; perform in a play; or work in theater behind the scenes. Some campus groups serve the community by performing in local schools or reading in library story hours.

- **Join the school newspaper.** Write stories or work in the office, which will also help build your portfolio of work samples.

- **Join a political group.** Campus and community political groups are a great way to meet people, become better informed, and support a cause.

- **Attend campus events.** Go to lectures, political debates, sporting events, and the many rich cultural, musical, intellectual, and fun events that are offered.

- **Attend community events.** There are so many wonderful organizations that can help you professionally and many offer scholarships. Check out Rotary, Kiwanis, AAUW (American Association of University Women), Boys and Girls Clubs, the City Council, and Board of Supervisors. In addition, there are many musical, theater, and art events.
- **Consider creative living situation.** You may be interested in living in a learning community, housing sponsored by the Greek system, or training for a dorm position.

Program Resources

Depending on the type of institution you attend, your school may have a variety of programs, departments, and offices that provide services and help. The people you meet in these offices can provide key information and help you find, evaluate, and use information of all kinds. A good place to start is the advising center.

ADVISING CENTER

An advising center provides general education advising and answers questions about policies, procedures, graduation requirements, and deadlines. The center has professional advisors who work closely with other departments, such as admissions, records, registration, learning centers, exchange and study abroad programs, and the cashier's office. You will want to verify if your advanced placement classes have been credited appropriately. If you are a transfer student, you need to know what upper-division and general education courses are required, what credits were transferred from your previous school, and whether they were accepted as general education or as electives.

While your academic advisor is responsible for helping you prepare a major contract and guiding you through your major's requirements, at most schools an evaluator does a degree check to make certain you have met not only your major's requirements but also all the university requirements, such as general education, diversity and common ground requirements, credit and no-credit guidelines, the institution's requirements, the required tests, and the number of college units. You may want to make an appointment once you have submitted your academic major contract and have applied for graduation (about three semesters before you graduate). You don't want to find out a month before graduation that you are short two units or have failed to meet a basic requirement.

ADMISSIONS, RECORDS, AND REGISTRATION

This office will have your transcripts, including information about grades, transfer credits, and the dropping or adding of classes. The registrar and staff can also assist you with graduation deadlines and requirements. You should keep your own copies of your transcripts, grades, grade changes, and other requirements.

LEARNING CENTERS

Explore learning centers designed to help with academic problems and grade improvement. Check out workshops in test-taking skills, time management, reading skills, note taking, math and science study strategies, individual or group tutoring, and study groups. They also do diagnostic testing to determine learning styles, difficulties, and differences. If you are diagnosed with a learning disability, you may be eligible for additional time on tests, tutors, or other services. They help students on probation by creating an academic success plan. Probation is a warning that you are doing substandard work—typically, a GPA below 2.0. If your GPA remains below 2.0 or falls to a certain level, you may be disqualified. Disqualification means being denied further school attendance until you are reinstated. Many resources are available to help you stay in school, avoid probation, and raise your GPA. Get Help Early!

LIBRARY

The library is a rich source of books, journals, periodicals (magazines and newspapers), encyclopedias, dictionaries, pamphlets, directories, and online databases. Libraries also offer many services besides the written and spoken word. Librarians and media center staff are trained to find information about almost every subject. They can often order special materials from other libraries or direct you to other sources. All libraries have electronic access to books and periodicals, and even more material is available via interlibrary loans. Checkout:

● **Use the Library**

Although you can do research online, your school may have an excellent library, which you should explore. *What assistance or resources can you get at the library that may be difficult to find online?*

GaudiLab/Shutterstock

- **The library's website.** Find out what the library offers and what research you can do from your own computer. (If access to materials is password protected, ask a librarian or an instructor for help.) Many libraries offer online tutorials and tips on evaluating information and citing material.
- **The catalog.** Look up the library's collection of print and online encyclopedias, biographies, and government works, as well as all the other available materials.
- **Searchable databases.** Find out what's available online. Ask about policies regarding use of the Internet on the library's computers.
- **DVDs, CDs, and digital recordings in the media center.** This is a wonderful way to access information, especially if you are a commuter student and want to listen to recordings on your commute or watch campus speakers you missed.
- **Reserves.** Many instructors put textbooks, supplemental readings, sample tests, and study aids on reserve.
- **Specialized libraries.** Specialized libraries may be available for your use, such as a medical or health sciences, law, journalism, or engineering library. Check the main library's website or ask a librarian.

CAREER CENTER

Check out the career center during your first semester. The staff will help you explore how academic majors relate to careers and explore internships, part-time jobs, and co-ops related to your major. These opportunities are very helpful for gaining experience and getting a job. The career center helps with career counseling, job fairs, and interview and résumé workshops. Keep a copy of personal inventories, assessments, and possible majors and careers in your Career Development Portfolio.

● **The Co-Curriculum**

Activities outside of the classroom are no longer considered "extra"—at least to employers looking for job candidates with real-life experiences. Find co-curricular activities that provide opportunities to meet new people and apply a variety of skills, such as communication, team-building, and leadership.

Bill Cheyrou/Alamy

HEALTH CENTER

Take advantage of free or low-cost medical services for illnesses, eating disorders, alcohol or drug misuse, anxiety, stress, birth control, and sexually transmitted diseases. If you have a high fever, nausea, severe headache, or stiff neck, go immediately to the health center or the emergency room because you might have meningitis or another serious illness. Many colleges are requiring students and staff to be fully vaccinated from COVID. Make certain you have the necessary vaccinations, or a hold may be placed on your registration. Check out your health insurance and carry your insurance card.

MEDIATION AND CONFLICT RESOLUTION

If you need help solving conflicts with instructors, roommates, neighbors, or your landlord, go to student resources and ask for an ombudsperson, mediation services, or legal aid.

COUNSELING CENTER

Adjusting to the demands of college life can be challenging. Professional counselors are trained to help with personal problems, such as loneliness, shyness, eating disorders, addictions, depression, and relationship problems. They often offer group counseling and classes, as well as individual support. They also refer students to agencies for specific problems. Go if you just need a caring and knowledgeable person to talk to.

STUDENT ACTIVITIES OFFICE

Working with other offices, student services provide many programs and activities, starting with an orientation program and campus tour. Sometimes these orientation programs are offered online for first-time, transfer, and reentry students. There are usually many activities for students to participate in, such as

- **Multicultural centers.** Classes, activities, and events are offered to celebrate diversity and provide support for racial and ethnic groups and the LGBT community. A women's center may offer classes and support for women.
- **International and exchange programs.** Check out exchange programs that allow you to stay enrolled at your own school but study for a term or a year at a designated school in this country or abroad. There may also be a center for international students.

Use **Personal Evaluation Notebook 5.1** to record activities or clubs you want to check out, and determine which ones would fit in your weekly schedule.

SERVICE LEARNING

Check out creative ways to incorporate service learning into your education. You may earn college credits and obtain valuable experience while integrating what you learn in classes into practical, on-the-job problem solving, directed study, and field experience. Some students tutor or work with the homeless, the elderly, or people with disabilities. (Learn more about incorporating service learning into your coursework in Chapter 14.)

STUDENT UNION

Check out the student union or center, which may include a dining hall, a bookstore, lounges, a post office, ATMs, and bulletin boards for information on clubs

Personal Evaluation Notebook 5.1

Activities and Clubs

Visit the student activities office or review your school's website to see what clubs or activities sound interesting. Look for activities that will increase your knowledge about your field of study, help you network and build business contacts, introduce you to people with similar interests, and give you a chance to enjoy your discretionary time, physically and emotionally.

1. Club/activity:_____ Day/time:_____

   Contact person:_____ Phone/e-mail:_____

   Meeting place:_____

2. Club/activity:_____ Day/time:_____

   Contact person:_____ Phone/e-mail:_____

   Meeting place:_____

3. Club/activity:_____ Day/time:_____

   Contact person:_____ Phone/e-mail:_____

   Meeting place:_____

4. Club/activity:_____ Day/time:_____

   Contact person:_____ Phone/e-mail:_____

   Meeting place:_____

and activities, student government, transportation, and off-campus housing. The bookstore sells textbooks, electronics, general interest books, and supplies.

RECREATIONAL CENTERS

If a recreation center is available on campus, you are probably already paying for access within your tuition costs. Check out classes, the pool, the weight room, and walking and running facilities. This is a great way to reduce stress and meet other students. Engage!

ALUMNI ASSOCIATION

Alumni associations and centers offer benefits and services to both current and former students, including connecting students with graduates in related career fields.

SECURITY

Security or police departments provide information about safety, parking, traffic rules, and lost and found items. Some provide safe escort for night-class students, classes in self-defense, and information on alcohol and drugs. See **Peak Progress 5.2** on personal safety issues.

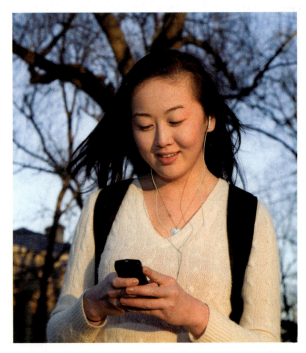

• Eyes Up

Although cell phones can be a communication and safety necessity, related thefts and injuries are on the rise. Reported injuries from texting while walking (TWW) have quadrupled in eight years. And more than 40 percent of robberies in major cities are of cell phones, often involving violent acts. *Is your phone password protected? Unplug and enjoy nature.*

Frederick Bass/fStop/Getty Images

Peak Progress

5.2

Staying Safe

Knowing your surroundings is key to your safety in any situation, be it at school, home, work, the mall, or a parking lot. Know where the exits are—from the room and the building—and plan how you would react to and where you should go in an emergency, be it a violent threat or natural disaster. Keep your cell phone handy.

Fortunately, school-associated homicides are very infrequent. The School-Associated Violent Death Study found that school-associated homicide rates decreased significantly from 1992 to 2006. Rarely does an individual just "snap." Rather, a series of behavior over time may lead to someone physically acting out. If you observe something that doesn't seem right, report it to the police or mental health professional.

Most schools have implemented "e-lert" systems for contacting students regarding safety emergencies at school, via e-mail, phone, or text. Determine if you need to sign up to be alerted (and, if so, sign up within the first week of school or earlier if possible). Find out where at school you should go if an emergency does occur.

Many schools also offer "call a ride" services that are staffed by approved volunteer students who will drive you, and even your car, home from an evening out—usually for free and with no questions asked. Be alert and aware of your surroundings, and go with a friend or two. Watch out for each other. Have a plan and use available resources.

Additional Online and Information Resources

Schools offer many resources on their website, such as the descriptions and schedule of classes, a phone and e-mail directory, links to departmental websites, and many financial transactions, such as financial aid applications, payment of fees, and bookstore purchases. You can register for classes, go through an orientation, and access your grades online. Many instructors distribute course materials, the syllabus, and assignments via e-mail or a course website. Online courses may include a blend of online instruction, websites, chat rooms, video conferencing, podcasts, and e-mail to ask questions and respond to lectures. See **Peak Progress 5.3** for some tips on using technology to your advantage.

Peak Progress

5.3

Using Technology at School

You will no doubt use technology in your coursework, from researching papers to viewing simulations to submitting homework assignments online. However, don't overlook basic tasks and resources that you may need to follow up on to make sure the technology is working for you:

- Thoroughly search the school's main website and periodically review it for recent postings.
- Register for a school e-mail account and check it often. You may decide to forward this e-mail account to another one, but make sure you look

for messages daily as this is how your school and instructors will communicate with you.

- Investigate if your school offers online courses you may be interested in. (Remember, though, that taking online courses requires an even greater commitment because you will be responsible for keeping up with assignments and reading materials on your own.)
- Contact or visit the computer lab and ask about support, including available hours and any courses or workshops.

(continued)

- Check to see if your school offers discounts on computers for students.
- Find out what and how technology will be used and required in your courses. Did your textbook come with a DVD or website that will be used? Does your course require a CPS (Classroom Performance System) device, and will you reuse it in future classes?
- Make sure you understand how to do quick searches on the Internet using search engines such as Yahoo!, Bing, and Google.
- Don't assume that everything you see on the Internet is true. Check out sources and think through opinions versus facts. If you are unsure about the reliability of the material you find on a website, ask your instructor. Be especially careful about Wiki sites.
- Respect copyrights and credit all sources.

SCHOOL CATALOG

However you access resources—online or in print—the school catalog is a key resource to review thoroughly. The catalog includes procedures, regulations, guidelines, academic areas, basic graduation requirements, and information on most of the services offered at your school. Most school catalogs contain the following information:

- Welcome from the president and a general description of the school and area
- Mission of the college and information about accreditation
- Support services and main offices in the campus community
- Admissions information, including placement tests and estimated expenses
- Academic regulations, such as auditing of a course, credit/no-credit, class level, academic standing, educational leave, drop/add, and withdrawal
- Fees and financial aid
- List of administrators, trustees, faculty, and staff
- Academic programs, minors, credentials, and graduate degrees
- Components of the degree, such as major, general education, institutions, diversity and common ground, and electives
- Course descriptions
- Expectations regarding academic honesty and plagiarism, discipline for dishonesty, class attendance, disruptive behavior, student responsibility, privacy act and access policy, grievance procedures, safety and security, substance abuse policy, and so on

Look up answers to questions before asking for help, and take responsibility for your own education. If someone gives you advice about a policy, ask where the rule is covered in the catalog so that you can review it. Look up academic areas. What fields of study interest you most or least? Which areas are so unusual you didn't even know they existed?

ORIENTATION GUIDE

Many colleges provide a student handbook or an orientation guide that familiarizes you with the school and basic requirements. If you attended an orientation program, keep your information packet and refer to planning guides and requirements before you register.

Obtain a new schedule of classes each term either in hard copy or by going online. You will need to review it carefully not only to register for classes, but also for other up-to-date information, such as an exam schedule, deadlines for adding and dropping classes and paying fees, and a calendar of events. Go through it carefully when you're planning and adjusting your schedule. Jot down deadlines in your phone or on your calendar.

Students with Disabilities

As we talked about in Chapter 1, all students have different learning styles and some students have difficulties that affect their success. Under the Americans with Disabilities Act, colleges are legally obligated to provide services and resources for students with disabilities, including physical disabilities, mental disabilities (such as depression, anxiety, or chronic illness), physical limitations (such as visual impairment), and learning disabilities (such as dyslexia or attention deficit hyperactivity disorder). Students should disclose disabilities, register with the campus disability office, and provide required documentation. Ask for assistance and advocate for yourself.

1. **Check out resources.** The first step is to see what is available at your school, such as a center for students with disabilities or a learning skills center. Special services may be provided by student services or counseling. The staff will inform you of services offered by the state and resources in the library. Some services to ask about include

   - Parking permits
   - Ramps and accessibility to buildings
   - Audio recordings and books in Braille
   - Extended time for test taking
   - Help in selecting courses, registering, and transcribing lectures
   - Lab course assistance
   - Availability of a sign language interpreter, note taker, and tutors

   A learning disability is a neurological disorder that can affect reading, writing, speaking, math abilities, and social skills. If you think you have persistent problems in these areas, you can contact the learning center or student health center for a referral to a licensed professional. Students whose learning disabilities are properly documented are entitled to certain accommodations. For more information, visit the National Center for Learning Disabilities at www.ncld.org.

2. **Meet with all of your instructors.** You are not asking for special favors or treatment but, rather, for alternatives for meeting your goals. You may want to sit in the front row, record lectures, take an oral test, or use a computer instead of writing assignments longhand, or you may need extra time taking a test. Don't try to tough it out in hopes that you won't have to talk with your instructor about your needs. This will only slow down your progress. Be calm and candid and ask for the help you need.

3. **Meet with your advisor.** Discuss your concerns with your academic advisor or an advisor from the learning center. Get help early, focus on your strengths, get organized, and map out a plan for success. Don't wait. Be proactive and get help early on.

4. **Be assertive.** You have a right to services and to be treated with respect. Ask for what you need and want in clear, polite, and direct language. If you don't get results, go to the next administrative level.

5. **Be positive and focus on your goals.** Realize that, even though your mountain may be steeper, you have what it takes to adapt and succeed. Use the ABC Method of Self-Management to dispute negative thinking and visualize yourself succeeding.

Commuter Students: Get Involved!

Commuters make up the largest number of college students. To get the most out of their college experience, commuter students (all students, for that matter) should get engaged and involved with school events and use available resources. Whenever possible, study on campus and join a club.

Returning Students

If you are a returning or reentry student, you have lots of company. More than one-third of all students are over age 25, and many are well over 40. These students are sometimes referred to as nontraditional students (with a traditional student defined as 18 to 25 years old, usually going from high school directly to college). The number of nontraditional students is growing every year as more and more people return to school to complete or further their education. Some returning students are veterans or single parents, some work full time, and almost all have other commitments and responsibilities. Returning students often do better than younger students because they have a sense of purpose, discipline, and years of experience to draw upon. Practice saying, "I belong. I'm good enough. I will succeed!"

Schools are offering more and more services geared for the older, returning student, such as special orientation programs, support groups, on-campus child care,

PhotoAlto/SuperStock

FOR COMMUTERS

1 **Participate in school activities**
Students who get involved are more likely to graduate and have a positive college experience.

2 **Use on-site resources**
Find the library, computer lab, and the best places to study.

3 **Connect with others**
Build relationships with students, instructors, advisors, and study groups.

4 **Listen to recorded lectures**
But don't let a podcast, music, or your thoughts distract you from driving safely.

5 **Pack snacks**
Bring your lunch and handy treats for long hours on campus.

6 **Carry an emergency kit**
If commuting by car, be prepared for accidents and weather emergencies.

7 **Get support from your family**
Make sure everyone understands your new responsibilities, expectations, and deadlines.
Delegate duties and ask for help and support.

tutoring and resources for brushing up on math or writing skills, credit for work or life experiences, and special classes. Other resources that are especially important for returning students include

- Adult reentry center
- Continuing education
- Distance learning office
- Veterans Affairs
- Office for credit for prior experience
- Women's center
- Counseling center
- Job placement center
- Information/referral services
- Financial aid office

No matter what your situation, take full advantage of all the resources available to help you succeed in school and all aspects of your life. See **Peak Progress 5.4** on community resources you should also explore.

Peak Progress
Explore Your Community's Resources

5.4

As a college student, you have a chance to get to know a city and make a contribution to the community. Even if you've always lived in the same city, you may not be aware of its rich resources and opportunities:

PEOPLE RESOURCES

- **Business professionals:** Connect with professionals in your field of study who can offer valuable information and advice, internships, scholarships, contacts, jobs, and career opportunities. Make contacts by volunteering your services or joining professional organizations. Many professional groups have student memberships.

- **Government officials:** Learn the names of your local political leaders, go to a city council meeting, or meet the mayor. Some city, county, and state governments have programs, internships, and fellowships for students. Do you know who your state senators and your state and local representatives are?

- **Political parties:** Political activity is one way to meet people, become informed about local issues, and contribute your organizational talents.

PROGRAM RESOURCES

- **Chamber of commerce:** The chamber of commerce has information about local attractions, special

events, museums, hotels, restaurants, libraries, clubs, businesses and economic development, environmental and political issues, and organizations.

- **Clubs and organizations:** Many clubs, such as the Rotary, Lions, Elks, Soroptimist, and Kiwanis, offer scholarships. Clubs such as Toastmasters and the Sierra Club offer programs for people with specific interests. Big Brothers, Big Sisters, YWCA, YMCA, Girls Clubs, and Boys Clubs are always looking for suitable volunteers and lecturers, and they offer many free and low-cost services. (Note that most volunteer work with children requires completing a background check.)

- **Recreation centers:** Fitness centers, swimming pools, parks, and community education programs offer classes and locations to participate in enjoyable physical activity.

- **Health care:** Hospitals and health clinics may provide vaccinations, birth control, gynecological exams, and general health care at a reduced cost. Some may sponsor support groups and offer classes on specific health conditions, CPR training, and diet and exercise for free or a nominal charge. Counselors and therapists can help with personal problems, such as depression, excessive shyness, or destructive behavior.

(continued)

Explore Your Community's Resources *(concluded)*

- **Houses of worship:** Great places to meet new friends, houses of worship hold social events, workshops, support groups, and conferences.
- **Job placement services:** Get career counseling, job listings, and help with interviewing skills and résumé writing.
- **Small Business Association (SBA):** Most cities have an SBA that provides free advice and essential contacts for those getting a business off the ground or just considering the feasibility of starting a business.
- **Crisis centers:** Hot lines are usually available 24 hours a day for such crises as suicidal feelings, physical and/or emotional abuse, rape, AIDS, and depression.
- **Support groups:** Whatever your needs, there may be a support group to share your concerns and offer help.
- **Helping organizations:** The American Cancer Society, American Heart Association, Red Cross, Salvation Army, and animal protection agencies, such as the Humane Society and ASPCA, provide information, services, and help. These organizations always need volunteers.

ADDITIONAL ONLINE AND INFORMATION RESOURCES

- **City website:** Almost every community has a website that highlights local areas of interest, schools, housing, businesses, and upcoming events.
- **Local newspapers, magazines, and newsletters:** Many communities have publications describing the area, featuring local interest stories, and advertising community events and resources.
- **Libraries:** Apply for a library card at the city or county library and check out free resources, such as DVDs and music CDs, as well as special interest classes, seminars, and book clubs.
- **2-1-1:** The United Way offers a service in many communities that provides assistance and links you to related support agencies. Dial 2-1-1 or look online to see if this service is available in your area.

Manage Your Financial Resources

In this section, we will analyze how to manage a very important resource—your money. Did you know the following facts?

- The average graduating senior of a public university has more than $30,000 in student loans, more than $5,000 since 2020.
- The average college student has almost $3,280 in credit card debt.
- The average college student spends about $900 on alcohol each year (and an average of $450 on textbooks). collegefinance.com Aug. 2021

To get control over your finances, plan ahead, create a budget, get financial assistance, limit or eliminate credit card debt, protect your identity, save, and create a positive, open mindset. Be aware of your thoughts and beliefs about money.

Keep a Budget

The first step in handling your finances is to write a budget. Calculate how much you earn and how much you spend. Write a short-term monthly budget, one for the school term, and a long-term budget for a year or more. (See **Worksheet 5.4** for samples.)

It All Adds Up

Bottled water	$1.20
Grande coffee	$4.50
"Value" meal	$5.39
Music download	$1.29
Movie and popcorn	$18
Pizza delivery	$20

Ryan McVay/Getty Images

Personal Evaluation Notebook

Money In/Money Out

1. Monitor your spending for a month. To keep it simple, list money in and money out. Record everything, including earnings, food, travel, and school items. At the end of the month, total your monthly income and your monthly expenses. Put them in the appropriate categories. Subtract your total expenses from your total income. The money left is your monthly surplus. If you have a deficit, you will need to explore ways of increasing revenue or decreasing expenses. Download free budget apps. Following is a sample assessment.

Date	Money In	Money Out
Jan. 2	$28.00 (edited paper)	
Jan. 3		$20.00 (dinner/movie)
		$50.00 (gas for car)
Jan. 4	$50.00 (house cleaning)	

2. How can you increase your earnings?

_____

_____

_____

3. How can you decrease your spending? Note the small items you buy every day.

_____

_____

_____

_____

4. List all the free or inexpensive entertainment available in your community.

_____

_____

_____

_____

Use **Worksheet 5.4** as a guide for planning your budget for the school term.

You will then have a big picture of large expenses, such as tuition, and will be able to monitor and modify your expenses each month. Your budget needs to include not only the big expenses, but also the "little" costs that quickly add up under the categories of "food" and "entertainment." Think of simple ways you can save. For example, instead of buying expensive coffee and a scone every day, brew your own. Bake a batch of scones or cookies and freeze them. Keep receipts, bills, canceled checks, and credit card statements in a digital file, in case you want to exchange your purchases or revise your budget for accuracy. Keep a file for taxes, and file applicable receipts. Complete **Personal Evaluation Notebook 5.2** to determine where you spend your money.

Research Financial Assistance

Student loan debt has tripled in the last decade, with 37 million students owing more than $1.1 trillion. This exceeds credit card debt and is second only to housing costs. Because of this mounting debt and lack of realistic plans to pay it back, more than 13 percent of graduates are defaulting on their loans within three years. This results in damaged credit that will linger for years. Thus, in order for your financial plan to truly "aid" you, you must not only find the necessary dollars to complete your education, but also develop a plan to pay back any loans in a reasonable amount of time. The source of your loan (government or private), total amount, and other factors will determine the time frame for your payback as well as the interest rate and how it accrues. Plus, government legislation is continually changing regarding student loan availability, interest rates, payback parameters, and debt forgiveness—all of which can be a confusing process to understand. However, before you incur debt, you need to calculate how much of your monthly income will need to be allocated toward your student loan (see **Figure 5.1**).

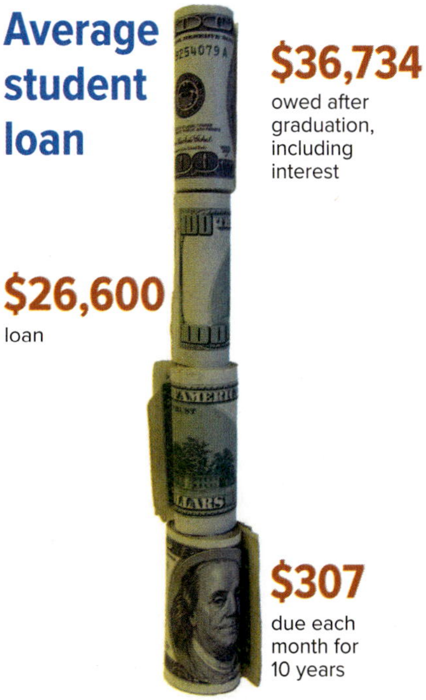

Check out a variety of financial aid options, including visiting the U.S. government's financial aid site at studentaid.ed.gov. Apply for FAFSA (Free Application for Federal Student Aid), which creates a personal identification number (PIN) and connects you with the main portal for detailed information on federal financial assistance.

Meet with your school's financial aid officer periodically to find out about loans, grants, scholarships, and job opportunities. Some sources of financial aid are included in **Table 5.1**.

Average student loan

$36,734 owed after graduation, including interest

$26,600 loan

$307 due each month for 10 years

Figure 5.1

Student Loan Payback

Go to studentaid.ed.gov/repay-loans/understand/plans/standard/comparison-calculator (or search "repayment comparison calculator" on the home page) and scroll down to use the standard payback calculator. Plug in your anticipated loans to see what your monthly payback will be. *How much will you need to allocate each month for your student loan?*

Mark Dierker/McGraw-Hill Education

Avoid Credit Card Debt

Get your credit report and take responsibility for your finances. When used wisely, credit cards are convenient and help establish a credit rating. Unfortunately, thousands of students fall into debt every year by using a credit card for everyday expenses without backup funds or a plan for repaying the balance. Besides having to pay the interest (usually from 10 to 18 percent), you can rack up additional charges by exceeding your credit limit or making payments late (which adds up fast if you use more than one card). The 2009 Credit Card Responsibility and Disclosure Act has made it more difficult for young adults to obtain credit cards because persons under 21 must have either an independent income or a co-signer. Although this has resulted in lower average debt for college students, it has been replaced by student loan debt.

It's important to pay off the credit card balances as fast as possible. When you develop your monthly budget, don't just add the minimum balance that's due on each card because interest will accrue for years. Suppose you have a credit card balance of $3,000 at a rate of 10 percent (which is at the very low end). Paying it off at $100 per month would take three years, assuming you don't charge another

Table 5.1

Sources of Financial Aid	
Financial Aid Source	**Description**
Scholarships and Grants Financial aid awarded according to criteria as designated by donor	Scholarships and grants are awarded at most schools on the basis of academic achievement, athletics, music, art, or writing and usually do not have to be paid back. Look on your school (or department) scholarship page for scholarships offered through, or in cooperation with, your school. Many companies and organizations (such as the Rotary, Kiwanis, Lions, Elks, Soroptimist, and American Association of University Women) also offer scholarships that fit a wide variety of interests and backgrounds. **For More Information** https://bigfuture.collegeboard.org/scholarship-search; www.fastweb.com; www.princetonreview.com/scholarships-financial-aid.aspx
Pell Grants Need-based grants that do not have to be repaid	This is the largest student aid program financed by the federal government. Students will need to complete the FAFSA before being considered for these grants. Filing for the FAFSA is free and can be done online. **For More Information** www2.ed.gov/programs/fpg/index.html; www.fafsa.ed.gov; studentaid.ed.gov/types/grants-scholarships/pell
Loans Payment for school from government (or other lender) that must be repaid, usually with interest	The extent of your financial need and status (undergraduate, graduate student, or parent) determines your eligibility for Perkins, Direct Subsidized or Unsubsidized, or PLUS loans offered by the federal government. Interest rates and repayment terms vary. **For More Information** studentaid.ed.gov/types/loans
Work Study Aid program that allows students to work on campus or at an approved off-campus organization to earn money to pay for college expenses	Individual colleges administer these federal funds to students participating in the Federal Work-Study (FWS) program. While on campus, workers normally work for the school; off-campus workers may be able to work for local nonprofit organizations or in a job relevant to their course of study. Student employment, or work study, is an excellent way to earn money and gain valuable experience while still in school. **For More Information** studentaid.ed.gov/types/work-study
Veterans' Programs Financial support and housing provided to military veterans and their dependents	Bills such as the Post-9/11 GI Bill and the Montgomery GI Bill provide financial assistance for the cost of tuition (including undergraduate, graduate, and vocational/technical training), housing, and books to eligible veterans. Scholarships and financial assistance are also available for veterans, military personnel, and their children. **For More Information** www.studentaid.ed.gov/types/grants-scholarships/military; www.gibill.va.gov
Programs for Native American Students Aid from federal or private institutions provided to Native American students	Native American students can find financial aid from the U.S. Bureau of Indian Education or many private donors and organizations, including the American Indian College Fund. **For More Information** www.bie.edu/Parentsstudents/Grants/index.htm Contact your financial aid office or search online for aid programs designed for specific cultural or ethnic groups.

Other Sources Loans, assistance programs, and aid programs may be available if you have disabilities or require additional help, such as visual impairments, hearing problems, or speech difficulties; are unemployed; or have a deceased parent. Search the Internet by using key words such as *college scholarship* or *college loans* to find available programs. While there are many valuable financial aid resources on the Internet, some websites are not reliable. Be especially wary of any websites that ask for money or unsecured personal information.

dollar to the credit card. On your monthly statement, credit card companies are required to indicate how many months it will take you to pay off your balance based on making just the minimum payments.

Protect Your Identity

Incidences of identity theft are increasing. Periodically check your account balances and always review your bank and credit card statements. If you handle your transactions online, carefully read the procedures on the bank's or company's website. Never respond to phone calls and e-mails asking for personal information, such as your Social Security number or bank account numbers, and do not post personal information on websites that can be viewed by persons you don't know or have only met online. Report any suspicious activity to your bank or credit card company immediately and you can also contact the National Consumers League's Fraud Center for help at www.fraud.org.

By law, you are entitled to access your credit report for free every 12 months from each of the three consumer credit reporting companies (Equifax, Experian, and Trans Union). Check your credit report for accuracy by accessing it at www.annualcreditreport.com. You do not need to sign up for additional services in order to access your credit report (although you may have to pay attention to your credit score, which is optional).

Save for the Future

Make a habit of living below your means. The U.S. Department of Commerce reports that most Americans save less than a penny for every $10 earned. And 35 percent of people under age 35 have less than $500 in the bank, leaving little cushion for unexpected expenses, such as car repairs or medical costs. Live simply. If you were to save and invest just $1 every day—the price of a small soft drink at a fast-food restaurant—you could have $90,000 in the bank at your retirement. For a traditional-aged college student, $25,000 today earning 8 percent interest will equal $800,000 at retirement. **Figure 5.2** shows how saving early—even for a shorter period of time—pays off later. (See **Peak Progress 5.5** for applications to the Adult Learning Cycle.)

Let's say you want to learn to save money. There are many ways you can cut expenses and build your savings:

1. **Pay yourself first.** If you get a paycheck, determine a percentage of your income to go directly into a savings account, your company's 401(k) plan, or an individual retirement account (IRA). If your employer offers direct deposit, see if you can split it between your checking and savings accounts so that saving is automatic. When creating your budget, add an expense entitled "me" and set a dollar amount.

2. **Shop wisely.** Research expensive purchases, such as a car, furniture, or a laptop. Take into account warranties, payment options and interest, delivery expenses, features, and what you will be using it for, and ask yourself if it is a necessity. A big screen TV may be nice to have, but you shouldn't buy it if it's beyond your means. For everyday items, refer to a list when you shop and don't buy on impulse or because something is on sale.

3. **Pay cash.** Limit credit card use to emergencies or special items, such as airline tickets. You will be tempted to buy more with credit, and it may be more difficult to monitor how much you spend. The same is true for debit

	TONYA	BEN
Invests $1,000 per year beginning: (About $84 per month in a tax-deferred retirement plan)	age 21	age 34
Stopped last contribution	age 31	age 65
Number of years contributing	10 years	31 years
Retirement	age 65	age 65
Total invested	$10,000	$31,000
Total investment value at retirement (based on 8% annual return, compounded monthly)	$249,000	$136,000

Figure 5.2

The Power of Compound Interest

There is a huge benefit to saving early. *Can you figure out how much Tonya would have had if she had not stopped after 10 years but continued investing until age 65?*

Rubberball/Getty Images

Peak Progress

Applying the Adult Learning Cycle to Managing Financial Resources

1. **FEEL and LISTEN.** *Why do I want to learn this?* I know if I start a habit of wise spending, successful saving, and investing now, it will pay off later. I want to stay debt-free and maintain a good credit rating. I will listen to advice from experts on money management and save money by going to free or inexpensive concerts and activities at the college or in the community.

2. **OBSERVE and VISUALIZE.** *How does this work?* Who do I know that appears to be in good financial shape? What can I learn from resources such as investment websites and money counselors? What online tools can I explore to determine what my goals should be? Observe when you have a craving to shop. Are you feeling anxious or lonely? Visualize yourself feeling financially secure and abundant. Feel the prosperity of knowledge, opportunity, good health, friends, and family.

3. **THINK and WRITE.** *What does this mean?* Where can I further limit my expenses? I'll keep track of my progress and see what strategies work for me. I keep a budget, write out obstacles, and a plan for overcoming them. I explore creative ways I can save money and use critical thinking when I'm tempted to spend on credit.

4. **DO and PRACTICE.** *What can I do with this?* I will practice reducing my spending every chance I get.

I'll make a commitment to paying my obligations on time. Each day, I'll work on one area to save. For example, I'll pack my lunch, rather than buying it on the run. I'll make my own coffee and buy in bulk. I will save every day.

5. **TEACH and PRACTICE AGAIN.** *Whom can I share this with?* I'll ask others for tips and share my progress with a financial counselor. I live beneath my means every day.

Use the **VARK** system to integrate your learning and help you think through and apply the Adult Learning Cycle. *Visualize* yourself feeling financially secure. Make a collage of what you want to save for—education, a car, house, travel—and also what makes you feel prosperous such as good health, friends, family, and knowledge. Illustrate your budget; collect stories of how people became financially secure. Use music to calm and soothe yourself when you feel anxious (instead of shopping) or exercise, get out in nature or visit with friends. There are many apps available on advice from financial advisors. *Write out* your goals and *read them* aloud. *Apply* what you've learned and do it every day. *Practice* saving money each day by making your own coffee, making home-made gifts, and going for walks instead of spending money.

---

cards, Apple pay, etc.; twice as many college students have debit cards than credit cards because they are easier to obtain. Keep a tally of your withdrawals, but also limit the amount of cash you carry or keep in your home. You will be less tempted to spend if money isn't readily available.

4. **Inventory your everyday expenses.** Just as you plan your monthly budget and write down anticipated expenses, jot down the many expenses you dole out each day (see your spending record from **Personal Evaluation Notebook 5.2**). Pack your lunch rather than eating out, make your coffee at home, buy in bulk, and take your water bottle and snacks rather than stopping at a convenience store.

5. **Pay bills and taxes on time.** Almost every credit card and utility bill incurs a late fee (on top of any interest) when not paid on time. The fee may be a percentage of the balance or a flat fee, which can be substantial (often $25 or more for credit cards). Besides adding up quickly, late fees can hurt your credit rating.

6. **Avoid payday loans.** Unless it's an emergency, avoid borrowing against your next paycheck. These types of loans have excessively high interest rates. For example, if you borrow $100 with the intention of paying it off when your

check comes in two weeks, you may incur an immediate $20 interest fee—that's a 520 percent annual percentage rate (APR). If you ask for an extension and incur a $25 late fee on top of the interest, the APR goes up to 1,170 percent.

7. **Use public transportation, if possible.** Many cities have public transportation. Biking or walking when you can is cheaper, gives you exercise, and is better for the environment. A car can be expensive, and the purchase price is only the initial cost. Also consider the cost of insurance, sales and personal property taxes, annual inspections and license plate renewal, maintenance, gasoline, and parking.

8. **Stay healthy.** Illness is costly in terms of time, energy, missed classes, and medical bills. Eat healthy, get exercise and rest, and avoid harmful substances. Not only is cigarette smoking expensive (a pack-a-day habit averages more than $31 per week), but smokers are sick more often than nonsmokers, pay higher health insurance premiums, and have more difficulty getting roommates and even employment.

9. **Look for free opportunities.** Take advantage of free concerts in the park, check out DVDs from the library, sign up for free birthday specials or frequent buyer cards, and visit your city's website to download discount coupons for local attractions. You may be surprised what you'll find with just a little bit of research.

10. **Conserve energy.** To save money on utilities, turn down the heat, turn off lights and switch to energy-efficient lightbulbs, unplug unused appliances, take quick showers, and turn the water off while you brush your teeth.

11. **Get a job.** Check with the career center for a list of on- and off-campus jobs.

12. **Exchange room and board for work.** Some students exchange room and board for lawn care, child care, or housecleaning. Because rent is expensive, an exchange situation can save you thousands of dollars over a few years. Explore creative options.

13. **Spend less than you earn.** It's as simple as that. Once you have a habit of living below your means, you will reap the rewards of confidence and control for life.

Get Financial Help If You're in Trouble

If you are having financial problems and your credit rating might be in jeopardy, get help.

1. **Admit that you have a problem.** Denial only makes the problem worse. If you experience two or more of these warning signs, you need to take action:
   - You make only the minimum monthly payments on credit cards.
   - You struggle to make even the minimum monthly payments.

Brain researchers have found that the brain scans of people with gambling addictions who had near misses reacted the same way as if they won. The brain areas related to emotion and reward were as active as if they had won. They would keep gambling because "they almost won."[1]

Luis recently moved into an unfurnished apartment from his parent's basement. He has been contributing to his company's 401(k) and putting money aside each month into a savings account. As a draftsman for a small architectural firm, he has a good job, but he wants to invest for a house and not just blow money on cars and furnishings. Two friends like to go out gambling at the local casino. They insist that they lose only a little and, in fact, almost always win. Luis has been going out with them occasionally and enjoys socializing. Do you think Luis should follow his financial plan or let loose and join his friends out more often.

- Should Luis continue to go out and spend a night or two gambling with his friends?
- What are some creative ways Luis could furnish his apartment for less money?
- What else can Luis do now (educationally, financially, socially) that will help him save more money to buy his first house?

THINK
CREATIVELY AND CRITICALLY

If your financial obligations are shared by a spouse or partner, be aware of each other's spending habits. *How can financial problems affect a relationship?*

Iakov Filimonov/123RF

- The total balance on your credit cards increases every month.
- You miss loan payments or often pay late.
- You use savings to pay for necessities, such as food and utilities.
- You receive second or third payment-due notices from creditors.
- You borrow money to pay off old debts.
- You exceed the credit limits on your credit cards.
- You've been denied credit because of a bad credit bureau report.

2. **Get professional help.** Contact the local chamber of commerce and ask if your community has a consumer credit agency that helps with credit counseling. Take all your financial information, including your budget, assets, bills, resources, loans, and any other requested items. Local branches of the Consumer Credit Counseling Service (CCCS) provide debt counseling for families and individuals, and they charge only a small fee when they supervise a debt-repayment plan. Universities, credit unions, the military, and state and federal housing authorities also provide financial counseling for a little or no charge.

You Are a Great Resource!

Your most powerful resource is a positive, open mindset. You already possess the power to change your life; you just need to claim it and use it consistently by focusing on growth and learning. A positive mindset takes advantage of opportunities. A negative, fixed mindset blames others and looks for excuses, "Why didn't someone tell me?" "If I had only known, I would have . . ."—these beliefs keep you stuck. A positive mindset is curious, asks questions, and sees setbacks as opportunities for growth. Positive, open people don't throw up their hands in frustration, but focus on learning ways to tolerate distress and manage their emotions. They choose positive thoughts and actions to move forward.

Overcoming Obstacles

You can use the power of habits to overcome obstacles. The opening Self-Management feature illustrates how many students feel about being overwhelmed by debt and money worries. Your habits are what you choose them to be and positive habits can guide you in how you spend money and save. Let's say that you want to save money. You have made it a habit to stop in at the coffee shop, which is right on the way to your 8:00 class. It's so easy to get a latte and scone. This simple habit can add up to $50 a week. So let's change your routine. You set out your mug. The mug becomes the *trigger,* and the *routine* is setting up the coffee machine every night before bed so you simply have to press the button when you wake up. If you want to froth milk for a latte, it takes just a minute and you

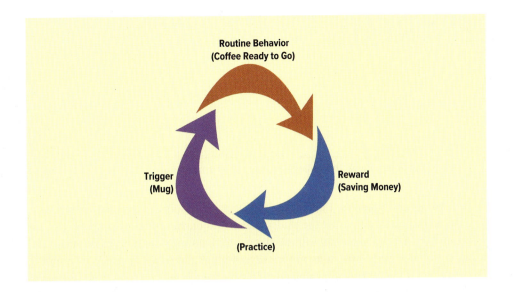

have a steaming cup of coffee to carry with you along with a healthy energy bar or piece of fruit. Your *reward* is great-tasting coffee, a healthy snack, and the sense of accomplishment at saving money in simple ways. Stay positive and practice until this becomes automatic.

TAKING CHARGE

Summary

In this chapter, I learned to

- **Explore and understand the college system.** It is important to understand the rules, regulations, deadlines, policies, procedures, requirements, and resources for help.

- **Seek out people resources.** I appreciate the faculty, advisors, administrators, and study team members, as well as all the students and relationships that make up the campus community. I build networks with all the people who provide information, help, and support. I meet with instructors and my advisor often to review and clarify my progress. I understand that having a mentor for guidance, knowledge, and advice is essential to my personal and academic growth as a person and my field of study.

- **Use program and online resources.** I explore various programs that offer help, support, and opportunities, such as the advising center, the career development center, counseling, the tutoring and learning center, exchange programs, the job placement office, clubs, campus events, and other activities. I spend time in the library exploring books, magazines, newspapers, technology, visit the bookstore and computer labs, read or go online to check out the catalog, look at school material, and read the school newspaper. I explore service learning opportunities and resources available for my unique needs, such as the adult reentry center, legal aid, child care, and veterans programs. As a commuting student, I check out carpooling boards, online classes, and look for programs that can help me be more involved.

- **Use technology to my advantage.** I determine how technology will be used in my courses and what opportunities and resources my school provides.

- **Explore community resources.** I go to city meetings and become familiar with community leaders and projects. I check into internships and part-time jobs. I check out the community's website and local publications to become familiar with local topics and opportunities for service, resources, and special support groups and agencies offering counseling and health services.

- **Manage my money.** I take full responsibility for my finances. I know how to make and stick to a budget, save money, and spend less than I earn. I limit my credit card use, alert to identity theft, and seek help managing my money when necessary.

- **Explore financial resources.** I explore scholarships and grants, loans, work study, and special assistance programs, campus jobs, and student assistance programs.

- **I am my best resource.** A positive, open mindset focuses on growth, learning, and perseverance. Being willing to change, grow, and cultivate positive qualities and habits is key for success. I focus on effort, make the most of my opportunities, and am proactive, diligent, and resourceful in order to motivate myself and reach my goals.

Performance Strategies

Following are the top 10 tips for maximizing your resources:

- A positive, open mindset that focuses on growth is the number one resource for success.
- Join clubs and activities and widen your circle of friends.
- Explore campus resources and investigate a new one each week.
- Get involved and volunteer at school and in the community.
- Seek help at the first sign of academic, financial, health, or emotional trouble.
- Know where your money goes, create a budget, and live beneath your means.
- Use the power of perseverance to create change and stick with your goals.
- Use a credit card for convenience only and don't go into debt for unnecessary items.
- Protect your identity from fraud.
- Look for creative ways to reduce spending and save money.

Tech for Success

- **Websites and textbooks.** Check out free websites that provide additional resources and study tools, such as online study guides, lab manuals, resources for research projects, and materials to study for certification exams. Read the book's preface, ask your instructor, or visit the publisher's website to see what is available.

- **Bill paying online.** Most financial institutions offer a service that lets you pay your bills through their website and may help you keep up with your financial obligations.

Endnote

1 Charles Duhigg, *The Power of Habit: Why We Do What We Do in Life and Business* (New York: Random House, 2012).

Study Team Notes

Career *in* Focus

Royalty-Free/Corbis

Donna Washington
SCHOOL SOCIAL WORKER

Related Majors: Social Work, Psychology, Sociology

Benefits of Community Resources

Donna Washington works as a social worker at an elementary school. School social workers help students, teachers, and parents cope with problems. Their work involves guidance and counseling regarding challenging issues in the classroom, as well as in the home. They diagnose behavior problems and advise teachers on how to deal with difficult students. They work with families to improve attendance and help working parents find after-school child care. They also help recent immigrants and students with disabilities adjust to the classroom.

A long list of community resources helps Donna provide appropriate referrals. She arranges services for children in need, such as counseling or testing. Other services on her list include legal aid societies, crisis hot lines, immigrant resource centers, and tutoring. Donna has developed her list over a 20-year career span and remains in touch with key community leaders to keep her list up-to-date.

Donna chose to be a school social worker because of a strong desire to make a difference in the lives of children. She possesses all the qualities that make her an excellent social worker: She is responsible, emotionally stable, warm and caring, and able to relate to a wide variety of clients, and she can work independently. Because of budget cuts, agencies in her district are understaffed, and Donna struggles with a huge caseload. Although she finds the work emotionally draining at times, Donna finds tremendous satisfaction when she sees the lives of her students improve due to her care.

CRITICAL THINKING What qualities make a good social worker? Why?

Peak Performer Profile

Eric Greitens

It's not a charity. It's a challenge. That's the motto of The Mission Continues, founded by Navy SEAL officer Eric Greitens. The group's goal is to help post-9/11 veterans' transition from military service by redeploying them on new missions at home. Greitens formulated the plan for The Mission Continues after visiting wounded colleagues. "Every single one of them said he wanted to find a way to continue to serve. They needed to know that when they came home, we saw them as vital."*

Returning veterans may face special challenges that affect their health and well-being after their service and combat have ended. According to the Department of Veterans Affairs, veterans who served in the wars in Iraq or Afghanistan have a much higher rate of dying in vehicle crashes at home, which in part can be attributed to post-traumatic stress disorder, which increases aggressive driving.

Sometimes, the violence of war also comes home, with veterans committing higher rates of spousal and child abuse and some turning to alcohol and drug use to deal with the trauma of war. Also, a U.S. military veteran commits suicide, on average, every 65 minutes. A study of veteran suicides from 1999 to 2010 showed that 22 vets were dying every day. More active-duty soldiers die from suicide than combat.

Starting a new career after leaving military duty can also be a challenge. An estimated 250,000 recent veterans are searching for jobs. Many vets face the additional challenge of rehabilitating and finding employment after a serious life-altering injury.

These statistics prove that it's critical for returning veterans to find and utilize resources that will help them apply core skills they acquired in the military, such as team building, dependability, strategic critical thinking, and leadership. They also need support to help them adjust to home and family life after serving in tense, unpredictable combat situations.

Programs such as The Mission Continues are vital resources for giving veterans a sense of purpose, assimilating their skills and leadership abilities into the community, and helping them make personal and professional connections. This is a win–win for everyone—returning veterans needing to transition their life purpose and welcoming communities needing their skills and abilities to tackle any challenge presented them. With The Mission Continues, Greitens, a Rhodes scholar and best-selling author, has used his vast education and military experience to continue his mission of providing opportunities for today's veteran.

PERFORMANCE THINKING Do you know anyone struggling with the after-effects of military service? What resources does your college offer that help returning veterans further their education and participate in school and community affairs?

CHECK IT OUT The Mission Continues is one of many organizations focused on issues related to active and returning military personnel. Go to www.missioncontinues.org to see what volunteer opportunities are in your area. Think of local "missions" that would benefit from the services of returning veterans.

*Tony Perry, "To Ease Veterans' Return to Civilian Life, Program Offers Purpose," *Los Angeles Times,* February 18, 2013. http://articles.latimes.com/2013/feb/18/local/la-me-veterans-mission-20130218.

Starting Today

At least one strategy I learned in this chapter that I plan to try right away is

_____

_____

_____

What changes must I make in order for this strategy to be most effective?

_____

_____

_____

Review Questions

Based on what you have learned in this chapter, write your answers to the following questions:

1. What are some of the benefits of participating in a study group?

_____

_____

2. What type of school programs would you contact to find a full- or part-time job while attending school?

_____

_____

3. Name two college financial resources cited in this chapter that you would like to investigate, and explain why.

_____

_____

4. How can staying healthy help you financially?

_____

_____

5. What is your most important resource? Why?

_____

_____

Using Resources

In the Classroom

Lorraine Peterson is a returning student at a two-year business school. She also works part time selling cosmetics at a retail store and would like to advance to a managerial position. She was away from school for several years. During that time, she started a family and is now eager to become involved in school and its activities. On returning to school, she happily discovered other returning students. Several of them get together for coffee on a regular basis. Lorraine is

Fancy/Alamy Stock Photo

especially interested in international students and global business opportunities. She also wants to learn more about available computer services, guest speakers, marketing associations, and scholarships.

1. What suggestions do you have for Lorraine about involvement in campus and community events?

    _____

    _____

2. How can she find out about scholarships and explore all the resources that would increase her success as a returning student?

    _____

    _____

In the Workplace

Lorraine has been a salesperson for several years with a large cosmetics firm. She recently was promoted to a district sales manager position. Part of her job is to offer motivational seminars on the benefits of working for her company. She wants to point out the opportunities and resources available to employees, such as training programs, support groups, demonstrations, sales meetings, and conferences. The company also sponsors scholarships and community events. An elaborate incentive system offers bonuses and awards for increased sales.

3. How can Lorraine publicize these resources to her sales staff?

    _____

    _____

4. What strategies in this chapter would help her communicate the importance of contributing time and talents to the community and the company?

    _____

    _____

Applying the ABC Method of Self-Management

In the Journal Entry at the beginning of the chapter, you were asked to write about a time when you set a financial goal. How would having a positive, open mindset have helped?

Let's apply the ABC Method and write a script.

_____

_____

A = Acknowledge reality and pay attention to your emotions.

_____

_____

B = Breathe: Take a deep breath and feel beloved and calm.

_____

_____

C = Choose: Knowing you have many options, choose the most appropriate behavior which will result in long-term positive consequences.

_____

_____

Sample Script: Even though I'm embarrassed and feel guilty that I cannot manage my money, I love and accept myself and want to grow. I breathe deeply and know that these feelings will pass. I'm not my emotions. Financial management is a skill that requires attention and good habits. I choose to learn these skills and know that they will help me in my future career and in all areas of my life. First I'll go to the financial aid office and check out other resources that can help me learn good financial management skills. Next, I'll keep a record of everything I spend even snacks, coffee, and other small items. I'll take small steps to find creative ways to save money and live simply.

Networking

Using your contacts is especially important when looking for a job. Write information about your network of people on the following form. You can copy this worksheet form to extend your list of contacts.

Name _____   **How I met/know this person** _____

Company _____   Position _____

Phone _____   E-mail _____

Type of work _____

Name _____   **How I met/know this person** _____

Company _____   Position _____

Phone _____   E-mail _____

Type of work _____

Name _____   **How I met/know this person** _____

Company _____   Position _____

Phone _____   E-mail _____

Type of work _____

Name _____   **How I met/know this person** _____

Company _____   Position _____

Phone _____   E-mail _____

Type of work _____

Community Resources

Research and list the various resources your community has to offer. Make a point to visit at least a few of them, and place a check mark by those you have visited. You can copy this worksheet form to extend your list of resources.

CHECK

_____Resource _____ Website _____

Service offered _____

Contact person _____ Title/Position _____

Phone _____ E-mail _____

_____ Resource _____ Website _____

Service offered _____

Contact person _____ Title/Position _____

Phone _____ E-mail _____

_____ Resource _____ Website _____

Service offered _____

Contact person _____ Title/Position _____

Phone _____ E-mail _____

_____ Resource _____ Website _____

Service offered _____

Contact person _____ Title/Position _____

Phone _____ E-mail _____

_____ Resource _____ Website _____

Service offered _____

Contact person _____ Title/Position _____

Phone _____ E-mail _____

REVIEW AND APPLICATIONS | CHAPTER 5

Monthly Budget

Creating a budget is the first step to financial success. Complete the following list and review it every month to keep track of your expenses. Many of the expenses will vary per month or will be paid periodically rather than monthly. Include monthly estimates in your budget in order to plan ahead. Modify the list to fit your needs.

Monthly Expense	Projected Cost	Actual Cost	Annual Cost
Savings account			
Housing (mortgage, rent)			
Utilities (gas, electric, water, sewer)			
Phone			
Internet/cable			
Transportation (bus, metro, car loan, taxes)			
Gasoline			
Insurance (including homeowner's, renter's, car)			
Health care (including health insurance, co-pays, prescriptions)			
Credit card(s)			
Food			
Household items			
Clothing (including laundry)			
Entertainment			
Tuition (including fees)			
Books and supplies			
Student loan			
Other			
Other			
Other			
Other			
TOTAL			
Financial Resources	**Projected Income**	**Actual Income**	**Annual Income**
Employment (include full- and part-time, work study, contract work)			
Loan(s)			
Savings			
Parental contribution			
Other			
Other			
TOTAL			

Managing Resources

Exploring your personal resources and abilities is important for your career development. Answer the following questions, and relate your community participation to your leadership skills. Add this page to your Career Development Portfolio.

1. Describe your ability to manage resources. What are your strengths in managing time, money, and information and in determining what resources are available to solve various problems?

   _____

   _____

   _____

   _____

2. Indicate how you would demonstrate to an employer that you have made a contribution to your school or community.

   _____

   _____

   _____

   _____

3. Indicate how you would demonstrate to an employer that you know how to explore and manage resources.

   _____

   _____

   _____

   _____

4. Indicate how you would demonstrate to an employer that you have learned leadership skills.

   _____

   _____

   _____

   _____

REVIEW AND APPLICATIONS | CHAPTER 5

Listen and Take Effective Notes

LEARNING OUTCOMES

In this chapter, you will learn to

6-1 List effective listening strategies

6-2 Describe the various note-taking systems

6-3 Identify ways to overcome note-taking obstacles with better habits

SELF-MANAGEMENT

I am having trouble staying focused and alert in my afternoon classes. The instructors speak in a monotone and I can hardly follow their lectures. How can I listen more effectively, be more alert, and take better notes?

Hero/Corbis/Glow Images

Have you had a similar experience? Have you left a class feeling frustrated because you couldn't stay focused and your notes were unreadable? In this chapter, you will learn how to be an attentive listener and take clear and organized notes.

JOURNAL ENTRY In **Worksheet 6.1**, describe a time when you had difficulty making sense out of a lecture and staying alert. Are there certain classes in which it is harder for you to listen attentively?

Attending lectures or meetings, listening, taking notes, and gathering information are a daily part of school and work. However, few people give much thought to the process of selecting, organizing, and recording information. Attentive listening and note taking are not just tools for school. They are essential job skills. Throughout your career, you will process and record information. Technology has dramatically expanded the volume of accessible information, but it has also compounded the number of distractions you may face. The career professional who can stay focused and can organize and summarize information will be valuable. This chapter addresses the fine points of attentive listening and note taking.

Attentive Listening Strategies

Before you can be an effective note taker, you must become an effective listener. Most people think of themselves as good listeners. However, listening is more than ordinary hearing. **Attentive listening** means being fully focused with the intent to understand the speaker. It is a consuming activity that requires physical and mental attention, energy, concentration, and discipline. It also requires respect, empathy, genuine interest, and the desire to understand. Researchers say we spend about 80 percent or more of our time communicating; of that time, almost half—45 to 50 percent—is spent listening, yet few of us have been trained to listen. The first place to start is with an open, positive attitude.

Not only is listening fundamental to taking good classroom notes, but it is also directly related to how well you do in college, in your career, and in relationships. Students are expected to listen attentively to lectures, to other student presentations, and in small-group and class discussions. Career professionals attend meetings, follow directions, work with customers, take notes from professional journals and lectures, and give and receive feedback. Many organizations have developed training programs to improve their employees' listening, attitude, and communication habits.

Apply the following attentive listening strategies for building effective relationships at school, at work, and in the rest of your life.

Prepare to Listen

1. **Have a positive, open mindset.** *The first place to start is with a positive, open attitude that focuses on growth and learning.* With effort and practice, you can learn to be a better listener. Is your intention to learn and understand the other person or is your intention to prove how smart you are and how wrong the other person is? The best listening strategies in the world won't help if you are unwilling to listen and understand another's viewpoint. Prepare mentally by creating a positive, open attitude that focuses on understanding and learning. Stretch yourself to remain alert, curious, and attentive.

2. **Be open to new ideas.** Many people resist change, new ideas, or different beliefs. This resistance gets in the way of actively listening and learning. *It is easy to misinterpret a message's meaning if you are negative, defensive, judgmental, bored, or upset.* Be curious and open to different points of view

"The reason why we have two ears and only one mouth is that we may listen the more and talk the less **"**
ZENO OF CITIUM, PHILOSOPHER

and styles of lecturing. With practice and discipline, you can create interest in any subject. "My professor is presenting an interesting idea that I'll share later with my roommate." "My boss has a lot of experience and I am open to her ideas." A growth mindset is curious.

3. **Position yourself to listen.** In the classroom, this may mean leaning forward to focus on the message and create a more personal relationship with the speaker. At work, use attentive body language, eye contact, nodding, smiling, and other cues that indicate to your co-workers that you are listening. Unplug. Put away your phone. Sit up straight. Find creative ways to position yourself to listen more attentively.

4. **Reduce distractions.** Avoid sitting next to a friend or someone who likes to talk or is distracting. Take a sweater if it is cold in the classroom or sit by an open window if it is warm. Carry a bottle of water with you to drink when your energy starts to lag. Don't do other activities (texting, doing math homework, making a to-do list, and so on). At work, focus on the task at hand and reward yourself for intense concentration by socializing briefly with co-workers. Learn to be mindful of the present moment.

5. **Show you are listening.** Attentive listening requires focus. It is easy to get distracted, but do what you are able to do to stay alert and attentive. Sit up, keep your spine straight, and uncross your legs. Maintain eye contact and lean slightly forward. Your body language is important—whether you are in a chair or engaged in a dialogue with others. Your body language indicates your interest both in class and in the workplace. Taking notes helps you focus. If you have trouble paying attention or have ADHD, visit the Learning Center for additional help and resources. Mindfulness training can benefit everyone.

6. **Create an alert and healthy state of mind.** You cannot be alert and awake if your glucose level is low or you are not rested. *Eat healthy meals and snacks every few hours and drink water throughout the day.* A handful of nuts or seeds, or a piece of cheese, will keep your glucose level much more even all day than candy or a soft drink. Make sure you get enough sleep each night to stay alert during the day. Breathe deeply.

Stay Attentive

1. **Be quiet.** The fundamental rule of listening is to be quiet while the speaker is talking. Don't interrupt or talk to classmates. The listener's role is to understand and comprehend. The speaker's role is to make the message clear and comprehensible. Observe and notice the environment and your thoughts and emotions. When they wonder, gently bring your attention back to the speaker.

2. **Stay focused and mindful.** Everyone's mind wanders at times during a long lecture, but being mentally preoccupied is a major barrier to effective listening. Mindfulness is the ability to be in the present moment. Mindfulness is an important skill that helps focus your attention, concentrate on the subject, and bring your mind back to the present. If you need additional help, visit the Learning or Counseling Center.

3. **Show empathy, respect, and genuine interest.** Focus on understanding the speaker's message and viewpoint. Look for common views and ways in which you are alike.

4. **Observe the speaker.** Watch for verbal and nonverbal clues about what information is important. If your instructor uses repetition, becomes more animated, or writes information on the board, it is probably important.

PowerPoint presentations or handouts may include important diagrams, lists, drawings, facts, or definitions. Pay attention to phrases, such as "One important factor is. . . ."

5. **Predict and ask questions.** Keep yourself alert by predicting and asking yourself questions. What are the main points? How does the example clarify the material you read prior to class? What test questions could be asked about the main points? Ask your study team or instructor to elaborate, give examples, or explain certain points. *Asking questions not only helps clarify principles, but also shows interest and curiosity.*

6. **Experiment with various** learning styles and use as many senses as possible. If you are primarily an *auditory* learner, consider recording lectures (be sure to ask the instructor first). Record yourself *reading* your book notes aloud and play it back several times. *Write* out a summary. If you are primarily a *visual* learner, visualize what your instructor is talking about, and supplement your lecture notes with drawings, illustrations, and pictures. If you are a *kinesthetic* learner, write as you listen, draw diagrams or pictures, rephrase what you hear in your own words, and take special note of material on the board, screen, and handouts. Read aloud and while standing up or walking around. Write key points on the board and present them to your study group. Be aware and shift body position so that you're comfortable, roll your shoulders and breathe deeply.

7. **Postpone judgment.** Don't judge the speaker or the person's message based on clothes, reputation, voice, or teaching style. Listen with an open and curious mind and focus on the message, the course content, and your performance. Talk in private if you disagree, but do not embarrass or unnecessarily challenge the person in front of others. Of course, you should use critical thinking, but be respectful and open to new ideas.

Review What You Have Heard

1. **Paraphrase.** Clarify the speaker's message by paraphrasing what you think the speaker said to you—for example, "Professor Keys, it is my understanding that the paper should be four to five pages long, is due on Friday, and should include supporting documentation. Is that correct?" or "Jan, do I understand that you feel you are doing more than your share of cleaning the apartment?" After a lecture, write a summary of the key points and main ideas. Compare notes and summarize with your study team.

2. **Assess.** Evaluate how effective your listening skills are for recall, test taking, and studying with your study group. Reflect on conflicts, misunderstandings, and others' reactions to you. Notice nonverbal cues. If there is a misunderstanding, assess your part. Did you jump to conclusions or misunderstand nonverbal clues? Did you fail to clarify the message or to follow up? When there is a misunderstanding or something is missing, ask simple, direct questions with the intent to understand.

3. **Practice awareness.** Changing old habits takes time. For example, do you continue to interrupt? Think about how you feel when that happens to you, and make a commitment to change. It won't happen overnight, but with awareness and consistent practice you can learn to improve your listening skills. You may want to visit the learning center or talk with a counselor for additional help.

Peak Progress 6.1 explores how you can become a more attentive listener by applying the Adult Learning Cycle. Then, **Personal Evaluation Notebook 6.1** asks you to think critically about your listening skills and how you can improve them.

Peak Progress

Applying the Adult Learning Cycle to Becoming an Attentive Listener

Learning to be an attentive listener and taking good notes requires time and effort.

1. **FEEL and LISTEN.** *Why do I want to learn this?* I know that being an attentive listener will help me in school, work, and life. People are naturally drawn to attentive listeners. I will listen with cultural sensitivity and respect. I will be aware of what other people are feeling and take time to understand their concerns. I will listen attentively in class to my professors and other students and at work to co-workers, relate to their concerns, and acknowledge their successes and new ideas.

2. **OBSERVE and VISUALIZE.** *How does this work? Who is an attentive listener?* I can learn a lot about attentive listening by watching others. I'll observe people who are good listeners and take good notes and those who are not good listeners. What happens when I'm an attentive listener? I will visualize myself being successful.

3. **THINK and WRITE.** *What does this mean?* I will gather information about listening and note taking and write out the best strategies for me to apply. I will ask for clarification. I'll explore creative ways to listen and take notes and evaluate what works and doesn't work. I will write out summaries and read them aloud to stay attentive and engaged.

4. **DO and PRACTICE.** *What can I do with this?* I will commit to being a more attentive listener and do it every day. For example, I'll choose one class in which I'm having trouble listening and experiment with new strategies. I will be actively engaged and attentive.

5. **TEACH and PRACTICE AGAIN.** *Whom can I share this with?* I will practice attentive listening skills. When I'm asked, I'll demonstrate and teach others in my study group the methods I've learned.

Use the VARK system to help you think though and apply the Adult Learning Cycle and integrate learning styles. *Visualize* yourself actively listening and taking good notes. Sketch or illustrate in the margins. *Observe* how the professor is talking and note tone, inflection, and emphasis. Observe effective listeners at college and work. *Write out* your notes and *read them* aloud. Rewrite or add to them as you read your textbook. Write summaries both for class and at work. Enhance *kinesthetic* learning by modeling what an attentive listener looks like. Lean in slightly, respond with facial expressions, and have direct eye contact. Be aware of your writing and your muscles as you take notes. *Experiment* with mind maps. *Practice* listening every day and *apply* concepts through trial and error. Stand or walk as you read notes or explain them to your study buddy. Explain directions or review with co-workers and teach them information you've learned. Now return to Stage 1 and think about how it feels to learn this valuable skill.

Recording the Message

Now that you are prepared and have sharpened your listening and observation skills, let's look at how to outline your notes so that you can organize material. **Note taking** is a method of creating order and arranging thoughts and materials to help a person retain information. You can use either a formal or an informal outline (see **Peak Progress 6.2**). The point of all note-taking systems is to distinguish between major and minor points and to add order to material. Let's start with one of the most widely used and effective systems—the Cornell System of Note Taking.

> **"He listens well, who takes notes."**
> DANTE ALIGHIERI (1265–1321)

The Cornell System of Note Taking

The Cornell System of Note Taking was developed in the 1950s by Walter Pauk at Cornell University. It is effective for integrating text and lecture notes. Start with a sheet of standard loose-leaf paper and label it with the class, date, and title of the lecture. Divide your notepaper into three sections ("Notes," "Cues," and

Personal Evaluation Notebook

Attentive Listening

Use critical and creative thinking to answer the following questions.

1. Do you go to class prepared and in a positive and receptive state of mind? Write down one tip you would be willing to try to improve your listening.

   _____

   _____

   _____

2. Jot down the name of a person you consider to be a good listener. Consider your feelings toward this person. Attentive listening shows respect and caring. Does that describe this person?

   _____

   _____

   _____

3. Write a list of daily situations that require attentive listening, such as talking to your child about their day at school, listening to your partner's views on politics, and meeting with a community group to plan a fund-raising event. What listening strategies would increase your attention and responsiveness in the situations you listed?

   _____

   _____

Take any one of the above and create a habit. For example, let's take number 3 since listening is so important for healthy relationships. The trigger to be an attentive listener may be the statement from a roommate, friend, child, or spouse who says, *"I need to talk to you about my day."* You are not being asked to say anything or give advice. Just listen. Use this trigger to set aside your problems or your project and resist the impulse to say, *"I'm too busy."* or *"Hey, I've had a bad day too."* Your consistent routine of being aware, sensitive, and attentive will pay off with cultivating empathy and kindness and creating healthy relationships.

"Summary") by drawing a vertical line about two inches from the left-hand margin; then draw a horizontal line below that. (See **Figure 6.1**.)

Notes. The right side is the largest section. Record information from class lectures in whatever format works best for you. You can use a formal system with standard Roman numerals or an informal system of indentation to distinguish between major and minor points and meaningful facts.

Cues. Then use the left side to jot down cues, main ideas, phrases, key words, or clarifications. List any pertinent examples or sample test questions from the lecture or the book. Try to pose questions that are answered by your notes.

Peak Progress

Formal (Traditional) versus Informal (Creative) Outlines

Your learning style can affect what outline style works for you. You may like a traditional outline that uses a logical, step-by-step, sequential pattern of thought and focuses on words and order. **Formal outlines** may use Roman numerals and capital letters to outline headings, main topics, and points, then list supporting points with lowercase letters and numbers. This system requires consistency. For example, the rules require at least two headings on the same level; if you have IA, you should also have IB. If you have IIIA1, you must also have IIIA2.

Some students find that formal outlines are too time-consuming and restrictive for classroom lectures.

However, they like using an outline because it organizes ideas and illustrates major points and supporting ideas. They prefer a free-form, or **informal outline**. This system shows headings, main points, and supporting examples and associations, but it uses a more flexible system of dashes, bullets, numbers, and/or indenting—whatever works for the note taker. Many students find an informal method easier for in-class note taking because it lets them focus on main ideas and supporting examples instead of worrying about rules.

Following are examples of formal (top) and informal (bottom) outlines.

Formal (Traditional) Outline

Example 1:   Jana Rosa
                                                          April 9, 2022

Topic: Note Taking

Effective Strategies for Taking Notes

I. The traditional outline for note taking

   A. Advantages

      1. Occupies your attention totally

      2. Organizes ideas as well as records them

   B. Disadvantages

      1. Too structured for right-brain-dominant person

      2. Time-consuming

II. The mapping system for note taking

   A. Advantages

      1. Presents a creative and visual model

      2. Can start anywhere on the page

   B. Disadvantages

      1. Too busy for a left-brain-dominant person

      2. Too unorganized for a left-brain-dominant person

Informal (Creative) Outline

Example 2:   Jana Rosa
                                                          April 9, 2022

NOTE TAKING

1. Summarize
2. Organize ——— Traditional / Mind map / Cornell
3. Visualize and illustrate
4. Shorthand
5. Notebook
6. One side of paper
7. Write down blackboard notes
8. Review
   —10 minutes
   —24 hours
   —Weekly

Figure 6.1

The Cornell System

This method integrates text and lecture notes and includes a summary section. *Which personality type might prefer the Cornell System?*

	Seminar	Jana Rosa
Peak Performance 101		April 9, 2022
Topic: Note taking		

Cues:

What is the purpose of note taking?

Different systems can be combined.

Notes:

I. Purpose of Note Taking
  A. To accurately record information
  B. To become actual part of listening
  C. To enhance learning

II. Note-Taking Systems
  A. Formal outline
  B. Cornell System
  C. Mind map

Summary:
Note taking is an important learning and communication tool. Use the note-taking system that is right for you or create a combination.

When you review, cover up the right side (the "Notes" section) and try to answer the questions you have written.

Summary. On the bottom of the page, include a "Summary" section. This is an effective way to summarize each class session in your own words. Fill in with details from the book, and elaborate after discussions with your study team or instructor.

The Cornell System is a great tool for reviewing and comparing notes for lectures and books. (In Chapter 7, we'll look further at taking notes while reading.) Notes can be taken sequentially to preserve the order decided upon by the lecturer. It is an effective method for study teams because you can compare class notes, review summaries, and use the sample test questions on the left. One student can recite his or her notes on the right while another uses the cues on the left for possible test questions and examples. Each can recite his or her class and chapter summaries. Many people who are left-brain dominant prefer the logical, sequential, step-by-step Cornell System.

Mind Maps

A **mind map** (or "think link") is a visual, holistic form of note taking that starts with the main idea placed in the center of a page and branches out with subtopics through association and patterns (see **Figures 6.2** and **6.3** for two examples). The advantage is that you can see the big picture, including connections to the main idea. You may find that mapping increases your comprehension, creativity, and recall. Mind maps can be useful in brainstorming ideas for speeches or papers, serving as a framework for recalling topics, or helping you review or for adding points and details to the main topic.

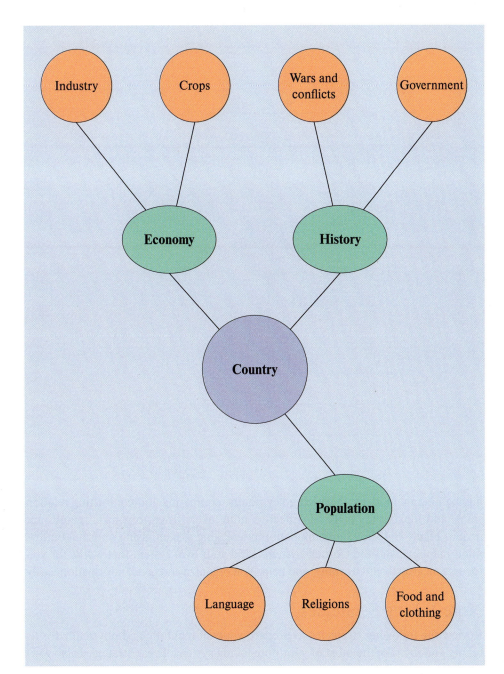

Figure **6.2**

Sample Mind Map
This template can be adapted for many subjects. *In which of your courses would this format be useful for note taking?*

Some students like to use a one-page mind map as a visual, creative design. Other students may favor an outline that is sequential and orderly. You can use both—a mind map to illustrate an entire chapter and a traditional outline for daily notes. Be flexible.

See **Worksheet 6.3** for a blank mind map template, which you can use or adapt for many situations.

Combination Note-Taking Systems

Because no two people take notes in the same way, you will want to experiment with several note-taking systems or a combination of systems. Effective note takers vary their strategies, depending on the material covered. These strategies include

Figure 6.3

Another Sample Mind Map

This type of mind map uses branches to reveal concept connections and patterns. *Which mind map design do you prefer?*

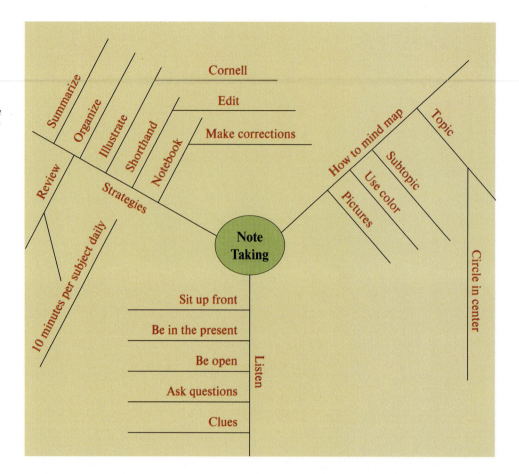

highlighting main ideas, organizing key points, comparing and contrasting relationships, and looking for patterns. Effective note takers listen, organize, record, and review. **Figure 6.4** shows a combination note-taking system, using a formal outline, mind mapping, and the Cornell System. Find your own system that works for you, focuses on growth and learning, and helps you organize and recall information easily.

Note-Taking Strategies

Review the following strategies to prepare yourself mentally and physically for listening and to make the most of your note-taking system. These strategies also work if you are taking your notes on a laptop or tablet.

1. **Preview the material.** Go to classes prepared, even if you have only a few minutes to prepare the night before or right before class. Preview or skim textbook chapters for main ideas, general themes, and key concepts. Previewing is a simple strategy that enhances your note taking and learning. In a sense, you are priming your brain to process information efficiently and effectively. Also review previous notes and connect what you have learned to new ideas. Have the supplies you need.

2. **Go to every class and be on time.** You cannot take effective notes if you are not there. Having someone else take notes for you is not the same as being in class. Of course, this doesn't mean "If I just show up, I should get an *A*." Being late for class indicates a similar attitude that class is not important to you, and it disrupts the instructor and other students. You have to invest in every class by showing up—on time—prepared, alert, and ready to participate.

Jana Rosa
April 9, 2022

Formal Outline

I. Selective Perception
  A. External
    1. Larger, brighter, louder
    2. Different
    3. Repetitive
    4. Contrast
  B. Internal
    1. Needs
      a. Hunger
      b. Fatigue
    2. Motives
      a. Food
      b. Lodging
      c. Entertainment

Mind Map

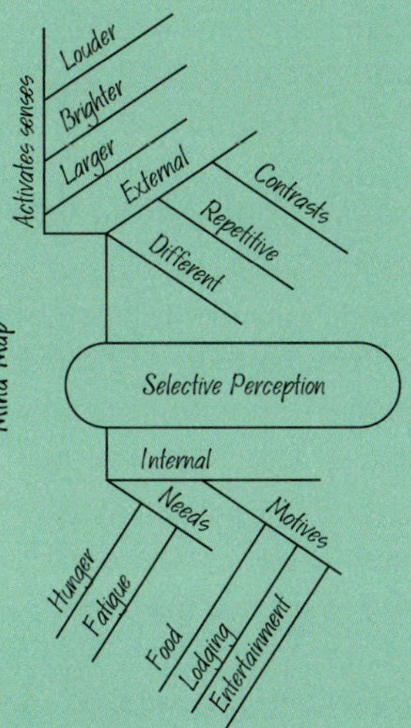

Louder, Brighter, Larger — Activates senses
External — Contrasts, Repetitive, Different

Selective Perception

Internal — Needs (Hunger, Fatigue), Motives (Food, Lodging, Entertainment)

Cornell Summary

Summary: Selective perception is the process by which information is selected for our attention. Both external and internal factors affect perception. External factors include stimuli that are larger, brighter, louder, unusual, unfamiliar, colorful, or intense. Internal factors include our motives and needs, such as hunger, anger, or attitude.

What is *Selective Perception*?

Selective perception is the *process by which certain events, objects, or information are selected for our attention*. Because of selection, we do not process the information required to make decisions or initiate behavior. Perception is selective. We all have the ability to tune out certain stimuli and focus on others or to shift our attention at will. We tend to hear and see what meets our *needs, interests, and motivation*. We fill in what is missing. We choose what we want to perceive and organize information into meaningful pictures. We block out some information and add to others. What are the factors that cause us to focus on and select certain events and ignore others? These factors fall into *two* categories: *external* and *internal*.

First let's look at *External Factors*.

External factors are *certain events* around us that determine whether we notice something or not. Many factors affect which objects will receive our attention and focus. Stimuli that activate our *senses* are noticed more (larger, brighter, louder). Anything that is out of the ordinary, colorful, or unfamiliar or that contrasts a background receives more attention. We notice what is *different* and incongruent (such as wearing shorts in church) and what is more *intense*. We also notice objects that are in motion and messages that are repetitive. The *more* information presented—or the frequency—the greater the chances that the information will be selected.

Marketing experts study these external factors and use them in advertisements. If a message is loud or bright, it increases the chance that it will be selected. We even use external factors in our daily life. For example, John is a public relations executive and wants to be noticed at his large company. He wears expensive suits and unusual, interesting ties. Even his office is decorated in a unique, colorful, yet professional style.

The second category is *Internal Factors*.

Several internal factors affect perception. What we focus on is affected by our current *motives or needs*. If you've ever attended a meeting close to lunchtime, you may have found yourself concentrating on the smells coming from a nearby restaurant. You tend to respond to stimuli that relate to your immediate needs (hunger or fatigue, for example). If you are driving down the highway and see a host of signs and billboards, you will notice the ones that are directed at your current motivational state, such as those for food, lodging, or entertainment.

Figure 6.4

Combination Note-Taking System

Note the various note-taking systems on the left, reflecting the lecture on the right. (The italicized words in the lecture side denote inflection by the speaker.) *Which note-taking system do you prefer?*

3. **Sit up front.** You will be more alert and will see and hear better if you sit in the front of the class if possible. You will also be more likely to ask questions and engage the instructor in eye contact. You will be less likely to talk with other students, text, or daydream. Explore creative ways to focus and make this class important. (See **Peak Progress 6.3** for tips on getting the most out of your instructor's presentation.)

4. **Use all your senses and the VARK systems.** Many people view note taking as an exclusively auditory activity. Actually, note taking is more effective if you integrate learning styles and use all your senses. For example, be a

Peak Progress

Getting the Most Out of a Class Lecture

In the classroom and in meetings you attend on the job, you will come across many styles of presenters, from dynamic and succinct to agonizingly vague and verbose. As discussed in Chapter 1, you can adjust your learning style to your instructor's teaching style, just as you would need to adjust your work style to that of your boss. But what if your instructor's style presents specific challenges to your learning? Following are some tips if your instructor

- **Talks too softly.** If you can't hear your instructor, first ask other students if they are having the same problem (to make sure it's not just your hearing). Then, try a seat in the front. If you still can't hear well, tell your instructor outside of class. Your instructors may not be aware it's a problem and may be able to adjust their speaking level or use a microphone. If you are hearing impaired, ask the Learning Center for help with recording devices or if you have different disabilities or challenging circumstances.

- **Talks too fast.** If you find you can't keep up with your instructor as you take notes (or you are missing points), you might be a little slower jotting down notes than others and may have to speed it up. Focus on writing just key words. If you miss a section, leave a space in your notes with a notation (such as an asterisk or "missed") and ask another student or your study group about the missing material.

- **Is hard to understand because their native language is different from yours.** As our world becomes more globally connected, you will encounter instructors, colleagues, physicians, neighbors, and others with various native languages, cultures, and experiences. No matter what language you or your instructor is most accustomed to, you are both in the room for the same reason—to teach and learn the material. Clarify and ask questions so you fully understand the material.

- **Never allows time to ask questions.** Find out your instructor's e-mail or office hours and contact them directly with your questions. Be proactive.

- **Never addresses material from the text.** Some students get frustrated when they buy a text and then the instructor doesn't cover the same material during lecture. The instructor might be expecting you to read the text on your own and is using lecture time for other topics. If you have difficulty with any of the text material, ask the instructor if you should bring that up during or outside of class.

- **Only lectures, never writes on the board or uses PowerPoint.** Listen for verbal cues (such as a louder voice) and nonverbal cues (such as hand gestures) that suggest more important points to remember. Ask for examples that illustrate key points.

- **Puts a lot of content in the PowerPoint presentation.** If the whole lecture is on a few slides, ask the instructor if the presentation is available online. If so, bring a copy to class and take notes on it. Look at slide headings for key words or phrases as the instructor speaks.

- **Never follows the lecture outline or PowerPoint.** Not everyone stays on course when speaking, especially if questions or new topics sidetrack the discussion. Remember that the PowerPoint presentation is just a blueprint, and try to balance your notes with the key points from it and the instructor's discussion.

- **Seems to ramble and never gets to a point.** Some speakers are better than others. Here's where you have to be proactive and ask clarifying questions ("So what you are saying is _____, correct?"), and confer with fellow classmates to put the pieces together.

- **Uses too many personal anecdotes that may or may not be relevant.** Everyone loves stories and they are an opportunity to connect personally with the instructor. Keep an open mind and ask for clarification or connections to the class material.

In every situation, if you still have difficulties listening and taking notes, you should promptly and politely talk with your instructor and ask what you can do to be more effective. Adapt to your instructor and use your study team to clarify and pretest.

POWERPOINT PRESENTATIONS AND NOTE TAKING

PowerPoint presentations are used by many professors. They can be a visual way of organizing a lecture and showing key illustrations. Each slide usually creates a transition. Pay attention because the PowerPoint doesn't usually include everything. Your professor will usually add examples, stories, facts, answers, and explanations. Plus you'll want to add notes from class discussion. You'll want to be attentive and take good notes.

(continued)

Getting the Most Out of a Class Lecture *(concluded)*

Record key ideas, main points, dates, names, places, facts, diagrams, formulas, and problems. Writing and taking notes enhance learning by using your kinesthetic style to help you remember ideas and main points. In a sense, your body helps you stay attentive. So sit up straight and focus.

- **Be prepared.** First, come to class prepared. Let's say you decide to use the Cornell System of Note Taking. Create a template the night before when you are skimming the chapter and getting a general idea of the chapter. Now you'll be ready for active note taking in class. As you read the chapter, take notes using the template and leave room for class notes. Next, write a quick summary and leave room to add to after class. Get a copy of the PowerPoint presentation before class, if possible. Many professors have them available online. If you use your computer for note taking, just open the file and type your notes in the window. Print them out and bring them to class to write on and take notes (print out the slides in Note view). Now you are prepared and ready to go. This small action will result in big payoffs!

- **Stay alert and focused.** When you are rested and hydrated and have had a healthy snack, you'll be more alert. Go beyond the slides and record main points and key concepts. Make certain you take note of questions and answers, explanations, and important points brought up in class discussion.

- **Review, reflect, and summarize.** As soon as possible after class, review your notes. Write a quick summary of key ideas, general ideas, and main points. Integrate your class notes with notes you took while reading and during discussions with study groups.

Reflect on key points and how they relate to your life and other classes. Make up test questions and review with your study team. You can also make up your own power point or slide show.

TAKING NOTES ONLINE

When you're taking an online course or a course with a lot of online information, you'll want to follow these strategies:

- **Keep up with the class.** It's easy to put off dealing with the course and procrastinate. Put it on your schedule and make time to "attend" the class just as you would for other classes and schedule in study time.

- **Create a detailed schedule.** Include lectures, assignments, discussion forums, and any meetings that are scheduled.

- **Meet with the instructor.** Meet in person if possible. E-mail often (include picture) and be aware that many professors have a busy schedule of classes. Develop a relationship and let your professor know that you're interested, engaged, and involved in the class.

- **Get organized.** Print out course materials as soon as they are posted and keep everything in a course folder. Turn in assignments on time.

- **Form a study team.** Ask the professor if you can create a study team with other interested students. You can call or meet in person if on campus or in the community. This connection is very important for success in online classes.

- **Check for e-mails.** Check every day and respond with questions. Ask for clarification and examples or if additional reading is available. Be persistent and follow up.

visual learner, develop mental pictures and use your right-brain creativity. Draw and illustrate concepts. Practice *visualizing* images while the speaker is talking, form mental pictures of the topic, and associate the pictures with key words. Use colored pencils, cartoons, or any other illustrations that make the material come alive. Supplement your lecture notes with drawings, and take special note of material in PowerPoint presentations and handouts. Be an *auditory* learner, listen attentively, and consider recording lectures. *Read* your notes and recite aloud the main points of the lecture and *write summaries* of the chapter and lecture. Explain your notes to your study group, so that you can hear the material again. Be a *kinesthetic* learner, by writing and rephrasing material, working with your study team or partner, collecting examples, creating stories and diagrams, using note cards, and standing when taking notes from your textbook. Use your body to model an attentive listener

Figure 6.5

Note-Taking Shortcuts

This chart lists some common symbols and abbreviations you can incorporate into your own note-taking system. *What is the essential element in taking effective notes?*

Symbol	Meaning	Abbreviation	Meaning
>	greater than; increase	i.e.	that is
<	less than; decrease	etc.	and so forth
?	question; unclear	lb.	pound
w/	with	assoc.	association
w/o	without	info	information
V or *	important ideas	e.g.	example
+	positive; benefit; pro(s); added; additional	p.	page
—	negative; con(s); lost	pp.	multiple pages
X	times		
~	gaps in information		
→	leads to (e.g., motivation →success)		
^	bridge of concepts; insert		
#	number; end		

(direct eye contact, sitting up straight). Be aware of your body and especially your hands. Be mindful of how they move and all the ways you use them to communicate. Mindfulness will help you by being in the present moment.

5. **Make note taking active and physical.** Sit up straight as slouching produces fatigue and signals the brain that this activity is not important. Show attention with eye contact. If you have ADHS, check with the Learning Center for recording devices that can help you be more effective.

6. **Link information.** Look for patterns that connect ideas as well as information that is different. Develop associations between what you know and don't know. When you link new knowledge to what you already know, you create lasting impressions. Ask yourself how this information relates to other classes or to your job.

7. **Reduce to the essential.** Don't make the mistake of trying to write down everything the instructor says. Notes are like blueprints: They represent a larger subject and highlight main details. Jot down only main points and key words. Add illustrations, statements, stories, introductions, and transitions that are important for depth, interest, and understanding. Devise a system for note taking that includes abbreviations and symbols. If you text, you may have already developed your own "shorthand vocabulary," which may be helpful when taking notes. See **Figure 6.5** for common note-taking shortcuts.

8. **Organize your notes.** Use large, bold headlines for main ideas and large print for key words, important points, facts, places, and other supporting data. Write your name, the topic, and the date on each sheet of paper. Consider getting a binder for each class to organize notes, syllabi, handouts, tests, and summaries. Leave wide margins and plenty of space to make corrections, add notes, clarify, and summarize. If you crowd your words, the notes will be hard to understand. Keep all handouts you receive in class. Use a question mark in areas that need clarification.

9. **Use flash cards.** Use index cards to jot down key words, formulas, and definitions. Note cards and flash cards help you integrate all learning styles. Write down key words and main points, use them throughout the day, and review for tests. Read out loud.

10. **Expand on notes from others.** Many instructors lecture in conjunction with a PowerPoint presentation. Ask your instructor if the lecture outline is available online and if so preview it before class, take a copy of the printout to class, and add notes and detail as the instructor talks. This is a handy note-taking tool that helps you follow the discussion, organize your notes, and read the text. If you missed class and borrowed notes from someone else, thoroughly review the notes, mark anything that is unclear and needs follow-up, and compare them with the textbook.

11. **Use your electronic device.** Your instructor may allow you to take notes in class on a laptop, tablet, or other electronic device. This can be a convenient way to store, organize, review, and share notes after class and may work for you. Be focused on discussions, nonverbal cues, and visual illustrations instead of just looking at your keyboard or screen. If your power fails or you forget to save your work, you may have no backup notes. Another way you may be able to use it outside of the physical classroom is to download podcasts of lectures if the instructor makes them available. These offer a way to review lectures on your own. Clarify questions with your instructor or team.

Research suggests that people listen more intently when they agree with an idea or even like a song. They tend to be offended with something that is different or unfamiliar. The brain seems to crave familiarity. What implications does this concept have to do with college and work?[1]

Selena loves to participate in her women's studies class—so much so that, by the end of the lecture, she has done more talking and arguing than listening or note taking. Although she feels energized by the debates, she has little to refer to when reviewing for the weekly quizzes. Sometimes she tunes out ideas that she disagrees with.

- How can Selena balance joining the discussions with taking good notes to refer to later? How can she be more open to new ideas?
- How can she listen more attentively to her classmates?
- What could Selena do immediately after class to make sure she understands the main points and is open to new ideas?

Assess and Review Your Notes

Don't just file your notes away after class. Instead, reinforce your memory and understanding of the material by assessing and reviewing your notes. Research indicates that, even after only one hour, you will retain less than 50 percent of the lecture. (See **Figure 6.6**.) Thus, it's important to revisit your notes as soon as possible.

1. **Summarize in your own words.** When you finish taking text and lecture notes, summarize in your own words. You might write summaries on index cards. If you used the Cornell System, make sure you complete the summary section. Summarizing can be done quickly and can cover only main concepts. *This one small action will greatly increase your comprehension and learning.* It is even more effective when you read your summary out loud to others; teaching is a good way to learn.

2. **Edit and revise your notes.** Set aside a few minutes as soon as possible after the lecture to edit, fill in, or copy your notes. (If possible, avoid scheduling classes back to back so you can spend time with your notes right after class.) Underline what the instructor indicated is important. Clean up, expand, and rewrite messy or incomplete sections. Compare your notes with the material in the textbook. If you are unclear on a point, leave a space and mark it with a question mark or a colored highlighter. Ask for verification from other students or your instructor and ask questions.

3. **Create a sample test.** Make up test questions and take sample tests with your study team. *This is a powerful, proven strategy.* Review results with your team.

Figure **6.6**

Ebbinghaus's Forgetting Curve

German philosopher Hermann Ebbinghaus determined that after only nine hours you remember about 36 percent of what you just learned. At 31 days, that amount drops to 21 percent. Thus, constant review is critical. *If you wait until midterm to review your lecture notes, how much will you remember from the first days of class?*
Source: Hermann Ebbinghaus, *Memory: A Contribution to Experimental Psychology,* 1885/1913.

Photo: Valueline/PunchStock

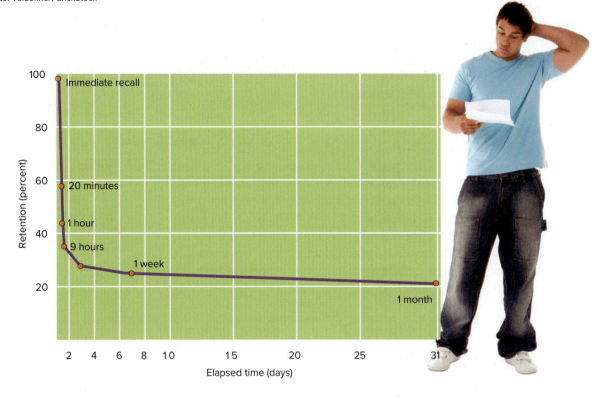

Retention (percent) — 100 · 80 · 60 · 40 · 20

- Immediate recall
- 20 minutes
- 1 hour
- 9 hours
- 1 week
- 1 month

Elapsed time (days) — 2 4 6 8 10 15 20 25 31

• **Taking Notes on the Job**

Note taking is an essential skill in many professions. *What are some jobs or professions in which taking notes is a critical, daily task?*
Corbis Super RF/Alamy Stock Photo

4. Use visual cues. Consider drawing a mind map of your notes to display the main points and their connections. For math and science classes, creating flowcharts may help visually reinforce processes or systems. Write out questions.

5. Review your notes. Develop a review schedule that supports continual reviewing and reflects on material you have already learned. Think of how you can review your notes within the first hour, the first day, and each week. Add this to the daily planner you created in Chapter 4.

There are many ways to work reviewing into your day:

- *Arrive at class early* and spend five minutes reviewing your notes from the previous class. Or review while the instructor passes out handouts or organizes the lecture.

- *Review right before you go to sleep* because your mind is receptive to new information.
- *Compare notes with your study group members* to make sure you recorded and understood all the key points.

6. **Monitor and evaluate.** Periodically assess your note-taking system and different strategies until you find the one that works best. Feedback from study group members, your instructor, and tests will help you assess how well your system is working. (See **Peak Progress 6.4** for note-taking tips for students who face special challenges.)

Peak Progress   6.4

Taking Note of Special Challenges

For some students, note taking may be a more challenging skill. Students with learning disabilities often have more difficulty identifying the important information they should record. They often cannot write fast enough to keep up with the lecturer or decipher their notes after the lecture. Sitting through long lectures in which the instructor uses few visual cues (such as words or illustrations on the board or PowerPoint) can be especially tough, as visuals help students focus on important concepts and examples.

However, the act of taking notes has many benefits. Students with learning disabilities tend to be passive learners, and taking notes is one way to actively engage in the learning process. Note taking also encourages them to clarify confusing information and helps them recall it later.

The strategies discussed earlier in this chapter apply to all students. Also, the following tips may be helpful to those with specific challenges (although any student can benefit from trying them as well):

1. **Sit in the front of the room.** Although this is a good tip for any student, it's especially important for those who have trouble sitting or focusing for long periods of time. Put yourself where you are forced to pay attention and keep distractions, such as books and cell phones, out of your hands.

2. **Use a binder instead of a traditional notebook.** This will help you keep everything organized, including lecture and reading notes, handouts, and assignments, and make studying for exams much easier. Write on loose-leaf paper, and three-hole punch everything.

3. **Put headings, your name, and dates at the top of all papers.** This makes them easier to identify and organize.

4. **Set up your paper in advance.** Create a note-taking form that helps you focus on the main points of the lecture. Include these items:
   - Today's topic
   - What you already know about the topic
   - Three to seven main points, with details of today's topic as they are being discussed (and then number each line)
   - A summary (quickly describe how the ideas are related)
   - New vocabulary or terms (write these terms in this section as they come up during class; repeat the previous sections as much as necessary)
   - The five main points of the lecture (describe each point)

5. **Cluster ideas as they are presented.** Write them with similar indentation or formatting, and separate clustered ideas by lines if that helps. Clustering information makes it easier to remember later.

6. **Leave space between notes.** Later, you can fill in comments, material you may have missed, or material from the text.

7. **Type your notes afterward.** Typed notes are more legible to study from, and an additional chance to think about the material and make sure you understand it.

8. **Clarify points with your instructor.** Students with learning disabilities often realize something is important to note after the instructor is well into the discussion, so they've already missed recording key points. Talk with your instructor outside of class and go over your notes together. Your instructor will appreciate that you are actively trying to improve your note-taking skills and may be able to provide additional tips related to his or her class.

Taking Notes with New Technology

There are many new note-taking features that allow you to create notes and have them at your fingertips wherever you go. Some of the best known free services include Evernote (www.evernote.com), Google Keep (www.google.com/keep), OneNote (www.onenote.com/), and Simplenote (http://simplenote.com). These popular services are usually available for free and then charge for more features if you want them. Some of them can even record audio lectures. They're usually available on the web, your desktop, and your smartphone. If these make you nervous, there is always a plain old word-processing document or pen and pencil. Just remember to keep your notes for each class in one place. The last thing you want to do is lose your notes. You can also use online outlines and mind maps. Try The Brain (www.thebrain.com).

Remember that if you're watching a recorded lecture, you can pause and revisit it. Jot down notes that you can ask your professor or study team later, just as you would if you were watching the lecture in person. *Continually asking questions is a good way to create understanding and clarification is key to effective note taking.*

Overcoming Obstacles to Better Notes

A positive, open mindset that focuses on growth and learning is the best way to overcome obstacles to note taking. An open mindset knows the importance of note taking to school and job success and wants to improve. A negative, fixed mindset doesn't see the value in putting in the effort to have organized, complete, and legible notes. Effective note taking helps you create test questions and changes information you hear into information that is distinctly yours and applicable. Use the power of positive habits to practice perseverance.

Build a Better Note-Taking Habit

Your pen and notebook, computer or tablet become the *trigger* for taking more organized notes. You should get to class a few minutes early so you are ready. Before class starts, prep your notepad with the note-taking system you've chosen; sit in the front row so you can see and hear. This preparation is the *routine* you're going to build. You listen for meaning and for key words and points. If you're

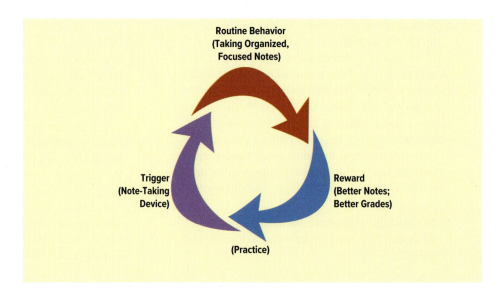

reading, you highlight the essential ideas. Write a brief summary as soon as you can. Your *reward* is the pride that you feel when you go to study and your notes are detailed, relevant, and focused. You know it will be much easier to study for tests and are willing to put in more effort. Feel satisfaction that this valuable skill will spill over into other areas of your life. Celebrate with your team.

Not only is mastering this process essential to improving your study skills, but it is a necessary job and life skill, whether you are learning how your job contributes to your company's objectives or listening to a presentation about employee health benefits. If you don't listen carefully or take complete, helpful notes and summarize main points, you have nothing to fall back on if the results aren't what you expected. Practice and effort are key!

TAKING CHARGE

Summary

In this chapter, I learned to

- **Create a positive, open mindset.** Being willing to put in effort to learn and grow is the first step in becoming an attentive listener. I am open to new information, new ideas, and different beliefs. My intent is to understand others and focus on the message. It is especially important and challenging to pay attention if you are taking a class online.

- **Go to every class.** I know I must make a commitment to go to every class and form a relationship with my instructor and other students. I'm on time and sit in front, where I'm alert and aware. I sit up straight, maintain eye contact, and show I'm listening and engaged. I reduce distractions, focus, and am in the present moment when I am taking a class online.

- **Observe my instructor and watch for verbal and nonverbal clues.** I watch for examples, words, and phrases that signal important information or transitions. I take note of handouts and visuals. I postpone judgment and focus on the message, not the presentation, clothes, voice, or teaching style. My willingness to grow and learn helps me look for supporting information and facts and ask questions.

- **Prepare before class.** I preview chapters before class so that I have a general idea of the chapter, and I make notes of questions to ask or concepts I want the instructor to give examples of or elaborate on. I do homework and use index cards to jot down and memorize key words, formulas, and definitions. I ask questions or use a chat room when taking a class online.

- **Focus on essential information.** I don't try to write down everything, but look for patterns, link information, and connect ideas in a way that makes sense and organizes the information. I leave space for corrections, additions, and questions.

- **Integrate learning styles.** I not only use my preferred learning style but also integrate all styles. I make note taking active and physical. I draw illustrations, use outlines, supplement my notes with handouts, create models, and summarize out loud. I check out google documents for creative ideas such as using pictures, etc.

- **Get organized.** I know that information that is not organized is not remembered. I write the date and topic on each sheet and organize notes in a folder or binder.

- **Experiment with note-taking styles.** I use a formal outline that follows sequential order, and an informal outline to see connections and the big picture. The Cornell System of Note Taking is organized into three sections: "Notes," "Cues," and "Summary." A mind map is more visual and includes main points connected to supporting points or examples. I experiment with elements of various note-taking systems for success and try creative ideas such as making slideshows.

- **Summarize in my own words when I am finished taking notes in class or from the text.** This tip improves my comprehension and learning. I compare this summary with the material in my book, review it with my study team, and fill in essential information. Online chatrooms are a great way to share summaries.

- **Review, monitor, and evaluate.** I review my notes for main ideas as soon as possible after class, within 24 hours. This increases my memory and helps me make sense of my notes. I edit and add to my notes. I evaluate my note-taking skills and look for ways to improve them. I study in blocks and review often overtime.

Performance Strategies

Following are the top 10 strategies for attentive listening and effective note taking:

- Create a positive, open mindset that focuses on growth and learning.
- Seek to understand and show respect to the speaker.
- Reduce distractions and be alert and focused.
- Postpone judgement, maintain eye contact, and look interested.
- Observe the speaker and listen for clues, examples, signal words, and phrases.
- Predict and ask questions to clarify main points.
- Look for information that is similar to what you know and information that is new.
- Use a note-taking system that suits your learning style.
- Summarize in your own words and review often.
- Edit and revise while information is still fresh.

Tech for Success

- **Your instructor's visual presentation.** Many instructors lecture in conjunction with a PowerPoint presentation. Ask your instructor if the lecture outline is available as a handout, on a course website, or in a bookstore. Take a copy of the printout to class with you and add notes and detail as the instructor talks. This is a handy note-taking tool that helps you follow the discussion, organize your notes, and read the text.

- **Summarize on your computer.** Some people type faster than they write. It's important to summarize your notes as soon as possible after class to make sure you understand the main points. If that sounds like a daunting task, simply write incomplete sentences first and then flesh out the sentences. If you aren't sure if you really understand the main points of the lecture, consider e-mailing your recap to your instructor or study team.

Endnotes

[1]Charles Duhigg, *The Power of Habit: Why We Do What We Do in Life and Business* (New York: Random House, 2012).

Study Team Notes

Career *in* Focus

Ryan McVay/Getty Images

Danielle Sievert
PSYCHOLOGIST

Related Majors: Psychology, Counseling

Listening in the Workplace

Danielle Sievert provides mental health care as an industrial-organizational psychologist for a *Fortune* 500 company. Most industrial-organizational psychologists hold master's degrees in psychology. Psychology is the study of human behavior and the mind and its applications to mental health. When most people think of psychologists, they think of clinicians in counseling centers or hospitals, but many large companies hire psychologists to tend to the needs of staff on all levels. Danielle and other industrial-organizational psychologists use psychology to improve quality of life and productivity in the workplace.

Danielle conducts applicant screenings to select employees who will work well within the company. She provides input on marketing research. She also helps solve human relations problems that occur in various departments. Danielle occasionally conducts individual sessions with employees who face problems within or outside the office. Danielle works a 9-to-5 schedule and is occasionally asked to work overtime. She is often interrupted to solve pressing problems.

Active listening is an important part of Danielle's job. Managers and other employees will ask for her help, she says, only when they sense that she is empathetic and wants to help. To hone her listening skills, Danielle asks questions to make sure she understands exactly what the person is saying. She also takes notes, either during or after a session. These skills help Danielle fulfill her role as a psychologist in the workplace.

CRITICAL THINKING What kinds of problems might occur at the workplace that could be addressed by a firm's psychologist?

Peak Performer Profile

Anna Sui

"What should I wear?" Many people ask this question almost daily. For international fashion and fragrance designer Anna Sui (pronounced *Swee*), the answer is simple: "Dress to have fun and feel great." Her first boutique, on Greene Street in Soho, New York, illustrated her attitude with a Victorian-inspired mix of purple walls, ornate clothing racks, glass lamps, and red floors.

To the second of three children and only daughter born to Chinese immigrants, the Detroit suburbs of the early 1960s were a long way from the fashion mecca of New York City. However, even then Sui seemed to be visualizing success. Whether designing tissue-paper dresses for her neighbor's toy soldiers or making her own clothes with coordinating fabric for shoes, Sui had flair.

After graduating from high school, Sui headed for the Big Apple. She eventually opened her own business after studying for two years at Parson's School of Design and working for years at various sportswear companies. Sui premiered her first runway show in 1991 and today has 300 stores in more than 30 countries.

To create her acclaimed designs, Sui takes note of the world around her. She continues to collect her "genius files"—clippings from pages of fashion magazines—to serve as inspiration. She listens to her clients, to music, to the street, and to her own instincts. Sui is quick to say that, although her moderately priced clothes are popular with celebrities, they are also worn by her mother. It's

Gregory Pace/Shutterstock

not about age and money, she explains, but about the "spirit of the clothing." By listening actively and staying attuned to the world around her, Sui continues to influence trends and enchant with her designs.

PERFORMANCE THINKING For the career of your choice, how would attentive listening and note taking contribute to your success?

CHECK IT OUT Anna Sui's "genius files" have included people from a variety of creative professions, including photographers, illustrators, filmmakers, theater and movie actors, musicians, and, of course, fashion designers and trendsetters. She includes many of these people on her website at **www.annasui.com** (click on the "About Anna" and then "Anna's Favorite Things"). Consider starting your own "genius file" of people and words that inspire you. Who would you include?

Starting Today

At least one strategy I learned in this chapter that I plan to try right away is

_____

_____

_____

What changes must I make in order for this strategy to be most effective?

_____

_____

_____

Review Questions

Based on what you have learned in this chapter, write your answers to the following questions:

1. What is attentive listening?

_____

_____

2. Why are listening and note-taking skills critical to job success?

_____

_____

3. Name two types of note-taking systems and describe how to use them.

_____

_____

4. Why is "Go to every class" an important note-taking strategy?

_____

_____

5. What should you do with your notes after attending class?

_____

_____

6. Reflect on this chapter and choose one thing you're ready to commit to that will improve your note-taking skills.

_____

_____

Developing Attentive Listening Skills

Camille Etan/Image Source

In the Classroom

Max Jackson is a fashion design student who works part time at a retail clothing store. He is outgoing, enjoys being around people, and loves to talk and tell stories. However, Max is a poor listener. In class, he is often too busy texting or talking with the person next to him to pay attention to class assignments. When he joins a study group, he starts off as popular but turns in assignments that are late and incorrect. His study team members feel they spend too much time reminding Max about class projects and expectations.

1. What strategies in this chapter can help Max be a more effective listener?

   _____

   _____

2. What should he do to improve his relationships with others and stay on top of class expectations?

   _____

   _____

In the Workplace

Max is now a buyer for a large department store. He enjoys working with people. He is a talented, responsible employee when he is actively aware and tuned in to others. People respond to him favorably and enjoy being around him. However, he is often too busy or preoccupied to listen attentively or take notes. He often forgets directions, misunderstands conversations, and interrupts others in his haste and enthusiasm.

3. What would you suggest to help Max become a better listener?

   _____

   _____

4. What strategies in this chapter would help him become more aware, more sensitive to others, and able to record information more effectively?

   _____

   _____

Applying the ABC Method of Self-Management

In the Journal Entry, you were asked to describe a time when you had difficulty making sense out of a lecture and staying alert. How would having a positive, open mindset help you to be a better listener?

_____

_____

_____

Now apply the ABC Method to the situation and write a script.

A = Acknowledge: Accept reality and pay attention to your emotions.

_____

_____

_____

B = Breathe: Take a deep breath and feel calm and beloved.

_____

_____

_____

C = Choose: Knowing you have many options, choose the most appropriate behavior which has the most positive long-term consequences.

_____

_____

_____

Sample Script: Even though I'm feeling frustrated and anxious, I still love and accept myself and want to grow. I breathe deeply, acknowledge my emotions, but know I am not them. I can tolerate them and allow them to float away. I put the situation into perspective. I choose to resist the urge not to go to class. Instead, I choose to increase my attentiveness and practice mindfulness skills by being quiet, noticing my thoughts, emotions, and surroundings, and focus my attention on my instructor. When my mind wanders, I bring it back to the lecture. I ask questions mentally and take notes to help organize my thinking. When class is over, I write a brief summery and jot down questions. I practice increasing my observations and listening skills when I'm with friends and family. I practice healthy living and get enough sleep so that I'm alert and mindful. I know that increasing my listening skills will help me in my career and in all areas of life. Most of all, I'm motivated to learn and grow.

Listening Self-Assessment

This simple assessment tool will give you an idea of your attentive listening skills. Read each statement. Then, check Yes or No as to whether these statements relate to you.

	Yes	No
1. My intention is to be an attentive and effective listener.	_____	_____
2. I concentrate on meaning, not on every word.	_____	_____
3. I focus on the speaker and use eye contact.	_____	_____
4. I am aware of emotions and nonverbal behavior.	_____	_____
5. I withhold judgment until I hear the entire message.	_____	_____
6. I am open to new information and ideas.	_____	_____
7. I seek to understand the speaker's point of view.	_____	_____
8. I do not interrupt, argue, or plan my response; I listen.	_____	_____
9. I am mentally and physically alert and attentive.	_____	_____
10. I paraphrase to clarify my understanding.	_____	_____
11. When I'm in class, I sit in the front so that I can hear and see better.	_____	_____
12. I mentally ask questions and summarize main ideas.	_____	_____
13. I increase the value of my listening by previewing the textbook before class.	_____	_____
14. I adapt to the instructor's speaking and teaching style.	_____	_____
Total Responses:	_____	_____

If you checked Yes to 10 or more questions, you are well on your way to becoming an attentive, effective listener. If you did not, you have some work to do to improve those skills. Which areas are the most difficult for you?

REVIEW AND APPLICATIONS | CHAPTER 6

Mind Map a Lecture

Create a mind map of one of your class lectures (see **Figures 6.2 and 6.3** for examples). Compare your mind maps with those drawn by other students in your class. Are there key points that you or other students missed? Did some include too much (or too little) detail?

REVIEW AND APPLICATIONS | CHAPTER 6

Use the Cornell System of Note Taking

Take notes in one of your class lectures by using the Cornell System in the space provided here (see **Figure 6.1** as a guide). Compare your notes with those from other students in your class. Are there key points that you or other students missed? Did some include too much (or too little) detail? Did you summarize your notes? Experiment for a week or so and see how this system works for you.

Cues: **Notes:**

Summary:

Listening and Note Taking in the Workplace

Write how you will demonstrate the listed listening and note-taking skills for future employers.

1. Finding meaning and interest in new information and projects

_____

2. Showing interest and being prepared

_____

3. Listening attentively

_____

4. Observing and asking questions

_____

5. Acquiring information

_____

6. Thinking through issues

_____

7. Organizing information and taking good notes

_____

8. Staying alert and in the present

_____

9. Being willing to test new strategies and learn new methods

_____

10. Practicing attentive listening and note taking again and again

_____

11. Teaching effective methods to others

_____

Actively Read

LEARNING OUTCOMES

In this chapter, you will learn to

7-1   Explain the importance of active reading

7-2   Identify the differences in the various reading systems

7-3   Identify the various reading strategies

7-4   Identify the various reviewing strategies

7-5   Identify the strategies for building a better vocabulary

7-6   Identify the strategies for succeeding in a language course

7-7   Identify the strategies for reading technical material and manuals and completing forms

7-8   Identify strategies for overcoming reading obstacles

SELF-MANAGEMENT

I usually love to read, but lately I feel like I'm on information overload. Sometimes I read several pages and realize I haven't understood a word I've read. What can I do to read more effectively and actually remember what I've read? Maybe I'm just not a good reader and can't handle college.

Chansom Pantip/Shutterstock

Do you ever close a book and feel frustrated because you don't remember what you've just read? In this chapter, you will learn how to become an active reader and maximize your reading. You will visualize yourself reading quickly, comprehending, and recalling information. You will see yourself discovering new information, building on facts and concepts, developing memory skills, and feeling the joy of reading.

JOURNAL ENTRY   Have you ever felt frustrated with too much reading? Use **Worksheet 7.1** to practice the ABC's of self-management and write a script to guide you.

207

The challenge is not just the volume of reading required in college; you are also expected to comprehend, interpret, and evaluate what you read. **Comprehension** is understanding main ideas and details as they are written. **Interpreting** is developing ideas and summarizing material. This requires noting the difference between fact and opinion, recognizing cause and effect, and drawing inferences and conclusions.

Because the amount of reading required in school can be enormous and demanding, it is easy to get discouraged and put it off until it piles up. *This is why a positive, open mindset that focuses on growth and learning can cultivate effective reading skills. Y*ou will learn to create an effective reading system that helps you keep up with your reading assignments and increase your comprehension.

The Importance of Active Reading

When you were a child at home, you may have been told, "This is quiet time; go read a book" or "Curl up with a book and just relax." In school, your instructor may have said, "Read Chapters 1 through 5 for tomorrow's test" or "You didn't do well on the test because you didn't read the directions carefully." On the job, someone may have said to you, "I need your reactions to this report. Have them ready to discuss by this afternoon."

Whether you are reading for enjoyment, for a test, or for a project at work, to be an effective reader you must become actively involved with what you are reading. If you approach reading with a lack of interest or importance, you read only what's required and are less able to retain what you have read. **Retention** is the process by which you store information. If you think something is important, you will retain it.

READING INVOLVES:
✔ Previewing
✔ Taking notes
✔ Outlining main points
✔ Digging out ideas
✔ Jotting down key words
✔ Finding definitions
✔ Asking and answering questions
✔ Underlining important points
✔ Looking for patterns and themes
✔ Summarizing in your own words
✔ Reviewing for recall

Andersen Ross/Getty Images

Reading Systems

Many factors affect your reading comprehension, but a positive, growth mindset is the foundation. A passion for stretching yourself and sticking to it even when reading is hard is the hallmark of a positive mindset. It will help you improve your vocabulary, ability to concentrate, and help you focus. It will also help you reduce your distractions and increase your comprehension and recall. You know you can grow and learn with effort and perseverance. Two helpful reading systems are the Five-Part Reading System and SQ3R.

The Five-Part Reading System

The Five-Part Reading System (see **Figure 7.1**) is similar to the Adult Learning Cycle, which is explored throughout this text (see **Peak Progress 7.1**). To remember the five parts, think of them as the five **P**s. As with many reading systems or strategies (and, in fact, many tasks in college), your first step is to prepare. Then you preview, predict questions, process information, and paraphrase and review.

1. **Prepare.** Prepare yourself mentally for reading by creating a positive, interested attitude. Look for ways to make the subject matter meaningful. Instead of telling yourself that the book is too hard or boring, say, "This book looks interesting because . . ." or "The information in this book will be helpful because. . . ." Clarify your purpose and how you will use the information. Think about what you already know about the subject. Prepare yourself physically by being rested, and read during high-energy times (refer to your Time Log in **Personal Evaluation Notebook 4.1**). Eliminate distractions by choosing a study area that encourages concentration. Experiment and make reading physical whenever possible. Take notes while reading and read aloud.

2. **Preview.** A quick survey of the chapter you are about to read will give you a general overview. Pay attention to the title, chapter headings, illustrations, and key terms. Look for main ideas connecting concepts, terms, and formulas. Gaining a general understanding of the assignment prepares you

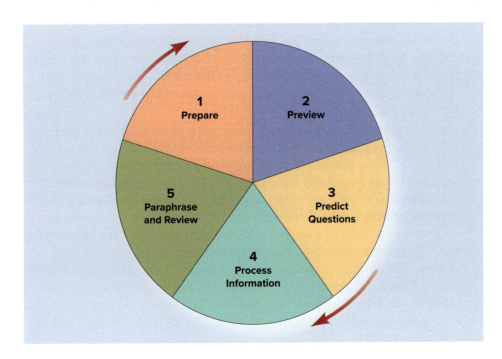

Figure 7.1

The Five-Part Reading System

This system can be useful for increasing your reading comprehension and recall. *In what ways is this system similar to your own reading system?*

Peak Progress

Applying the Adult Learning Cycle to Becoming a Better Reader

Becoming an active reader and learning to like reading take time, effort, and practice. Let's say you want to become a better reader and you also want to read for fun and enjoyment.

1. **FEEL and LISTEN.** *Why do I want to learn this?* Being an effective reader can help me get ahead in school, work, and life. Through reading, I continually learn and explore new ideas. I can also escape through fiction, relieving the stress of the day. I want to improve my comprehension. I will listen attentively to lectures and compare them with the textbook. I will listen to the intent of the author and look for ways that I relate to the subject.

2. **OBSERVE and VISUALIZE.** *How does this work?* I can learn a lot about active reading by watching, listening, and observing people who are avid readers. I will try new techniques to increase my comprehension and visualize myself succeeding.

3. **THINK and WRITE.** *What does this mean? Which techniques work and which ones don't work for me?* I will find creative ways to make reading more enjoyable and effective. I will use critical thinking to stay alert and question concepts. I will write a summary after each section and read it aloud. Reflect on what this

reading means and how it can be connected to other classes and to areas of your life.

4. **DO and PRACTICE.** *What can I do with this?* I will make a commitment to be a more active reader and practice. I'll choose one class and experiment with new strategies to improve my comprehension. I will use effort and perseverance.

5. **TEACH and PRACTICE AGAIN.** *Whom can I share this with?* I'll talk with others and share my tips and experiences. I'll demonstrate and describe the methods I've learned. I'll pretend I'm giving a lecture on what I've read. I'll read more for pleasure and read to others when possible. I will stress how important effort is.

Use the VARK system to integrate learning styles and help you think through and apply the Adult Learning Cycle. *Visualize* yourself digging out main ideas and developing questions. Note all the visuals in the chapter including illustrations, pictures, graphs, and features. How do they enhance the material? *Read* sections of the book aloud. If it works, *listen* to soft music while you read. Take notes, *write out* summaries, and read them aloud. *Read* every day. *Experiment* with your *body. Stretch, read aloud, and stand up if able* to explain the chapter or summarize to your study team. Explore creative ways to stay alert.

to read the material actively and understand the classroom lecture. When you have been exposed to a subject before, your brain is far more receptive to taking in more information, so jot down in the margins everything you can think of that you already know about the topic, even just a word or an image. Investing small amounts of time pays off.

3. **Predict questions.** Make questions out of chapter headings, section titles, and definitions. For example, if a section is titled "Groupthink," ask, "What is groupthink? What conditions are required for it to occur? What key word(s) defines it? *What are possible test questions?*" Ask what, who, when, where, why, and how. You will make **inferences** (drawing conclusions based on previous information) and interpretations as you read. Which ones are based on your experiences or background? Which ones are logical and based on fact? The more questions you ask, the better prepared you will be to find answers. If there are sample questions at the end of the chapter, review them and tie them in with your other questions. Asking questions gets you more involved and focused, organizes information, and helps you prepare for tests. Create possible test questions on note cards, test yourself, and share with your study team.

4. **Make flash cards.** Outline, underline, and highlight key words, main ideas, definitions, facts, and important concepts. Highlighting is just the start. *Turn highlighted information into flash cards and use for self-testing.* Look for supporting points, connections, and answers to the questions you have raised. Develop an outline to help you organize the information. Integrate what you are reading into classroom lectures, notes, field trips, study group discussions, models, and graphs. Summarize with the study team.

5. **Paraphrase and review.** Summarize in your own words and recite your summary out loud right after class and again within 24 hours of previewing the chapter. Share it in your study group. Review until you understand the material and can explain it to someone else. This helps you integrate learning styles and remember the main points at the end of each major section. Review in your study group and take turns listening to each other's summary. The best way to learn is to teach. Carry your note cards so that you can review questions and answers. This is also the *reflective* stage. Pause and reflect on main points, what this reading has meant, how it relates to your life or to other classes, and what images come up when you summarize the reading. Practice.

The SQ3R Reading System

The SQ3R Reading System is a five-step method that has helped many students improve their reading comprehension since it was developed by Professor Francis Robinson in 1941. It breaks reading down into manageable segments so that you understand the material before proceeding to the next step.

1. **S = Survey.** Quickly peruse the contents, scan the main heads, take note of illustrations and captions, and become familiar with the special features in each chapter. Surveying, or previewing, reflects on how the chapter is organized and supports the main concept. You get an overview of where the material is going. Previewing works!

2. **Q = Question.** Find the main points and begin to formulate questions. This helps you determine if you really understand the material. Here are a few questions:

   • What is the main idea of this chapter?
   • What is the main idea of this section?
   • What are examples that support this main idea?
   • Who are the main people or what key events are discussed in this chapter?
   • Why are they important?
   • What are possible test questions?
   • What points don't I understand?

• Preview Your Reading
You get the big picture by quickly scanning through an ebook or book, and you enhance your learning. *Besides identifying key concepts, what else should you look for when previewing?*

Hill Street Studios/Blend Images

3. **R = Read.** Actively read the material and search for answers to your questions. Even when you read a novel, you will ask such questions as "What is the main theme of this novel? Who is this supporting character? Why did they turn up at this time in the novel? How does this character relate to the main characters? What are their motives?"

4. **R = Recite.** Recite the main ideas and key points in your words after each section. Paraphrase what you have just read in your own words. Reciting promotes concentration, creates understanding, and helps raise more questions.

5. **R = Review.** Review the chapter summary and then go back over each section. Jot down additional questions. Review and clarify questions with your study group or instructor.

The exercise in **Personal Evaluation Notebook 7.1** gives you an opportunity to try the SQ3R Reading System.

Reading Strategies

The Five-Part and SQ3R Reading Systems include strategies such as previewing the material and reciting or paraphrasing main concepts in your own words. Let's review:

1. **Determine your purpose.** Reading assignments vary in terms of difficulty and purpose. Some are technical and others require imagination. (See **Peak Progress 7.2** for tips on reading in different disciplines.) Ask yourself, "Why am I reading this?" Whether you are reading for pleasure, previewing information, reviewing background information, understanding ideas, finding facts, memorizing formulas and data, or analyzing a complex subject, you will want to know your purpose.

2. **Ask questions.** The key to effective reading is to be an active, curious reader. *Continually ask questions that will help you lead to a full understanding of the material.* Pace your reading, not only to make sure you complete it but also to give yourself time to ask questions, be sure you understand the material, and review it—again and again if necessary. Just as you map out the semester's exams, plan your reading assignments in your daily planner or calendar (see Chapter 4 for many handy forms). Be realistic as to how long it takes you to read a certain number of pages, especially for difficult courses. Check off reading assignments as you complete them, and rearrange priorities if need be. Schedule blocks of time to review reading assignments and prepare for exams—mornings or afternoon. Read, review, and then review again in a few weeks.

3. **Concentrate.** Whether you are playing a sport, performing a dance, giving a speech, acting in a play, talking with a friend, or focusing on a difficult book, *being in the present is the key to concentration.* Keep your reading goals in mind and concentrate on understanding main points as you prepare to read. Stay focused and alert by reading quickly and making it an active experience. If your mind wanders, become aware of your posture, thoughts, and surroundings and then gently bring your thoughts back to the task at hand. Reduce distractions and really concentrate for 30 minutes or so. Finish one section of a book and then get up and stretch for even a minute or less.

4. **Create an outline.** Use a traditional or an informal outline to organize the main points. (See Chapter 6 for examples of outlines.) The outline can add meaning and structure to material, and it simplifies and organizes complex information. The physical process of writing and organizing material creates

Personal Evaluation Notebook   7.1

Using the SQ3R Reading System

Follow the SQ3R Reading System as you read the following passages. Then complete the questions that follow.

ORGANIZED INTERESTS: WHO ARE THEY?

Accomplishing broad yet shared goals is always easier when a number of people pitch in to help. Both joining with neighbors to clean up a community after a storm and banding together with friends to convince your college cafeteria to purchase "free trade" coffee are examples of cooperative action. Group activity is a hallmark of America's volunteer ethic. The same is true in politics. Organized groups are nearly always more effective in attaining common goals than individuals acting alone. The term **interest group** refers to those formally organized associations that seek to influence public policy. In America, it applies to a dizzying array of diverse organizations reflecting the broad spectrum of interests that make up our **pluralistic society.** They include corporations, labor unions, civil rights groups, professional and trade associations, and probably some of the groups with which you are associated as well.

Neighbors or Adversaries?

Theorists from Alexis de Tocqueville to Robert Putman have praised voluntary associations as training grounds for citizen involvement. de Tocqueville saw collective action as evidence of democracy at work. Putnam extols organized interests for creating social capital, the glue that binds the citizenry so they can achieve collective goals. Not all political theorists, however, share these views. In *The Federalist* No. 10, James Madison warned against factions—groups of individuals, "whether amounting to a majority or minority of the whole, who are united by some common impulse of passion, or of interest, adverse to the rights of other citizens, or to the permanent and aggregate interests of the community." Although opposed to factions, Madison felt that they could not be eliminated because they expressed the innately human drive for self-interest. Instead, he argued, the government must dilute their influence by filtering their views through elected officials and submerging their interests in a sea of competing interests. Only by countering the ambition of such groups with the ambition of others, he believed, could government fashion the compromise necessary to accommodate interests common to all.

Distinctive Features

Like the political movements of the past that advanced causes such as abolition or civil rights, interest groups seek to use the power of government to protect their concerns. However, although political movements promote wide-ranging social change, interest groups are more narrowly focused on achieving success with regard to specific policies. Where the Women's Movement of the 1960s sought to change Americans' views about the role of women at home and in the workplace, interest groups like the National Organization for Women (NOW) focus on solving specific problems faced by women in a world that has already grown more accepting of the diverse roles women play.

Interest group causes may be purely economic, as in the case of a business seeking tax breaks or a union seeking negotiating clout; they may be ideological, as in the case of those favoring or opposing abortion rights. Some, known as **public interest groups,** advocate policies they believe promote the good of all Americans, not merely the economic or ideological interests of a few. Environmental groups such as the Sierra Club fall into this category. Some interest groups, such as trade associations and labor unions, have mass memberships; others represent institutions and have no individual membership at all. One example of the latter is the American Council on Education (ACE), a collective institution of higher education that promotes policies that benefit colleges and universities.

Source: Joseph Losco and Ralph Baker, *AM GOV 2009* (New York: McGraw-Hill, 2009).

(continued)

a foundation for committing it to memory. Use section titles and paragraph headlines to provide a guide. Continue to write questions in the margin. (See **Worksheet 7.5** for a blank format to use for a formal outline.)

5. **Identify key words and concepts.** Underline and highlight key words, definitions, facts, and important concepts. Write them in the margins and on note cards. Draw illustrations (or embellish those in the book) to help clarify the text. Use graphics and symbols to indicate difficult material, connections,

Personal Evaluation Notebook

Using the SQ3R Reading System *(concluded)*

S—Survey

1. What is the title of the selection?

   _____

2. What is the reading selection about?

   _____

3. What are the major topics?

   _____

4. List any boldface terms.

   _____

Q—Question

5. Write a question for the first heading.

   _____

6. Write a question for the second heading.

   _____

3 Rs

R—Read

Read the selection section by section.

R—Recite

Briefly summarize to yourself what you read. Then share your summary with a study team member.

R—Review

7. Can you recall the questions you had for each head?   Yes _____ No _____
8. Can you answer those questions?   Yes _____ No _____

Write your answers for each section head question on the following lines.

9. Head 1

   _____

10. Head 2

   _____

Once you're finished, go back and check your answers. For those that you got wrong, consider how SQ3R or other reading methods could help. Now take a moment to *reflect* on what this reading assignment means to you. How does it connect with other classes? What images does it bring up? Be aware of visual images, body sensations, feelings, memories, thoughts, and perceptions.

Peak Progress

Reading for Different Courses

Sometimes even successful students resist reading in disciplines they find difficult or uninteresting. Your goal is to make difficult material easy to understand. Check out supplemental reading or check out other books or sources from the library to get a different view and approach. Also try the following tips:

Literature: Make a list of key figures and characters. Think about their personalities and motives. See if you can predict what they will do next. Allow your imagination to expand through your senses; taste, smell, hear, and see each scene in your mind. What is the story's main point? What are supporting points? What is the author's intent?

History: Use an outline to organize material and create a time line and place dates and events as you read. Notice how events are related. Connect main people to key events. Relate past events to current events. Picture yourself living during the time period of the event and what your circumstances and beliefs might be.

Mathematics and science: When reading a math book, work out each problem on paper and take notes in the margin. Spend additional time reviewing graphs, tables, notations, formulas, and the visuals used to illustrate points and complex ideas. These are not just fillers; they are important tools you use to review and understand the concepts behind them. Ask questions when you review each visual, and write down formulas and concepts on note cards. Come up with concrete examples when you read about abstract and difficult concepts.

(We will further explore critical thinking and problem solving in math and science in Chapter 11.)

Psychology and sociology: Jot down major theories and summarize them in your own words. You will be asked how these theories relate to topics in other chapters. Use the margins to analyze research conclusions. Pay attention to how the research was conducted, such as sample size and the sponsors of the research, biases and arguments, scientific evidence presented and if study was duplicated? Key terms and definitions are also important for building on additional information.

Anthropology (social-cultural): You may want to use a mind map to compare various cultures. For example, under the culture, you may look at religion, customs, food, and traditions. Ask yourself if the ideas apply to all people in all cultures or in all situations. Is the author's position based on observation, research, or assumptions? Is there a different way to look at these observations? What predictions follow these arguments?

Trade and technical: These courses tend to be very hands-on and the text materials will include background information, instructions, and key illustrations with multiple labels. As much as possible, read and reread the material while working with the equipment to make sure you understand the process. Identify each component and its relevance. How does this information translate to working on the job? Working through the details with a study partner or reading aloud can help you see how all the pieces fit together.

and questions you need to go over again. (Refer to **Figure 6.5** for common symbols used in note taking and reading.) A highlighter may be useful for calling out main points and marking sections that are important to review later. (See **Peak Progress 7.3** on using a highlighter.)

6. **Make connections.** Link new information with what you already know. Look for main ideas, supporting points, and answers to the questions you have developed. Integrate what you are reading into lecture notes and study group discussions. Asking yourself these questions may help you make associations and jog your memory:

   • What conclusions can I make as I read the material?

   • How can I apply this new material to other material, concepts, and examples?

   • What information does and does not match?

   • What do I know about the topic that may influence how I approach the reading?

Peak Progress

To Highlight or Not to Highlight?

The point of highlighting is to determine main points and key words. The simple act of highlighting makes you reread the information, helping you improve your comprehension. Research has also shown that recall increases when you write these key words on *note cards*. Students with learning disabilities or ADHD demonstrate a marked increase in their learning ability when they use a highlighter while reading and use notecards.

Highlight?

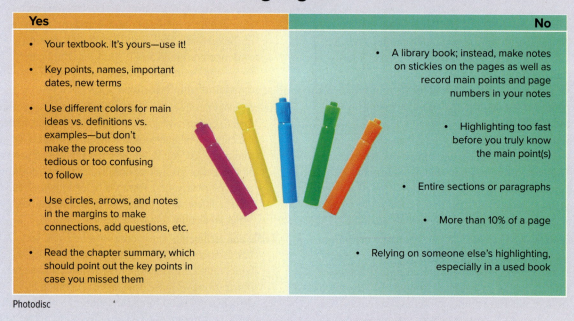

Yes	No
• Your textbook. It's yours—use it!	• A library book; instead, make notes on stickies on the pages as well as record main points and page numbers in your notes
• Key points, names, important dates, new terms	
• Use different colors for main ideas vs. definitions vs. examples—but don't make the process too tedious or too confusing to follow	• Highlighting too fast before you truly know the main point(s)
• Use circles, arrows, and notes in the margins to make connections, add questions, etc.	• Entire sections or paragraphs
	• More than 10% of a page
• Read the chapter summary, which should point out the key points in case you missed them	• Relying on someone else's highlighting, especially in a used book

Photodisc

7. **Talk with the author.** Pretend you are talking with the author and jot down points with which you agree or disagree. This exercises your critical thinking skills and helps you connect new information to what you already know. If there are points you disagree with, consider bringing them up in your study group and discuss their reactions.

8. **Compare notes.** Compare your textbook notes with your lecture notes and with those of your study team members. Make test questions. Instructors often highlight important information in class and want students to read the text for a broad overview.

9. **Take frequent breaks.** To enhance your attention, schedule short stretching breaks about every 40 minutes. A person's brain retains information best when you have a block of time, but take regular breaks. Don't struggle with unclear material, but use question marks and review with your study team. Ask your professor to clarify. You may need several readings to comprehend material. It takes effort and perseverance to grow and learn. Preview, ask questions, listen, summarize, and discuss with your study team.

10. **Integrate learning styles.** Take special note of pictures, charts, and diagrams. Develop mental pictures in your mind and actively use your imagination. Compare what you are reading with course lectures, overhead material, and notes on the board. Read out loud or into a digital recorder and then

Using Your Textbook

Textbooks are developed with many features to help you preview, understand, review, and apply the material. As soon as you purchase your text, take a few minutes to flip through it to see how it is put together.

Preface. Read through the preface, message to students, and other information to help you get off on the right foot. For example, at the beginning of this text, you will find a **Getting Started** section that explores many issues you may be facing the first few weeks of school (or even before the first day of school).

Preview features. Many texts include features that let you know what you will learn in the chapter, such as learning outcomes, chapter outlines, and introductory statements or quotes. *What types of preview features can you find in this text?*

Applications. More effective texts not only provide the essential information but also give you opportunities to apply it. These applications can take the form of case studies, exercises, assessments, journal activities, websites, and critical thinking and discussion questions. *What are some features in this text that help you apply what you are learning?*

Review material. You may find features that reinforce and help you understand and review the material, such as section or chapter summaries; glossaries; important key points or words; bulleted lists of information; comprehensive tables; and review questions. *What features in this text are useful for reviewing the material?*

Resources beyond the text. Many texts have accompanying websites, workbooks, and DVDs that reinforce and apply what you are learning in the text and course. Often, connections to these resources appear in the text, reminding you to use the resource for specific information. *What resources are available with this text?*

---

listen to it. Read with a highlighter in hand to mark important passages and key words. Work out problems on paper and draw illustrations. Write your vocabulary, formulas, and key words on note cards. Read while standing up or recite out loud. The physical act of mouthing words and hearing your voice enhances learning. Using all your senses increases your comprehension and recall. Take charge of your reading and comprehension.

11. **Use the entire text.** As discussed in Chapter 5, a peak performer seeks out and uses available resources. Many textbooks include a number of resources that sometimes get overlooked, such as a glossary, chapter objectives, and study questions. Make sure you read all the elements in your textbook, as they are included to help you preview, understand, review, and apply the material. (See **Peak Progress 7.4**.) After all, you've paid for the text, so use it! (Also see **Peak Progress 7.5** for tips on reading digital material.) *You might want to take a speed-reading course. Not only will you increase your words per minute, but you'll also learn to look at the table of contents, graphs, and pictures.*

12. **Use technology.** There are many programs to help you read. Check out resources and these apps: Kindle, Elevate—Brain Training, Nook, Audiobooks.

For practice on taking notes, take a look at **Figure 7.2** and compare it with your notes for this page.

Reviewing Strategies

Reading isn't over with the turn of the last page. Take the time to review what you have read to make sure you understand and retain the information.

Digital Reading Material

As a student today, you have many digital options available that weren't offered even just a few years ago. Books, journals, newspapers, and textbooks are often delivered in a digital format. Communication media, such as Facebook, Twitter, and Wikipedia, have changed how we learn and interact.

Digital readers have become a popular alternative to print books. Amazon's Kindle, which sold out in 5½ hours upon its release in 2007, allows you to store and read digital media for use anywhere and features "electronic paper." Apple's iPad offers numerous applications, including the Internet, iTunes, and iBooks, in a portable format. Many textbooks are offered for use with these digital readers, as are subscriptions to newspapers and magazines. Audio books are another option.

As online reading and audio books become more popular, consider these reading strategies:

- **Pace your reading.** Research indicates the average person reads from a computer screen about 10 percent slower than from a printed text. If that's true for you, plan your reading schedule accordingly.
- **Adjust the page.** Change the type size and font to one that is easier to read.
- **Use the built-in functions.** Learn how to use the highlighter.
- **Print.** Make backup copies of your digital notes and print key sections, in case you run into technical issues later. Annotate the hard copies for reinforcement.
- **Avoid ads.** Many articles are surrounded by advertisements and pop-up ads that can distract you. Turn on a pop-up blocker.
- **Protect against theft.** Store your tablet in a secure place.
- **Reduce use before bedtime.** The bright LED light of a computer screen or Kindle over stimulates eyes, suppresses melatonin, and affects sleep. Read a book instead.[1]

1. **Summarize in writing.** After you finish reading, close your book and write a summary in your own words. Writing down everything you can recall about the chapter increases comprehension and recall. Write quickly and test yourself by asking questions:

   - What is the major theme?
   - What are the main points?
   - What are the connections to other concepts?

2. **Summarize out loud.** Summarizing out loud can increase learning. Some students use an empty classroom and pretend they are lecturing. Recite quietly to yourself and review several times until you understand the material and can explain it to someone else. Review in your study team and take turns listening to each other's summary. As you recite and listen to each other, you can ask questions and clarify terms and concepts. Summarizing is a small amount of effort that results in a big payoff!

3. **Review and reflect.** You have previewed, developed questions, outlined main points, read actively, highlighted and underlined, written key words, and summarized in writing and aloud. Now it is important to review for understanding main ideas and to commit the information to long-term memory. You can increase your comprehension by reviewing the material within 24 hours of your first reading session. Reflect by bringing your own experience and knowledge to what you have learned with readings, lectures, field trips, and work with your study team. Review headings, main topics, key ideas, first and last sentences in paragraphs, and summaries. Make sure you

Figure **7.2**

Sample Notes

This illustration shows study notes you might take when reading the Reading Strategies and Reviewing Strategies sections of this chapter. Compare it with the notes you took on those pages. *What are the similarities? What did you do differently? Do you have unique note-taking strategies that work for you?*

Integrate VAK

vocabulary, formulas, and key words on note cards. Read while standing up or recite out loud. The physical act of mouthing words and hearing your voice enhances learning. Using all your senses increases your comprehension and recall. Take charge of your reading and comprehension.

Use textbook features

11. <mark>Use the entire text.</mark> As discussed in Chapter 5, a peak performer seeks out and uses available resources. Many textbooks include a number of resources that sometimes get overlooked, such as a glossary, chapter objectives, and study questions. Make sure you read all the elements in your textbook, as they are included to help you preview, understand, review, and apply the material. (See **Peak Progress 7.4.**) After all, you've paid for the text, so use it! (Also see **Peak Progress 7.5** for tips on reading digital material.) *You might want to take a speed-reading course. Not only will you increase your words per minute, but you'll also learn to look at the table of contents, graphs, and pictures.*

What's in this book?

12. **Use technology.** There are many programs to help you read. Check out resources and these apps: Kindle, Elevate—Brain Training, Nook, Audiobooks.

For practice on taking notes, take a look at Figure 7.2 and compare it with your notes for this page.

Reviewing Strategies

Reading isn't over with the turn of the last page. Take the time to review what you have read to make sure you understand and retain the information.

1. <mark>Summarize in writing.</mark> After you finish reading, close your book and write a summary in your own words. Writing down everything you can recall about the chapter increases comprehension and recall. Write quickly and test yourself by asking questions:

questions to ask

- What is the major theme?
- What are the main points?
- What are the connections to other concepts?

Good for AK — **2.** <mark>Summarize out loud.</mark> Summarizing out loud can increase learning. Some students use an empty classroom and pretend they are lecturing. Recite quietly to yourself and review several times until you understand the material and can explain it to someone else. Review in your study team and take turns listening to each other's summary. As you recite and listen to each other, you can ask questions and clarify terms and concepts. Summarizing is a small amount of effort that results in a big payoff!

3. <mark>Review and reflect.</mark> You have previewed, developed questions, outlined main points, read actively, highlighted and underlined, written key words, and summarized in writing and aloud. Now it is important to review for understanding main ideas and to commit the information to long-term memory. You can increase your comprehension by reviewing the material within 24 hours of your first reading session. Reflect by bringing your own experience and knowledge to what you have learned with readings, lectures,

have answered the questions you created as you read the material. Carry your note cards with you and review main topics, key words, and summaries.

4. Read and review often. Reviewing often and in blocks of time kicks the material into long-term memory. Review weekly and conduct a thorough review a week or so before a test. Keep a list of possible test questions and pretest yourself. The key is to stay on top of reading so it doesn't pile up so you can review effectively.

Research indicates that the brains of beginning college students have the quality of novelty seeking and visual cues. They want to engage in life and dislike reading when they can use their phone, watch YouTube videos, and use other exciting ways to communicate. What implications does this have for college and work?[2]

Evan always waits until the last minute to tackle his reading assignments. At the eleventh hour—literally—he finally plops into an easy chair and begins to read. Not a morning person, Evan is sure he can focus and whip through it, until 30 minutes later, when his eyes are half closed and he realizes he doesn't remember a word. He has his phone with him constantly, so interruptions are frequent.

- If Evan truly does his best work at night, what strategies should he use while reading to make sure he's alert, focused, learning, and retaining the material?
- Do you think Evan's last-minute strategy is an effective method of reading for class? What important steps from the Five-Part Reading System might he end up skipping for time's sake?
- Does Evan really understand the purpose of reading assignments? If not, can you explain it to him? How can he concentrate on reading and unplug periodically?

THINK
CREATIVELY AND CRITICALLY

Build Your Vocabulary

You will need a fundamental vocabulary to master any subject. To succeed in a career, you must know and understand the meaning of words you encounter in conversations, reports, meetings, and professional reading. People often judge the intelligence of another person by the ability to communicate through words, and an effective speaker who has a command of language can influence others. Try the following methods for building your vocabulary:

1. **Observe your words and habits.** You may be unaware that you fill your conversations with annoying words, such as *you know, OK, like,* and *yeah,* or inappropriate expletives.
2. **Be creative and articulate.** Use precise, interesting, and expressive words.
3. **Associate with articulate people.** Surround yourself with people who have effective and extensive vocabularies.
4. **Look up words you don't know. Peak Progress 7.6** shows you how to navigate around a dictionary.
5. **Write down new words.** Listen for new words; observe how they are used; how often you hear them and see them in print. Record them in your journal or on note cards.
6. **Practice mentally.** Say new words again and again in your mind as you read, and think of appropriate settings where you could use the words.
7. **Practice in conversation.** Use new words until you are comfortable using them.
8. **Read widely.** Read newspapers, magazines, trade journals, nonfiction, and fiction. You build your vocabulary as you read.
9. **Look for contextual clues.** Try to figure out a word by the context in which it is used.
10. **Learn common word parts.** Knowing root words, prefixes, and suffixes makes it easier to understand the meaning of many new words. Also, in fields such as biology, knowing prefixes and suffixes helps you learn many new terms, such as *cardi* means "heart" (as in *cardiovascular*) and *calor* means "heat" (as in *calorie,* which is the energy content of food in the form of heat). Other examples follow:

Root	Meaning	Example
auto	self	autograph, autobiography
sub	under	submarine, submerge
circum	around	circumference, circumspect
manu	hand	manuscript, manual, manufacture

Also, learn to recognize syllables. Dividing words into syllables speeds up learning and improves pronunciation, spelling, and memory recall.

11. **Review great speeches.** Look at how Thomas Jefferson, Abraham Lincoln, John F. Kennedy, and Margaret Thatcher chose precise words. Read letters

Look It Up! Using a Dictionary

Depending on the source you are using, many dictionary resources will provide at least some of the following:

Guide words: In a printed dictionary, boldface words at the top of the page indicate the first and last entries on the page. Online dictionaries will often provide the previous and subsequent words.

Pronunciation: This key shows how to pronounce the word. Online dictionaries will often provide an audio pronunciation.

Part of speech: If not spelled out, the following are abbreviations for the parts of speech:

- n.—noun
- adj.—adjective
- v.i.—intransitive verb
- adv.—adverb
- conj.—conjunction
- prep.—preposition
- v.t.—transitive verb
- pron.—pronoun
- interj.—interjection

Etymology: This is the origin of the word, which is especially helpful if the word has a Latin or Greek root

from which many other words are derived. Knowing the word's history can help you remember the word or look for similar words.

Syllabication: This shows how the word is divided into syllables.

Capital letters: This indicates if a word should be capitalized.

Definition: Definitions are listed chronologically (oldest meaning first).

Restrictive labels: Three types of labels are used most often in a dictionary. Subject labels tell you that a word has a special meaning when used in certain fields (mus. for music, med. for medicine, etc.). Usage labels indicate how a word is used (slang, dial. for dialect, etc.). Geographic labels tell you the region of the country where the word is used most often.

Homographs: A single spelling of a word has different meanings.

Variants: These are multiple correct spellings of a single word (example: *ax* or *axe*).

Illustrations: Drawings or pictures can help demonstrate or explain a word.

---

written during the Revolutionary and Civil Wars. You may find that the common person at that time was more articulate and expressive than many people today.

12. **Invest in a vocabulary book.** Many are available, so you may want to ask your instructor for guidance. Also, if you have decided on your future career, see if any books are written for that field.

13. **Read.** The best way to improve your vocabulary is simply to read more.

Manage Language Courses

If you have the opportunity, learn another language. This builds neural connections that keep your brain active. Building vocabulary is important if you are learning a new language. Following are a number of reading and study tips.

1. **Do practice exercises.** As with math and science, doing practice exercises is critical in learning any language.

2. **Keep up with your reading.** You must build on previous lessons and skills. Therefore, it is important to keep up with your reading; preview chapters, so

that you have a basic understanding of any new words; then complete your practice sessions several times.

3. **Carry note cards with you.** Drill yourself on the parts of speech and verb conjugation through all the tenses, which is a significant part of learning a new language. Keep related terms grouped together on cards (such as "In the Kitchen" or "In the Home").

4. **Recite out loud.** This is especially important in a language course, as knowing a word's pronunciation is as important as understanding its meaning. Record yourself.

5. **Form study teams.** Meet with a study team and speak only the language you are studying. Recite out loud to each other and use words in various contexts.

6. **Listen to recordings.** Plug into CDs, podcasts, apps, etc., and downloads while commuting and exercising.

7. **Model and tutor.** Meet with a student whose primary language is the one you are studying and speak only in the native language. You can meet international students in classes for English as a second language.

8. **Have fun.** Do research on the country of the language you're studying. Invite your study group for an authentic meal, complete with music and costumes. The key to learning a new language is to practice, practice, and practice.

9. **Check out apps.** There are free apps that can help you with languages. Duolingo, for example, helps you learn a number of foreign languages in fun, interactive bits. It was voted iPhone's free App of the Year in 2013 and several more apps have been added.

The same principles and strategies you use for reading English can be applied to reading and learning a different language. Your efforts will be worthwhile, especially when you are able to speak, read, and understand another language as you communicate in the real world. Remember, as you become a better reader, you will enjoy the new language more and more. (**Figure 7.3** offers additional tips for students whose first language is not English.)

Figure 7.3

Tips for ESL Students

Students whose first language is not English can try additional strategies for reading success. Also, there is a wealth of resources on the Internet for ESL readers. Search "ESL reading activities" or a similar phrase. *What challenges do you face if your home language is different from a community's prominent language?*

Image Source/Getty Images

Get the "gist" of it: Don't worry about every word. Focus on main ideas, concepts, and key words.

Vary your reading materials: Language "styles" vary based on the purpose, such as a textbook vs. a magazine vs. a blog. The more variety you are exposed to, the more fluent you will become.

Discuss in your first language: Talk about the topic with family and friends, who will offer additional perspectives and questions to explore.

Make a list: Jot down unfamilliar words that seem important and look them up.

Specialized Reading

Comprehending Technical Material

During your career workday, you will have specialized and technical reading such as workbooks, reference manuals, documents, brochures, training materials, annual reports, technical websites, job descriptions and applications, and much more. Many courses present their data in specialized formats and you'll need to interpret graphs, charts, diagrams, tables, and spreadsheets. You may read technical material, such as the directions for a chemistry experiment, a flowchart in a computer program, the steps for administering medication, or the statistical analysis of a financial statement. Don't get discouraged and give up. Realize that with effort and perseverance, you are capable of growth and learning.

Try these strategies:

1. Identify the type of graphic you are looking at. Is it a table, chart, graph, or other type of illustration? (See **Figure 7.4**.)
2. Read each element:
   - Graphic title
   - Accompanying captions
   - Column titles
   - Labels or symbols and their keys (usually provided at the bottom of the graph)
   - Data (percentages, totals, figures, etc.)
3. Identify the purpose of the graphic. Is it demonstrating similarities or differences, increases or decreases, comparisons or changes?
4. See a connection between the topic of the graphic and the chapter in which it appears.

Figure 7.4

Illustration Examples

The table (left) and graph (right) include the same information but present it differently. *What key elements would you look for to understand the material? Which presentation is easier to understand—the table or the graph? Which one might be easier to remember? What conclusions might you draw from this information regarding future statistics?*

Source: 2007–2008 National Health and Nutrition Examination Survey (NHANES).

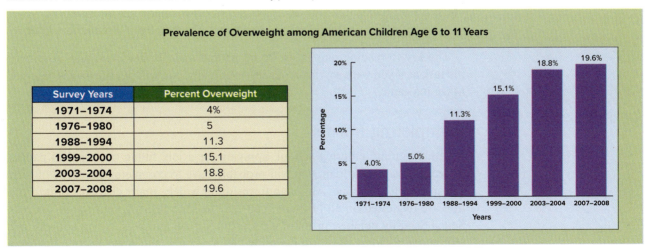

Prevalence of Overweight among American Children Age 6 to 11 Years

Survey Years	Percent Overweight
1971–1974	4%
1976–1980	5
1988–1994	11.3
1999–2000	15.1
2003–2004	18.8
2007–2008	19.6

5. Explain in your own words the information depicted on the graphic.
6. Share your interpretation of the graphic with your study group members.
7. Like any reading material, check the source for dates, author, credentials, and so on.

Reading Manuals

Technical writing professionals spend hundreds of hours writing instructions for everything from using your new toaster to troubleshooting why engine lights are coming on (i.e., your car's owner's manual). However, many people resist opening up the manual or give up. A closed mindset says, "I can figure it out on my own!" A positive, open mindset says, "With effort and perseverance, I can learn this information. I welcome the opportunity to learn and grow. I've got what it takes to stretch myself and bounce back."

First scan the step-by-step instructions and review the table of contents to see how the instructions are set up (such as a description or an illustration of product components, assembling or starting the product, caution or warning signs, and maintenance issues). After that, follow these time-saving tips:

1. Compare the description with what you received and make sure all the pieces are there.
2. Follow step-by-step installation or assembly instructions. Often it is helpful to read the instructions aloud to yourself or someone else as you go along. Assembling a product incorrectly can cause it to fail, break, or become dangerous.
3. Go to the index and look up key words related to problems you encounter or specific tasks you want to do. For example, if you need to change the time on your car clock, the index will show the page where the manual explains the procedure.
4. If the manual that came with the product is too brief or doesn't address a problem you are having, look online by checking the company's website or searching the product's name. You may find more detailed instructions, as well as tips from other users.
5. The manual (or website) may include a frequently asked questions (FAQs) section, which includes issues you may encounter using the product. Read this even if the product appears to be working correctly, as it may warn you of potential problems or maintenance issues.
6. If the product came with access codes or other important information, record that in the manual and keep it in a place that you'll remember later.

The key to reading manuals is to be patient and not get frustrated. Approach the task as if you were solving a puzzle—eventually, you will put the pieces together. Make it a game.

Completing Forms

Whether you are entering school, applying for a job, filling out medical papers, or requesting a bank loan, you will probably have to complete some type of form and many will be online. Although forms differ widely, many elements of information are requested on all of them. You may need to provide your name, address, Social Security number, proof of citizenship, phone numbers, e-mail address, and references. Reading the form carefully can save time and prevent complications.

AVOID CARELESSNESS

1 Scan the entire form before you begin to fill it out.

2 When filling out the form, read the small print directions carefully. Often, these directions appear in parentheses below a fill-in blank.

3 Fill in all the questions that pertain to you. Pay attention when you read the directions that tell you which sections of the form or application you should fill out and which sections are to be completed by someone else.

4 Write clearly—particularly numbers.

5 Reread your responses before submitting your form or application. If you are filling out a form online, check and recheck more than once before clicking "send" because you probably can't retrieve your form.

Hill Street Studios/Getty Images

For example, if the directions say to print your name in black or blue ink, do not use a pencil or write your name in cursive handwriting. And fill in all required boxes. Failure to "follow the rules" could result in you missing a deadline or losing out on a job offer or other opportunity. Ask a friend to read it carefully and proof for errors. If completing a form online, before you push the send button, read it through carefully several times out loud. If possible, make a copy.

Overcome Obstacles to Better Reading

A positive, open mindset that focuses on growth and learning can help you overcome obstacles to reading. Positive habits grow out of this empowering mindset.

Build a Better Reading Habit

Challenge Let's say that you start to read and then crave a snack or want to watch TV. In this case, you might want to experiment with where you are sitting, what time it is, and your emotional state. You might discover that when you are reading in the library, you can concentrate better and do not have as much of a craving for snacks and other distractions. You may read with more concentration earlier in the day and cultivate this practice.

Better Habit Build a habit around when and where you do your reading and studying. Try to choose a specific place and time each day and go there explicitly to read and study; this will act as the *trigger* that activates your *routine* (your reading strategies described earlier in this chapter). Set a time to concentrate fully; usually this is best in the morning or early afternoon after a lunch and a little exercise. You want to be fully awake and able to concentrate. After you have spent an hour or so, take a break. When you have completed your reading assignment, get up and call a friend or arrange to meet for a snack and chat. Socializing for a few minutes will be your *reward.* Plus you'll find the reading and studying all go by faster and you'll get more out of them.

Reading Difficulties

If you have created a positive mindset and you still have reading challenges, they may be related to decoding, comprehension, and retention. **Decoding** is the process of breaking words into individual sounds. Those with decoding problems may have trouble

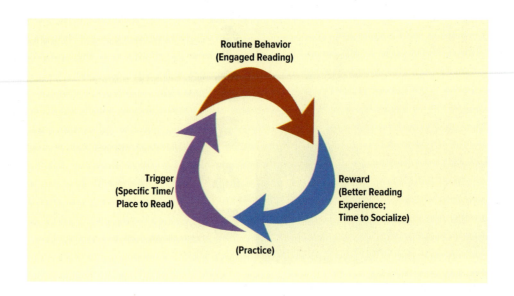

Routine Behavior
(Engaged Reading)

Trigger
(Specific Time/
Place to Read)

Reward
(Better Reading
Experience;
Time to Socialize)

(Practice)

sounding out words and recognizing words out of context, can confuse letters and the sounds they represent, and may ignore punctuation while reading. People with dyslexia have difficulty decoding. Dyslexia affects as many as 15 percent of all Americans, including celebrities Jay Leno, Tom Cruise, Whoopi Goldberg, and Albert Einstein.

Although reading speeds vary, the average adult reads 250 to 300 words per minute. The key, however, is to balance your pace with comprehension. Flying through pages at lightning speed will do you no good if you can't articulate the main points of what you've just read. The following concerns also could signal reading difficulties:

- Making poor grades despite significant effort
- Needing constant, step-by-step guidance for tasks
- Having difficulty mastering tasks or transferring academic skills to other tasks

The good news is that you can improve your reading abilities. As discussed in Chapter 5, many resources are available, such as your school's learning center if you are struggling with reading. Professionals will help you understand your difficulty and provide specific tips to help you improve.

Create a Positive Attitude

One of the greatest barriers to effective reading is attitude. Those with a negative, fixed mindset are not willing to invest the effort it takes to become better readers. They give up and believe they can't change. If the material is difficult, boring, or requires concentration, they may not complete the assignment. So much instant entertainment is available in their phone instead of reading a newspaper or news magazine. A person with a positive, open mindset has a passion for stretching and sticking to it even when the reading is difficult. They know it takes time, effort, concentration, perseverance, and practice to learn and improve. They see the value in learning to be a better reader and invest the effort to grow.

• **Finding Time to Read**
Investing time in reading pays off. Your reading skills improve when you read more. *How can you make time to read for pleasure?*

Prostock-studio/Shutterstock

To create a positive attitude about reading, first pinpoint and dispel illogical thoughts, such as "I have way too much reading; I can never finish it all"; "I'm just not good at math"; or "I never will understand this material!" It takes time and patience to learn to ski, drive a car, become proficient with computers, or become a more effective reader. Be positive as you say: "With patience and practice, I will understand this material." Use the ABC Method of Self-Management to dispel negative thinking and create a "can do" attitude.

Let's say that you study every afternoon and feel a craving around 4:00 p.m. You may want to write out a plan: At 4:00 p.m., every day, I will drink a glass of water and walk with a friend for 15 minutes or so and enjoy socializing and a chance to stretch and breathe deeply. Then I'll go back and study for another hour or so and then reward myself with a good dinner and more socializing. If you have an hour or so break in the mornings between classes, use that time to read while you're alert.

Some students and career professionals say they have too much required reading and too little time for pleasure reading. Returning students have difficulty juggling reading, lectures, homework, job, and kids. They can't even imagine having time to read for pleasure. However, it is important to read for pleasure, even if you have only a few minutes a day you can read while waiting. (See **Peak Progress 7.7** for ways to fit in reading with children around.) If you're a commuting student, use audiobooks in your car and read for pleasure each night before turning in. Audiobooks are great for road trips too.

The more you read, the more your reading skills will improve. As you become a better reader, you will find you enjoy reading more and more. You will also find that, as your attitude improves, so does your ability to keep up on assignments, build your vocabulary, understand and retain what you have read, and learn more about areas that interest you.

> **❝** My alma mater was books, a good library . . . I could spend the rest of my life reading, just satisfying my curiosity. **❞**
> **MALCOLM X**
> *Civil rights leader*

WORDS TO SUCCEED

Peak Progress   7.7

Reading with Children Around

Concentrating on your reading can be challenging with children at your feet. However, it's essential to fit reading into your daily routine (as well as theirs). Try these ideas:

1. **Read in short segments.** Provide activities for your children and set a timer. Tell them that, when it goes off, you'll take a break from reading and do something enjoyable with them. Then set the timer again. In 10 or 15 minutes, you can preview a chapter, outline main ideas, recite out loud, or review. Don't fall into the trap of thinking you need two uninterrupted hours to tackle a chapter, or you'll give up.

2. **Read while they sleep.** Get up early and read, or try reading at night when your kids are sleeping. Even if you're tired, outline a chapter before you turn in. Resist doing the dishes or cleaning and save

those activities for when reading and concentrating would be very difficult. Read a little each night and notice how it pays off.

3. **Take reading with you.** If your children are in after-school activities, such as sports or music, take your reading with you and make the most of your waiting time. Chat with other parents for a few minutes and then read and review.

4. **Read to your children.** Get your kids hooked on reading by reading to them and having them watch you read out loud. Have family reading time, when everyone reads a book. After you read your children a story, ask them to read by themselves or look at pictures while you read your assignments. Remember to approach reading with a positive attitude so that they will connect reading with pleasure.

TAKING CHARGE

Summary

In this chapter, I learned to

- **Apply the Five-Part Reading System.** Like the Adult Learning Cycle, this system is useful for increasing my comprehension and recall. The steps are (1) prepare, (2) preview, (3) predict questions, (4) process information, and (5) paraphrase and review. Scanning chapters gives me a quick overview of main concepts and ideas. I look for information I already know and link it to new information. I look for key words, main ideas, definitions, facts, and important concepts. I make questions out of chapter headings and definitions. I review the chapter to find answers and write them in the margin or on note cards and compare my answers with those of my study team.

- **Apply the SQ3R Reading System.** A five-step process, this method can improve my reading comprehension: S = Survey; Q = Question; R = Read; R = Recite; R = Review.

- **Be an active reader.** I clarify how I will use the information and set goals. I concentrate on main points and general understanding. I read difficult material out loud or standing up. I write in the margins, draw illustrations, underline, sketch, take notes, and dig out key points and key words. I pretend I'm talking with the author and jot down questions.

- **Outline main points and make connections.** Organizing information in an outline creates order, meaning, and understanding and helps me recall the material. It simplifies difficult information and makes connections clear. I link new information with what I already know and look for connections to what I don't know. I search for similarities and differences. I look for examples and read end-of-chapter summaries.

- **Summarize.** Summarizing in writing and out loud are powerful reading and memory strategies. I close the book at various times to write summaries and then check my brief summaries with the book. I summarize in writing after I finish a quick read.

- **Review.** I increase my comprehension by reviewing my outline, note cards, key words, main points, and summaries within 24 hours of reading and after lectures.

- **Build a strong vocabulary.** A good vocabulary is critical to success in school and my career. I improve my vocabulary by learning and incorporating new words into my writing and conversations and using resources such as a dictionary or vocabulary books.

- **Manage language courses.** Many of the same vocabulary-building strategies work for second-language courses. I can focus on key words, recite out loud, carry note cards, listen to recordings, keep up with the reading assignments, and use practice exercises.

- **Tackle specialized reading.** Thoroughness and precision are critical for reading technical information, graphs, manuals, and forms. Tips for technical information include identifying the purpose of the material, looking for connections, and explaining in my own words. Tips for manuals include reviewing the table of contents, looking up key words in the index, following step-by-step instructions, and reading aloud if necessary. Tips for forms include scanning before I begin, reading the small print, knowing what pertains to me, and asking questions when I'm unsure.

- **Address reading challenges.** I know to seek help with reading difficulties and create a positive attitude about improving my reading abilities, including reading for pleasure.

Performance Strategies

Following are the top 10 strategies for active reading:

- Create a positive, open mindset that is focused on growth and learning.
- Outline the main points, identify key words, and predict questions.
- Stretch yourself and stick to reading even if it's difficult.
- Take breaks and make reading physical.
- Reduce distractions and stay alert. Create interest in the subject.
- Make connections and link information.
- Create a relationship with the author.
- Summarize in writing in your own words.
- Review consistently and as soon as possible.
- Teach by summarizing out loud and explaining the material to others.

Tech for Success

- **Books online.** Many of your textbooks can be purchased online and downloaded to your computer or electronic device. Most of these books are formatted to be read online, rather than printed. Do you prefer this format over reading from a printed text? List some of the advantages and disadvantages of both options.

- **All the news that's fit to click.** What's your source for the latest news? Most major newspapers are available online and archive previous articles. Take a poll of your classmates to see who still opts for newsprint, who prefers the local and cable networks, and who relies on the Web. Discuss the pros and cons. Do your classmates' preferences match their learning styles? Which sources do the more avid readers prefer?

Endnotes

[1]D. Bavelier and H. Neville, "Neuroplasticity, Developmental," in *Encyclopedia of the Human Brain,* vol. e, ed. V. S. Ramachandran (Amsterdam: Academic Press, 2002), p. 561.

[2]Daniel J. Siegel, *Brainstorm: The Power and Purpose of the Teenage Brain* (New York: Penguin Random House, 2015).

Study Team Notes

Career *in* Focus

Blend Images/Getty Images

Brian Singer
INFORMATION TECHNOLOGY SPECIALIST

Related Majors: Computer Science, Mathematics, Information Systems

Keeping Up-to-Date

Brian Singer is an information technology specialist, or computer programmer, for a major hospital group. His job is to write computer instructions that update financial records.

When writing a program, Brian must first break the task into various instructional steps that a computer can follow. Then he must code each step into a programming language. When finished, Brian tests the program to confirm it works accurately. Usually, he needs to make some adjustments, called debugging, before the program runs smoothly. The program must be maintained over time and updated as the need arises. Because critical problems can be intricate and time-consuming and must be fixed quickly, Brian usually works long hours, including evenings and weekends. Although his office surroundings are comfortable, Brian must be careful to avoid physical problems, such as eyestrain or back discomfort.

To stay current in his field, Brian reads about 300 pages of technical materials each week. Brian also took a class on reading technical information to improve his reading skills. Because he concentrates best when he is around people, Brian likes to read and study in a coffeehouse. When he has difficulty understanding what he reads, he gets on the Internet and asks for help from an online discussion group. To help him remember and better understand what he has read during the week, Brian tries to implement the new information in his work.

CRITICAL THINKING What strategies might help an information technology specialist when reading technical information?

Peak Performer Profile

Sonia Sotomayor

A culmination of a successful career in law and an early love of books led Sonia Sotomayor, born to and raised in the Bronx by Puerto Rican parents, to a U.S. Supreme Court nomination in 2009. In this historic appointment, Sotomayor was the first Hispanic person and third woman to become a justice on the Supreme Court. Sotomayor believes that the law and its inherent fairness enabled her to rise from the Bronx housing project where she grew up to become a member of the Supreme Court today. She is credited as being a "role model of aspiration, discipline, commitment, intellectual prowess, and integrity."

It was a love of books that initially led Sotomayor into pursuing law. She became an avid reader when, at the age of 9, she turned to books for solace after her father died. Nancy Drew mysteries especially captivated her and inspired her to want to become a detective. She soon discovered the *Perry Mason* television show. Because the lawyers were often involved in investigative work like Nancy Drew, she decided at the age of 10 that she would become a lawyer.

Sotomayor graduated valedictorian of her high school and attended Princeton University, where she felt like "a visitor landing in alien country," given the lack of female and Hispanic students at the time. With hard work and perseverance, Sotomayor excelled in her classes and attended Yale Law School on a scholarship, where she graduated with a J.D. in 1979.

Shutterstock

As an assistant district attorney in New York and later as the first Latina woman on the U.S. Court of Appeals for the Second Circuit, Sotomayor was known for her preparedness, fairness, and adherence to the law. In the courthouse, she works to empower young people with her Development School for Youth program, which sponsors workshops that teach inner-city students how to function successfully in a work setting. By following her own dreams from a very early age, Sotomayor hopes to encourage the next generation of lawyers, doctors, and, perhaps, detectives.

PERFORMANCE THINKING Books and other media not only offer opportunities for escape and personal reflection but also allow us to see a different view of a particular occupation we may not have seen before. When have you learned more about a career while reading a book or an article?

CHECK IT OUT Websites such as Flashlight Worthy Book Club Recommendation (**www.flashlightworthybooks.com/**), LitLovers Online Book Community (**www.litlovers.com**), and Book Movement Book Club Resources (**www.bookmovement. com/**) recommend book clubs and publish book reviews. Some connect members through forums, reading guides, or online courses. Find inspiration for what you'll read next. Through reading, you, too, may discover something new about yourself, as Sotomayor did with the Nancy Drew series.

Starting Today

At least one strategy I learned in this chapter that I plan to try right away is

_____

_____

_____

What changes must I make in order for this strategy to be most effective?

_____

_____

_____

Review Questions

Based on what you have learned in this chapter, write your answers to the following questions:

1. Name and describe each part of the Five-Part Reading System.

_____

_____

2. How does outlining the main points help you improve your reading?

_____

_____

3. Name three strategies for managing language courses.

_____

_____

4. Explain how building your vocabulary can be important to your career success.

_____

_____

5. What are important elements to look for when reading graphics?

_____

_____

Effective Reading Habits

In the Classroom

Chris McDaniel struggles to keep up with her reading. She is overwhelmed by the amount of reading and the difficulty of her textbooks. She has never been much of a reader, spending most of her free time watching television. She sometimes reads in bed but often falls asleep. She realizes this is not the most productive way to study, but it has become a habit. Chris has noticed that, after reading for an hour or so, she can recall almost nothing. This has frustrated her, and she doubts her ability to succeed in college.

Shutterstock

1. What habits should Chris change to improve her reading skills?

_____

_____

_____

2. Suggest one or two specific strategies Chris could implement to become a better reader.

_____

_____

In the Workplace

Chris is now a stockbroker. She never thought she would work in this business, but a part-time summer job led her to a career in finance, and she really likes the challenge. She is surprised, however, at the vast amount of reading involved in her job: reports, magazines, and articles. She also reads several books and blogs on money management each month.

3. What strategies in this chapter would help Chris manage and organize her reading materials?

_____

_____

4. What are some specific reading strategies that apply to both school and work?

_____

_____

Applying the ABC Method of Self-Management

In the **Journal Entry**, you were asked to describe a time when you were frustrated with information overload and comprehension. How would having a positive, open mindset help you with reading?

_____

_____

_____

_____

Apply the ABC steps to enhance your reading skills and write a script.

A = Acknowledge: Accept reality and pay attention to your emotions.

_____

_____

B = Breathe: Take a deep breath to calm down and feel beloved.

_____

_____

C = Choose: Knowing you have many options, choose the most appropriate for the situation and that will result in positive long-term consequences.

_____

_____

Sample Script: Even though I'm feeling frustrated, I still love and accept myself and want to grow and learn. I breathe deeply, calm down, and know that I can tolerate these frustrating feelings. I allow them to pass as I calm down and resist the urge to skip reading. I choose to increase my reading and comprehension skills. I choose to go to the learning center for tips and workshops on reading comprehension. I choose to take notes while I'm reading, ask questions, and give a summary out loud. I choose to test myself after each chapter. I also increase my reading skills by always having a fun book to read. I reward myself with reading for pleasure and listen to audio books while driving. I'll join a book club in the summer and have a reading list of a variety of good books. I know that being open to new ideas and learning reading and comprehension skills will help me in my career and in all aspects of my life.

Attitudes and Reading

Read the following questions and write your answers on the lines provided.

1. What is your attitude toward reading?

_____

_____

2. What kind of books do you most like to read?

_____

_____

3. Do you read for pleasure?

_____

_____

4. Do you read the daily newspaper? (print or online)   Yes _____ No _____

If yes, what section(s) do you read?

_____

_____

5. Do you read magazines?   Yes _____ No _____

If yes, which magazines?

_____

_____

_____

6. How would it benefit you to read faster?

_____

_____

7. What techniques can you learn to read faster and remember more?

_____

_____

_____

8. What is one thing you want to practice to improve your reading?

_____

Different Types of Reading

Find a sample of each of the following sources of reading material:

- Newspaper
- Chapter from a textbook
- Instructions such as for an appliance, an insurance policy, or a rental contract

Read each sample. Then answer the following questions.

1. How does the reading process differ for each type of reading?

_____

_____

_____

_____

_____

_____

_____

_____

_____

_____

2. How does knowing your purpose for reading affect how you read? Why?

_____

_____

_____

_____

_____

_____

_____

_____

_____

_____

_____

Summarize and Teach

1. Read the following paragraphs on Title IX. Underline, write in the margins, and write a brief summary of the paragraph. Compare your work with a study partner's work. There are many ways to highlight, so don't be concerned if yours is unique.

THE IMPACT OF TITLE IX

When Title IX of the Education Amendments was passed, gender was added to the list of categories protected by federal law. From then on, schools and colleges receiving any federal funds were prohibited from discriminating against either employees or students on the basis of their sex. Despite resistance in many forms, Title IX has slowly transformed education in the United States.

When people hear the words *Title IX,* they usually think of athletics and sports facilities. Indeed, in 1972, only about 294,000 American high school girls took part in interscholastic sports; today, about 3 million girls play sports. But Title IX is much more far-reaching than sports.

Prior to Title IX, girls who became pregnant were often forced to leave school or, at best, to attend segregated—and well-hidden—classes. Title IX prohibited that practice. Although schools can still offer voluntary classes for pregnant and parenting teens, no girl can be kept out of any program, class, or extracurricular activity because of bearing a child. These were no small victories in schools where girls who became pregnant were routinely expelled.

Source: James W. Fraser, *Teach: A Question of Teaching* (McGraw-Hill, 2011).

SUMMARY

_____

_____

_____

_____

_____

_____

2. Work with a study partner in one of your classes. Read a chapter and write a summary. Compare your summary with your study partner's summary. Then summarize and teach the main concepts to your partner. Each of you can clarify and ask questions.

SUMMARY

_____

_____

_____

_____

_____

_____

_____

Creating a Reading Outline

Outlining what you read can be a helpful study technique. Develop the habit of outlining. Use the following form as a guide. You may also develop your own form (see Chapter 6 for examples). Outline Chapter 7 on the following lines (or select another chapter in this or one of your other texts).

Course _____ Chapter _____ Date _____

I. _____

   A. _____

      1. _____

      2. _____

      3. _____

   B. _____

      1. _____

      2. _____

      3. _____

II. _____

   A. _____

      1. _____

      2. _____

      3. _____

   B. _____

      1. _____

      2. _____

      3. _____

III. _____

   A. _____

      1. _____

      2. _____

      3. _____

   B. _____

      1. _____

      2. _____

      3. _____

IV. _____

   A. _____

      1. _____

      2. _____

      3. _____

   B. _____

      1. _____

      2. _____

      3. _____

Analyzing Chapters

As you start to read the next chapter in this book, fill in this page to prepare for reading. You may need to add additional headings. List each heading and then phrase it as a question. Then summarize as you complete your reading. Use a separate sheet of paper if needed.

Course _____ Textbook _____

Chapter _____

Heading 1 _____

Question _____

Heading 2 _____

Question _____

Heading 3 _____

Question _____

Heading 4 _____

Question _____

SUMMARY OF SECTION

_____

_____

_____

_____

_____

SUMMARY OF CHAPTER

_____

_____

_____

_____

_____

Mind Map Your Text

Make a mind map of a section or chapter of one of your textbooks using the format provided here (and edit/change as necessary). Use **Figure 6.2** as a guide.

For example, let's say you will map out a section from **Chapter 4** of this text: "Manage Your Time." In the middle circle, you might put "Time-Management Strategies." In one of the surrounding circles, you might enter "Study everywhere and anywhere." In offshoot circles from that, you might put "Carry note cards," "Listen to recorded lectures," and "Avoid peak times in the library." Compare your mind maps with those drawn by other students in your class.

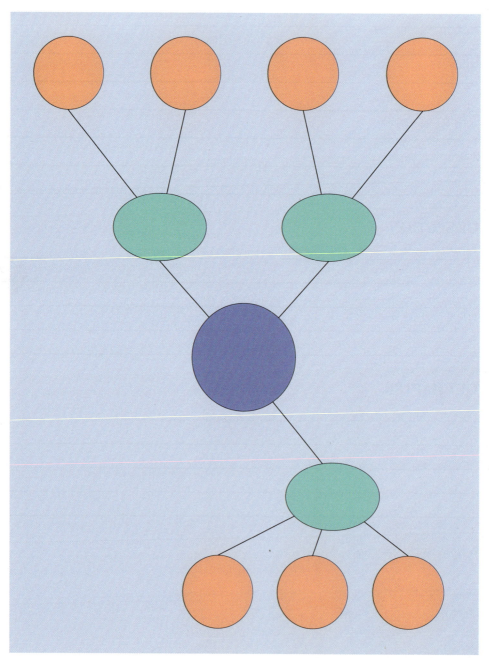

Breaking Barriers to Reading

Following is a list of the common reasons that some students use for not reading effectively. Read this list; then add to it on the lines provided. Use creative problem solving to list strategies for overcoming these barriers.

Reasons for Not Reading	**Strategies for Overcoming Reading Barriers**
1. My textbooks are boring.	_____
	_____
	_____
	_____
2. I can't concentrate.	_____
	_____
	_____
	_____
3. I'm easily distracted.	_____
	_____
	_____
	_____
4. I fall asleep when I read.	_____
	_____
	_____
	_____
5. I never study the right material.	_____
	_____
	_____
	_____
6. There is too much information, and I don't know what is important.	_____
	_____
7. I read for hours, but I don't understand what I have read.	_____
	_____
	_____
8. I don't like to read.	_____
	_____
	_____

Demonstrating Competencies

Follow these steps and fill in the blanks to demonstrate your competencies. Then add this page to your Career Development Portfolio.

1. **Looking back:** Review your worksheets from other chapters to find activities from which you learned to read and concentrate.
2. **Taking stock:** Identify your strengths in reading and what you want to improve.
3. **Looking forward:** Indicate how you would demonstrate reading and comprehension skills to an employer.
4. **Documentation:** Include documentation of your reading skills.
5. **Inventory:** Make a list of the books you've read recently, including any classics. Use a separate sheet of paper.

Explain how you demonstrate these competencies:

Competencies	Your Demonstration
Active reading	_____
Critical reading	_____
Willingness to learn new words	_____
Improvement in technical vocabulary	_____
Articulation	_____
Expressiveness	_____
Ability to use a dictionary	_____
Positive attitude toward reading	_____
Technical reading	_____
Form reading	_____

Improve Your Memory Skills

8

LEARNING OUTCOMES

In this chapter, you will learn to

8-1 Describe the five-step memory process

8-2 Describe memory strategies, including mnemonic devices

8-3 Identify strategies to overcome obstacles for better habits

SELF-MANAGEMENT

> *I have been meeting so many new people. I wish I could remember their names, but I just don't have a good memory. How can I increase my memory skills and remember names, facts, and information more easily?*

Dean Drobot/Shutterstock

Do you ever feel embarrassed because you cannot remember the names of new people you've met? Do you ever get frustrated because you don't remember material for a test?

JOURNAL ENTRY Worksheet 8.1 will help you apply the ABC's of self-management and practice writing a script.

Technology has provided ample ways to store and retrieve information. No longer do we memorize and recite long stories in order to pass them down, as was done hundreds of years ago. In fact, many people don't even know their best friend's phone number because it's programmed into their cell phone.

However, you can't whip out your phone when you take a test or run into a business acquaintance and can't remember his name ("Is it Bob or Bill? I know it starts with a *B*."). Although you may search the Internet to find information, you still need to determine what the information means, how it relates to other material, and how you will use it now and in the future. For this, your brain—not your computer, smartphone, or calculator—is the most essential "device."

Do you think some people are born with better memories than others? *You will discover in this chapter that memory is a complex process that involves many factors you can control, such as your attitude, interest, intent, awareness, mental alertness, observation skills, senses, distractions, memory techniques, and willingness to practice.* Most people with good memories say they mastered the skill by learning and continually practicing the strategies for storing and recalling information. Research on neuroplasticity has shown that the brain can be exercised as though it were a muscle and grow in memory skills through visual, auditory, reading and writing, and kinesthetic exercises.[1] This chapter will describe specific strategies that help you remember information in college and at work.

The Memory Process

Memory Research

The teen years are the time when your brain is learning at peak efficiency. So college is the time to identify strengths and cultivate talents and interests and to explore areas to improve. There are resources available to help with remediation, learning, and emotional issues. An open, growth-oriented mindset can help you increase your discipline, task completion, attention, and focus. The most successful students do not ruminate about setbacks but think of mistakes as problems and challenges to be solved. Exercising, eating well, getting enough sleep, and meditation and mindfulness are key. Exercise increases blood flow to the areas of the brain involved in memory, which is so important to the adolescent and young adult brain.[2] It is important to stress that even though your brain is learning at peak efficiency, attention, task completion, emotions, and self-discipline are often inefficient. This is where creating positive habits can help. Planning and focusing on one thing at a time helps increase blood flow to the areas of the brain involved in organizing tasks and memory. Focus is key to memory.

The memory process involves five main steps:

1. Intention—you are interested and have a desire to learn and remember
2. Attention—you are attentive, observing information, and concentrating on details

3. **Association**—you organize and associate information to make sense of it
4. **Retention**—you practice until you know the information
5. **Recall**—you remember, teach, and share information with others

As you can see, this process is similar to the Adult Learning Cycle, which is explored throughout this text. (Read **Peak Progress 8.1** to see how you can use this cycle to improve your memory skills.) Let's say that you want to remember names.

1. **Intention.** *The first step in using memory effectively is to prepare mentally. As with learning any skill, a positive, open mindset focuses on growth.* You know that with effort you can cultivate a good memory by being interested and willing to learn. You intend to remember by finding personal meaning and interest. Instead of, "I wish I could remember names" or "I can't remember formulas for math," say, "I really want to remember JoAnne's last name. I intend to improve my memory. I remember names."

    If you have a negative, fixed mindset, you believe you are born with a good memory and won't even try to improve. If you have a positive, open mindset you believe that with effort, memory can improve. You make a conscious intention to remember and are curious and interested. Be willing to learn new information and skills at work even if your part-time job isn't in

Peak Progress 8.1

Applying the Adult Learning Cycle to Increasing Your Memory Skills

1. **FEEL and LISTEN.** *Why do I want to learn this?* I really want to become more proficient at remembering names, facts, and information. This is critical for success not only in school but also in work and social situations. First I'll review the strategies I already use to remember information and relate it to new tips. I will listen carefully as names are said.

2. **OBSERVE and VISUALIZE.** *How does this work?* I'll observe who is good at remembering names and information. What tips can I pick up? Who seems to struggle with remembering important information? I'll observe the information I want to remember and visualize it.

3. **THINK and WRITE.** *What does this mean?* I will think about the strategies that work best for me? I will eliminate negative and defeating self-talk. I'll look for connections and associations. I use humor, songs, rhymes, and other mnemonic techniques. I write down names and read them out loud.

4. **DO and PRACTICE.** *What can I do with this?* I will practice remembering names every day. I'll make games out of my practice and have fun. I'll find practical applications and use my new skills in everyday life. Each day, I'll work on one area. For example, I'll choose one class in which to get to know one or two new students.

5. **TEACH and PRACTICE AGAIN.** *Whom can I share this with?* I'll talk with others and share my tips and experiences. I'll ask if they have any strategies they find useful that I might also try. I will demonstrate how I remember information using all my senses and practice over and over again.

Use the VARK system to help you think through and apply the Adult Learning Cycle. Use all your senses to integrate learning and leverage your success. *Visualize* the name and make associations with your imagination. Use fantasy and imagery to bring the name to life. *Listen* carefully to names and pronunciation. Ask how the name is spelled. *Repeat* the word to yourself and say it aloud. *Write* out the name and *read* it again and again. Summarize the information. *Actively practice* your memory skills and teach them to others. Create a positive, open mindset. Don't say that you're bad at remembering names and just *do it!* Congratulate yourself when you improve.

Personal Evaluation Notebook

Being Observant

Try the following experiments to determine if you are really observing the world around you.

EXPERIMENT 1

1. Look around the room or use other senses to determine the environment.
2. Close your eyes. What is it that you sense?
3. Mentally picture what is in the room.
4. Open your eyes. Now take what is in the room through various senses.
5. Now take in the room slowly. Take note of what you remembered. Is there a pattern? Take note of what you didn't remember. Is there a pattern? What about sound, texture, smells, color? What now stands out?

_____

_____

_____

If you missed items, what were the possible causes? Were you distracted? Were you focused on only one item? What can you do to bring your mind back to the present moment, be alert, and aware of your surroundings, sights, sounds, smells, textures, and tone? Being mindful is a skill that can be enhanced with practice. Choose one event today for which you choose to practice mindfulness.

EXPERIMENT 2

1. Look at a painting, photo, or poster for one minute.
2. Without looking back, write down the details you remember.
3. Compare your list of details with the painting, photo, or poster.
   a. What details did you remember? Colors? Faces? Clothing?

_____

_____

_____

   b. What details didn't you remember?

_____

_____

_____

   c. Did you remember the obvious things or did you remember subtle details?

_____

(continued)

Personal Evaluation Notebook

Being Observant   (*concluded*)

d. Why do you think those were the details you remembered?

_____

_____

_____

_____

After you've completed this exercise, you'll have a better idea of your observation skills and can choose to create a habit for heightening your awareness. Your trigger might be saying, "What an interesting room" *or* "What an interesting person." This helps you to be more aware of color, photos, features, clothing, body language, and so on.

your field. Once you make it a habit to remember names and information, it will become a positive habit.

2. **Attention.** *Mindfulness helps you to concentrate, observe, and be attentive to details.* How often have you physically been in one place but mentally and emotionally thousands of miles away? **Mindfulness** is the state in which you are totally in the moment and part of the process. Learning occurs when your mind is relaxed, focused, receptive, and alert. Focus your attention by concentrating briefly on one thing. Visualize details by drawing mental pictures. Observe and pay attention. **Personal Evaluation Notebook 8.1** helps you practice your observation skills.

3. **Association.** Nothing is harder to remember than unconnected facts, dates, or theories. How is this information similar to other information? How is it different?

   By associating and linking new material with old material, you make it meaningful. You cannot retain or recall information unless you understand it. Understanding means being able to see connections and relationships in information. Summarize and explain the material in your own words. Make associations by looking for similarities or differences. Create understanding by finding out why this information is important and how it relates to other information. Sustained effort creates interest and understanding. (See **Peak Progress 8.2** on short-term versus long-term memory.)

   One way to organize material to look for connections is by outlining each chapter. As discussed in Chapter 6, use whatever outline method works for you to organize information. (See **Personal Evaluation Notebook 8.2** for a sample of a mind map.)

4. **Retention.** *Repetition and practice help you retain information.* Do it, and do it again. Repeat names or information aloud. Practice what you have learned, find new applications, and connect this information to other information you already know. Continue to ask questions and look for more examples.

> **"**An education isn't how much you have committed to memory, or even how much you know. It's being able to differentiate between what you know and what you don't.**"**
>
> **ANATOLE FRANCE**
> *Author*

WORDS TO SUCCEED

Peak Progress

Short-Term and Long-Term Memory

People have two basic types of memory: short-term, or active, memory and long-term, or passive, memory. Each type plays an important role in learning.

Before short-term memory can perform its wonders, information must flow into it. This can be new information entering through your natural senses, stored information you retrieve from long-term memory, or a combination of both. You might equate your natural senses with the zoom-in button on your camera, while you may think of long-term memory as your computer hard drive where you download and save your pictures. (See **Figure 8.1**.) Just as you make choices about which pictures to save on your computer, you determine which information becomes stored in your long-term memory. The information you choose to save in long-term memory has great value. It can be retrieved and used as it is, or it can be retrieved and combined with other information to create something entirely new. Research has shown that when a single neuron develops a long-term memory for sensitization, it can more than double synaptic connections. Neuroplastic changes occur when neurons are turned on.[3]

When we consider the transfer of information back and forth in our memory system, think of the mind as a vast relational database. It is not enough merely to store information; for any database to be useful, the information stored in it must be organized and indexed for retrieval. This occurs naturally when we are predisposed to remember something, but what happens when we have to memorize information we just don't care about? Not only is that information more difficult to memorize but also it becomes nearly impossible to recall. The good news is that we can make such information more memorable by personally relating to it. For example, ask yourself, "How can I use this information in my life?" Answers to such questions can create meaning, which helps our mind to naturally organize information. When it comes time to use that information, such as during an examination, it will have been naturally indexed for easier recall.

Figure **8.1**

Short-Term and Long-Term Memory

Think of your memory like taking pictures. First, you input information through your natural senses (such as pointing the camera and clicking). Your short-term memory is like the group of pictures in your camera, which can be deleted easily and gone forever. But, instead, you want to download your pictures onto your computer for long-term access, which can be organized, retrieved, printed, and viewed later (recall). *What material from this course may be in your short-term memory? In your long-term memory?*

(left) Mark Dierker/McGraw-Hill Education; *(center)* Gregor Schuster/Photographer's Choice/Getty Images; *(right)* Tero Vesalainen/Shutterstock

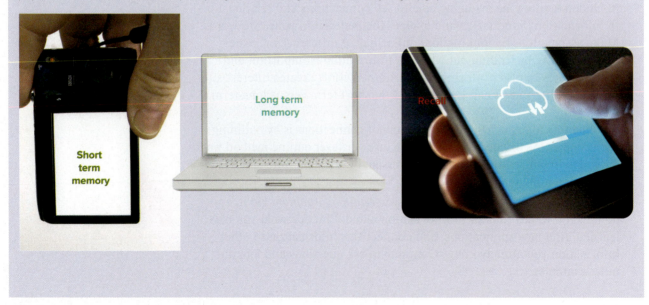

Personal Evaluation Notebook

Using a Mind Map to Enhance Memory

A mind map helps you organize information, and the physical act of writing will help you commit the material to memory. Use the map figure that follows as a guide, and in the space provided create a mind map of this chapter.

- Write the main topic in the middle and draw a circle or box around it.
- Surround the main topic with subtopics.
- Draw lines from the subtopics to the main topic.
- Under the subtopics, jot down supporting points, ideas, and examples.

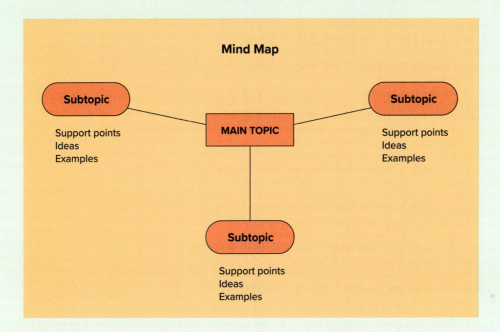

Create your own mind map.

Think of an essay question from an exam you have taken. How would using a mind map have helped you answer the question?

5. **Recall. Memorization** is the transfer of information from short-term memory into long-term memory so you can retrieve it in the future. To **recall** information means you not only have retained it but also can remember it when you need to. The more often you recall information, the stronger your memory becomes. For example, if you cannot recall a friend's name, you can jog your memory by recalling the name of her husband or boyfriend. Unblock your recall by stimulating a similar area of your memory.

Share information with others; introduce a person you have just met; practice giving summaries of chapters to your study team. Teach the information, write about it, talk about it, apply it to new situations, and demonstrate that you know it. This will make you more interested in the information, create more meaning for you, and build your confidence. Repeating this cycle will build your memory skills.

Memory Strategies

The following strategies will help you improve your memory skills.

1. **Write it down.** Writing is physical and enhances learning. When you write information, you are reinforcing learning by using your eyes, hand, fingers, and arm. *Writing uses different parts of the brain than do speaking and listening.*

   - Write down information to reinforce learning.
   - Plan your time and create a to-do list to trigger memory later in the day when you may have become overwhelmed with distractions.
   - Take notes in class to organize and fill in memory gaps.
   - Underline important information to reinforce learning.
   - Write a summary to transfer information to long-term memory.

2. **Go from the general to the specific.** Many people learn and remember best by looking at the big picture and then learning the details. Try to outline from the general (main topic) to the specific (subtopics). Preview a chapter to give you an overview. *Your brain is more receptive to details when it has a general idea of the main topic.* Preview, read, listen, and look for general understanding; then add details and summarize.

3. **Reduce written information.** You don't have to memorize certain types of information, such as deadlines, telephone messages, and assignment due dates. You just have to know where to find this information. Use digital ways to keep track of deadlines, set reminders, and keep digital task lists or easy access.

4. **Eliminate distractions.** Distractions keep you from paying attention and remembering what you're trying to learn. One way to avoid distractions is to study in an uncluttered, quiet area, such as a library or designated study room. If it is noisy in class, move closer to the front and focus your attention, create associations, and recall information.

5. **Take regular breaks.** You will use the power of concentration more fully, and the brain retains information better, when you take short breaks. After about 60 minutes, the brain needs a break to process information effectively. Read your textbook for 30 minutes, outline and make test questions for 30 minutes.

Then take a 10-minute break. Stretch, drink a glass of water, or eat a small snack. Then return to studying.

6. **Use all your senses if possible.** Memory is sensory, so using all your senses (sight, hearing, touch, smell, and taste) will give your brain a better chance of retaining information. Be creative and adaptive to what works best for you.

   • *Visualize.* Because much of what you learn and remember reaches you through sight, it is important to visualize what you want to remember. The art of retention is the art of attention. Be a keen observer of details and notice differences and similarities. Suppose you are taking a medical terminology or vocabulary-building course. You may want to look at pictures and visualize images with the new terms or words. Look at illustrations, pictures, and information on the board.

   • *Listen.* You cannot remember a name or information in class if you are not attentive and listening. Actively listen in class, record lectures (ask for the instructor's permission), and play them back later. Recite definitions and information aloud.

   • *Move.* Whether you learn best by reading or listening, you will retain information better if you use all your senses and make learning physical. Read aloud; read while standing; jot down notes; lecture in front of the classroom to yourself or your study team; draw pictures, diagrams, and models; and join a study group. Practice reciting information while doing physical activity, such as showering or jogging. The more you use all your senses, the more information you will retain.

   Complete **Personal Evaluation Notebook 8.3** to assess your memory and how your senses relate to your childhood memories. Complete **Personal Evaluation Notebook 8.4** to determine how to use learning styles to improve recall.

7. **Use technology.** There is a lot of new technology that can help you organize and enhance your memory. Check out *outlining software* to encode and outline information from your textbooks and lecture notes. There are *websites* for bookmarking that allow you to store, share, and search links to pages. Check out http://pinboard.in, http://draggo.com/ and www.diigo.com. There are *online notebooks,* such as *Evernote, Google Keep,* and *One Note.* There are *apps* that let you create digital flash cards to use on your smartphone, tablet, and computer: Luminosity, Elevate, Brain Trainer, iCue Memory, and Memory Trainer. When you store documents either on your digital device or online, name them with something specific so you'll remember and be able to find them. Just remember that the best technology and app is your own brain. Continue to exercise your memory muscle so that you can deliver presentations with few notes and remember people's names. Now that's impressive!

• Learning Memory

Focusing on your preferred learning style strengthens your memory skills. *How does your learning style affect the way in which you memorize?*

Marc Romanelli/Blend Images LLC

Personal Evaluation Notebook 8.3

Memory Assessment

1. Sometimes your perceptions differ from reality, particularly when you are assessing your skills and personal qualities. Check Yes or No as it pertains to you.
   a. Do you remember names easily?   Yes _____ No _____
   b. Do you remember important information for tests?   Yes _____ No _____
   c. Do you often forget about due dates and appointments?   Yes _____ No _____
   d. Do you often "lose" things around the house?   Yes _____ No _____
   e. Did you use your senses more as a child?   Yes _____ No _____

2. Write a few lines about your earliest memory.

   _____

   _____

   _____

   _____

3. Does it help your memory to look at family photos or hear about your childhood? Why?

   _____

   _____

   _____

   _____

4. What sounds and smells do you remember most from home?

   _____

Take stock of your memory on a daily basis and see what patterns emerge and what works. Do visual cues such as photos help, or sounds such as a song or smells such as fresh bread baking, or taste? When you remember early memories, jot them down in a journal. What techniques would help you on a daily basis, such as having a specific place for keys or keeping notes on new people you have met and saying their names again and again before you attend a class or party? Create a plan.

8. **Use mnemonic devices. Mnemonic** (neh-mon-nik) devices are memory tricks that help you remember information. Because mnemonic devices don't help you understand the information or develop skills in critical thinking, they are best used for sheer rote memorization. Follow up by looking for associations, making connections, and writing summaries. Some mnemonic devices are

   • *Rhymes and rhythms.* In elementary school, you might have learned the rhyme "In 1492 Columbus sailed the ocean blue" to remember the date of Columbus's voyage. Rhythms can also be helpful. Many people have learned to spell the word *Mississippi* by accenting all the *i*s and making the word rhythmic. This is similar to the technique used in rap music and poetry, in which syllables are accentuated on an established beat.

Personal Evaluation Notebook 8.4

Learning Styles and Memory

Answer the following questions on the lines provided.

1. What is your preferred learning style? How can you use this information to enhance your memory?

   _____

   _____

   _____

   _____

   _____

2. How can you incorporate other learning styles to help you improve your recall?

   _____

   _____

   _____

   _____

   _____

- *Acronyms.* **Acronyms** are words formed from the first letters of a series of other words, such as HOMES for the Great Lakes (Huron, Ontario, Michigan, Erie, and Superior) and EPCOT (Experimental Prototype Community of Tomorrow).

- *Acrostics.* **Acrostics** are similar to acronyms, but they are made-up sentences in which the first letter stands for something, such as Every Good Boy Deserves Fun for remembering the sequence of musical notes on the lines of the treble clef: E, G, B, D, F. Another is My Very Easy Memory Jingle Seems Useful Now, which helps you remember the order of the planets from the sun. (This assumes you know that the first planet is Mercury and not Mars and that Pluto is no longer considered a planet. Can you name the rest with the help of the acrostic?) Acrostics are often used in poetry, where the first letter of every line combines to spell something, such as the poem's title. (See **Personal Evaluation Notebook 8.5** to practice creating acronyms and acrostics.)

- *Association.* Suppose you are learning about explorer Christopher Columbus's three ships. Think of three friends whose names start with the same first letters as the ships' names: *Pinta, Santa Maria,* and *Nina* (e.g., Paul, Sandy, and Nancy). Vividly associate your friends' names with the three ships, and you should be able to recall the ships' names. Using associations can also be helpful in remembering numbers. For example, if your ATM identification number is 9072, you might remember it by

Personal Evaluation Notebook

8.5

Acronyms and Acrostics

An *acronym* is a word formed from the first letters of a series of other words. An *acrostic* is a made-up sentence, with the first letter of each word standing for something. Create one or more acronyms and acrostics based on information you are learning right now in your courses.

Acronym example: "NATO" stands for North Atlantic Treaty Organization.

Acronym _____

Stands for _____

Acrostic example: "Old People From Texas Eat Spiders" stands for the bones of the skull (occipital, parietal, frontal, temporal, ethmoid, sphenoid).

Acrostic _____

Stands for _____

Apply this to your major or any class. For example, let's say you're taking a geography class and want to remember the Great Lakes. HOMES will help you remember Lakes Huron, Ontario, Michigan, Erie, and Superior. If you're taking a music class, the sentence *Every good boy does fine* will help you remember the music notes of the lines of the treble clef staff (E, G, B, D, and F). Compare these with your study team and ask the professor for tips.

creating associations with dates. Maybe 1990 is the year you graduated from high school and 1972 is the year you were born.

- *Chunking.* **Chunking**, or grouping, long lists of information or numbers can break up the memory task and make it easier for you. Most people can remember up to seven numbers in a row, which is why phone numbers are that long.

- *Stacking technique.* Visualize objects that represent points, and stack them on top of each other to remind you of key points. For example, if you were giving a speech on time management, you would start with a clock with a big pencil on it to represent how much time is saved if you write information down. On top of the clock is a big calendar, which reminds you to make the point that you must set priorities in writing. On the calendar is a Time Log with the name Drucker on it. This will remind you to present a quote by Peter Drucker that you must know where your time goes if you are to be effective in managing your life.

- *Method-of-place technique.* As far back as 500 BCE the Greeks were using a method of imagery called loci–the method-of-place technique. (*Locus* is Latin for "place"; *loci* is the plural.) This method, which is similar to the stacking technique, is still effective because it uses imagery and association to aid memory. Memorize a setting in detail and then place the item or information you want to remember at certain places on your memory map. Some people like to use a familiar street, their home, or workplace as a map on which to place their information. Memorize certain places on your map and the specific order or path in which you visit each place. Once you have memorized this map, position various items to remember at different points. **Personal Evaluation Notebook 8.6** gives you a chance to practice this technique.

9. **Recite.** Recite and repeat information, such as a name, poem, date, or formula. When you say information aloud, you use your throat, voice, and lips, and you hear yourself recite. This recitation technique may help when you are dealing with difficult reading material. Reading aloud and hearing the material will reinforce it and help move information from your short-term memory to your long-term memory. Use the new words in your own conversations. Write summaries in your own words and read to others. Study groups are effective because you can hear each other, clarify questions, and increase understanding as you review information. Practice again and again.

To remember names, when you meet someone, recite the person's name several times to yourself and out loud. **Peak Progress 8.3** provides more tips for remembering names.

10. **Make flash cards.** Use note cards to condense information The act of writing is kinesthetic and holding cards is tactile. Flash cards are visual and, when the information is recited out loud or in a group, the auditory element enhances learning. They're a great way to organize information, highlight key words, and test yourself.

11. **Practice, practice, practice!** You must practice information you want to remember. For example, when you first start driver training, you learn the various steps involved in driving. At first, they may seem overwhelming. You may have to stop and think through each step. After you have driven a car for a while, however, you don't even think about all the steps required to start it and back out of the driveway. You check your mirror automatically before changing lanes, and driving safely has become a habit. *Through repetition, you put information into your long-term memory.* The more often you use the information, the easier it is to recall. You could not become a good musician without hours of practice. Playing sports, speaking in public, flying an airplane,

Research has shown not only that multitasking is a myth but that engaging in simultaneous tasks harms memory. Missouri scientists tested college students when memorizing and recalling. Students performed poorly when multitasking during recall, but even worse when they multitasked while memorizing.[4]

Definitely a "people person," Aleah is plugged in and stays in touch with her friends by texting and phone. She's just begun her nursing program and is enjoying working with patients. She enjoys the hands-on lab section of her anatomy and physiology course but worries she'll never master all the basic terminology—there is a lot to memorize. She studies with the television on, with headphones attached to an iPod, and while texting friends on her smartphone. She insists she can concentrate and multitask, but her test scores have been poor. Can you offer Aleah tips to help her focus and concentrate?

- Use the Habit Cycle to illustrate how Aleah can focus on one task at a time.
- Give Aleah tips for remembering information and names of patients and co-workers.
- How can Aleah integrate the VARK system of learning styles to enhance her memory?

Multitasking and Memory
Students will often say that their studying is not affected by their distractions of messaging, texting, and watching television. Research has shown, however, that students perform poorly on memory tests while distracted. The ability to successfully switch attention among multiple tasks reduces performance in all areas. Multitasking is not only a myth, but a dangerous one. Of the nearly 6,000 adolescents who die every year in automobile accidents, nearly 90 percent die because of distracted driving.[5]

THINK
CREATIVELY AND CRITICALLY

✔ Use index cards for recording information you want to memorize. Write brief summaries and indicate the main points of each chapter on the backs of note cards.

✔ Carry the cards with you and review them during waiting time, before going to sleep at night, or any other time you have a few minutes to spare.

✔ Organize the cards according to category, color, size, order, weight, and other areas.

Personal Evaluation Notebook

A Walk Down Memory Lane

Creating a memory map is a visual way to enhance and practice your memory skills. The key to this method is to set the items clearly in your memory and visualize them. For example, a familiar memory map involves remembering the 13 original colonies. The memory map in this case is a garden with several distinct points. There is delicate chinaware sitting on the garden gate (Delaware); the birdbath contains a large fountain pen (Pennsylvania); in the gazebo is a new jersey calf (New Jersey); and sitting on the calf is King George (Georgia) with a cut on his finger (Connecticut). The flowerbed has a mass of flowers (Massachusetts); in the fountain, splashing, is Marilyn Monroe (Maryland); the garden sun dial is pointing south (South Carolina); a large ham is sitting on the garden bench (New Hampshire); and the gardener, named Virginia (Virginia), who is wearing an empire dress (New York), is watering the northern flowerbed (North Carolina). In the middle of the flowerbed is an island of rocks (Rhode Island). There you have the 13 original colonies in the order in which they joined the union.

YOUR MEMORY MAP

Create your own memory map using a familiar place, such as your neighborhood, the mall, or a store you often visit, such as a grocery store. Chances are, you navigate around these places the same way every time. You start out on the same path; you park near or enter the same door. You are very familiar with what you will see at each point. For example, you may enter the grocery store near the courtesy counter, grab a cart, and turn right toward the produce section. You can easily visualize where everything is located and what you will see along the "path." Draw a picture of your map in detail in the space provided.

(continued)

Personal Evaluation Notebook 8.6

A Walk Down Memory Lane (*concluded*)

Using your map, imagine you have a test coming up in your American government class and need to remember the first 4 (out of 10) amendments that make up the Bill of Rights:

1. Freedom of speech, press, religion, assembly, and petition
2. Right to keep and bear arms
3. Quartering of soldiers
4. Search and arrest

Now, follow these steps in the method-of-place technique:

1. Imagine your memory location and think of each distinctive detail within the location.
2. Create a vivid image to help you remember each amendment. (If you are unfamiliar with the meaning of any of the amendments, do a quick search online or at the library.)
3. Associate each of the images representing the amendments with points in your map and see the images at each location. Draw them in your map.
4. As you "stroll" through your map, create mental pictures of each of your items through association. Recite each one aloud as you visualize them.

To help you get started, you may think of a newspaper stand to remind you of freedom of speech or of the press, or protesters with signs to remember the right to assemble or petition. Place these images within your memory map, such as at the front door (so that you have to walk around the protesters to get in the door).

Be creative and make the images meaningful to you. If you really want to stretch your critical thinking skills, add images for Amendments 5 through 10:

5. Rights concerning prosecution in criminal cases
6. Right to a speedy and fair trial
7. Right to a trial by jury
8. Bail, fines, and punishment
9. Rights retained by the people
10. States' rights

and learning to drive all require skills that need to be repeated and practiced many times. Repetition puts information into long-term memory and allows for recall.

These strategies are very effective in strengthening your memory skills. Certain strategies might work better for you than others, depending on your personality and learning styles, personal strengths, and abilities. You can master the use of memory strategies with effort, patience, and practice. As you build your memory skills, you will also enhance your study habits and become more disciplined and aware of your surroundings.

Remembering Names

Techniques that help you remember names can also be used to remember material in class, such as key people and events.

1. **Imagine the name.** Visualize the name clearly in your mind: Tom Plum. Clarify how the name is spelled: P-l-u-m.

2. **Be observant.** Pay attention to the person's features, stance, and mannerisms.

3. **Use exaggeration.** Caricaturing the features is a fun and effective way to remember names. Single out and amplify one outstanding feature. For example, if Tom has red hair, exaggerate it to bright red and see the hair much fuller and longer than it is.

4. **Visualize the red hair and the name Tom.** See this vision clearly.

5. **Repeat Tom's name to yourself several times** as you are talking to him.

6. **Recite Tom's name aloud** during your conversation. Introduce Tom to others.

7. **Use association.** Associate the name with something you know ("Tom is the name of my cat") or make up a story using the person's name and add action and color. Tom is picking red plums that match his hair.

8. **As soon as you can, jot down the name.** Use key words, write, draw descriptions.

9. **Use rhyming to help you recall:** "Tom is not dumb; he's a plum."

10. **Integrate learning styles.** It may help if you see the name (visual), hear it pronounced (auditory), or practice saying it and writing it several times and connecting the name with something familiar (kinesthetic).

11. **Ask people their names.** If you forget, say your name first. "Hi, I'm Sam and I met you last week." If they don't offer their names, ask.

Overcome Obstacles

A barrier to memory is *disinterest.* You have to *want* to remember. People often say, "If only I could remember names" or "I wish I had a better memory." Avoid using words such as *try, wish,* and *hope.* Overcome the barrier of disinterest by creating a positive, curious attitude; intend to remember; use all your senses; and use memory techniques. Related to disinterest is *lack of attentiveness.* You must be willing to concentrate by being an attentive listener and observe. Listen for overall understanding and for details. A shorter period of intense concentration will help you remember more than reading for hours. Review often.

Build Better Memory Habits

Let's say you want to get better at remembering names. When a person is introduced to you, their name is the *trigger.* Create a *routine* of specific behaviors. Look at the person and mentally say the name. Observe any particular features. Jack has red hair just like your Uncle Jack. Say the name while you're talking to Jack. When you have a minute alone, jot down the name and say it out loud. Your *reward* will be the emotional payoff of feeling pride that comes with remembering names. You'll gain confidence when you see results and realize that it's worth the effort. You'll also receive praise because people are impressed with those few who actually remember names. It makes a person feel special and listened to. People will notice!

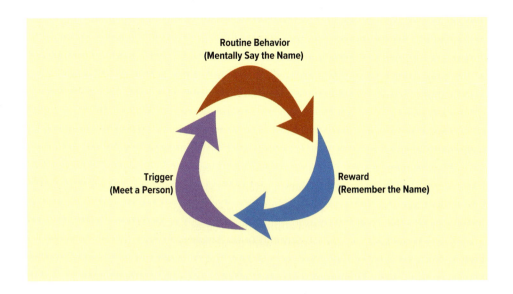

Routine Behavior
(Mentally Say the Name)

Trigger
(Meet a Person)

Reward
(Remember the Name)

Finally, relax. Anxiety and stress can make you forget. For example, let's return to remembering names. Suppose you see Alex when you are with a good friend. You may be so anxious to make a good impression that Alex's name is lost for a moment. Relax by being totally in the moment instead of worrying about forgetting, how you look, what others may think, or your nervousness. Take a deep breath. Try introducing your friend to Alex, "Hi, I'd like you to meet Blaise." Often the other person will jump in with, "Hi, I'm Alex." If that doesn't happen and you still can't remember, laugh and say, "My mind just went blank. I'm Jamel; please refresh my memory. Good to see you again, Alex." Practice your routine until it's automatic.

Just as you need to exercise your physical body, keep your memory skills sharp by exercising your brain—stretch your imagination, flex your interest, and jog your memory!

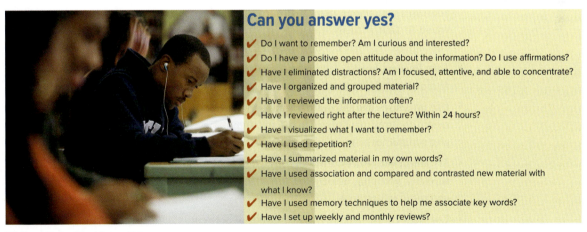

Can you answer yes?

✔ Do I want to remember? Am I curious and interested?
✔ Do I have a positive open attitude about the information? Do I use affirmations?
✔ Have I eliminated distractions? Am I focused, attentive, and able to concentrate?
✔ Have I organized and grouped material?
✔ Have I reviewed the information often?
✔ Have I reviewed right after the lecture? Within 24 hours?
✔ Have I visualized what I want to remember?
✔ Have I used repetition?
✔ Have I summarized material in my own words?
✔ Have I used association and compared and contrasted new material with what I know?
✔ Have I used memory techniques to help me associate key words?
✔ Have I set up weekly and monthly reviews?

Hill Street Studios/Blend Images LLC

CHAPTER 8   Improve Your Memory Skills   **259**

TAKING CHARGE

Summary

In this chapter, I learned to

- **Apply the five-step memory process.** Similar to the Adult Learning Cycle, the memory process consists of five steps: intention, attention, association, retention, and recall.

- **Intend to remember.** People who have better memories *want* to remember and make it a priority. I create a positive, open attitude that focuses on effort, growth, and learning. I create interest and meaning in what I want to remember. I stick with it until I learn.

- **Be observant and alert.** I observe and am attentive to details. I am relaxed, focused, and receptive to new information. I reduce distractions, concentrate, and stay focused and mindful of the present. I look at the big picture, and then I look at details.

- **Organize and associate information.** Organization makes sense out of information. I look for patterns and connections. I look for what I already know and jot down questions for areas that I don't know. I group similarities and look for what is different.

- **Retain information.** I write summaries in my own words and repeat out loud. I jot down main points, key words, and important information on note cards. I review often.

- **Recall.** I increase my recall through effort, concentration, and discipline. I also write down information, recite out loud, and teach others. Practicing and reviewing information weekly and monthly are key to increasing recall.

- **Write it down.** The simple act of writing helps me create a mental picture.

- **Go from the general to the specific.** I first look at the big picture for gaining general, overall understanding and meaning. I then focus on the details and specific supporting information.

- **Reduce information and eliminate distractions.** Some information (such as e-mail addresses and phone numbers) does not have to be memorized; I just need to know where to find it easily. I also need to eliminate distractions that affect my ability to concentrate on what I'm trying to learn and remember.

- **Take frequent breaks.** I study in 40- to 60-minute sessions because I know that the brain retains information best in short study periods. I take breaks to keep up my motivation.

- **Use my senses and integrate learning styles.** I draw pictures and illustrations, use color, record lectures, play music, write out summaries, jot down questions, collect samples, give summaries to my study group, and recite out loud.

- **Try mnemonic devices.** I use various techniques, such as rhymes and rhythms, acronyms, acrostics, grouping, association, and the method-of-place technique to help me memorize and recall information.

- **Use flash cards.** Making flash cards out of note cards is an easy and convenient way for me to review important facts, terms, and questions. I test myself with them.

- **Find connections and recite.** I link new information with familiar material, and I summarize what I have learned, either out loud or in writing.

- **Practice!** If I want to understand and remember information, I must practice and review it again and again. I realize that it takes practice and persistence to learn.

Performance Strategies

Following are the top 10 strategies for improving memory:

- Intend to remember and prepare yourself mentally. Be positive and curious.
- Be observant, be alert, and pay attention.
- Organize information to make it meaningful.
- Look for associations and connections.
- Write down information.
- Integrate learning styles.
- Review often.
- Use mnemonic devices.
- Summarize information in your own words.
- Practice, use repetition, and relax.

Tech for Success

- **Acrostics online.** Many disciplines (especially in the sciences) have well-known acrostics that students and professionals use to remember key information (such as human anatomy). There are a number of online sites that have collected hundreds of useful acrostics.

- **Stored memory.** Your computer is one big memory tool, storing thousands of hours of your work and contact information. For example, if you use the "Favorites" feature in your Web browser to catalog websites, consider how long it would take for you to reconstruct this information if it were suddenly wiped out. Do you have backup plans in case your hard drive becomes inaccessible, or if you lose your cell phone containing countless stored numbers? Use these many tools and features to help you organize and save time, but don't forget to write down or keep hard copies of very important documents and contact information.

Endnotes

1 D. Bavelier and H. Neville, "Neuroplasticity, Developmental," in *Encyclopedia of the Human Brain,* vol. e, ed. V. S. Ramachandran (Amsterdam: Academic Press, 2002), p. 561.

2 A. M. Brant et al., "The Nature and Nurture of High IQ: An Extended Sensitive Period of Intellectual Development," *Psychological Science* 24, no. 8 (August 2013), pp. 1487–95.

3 E. R. Kandel, "The Molecular Biology of Memory Storage: A Dialog between Genes and Synapses," in *Nobel Lectures in Physiology or Medicine 1996–2000,* ed. Hans Jornvall (Singapore: World Scientific Publishing Co., 2003), p. 402.

4 M. Naveh-Benjamin, A. Kilb, and T. Fisher, "Concurrent Task Effects on Memory Encoding and Retrieval: Further Support for Asymmetry," *Memory & Cognition* 34, no. 1 (January 2006), pp. 90–101.

5 Allstate/Sperling's Best Places, "'Allstate America's Teen Driving Hotspots' Study," Executive Summary (May 2008).

Study Team Notes

Career *in* Focus

BAZA Production/Shutterstock

Diana Tanaka
JOURNALIST

Related Majors: Journalism, Communications, English, Social Studies

Integrating Learning Styles

As a journalist, Diana Tanaka's job is to find newsworthy local issues, collect accurate information from both sides of the story, and write an article that treats the subject fairly. As a general assignment reporter for an online news service, she covers stories on politics, crime, education, business, and consumer affairs.

Diana works closely with her editor when selecting a topic for an article. She often investigates leads for a story, only to realize later that she does not have enough information to make a strong story. She organizes the information she gathers, not knowing how or if it will fit into the article. Diana usually works on more than one story at a time, as some stories take weeks of research. Her hours are irregular. Diana might attend an early morning political breakfast and a school board meeting that evening.

Each week, Diana interviews a wide variety of people, including the mayor, the police chief, the school supervisor, and other community leaders. She always says hello to people, using their names. She prides herself on being able to remember names after only one meeting. When conducting an interview, the first thing Diana does is write down the name of the person, asking for the correct spelling. By doing this, she not only checks spelling but also sees the name in print. Because Diana is a visual learner, this helps her remember it. After an interview, Diana types her notes and memorizes pertinent information, such as the names of people, businesses, and locations and determines key follow-up questions. Diana knows that having good memory skills is essential for being a capable journalist.

CRITICAL THINKING Which learning styles help Diana remember pertinent information?

Memory

A. Quickly read these lists once. Read one word at a time and in order.

1	2
the	Disney World
work	light
of	time
and	and
to	of
the	house
and	the
of	packages
light	good
of	praise
care	and
the	coffee
chair	the
and	of

B. Now cover the lists and write as many words as you can remember on the lines that follow. Then check your list against the lists in Part A.

_____   _____

_____   _____

_____   _____

_____   _____

_____   _____

_____   _____

_____   _____

_____   _____

_____   _____

_____   _____

_____   _____

(continued)

1. How many words did you remember from the beginning of each list? List them.

_____

_____

2. How many words did you remember from the middle of each list? List them.

_____

_____

3. How many words did you remember from the end of each list? List them.

_____

_____

4. Did you remember the term *Disney World?*   Yes _____ No _____

Most people who complete this exercise remember the first few words, the last few words, the unusual term *Disney World,* and the words that were listed more than once (*of, the,* and *and*). Did you find this to be true about yourself?   Yes _____ No _____

C. Remembering names
   1. Do you have problems remembering names?   Yes _____ No _____
   2. What are the benefits of remembering names now and in a career?

_____

_____

_____

D. Which memory techniques work best for you and why?

_____

_____

_____

_____

_____

_____

_____

_____

Have fun with this and just gently notice when you are relaxed and remembering and when your mind goes blank.

Mental Pictures

Use various techniques to recall the following information:

In World War II, the major Axis powers were Germany, Italy, and Japan. The Allied powers were led by Great Britain, the Union of Soviet Socialist Republics (USSR), and the United States of America.

1. Think of mental images that would help you remember each of the following during an exam:

Axis Powers

Germany _____

_____

Italy _____

_____

Japan _____

_____

Allied Powers

Great Britain _____

_____

USSR _____

_____

USA _____

_____

2. Create a memory map using the method-of-place technique. Either place these mental images in the map or create new images that may work better using this technique.

3. Now create an acrostic or acronym to remember each grouping (all three Axis powers and all three Allied powers). Refer to item 8, "Use mnemonic devices," under **Memory Strategies** to refresh your memory on these mnemonic devices.

- Axis powers: _____

- Allied powers: _____

Collect exercises and tips for remembering. Think of it as a game and have fun with exercising your memory muscles.

Applying Memory Skills

Assess your memory skills by answering the following questions. Add this page to your Career Development Portfolio.

1. **Looking back:** Review an autobiography you may have written for this or another course. Indicate the ways you applied your memory skills.

   _____

   _____

2. **Taking stock:** What are your memory strengths and what do you want to improve?

   _____

   _____

3. **Looking forward:** How would you demonstrate memory skills for employers?

   _____

   _____

4. **Documentation:** Include examples, such as poems you have memorized, literary quotes, and techniques for remembering names.

   _____

   _____

5. **Assessment and demonstration:** Critical thinking skills for memory include the following. When have you demonstrated these?
   - Preparing yourself mentally and physically
   - Creating a willingness to remember
   - Determining what information is important and organizing it
   - Linking new material with known information (creating associations)
   - Integrating various learning styles
   - Asking questions
   - Reviewing and practicing

   _____

   _____

   _____

   _____

   _____

   _____

Excel at Taking Tests

LEARNING OUTCOMES

In this chapter, you will learn to

9-1   Create a positive, open mindset for taking tests

9-2   Describe strategies for taking different types of tests

9-3   Identify the number one tip for test taking

9-4   Identify ways to overcome test anxiety and obstacles

SELF-MANAGEMENT

I studied very hard for my last test, but my mind went blank when I tried to answer the questions. How can I reduce my anxiety and be more confident about taking tests? Maybe I'm just not good at taking tests.

Paul Bradbury/Calaimages/Getty Images

Have you ever felt anxious and worried when taking tests? Do you suffer physical symptoms, such as sweaty palms, an upset stomach, headaches, or an inability to sleep or concentrate? Everyone experiences some anxiety when faced with a situation involving performance or evaluation. Peak performers know that the best strategy for alleviating feelings of panic is to be prepared. In this chapter, you will learn ways to decrease your anxiety and test-taking strategies that will help you before, during, and after tests. First step, let's create a positive mindset that focuses on growth.

JOURNAL ENTRY In **Worksheet 9.1**, describe a time when you felt anxious about a performance, sporting event, or test. What factors helped you be calm, feel confident, and remember information? Apply the ABC's of self-management and write a script.

Successful athletes and performers know how important it is to monitor their techniques and vary their training programs to improve results. Taking tests is part of school; performance reviews are part of a job; and tryouts and performing are part of being an athlete, a dancer, or an actor. In fact, just about any job involves some assessment of skills, attitudes, and behavior. Many fields also require you to pass rigorous exams before you complete your education (such as the LSAT for law) and certification exams (as in athletic training). In this chapter, we explore specific test-taking strategies that will help you in both school and your career.

Test-Taking Strategies

Before the Test

Test taking starts long before sitting down in front of a computer or alongside pencil to tackle an exam. These strategies are no panacea. *They benefit only students who are motivated and have a positive mindset that focuses on effort, growth, and learning.*

1. **Start on day one.** The best way to do well on tests is to begin preparing from the first day of class. Set up a review schedule and attend all classes, on time, prepared, and stay until the end of class. Create a positive, open mindset about succeeding. *Make a habit of using flash cards and answering sample questions at the end of the chapter.*

Test-Taking Skills

1 Prepare yourself both mentally and physically

2 Determine what information is important

3 Pretest yourself using flash cards and practice tests. This is the #1 tip!

4 Link new material with known information

5 Create associations and interleave new problems with related ones

6 Create a willingness to remember and a commitment to learn

7 Stay focused on effort and growth

8 Reason logically and use creative approaches to recall

9 Overcome fear by rehearsing and testing yourself

10 Evaluate test results

11 Be open to feedback as an opportunity to grow

Hero/Corbis/Glow Images

Personal Evaluation Notebook

9.1

Test Taking

Your instructor will often give clues in class as to what will be covered on tests. Watch for

- Information that is repeated or emphasized
- Illustrations on the board, PowerPoint presentations, or handouts
- Intensified voice or hand gestures and eye contact
- Examples and pauses for students to take notes
- Points covered while introducing or summarizing a topic

1. With classmates or study team members, use the list of clues as a guide to create a list of topics you think might be covered on the next exam.

_____

_____

_____

2. As a team, approach your instructor to see if your list is on target. Ask your instructor what kinds of questions to expect on the test. Write that information on the following lines. (See the section **"Taking Different Types of Tests"** for types of test questions.)

_____

_____

_____

2. **Know expectations.** On the first day of class, most instructors outline the course and clarify the syllabus and expectations concerning grading, test dates, and types of tests. During class or office hours, ask your instructors about test formats, sample questions, a study guide, or additional material that may be helpful. Ask how much weight the textbook has on tests. Some instructors cover key material in class and assign reading for a broad overview. Observe your instructors to see what they consider important and what points and key words they stress. *As you listen to lectures or read your textbook, ask yourself what questions might be on the tests.* A large part of fear and anxiety comes from the unknown, so the more you know about what is expected, the more at ease you will be. **Personal Evaluation Notebook 9.1** gives you a guide for approaching your instructors about upcoming tests. (**Worksheet 9.3** also provides a detailed guide for tracking test information.)

3. **Ask questions.** *Ask why and how questions.* Why does this make sense? Why is this true? How is this information new and how it is different? *Ask questions in class.* If you are unclear about a point, raise your hand and ask for clarification. Or ask your instructor or another student at the end of class. Don't assume all of the lecture will be covered in the textbook. Asking questions gives explanations to information and explains facts. Interrogation improves memory for facts and increases understanding.

4. **Keep up and interleave practice.** Keep up with daily reading and assignments and use creativity to reflect and compare. (Use your time-management strategies from Chapter 4. **Worksheet 9.2** is a handy form for keeping track of your exams.) *Interleave new problems with related ones from preceding units. Before moving on from one topic to another, reflect and intermix.* Look for comparisons between sections. Interleaving helps you distinguish among similar concepts by comparing different kinds of problems. *Ask what is new or similar and what is different and why it is important.* Self-explanation and reflection boost recall by asking questions and practice testing.

5. **Review immediately and often.** Start the review process by quickly previewing chapters before classes and taking a few minutes to review your notes right after class. When information is fresh, you can fill in missing pieces, make connections, and raise questions to ask later. When reviewing each day, scan reading and lecture notes and make up questions. *Take a few minutes every day to use flash cards.*

6. **Spread your study over time.** Students often cram, but *distributing studying over time is much more effective.* One study showed that students who spread reviews 30 days apart remembered the best. You actually retain information during these long intervals and you quickly relearn what you forgot. Distributed practice is effective because it reintroduces major concepts over a period of time. These review sessions can include class notes, reading notes, chapter questions, note cards, mind maps, flash cards, and summaries written in your own words. Review often.

7. **Do a final review.** A week or so before a test, commit to a major review. (Some instructors recommend allocating at least two hours per day for three days before the exam.) This review should include class and book notes, note cards, and summaries. *You can practice test questions, compare concepts, review major points, and pretest with your study team.* Long-term memory depends on organizing the information. Fragmented information is hard to remember or recall. When you understand the main ideas and connect and relate information, you transfer the material into long-term memory.

8. **Use memory techniques.** Determine which memory techniques will help you recall information, especially if you need to remember key dates, names, or lists. (Refer to Chapter 8 for descriptions of effective memory techniques.)

9. **Create sample tests.** *Make up a sample test and pretest yourself.* Unlike classroom tests, practice tests are done outside of class by yourself or with your study team. Have each person in your study group make up a test and share with each other. *Quizzing yourself is the number one proven tip to improve learning and retention.* Self-testing also reduces anxiety. One theory is that practice testing triggers a mental search of long-term memory that sparks related information and this forms memory pathways that increase recall. Use *flash cards* to test recall or answer sample questions at the end of the chapter. Key words and end-of-chapter questions provide examples of possible test questions. Many textbooks have accompanying DVDs or websites that include sample test questions. Review and rehearse until you have learned the material and feel confident. Save all quizzes, course materials, exercise sheets, and lab work. Ask your professor if old tests or sample tests are available online or at the library.

10. **Summarize.** After you read a section, close your book and write a summary. Check to see what needs filling in and then review. Pretend the professor allows you to take one note card to the test. Choose the most important

concepts, formulas, key words, and points, and condense them onto one note card. Turn it over and write a summary of main points. Even better, take your summary and review with your professor. *Have you covered all the main points?* Summarizing helps you organize information.

11. **Use your study team.** You may be tempted to skip studying one night, but you can avoid temptation if you know other people are depending on your contribution. Have each member of the study team provide 5 to 10 potential test questions. Share these questions and discuss possible answers. Word the questions in different formats—multiple-choice, true/false, matching, and essay. *Then simulate the test-taking experience by taking, giving, and correcting each other's timed sample tests.*

12. **Use all available resources.** If your instructor offers a review before the exam, attend it, take good notes, and ask clarifying questions. Check out the tutorial center and consider getting a tutor; check with the learning center, academic departments, or student services. A tutor will expect you to attend all classes, keep up with reading and homework assignments, and be motivated to learn. Your tutor will not do your work for you but will review assignment expectations, explain concepts, help you summarize and understand terms and definitions, and help you study for tests. Use the learning center for help with general study strategies, taking sample tests, and help with test taking in specific classes.

13. **Assemble what you will need.** Pack sharpened pencils, pens, paper clips, and any other items you may need, such as a watch or calculator, and flash cards. Get a good night's sleep, eat a light breakfast, and make sure you set an alarm. You don't want to be frantic and late for a test. Arrive a few minutes early and review flash cards. Relax.

14. **Use technology.** Web-based flash cards are easy to create using your computer, smartphone, or tablet. Check out www.flashcardmachine.com, www.quizlet.com, and www.studyblue.com. Check out the apps *Flashcards* and *Study Blue.* Either digital or simple flash cards are easy to carry with you to review definitions, key words, dates, formulas, and sample problems.

During the Test

The following strategies will help you take a test. See **Peak Progress 9.1** for specific tips on taking online exams.

1. **Read and listen to all instructions.** Many mistakes result from a failure to follow directions correctly. For example, your instructor may require that you use a pen and write on only one side of the paper. Make sure you understand what is expected in each section of the test. If you are unsure, ask your instructor immediately. (See **Figure 9.1** on how to take a Scantron test.)

2. **Write down key information.** As soon as you get the test, write your name on it and jot down key words, facts, formulas, dates, ideas, concepts, statistics, and other memory cues in pencil on the back of your paper or in the margins. If you wait until you are reading each question, you may forget important material while under pressure.

3. **Scan the entire test.** Before you start answering questions, you need to
   - Look at the point value for each question and determine the importance of each section. For example, you will want to spend more time on an essay worth 25 points than on a multiple-choice section worth 5.

Figure 9.1
Fill in the Bubbles

You have probably taken a number of Scantron tests (named after the company that distributes them), or "bubble" tests. Using a #2 pencil, you must completely fill in the circles. Fill in only one bubble per line, and completely erase any changes. Be careful not to skip a line, or all the rest of your answers may be wrong. *Would all of the answers in this figure be acceptable?*

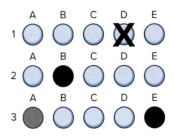

Although the preparation may be similar, taking an online exam may involve more coordination than a traditional pencil-and-paper exam.

- Double-check your computer's settings before you start the test so that you avoid problems.
- Unless the test must be taken at a certain time or on a specific date, do not wait until the last day to take it. If you have technical difficulties or lose your connection, you may not have time to solve the problem.
- Shut down all other programs not needed during the exam, including e-mail.
- If your test is timed, make sure you can easily see the timer or the computer's clock.
- If allowed, have your text and any other materials nearby and easily accessible. Put key information, dates, or formulas on sticky notes next to the screen.

- Wait until the test is fully loaded before answering questions.
- Set the window size before you start. Resizing later may refresh your screen and cause the test to reload and start over.
- To avoid being accidentally kicked out of the exam, do not click outside the test area or click the back arrow. Only use functions within the testing program to return to previous questions.
- If there is a save option, save often throughout the exam.
- If more than one question is on a page, click "Submit" or the arrow button only after all questions on that page have been answered.
- Review carefully. If time permits, read it all over once more.
- Click "Submit" only once at the end of the test, and confirm that the test was received.

- See which questions are easiest and can be answered quickly.
- Underline or put a star by key names and themes that pop out. These may stimulate your memory for another question.
- Set a plan and pace yourself based on the amount of time allowed.

4. **Answer objective questions.** Sometimes objective questions contain details you can use for answering essay questions. Don't panic if you don't know an answer right away. Answer the easiest questions, and mark questions you want to go back to later.

5. **Answer essay questions.** Answer the easiest subjective or essay questions first, and spend more time on the questions with the highest value. Underline or circle key words or points in the question. If you have time, do a quick outline in pencil, so that your answer is organized. Look for defining words, and make sure you understand what the question is asking. For example, are you being asked to justify, illustrate, compare and contrast, or explain? Write down main ideas and then fill in details, facts, and examples. Be complete, but avoid filler sentences that add nothing.

6. **Answer all remaining questions.** Unless there is a penalty for guessing, answer all questions. Rephrase questions you find difficult. It may help if you change the wording of a sentence. Draw a diagram, use a different equation, or make a mind map and write the topic and subtopics. Use association to remember items that are related.

7. **Review.** Once you have finished, reread the test carefully and check for mistakes or spelling errors. *Stay the entire time,* answer extra-credit and bonus questions, fill in details, and make any necessary changes. (See **Peak Progress 9.2** to learn specific strategies for math and science tests.)

Peak Progress

Special Strategies for Math and Science Tests

1. **Use note cards.** Write formulas, definitions, rules, and theories on note cards and review them often. Write out examples for each theorem.

2. **Write key information.** As soon as you are given the test, jot down theorems and formulas in the margins.

3. **Write the problem in longhand.** Translate into understandable words—for example, for $A = 1/2bh$, "For a triangle, the area is one-half the base times the height."

4. **Make an estimate.** A calculated guess will give you an approximate answer. This helps you when you double-check the answer.

5. **Illustrate the problem.** Draw a picture, diagram, or chart that will help you understand the problem—for example, "The length of a field is 6 feet more than twice its width. If the perimeter of the field is 228 feet, find the dimensions of the field."

   Let l = the length of the field
   Let w = the width of the field
   Then $l = 2w + 6$

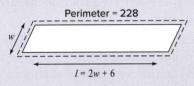

Perimeter = 228

$l = 2w + 6$

$w + 2w + 6 + w + 2w + 6 = 228$

   So $w + 2w + 6 + w + 2w + 6 = 228$
   $6w + 12 = 228$
   $6w = 216$

$w = 36$

So $l = 2w + 6 = 2(36) + 6 = 78$

Translating: The width of the field is 36 ft. and its length is 78 ft.

Checking: The perimeter is $2w + 2l = 2(36) + 2(78) = 72 + 156 = 228$

6. **Ask yourself questions.** Ask, "What is being asked? What do I already know? What are the givens? What do I need to find out? How does this relate to other concepts? What is the point of the question?"

7. **Show your work.** If allowed, write down the method you used to get to the answer, which will help you retrace your steps if you get stuck. Your instructor may give you partial credit, even if the answer is incorrect. In some cases, you are expected to show your work (and will lose points for not showing complete or accurate work). Make sure you know what your instructor requires.

8. **Do a similar problem.** If you get stuck, try something similar. Which formula worked? How does this formula relate to others?

9. **State answers in the simplest terms.** For example, 4/6 instead should be answered as 2/3.

10. **Pay attention to the sign.** Note if a number is actually a negative number.

11. **Check your work.** Does your answer make sense? Is your work correct and systematic?

12. **Review.** Review your test as soon as you get it back. Where did you make mistakes? Did you read the problems correctly? Did you use the correct formulas? What will you do differently next time?

After the Test

The test isn't over when you hand it in. Successful test taking includes how you use the results.

1. **Analyze and assess.** When you receive the graded test, analyze the grade and your performance for many things, such as the following:

   - *Confirm your grade.* Confirm that your score was calculated or graded correctly. If you believe there is a mistake in your grade, see your instructor immediately and ask to review it.

   - *Determine common types of mistakes.* Were your mistakes due to carelessness in reading the instructions or lack of preparedness on certain topics? **Figure 9.2** identifies common reasons for incorrect answers on tests. Are there patterns in your mistakes? If so, determine how to correct those patterns.

Figure 9.2

Reasons for Incorrect Test Answers

As you review your test results, check if any of these problems affected your performance. *How can you use this list to prepare for future exams?*

Common errors

- ✔ I did not read and/or follow the directions.
- ✔ I misread or misunderstood the question.
- ✔ I did not demonstrate reasoning ability.
- ✔ I did not demonstrate factual accuracy.
- ✔ I did not demonstrate good organization.
- ✔ My answer was incomplete.
- ✔ My answer lacked clarity.
- ✔ My handwriting was hard to read.

- ✔ I used time ineffectively.
- ✔ I did not prepare enough.
- ✔ I studied the wrong information.
- ✔ I knew the information but couldn't apply it to the questions.
- ✔ I confused facts or concepts.
- ✔ The information was not in my lecture notes.
- ✔ The information was not in the textbook.

❝ We learn more by looking for the answer to a question and not finding it than we do from learning the answer itself. ❞

LLOYD ALEXANDER
Author

- *Learn what to do differently next time.* Your test will provide valuable feedback, and you can learn from the experience. Be a detached, curious, receptive observer and view the results as feedback that is essential for improvement. (See **Peak Progress 9.3** for a checklist on how to assess your testing performance in order to improve your skills.) View evaluations as a chance to grow.

2. **Review with your instructor.** If you honestly don't know why you received the grade you did, ask your instructor to review your answers with you. Approach the meeting with a positive attitude, not a defensive one. Ask for clarification and explain your rationale for answers. Ask for advice on preparing for the next test. Show that you want to learn.

3. **Review the test with your study team.** This will help you see common errors and how others approached answering the questions, which will give you insights into how to study more effectively and answer questions better on the next test.

Remember, a test is feedback on how you are doing, not an evaluation of you as a person. You cannot change unless you understand your mistakes. Assess what you did wrong and what you will do right the next time. *This is a chance to grow and learn.*

Peak Progress   9.3

Using Test Results

Determine if your study strategy is working and what to do differently next time. Ask yourself the following questions:

1. Did I read the test before I started?
2. What were my strengths? What did I do right?
3. What questions did I miss?
4. Did I miss clues in the test? Did I ask the instructor for clarification?
5. How well did I know the content on which I was being tested?
6. What should I have studied more?
7. Did I anticipate the style and format of the questions?
8. What didn't I expect?
9. Did I have trouble with certain types of questions?
10. Did I use the power of self-testing? How did I quiz myself?
11. Did I handle test anxiety well?
12. Would it have helped if I had studied with others?
13. What changes will I make in studying for the next test?

Taking Different Types of Tests

Objective Tests

TRUE/FALSE TESTS

1. **Read the entire question carefully before answering.** For the question to be true, the entire question must be true. If any part of the statement is false, the entire statement is false.

2. **Pay attention to details.** Read dates, names, and places carefully. Sometimes the numbers in the dates are changed around (1494 instead of 1449) or the wording is changed slightly. Any such changes can change the meaning.

3. **Watch for qualifiers.** Watch for such words as *always, all, never,* and *every.* If you can think of just one exception, then the statement is false. Does the statement over- or understate what you know is true?

4. **Watch for faulty cause and effect.** Two true statements may be connected by a word that implies cause and effect, and this word may make the statement false—for example, "Temperature is measured on the centigrade scale *because* water freezes at zero degrees centigrade."

5. **Always answer every question.** Unless there is a penalty for wrong answers, answer every question. You have a 50 percent chance of being right.

6. **Trust your instincts.** Often, your first impression is correct. Don't change an answer unless you are certain it is wrong. Don't spend time pondering until you have finished the entire test and have time to spare.

MULTIPLE-CHOICE TESTS

1. **Read the question carefully.** Are you being asked for the correct answer or the best choice? Is there more than one answer? Preview the test to see if an answer is included in a later statement or question.

2. **Rephrase the question.** Sometimes it helps to rephrase the question in your own words, which may trigger reading or hearing the initial discussion.

3. **Cover the potential answers.** Cover the answers (called "distractors") as you read the question and see what answer first comes to you. Then look at the answers to see if your answer is one of the choices.

4. **Eliminate choices.** Narrow your choices by reading all of them and eliminating those you know are incorrect so that you can concentrate on real choices.

5. **Go from easy to difficult.** Go through the test and complete the questions for which you know the answers. Don't spend all your time on a few questions. With a pencil, mark the questions that you are unsure of, but make certain you mark your final answer clearly.

6. **Watch for combinations.** Read the question carefully; don't just choose what appears to be the one correct answer. Some questions offer a combination of choices, such as "all of the above" or "none of the above."

7. **Look at sentence structure.** The grammatical structure of the question should match that of your choice.

MATCHING TESTS

1. **Read carefully.** Read the question carefully before matching items, and make sure you understand what you are being asked to match.

Sample True/False Question

You can't get skin cancer if your routine (work, hobbies, and vacations) doesn't include any outdoor activities.
_____ True
_____ False

Does this statement overstate what you know to be true?

Sample Multiple-Choice Question

Which of the following is an example of a government providing foreign aid?
1. Placing an embargo on foreign sugar
2. Signing a nuclear arms control treaty
3. Sending medical supplies to foreign doctors
4. Increasing immigration restrictions

What is the key word(s) in the question that helps you determine the answer?

Sample Matching Question

Match the following mnemonic devices with their definition:
A. Acronym
B. Acrostic
C. Rap
D. Chunking
E. Method-of-place
1. grouping information
2. uses rhythm
3. words formed from first letters of other words
4. sentences in which the first letter of each word stands for something
5. memory map

Which are the easiest answers to match up first?

2. **Eliminate.** Go through and match all the items you are absolutely sure of first. Cross out items as you match them unless the directions mention that an item can be used more than once.

3. **Look for clues.** Should the pair include a person's name, a date, or an event? Is chronological order important? Look for commonalities in sentence structure. Does it make sense?

FILL-IN-THE-BLANK TESTS

1. **Watch for grammatical clues.** If the word before the blank is *an*, the word in the blank generally begins with a vowel. If the word before the blank is *a*, it probably begins with a consonant.

2. **Count the number of blanks.** The number of blanks often indicates the number of words in an answer. Think of key words that were stressed in class.

3. **Watch for the length of the blank.** A longer blank may indicate a longer answer.

OPEN-BOOK TESTS

Students often think open-book tests will be easy, so they don't study or prepare their book. Generally, these tests go beyond basic recall and require critical thinking and analysis. Put markers in your book to indicate important areas. Write formulas, definitions, key words, sample questions, and main points on note cards. Bring along your detailed study sheet. You will need to find information quickly. However, use your own words to summarize—don't copy from your textbook.

ONLINE TESTS

Be strategic and careful when you take online tests. Make certain you check to see when the test has been posted. Look for e-mail announcements about when the test is available, time allowed, and when it expires. Online tests are often timed. Check to see if you can re-enter the test site and redo answers before you hit Submit. Find out all this information before the day of the test and be at your computer a half-hour or so early to get prepared and ready. Read through the entire test before you begin. Follow directions. Have textbook, notes, water, snacks, and summaries in easy reach. Take a break every hour or so to stretch. Read directions carefully and review before you hit Submit.

Essay Tests

Being prepared is essential when taking an essay test. Make certain you understand concepts and relationships, not just specific facts. (See **Figure 9.3** for a sample essay test.) In addition, use the following strategies to help you take an essay test.

1. **Budget your writing time.** Review the whole test, noticing which questions are easiest. Allot a certain amount of time for each essay question, and include time for review when you're finished.

2. **Read the question carefully.** Be sure you understand what the question is asking. Respond to key words, such as *explain, classify, define,* and *compare*. Rephrase the question into a main thesis. Always answer what is being asked directly—don't skirt around an issue. If you are asked to compare and contrast, do not describe, or your answer will be incorrect. **Peak Progress 9.4** lists key words used in many essay questions.

Sample Fill-in-the-Blank

Question
The term that describes when it is legal and ethical to use a direct quote from the Internet or another source is
_____.

What clues help you determine the answer?

Figure 9.3

Sample Essay Test

When answering an essay question, a detailed outline may also be required, as in this example. *In what situations would a mind map work better to develop your thoughts rather than a formal outline?*

Intro to Economics Quiz   March 16, 2022

Steve Hackett

ESSAY QUESTION: Describe the general circumstances under which economists argue that government intervention in a market economy enhances efficiency.

THESIS STATEMENT: Well-functioning competitive markets are efficient resource allocators, but they can fail in certain circumstances. Government intervention can generate its own inefficiencies, so economists promote the forms of government intervention that enhance efficiency under conditions of market failure.

OUTLINE:

I. Well-functioning competitive markets are efficient.
    A. Firms have an incentive to minimize costs and waste.
    B. Price approximates costs of production.
    C. Effort, quality, and successful innovation are rewarded.
    D. Shortages and surpluses are eliminated by price adjustment.

II. Markets fail to allocate scarce resources efficiently under some circumstances.
    A. Externalities affect other people.
        1. Negative externalities, such as pollution
        2. Positive externalities and collectively consumed goods
    B. Lack of adequate information causes failure.
    C. Firms with market power subvert the competition.

III. Government intervention can create its own inefficiencies.
    A. Rigid, bureaucratic rules can stifle innovative solutions and dilute incentives.
    B. Politically powerful groups can subvert the process.

IV. Efficient intervention policy balances market and government inefficiencies.

ESSAY RESPONSE:

Well-functioning competitive markets allocate resources efficiently in the context of scarcity. They do so in several ways. First, in market systems, firms are profit maximizers and thus have an incentive to minimize their private costs of production. In contrast, those who manage government agencies lack the profit motive and thus the financial incentive to minimize costs. Second, under competitive market conditions, the market price is bid down by rival firms to reflect their unit production costs. Thus, for the last unit sold, the value (price) to the consumer is equal to the cost to produce that unit, meaning that neither too much nor too little is produced. Third, firms and individuals have an incentive to work hard to produce new products and services preferred by consumers because, if successful, these innovators will gain an advantage over their rivals in the marketplace. Fourth, competitive markets react to surpluses with lower prices and to shortages with higher prices, which work to resolve these imbalances.

    Markets can fail to allocate scarce resources efficiently in several situations. First, profit-maximizing firms have an incentive to emit negative externalities (uncompensated harms generated by market activity that fall on others), such as pollution, when doing so lowers their production costs and is not prevented by law. Individual firms also have an incentive not to provide positive externalities (unpaid-for benefits) that benefit the group, such as police patrol, fire protection, public parks, and roads. A second source of market failure is incomplete information regarding product safety, quality, and workplace safety. A third type of market failure occurs when competition is subverted by a small number of firms that can manipulate prices, such as monopolies and cartels. Government intervention can take various forms, including regulatory constraints, information provision, and direct government provision of goods and services.

    Government intervention may also be subject to inefficiencies. Examples include rigid regulations that stifle the incentive for innovation, onerous compliance costs imposed on firms, political subversion of the regulatory process by powerful interest groups, and lack of cost-minimizing incentives on the part of government agencies. Thus, efficient government intervention can be said to occur when markets fail in a substantial way and when the particular intervention policy generates inefficiencies that do not exceed those associated with the market failure.

Peak Progress

Important Words in Essay Questions

Analyze	Explain the key points, parts, or process and examine each part.	**Enumerate**	Present the items in a numbered list or an outline.
Apply	Show the concept or function in a specific context.	**Evaluate**	Carefully appraise the problem, citing authorities.
Compare	Show similarities between concepts, objects, or events.	**Explain**	Make an idea or a concept clear, or give a reason for an event.
Contrast	Show differences between concepts, objects, or events.	**Identify**	Label or explain.
Critique	Present your view or evaluation and give supporting evidence.	**Illustrate**	Clarify by presenting examples.
Define	Give concise, clear meanings and definitions.	**Interpret**	Explain the meaning of a concept or problem.
Demonstrate	Show function (how something works); show understanding physically or through words.	**Justify**	Give reasons for conclusions or argue in support of a position.
Describe	Present major characteristics or a detailed account.	**List**	Enumerate or write a list of points, one by one.
Differentiate	Distinguish between two or more concepts or characteristics.	**Outline**	Organize main points and supporting points logically.
Discuss	Give a general presentation of the issue with examples or details to support main points.	**Prove**	Give factual evidence and logical reasons for why something is true.
		Summarize	Present core ideas in a brief review that includes conclusions.

3. **Create an outline.** Organize your main points in an outline so that you won't leave out important information. An outline will provide a framework to help you remember dates, concepts, names, places, and supporting material. Use **Personal Evaluation Notebook 9.2** to practice outlining key words and topics.

4. **Focus on main points.** Your opening sentence should state your thesis, followed by supporting information.

5. **Write concisely and correctly.** Get directly to the point, and use short, clear sentences. Remember that your instructor (or even teaching assistants) may be grading a pile of tests, so get to the point and avoid filler sentences.

6. **Use key terms and phrases.** Your instructor may be looking for very specific information in your answer, including terms, phrases, events, or people. Make sure you include that information—don't just assume the instructor knows to whom or what you are referring.

7. **Answer completely.** Reread the question and be sure you answered it fully, including supporting documentation. Did you cover the main points thoroughly and logically?

8. **Count your words.** Double-check that your response meets any required length criteria. Note if the essay must meet a minimum or maximum word count, number of paragraphs, or pages.

Personal Evaluation Notebook 9.2

Essay Test Preparation

Pretend you are taking an essay test on a personal topic—your life history. Your instructor has written the following essay question on the board:

Write a brief essay on your progress through life so far, covering the highs and lows, major triumphs, and challenges.

1. Before you begin writing, remind yourself of the topics you want to cover in this essay. List key words, phrases, events, and dates you would jot in the margin of your paper on the lines provided.

   _____

   _____

   _____

   _____

   _____

   _____

2. In the following space, create a mind map or an outline of the events or topics you would cover in your essay.

9. **Write neatly.** Appearance and legibility matter. Use an erasable pen. Use wide margins and don't crowd your words. Write on one side of the paper only. Leave space between answers so that you can add to an answer if time permits.

10. **Use all the available time.** Don't hurry. Pace yourself and use all the available time for review, revisions, reflection, additions, and corrections. Proofread carefully. Answer all questions unless otherwise directed. Focus on showing what you know.

Research has shown that one of the brain structures that suffer the most damage from stress and anxiety is the hippocampus, which is critical for learning and memory. Test taking can be extremely stressful for some students.[1]

Silas failed his midterm. He thought he had studied enough before the test, but he quickly realized he should have paid more attention to the online readings. He was so anxious that his mind went blank when he tried to formulate an answer to the essay question that was worth 50 percent of the total exam.

- What questions could he have asked his instructor before the test to clarify expectations?
- What could Silas have done as he started the essay section to help him formulate his thoughts?
- How could taking practice tests and working with a study team help Silas?

THINK
CREATIVELY AND CRITICALLY

Last-Minute Study Tips

Cramming is not effective if you haven't studied or attended classes. The following activities, however, will help you make the most of the last hours and minutes before a test. Remember the 80/20 rule and invest in top-priority activities that create big returns in a small amount of time. *Flash cards and pretesting can result in big benefits.*

1. **Pre-test yourself.** You can use physical or digital flash cards, answer questions at the end of each chapter, making questions out of your notes or make questions out of chapter headings. *Self-testing improves learning and retention.*

2. **Focus on a few points.** Instead of trying to cram everything into a short study session, decide what are the most important points or formulas, key words, definitions, and dates. Preview each chapter quickly; read the chapter objectives or key concepts and the end-of-chapter summary.

3. **Review your note cards.** The physical (and visual) act of reading and flipping note cards will help you review key information. Self-test yourself with your notecards.

4. **Review your notes.** Look for words or topics you have highlighted or written on the side. Reread any summaries or mind maps you created after class.

5. **Affirm your memory.** The mind is capable of learning and memorizing material in a short time if you focus and apply it. Look for opportunities to connect information.

6. **Focus on healthy habits.** Focus on healthy solutions. Exercise and get out in nature. Get a good night sleep. Eat breakfast. Have a cup of coffee. Relax. Meditate to stay calm. Stay positive.

Overcome Obstacles

People with a negative, fixed mindset see tests and performance assessments as huge mountains—one slip and they tumble down the slope. Tests undermine their confidence, cause anxiety, and instill a fear of looking dumb. *People with a positive, open mindset have a passion for learning and they know they can grow and change through effort and application.* They learn how to manage anxiety and know that being prepared and pretesting are key to test-taking success. They welcome feedback as a way to improve. Focus and keep your life simple on days you have tests. Don't make unnecessary big decisions (such as breaking up or creating conflict with roommates) during test week. Focus. It's critical to keep your glucose level high with frequent healthy snacks, plenty of water, exercise, and rest. Use the 80/20 rule by putting time into areas that create high results. For example, if you summarize, study early with a group, and take sample tests, you'll do much better than cramming and staying up late.

Build Better Test Habits

Let's say that when you sit down to study or even when you think about upcoming tests, you become aware that you're feeling anxious. The *trigger* is the emotion of anxiety. Your current *routine* may be to avoid thinking of studying and tests by distracting yourself with television or socializing. However, you know this will only make the stress worse on test day (or on grade day). So you need to change your routine to help you cope with stress and anxiety. Your new *routine* includes preparing for your test well in advance. It includes planning out study times and taking pretests. Practice until the day of the test is just part of the routine. Your *reward* is a good grade, socializing with your friends, going out for pizza after the test, and the pride of knowing that you have control over your anxiety.

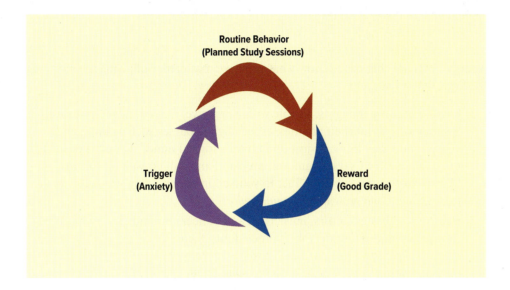

BETTER HABITS HELP MAKE DECISION MAKING EASIER

Research has found that when we make decision after decision, we become low on mental energy and tend to look for shortcuts. One is to act impulsively instead of thinking through consequences and the other is to do nothing and avoid making a choice. Since too many choices can sap our willpower, habits make for fewer decisions. Students who create regular study plans, pretest, get enough rest, take frequent breaks, and keep glucose levels steady through protein and healthy snacks do better on tests and make better decisions. These simple habits lead to better decisions and clearer thinking during tests.[2]

Test Anxiety

Test anxiety is a learned response to stress. The symptoms include nervousness, upset stomach, sweaty palms, and forgetfulness. *Being prepared is the best way to reduce anxiety.* As we discussed earlier in this chapter, you will be prepared if you have attended every class; previewed chapters; reviewed your notes; and written, summarized, and studied the material each day. Studying with others is a great way to rehearse test questions and learn through group interaction. *Testing yourself is a proven tip.*

The attitude you bring to a test affects your performance. Approach tests with a positive attitude. Tests let you practice facing fear and transforming it into positive

energy. Tests are chances to show what you have mastered. Following are more suggestions that might help:

1. **Dispute negative thoughts.** People with a negative, fixed mindset have faulty assumptions about their abilities, especially in courses such as math and science, and may think, "I just don't have a logical mind." Create a positive, open mindset that says, "I am well prepared and will do well on this test" or "I can excel in this subject." Talk to yourself in encouraging ways. *You know you can learn and grow with sustained effort.*

2. **Rehearse.** Athletes, actors, musicians, and dancers practice for hours. When they perform, their anxiety is channeled into focused energy. *If you practice taking sample tests with your study team, you should be more confident during the actual test.*

3. **Get regular exercise.** Aerobic exercise and yoga reduce stress and tension and promote deeper, more restful sleep. Build regular exercise into your life, take walks, renew yourself in nature, breathe deeply, and meditate before a test, if possible.

4. **Eat breakfast.** Eat a light, balanced breakfast that includes protein, such as cheese or yogurt. Keep a piece of fruit, cheese, nuts, and bottled water in your backpack for energy and to keep your glucose level steady. Have a few cups of coffee, but not enough to make you more nervous or agitated.

5. **Visualize success.** See yourself taking the test and doing well. Imagine being calm and focused. Before getting out of bed, relax, breathe deeply, and visualize your day unfolding in a positive way. Remind yourself that you've taken a pretest and done well.

6. **Stay calm.** Make your test day peaceful by assembling your books, supplies, pens, chargers, spare battery packs for your laptop, and keys the night before. Review your note cards just before you go to sleep, repeat a few affirmations, and get a good night's rest. Set an alarm so that you'll be awake in plenty of time. Last-minute, frantic cramming creates a hectic climate and increases anxiety. To alleviate stress, practice relaxation techniques (see Chapter 12). Breathe.

7. **Get to class early.** Get to class early enough that you are not rushed and can use the time before the test to take a few deep breaths and review your note cards. While waiting for the start of class, the instructor will sometimes

answer questions or explain material to students who arrived early. You want to be relaxed, calm, and centered.

8. **Focus.** When your attention wanders, bring it gently back. Stay in the present moment by focusing on the task at hand. Concentrate on answering the questions, and you won't have room in your mind for worry. Take time to review.

9. **Keep a sense of perspective.** Don't exaggerate the importance of tests. Tests do not measure self-esteem, personal qualities, character, or ability to contribute to society. Even if the worst happens and you do poorly on one test, it is not the end of your college career. You can meet with the instructor to discuss options and possibly do extra work, retake the test, or retake the class, if necessary. Assess and use feedback to improve your test-taking skills.

10. **Get help.** If you are experiencing severe anxiety that prevents you from taking tests or performing well, seek professional help from the learning center or see a counselor at your school. Services often include support groups, relaxation training, and other techniques for reducing anxiety. Taking tests and being evaluated are essential parts of school and work, so it's important to get your fears under control. (See **Peak Progress 9.5** on preparing for a performance appraisal.)

Peak Progress   9.5

Preparing for a Performance Appraisal

If you are employed, at some time you will probably receive a performance appraisal. This can be a valuable tool for informing you about how your employer perceives the quality of your work, your work ethic, and your future opportunities. It also allows you to ask similar questions of your manager or reviewer. Often, employees are asked to evaluate their own performance, which is similar to answering an essay question. You want to address the question fully and provide supporting, factual evidence (and often suggest outcomes, such as new goals and challenges).

Start with a positive mindset that focuses on growth and the willingness to learn. The following questions will help you focus on getting the most out of your appraisal:

- Review your job description, including the duties you perform. What is expected of you? What additional duties do you perform that are not listed?
- How do you view your job and the working climate?
- List your goals and objectives and the results achieved.
- What documentation demonstrates your results and achievements?
- What areas do you see as opportunities for improvement?

- What are your strengths, and how can you maximize them?
- What are your advancement possibilities?
- What additional training would be helpful for you?
- What new skills could assist in your advancement?
- How can you increase your problem-solving skills?
- How can you make more creative and sound decisions?
- What can you do to prepare yourself for stressful projects and deadlines?
- How have you specifically contributed to the company's profits?
- What relationships could you develop to help you achieve results?
- Do you work well with other people?
- What project would be rewarding and challenging this year?
- What resources do you need to complete this project?
- Do you have open and effective communication with your supervisor and co-workers?
- How does your assessment of your work compare with your supervisor's assessment?

Personal Evaluation Notebook

Reflection on Test Anxiety

The purpose of this mindful exercise is to reflect on your level of test anxiety. This insight will help you have a clear sense of your thoughts and feelings and help you write out a plan for overcoming anxiety. It is normal to have some anxiety when taking a test at college or having a performance review at work.

1. In what classes do you experience the most anxiety? Why?

   _____

   _____

   _____

2. What physical symptoms do you most often experience? (Examples include headaches, nausea, extreme body temperature changes, excessive sweating, shortness of breath, light-headedness or fainting, rapid heartbeat, and dry mouth.) Do you have trouble sleeping the night before a test? Do you experience mild examples of the above physical symptoms or are they serious enough to affect your health?

   _____

   _____

   _____

3. Which emotional symptoms do you most often experience? (Examples include excessive feelings of fear, disappointment, anger, depression, helplessness, or uncontrollable crying or laughing.) Does your mind go blank during a test? Are these symptoms occasional or do they affect your life on a regular basis?

   _____

   _____

   _____

4. Do you have different feelings about nonacademic tests, such as a driving test, job interview or review, or a medical test, than academic tests such as quizzes and exams? If so, why?

   _____

   _____

   _____

(continued)

Personal Evaluation Notebook

9.3

Reflection on Test Anxiety   *(concluded)*

5. Describe any other reactions you have before, during, or after taking a test.

_____

_____

_____

If your anxiety level is high enough to affect your physical and mental well-being, you may want to talk with a counselor in the counseling center, career center, or health center. Anxiety can exhaust your physical and mental reserves. Create positive habits by creating structure in your routine and keeping your life simple during a week of several tests and exams. At the first trigger of anxiety or depletion, eat an apple and some cheese or protein. Keep your glucose level steady with healthy food every few hours and get plenty of rest and downtime through music, rest, and exercise. Study during morning hours whenever possible and study with a group for effectiveness and socialization. Reward yourself for reducing anxiety.

Reflect and use critical thinking to describe your test anxiety experiences in **Personal Evaluation Notebook 9.3**. **Peak Progress 9.6** explores how you can apply the Adult Learning Cycle to improve your test-taking skills and reduce anxiety.

Cheating

A central theme of this book is that character matters. Honesty during test taking demonstrates to your instructor, your classmates, and, most important, yourself that you are trustworthy—a person of integrity. Cheating hurts only you and includes:

- Looking at someone's paper during a test
- Passing or texting answers back and forth
- Getting notes from someone who has just taken the same test
- Stealing tests from an office
- Using electronic devices (such as a calculator) when not allowed
- Taking or receiving pictures of test questions via cell phone
- Having someone else complete online work for you

Even if you haven't fully prepared for an exam, there is no excuse for cheating. Cheating hurts only you because it

- **Violates your integrity.** You begin to see yourself as a person without integrity; if you compromise your integrity once, you're more likely to do it again.
- **Erodes confidence.** Cheating weighs on your conscience and sends you the message that you don't have what it takes to succeed. Your confidence and self-esteem suffer.

- **Cheating Hurts Only You**
There is never an excuse to cheat. *If this student is caught cheating, what are some of the repercussions they could face?*

- **Creates academic problems.** Advanced courses depend on knowledge from earlier courses, so cheating creates only future academic problems. You are paying a lot of money not to learn essential information.

- **Increases stress.** You have enough stress in your life without adding the intense pressure of worrying about being caught.

- **Brings high risks.** Possible consequences of cheating and plagiarism include failing the class, being suspended for the semester, and even being expelled from school permanently. Cheating can mess up your life. It is humiliating, stressful, and completely avoidable.

There is never a legitimate reason to cheat. Instead, be prepared, use the resources available to help you succeed, and practice the strategies offered in this book to become a peak performer.

Peak Progress 9.6

Applying the Adult Learning Cycle to Improving Your Test-Taking Skills and Reducing Test Anxiety

1. **FEEL and LISTEN.** *Why do I want to learn this?* I need to reduce my test anxiety and want to do better on tests. Knowing how to control anxiety will help me when taking tests and in other performance situations such as public speaking. Overcoming my anxiety will also help in job interviews and performance reviews. I will listen and acknowledge my anxiety and how it affects my body and mind. I will listen to advice on test-taking strategies.

2. **OBSERVE and VISUALIZE.** *How does this work?* Who does well on tests, and does that person seem confident when taking tests? What strategies can I learn from that person? Who does poorly on tests or seems full of anxiety? Can I determine what that person is doing wrong? I can learn from those mistakes. I will observe and review some of my bad habits, such as last-minute cramming. I'll reflect and try new strategies for test taking and observe how I'm improving.

3. **THINK and WRITE.** *What does this mean?* I will use critical thinking to review what strategies are working for me and which ones are not working. I will use creativity to explore ways to reduce my anxiety. I will write out a plan for overcoming anxiety and for creating positive habits and read it aloud.

4. **DO and PRACTICE.** *What can I do with this?* I will follow the plan I wrote and apply these strategies before each major test. I will be prepared and confident. I will prepare every day and won't wait until the last minute to study. Each day, I can practice reducing my anxiety in many stressful situations. I'm going to jump in and practice taking tests.

(continued)

Applying the Adult Learning Cycle to Improving Your Test-Taking Skills and Reducing Test Anxiety *(concluded)*

5. **TEACH and PRACTICE AGAIN.** *Whom can I share this with?* I'll talk with others and share what's working for me and share my effective strategies.

Use the VARK system to integrate learning styles and help you think through and apply the Adult Learning Cycle. *Visualize* yourself successfully taking tests. Imagine yourself calm, centered, and prepared. Observe how others prepare and take tests. *Listen* to yourself as you read summaries. Listen to others in your study group. *Write out* summaries and *read them* out loud. *Practice* taking sample tests until the routine is automatic. *Teach others* in your study group. This is really the best way to learn anything. Each of you can develop test questions, take a topic, and then fill in gaps. Now return to Stage 1 and think about how it feels to learn this valuable new skill. Remember to congratulate and reward yourself when you achieve positive results.

TAKING CHARGE

Summary

In this chapter, I learned to

- **Prepare for test taking.** The time before a test is critical. I must prepare early, starting on the first day of class. I keep up with the daily reading and ask questions in class and while I read. I review early and often, previewing the chapter before class and reviewing the materials after class. I save and review all tests, exercises, and notes and review them weekly.

- **I rehearse by taking pretest.** I quiz myself often. I predict questions by reviewing the text's chapter objectives and summaries. I summarize the chapter in my own words (in writing or out loud), double-checking that I've covered key points. I take tests with my study team and compare notes after we test each other. I also use flash cards, answer sample questions at the end of the textbook. *Self-testing works!*

- **Take a test effectively.** Arriving early helps me be calm and focused on doing well. I get organized by reviewing key concepts and facts. I write neatly and get to the point with short, clear responses. I read all the instructions, scanning the entire test briefly and writing formulas and notes in the margins. I pace myself by answering the easiest questions first, and I rephrase difficult questions and look for associations to remember items. At the end, I review to make certain I've answered what was asked and check for mistakes or spelling errors. I stay the entire time that is available.

- **Follow up a test.** I will analyze and assess how I did on the test. Did I prepare enough? Did I anticipate questions? What can I do differently for the next test? I'll use creative problem solving to explore ways to do better on future tests.

- **Be successful on different kinds of tests.** Objective tests include true/false, multiple-choice, matching, fill-in-the-blank, and open-book. I must read the question carefully, watch for clues, and look at sentence structure. Essay tests focus on my understanding of concepts and relationships. I outline my response, organize and focus on the main points, and take my time to deliver a thorough, neat, well-thought-out answer.

- **Use last-minute study tips.** I know it's not smart to wait until the last minute, but a few important things I can do include focusing on a few key points and key words, reviewing note cards, looking for connections to memorize, and not wasting time by panicking.

- **Overcome test anxiety.** *A positive open mindset alleviates anxiety before and during a test.* I am focused on growth and learning. I welcome feedback. I'm prepared, avoid last-minute cramming, practice taking a sample test, get to class early, stay calm, listen carefully to instructions, preview the whole test, and jot down notes. I have grit.

- **Practice honesty and integrity when taking tests.** I know that cheating on exams hurts me by lowering my self-esteem and others' opinions of me. Cheating also has long-term repercussions, including possible expulsion from school. I will never cheat.

Performance Strategies

Following are the top 10 strategies for successful test taking:

- Prepare early.
- Clarify expectations.
- Observe and question.
- Review.
- Apply memory techniques.
- **Self-test.** Use flash cards and answer sample questions at the end of the chapter.
- Use your study team for pretesting and review.
- Answer easier questions first.
- Spend more time on questions worth the most points.
- Analyze your test results to learn how to improve.

Tech for Success

- **Online tutors.** Various organizations provide online tutors and live tutorial services. Your school or public library may also offer access to this kind of service. Often, these are paid services and may be worth the fee. However, you may be able to get limited assistance for free through a professional organization or related site. Ask your librarian for advice and explain how much help you think you need and in what content areas.

- **Textbook accompaniments.** Many of your textbooks have accompanying websites that provide study materials, such as online study guides, animated flash cards, and possible essay questions. Often, this material is free when you purchase a new text. Take advantage of these resources to test your understanding of the information prior to taking the real test.

Endnotes

[1] B. Casey, N. Tottenham, et al., "Transitional and Translational Studies of Risk for Anxiety," *Depression and Anxiety* 28, no. 1 (January 2011), pp. 18–28.

[2] Roy F. Baumeister, *Willpower: Rediscovering the Greatest Human Strength* (New York: Penguin Press, 2011).

Study Team Notes

Answers to **Taking Different Types of Tests**
True/False: False
Multiple choice: C
Matching: A/3; B/4; C/2; D/1; E/5
Fill-in-the-blank: fair use

Career *in* Focus

Keith Brofsky/Getty Images

Carlos Fuentes
PHYSICAL THERAPIST

Related Majors: Physical Therapy, Athletic Training, Biology

Tests in the Workplace

Carlos Fuentes is a physical therapist. A physical therapist works closely with physicians to help patients restore function and improve mobility after an injury or illness. Their work often relieves pain and prevents or limits physical disabilities.

When working with new patients, Carlos first asks questions and examines the patients' medical records, then performs tests to measure such items as strength, range of motion, balance and coordination, muscle performance, and motor function. After assessing a patient's abilities and needs, Carlos implements a treatment plan, which may include exercise, traction, massage, electrical stimulation, and hot packs or cold compresses. As treatment continues, Carlos documents the patient's progress and modifies the treatment plan.

Carlos is self-motivated and works independently. He has a strong interest in physiology and sports, and he enjoys working with people. He likes a job that keeps him active and on his feet. Carlos spends much of his day helping patients become mobile. He often demonstrates an exercise while teaching how to do it correctly. His job sometimes requires him to move heavy equipment or lift patients. Because Carlos is pursuing a master's degree in physical therapy, he works only three days a week.

Although his job does not require him to take tests, Carlos does undergo an annual performance appraisal with his supervisor. After eight years of service, Carlos is familiar with the types of questions his supervisor might ask and keeps those in mind as he does his job throughout the year.

CRITICAL THINKING How might understanding test-taking skills help Carlos work more effectively with his patients? How would test-taking skills help him prepare more effectively for performance appraisals?

Peak Performer Profile

Ellen Ochoa

When astronaut Ellen Ochoa was growing up in La Mesa, California, in the 1960s and early 1970s, it was an era of space exploration firsts: the first walk in space, the first man on the moon, the first space station. Even so, it would have been difficult for her to imagine that one day she would be the first Hispanic woman in space because women were excluded from becoming astronauts.

By the time Ochoa entered graduate school in the 1980s, however, the sky was the limit. Having studied physics at San Diego State University, she attended Stanford and earned a master's of science degree and a doctorate in electrical engineering. In 1985, she and 2,000 other potential astronauts applied for admission to the National Aeronautics and Space Administration (NASA) space program. Five years later, Ochoa, 18 men, and five other women made the cut. The training program at the Johnson Space Center in Houston, Texas, is a rigorous mix of brain and brawn. Ochoa tackled subjects such as geology, oceanography, meteorology, astronomy, aerodynamics, and medicine. In 1991, Ochoa officially became an astronaut and was designated a mission specialist. On her first mission in 1993, Ochoa carried a pin that read "Science Is Women's Work."

NASA

From 1993 to 2002, Ochoa logged in four space shuttle missions. Her first and second missions focused on studying the sun and its impact on the earth's atmosphere. Her third mission involved the first docking of the shuttle *Discovery* on the International Space Station. Her latest flight experience was the first time crewmembers used the robotic arm to move during spacewalks.

Ochoa enjoys talking to young people about her experiences. Aware of her influence as a woman and a Hispanic, her message is that "education is what allows you to stand out"—and become a peak performer.

PERFORMANCE THINKING Ochoa had to excel in many difficult academic courses in order to realize her dream of becoming an astronaut. What are some important personal characteristics that helped her reach the top? What are some specific testing strategies she may have used to get through her coursework, as well as to prove she had the "right stuff"?

CHECK IT OUT Ochoa is among a number of space pioneers profiled by NASA at **www.nasa.gov**. This site includes a wealth of media downloads, news articles, and activities for young and old space adventurers. Also visit the "Careers@NASA" section, which describes the types of internships, cooperative programs, and positions available. According to the first female astronaut in space, Sally Ride, the "most important steps" she followed to becoming an astronaut started with studying math and science in school.

Starting Today

At least one strategy I learned in this chapter that I plan to try right away is

_____

_____

_____

What changes must I make in order for this strategy to be most effective?

_____

_____

_____

Review Questions

Based on what you have learned in this chapter, write your answers to the following questions:

1. Describe five strategies for preparing for a test.

_____

_____

2. Why is it important to pace yourself while taking a test?

_____

_____

3. What should you do after taking a test?

_____

_____

_____

4. Describe three strategies for taking math and science tests.

_____

_____

5. Describe three ways in which cheating hurts you.

_____

_____

Coping with Anxiety

In the Classroom

Sharon Martin is a bright, hardworking student. She studies long hours, attends all her classes, and participates in class discussions. Sharon is very creative and especially enjoys her typography course. When taking tests, however, she panics. She stays up late, cramming; tells herself she might fail; and gets headaches and stomach pains. Her mind goes blank when she takes the test, and she has trouble organizing her thoughts. Sharon could get much better grades and enjoy school more if she reduced her stress and applied some test-taking strategies.

1. What techniques from this chapter would be most useful to Sharon?

   _____

   _____

   _____

Stockbyte/Getty Images

2. What one habit could she adopt that would empower her to be more successful?

   _____

   _____

   _____

In the Workplace

Sharon now works as a graphic designer for a large company. She likes having control over her work and is an excellent employee. She is dedicated, competent, and willing to learn new skills. Her job involves great pressure to meet deadlines, learn new techniques, and compete with other firms. She handles these responsibilities well unless she is being evaluated. Despite her proficiency, Sharon panics before performance appraisals. She feels pressure to perform perfectly and has trouble accepting criticism or even advice.

3. What strategies in this chapter would be most helpful to Sharon?

   _____

   _____

   _____

4. What would you suggest she do to control her performance anxiety?

   _____

   _____

   _____

REVIEW AND APPLICATIONS | CHAPTER 9

Applying the ABC Method of Self-Management

In the **Journal Entry**, you were asked to describe a time when you felt anxious in a performance, sporting event, or test. How did a positive, open mindset help?

_____

_____

_____

_____

Apply the ABC Method and write a script.

A = Acknowledge: Accept reality and pay attention to your emotions.

_____

_____

_____

B = Breathe: Take a deep breath to calm down and feel beloved.

_____

_____

_____

C = Choose: Knowing you have many options, choose the most appropriate for the situation and that will result in positive long-term consequences.

_____

_____

_____

Sample Script: Even though I'm feeling anxious, I love and accept myself and want to learn and grow. I breathe deeply and see myself calm, centered, and relaxed as I take a test or give a performance. I choose to practice positive self-talk and see myself recalling information easily and being calm and at ease. I choose to practice taking tests which is a proven method of remembering information. I join a study team so we can each do self-tests and discuss answers. Learning to control anxiety and feel comfortable taking tests and giving performances will help me in my career and in all aspects of life. I stay positive.

Exam Schedule

Fill in the following chart to remind you of your exams as they occur throughout the semester or term.

Course	Date	Time	Room	Type of Exam
Student Success 101	November 7	2:15 p.m.	1012A	Essay

Preparing for Tests and Exams

Before you take a quiz, a test, or an exam, fill in this form to help you plan your study strategy. Certain items will be more applicable, depending on the type of test.

Course _____

Date of test _____ Test number (if any) _____

- Pretest(s)   Date given _____   Results _____
                    Date given _____   Results _____
                    Date given _____   Results _____

- Present grade in course _____

- Met with instructor   Yes _____ No _____ Date(s) of meeting(s) _____

- Study team members   Date(s) of meeting(s) _____

     Name _____   Phone/e-mail _____

     Name _____   Phone/e-mail _____

     Name _____   Phone/e-mail _____

     Name _____   Phone/e-mail _____

- Expected test format (circle; there can be more than one test format)

     Essay   True/false   Multiple-choice   Fill-in-the-blank

     Other _____

- Importance (circle one)

     Quiz   Midterm   Final exam   Other

- Chapters covered in the test _____

     Date for chapter review _____

- Chapter notes (use additional paper)

     _____

     _____

     _____

- Date for review of chapter notes _____

- Note cards   Yes _____ No _____ Date note cards reviewed _____

- List of key words

Word _____   Meaning _____

Word _____   Meaning _____

Word _____   Meaning _____

Word _____   Meaning _____

- Possible essay questions

1. Question _____

   Thesis statement _____

   Outline _____

    I. _____

       A. _____

       B. _____

       C. _____

       D. _____

    II. _____

       A. _____

       B. _____

       C. _____

       D. _____

   - Main points

     _____

     _____

   - Examples

     _____

     _____

2. Question _____

   Thesis statement_____

   Outline_____

    I. _____

       A. _____

       B. _____

       C. _____

       D. _____

    II. _____

       A. _____

       B. _____

       C. _____

       D. _____

   - Main points

     _____

     _____

   - Examples

     _____

     _____

   Summarize: _____

Assessing Your Skills and Competencies

The following are typical qualities and competencies that are included in many performance appraisals.

- Communication skills (writing, speaking, reading)
- Integrity
- Willingness to learn
- Decision-making skills

- Delegation
- Planning
- Organizational skills
- Positive attitude
- Ability to accept change

- Working with others
- Quality of work
- Quantity of work
- Personal growth and development
- Use of technology

On the following lines, describe how you currently demonstrate each of the listed skills and competencies to an employer. Consider how you can improve. Add this page to your Career Development Portfolio.

1. How do you demonstrate the listed skills?

_____

_____

_____

_____

_____

_____

_____

_____

_____

_____

2. How can you improve?

_____

_____

_____

_____

_____

_____

_____

_____

_____

_____

Express Yourself in Writing and Speech

LEARNING OUTCOMES

In this chapter, you will learn to

10-1 Explain the importance of writing and speaking

10-2 Explain the five-step writing process for developing effective papers and speeches

10-3 Research information through the library and online

10-4 Use strategies for giving effective presentations

10-5 Identify strategies to overcome speech anxiety

SELF-MANAGEMENT

I put off taking the required public speaking class because I hate getting up in front of people. My mind goes blank, I get butterflies, and my palms sweat. How can I decrease stage fright and be more confident about speaking in public?

Steve Debenport/E+/Getty Images

Have you ever had a similar experience? Do you feel anxious and worried when you have to make a presentation or give a speech? Do you suffer physical symptoms, such as sweaty palms, upset stomach, headaches, or an inability to sleep or concentrate, even days before the event? In this chapter, you will learn how to communicate effectively and develop public speaking skills.

JOURNAL ENTRY In **Worksheet 10.1**, describe a time when you felt anxious giving a speaking assignment or leading a discussion. What factors helped you remain calm and confident?

Famed sportswriter Red Smith once commented, "Writing is very easy. All you do is sit in front of a typewriter keyboard until little drops of blood appear on your forehead." For some people, few things in life cause as much anxiety as writing research papers and public speaking. Just the thought of speaking in front of a group can produce feelings of sheer terror. In fact, research indicates that public speaking is the greatest fear for most people, outranking even fear of death. For many students, writing not only produces feelings of doubt but also demands their focused attention, intense thinking, and detailed research. You can't avoid writing or speaking in school or at work, but you can learn strategies that will make them easier and more effective.

The Importance of Writing and Speaking

The ability to communicate clearly, both orally and in writing, is the most important skill you will ever acquire. Peter Drucker, a noted management expert and author, remarked, "Colleges teach the one thing that is perhaps most valuable for the future employee to know. But very few students bother to learn it. *This one basic skill is the ability to organize and express ideas in writing and speaking.*" This skill can be learned with effort and practice.

You may be asked to do research on new ideas, products, procedures, and programs and compile the results in a report. You will most likely write business correspondence. You may give formal speeches before a large group, preside at meetings, or present ideas to a project team. You will be expected to present written and spoken ideas in a clear, concise, and organized manner. Writing papers and preparing speeches in school give you a chance to show initiative, use judgment, apply and interpret information, research resources, organize ideas, and polish your style. Public speaking skills also help you inform and persuade others. Good writers and speakers are not born, and there is no secret to their success. A positive, open mindset that focuses on effort means you can grow and change.

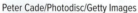
Peter Cade/Photodisc/Getty Images

The Writing Process

This chapter will give you strategies for handling every step of the paper-writing and speech-giving process. Remember, the best strategies in the world won't help if you are negative or unmotivated. Create a positive mindset that focuses on effort and growth. Keep learning in mind as you go through the five basic steps: (1) prepare, (2) organize, (3) write, (4) edit, and (5) review.

Term Paper for Criminal Justice 101, Due April 3	
Final Check. Print.	April 2
Edit, revise, and polish.	March 29 (Put away for one or two days)
Complete bibliography.	March 28
Revise.	March 26
Edit, review, revise.	March 24 (Confer with instructor)
Final draft completed.	March 22 (Proof and review)
Complete second draft.	March 20
Add, delete, and rearrange information.	March 17
First draft completed.	March 15 (Share with writing group)
Write conclusion.	March 12
Continue research and flesh out main ideas.	February 16
Write introduction.	February 10
Organize and outline.	February 3
Gather information and compile bibliography and notes.	January 29
Narrow topic and write thesis statement.	January 23
Do preliminary reading.	January 20
Choose a topic.	January 16
Brainstorm ideas.	January 15
Clarify expectations and determine purpose.	January 14

Figure 10.1
Sample Schedule

This schedule for preparing a term paper starts where the paper is finished. *Why does this schedule begin at the due date of the term paper?*

Prepare

1. **Set a schedule.** Estimate how long each step will take, and leave plenty of time for proofing. Allot about half your time to steps 1, 2, and 3 and the other half to steps 4 and 5. To develop a schedule, consider working backward from the due date, allowing yourself ample time for each step. See **Figure 10.1** for an example.

2. **Choose a general topic.** Choose a topic that meets your instructor's requirements, interests you, and is narrow enough to handle in the time available. Talk with your instructor about any questions you have concerning expectations for the topic, length, format and style, purpose, and method of citation. Use the tips in **Peak Progress 10.1** to help you come up with a topic.

3. **Determine your purpose.** Do you want your reader or listener to think, feel, or act differently or be called to action? Is your purpose to entertain, inform, explain, persuade, gain or maintain goodwill, gain respect and trust, or gather information?

4. **Do preliminary reading and research.** Gather general information by reviewing reference materials, such as articles or an encyclopedia. Check the

Peak Progress

How to Generate Topic Ideas

- *Brainstorm.* Brainstorming is generating as many ideas as possible without evaluating their merit. You can brainstorm ideas alone, but the process works well in small groups. Your goal is to list as many creative ideas as you can in the allotted time without defending or judging ideas. Because ideas build on each other, the more ideas the better. Within 10 minutes, you can often generate a sizable list of potential topics.

- *Go to the library.* Look in the *Readers' Guide to Periodical Literature* for possible ideas or check out digital resources and websites. Look through newspapers, magazines, and new books.

- *Search online.* Do a number of key word searches to see what topics pop up.

- *Keep a file.* Collect articles, quotes, and a list of topics you find interesting. Listen to good speeches and collect stories or ideas from current newspapers that you could research and write about from a different perspective. Think of possible topics as you read, watch television and movies, and talk with friends. What topics are in the news? What are people talking about?

- *Complete a sentence.* Brainstorm endings to open-ended sentences such as these:

  The world would be better if _____
  Too many people _____
  In the future _____
  A major problem today is _____
  The best thing about _____
  What I enjoy most is _____
  I learned that _____
  It always makes me laugh when _____
  If I had unlimited funds, I would buy _____
  I get through a tough day by _____

- *Free write.* For one or more potential topics, start jotting down as many related items as you can as fast as you can. Include examples, descriptions, and key events. Sometimes the original topic leads to a better topic.

- *Mind map.* For a potential topic, sketch a mind map (described in Chapters 6 and 7). Include supporting points and examples.

list of related references at the end of reference books and articles. Your initial research is intended to give you an overview of the subject and key issues. Later, you will want to look at specific facts and data. Develop a list of questions that can lead to new directions and additional research:

- What do I already know about the topic? What do I want to know?
- What questions do I want to explore? What interests me most?
- What is the point I want to research?

5. **Narrow your topic.** After you have finished your preliminary reading, you can focus on a specific topic. For example, instead of "health problems in America," narrow the subject to "cigarette smoking among teenage girls" or "should cigarette advertising be banned?"

6. **Write a thesis statement.** The thesis is the main point, or central idea, of a paper. In one sentence, your thesis should describe your topic and what you want to convey about it. A good thesis statement is unified and clear—for example, "Smoking among teenage girls is rising due to influences by peers and advertising that glamorizes smoking." Remember, you can always revise your thesis statement as you do more research.

7. **Take notes.** Determine the most convenient way to record support, such as quotations, ideas, reports, and statistics that clarify your research topic. An "old school" way is to use 3×5 note cards, writing the topic at the top and one idea per card so that you can organize your ideas easily. (This

method may be effective for kinesthetic learners or if you are unsure of your overall outline or where your research may lead you.) You can also keep your research documented in a notebook or on a computer or tablet. (Having a digital file is probably best to avoid misplacing your work.) No matter which method of organization works best, you will need exact information for your final bibliography or footnotes (discussed in more detail later); thus, the more complete you can be in your initial research, the less backtracking you will need to do to plug in holes. Record the following information in your research notes (examples are provided here):

- **Topic:** Indicate what this source supports, which can be general at this point.

  Example: Food addictions: Caffeinated drinks

- **Author's full name:** Include all authors and the order in which they are listed. If it is an image, include the photographer or right's owner.

  Example: Mayo Clinic Staff (no individuals listed)

- **Title of article, book, or report:** Include any subtitles as well.

  Example: Caffeine content for coffee, tea, soda, and more

- **Publisher:** Include the main source for the material, such as the publishing company, journal, news service, or website. Copy the direct link to the article if it's from an online source and the date you accessed it. Also include any original research sources cited in the article.

  Example: Mayo Clinic website (Nutrition and Healthy Eating section) https://www.mayoclinic.org/healthy-lifestyle/nutrition-and-healthy-eating/in-depth/caffeine/art-20049372; retrieved on March 7, 2020.

- **Summary:** In your own words, summarize the point of the source.

  Example: The amount of caffeine in everyday drinks varies widely. One popular energy drink has about 10 times the caffeine content of other energy drinks—more than 200 milligrams per 2-ounce serving. In comparison, a 12-ounce cola has 35 milligrams. High amounts of caffeine can cause headaches and anxiety. Experts recommend no more than 500 milligrams for adults and 100 milligrams for adolescents per day.

- **Relevance:** Include why you think this makes sense to include.

  Example: Article provides compiled data on caffeine content, which most likely is much higher than the average consumer realizes. Specific energy drinks and espresso have extremely high amounts of caffeine, which have become popular drinks for teens as well as adults.

- **Quotations:** If you are quoting, record the author of the quote or comment, use quotation marks, and write the words exactly as they appear in the source, including the page number or date if applicable. If there is an error in the text (such as the speaker used a word incorrectly or there was a grammatical mistake in the text), in brackets write the term *sic,* which means "thus in the original." If you omit words, indicate missing words with ellipsis points (three periods).

  Example: November 1, 2013: Personal interview with Ava Simpson, age 19, who has drunk energy drinks since high school: "At first, I drank them for the novelty—the buzz you would feel. Now, I can barely make it through the day without a couple cans. Sometimes I'm so wired at night, I can't sleep. I feel like a yo-yo, bouncing around all day. I hate it."

Along with your notes, print or make a copy of the original article or book section. This isn't usually required but is tremendously helpful if the online source moves or is taken down or if the book you used is checked out and you need to read the material again. (Conducting your research is discussed in further detail later in this chapter.)

8. **Don't just cut and paste.** As we'll discuss further in this chapter in regard to plagiarism, be careful about simply cutting and pasting material, especially from online sources. Reword the material as you write it and summarize in your own words.

9. **Prepare a bibliography.** A bibliography is a list of books, articles, Internet sources, interviews, and other resources about a subject or by a particular author that you plan to use as support for information in your paper. A bibliography page or section appears at the end of a research paper or book. Most instructors expect you to include a complete list of your source. Record them accurately and thoroughly as you research.

10. **Create a credibility checklist.** It is important to be able to separate opinions and beliefs from facts and data. When you are doing evidence-based writing versus narrative writing, which is based on your opinion or beliefs, it is important to make sure that the information and author are credible, valid, accurate, and reliable. The information should be factual, up-to-date, logical, and fair; have depth; and cite sources. Evidence-based writing takes time, effort, and critical thinking. These are essential college and career skills and will also make you a better citizen and informed voter.

Sample Outline

Thesis statement: Smoking among teenage girls is rising due to influences by peers and advertising that glamorizes smoking.

I. Smoking among teenage girls is increasing.
  A. Smoking has increased by 24 percent.
    1. Supporting information
    2. Supporting information
  B. Girls are smoking at younger ages.
    1. Supporting information
    2. Supporting information
II. Advertising targets young girls directly.
  A. Examples of advertising
    1. Supporting information
    2. Supporting information
  B. Effects of advertising
    1. Supporting information
    2. Supporting information

Organize

Now that you have done the preliminary legwork, you'll want to create a writing plan.

1. **Develop an outline.** Organize your notes into a logical order using either a traditional or mind map outline. This outline should contain main points and subtopics and serve as a road map that illustrates your entire project and keeps you focused. (See the sample outline nearby.) Use **Personal Evaluation Notebook 10.1** to help you organize your paper.

2. **Do in-depth research.** Look for specific information and data that support your main points and thesis. Research further the books and articles you recorded in your initial research. Make certain that the information and author are credible, valid, accurate, fair, current, and reliable.

3. **Revise your outline as needed.** You may also refine your writing strategy by considering how best to accomplish your purpose. What is your major topic? What subtopics do you want to include? What examples, definitions, quotations, statistics, stories, or personal comments would be most interesting and supportive and support your thesis?

Write

Now is the time to organize all your notes according to sections and headings and write your first draft in your own words according to your revised outline. Write freely and don't worry about spelling, grammar, or format. The key is to begin writing and keep the momentum going. Both papers and speeches should have three sections: an introduction, a main body, and a conclusion.

Personal Evaluation Notebook 10.1

Preparing Research Papers

Use this form to prepare and organize your upcoming paper. Jot down preliminary notes to get started.

Topic _____   Due Date _____

Main Point (Thesis) _____

_____

_____

How do the topic and thesis fulfill the assignment?

_____

_____

Review your outline and notes for these elements and provide examples or descriptions of how they will be addressed in the paper:

MAIN BODY

• Background of topic _____

• Main points and arguments _____

• Supporting points _____

• Terminology, facts, data _____

• Key words _____

CONCLUSION

• Restate thesis. _____

• Summarize key points. _____

• Present a clear and strong conclusion. _____

1. **Introduction.** The introduction should be a strong opening that clearly states your purpose, captures the audience's attention, defines terms, and sets the stage for the main points. Use an active, not a passive, voice. For example, "More than 450,000 people will die this year from the effects of cigarette smoking" is a stronger introduction than "This paper will present the dangers of smoking."

2. **Main body.** The main body is the heart of your paper or speech. Each main point should be presented logically, in your own words, and stand out as a

unit (see **Figure 10.2**). Use direct quotes when you want to state the original source. Your research notes will help you find supportive elements for main points.

3. **Conclusion.** Your final paragraph should tie together important points. The reader or listener should now have an understanding of the topic and believe that you have achieved your purpose. You might use a story, quotation, or call to action. You may want to refer again to the introduction, reemphasize main points, or rephrase an important position. Keep your conclusion brief, interesting, and powerful. (**Figure 10.3** provides hints on overcoming writer's block.)

Edit

A thorough edit can turn good papers into excellent papers.

1. **Revise.**
   - Do a word count. Most papers have a minimum or maximum word count objective or may require a specific number of paragraphs or pages, either single- or double-spaced. Check to make sure you are within these parameters. Keep this objective in mind throughout all stages of revision. Not meeting length criteria set by your instructor may result in lost points.
   - Read your paper out loud to get an overall sense of meaning and the flow of words. Vary sentence lengths and arrangements to add interest and variety. For example, don't start each sentence with the subject or overuse the same words or phrases.
   - Rework paragraphs for clarity and appropriate transitions. Does each paragraph contain one idea in a topic sentence? Is the idea well supported and does a sentence support the purpose? Transitions should be smooth and unobtrusive. In a speech, they should be defined clearly, so that listeners stay focused. Be concise.
   - Recheck your outline. Have you followed your outline logically and included supporting information in the correct places? Break up the narrative with lists if you are presenting series of data. As you revise, stay focused on your purpose, not on the ideas that support your conclusion. Be sure your points are clearly and concisely presented with supporting stories, quotes, and explanations.
   - Review sentence structure, punctuation, grammar, and unity of thought. Correct typographical and spelling errors, grammatical mistakes, and poor transitions. As you work, remember to save your work frequently.

2. **Revise again.** Set your paper aside for a day or two before you give it a final revision with a fresh view. Go through your entire paper or speech. Is your central theme clear and concise? Read your paper out loud. Does it flow? Could it use more stories or quotes to add flair? Is it too wordy or confusing? Does it have an interesting introduction and conclusion? Share your paper with a friend or member of your study team, to proofread and provide a fresh viewpoint. Sometimes you can't see your own errors.

3. **Confer with your instructor.** If you have not done so earlier, make an appointment with your instructor to review your paper. Some students make an appointment after completing their outline or first draft, while others like to wait until they have proofed their second draft. Most instructors will

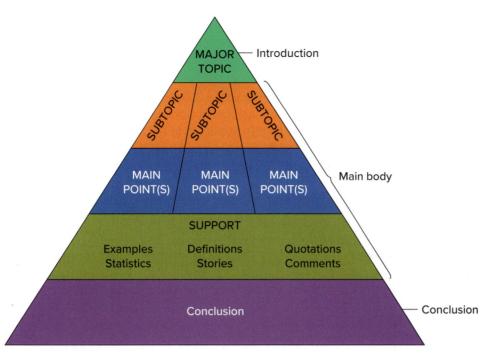

Figure **10.2**

Writing Pyramid

Start at the top of the pyramid with your major topic and move down to each subtopic and its main points. Provide support for your main points, including examples and statistics. End with a powerful conclusion that summarizes the paper or speech. *Why are "support" elements so important?*

Figure **10.3**

Overcoming Writer's Block

There are a number of ways to jump-start your writing. *Which tips have worked best for you?*
Brand X/JupiterImages/Getty Images

Read Expand your vocabulary by reading novels, classic literature, biographies, and news articles. Exchange papers within your study team.

Write in a conversational tone Avoid technical, artificial, or stilted language. Use everyday words as if you are talking to someone.

Write in short blocks of time Write for 5 minutes before bed, in the morning, or between classes. Write a little every day—anywhere you happen to be.

Understand your purpose Make a list of key points you want to make, and write in a few words or phrases what you want to accomplish.

Find an empty room You may need space to be alone, spread out papers, and work without interruptions.

Create a mind map A map frees your ideas to flow and helps you see connections between topics. Start with your central purpose and topic. Outline main points, subtopics, and so on, and fill in with additional ideas.

Free write After you have completed your map outline, write for 30 or 40 minutes. Don't worry about spelling, organization, or grammar. Free writing is especially useful if you start early, let the first draft sit for a few days, and then revise.

Vary your routine Skip the introduction, work on your conclusion, or write about the supporting points you know the best.

Set a deadline Create a schedule and stick to it. Complete each task, even if it isn't perfect. You can revise later.

review your paper with you and make suggestions—discuss what to add, what to revise, and the preferred method of citation. Also, many colleges have a writing center staffed with English majors who will read your rough drafts and help you revise.

4. **Prepare your final draft.** Following your instructor's guidelines, prepare your final draft. Leave a margin of 1 inch on all sides, except for the first page, which should have a 3-inch margin at the top of the paper. Double-space your entire paper, except for the footnotes and bibliography, which are often single-spaced. Make corrections, revise, run a spell-check, and print out a clean, corrected copy on good-quality paper (if submitting a hard copy versus online). Also, proofread this hard copy, as it's easy to miss errors on a computer screen. See **Peak Progress 10.2** for writing tips. (Also see **Peak Progress 10.3** if you are writing online.)

5. **Cite your sources.** Always cite your sources when you quote or use another person's words or ideas. **Plagiarism** is using someone else's words or ideas and trying to pass them off as your own. It can have serious consequences, such as a failing grade or expulsion from school. You can put the person's exact words in quotation marks, or you can **paraphrase** by using your own

Peak Progress 10.2

Writing Do's: The Seven C's of Effective Writing

Be concise. Eliminate unnecessary words. Write in plain language and avoid wordiness. Cut any phrases that do not support your purpose.

Be concrete. Use vivid action words rather than vague, general terms. The sentence "Jill wrote the paper" is in the active voice and is easy to understand; "The paper was written by Jill" is in the passive voice and sounds weak. Avoid vague adjectives and adverbs, such as *nice, good, greatly,* and *badly.*

Be clear. Never assume that the audience has prior information. Avoid technical terms, clichés, slang, and jargon. If you must be technical, include simple definitions for your audience.

Be correct. Choose precise words and grammatically correct sentences. Verify that supporting details are factual and correctly interpreted. Make certain you cite another's work. Check spelling and punctuation carefully.

Be coherent. Your message should flow smoothly. Transitions between topics should be clear, logical, and varied in word choice. Also, vary the length of sentences for interest and a sense of rhythm. Include stories, examples, and interesting facts.

Be complete. Include all necessary information. Will your listeners or readers understand your message? Reread your speech or paper from their point of

view. What questions might the audience have? Answer any unanswered questions.

Be considerate. Respect your reader by presenting a professional paper. Neatness counts, and papers should always be typed. Use a respectful tone; don't talk down to your audience or use pompous or prejudiced language. Write with courtesy and consideration, and avoid using words that are biased in terms of sex, disabilities, or ethnic groups.

Instead of	You Can Substitute
mankind	humanity, people, humankind
manmade	manufactured, handcrafted
policeman	police officer
fireman	firefighter
housewife	homemaker
crippled, disabled	physically challenged
Indian (American)	Native American
Oriental	Asian
Chicano	Latino

Peak Progress

Online Writing and Social Networking

Websites such as Facebook, Google, Twitter, and LinkedIn are popular places to share photos and news and a great way to stay in touch with friends and family. The downside is that they can eat up an enormous amount of time and replace face-to-face communication and personal notes. They are also a public medium and this information will be public forever. Think about the information you post and ask yourself if you would want your future employer to see it or how it would affect your image if you were running for public office. Avoid personal information such as your birth date or class schedule, do not offer financial information or plans for vacations, or post provocative pictures or messages. Do not post photos of others without their permission. Avoid meeting in person someone you've only known online unless it's a public place or you bring a friend along.

E-mails and texts may be a major part of your writing. Like all business writing, these guidelines can help you be more effective. When writing e-mails, be specific in your subject line, get to the point quickly in your text, and highlight important information about date, time, and purpose. Keep it concise, complete, and correct. It should be easy for your reader to skim quickly and find information. Use complete, grammatically correct sentences. Don't send the e-mail until you've read it over again.

Text messages are more casual but should still be concise, accurate, and limited. Be respectful of your reader. People get way too many messages and use a lot of valuable time responding. Ask yourself if the e-mail or text is necessary because you don't want to add to their fatigue. Respect others' time. Remember that your message is missing emotion and can be easily misinterpreted. Ask yourself, "Would I say this to this person's face?" Keep important messages for face-to-face communication.

The Internet opened the floodgates of communication opportunities, as **blogging** (writing personal thoughts online, usually about a specific topic, for others to view and often comment on) and chatting on social networking sites have become popular writing activities. Many courses require students to manage their own blogs (for example, to report on service learning experiences) or to communicate with other class members via discussion boards.

When posting material online, the purpose is usually the same as for writing a class paper—to succinctly communicate your main message—and the techniques are very similar, including providing supporting material and examples. Following are some specific tips to help focus your online writing:

1. **Be respectful.** The point of your writing (especially with a blog) is to express your own opinion, so do it respectfully (without slander or profanity) and as briefly as possible. Be civil and use etiquette.

2. **Be direct.** Write a creative headline that conveys your main message.

3. **Be concise.** Limit your words to no more than 250.

4. **Make it easy to scan.** If your message is longer than three paragraphs, break it up with subheads so that the post is easy to skim.

5. **Highlight important information.** Use bullets for examples or to stress information (dates, time, place), which catches the reader's attention.

6. **Use key words.** If your goal is to attract readers to your posting, include many key terms that would pop up during word searches.

7. **Be credible.** Make sure your information is credible. Be objective. Evidence-based writing is backed up by credible resources versus narrative writing, which is based on your opinions and beliefs. Link to supporting, credible websites.

8. **Copyedit before you post.** Nothing hurts your credibility more than typos and grammatical mistakes.

9. **Respond when appropriate.** Now that you've started the line of communication, be prepared to follow up on feedback, if necessary. Keep your communication respectful and brief if you receive an angry comment. Don't get caught up in an online battle.

10. **Use privacy features.** Check out options for restricting who can access your profile. Review and update your list of friends or followers on a regular basis.

11. **Unplug.** Take stock of the time you are taking away from family and friends to be attached to your devices. Set up times when you put your phone out of site. Look at the sky. Notice your surroundings. Be fully engaged in what you are doing without checking your phone. Look at people and listen attentively. Turn off digital objects and electronic screens at least an hour before you go to bed so your brain and body really rest.

words to restate the author's ideas. You can give credit in the text of the paper or in a note, either at the bottom of the page as a footnote or at the end of the paper as an endnote. (See **Peak Progress 10.4** for a discussion of citation styles.)

For example, you may choose to use the following source when writing a paper on the history of the funeral industry. This is the exact quote from the text along with one method of citation:

> "Simplicity to the point of starkness, the plain pine box, the laying out of the dead by friends and family who also bore the coffin to the grave—these were the hallmarks of the traditional funeral until the end of the nineteenth century."[1]

Instead, you may choose to paraphrase the information from the book:

> In her book *The American Way of Death,* Jessica Mitford says one myth that is sold by the funeral industry is that today's elaborate and expensive funeral practices are part of the American tradition. In truth, prior to the end of the nineteenth century, the average American funeral was inexpensive and often consisted of a pine box and a simple ceremony.

You do not need to credit general ideas that are considered to be part of common knowledge, such as the suggestion that people who exercise reduce their stress levels. However, when in doubt, it's best to cite your source. Read **Personal Evaluation Notebook 10.2** to get a better understanding of plagiarism and how to avoid it.

Peak Progress   10.4
Writing Citations

There are many ways to write citations. Ask your professor for specific instructions on how to cite sources and which documentation style is preferred. Each academic discipline has its preferred format. The Modern Language Association (MLA) of America format is often preferred for the humanities (philosophy, languages, arts, and so on). The American Psychological Association (APA) format is commonly used for the social sciences, psychology, and education. The style of the Council of Biology Editors (CBE) is primarily used for the natural and physical sciences. Computer programs are available to help you format citations according to some styles.

Reference notes can be placed at the bottom of a page as footnotes or listed together at the end of the paper as endnotes. A bibliography, which lists all the sources (such as books, articles, websites, and personal communication) referenced in a paper, may include works for background and further reading. A reference list, on the other hand, cites works that specifically support an article. Bibliographies and reference lists are found at the end of a paper after endnotes, if there are any. In the MLA format, the bibliography appears under the heading "Works Cited." You can find helpful guidelines in the *MLA Handbook for Writers of Research Papers.* For more information on MLA format, visit the MLA website at **https://style.mla.org/mla-format/**.

The various citation formats are similar. The MLA style uses the simplest punctuation and is acceptable in many situations. The elements of an MLA citation are author, book title, place of publication, publisher, year of publication, and page number.

The APA style generally uses a combination of in-text citations and a reference list. Text citations use an author-date system, such as (Nelson, 2004). Items in the reference list usually contain the following elements: author, year of publication, title of the work, place of publication, and publisher. For more information about APA style, visit the APA website at **www.apastyle.org/faqs.html**.

Several excellent websites can guide you through a generally acceptable way to cite sources. Your local or school library may also post citation information on its website. Following is a guide for most types of sources you will cite:

(continued)

Writing Citations   *(concluded)*

For Footnotes

MLA 1. Lee, Ann. *Office Reference Manual.* New York: Irwin, 1993.

APA (Lee, 1993) *Note:* In the APA's author-date system, the last name(s) of the author(s) and the year of publication are inserted in the text at the appropriate point.

For Reference List or Works Cited

Book: One Author

MLA Henley, Patricia. *Hummingbird House.* Denver: MacMurray, 1999.

APA Henley, P. (1999). *Hummingbird house.* Denver: MacMurray.

Book: Two or More Authors

MLA Gillespie, Paula, and Neal Lerber. *The Allyn and Bacon Guide to Peer Tutoring.* Boston: Allyn, 2000.

APA Gillespie, P., & Lerber, N. (2000). *The Allyn and Bacon guide to peer tutoring.* Boston: Allyn.

Government Publication

MLA United States Department of Health and Human Services. *Pressure Ulcers in Adults: Prediction and Prevention.* Rockville, MD: Publisher, 1992, 28.

APA U.S. Department of Health and Human Services. (1992). *Pressure ulcers in adults: Prediction and prevention* (AHCPR Publication No. 92-0047). Rockville, MD: Author.

Journal

MLA Klimoski, Richard I., and Susan Palmer. "The ADA and the Hiring Process in Organizations." *Consulting Psychology Journal: Practice and Research,* 45.2 (1993) 10-36.

APA Klimoski, R. I., & Palmer, S. (1993). The ADA and the hiring process in organizations. *Consulting Psychology Journal: Practice and Research,* 45(2), 10-36.

Nonprint Source (website)

MLA Stolley, Karl. "MLA Formatting and Style Guide." The OWL at Purdue. 10 May 2006. Purdue University Writing Lab. 12 May 2006 <http://owl.english.purdue.edu/owl/resource/747/01/>.

APA Stolley, K. (2006). MLA formatting and style guide. Retrieved May 12, 2006, from Purdue University Writing Lab website: http://owl.english.purdue.edu/owl/resource/747/01/

Nonprint Source (Online Journal)

MLA Wheelis, Mark. "Investigating Disease Outbreaks under a Protocol to the Biological and Toxin Weapons Convention." *Emerging Infectious Diseases* 6.6 (2000): 33 pars. 8 May 2006 <wwwnc.cdc.gov/eid/article/6/6/00-0607_article>.

APA Wheelis, M. (2000). Investigating disease outbreaks under a protocol to the biological and toxin weapons convention. *Emerging Infectious Diseases,* 6. Retrieved May 8, 2006, from wwwnc.cdc.gov/eid/article/6/6/00-0607_article

Nonprint Source (DVD)

MLA Reaven, Gerald, and Meenakshi Aggarwal. *Heart Disease and South Asians: A Population at Risk.* DVD. CustomFlix, 2006.

APA Reaven, G., & Aggarwal, M. (2006). *Heart Disease and South Asians: A Population at Risk.* [DVD]. CustomFlix.

Nonprint Source (App)

MLA Prentice, William E., Amanda Andrews Benson, and Linda Stark Bobo. *Athletic Trainer Plus.* Van Brien & Associates. 2013. Electronic application. June 19, 2013.

APA Van Brien & Associates. (2013). *Athletic Trainer Plus.* [Mobile application software]. Retrieved from http://itunes.apple.com

Letter to the Editor

MLA Berkowitz, A. D. Letter. "How to Tackle the Problem of Student Drinking." *The Chronicle of Higher Education.* 24 Nov 2000: B20.

APA Berkowitz, A. D. (2000, November 24). How to tackle the problem of student drinking [Letter to the editor]. *The Chronicle of Higher Education,* p. B20.

Encyclopedia or Other Reference Work

MLA Bergmann, Peter G. "Relativity." *The New Encyclopaedia Britannica.* 15th ed. 1993.

APA Bergmann, P. G. (1993). Relativity. In *The new encyclopaedia britannica* (Vol. 26, pp. 501-508). Chicago: Encyclopedia Britannica.

Personal Evaluation Notebook 10.2

That's Not Fair (Use)

One survey reported that 36 percent of teens admitted they had used the Internet to plagiarize an assignment. However, it's likely that even more are committing plagiarism without realizing it because of the confusion over what constitutes plagiarism versus "fair use."

Fair use is the legal and ethical use of a direct quote from the Internet or another source, including a book, in something you claim as your own work. According to the U.S. Copyright Office, fair use is limited to the "quotation of excerpts in a review or criticism for purposes of illustration or comment; quotation of short passages in a scholarly or technical work, for illustration or clarification of the author's observations; use in a parody of some of the content of the work parodied; summary of an address or article, with brief quotations," and similar use. Even when the quotation is within the fair use guidelines, it is essential to give a reference through a footnote or other indication that these words were written by someone other than you. Because of the prevalence of plagiarism, many instructors use online services to check for it, including having students deliver their papers via an online site, such as Turnitin.

To test your understanding, consider the following scenarios*:

1. This morning, you read an editorial in the local newspaper and totally agreed with the author's 10-step approach to improving high school graduation rates. You include all 10 suggestions in your presentation to your Introduction to Education class but reword each one slightly and don't cite the author. Is this plagiarism?

   yes _____ no _____

2. You cut and paste a lengthy article from a reputable online news service into your paper and add a new introduction and a brief summary. You include a complete citation in your source information. Is this plagiarism?

   yes _____ no _____

3. Last semester, you wrote a stellar paper for your English composition class, in which you compared and contrasted a number of local businesses. You decide to hand in the same paper this week for an Economics 101 assignment. Is this plagiarism?

   yes _____ no _____

If you answered "yes" to 1 and 2, you're right; it is plagiarism. In number 1, you need to cite the author and put the ideas into your own words, not just reword slightly. In number 2, you need to quote directly and give credit. Adding a new introduction and summary is not paraphrasing. Number 3 is not plagiarism since it is your own paper. However, it would be a better paper and fit with the intent of the class if you were to rework the paper to fit the economics class, conduct relevant interviews, and so on. That is the intent of the professor for the assignment.

Sources: Josephson Institute, Center for Youth Ethics, "The Ethics of American Youth—2008 Summary," **http://www.bentley.edu/sites/www.bentley.edu.centers/files/centers/cbe/cbe-external-surveys/the-ethics-of-american-youth-2008.pdf**, accessed September 12, 2016; U.S. Copyright Office, Fair Use Index, **www.copyright.gov/fls/fl102.html**, revised August 2016.

*Answers are in the section "Taking Charge."

6. **Stay current.** Most writing in college and in the workplace will be done on your computer. You'll want to stay up to speed on all new software. Check out free or low-cost software such as **drive.google.com** and **www.zoho.com/docs**. Check with your professors to see which formats and software they prefer. Also check out free apps for writing and speaking: Worksmith and Speech Jammer.

7. **Add a title page and page numbers.** If required, create a title page by centering the title one-third of the page from the top. Two-thirds from the top, center your name, the instructor's name, the course title, and the date. Do not number this page. Number all remaining pages in the upper right-hand corner 1/2 inch from the top of the page. Number your endnotes and bibliography as part of the text. (Refer to any guidelines your instructor may have given you regarding formatting preferences.)

Review

Proofread by carefully reading through your work one more time. **Peak Progress 10.5** provides a handy checklist to use as you finalize. Be prepared to submit your paper or give your speech by the due date. Delaying just adds to the anxiety and may result in a lower grade. Keep backup copies (a hard copy and a digital file) of your final paper or speech, in case your instructor loses the original.

Review your graded paper or speech when it is returned to you and make sure you understand what you could have done differently to have received a better grade. If you are unsure, ask your instructor for tips on improving your work. Keep copies of your major research papers in your Career Development Portfolio to show documentation of your writing, speaking, and research skills.

> 66 Proofread carefully to see if you any words out. 99
>
> AUTHOR UNKNOWN

Peak Progress   10.5

Checklists for Writing Papers and Giving Speeches

Papers and Speeches

_____ Appropriate and focused topic   _____ Good examples

_____ Attention-getting introduction   _____ Good visuals

_____ Clear thesis statement   _____ Sources credited

_____ Appropriate word choice   _____ Smooth transitions

_____ Plenty of factual support   _____ Effective summary/conclusions

Papers

_____ Spelling and grammar checked   _____ Neat appearance/format

_____ Proofread at least twice   _____ Deadline met

_____ Pages numbered

Speeches

_____ Eye contact   _____ Relaxed body language

_____ Appropriate voice level and tone   _____ Appropriate attire

_____ No slang or distracting words   _____ Access to watch or clock

---

Information Literacy

Information literacy is the ability to find, interpret, and use information to meet your research needs. Conducting research requires the same skills you've been learning throughout this book: observing, recording, reviewing, and using critical thinking to assess and evaluate. The purpose of research is to find information and ideas about a topic beyond what you already know. Research helps you support opinions and information with facts and data. Your initial research will give you an overview of the subject and help you define your thesis statement. Additional research will uncover specific facts about your subject. You will want to develop information literacy by learning to find information and evaluate it from appropriate sources.

You will be reading all kinds of material in the course of your college and career life. You'll read brochures, job descriptions, meeting minutes, training materials, annual reports, websites, ebooks, and research material. Think about the purpose of your reading and what you can do with it. Information is now available at your fingertips. This means that you will need to develop information literacy and be able to determine credibility. You can learn this with effort, practice, and a positive attitude. This includes:

- **Computer literacy** is the ability to use electronic tools including computers, digital devices, and social media to conduct your searches. It is being aware of new technology and having the mindset that says, "I'm willing to learn, stretch, and grow."
- **Media literacy** is the ability to use critical thinking when you read books or magazines, use the Internet, watch television or films, listen to the radio, listen to or read advertisements, or interact with any type of media. Is this bias? Is this true?
- **Cultural literacy** is being aware and having fundamental knowledge about what has gone on in the past and what is going on now in the world. It is understanding history and current events enough to carry on an intelligent conversation and in relating past and current issues to your studies. Create a sense of curiosity and wonder.

Using the Library for Research

As discussed in Chapter 5, the library contains a wealth of information. Reference librarians are trained to find information about every subject. They can often order materials from other libraries or direct you to other sources. Asking for their guidance at the beginning of your search can save you hours of time and frustration. College and university libraries are changing as information goes digital. Librarians are skilled in research technology and can help you explore searches for choosing a topic, find appropriate sources, and improve your research and writing skills. When planning your research strategy, remember the basic types of sources found in most libraries:

- **Books.** Books make up a large part of every library. They treat a subject in depth and offer a broad scope. In your research project, use books for historical context, detailed discussions of a subject, or varied perspectives on a topic.
- **Periodicals.** A periodical is a regularly issued publication, such as newspapers, news magazines, professional and scholarly journals, and trade

and industry magazines. For your research, use periodicals when you need recent data.

- **Reference materials.** Reference materials may be in print or digital. Examples include encyclopedias, dictionaries, chronologies, abstracts, indexes, and compilations of statistics. In your research strategy, use reference materials when you want to obtain or verify specific facts.

  The *Readers' Guide to Periodical Literature* is a helpful source for locating articles. Other standard reference materials that may give you a general understanding of specific topics and help you develop questions include the *Encyclopaedia Britannica* and the indexes of *The New York Times* and *The Wall Street Journal.*

  Check these sources for historical speeches:
  - *Speech Index*
  - *Index to American Women Speakers, 1828-1978*
  - *Representative American Speeches*
  - *Facts on File*
  - *Vital Speeches of the Day*
  - *Public Papers of the Presidents of the United States*

- **Interlibrary loan.** If your library doesn't have a book, journal, or article that you need, you can request an item at no charge from another library.

- **Ebooks and other resources.** Many new books are offered only as ebooks in the library. Check with the reference librarian for different accessibility needs, for example, audio and Braille. The same strategies for reading books apply to ebook readers. You may want to create a more readable page by adjusting the size and fonts. Look for a search box where you can enter key words and follow links to definitions and related information and material. Ebooks allow you to highlight and select words, sentences, or entire paragraphs and highlight them in a color of your choice. You can annotate a book by tying your notes to specific pages. Look for illustrations, charts, tables, diagrams, and photos. If they do not show well on a small screen, choose a printed copy. Most ebook readers will connect you to websites.

Search by author or subject through the library's online catalog. Often, the electronic source will include only a summary, so you may need to go to the library stacks or periodicals to read the book or article.

Taking Your Search Online

The reading strategies suggested in this chapter work for reading a web page, ebook, mobile phone, tablet, or computer. Eliminate distractions. Cut the clutter on web pages and cut ads, pop-up windows, and animations. Reduce distractions and focus by not getting sidetracked by other interesting, but unrelated, links. Look for the main ideas and content. Ask questions, find answers, and flag them in the text. Before you start a search online, think about a precise question you want to answer, such as "How does education affect smoking by college students?" Identify the key words and ideas in this question—for example, *smoking, education,* and *addiction.* Directories such as Yahoo! (**www.yahoo.com**) are often helpful when

• A Good Source

Libraries provide the most research options, with books, periodicals, reference materials, online access, and trained librarians. *What's the best source for recent data?*

Hill Street Studios/Blend Images

Brain research has shown that the brain of the adolescent (ages 12–15) is very creative and the circuits that create the inner motivation to try something new are connecting and firing. The key is to focus, harness that creative energy, and put in the effort necessary to succeed. Virtually any task can be made pleasurable if you approach it from a positive attitude.[2]

Bella's blog has become an instant hit with fans of local cuisine. Majoring in food science, Bella loves to give (and ask for) opinions on hot spots, new chefs, menu makeovers, and dining experiences—the good and the bad. However, as much as Bella enjoys voicing her thoughts online in elaborate detail, writing a term paper is as appealing to her as a trip to the dentist.

- How do Bella's personality and learning styles influence her online writing success?
- If Bella enjoys writing her blog, why does she view other writing opportunities differently? How can she create a positive attitude and discipline to write in many areas of life?
- What tips would you give Bella to help her tackle her more structured writing projects?

THINK
CREATIVELY AND CRITICALLY

starting your research because they are organized by subject. Other sites, such as Google (**www.google.com**), combine directories with search engines. Type your key words into the search box, select from the options that pop up, or hit the return key and wait for a list of web pages to appear. If they don't answer your question, rephrase your question and search again using other key words. Each search site offers links that will explain how to do advanced searches. Bookmark websites that you use often. You can use Google, Wikipedia, and IMDb (**www.imdb.com**) for casual research, but you'll want to extend your research for college research projects. Besides the free Web, there are other sites known as the deep Web that offer articles by recognized experts for an audience of scholars. Google Books (**books.google.com**) offers many more ways to find information. Google Scholar (**scholar.google.com**) is useful for finding peer-reviewed articles in professional journals. It is important to learn what research is objective and factual. You may also try peer-reviewed academic journals such as *Harvard Business Review,* newspaper websites such as *The New York Times,* or government websites ending in .gov.

Although searching for information on the Internet by using key words or key phrases may seem relatively easy and efficient, you must verify that what you choose to use comes from a reliable source. See **Peak Progress 10.6** for tips on evaluating online material. As with other sources, you must also cite material you find on the Internet.

Public Speaking Strategies

Public speaking is an essential school and job skill. In school, you will ask and answer questions in class, lead discussions, summarize topics, introduce other students, present your academic plan or thesis, and interview for internships or jobs. On the job, you may introduce a guest, present the results of a group project, make a sales pitch, demonstrate a new product, present goals, objectives, entertain clients, and talk with upper management.

Many of the strategies for choosing a topic and organizing and writing a speech are like those for writing papers. Strategies specifically for public speaking include:

1. **Understand the occasion.** Is your purpose to inform, entertain, inspire, or persuade? Is the occasion formal or informal? How much time do you have? Review your intent.

2. **Think about your topic.** If a topic hasn't been assigned, what are you interested in talking about? Prepare a thesis statement, such as "My purpose is to inform the Forestry Club on the benefits of our organization."

• Eye Contact
When you look at the audience as you speak, you create a rapport that makes everyone more comfortable. *What other strategies can help you become a good speaker?*

Skynesher/Getty Images

Peak Progress

Evaluating Online Information

With millions of web pages to choose from, how do you know which sites are reliable? Use the following checklist when evaluating online or library information for research and personal use.

Is It Credible?

- Is the page's author clearly identified? Does he or she have the credentials for writing about this topic? Make sure there is credibility. Look for educational degrees, training, and work experience that would show why this person is qualified to publish on the topic of your research.
- Is the author affiliated with an organization? If so, what is the organization's nature or purpose?
- Note the publication date. Is the reference current or time sensitive? What new information has been published on the topic in the last five years?
- Is there a link to the organization's home page or some other way to contact the organization and verify its credibility (a physical address, phone number, or e-mail address)?
- Is the page geared for a particular audience or level of expertise?
- Is it fair? Does the article present both sides of an argument or attempt to be balanced?
- Is there a bias? Is the primary purpose to provide information, sell a product, make a political point, or have fun? You should balance out your research with other sources on the topic. Why was this page put on the Web?
- Is it logical? Could the article be satire or humorous?
- Is the page part of an edited or peer-reviewed publication?
- Does the domain name provide clues about the source of the page?

- Does the site provide details that support the data?
- Is there a bibliography or other documentation to corroborate the information? When facts or statistics are quoted, look to see whether their source is revealed.

Is It Accurate?

- Are there obvious typographical or spelling errors?
- Based on what you already know or have just learned about this subject, does the information seem credible?
- Can factual information be verified?
- Is it comprehensive, or does it focus on a narrow range of information?
- Is it clear about its focus?
- Has the site been evaluated?
- Have you looked for peer-reviewed articles in professional journals?

Is It Timely?

- Can you tell when the information was published? Is it current?
- When was the page last updated?
- If there are links to other web pages, are they current?

Is It Objective?

- Is the source of factual information consistent and stated clearly?
- Does the page display a particular bias? Is it clear and forthcoming about its view of a particular subject?
- If the page contains advertisements, are they clearly distinguishable from the content of the information?

Source: The University of Texas System Digital Library, The University of Texas at Austin.

3. **Know your audience.** You don't need to know them personally, but you should have a sense of their backgrounds and why they are in the room. For example, if you are giving a speech on cutting-edge technology and the majority of your audience barely knows how to turn on a computer, chances are you are going to lose them quickly unless you present the topic at a level they can relate to, with benefits they can appreciate.

4. **Get the audience's attention.** Write an introduction that gets attention, introduces the topic, states the main purpose, and briefly identifies the main points.

5. **Get the audience involved.** Consider asking a question, which may help personalize the topic, encourage participation, or keep the audience interested.

6. **Look at the audience.** Establish eye contact, speak to the audience members, smile, develop rapport, and notice if your audience agrees or looks puzzled or confused.

7. **Outline your speech.** Organize the body of your speech to include supporting points and interesting examples. Could a good quote or story add interest?

8. **Write a good conclusion.** The audience should have a clear picture of what your main point is, why it's important, and what they should do about it. You may want to end with a story, strong statement, or question.

9. **Develop visuals.** When appropriate, use overheads, a PowerPoint presentation, handouts, and demonstrations to focus attention and reinforce your speech. Make sure the projection equipment works, and you have practiced working with the visual aids. See **Figure 10.4** for tips on creating effective PowerPoint presentations.

10. **Prepare your prompters.** Don't memorize the speech, but be well acquainted with your topic so that you are comfortable talking about it. Prepare simple notes to prompt yourself. Write key phrases, stories, and quotes in large letters on note cards.

11. **Practice.** Rehearsal is everything! Practice the speech aloud several times in front of a mirror, an empty classroom, or friends. Practice speaking slowly, calmly, and louder than usual. Vary the pitch and speed for emphasis. Practice will also help you overcome stage fright. (See the next section on speech anxiety.)

12. **Relax.** Take a deep breath as you walk to the front of the room. During the speech, speak loudly and clearly, don't rush, and gesture when appropriate to help you communicate.

13. **Watch your time.** If you have a time limit, make sure there is a clock you can glance at during your presentation. Pace yourself so that you finish on time.

14. **Be in the present.** Look at your audience and smile. Keep your purpose in mind and stay focused on the message and the audience. Pause at important points for emphasis and to connect with your audience.

15. **Avoid unnecessary words.** Use clear, concise wording. Don't use pauses as fillers or overused slang, such as *uh, er, you know, stuff like that, sort of,* and *like.*

Figure **10.4**

PowerPoint Presentations

When developing a PowerPoint presentation, include only essential words and images. The text has to be big enough to be read from the back of the room. Do not read from your presentation, but use it as a guide to follow as you speak. *Do you feel more comfortable giving a presentation with or without an accompanying PowerPoint?*

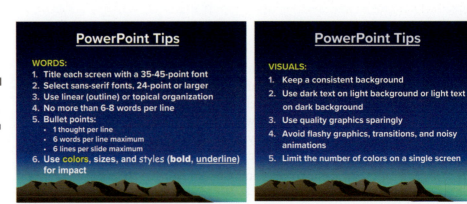

PowerPoint Tips

WORDS:
1. Title each screen with a 35-45-point font
2. Select sans-serif fonts, 24-point or larger
3. Use linear (outline) or topical organization
4. No more than 6-8 words per line
5. Bullet points:
   - 1 thought per line
   - 6 words per line maximum
   - 6 lines per slide maximum
6. Use colors, sizes, and styles (**bold**, underline) for impact

PowerPoint Tips

VISUALS:
1. Keep a consistent background
2. Use dark text on light background or light text on dark background
3. Use quality graphics sparingly
4. Avoid flashy graphics, transitions, and noisy animations
5. Limit the number of colors on a single screen

Figure **10.5**

Speech Evaluation Form

Feedback on your speaking skills can help you improve. *How would you assess your last speech in a class?*

Name _____	Topic _____	
Introduction	**Delivery**	**Suggestions**
__ Gained attention and interest	__ Spoke at an appropriate rate	_____
__ Introduced topic	__ Maintained eye contact	_____
__ Topic related to audience	__ Maintained volume and projection	_____
__ Established credibility	__ Avoided distracting mannerisms	_____
__ Previewed body of speech	__ Used gestures effectively	_____
	__ Articulated clearly	_____
Body	__ Used vocal variety and dynamics	_____
__ Main points clear	__ Presented visual aids effectively	_____
__ Organizational pattern evident	__ Departed appropriately	**General Notes**
__ Established need	__ Other: _____	_____
__ Presented clear plan		_____
__ Demonstrated practicality	**Conclusion**	_____
__ Language clear	__ Prepared audience for ending	_____
__ Gave evidence to support main points	__ Reinforced central idea	_____
__ Sources and citations clear	__ Called audience to agreement/action	_____
__ Reasoning sound	__ Used a vivid ending	_____
__ Used emotional appeals		_____
__ Connectives effective		_____

Key: Superior (1), Effective (2), Average (3), Weak (4)

16. **Review your performance.** Ask your instructor and fellow students for feedback. Use the sample speech evaluation form shown in **Figure 10.5** to help you improve your performance or as you are listening to others.

See **Peak Progress 10.7** to explore how you can apply the Adult Learning Cycle to become more proficient at public speaking.

Overcoming Obstacles with a Positive Mindset and Habits

The biggest obstacle for speaking is speech anxiety. If you have a fixed, negative mindset, you don't think you can change. "Good speakers just have a natural ability. I'm just not a natural good speaker." *If you have a positive, growth mindset, you know you can enhance your abilities with effort and practice.* Most people feel nervous about speaking in front of others. This kind of nervousness is called speech anxiety or stage fright and it is normal. Two researchers at the University of Nebraska asked over 800 students to select their three greatest fears from a list that included flying, deep water, financial problems, heights, speaking before a group, and death. Public speaking beat out all of the fears, even death.[3]

A little apprehension can add energy and sharpen your awareness and focus. Too much anxiety, however, can be harmful. Speech anxiety has both mental and physical components. Mentally, you might think of all the ways you will fail. As you worry about the speech, your negative thoughts can work you into a state of real anxiety. There is a feeling of exposure. Physical symptoms include butterflies in the stomach, irregular breathing, sweaty palms, dry mouth, nausea, mental blocks,

Peak Progress

Applying the Adult Learning Cycle to Improve Your Public Speaking

Increasing your public speaking skills takes time, effort, and practice.

1. **FEEL and LISTEN.** *Why do I want to learn this?* I admire people who are confident speaking in front of others, and I want to feel as confident, poised, and in control. Becoming an effective public speaker will be a valuable skill for both school and career. What areas do I need to work on? I will acknowledge, listen to, and feel my physical symptoms of anxiety and relate them to other times I've been nervous and overcame these feelings.

2. **OBSERVE and VISUALIZE.** *How does this work?* I can learn by observing people who confidently give effective speeches. What makes them successful? Do I understand the message? I'll also analyze ineffective speeches. Did stage fright play a role? Did the speaker seem nervous? I'll try using new techniques and strategies for dealing with stage fright and observe how I'm improving.

3. **THINK and WRITE.** *What does this mean?* What strategies are working for me? Am I more confident and relaxed? Am I reducing anxiety and negative self-talk? I will write out a plan for dealing with anxiety and read it. I will write out my speech and read it out loud.

4. **DO and PRACTICE.** *What can I do with this?* I will practice my public speaking skills whenever possible. I'll find practical applications for my new skills. Each day, I'll work on one area. For example, I'll choose less stressful situations, such as my study group or a club meeting, and offer to give a presentation on an interesting topic. I will ask for feedback.

5. **TEACH and PRACTICE AGAIN.** *Whom can I share this with?* I'll talk with others and share my tips and experiences and listen to theirs in return. I'll volunteer to help other students in my study group.

Use the VARK system to integrate learning styles and help you think through and apply the Adult Learning Cycle. *Visualize* yourself being calm and focused and giving an excellent speech. Record your speech and *listen* to it. *Write it out and read* it again and again. Now *practice.* Go to the classroom where you are giving the speech and stand up in front. *Practice* your speech in the room if possible. Give your speech to another student and listen to comments. Now, return to stage 1 and think about how it feels to learn this valuable new skill. Remember, the more you practice speaking in front of others, the more relaxed and confident you will become.

---

flushed skin, tense muscles, and shaky hands. In response to stress, the adrenal glands pump the hormone adrenaline into the bloodstream, causing a panic attack. Extreme anxiety can prevent you from doing your best. Instead of worrying and fretting about giving your speech, channel your anxiety into action and effort. *The best way to deal with speech anxiety is to prepare:* (1) *research* your speech, (2) *revise,* and (3) *practice* until you feel comfortable. The more you practice this routine, the more confident you'll feel and not only will you become a better public speaker, but you will also learn to manage stress. Focus on being positive and growing and learning. Being a good speaker requires effort and practice.

Build Better Public Speaking Habits

The podium at the front of the room is your *trigger.* When you see this, you automatically go into your *routine.* You know you have practiced and prepared and are

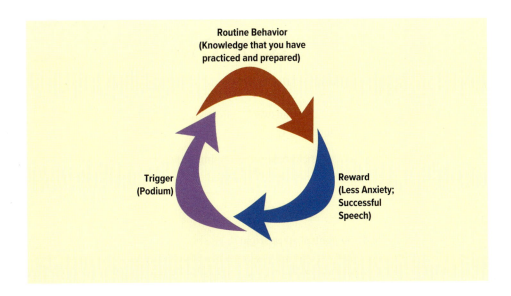

Routine Behavior
(Knowledge that you have
practiced and prepared)

Trigger
(Podium)

Reward
(Less Anxiety;
Successful
Speech)

focused. As a result, your anxiety is more under control. You go up to the podium and take a deep breath while slowly looking at the class. Your PowerPoint prompts your stories and you make sure that each point is covered. You know where to pause. The *reward* is the pride in accomplishment. You gave a good speech and controlled your speech anxiety.

Practice your routine often until it becomes automatic. Work the following strategies into your practice. You will soon become a more confident speaker.

1. **Practice.** The more prepared you are, the less nervous you're likely to be. Practice out loud, in front of a mirror, with a friend, and in the room where you'll be speaking, if possible.

2. **Use visuals.** Visual aids can prompt you during the presentation and direct the spotlight away from you.

3. **Dispute irrational thoughts.** You might think, "People will laugh at me" or "My mind will go blank." In reality, others are also apprehensive (and more concerned about their own performance) and want you to do your best. Counter your "catastrophic" thinking by considering, "What's the worst thing that can happen?" and follow with affirmations: "I am well prepared. I am relaxed. I am comfortable talking with others. The audience is on my side."

4. **Use stress-reduction techniques.** Relax your muscles by tensing and then quickly releasing them. Do head rolls. Put your shoulders way up and then drop them. Take deep breaths and concentrate on expanding your stomach with each breath and exhaling fully. Don't rush right into your speech. Take several slow, deep breaths before going up to speak. Relax and smile.

If your anxiety is severe and prevents you from succeeding, see the learning center or counseling center for individualized tips. Complete **Personal Evaluation Notebook 10.3** to determine how you handle stage fright and writer's block.

Personal Evaluation Notebook 10.3

Controlling Stage Fright and Writer's Block

A. Use your critical thinking skills to answer the following questions. Be prepared to discuss your answers in your study team.

1. Describe your typical physical reaction to giving a speech.

 ____

 ____

2. What has helped you control stage fright?

 ____

 ____

3. Describe the processes of writing that are easiest for you and those that are hardest.

 ____

 ____

B. Read the following common reasons and excuses that some students give for not writing effective speeches. Use creative problem solving to list strategies for overcoming these barriers.

REASONS/EXCUSES

1. I experience panic and anxiety before I write or give speeches.
 Strategy: ____

 ____

2. I can't decide on a topic.
 Strategy: ____

 ____

3. I don't know how to research.
 Strategy: ____

 ____

4. I procrastinate until the last minute.
 Strategy: ____

 ____

5. I don't know what my instructor wants.
 Strategy: ____

 ____

(continued)

Personal Evaluation Notebook 10.3

Controlling Stage Fright and Writer's Block   *(concluded)*

6. My mind goes blank when I start to write or give a speech.

Strategy: _____

_____

Now review your strategies and reflect on the trigger that can create a new habit. For example, let's take procrastination. It is easy to fall into the trap of putting off decisions because of irrational thinking that says, "There is a long time before the paper is due and everything will go according to plan." These beliefs trigger unrealistic expectations. In reality, there are always distractions and unplanned events that create a crisis unless planned for. Your new trigger is choosing a topic the day your paper is assigned. You create a project board and stick to the dates so that there is plenty of time to meet deadlines.

TAKING CHARGE

Summary

In this chapter, I learned to

- **Create a positive, open mindset.** I focus on growth, learning, and effort.

- **Become a more effective writer and speaker.** Being a good communicator is the most important skill I will ever acquire. Although public speaking can be stressful, I can learn to reduce my anxiety and become more successful if I prepare, organize, write, edit, and review my presentation carefully.

- **Prepare effectively.** When writing a paper or presentation, I first set a schedule. I carefully and thoughtfully choose my topic and do the preliminary reading and information gathering. I can then narrow my topic and write a thesis statement that clarifies what I plan to cover. I prepare a bibliography of references and original sources and take notes that support my topic.

- **Organize my writing plan.** I must organize my thoughts and research into a coherent outline. I continue to look for specific data that support my main points. I revise my outline as necessary as I consider the subtopics that support my main theme. I include interesting and supportive examples, definitions, quotations, and statistics.

- **Write a draft of my paper or presentation.** After finishing the preliminary research and outline, I prepare a draft, writing freely and with momentum. My draft includes an introduction, the main body, and a conclusion. The introduction clearly states the purpose or theme, captures attention, and defines terms. The main body includes the subtopics that support the main theme, as well as visual aids. The conclusion ties the important points together and supports the overall theme of the presentation.

- **Revise and edit my paper or presentation.** I revise my draft and make sure the overall theme and supporting points are clear and correct. I correct spelling and grammatical mistakes and review transitions and sentence structure. I read it out loud to make sure the writing is varied and interesting. I verify that I have accurately prepared the bibliography. I ask my instructor and study team to review my paper. I then finalize my paper, number the pages, and add a title page if required.

- **Review and assess my paper or presentation.** After a final check of my paper, I make a copy for my Career Development Portfolio. I submit it on time, go over my graded results, and ask my instructor for tips for improvement.

- **Use the library and Internet for research.** The library provides a wealth of resources, and reference librarians can assist in my search. The Internet is the world's largest information network, providing access to a myriad of resources, including databases.

- **Incorporate new strategies.** When I speak in public, it's important for me to be prepared, establish eye contact with my audience, develop visual aids, and prepare simple notes or cues to prompt myself. I avoid unnecessary words and fillers, and I connect with my audience. Rehearsing is key to a successful presentation.

Performance Strategies

Following are the top 10 strategies for writing papers and giving speeches:

- Determine your purpose and set a schedule.
- Choose and narrow your topic.
- Read and research. Prepare a bibliography.
- Organize information into an outline.
- Write a draft.
- Refine your purpose and rewrite the draft.
- Edit and proof.
- Use your study team to practice and review.
- Revise and polish.
- Practice. Practice. Practice.

Tech for Success

- **Visual aids.** As many of your instructors do, you will want to enhance your presentations with visual aids, such as handouts and PowerPoint presentations. Many employers do not provide training for presentation software but knowing how to incorporate them into business meetings and presentations is often expected. Thus, learning at least the basics of PowerPoint or a similar program will be a valuable skill you can use both in school and on the job.

- **Spell-check, spell-check, spell-check.** As e-mail has replaced the traditional memo, it's much easier to send out correspondence quickly to a group of people. However, it's not uncommon to receive important e-mails that are riddled with typos, grammatical mistakes, and texting jargon. Get in the habit of using the spell-check function before you send e-mails or any documents. The few seconds it takes to check your outgoing correspondence can save you from unnecessary embarrassment.

Endnotes

[1] Mitford, Jessica. *The American Way of Death*. New York: Simon & Schuster, 1963.

[2] Daniel J. Siegel, *Brainstorm: The Power and Purpose of the Teenage Brain* (New York: Penguin Random House, 2015).

[3] Karen K. Dwyer and Marlina M. Davidson, "Is Public Speaking Really More Feared Than Death?" *Communication Research Reports*, April–June 2012.

Study Team Notes

Answers to **Personal Evaluation Notebook 9.2**:

1. Yes. Using someone else's ideas and presenting them as your own—whether from a written or a verbal source—is considered plagiarism unless credit is given to the original source.

2. Yes. Even though the source is cited, a significant amount of material has been used and is being presented as original work. The ideas can still be included in your work (as long as the source is cited), but the material should be revised in your own words.

3. No. However, the paper should be adapted and reworked in your own words to the specific class. Each college has different rules about submitting the same paper multiple times. Check with your professor.

Career *in* Focus

sturti/Getty Images

Lori Benson
HUMAN RESOURCES DIRECTOR

Related Majors: Human Resources, Personnel Administration, Labor Relations

Communication Skills

Lori Benson is the human resources director for a small advertising firm. Lori is her company's only human resources employee. Besides recruiting and interviewing potential employees, Lori also develops personnel programs and policies. She serves as her company's employee benefits manager by handling health insurance and pension plans. Lori also provides training in orientation sessions for new employees and instructs classes that help supervisors improve their interpersonal skills.

Possessing excellent communication skills is essential for Lori's job. To recruit potential employees, Lori contacts local colleges to attract recent graduates and places ads on online job search sites. In addition, Lori often sends e-mails to the employees at her company to notify them about new policies and benefits. This kind of writing must be clear, accurate, and brief. She usually asks the CEO to review the ads and press releases sent to the media.

Lori does research to find out what programs and policies other companies are offering. She uses public speaking strategies when preparing for training and other classes. First she makes notes and then writes prompts to help her remember what she wants to say. Lori practices her presentation several times and reviews her notes before each class. She keeps her notes on file for the next time she gives a class on the same subject.

CRITICAL THINKING How does Lori incorporate the communication skills she learned in college into the workplace?

Peak Performer Profile

Toni Morrison

Her books have been described as having "the luster of poetry" illuminating American reality. However, one reader once commented to the late acclaimed novelist Toni Morrison that her books were difficult to read. Morrison responded, "They're difficult to write." The process, Morrison sums up, "is not [always] a question of inspiration. It's a question of very hard, very sustained work."

An ethnically rich background helped provide Morrison's inspiration. The second of four children, she was born Chloe Anthony Wofford in a small Ohio steel town in 1931 during the Great Depression. The family's financial struggle was offset by a home strengthened by multiple generations and traditional ties. Storytelling was an important part of the family scene and black tradition.

In the late 1940s, Morrison headed to the East Coast. After earning a bachelor's degree in English from Howard University and a master's degree from Cornell University, she was still years away from literary recognition. While working as an editor at Random House in New York City, she began her writing career in earnest, and in 1970 her first novel, *The Bluest Eye,* was published.

Since then, Morrison has produced a body of work described as standing "among the 20th century's richest depictions of Black life and the legacy of slavery." In 1987, she won the Pulitzer Prize for her fifth novel, *Beloved.* Based on a true incident that took place in 1851, this novel has been read by millions. Then, in 1993, Morrison was awarded the Nobel Prize in Literature. She is the first black woman and only the eighth woman to receive this supreme honor.

Through Morrison's writing skills and self-expression, she has provided insight into American cultural heritage and the human condition.

PERFORMANCE THINKING The novel *Beloved* is dedicated to "Sixty Million and more." What is Morrison trying to express?

CHECK IT OUT "Toni Morrison's novels invite the reader to partake at many levels, and at varying degrees of complexity. Still, the most enduring impression they leave is of empathy, compassion with one's fellow human beings," said Professor Sture Allén as he presented Toni Morrison with the Nobel Prize for Literature for 1993. At **www.nobelprize.org**, select "Nobel Prizes" and then choose the Literature section to read about the many laureates who have received this highest honor. You can also listen to acceptance speeches and Nobel lectures, including Morrison's eloquent prose, "We die. That may be the meaning of life. But we do language. That may be the measure of our lives."

Starting Today

At least one strategy I learned in this chapter that I plan to try right away is

_____

_____

_____

What changes must I make in order for this strategy to be most effective?

_____

_____

_____

Review Questions

Based on what you have learned in this chapter, write your answers to the following questions:

1. What is the one basic skill taught in college that Peter Drucker feels is the most valuable for a future employee to know?

_____

_____

2. How should you establish a schedule to research and write a paper?

_____

_____

3. What are three questions to ask when evaluating information on the Internet?

_____

_____

4. Describe four strategies you can use to overcome writer's block.

_____

_____

5. What are five public speaking strategies?

_____

_____

Learning Communication Skills

In the Classroom

Josh Miller is a finance student at a business college. He likes numbers and feels comfortable with order, structure, and right-or-wrong answers. As part of the graduation requirements, all students must take classes in speech and writing. Josh becomes nervous about writing reports or giving speeches and doesn't see the connection between the required class and his finance studies. One of Josh's biggest stumbling blocks is thinking of topics. He experiences writer's block and generally delays any project until the last possible minute.

Shutterstock

1. What strategies in this chapter would help Josh think of topics and meet his deadlines?

_____

_____

2. What would you suggest to help him see the value of speaking and writing well?

_____

_____

In the Workplace

Josh has recently been promoted to regional manager for an investment firm. He feels very secure with the finance part of his job but pressured by new promotion requirements. He will need to present bimonthly speeches to top management, run daily meetings, and write dozens of reports. He must also give motivational seminars at least twice a year to his department heads. Josh wants to improve his writing skills and make his presentations clear, concise, and motivational.

3. What suggestions would you give Josh to help make his presentations more professional and interesting?

_____

_____

4. What strategies could he use to improve his writing?

_____

_____

Applying the ABC Method of Self-Management

In the **Journal Entry**, you were asked to describe a time when you felt anxious in a speaking assignment or leading a discussion. How would having a positive mindset help you succeed?

Apply the ABC Method of self-management and write a script.

_____

_____

_____

A = Acknowledge: Accept reality and pay attention to your emotions.

_____

_____

_____

B = Breathe: Take a deep breath to calm down and feel beloved.

_____

_____

_____

C = Choose: Knowing you have many options, choose the most appropriate for the situation and that will result in positive long-term consequences.

_____

_____

_____

Sample Script: Even though I'm feeling anxious and fearful, I love and accept myself and want to grow and learn. I practice deep breathing and see myself as calm, centered, and relaxed as I give my speech. I put this situation in perspective and resist dropping the course or skipping class. Instead, I choose to practice giving my ideas in a clear, concise, and confident manner. I go to the learning center for tips and talk with my professor. I know that I can learn to control stage fright by being well-prepared and practicing in the actual classroom. I'm grateful that I have a chance to learn this valuable skill which will help me in my career and in all aspects of my life.

Practice Paraphrasing

Because it's so easy to cut and paste material from the Internet, it's also too easy to pick up someone else's work and use it as your own. It's essential to paraphrase (and cite) material originally developed by others.

Read the following excerpt and then attempt to rewrite in your own words what the author has said:

Are you among the millions of Americans who take vitamin supplements? If your answer is "yes," why do you use them? Many people take multiple vitamin/mineral supplements as an "insurance policy" in case their diets are not nutritionally adequate. Other people use specific vitamin supplements because they think this practice will result in optimal health. Vitamin supplements are effective for treating people with specific vitamin deficiency diseases, metabolic defects that increase vitamin requirements, and a few other medical conditions. However, scientific evidence generally does not support claims that megadoses of vitamins can prevent or treat everything from gray hair to lung cancer.

(Source: Wendy J. Schiff: *Nutrition for Healthy Living,* 2009, McGraw-Hill.)

Now, write the essence of what the author has said:

_____

_____

_____

_____

_____

_____

_____

_____

_____

_____

_____

_____

_____

_____

_____

_____

_____

_____

_____

_____

Your Writing and Speaking Skills

Looking Back

1. Recall any activities and events through which you learned to write and speak. Jot down examples of classes, presentations, essays, journals, and papers.

   _____

   _____

2. What are your strengths in writing and speaking?

   _____

   _____

3. What would you like to improve?

   _____

   _____

4. What are your feelings about writing and speaking?

   _____

   _____

Looking Forward

5. How can you demonstrate to employers that you have effective writing and speaking skills?

   _____

   _____

6. Include in your portfolio samples of speeches you have given. List the titles on the following lines.

   _____

   _____

7. Include in your portfolio samples of your writing. List the titles.

   _____

   _____

8. Include in your portfolio samples of your research. List the titles.

   _____

   _____

Add this page to your Career Development Portfolio.

Become a Critical Thinker and Creative Problem Solver

11

LEARNING OUTCOMES

In this chapter, you will learn to

11-1 Identify the essentials of critical thinking

11-2 Explain the problem-solving process

11-3 Identify critical thinking and problem-solving strategies

11-4 Describe common fallacies and errors in judgment

11-5 Explain the importance of creativity in problem solving

11-6 Identify problem-solving strategies for mathematics and science

11-7 Identify ways to enable creativity

SELF-MANAGEMENT

I dropped a class, thinking I could take it next semester, but it's offered just once a year, so I won't graduate when I had planned to. I didn't realize one decision could have such an impact. What was I thinking? I'm feeling embarrassed, sad, and frustrated.

Larry Washburn/Getty Images

Have you ever made a decision without thinking through all the consequences? How does your attitude affect your thinking and creativity? In this chapter, you will learn to use your critical thinking and creative problem-solving skills and learn strategies for making sound decisions in all areas of life.

JOURNAL ENTRY In **Worksheet 11.1** think of a decision you made that has cost you a lot of time, money, or stress. How would critical thinking and creative problem solving have helped you make better decisions? Practice applying the self-management method.

Problem solving is creating or identifying a potential answer or solution to a question or problem. **Decision making** is determining or selecting the best or most effective answer or solution. You have to make decisions to solve a problem; conversely, some problems occur because of a decision you made. For example, you may decide to smoke cigarettes; later, you face the problem of nicotine addiction, health problems, and a lot of your budget spent on cigarettes. In school, a decision not to study mathematics and science because they seem too difficult will close off the chance to choose certain majors and careers. *Many events in life do not just happen; they are the result of our choices and decisions.* We make decisions every day; even not deciding is making a decision. For example, if you avoid going to class, that shows you have decided the class is unimportant or not worth the time. You may have not formally dropped the class or not thought through the consequences, but the result of deciding not to go to class is an *F* grade.

In this chapter, you will learn to use critical thinking and creativity to help you solve problems and make effective and sound decisions. Mathematics and science will be discussed, as these are key areas that rely on your critical thinking and problem-solving skills. You will also learn to overcome math anxiety and develop a positive attitude toward problem solving. You will learn the power of resiliency.

Essential Critical Thinking Skills

As discussed in **Chapter 1**, *critical thinking is a logical, rational, systematic thought process necessary for understanding, analyzing, and evaluating information in order to solve a problem.* Peak performers use critical thinking to ask questions that lead to a deeper understanding of information. They also use creative thinking to find unexpected connections and create something new. In the 1956 text *Taxonomy of Educational Objectives,* Benjamin Bloom and his colleagues outlined a hierarchy of six critical thinking skills that college requires (from lowest to highest order): remembering, understanding, applying, analyzing, evaluating, and creating. (See **Figure 11.1**.)

Let's say you are taking a difficult political science class and want to give it your all. You're going to use the Bloom Taxonomy guide to help you ask questions and be a more creative and critical thinker. You know you can learn and grow with effort and practice.

1. **Remembering.** You know it is important to memorize, remember, and recall lists; identify facts; complete objective tests; and recognize terms and information. You keep up with your reading, take good class notes, and ask questions in the text and in class. You create flash cards of dates, events, and other key words and review right before bed. The major question at this level is: *Can you recall this information including key points, facts, names, dates, definitions, or events?*

2. **Understanding.** Your professor does not want you to just give back facts and terms, but to demonstrate that you understand and comprehend the material. You may be asked to state ideas in your own words, outline key ideas, and

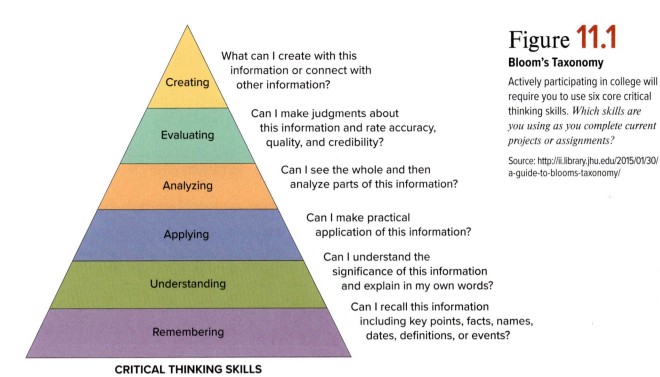

What can I create with this information or connect with other information?

Can I make judgments about this information and rate accuracy, quality, and credibility?

Can I see the whole and then analyze parts of this information?

Can I make practical application of this information?

Can I understand the significance of this information and explain in my own words?

Can I recall this information including key points, facts, names, dates, definitions, or events?

Creating

Evaluating

Analyzing

Applying

Understanding

Remembering

CRITICAL THINKING SKILLS

Figure **11.1**

Bloom's Taxonomy

Actively participating in college will require you to use six core critical thinking skills. *Which skills are you using as you complete current projects or assignments?*

Source: http://ii.library.jhu.edu/2015/01/30/a-guide-to-blooms-taxonomy/

translate an author's meaning. You begin by writing summaries to help you remember and understand the information. You discuss your understanding with others and listen to their views. The key question at this level is: *Can you understand the significance of this information and explain it?*

3. **Applying.** Apply what you've learned to a new situation. How do historical events apply to current events? You explore case studies about problem solving and provide examples to support your ideas. You can learn applications by applying ideas to your own life. For example, how can you apply political science concepts to issues in your community and state? You can discuss applications with your study group and ask how the information affects their lives. The questions to ask are: *Can you make practical applications of this information? What can you do with this information to produce results?*

4. **Analyzing.** Your professor will want you to have a general understanding of the information and to see the whole of an issue. You will also be asked to analyze and break apart ideas and relate them to other concepts, answer essay questions, identify assumptions, and analyze values. You will compare and contrast ideas or subjects, such as economic theories or how political issues affect many aspects of daily life. The question is: *Can you see the whole and then analyze parts of this information?*

5. **Evaluating.** You will be asked to use critical thinking to assess a position, form conclusions and judgments, list advantages and disadvantages of a project or an idea, and develop and use criteria for evaluating a decision. If you are doing research, you will be asked to review facts, relevancy, credentials, and accuracy of sources. You can also practice evaluation by evaluating speeches in class, evaluating group projects, and being open to suggestions from your study group and professors. The question to ask: *Can you make judgments about this information and rate accuracy, quality, and credibility?*

6. **Creating.** Synthesize and integrate ideas, build on other skills, identify connections and interconnections, create and defend a position, improve on an existing idea or design, and develop creative ideas and new perspectives. You may want to take an idea and create a small movement on campus or in your community. For example, you may create a recycling project, register eligible voters, or bring in a noted speaker. You might foster diversity and integrate socializing among minority students by creating a series of discussions or a potluck featuring foods and ideas from different cultures, or research ways that a community project affects other areas of the community. *What can you create with this information or connect with other information?*

To excel in school and make sound decisions at work and in life, you must move beyond simply remembering knowledge and be able to comprehend, apply, analyze, and evaluate questions and problems you are faced with and be able to synthesize and create new ideas and solutions. You need to understand what happens in your brain when you face setbacks.

Creative Problem-Solving Steps

Problem-Solving Steps

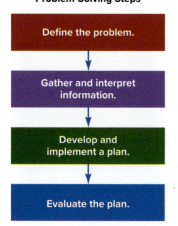

Define the problem.

Gather and interpret information.

Develop and implement a plan.

Evaluate the plan.

Problems are part of life, but when you acknowledge and face them squarely, even when it's uncomfortable, you can marshal all your creative energies and resources to solve them. You don't need to feel overwhelmed as you face confusing situations. Creativity and critical thinking can help you carefully think through any problem, gather information and create a plan, plot out your steps, and consider all possible outcomes and consequences. *You cannot always control your environment, but with a positive, growth mindset, you can create a calm, thoughtful, creative response.* The basic problem-solving process can be broken down into four major steps: (1) Define the problem, (2) gather and interpret information, (3) develop and implement a plan of action, and (4) evaluate the plan. You can weave creativity into each step. Ask, "How can I see this differently?"

1. **Define the problem.** Do you understand and can you clearly state the problem? What are you trying to find out? What is known and unknown? What is the situation, or context? What decision were you asked to make? Can you separate the problem into various parts? Can you see the big picture? Mindfulness can help you focus on the problem at hand without getting caught up in worrying about the future or locked into a plan. It can give you clarity and calm your anxious mind. Organize the problem or restate the decision or problem in your own words—for example, *"Should I go on a study abroad exchange or do an internship?"* How do the various programs compare in experience, location, and cost? Do some require another language or a specific major? What would the internship pay? What kind of work would I be doing? What are the chances that it might lead to a job upon graduation? *Creative problem solvers prepare and are able to manage their emotions.*

2. **Gather and interpret information.** Gather all the information you need to solve the problem and make a decision. *Pause* while you interpret these ideas. This will allow other possibilities and questions to emerge. You will be able to see the problem from different angles. From whom can you seek more advice (neighbors, parents, professors, advisor, alumni, business co-workers, professionals)? Are there other options, such as a paid internship or student

teaching abroad? When choosing a plan of action, consider all options and then narrow the list. *"I have gathered information and talked to professionals in the Career Center and Study Abroad Office and in my chosen field. Most career professionals have suggested that I go on an exchange as a way to broaden my worldview. I have listed pros and cons for each choice. I have included cost and expenses."* Eat a good dinner and get a good night's sleep. Let the ideas stew and incubate for a few days if possible or overnight at the least. Then come back to them fresh and renewed. *Creative problem solvers pause before they make a decision.*

3. **Develop and implement a plan of action.** How would this plan work? Eventually, you need to act on your decision and choose an appropriate strategy. Ask yourself what information would be helpful. Your intention to make this decision succeed is key. *"I found out I can apply for an internship for the following term. Because I can learn a second language and take valuable classes, I am going on the study abroad exchange and will do everything possible to make this experience valuable."* As your ideas and solutions rise and narrow, they are illuminated, which helps you make a sound decision. *Creative problem solvers allow insights to rise and perk.*

4. **Evaluate your plan.** Why is this plan better for you than other options? Is there one right answer? What consequences are likely if you choose this approach? Observe the consequences of this decision over time, and reflect on other options. *"I made valuable contacts and am learning so much from this experience. I'll do an internship when I return. This was the best choice for me at this time."* Reflect on the successes and failures you experienced. For example, the outcome may have been successful, but the process in making the decision could have been improved. What steps in the process would you do differently? What errors did you have to fix along the way? How would creativity have improved the process? Whom can you share this experience with and how can you persuade others to share your experience? Speak to first-year college students about the value of both exchange programs and internships and persuade them to expand their opportunities. See **Personal Evaluation Notebook 11.1** to explore the consequences of everyday decisions. *Creative problem solvers are able to communicate the value of their decision to others.*

Critical Thinking and Creative Problem-Solving Strategies

Creativity and critical thinking skills will help you make day-to-day decisions about relationships, courses to take, jobs to apply for, places to live, ideas for speeches and papers, and resolutions to conflicts. You can apply the following strategies to ensure you are fully using your creativity and critical thinking to enhance problem-solving capabilities:

1. **Create a positive, growth mindset.** Critical thinking requires a willingness and passion to explore, probe, question, learn, and search for answers and solutions. (See **Figure 11.2**.) Your attitude influences how you solve a problem or make a decision. Think of problems as puzzles to solve, rather than obstacles to avoid. Instead of delaying, making an instinctive decision, or looking for the one "right answer," *focus on growth and learning.* For example,

Personal Evaluation Notebook 11.1

Think It Through

Often we make decisions without considering the consequences. It may be because we're thinking only about the immediate result or benefit. Or maybe the decision seems so minor that the consequences are insignificant. However, a series of poor "small" decisions can lead to big problems later.

Exercise your decision-making and problem-solving skills by teaming up with classmates to consider decisions you make every day. For example, let's say you've missed a couple of classes lately. One person should state the problem or issue. Then go through the problem-solving steps, ask questions, explore possibilities, and use critical thinking to make a sound decision:

1. **Define the problem.**
   - I've missed three classes in the past 3 weeks.
   - Twice I overslept and one time I went home early for the weekend.
2. **Gather and interpret the information.**
   - The consequences for missing this class are getting a poor grade, or having to retake the class to bring up my GPA and to stay on track with my major classes.
   - If I drop the class, what could happen? Would I be able to take advance classes or graduate on time? Would my financial aid or eligibility be affected? Have I missed the deadline to drop a class without serious consequences?
   - If I keep missing the class, what could happen? I could be put on academic probation if I receive an F grade. The class may not be offered next semester, and my academic plan would be affected.
3. **Develop and implement a plan of action.**
   - What are some creative possibilities to help me get to class? For example, I will make a commitment, set two alarms, join a study group, see the professor about making up work, and make up assignments. I will make a college plan with my advisor so I can clearly see what classes and steps are necessary to graduate.
   - What is the best plan of action? It is clear that I should stay in class and become disciplined about attendance. I can turn this around by going to class every session, making up work, studying with a group, and getting a good grade. This will keep me on track for graduating on time.
4. **Evaluate the plan.**
   - What decision is best for my goals and priorities? I will stay in class, do well, and then take the next required class in my major. I realize that this just isn't a class but a necessary part of my long-term goals. I want to graduate and be successful in my career.
   - How will I ensure that this decision succeeds? I will go to every class, meet with my study team twice a week, keep up on assignments, meet with my advisor every week or so, and develop a relationship with my professor by meeting several times this term.

Come up with other situations you may encounter daily, such as relationship issues and spending decisions, and work through them using the problem-solving steps.

Copyright © 2023 McGraw-Hill Education

A Critical Thinker . . .

Admits a lack of information or understanding when necessary

Suspends judgment and tolerates ambiguity

Is curious and interested in seeking new solutions

Is open-minded and seeks opposing views

Clearly defines the criteria for analyzing ideas

Asks pertinent questions and assesses statements and arguments

Examines beliefs, assumptions, and opinions against facts

Figure **11.2**

Critical Thinking Qualities

Thinking critically is important for understanding and solving problems. *Do you apply any of the attributes of a critical thinker when you need to solve a problem?*

PhotoAlto/PunchStock

instead of avoiding taking a math or science course, choose to create curiosity, passion, and perseverance to stretch and grow. Complete **Personal Evaluation Notebook 11.2** to practice turning negatives into positives.

2. **Ask questions.** It's difficult to solve a problem without knowing all the facts and opinions—or at least as many as you can find out. **Peak Progress 11.1** offers tips for formulating effective questions. Ask often, "What's working and what's not working?" Take stock of all areas of your life and make positive changes. Sometimes it takes small changes to create big results. For example, "I'm feeling overwhelmed and scattered. What could I do to help this problem? I'm going to take a few minutes every night to get organized, go to bed a half hour earlier, wake up in time to walk to class, and pause a few times throughout the day to be mindful and meditate for a few minutes."

3. **Persistence pays off.** You won't solve every problem with your first effort; it requires effort, time, resiliency, and patience. What drives success is not genius, but hard work and perseverance. Creative problem solvers are not beaten by frustration but look for new ways to solve problems. Commit to overcome self-imposed limits. Grit pays off.

4. **Use creativity.** As we will explore later in this chapter, you should learn to think in new and fresh ways, look for interconnections, and brainstorm many solutions. Good problem solvers explore many alternatives and evaluate their strengths and weaknesses. We are all creative and can nurture our curiosity and sense of wonder at this amazing universe. Have the courage to try new things, explore new interests, and search for creative possibilities for living with more passion, growth, and learning.

Personal Evaluation Notebook 11.2

Using Critical Thinking to Solve Problems

Stating a problem clearly, exploring alternatives, reasoning logically, choosing the best alternative, creating an action plan, and evaluating your plan are all involved in making decisions and solving problems.

Look at the common reasons or excuses given by some students for not solving problems creatively or making sound decisions. Create strategies for overcoming these barriers.

1. I'm not a creative person.

   Strategy: _____

2. Facts can be misleading; I like to follow my gut instinct.

   Strategy: _____

3. I avoid conflict.

   Strategy: _____

4. I postpone making decisions.

   Strategy: _____

5. I worry that I'll make the wrong decision.

   Strategy: _____

Now, review your responses to these common excuses and add a few excuses of your own. Reflect on what you could do to change these excuses. What triggers can help you reshape your thoughts and behavior? For example, is there a certain pattern to the times you avoid conflict or making decisions? Are you tired or hungry? If you notice a problem at around 3:00 in the afternoon when your glucose level may be low, have an apple and piece of cheese and go for a short walk. Remember, critical thinkers know when they need to rest or eat before they can make sound decisions.

5. **Pay attention.** Creative people have the ability to see the big picture and pay attention to everything around them. Effective problem solvers also show concern for accuracy and for paying attention to details. They think about what could go wrong, recheck calculations, and look for errors. They gather all relevant information and proofread or ask questions. They are willing to listen to arguments, create and defend positions, and can distinguish among various points of view.

6. **See all sides of the issue.** Think critically about what you read, hear, and see in newspapers and on the Internet. As you read, question sources and viewpoints. For example, when you read an article about Social Security or tax cuts, ask yourself what biases politicians or special interest groups might have regarding these issues. Does the argument appeal to emotion rather than to logic? Talk to people who have different opinions or belong to a different political party. Really listen to their views, and ask them to explain their opinions and why they support certain issues.

Peak Progress

Asking Questions

"Why is the sky blue?" "Where do babies come from?" When we were children, our days were filled with endless questions, reflecting curiosity about the world around us. As adults, some of us have become reluctant and sometimes even nervous to ask for help or insightful answers. It's not that there are no questions left to ask—just the contrary. Attending college opens up the floodgates of new information to comprehend, process, apply, and question.

This reluctance can stem from possible embarrassment, as the information may have already been covered (and you were daydreaming, didn't read the assignment, didn't see the connections, etc.) and others will think you're behind for one reason or another. Or when simply talking with friends, you may think asking questions will seem like you are prying or are "nosey," or behind on the latest trends.

Whatever your reasons, you must overcome your reluctance and learn how to formulate questions. Most careers require asking questions and persistence in finding answers. A sales representative asks customers what their needs are and tries to fulfill those needs with his or her product. A competent physician asks patients questions about their medical history, symptoms, and reactions to medications. A patient who has critical thinking skills asks the physician questions as well.

Peak performers are critical and creative thinkers who ask a lot of questions. One of the most important questions to ask is, *"What's working and what's not working in my life?"* Look at your classes, your job, your relationships, your health, your energy, and your mood and ask the question, *"What small steps would create positive changes?"*

WHO CAN BEST ANSWER YOUR QUESTION?

Before asking a question, determine whom or what you should be consulting. Could the information be found more easily or quickly by looking it up online, in the library, or in another source? Is it a question more appropriate for your professor, advisor, or financial aid officer? Is there a local "expert" in this area? You may decide that in order to make a sound decision, you'll want to ask several people for advice. For example, before you choose a major, you might want to take an inventory test and seek advice from the career center, ask your advisor about required classes, and talk to key professors in specific departments and professionals in the field. Stay open

to suggestions. Do not discount ideas from unexpected sources. Creative ideas and inspiration can come from anyone, anywhere, at anytime. Be open.

WHAT TYPE OF QUESTION SHOULD YOU ASK?

State your question quickly and succinctly, and provide background information only if your question isn't clear. Based on the type of response you are looking for, there are several ways to formulate your question:

- **Closed question.** Use this type of question when you want either a yes/no answer or specific details—for example, "Which planet is closer to the sun—Earth or Mars?"
- **Fact-finding question.** This is aimed at getting information on a particular subject, usually when your core materials (such as the textbook or lecture) haven't provided the information—for example, "Which battle had the most casualties, and was that considered the turning point in the war?"
- **Follow-up question.** This question clarifies a point, gathers more information, or elicits an opinion—for example, "So, what side effects might I experience from this medication?"
- **Open-ended question.** Use this to invite discussion and various viewpoints or interpretations of an issue—for example, "What do you think about the ordinance to ban smoking in local restaurants?"
- **Feedback question.** Use this when you want someone to provide you with constructive criticism—for example, "What sections of my paper supported my main points effectively, and what sections needed more backup?"
- **Big questions.** Problems often exist right in front of your eyes, but you don't see them. The key to seeing clearer is to ask the big question, "What's working and what's not working?" Sometimes you need to step back and take a broad perspective view and ask other questions: "Does this choice get me closer to short-term goals or fit with my long-term goals and my life's purpose? Does it create other problems?"

WHEN SHOULD YOU ASK QUESTIONS?

Asking questions is the foundation for creative and critical thinking. Ask questions often to yourself and

(continued)

keep a list in a notebook. *Ask questions when you read your textbooks and jot them in the margin or in your notebook.* Each class will vary, so ask about preference. Most likely, your professor has guidelines for the class (such as saving questions for the last 10 minutes). If so, jot down your questions during the lecture so that you can return to them or add answers if the content is covered in the meantime. If you have a detailed question, you may want to see your professor or the speaker after class. Open-ended and feedback questions may be more appropriate outside a typical class discussion but can often provide the most thoughtful answers. Keep a list of questions for other situations. For example, you'll want to ask questions in your study group often and ask your advisor questions on deadlines and about your academic plan early in the semester and about possible majors and careers during your first year in college. Don't wait until your senior year to visit the career center. Remember, you don't have to have thought through your questions or an issue. Sometimes, you need to say, "I'm confused. Can you help me think this through?" Some people want their ideas and questions to be perfect before they share them with others. *It's fine to be vulnerable and simply take the risk involved with asking questions.* For example, "I'm uncomfortable about our discussions in our study group. I love hearing all about your personal lives, but could we do that later over soup and sandwiches during social time and get our work done during this study time? Does anyone else feel that we're being unproductive?"

7. **Use reasoning.** We are constantly trying to make sense of our world, so we make inferences to explain and interpret events. Check your inferences to see if they are sound, not based on assumptions, which often reflect your own experiences and biases. Ask yourself, "What makes me think this is true? Could I be wrong? Are there other possibilities?" Effective problem solvers do not jump to conclusions.

8. **Be rested and healthy.** We've talked about how important it is to take breaks and eat healthy. Research has shown that when you make too many decisions in too short of a time, you can create willpower fatigue. You may not realize that you're tired, but your decisions are not well thought out. Taking frequent breaks, getting enough sleep at night, drinking plenty of water, and eating a high-protein, healthy snack every few hours can keep your glucose level high and you'll be able to make better decisions. Remember, the best decision makers are people who know when they are not able to be critical thinkers because they're tired, hungry, or overwhelmed.

Inductive reasoning is generalizing from specific concepts to broad principles. Inductive reasoning can contain some errors such as coming to a conclusion too quickly. For example, you might have had a bad experience with a math class in high school and, based on that one experience, might reason inductively that all math classes are hard and boring. When you get into your college math class, you may discover that your conclusion was incorrect and that you actually like mathematics. In contrast, **deductive reasoning** is drawing conclusions based on going from the general to the specific. A classic example is: All men are mortal. Socrates is a man. Therefore, Socrates is mortal. However, there may be exceptions in some cases. For example, "Because all mathematics classes at this college must be taken for credit and this class is a math class, I must take it for credit." However, don't assume that the main premise is always true. In this example, there may be math labs, workshops, or special classes offered for no credit. Practice inductive versus deductive reasoning in **Personal Evaluation Notebook 11.3.**

Personal Evaluation Notebook 11.3

Inductive versus Deductive Reasoning

Practice creating inductive and deductive statements and assumptions that can influence decision making.

INDUCTIVE EXAMPLES

- No one should consider buying a car with a sunroof. Mine leaked every time it rained. (Hasty conclusion. One example does not offer enough evidence.)
- Nadia ended up in the hospital with food poisoning the day after the party. I'm sure that's why Kara said she was sick the next day, too. (This is an example of false cause. Just because something happened after the first event, doesn't mean that the first event caused the second event. Kara may have gotten the flu.)

_____

_____

_____

DEDUCTIVE EXAMPLES

- Everyone who attended the review session for the first test received an A. If I attend the next session, I'm bound to get an A. (You have a better chance if you attend the review session, but you may not get an A for a number of reasons, such as not having the same study skills or background as the other students).
- All the men in our family are over 6 feet tall. I'm sure my baby son will be as tall when he's an adult. (Likely, but genetics can be unpredictable.)

_____

_____

_____

Write a few more examples that you observe. Write a few examples of assumptions and how they influence your thinking. For example, I assume that professors don't want students coming to their office since they are very busy. I assume that the advising center will let me know if there is a deadline for dropping a class.

_____

_____

_____

Common Errors in Judgment

Some thoughts and beliefs are clearly irrational, with no evidence to support them. For example, if you believe that you are just not smart in math, you impose self-limiting beliefs. You may not become a mathematician, but that doesn't mean you can't pass a math class with effort and practice. Assess your thoughts and beliefs and hold fast to your goals. _To have grit means you stick with it and get up after_

Research has shown that college students experience a great deal of stress coping with demands and decisions, and one of them is the anxiety of choosing a major and career. During stressful times, it is important to take care of yourself, body and mind. Change your perspective and create curiosity and excitement about exploring various majors and careers with your advisor and career counselor.[1]

Brandon has really enjoyed his first semesters of college and has gotten good grades in the wide variety of classes he has taken. Now, at the end of his sophomore year, the pressure is on for him to choose a major and he finds it very stressful to be indecisive. Use creative and critical thinking tools to help Brandon.

- Which school resources are available to find out more about selecting a major?
- What questions should he ask his advisor or career counselor?
- Help Brandon walk through the problem-solving process to figure out which major best suits him. What steps should he set for meeting his goals?

THINK
CREATIVELY AND CRITICALLY

you fall down. Clarify your thinking and apply the ABC Method of Self-Management to dispel myths and irrational thoughts.

Here are some common errors in judgment or faulty thinking that interfere with effective critical thinking:

- *Stereotypes* are judgments held by a person or group about the members of another group—for example, "All instructors are absentminded intellectuals." Learn to see individual differences between people.

- *All-or-nothing thinking* means seeing events or people in black or white, such as turning a single negative event into a pattern of defeat: "If I don't get an *A* in this class, I'm a total failure." Be careful about using the terms *always* and *never*.

- *Snap judgments* are decisions made before gathering all the necessary information or facts. An example is concluding that someone doesn't like you because of one comment or because of a comment made by someone else. Instead, find out the reason for the comment. Perhaps you misinterpreted the meaning.

- *Unwarranted assumptions* are beliefs and ideas you assume are true in different situations. For example, your business instructor allows papers to be turned in late, so you assume that your biology instructor will allow the same.

- *Projection* is the tendency to attribute to others some of your own traits in an attempt to justify your own faulty judgments or actions—for example, "It's OK if I cheat because everyone else is cheating."

- *Sweeping generalizations* apply one experience to a whole group or issue. For example, if research has been conducted using college students as subjects, you cannot generalize the results to the overall work population.

- The *halo effect* is the tendency to label a person good at many things based on one or two qualities or actions. For example, Serena sits in the front row, attends every class, and gets good grades on papers. Based on this observation, you decide she is smart, organized, and a great student in all her classes. First impressions are important in the halo effect and are difficult to change. You can make this work for you. Suppose you start out the semester by giving it your all; you go to every class, establish a relationship with the instructor, participate in class, and work hard. Later in the semester, you may need to miss a class or ask to take an exam early. Your instructor has already formed a positive opinion of you as a good student and may be understanding.

- *Negative labeling* is focusing on and identifying with shortcomings, either yours or others'. Instead of saying, "I made a mistake when I quit going to my math study group," you tell yourself, "I'm a loser." You may also pick a single negative trait or detail and focus on it exclusively. You discount positive qualities or accomplishments: "I've lost my keys again. I am so disorganized. Yes, I did organize a successful club fund-raiser, but that doesn't count."

Creative Problem Solving

Creativity is not a fixed trait that is inherent in a few people. You don't have to be a poet, artist, writer, musician, or inventor to be a creative person. In fact, as the global economy gets more competitive, creativity will become more and more important to distinguish yourself. Creativity is a decision to live life with curiosity and wonder. It is finding an interest, hobby, pursuit, or way of engaging in life that unfolds a certain beauty and passion within you. This mindset amplifies life, expands the heart, and embraces the mystery of the unknown. Creativity is living large. Creative people think differently by shifting their perspective and breaking through limits and traditional thinking to reach that "aha!" experience. For example, Albert Einstein used many unusual approaches and "riddles" that revolutionized scientific thought. (Several websites include "Einstein's Riddle." Locate one and test yourself to see if you can answer "who owns the fish?")

Create a positive, open mindset that focuses on growth and effort. With practice, you can bring forth the talent, ideas, dreams, and passion that are within you. This not only takes courage and effort, but the discipline and the willingness to be vulnerable and criticized. Every creative person has been there. Get beyond the fear of rejection and look ahead to creating. Who knows what sorts of art projects, inventions, new ideas, writing, and speaking projects await you. Before you know it, you'll be writing your memoir and writing about a creative life lived with passion, wonder, and curiosity. So you might as well get going. Pick yourself up when you fall down. Invest day after day in practice. Grit works!

Use creativity to explore alternatives, look for relationships among different items, and develop imaginative ideas and solutions. Try the following strategies:

1. **Expect to be creative.** You were born creative, so tune into the creative spark within you, believe in yourself and with courage and discipline, and act with confidence. As the novelist, Sylvia Plath said, "The worst enemy to creativity is self-doubt."

   - I am a creative and resourceful person. Creative ideas flow to me.
   - I am open to the many imaginative and unusual ideas that come to me when I play, work, walk in nature, and just relax.
   - I am willing to put in effort and time to achieve and I act on many of these ideas.
   - I am flexible and pay attention. I observe and listen to hunches.
   - I ask lots of questions and am curious. I am filled with a sense of wonder.

2. **Challenge the rules.** A fixed negative mindset restricts you from trying new approaches to problem solving. Often, there is more than one solution, so be open-minded, positive, and flexible. *Focus on growth and learning.* List many alternatives and imagine the likely consequences of each. Empty your mind of the "right" way of looking at problems and strive to see situations in a fresh, optimistic way. How often have you told yourself you must follow certain rules and perform tasks a certain way? If you want to be creative, try new approaches, look at things in a new order, break the pattern, and challenge the rules. Practice a different approach by completing the Nine-Dot Exercise in **Personal Evaluation Notebook 11.4**. This exercise is a good reminder of how we make decisions based on assumptions and create barriers where none exist.

3. **Use games, puzzles, and humor.** Have fun! Rethinking an assignment as a puzzle, challenge, or game instead of a difficult problem opens your mind

Personal Evaluation Notebook 11.4

Nine-Dot Exercise

Connect the following nine dots by drawing only four (or fewer) straight lines without lifting the pencil from the paper. Do not retrace any lines. The solution is in the Taking Charge section.

and encourages your creative side. Life is full of absurdities and wonder. Laugh every day and see the humor in everyday events. Creative people embrace complexity and ambiguity. *Creative people often get fresh ideas while having fun engaging in an unrelated activity such as a game, hobby, or new interests.* When your defenses are down, your brain is relaxed and your subconscious is alive; creative thoughts can flow. An interesting book about creative thinking techniques is *Thinkertoys,* by Michael Michalko. Also try these apps: Peak, Brainwave, and other brain games.

4. **Brainstorm.** Brainstorming is a common strategy for freeing the imagination and generating ideas. Brainstorming encourages the mind to explore without judging the merit of new ideas. In fact, even silly ideas can lead to truly inventive ideas. One study group started joking about possible speech topics, and new ideas came from all directions. The key is to be free to express ideas and not be judgmental or critical. Another fun way to brainstorm is to divide the group into people who tend to be rational thinkers and ask them to come up with unconventional, fresh, impractical, and imaginative ideas. Ask intuitive thinkers to focus on useful, practical, logical, and practical ideas. Then bring the groups back and combine ideas and see what happens.

5. **Integrate the whole brain.** *You will be more effective and well-rounded if you integrate these various skills and ways to think and relate.* If you tend to be logical and analytical try fantasy, daydreaming, novelty, associations, and imagination to loosen up and enhance your thinking. If you tend to be more intuitive and inventive and to see the big picture, practice paying attention to details; using linear, practical, and useful solutions; and being disciplined and focused. Acknowledge how you normally think and respond to problems, assess if your personality style clouds or limits your thinking, and determine

how to expand your abilities. For example, as an introvert, you may be more comfortable brainstorming or working alone, but working with others occasionally can stretch your thinking. There are times and situations where you need to be an extrovert and other times when you need to tune into inner experiences and enjoy solitude. *Peak performers use their whole brain.* Focus on growth, learning, and curiosity.

6. **Be grateful.** *The simple act of living with gratitude can create a huge mind shift and allow you to see possibilities. With an open, flexible mindset you are open to growth and learning and other viewpoints.* You are also open to your inner life and aware of your strengths, shadows, beliefs, and assumptions. It is difficult to see another frame of reference if your mindset is fixed, negative, envious, and resentful. The exercise in **Personal Evaluation Notebook 11.5** is an "aha" exercise. It is exciting to watch people see the other picture. Perceptual exercises of this kind demonstrate that you see what you focus on; but when you reframe, a whole new image or viewpoint can appear. You are conditioned to see certain things, depending on your beliefs and attitudes. Rather than seeing facts, you may see your interpretation of reality. Perceptual distortion can influence how you solve problems and make decisions. For example, John was told that his Spanish instructor was aloof and boring, but he decided not to let that information influence his experience and was open and flexible. He sat in front, became engaged, and was grateful for the knowledge of this instructor. He chose to focus on the good. *Peak performers live with gratitude.*

7. **Embrace diversity and change.** Spend time with people who are different from you and develop empathy and sensitivity to different viewpoints and experiences. Really listen to opposing viewpoints. *Diversity really is key for creativity.* Broaden your experiences by exploring new music and movies; traveling; attending plays, sports, and classes; and reading a variety of books. Occasionally break away from your daily routine and take time to really explore and observe around you and within you. Be mindful. Look at unexpected events as a chance to retreat from constant activity and hurried thoughts. What new hobby or skill have you wanted to try? If you procrastinate, set a firm deadline to complete a specific project. If you are running frantically, take time to review your life's goals and set new priorities. If you feel shy and inhibited, clear some time to socialize and meet new people. Try a different route to work or school. Use your other hand to brush your teeth, try interesting new foods, or go to an event that is outside your comfort zone. *In other words, shake it up! Stretch yourself.*

8. **Collect ideas.** You may jot down quotes, notes, thoughts, and lots of innovative ideas on scraps of paper or put items in a shoebox. You may want to keep a journal where you jot down ideas, interesting quotes, designs, questions, words, dreams, and thoughts. Collect stories of creative people and what they do that is unique. Collect interesting questions and share them with others. Write in your journal about risks you take and what you have learned from the experience. Doodle and sketch. Use a file, online vision board, or save links to inspiring photos, cartoons, articles, pictures, or online content. These ideas may trigger other ideas by association. *Hang out with creative people who appreciate the offbeat and unusual, love to laugh, and see life with a sense of curiosity, wonder, and joy.*

Personal Evaluation Notebook   11.5

Mindsets

Look at the following figure. Do you see a poised young woman or an old woman with a hooked nose?

I see a(n) _____

Chronicle of World History/Alamy Stock Photo

If you saw the young woman first, it is very hard to see the old woman. If you saw the old woman first, it is just as hard to see the young woman. Why is that true?

Source: A. Maslow, "Emotional Blocks to Creativity," in *A Sourcebook for Creative Thinking*, eds. S. J. Parnes and H. F. Harding (New York: Scribner, 1962).

9. **Relax and trust.** *The biggest barrier to creativity is fear.* New ideas are fragile and you might feel vulnerable and exposed when suggesting or trying a new idea. Don't worry about being criticized; having a perfect, well-thought-out idea; or obsessing about a certain outcome. Creativity is messy. Jump in and trust it will all come out fine. Mindfulness, deep breathing, and meditation can help you become more relaxed. It takes courage, faith, focus, and trust to bring forth that creative force. *Trust is the best tool for driving out fear.* Trust that you have the necessary ability to create and the discipline to invest hours of devotion to your pursuit. Trust the creative process and that others will help you along the way. Relax. Often solutions come when you allow frustration to float away. Trust that the universe is full of ideas and be open to them or, as Rumi said, "Live life as if everything is rigged in your favor."

10. **Play.** It takes focus and intense attention to tap into creativity and bring forth new ideas and hours of devotion to bring a creative project to life. It also takes balance between work and play, isolation and socializing, and allowing yourself to have fun, relax, daydream, and renew your energy. Mindfulness isn't just about focusing on problems, but also allowing the unexpected. Many serendipitous discoveries have been made by accident. Albert Einstein came up with his best ideas while playing. Thomas Edison took frequent naps to balance his intense concentration. When rested, he was aware of new insights. Harriet Beecher Stowe had to juggle raising children and writing Uncle Tom's Cabin by writing in small chunks of time. Nina Simone said determination was a prerequisite for sustained creative work. *The key is balance and being open and alert to new ideas and possibilities.*

11. **Evaluate.** Creativity and critical thinking go hand-in-hand. Go through each step and examine your work. Turn a problem upside down. Go through the back door and work a problem backward. *Look at a problem before bed and let it rest overnight.* Jot down ideas as soon as you wake up. Your brain never sleeps and many people insist that they have woken to insightful and creative ideas. Examine relationships between facts and find ways to combine, connect, and relate what seems opposite or unrelated. Research has shown that reflection and self-awareness are very important for processing new ideas and result in balancing impulsiveness with critical thinking for better long-term results.[2] Look at what you know and don't know, and examine your hypotheses. Can you prove that each step is correct? Examine the solution carefully. Can you obtain the solution differently? Investigate the connections of the problem. What formulas did you use? Can you use the same method for other problems? Talk about problems with your study team, and see if there are other creative ways to solve them. Can you communicate your problem and ideas clearly to others? Can you persuade them? *Creative ideas almost always need refinement and follow-through.* Practice your decision-making skills by working through the case scenario in **Personal Evaluation Notebook 11.6**.

12. **Support, acknowledge, and reward creativity.** Surround yourself with creative people from all walks of life who challenge you to be your best. Get excited about new ideas and approaches, and acknowledge and reward yourself and others for creative ideas. Get involved with projects that encourage you to explore and be creative. How often do you put your creative ideas into action? Is there anything you want to change but keep putting it off? See people as supportive instead of critics. For example, if you're giving a speech in class, think of your professor and classmates as encouraging you to push boundaries and be successful. Think of them as cheerleaders. Support courage and creativity in others. Be open-minded and encourage new views. *Nothing shuts down creativity as concretely as being convinced you're right and shutting down other viewpoints.*

13. **Allow failure.** Failure doesn't need to strike fear in your heart. If you don't fail occasionally, you are not risking anything. Mistakes are stepping stones to growth and creativity. *Fear of failure undermines the creative process by forcing us to play it safe. Eliminate the fear and shame of failure experienced in earlier years, and learn to admit mistakes.* Ask yourself, "What did I learn from this mistake? How can I handle the same type of situation the next time? How can I prepare for a situation like this the next time? How can I balance impulsiveness with critical thinking?" Creative people aren't afraid to look foolish at times, generate unusual ideas, be nonconformists, or take risks. It takes courage to be creative. Create a climate in your life for mistakes.

> **❝ You can't use up creativity. The more you use, the more you have. ❞**
>
> **MAYA ANGELOU,**
> *Author*

CHAPTER 11 Become a Critical Thinker and Creative Problem Solver **353**

Personal Evaluation Notebook 11.6

Decision-Making Application

Use critical thinking and creative problem-solving skills to evaluate the following case scenario:

I am currently attending a career school and will soon earn my associate's degree in computer-aided design. Once I obtain my degree, should I continue my education or look for a full-time job? My long-term goal is to be an architect. My spouse and I have been married for 3 years, and we want to start a family soon.

- **Define the problem.** "Should I continue my education or get a job?"
- **Gather and interpret information.** Ask questions such as these: "What are the advantages and disadvantages? With whom should I talk (advisor, instructors, family members, alumni, and career professionals)?"
- **Develop and implement a plan of action.**

   1. *List the pros and cons for each choice:* "What are the factors I should consider, such as cost, opportunities, and time?"

Consider the following pros and cons for each solution, and list additional reasons that you think should be considered.

Solution: *Continue education at a local state university*

Pros	Cons
I'll get a better job with a 4-year degree.	I'll have to take out more student loans.
I'm enjoying school and the learning process.	I want to put my skills into practice in the job.
I'll meet new, diverse friends and contacts.	A lot of my time at home will be devoted to studying.

Solution: *Get a job*

Pros	Cons
I can make more money than I am now and start paying off debts.	The opportunities would be better with a 4-year degree.
We can start a family.	It will take longer to become an architect.
I get to put my skills to work.	Once I start working full-time, it may be hard to go back to school.

Now you can go through the pros and cons and see which column has the most value. See a professional in the career or counseling center and walk through your list. Ask for advice and then, weighing all the information, make your decision.

(continued)

Personal Evaluation Notebook 11.6

Decision-Making Application *(concluded)*

2. *Choose what you believe is the best solution:* "I have decided to get a job."

- **Evaluate the plan.** "My choice is reasonable and makes sense for me now in my situation. I won't have to work such long hours and juggle school and work, and I can pay back loans and save money. We can start our family. I can review my long-term goal and determine another way to achieve it."

Would you arrive at the same decision? What is your main reason?

_____

_____

Now set up a problem or decision you are facing, and follow the same steps.

- Problem

    _____

    _____

- Where can I get help or information?

    _____

    _____

POSSIBLE SOLUTIONS AND PROS AND CONS

Solution 1: _____

_____

	Pros	Cons
1.	_____	_____
2.	_____	_____
3.	_____	_____

Solution 2: _____

_____

	Pros	Cons
1.	_____	_____
2.	_____	_____
3.	_____	_____

SOLUTION CHOSEN AND WHY

_____

_____

14. **Be disciplined and persistent.** *Effort and plain hard work are more important than talent.* Problem solving requires discipline and focused effort. Invest every day in challenging practice. Be persistent. Create a work space that *triggers* the *routine* of practicing consistently. The *reward* is the discipline that comes out of this routine and the feeling of satisfaction when you complete projects. **Peak Progress 11.2** provides a handy checklist to help you think of new ways to be persistent and create grit.

15. **Be creative for job success.** Research has shown that employers want creative thinking in the workplace.[3] Every tip that has been presented in this chapter can be used to help you thrive and come up with new ideas for services, procedures, and customer satisfaction in any career you choose. Take each of these strategies as a starting point for prompting a deeper inquiry about how they can be related to the world of work. How can art and technology be integrated together? How can creativity help with communication problems? How can being mindful and focused help increase your imagination? Talk with co-workers and other professionals and ask them how important creativity has been in their career. Like any skill, the more you practice, the better you'll be at creativity. See college as a chance to practice your creativity skills so that this mindset creates daily habits that are as natural as breathing.

Math and Science Applications

Critical thinking and creative problem solving are essential for success in mathematics, science, and computer science courses—information that is also vital for

---

Peak Progress   11.2
Creative Ideas Checklist

Use this checklist of questions to challenge your usual thought patterns and explore alternative approaches. You can put each category on a separate card.

- What other idea does this situation suggest?
- How can I modify?
- What can I subtract? Can I take it apart?
- What can I streamline?
- What can I rearrange?
- Can I transfer?
- Can I combine or blend?
- What are other uses if modified?
- Have I written it out?
- Have I paused and allowed the idea to rest?
- Have I returned to it with a new perspective?
- Can I use another approach?
- Can I interchange components?
- Are there any opposites?

- What are the positives and negatives?
- Have I used a mind map, model, diagram, list, or chart?
- Have I used a drawing or picture?
- Have I acted it out?
- Have I talked it out?
- Have I tried it?
- Should I sleep on it?
- Have I persuaded others with it?
- List some of your own suggestions for creative problem solving:

  _____

  _____

  _____

  _____

---

job and life success. Studying mathematics and science develops such everyday skills as interpreting interest rates on credit cards, calculating your tuition, managing your personal finances, computing your GPA, and understanding how your body and the world around you work. Basic arithmetic can help you figure out a tip at a restaurant, algebra can help you compute the interest on a loan, basic probability can help you determine the chance that a given event will occur, and statistics can help you collect, analyze, and interpret data.

Problem-Solving Strategies for Math and Science

The basic problem-solving strategies discussed earlier in this chapter, in the Critical Thinking and Creative Problem-Solving Strategies section, also apply to math and science. Additional strategies, many of which will get you physically involved, integrate all learning styles and make learning active and personal. Included are sample problems to help you practice these strategies.

1. **Make a model or diagram.** Physical models, objects, diagrams, and drawings can help organize information and can help you visualize problem situations. Use objects, design a model, measure lengths, and create concrete situations—for example:

   Problem: What is the length of a pendulum that makes one complete swing in 1 second?

   Strategy: Make a model. With a 50-cm string and some small weights, make a pendulum tied to a pencil taped to a desk. To determine the length of the pendulum, measure the distance from the pencil to the center of the weight.

   Solution: Because it is difficult to measure the time period accurately, time 10 swings and use the average. The correct answer is approximately 25 cm.

   Evaluation: If the length is fixed, the amount of weight does not affect the time period. The amount of deflection does affect the period when large deflections are used, but it is not a factor for small amounts of 5 cm or less. The length of the pendulum always affects the time period.

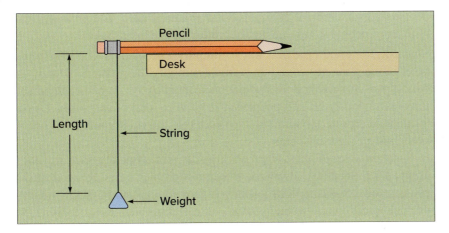

2. **Draw, illustrate, and make tables, charts, or lists.** This way of organizing data presented in a problem helps you look for patterns. For example, a fruit punch dispenser mixes 4 ml of orange juice with 6 ml of pineapple juice. How many ml of orange juice does it mix with 240 ml of pineapple juice?

			Answer
Orange juice ml	4	16	**160**
Pineapple juice ml	6	24	**240**

3. **Look for patterns and connections.** A pattern is a regular, systematic repetition that helps you predict what will come next. Field trips and laboratory work can help you find patterns and categorize information, and so can creating tables. For example, an empty commuter train is picking up passengers at the following rate: One passenger got on at the first stop, three got on at the second stop, and five got on at the third stop. How many passengers got on the train at the sixth stop?

						Answer
Stops	1	2	3	4	5	**6**
Number of passengers	1	3	5	7	9	**11**

4. **Act out the problem.** Sometimes it helps to physically act out the problem. For example, there are five people in your study group, and each person initiates a handshake with every member one time. How many total handshakes will there be? There will be 20 handshakes total because each person shakes hands four times (because you cannot shake your own hand). Thus, five people times 4 handshakes equals 20 total handshakes. You multiply the total number of people times one number fewer for the handshakes.

5. **Simplify.** Sometimes the best way to simplify a problem is first to solve easier cases of the same problem. For example, simplify the problem of study group handshakes by solving it for two people instead of five. When each person initiates a handshake, two people shake hands a total of two times. Using the formula determined in number 4, you see that the equation is $2 \times 1 = 2$. Fill in the rest of the table below.

   Along the same lines, when working on homework, studying in your group, or taking a test, always do the easiest problems first. Confident that you can solve one kind of problem, you gain enthusiasm to tackle more difficult questions or problems. Also, an easier problem may be similar to a harder problem.

6. **Translate words into equations.** Highlight visual and verbal learning by showing connections between words and numbers. Write an equation that

Number of People	Each Person Initiates Handshake × Times	Total Number of Handshakes
2	1	2
3	2	
4		
5	4	20
6		

models the problem. For example, Sarah has a total of $82.00, consisting of an equal number of pennies, nickels, dimes, and quarters. How many coins does she have in all? You know how much all of Sarah's coins are worth and you know how much each coin is worth. (In the following equation, p = pennies, n = nickels, d = dimes, and q = quarters.)

$p + 5n + 10d + 25q = 8,200$

We know that she has an equal number of each coin; thus, $p = n = d = q$. Therefore, we can substitute p for all the other variables:

$1p + 5p + 10p + 25p = 41p = 8,200$, so $p = 200$

Sarah has 200 pennies, 200 nickels, 200 dimes, and 200 quarters. Therefore, she has 800 coins.

7. **Estimate, make a reasonable guess, check the guess, and revise.** Using the example in number 6, if you were told that Sarah had a large number of coins that added up to $82.00, you could at least say that the total was no more than 8,200 (the number of coins if they were all pennies) and no less than 328 (the number of coins if they were all quarters).

8. **Work backward and eliminate.** For example, what is the largest 2-digit number that is divisible by 3 whose digits differ by 2? First, working backward from 99, list numbers that are divisible by 3:

    99, 96, 93, 90, 87, 84, 81, 78, 75, 72, 69, 66, 63, 60, . . .

    Now cross out all numbers whose digits do not differ by 2. The largest number remaining is 75.

9. **Summarize in a group.** Working in a group is the best way to integrate all learning styles, keep motivation and interest active, and generate lots of ideas and support. Explain the problem to your group and why you arrived at the answer. Talking out loud, summarizing chapters, and listening to others clarify thinking will help you learn.

10. **Take a quiet break.** If your group can't find a solution to the problem, take a break. Sometimes it helps to find a quiet spot and reflect. Working on another problem or relaxing for a few minutes while listening to music helps you return to the problem refreshed.

Some students are nervous about taking courses in math and science, even though the basic principles have many everyday applications. *What are some tasks you do daily that involve knowledge of basic math and science?*

image100 Ltd

Overcome Math and Science Anxiety

If you have fixed, negative mindset, you view the material as too difficult to learn or over your head, and you throw up your hands and quit. If you have an open, positive mindset, you focus on persistent effort. You know that with challenging practice you can learn and grow. As with the fear of public speaking, face these anxieties and persist. Commit to being gritty.

Anxiety is a learned emotional response—you were not born with it. Because it is learned, it can be unlearned. In **Chapter 10**, we explored strategies for overcoming speech anxiety, and many apply to math and science as well. Here are some additional strategies:

1. **Do your prep work.** Don't take a math or science class if you haven't taken the proper prerequisites. It is better to spend the summer or an additional semester gaining the necessary skills so that you don't feel overwhelmed and discouraged.

2. **Keep up and review often.** If you prepare early and often, you will be less anxious. Use the night before a test for reviewing and testing yourself, not for learning new material.

3. **Discipline yourself.** Focus your attention away from your fears and concentrate on the task at hand. Jot down ideas and formulas, draw pictures, and write out the problem. Reduce interruptions and concentrate fully for short periods. Time yourself on problems to increase speed and make the most of short study sessions. Make up tests.

4. **Study in groups.** A supportive, safe environment can reduce anxiety and encourage creativity, interaction, and multiple solutions. *Make up sample tests, take them, and compare results. Focus on learning.* You will build confidence as you learn to think out loud, brainstorm creative solutions, and solve problems. See **Peak Progress 11.3** for a comprehensive checklist of questions to use as you solve problems.

Peak Progress

Problem-Solving Checklist

When you enroll in any course, including math or science, consider these questions:

- Have you approached the class with a positive attitude?
- What do you want to know, and what are you being asked to find out?
- Have you separated essential information from the unessential?
- Have you separated the known from the unknown?
- Have you asked a series of questions: How? When? Where? What? If?
- Have you devised a plan for solving the problem?
- Have you gone from the general to the specific?
- Have you made an estimate?
- Have you illustrated or organized the problem?
- Have you made a table or a diagram, drawn a picture, or summarized data?
- Have you written out the problem?

- Have you discovered a pattern to the problem?
- Have you alternated intense concentration with frequent breaks?
- Have you tried working backward or solving small parts?
- Have you determined if you made careless errors or that you don't understand the concepts?
- Have you asked for help early?
- Have you been willing to put in the time required to solve problems?
- Have you analyzed the problem? Was your guess close? Did your plan work?
- Have you brainstormed ideas on your own? In a group setting?
- Have you rewarded yourself for facing your fears, overcoming anxiety, and learning valuable skills that will increase your success in school, in your job, and in life?

5. **Create a positive mindset.** A positive attitude is key to learning any subject. Do you get sidetracked by negative self-talk about your abilities or the reason for learning math skills? Choose to focus on effort, growing, and learning. Replace negative and defeating self-talk with positive "I can" affirmations. Math anxiety, like stage fright and other fears, is compounded by negative self-talk. You can succeed with sustained effort.

6. **Dispute the myths.** Many times, fears are caused by myths, such as "Men do better than women in math and science" or "Creative people are not good at math and science." There is no basis for the belief that gender determines math ability, nor is skill in math and science unfeminine. Success in math and science requires creative thinking. As mathematician Augustus De Morgan said, "The moving power of mathematics is not reasoning, but imagination."

7. **Ask for help.** Don't wait until you are in trouble or frustrated. Talk with the instructor, visit the learning center, get a tutor, and join a study group. If you continue to feel anxious or lost, visit the counseling center. Try taking a summer refresher course. You'll be prepared and confident when you take the required course later.

See **Peak Progress 11.4** to apply the Adult Learning Cycle to overcoming anxiety.

> **Man's mind, once stretched by a new idea, never regains its original dimensions.**
> **OLIVER WENDELL HOLMES**
> *Author*

WORDS TO SUCCEED

Peak Progress

Applying the Adult Learning Cycle to Overcoming Math and Science Anxiety

1. **FEEL and LISTEN.** *Why do I want to learn this?* I want to be confident in math and science and avoiding these classes closes doors and limits opportunities. More than 75 percent of careers use math and science, and these are often higher-status, better-paying jobs. This is essential knowledge I'll use in all facets of life. I will listen to my feelings, to my intuition, and to others who have succeeded at math and science.

2. **OBSERVE and VISUALIZE.** *How does this work?* I'll observe people who are good at math and science. What do they do? I'll also observe and learn from the mistakes of people who experience anxiety and don't do well. I will reflect on how I've dealt with fear in other situations and observe how I'm improving. I'll look for connections and associations with other types of anxiety.

3. **THINK and WRITE.** *What does this mean?* I'll apply critical thinking to mathematics and science. What works and doesn't work? I can learn a lot about applying creative problem solving to mathematics and science by trying new things. I'll think about and test new ways of reducing anxiety and break old patterns and negative self-talk. I will write out a script for dealing with anxiety and read it.

4. **DO and PRACTICE.** *What can I do with this?* I will practice reducing my anxiety. I'll find practical applications for connecting critical thinking and creative problem solving to math and science. Each day I'll work on one area. For example, I'll maintain a positive attitude as I approach math and science classes and practice it every day. I will go to the learning center and take a workshop on improving my math and science skills. I'll apply what I learn.

5. **TEACH and PRACTICE AGAIN.** *Whom can I share this with?* I'll form a study group and share my tips and experiences. I'll demonstrate and teach others the methods I've learned. I'll reward myself when I do well.

Use the VARK system for integrating learning styles and to help you think through and apply the Adult Learning Cycle. *Visualize* yourself as a creative person with excellent critical thinking skills and doing well in math and science. *Imagine* yourself in a career using math and science. Practice observing, paying attention to details, and seeing new connections. Use your *auditory* skills to really listen and see all sides of the issue. *Write out* the problem, pros, and cons and *read* possible solutions out loud. Use your *kinesthetic* skills to jump in and experiment, try new things, see how something works, and then demonstrate it to others. Practice every day again and again.

Overcoming Obstacles: Building Better Habits

Use the power of habits to make a routine. Reflect on what triggers your creativity.

- Are you in a certain *location* (taking a shower, playing, walking in nature, jogging, in the library, in class, or brainstorming with friends)?
- What is your *emotional state?* Are you relaxed, playful, stressed, lighthearted, or serious? Have you already made a lot of decisions and feel overwhelmed?
- What is your *physical state?* Are you rested? Did you have a healthy breakfast and are you eating protein snacks every few hours? Is your glucose level steady or are you running on empty? Are you well hydrated?
- What *time* do you seem to be most creative (early morning, evening, weekends, after lunch)? Are you around other people or by yourself?

These questions will help you identify patterns. Let's say that you seem to be most creative when you go for an early jog with a friend and you're brainstorming ideas. You're rested, relaxed, and playful and just having fun being outdoors and enjoying nature. Ideas just seem to come to you without trying. If that's the case, your jogging shoes become the *trigger* and your *routine* will include jogging outdoors and paying attention to nature. Your *reward* will be feeling relaxed, pumped up by the endorphins, and coming up with fresh, new ideas.

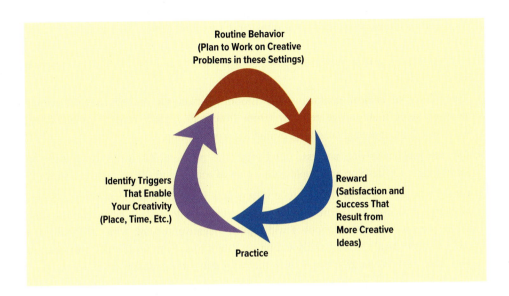

Remember, attitude is everything. If you keep an open mind, apply strategies you have learned in this chapter, and practice your creative and critical thinking skills, you will become more confident in your problem-solving abilities. Focus on growth and learning.

TAKING CHARGE

Summary

In this chapter, I learned to

- **Appreciate the importance of critical thinking.** Critical thinking is key to understanding and solving problems at school, at work, and in the rest of my life. I have learned to examine beliefs, assumptions, and opinions against facts; ask pertinent questions; and analyze data.

- **Apply essential critical thinking skills.** Bloom's Taxonomy outlines the six critical thinking skills that college requires (from lowest to highest order): remembering, understanding, applying, analyzing, evaluating, and creating.

- **Use the problem-solving process.** (1) Define the problem, (2) gather and interpret information, (3) develop and implement a plan of action, and (4) evaluate the plan.

- **Create a positive mindset.** My attitude affects how I approach problem solving. *I have developed a positive, inquisitive attitude and a willingness to explore, probe, question, and search for answers and solutions.* I will replace negative self-talk with affirmations. I will use my critical thinking skills and be persistent in solving problems. I will practice pretesting with my study group. I know that with effort and practice, I will learn.

- **Avoid errors in judgment.** I will avoid using stereotypes, all-or-nothing thinking, snap judgments, unwarranted assumptions, projection, sweeping generalizations, the halo effect, and negative labeling. I will not project my views onto others to justify decisions.

- **Use creative problem solving.** I will use creative problem solving to approach problems from a different direction and explore new options. What problems are similar? Is there a pattern to the problem? I will brainstorm various strategies. I will act out the problem, move it around, picture it, take it apart, translate it, and summarize it in my own words. I will solve easier problems before tackling harder problems.

- **Apply strategies to math and science courses.** What model, formula, drawing, sketch, equation, chart, table, calculation, or particular strategy will help? I choose the most appropriate strategy, outline my plan, and show all my work so that I can review.

- **Overcome anxiety for math and science.** A positive mindset focuses on growth and learning, which helps to reduce anxiety. Persistent practice and effort produces success.

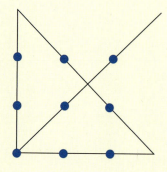

Solution to the Nine-Dot Exercise
Personal Evaluation Notebook 11.4

Most people try to solve this problem by remaining within the boundaries of the dots. However, when you move outside the confines of the dots and the boundaries are reset, you can easily solve the puzzle. This exercise helps illustrate that some problems cannot be solved with traditional thinking.

Performance Strategies

Following are the top 10 strategies for critical thinking and creative problem solving:

- Define the problem.
- Gather and interpret information.
- Develop and implement a plan of action.
- Evaluate your decisions.
- Ask questions.
- Brainstorm creative options.
- Pay attention to details.
- Consider all sides of an issue.
- Use reasoning and avoid errors in judgment.
- Create a positive mindset that focuses on effort, growth, and learning.

Tech for Success

- **Work on weak areas.** Various online programs can help you determine the mathematical areas where you need the most work. ALEKS (www.aleks.com/highered) is a tutorial program that identifies your less proficient areas and then focuses on improvement through practice and targeted problems.

- **Math at your fingertips.** In your studies, you will come across many standard calculations and formulas, most of which can be found online and downloaded. Although this should not replace working through the formulas yourself to make sure you understand their applications, it does make incorporating math into your everyday life much easier.

Endnotes

[1] Frances E. Jensen, *The Teenage Brain: A Neuroscientist's Survival Guide to Raising Adolescents and Young Adults* (New York: HarperCollins, 2015).

[2] Daniel J. Siegel, *Brainstorm: The Power and Purpose of the Teenage Brain* (New York: Penguin Random House, 2015).

[3] Ed Catmull, *Creativity, Inc.: Overcoming the Unseen Forces That Stand in the Way of True Inspiration* (New York: Random House, 2014).

Study Team Notes

Career *in* Focus

fotostorm/Getty Images

Marina and Josef Koshetz
RESTAURANT OWNERS

Related Majors: Restaurant and Food Service Management, Business

Creativity at Work

Marina Koshetz and her husband, Josef, have recently opened a small restaurant that serves foods from their homeland of Russia. Starting their restaurant was a great deal of work. They had to get the correct permits, remodel an existing building, purchase equipment, and plan the menu. The couple works long hours, six days a week. Before opening the restaurant at 11 a.m., Marina makes bread while Josef mixes together the traditional dishes they will serve. Then Marina remains in the kitchen to cook and prepare dishes while Josef waits tables and runs the cash register. At the end of the day, the couple washes the dishes and cleans the restaurant together. Although the restaurant is closed on Mondays, Marina and Josef use that day to plan the next week's specials and purchase food and other supplies.

Despite their hard work, the couple has made only enough money to cover costs. On a recent Monday afternoon, the two restaurateurs brainstormed ways to attract more customers. The restaurant is located in a quiet neighborhood on the edge of a district where many Russian immigrants live. So far, almost all of their customers have been Russian. Josef and Marina realized they needed to do more to attract other residents to their restaurant. They decided to host an open house and invite everyone living within a mile radius of the restaurant. Then they decided to add a couple of popular American dishes and offered a discount on Groupon. Soon their restaurant was attracting more customers, and the business began to show a profit.

CRITICAL THINKING How did Josef and Marina use creativity and critical thinking to improve their business?

Peak Performer Profile

Scott Adams

He's been described as a techie with the "social skills of a mousepad." He's not the sort of fellow you'd expect to attract media attention. However, pick up a newspaper, turn to the comics, and you'll find him. He's Dilbert. Cartoonist Scott Adams created this comic-strip character who daily lampoons corporate America and provides a humorous outlet for employees everywhere.

Though Adams was creative at a young age, his artistic endeavors were discouraged early on. The Famous Artists School rejected him at age 11. Years later, he received the lowest grade in a college drawing class. Practicality replaced creativity. In 1979, Adams earned a B.A. in economics from Hartwick College in Oneonta, New York, and, in 1986, an MBA from the University of California at Berkeley. For the next 15 years, Adams settled uncomfortably into a series of jobs that "defied description." Ironically, the frustrations of the workplace—power-driven co-workers, inept bosses, and cell-like cubicles—fueled his imagination. Adams began doodling, and Dilbert was born.

Encouraged by others, Adams submitted his work to United Media, a major cartoon syndicate. He was offered a contract in 1989, and *Dilbert* debuted in 50

Marcio Jose Sanchez/AP Images

national newspapers. Today, *Dilbert* appears in 2,000 newspapers in 70 countries and was the first syndicated cartoon to have its own website.

With such mass exposure, coming up with new ideas for cartoons could be a challenge. However, Adams found the perfect source: He gets hundreds of messages a day from workers at home and abroad. His hope is that, through his creative invention, solutions will develop for the problems he satirizes.

PERFORMANCE THINKING Of the creative problem-solving strategies in the Creative Problem Solving section, which one do you think has been most helpful for Scott Adams and why?

CHECK IT OUT According to Scott Adams, "Creativity is allowing yourself to make mistakes. Art is knowing which ones to keep." Adams is no stranger to taking chances and voicing his views on management—both in the workforce and in the government. At **www.dilbert.com**, you can read (and respond to, if you like) Adams's blog and "mash up" one of his comics by creatively inserting your own words into the frames.

Starting Today

At least one strategy I learned in this chapter that I plan to try right away is

_____

_____

_____

What changes must I make in order for this strategy to be most effective?

_____

_____

_____

Review Questions

Based on what you have learned in this chapter, write your answers to the following questions:

1. Name six critical thinking skills necessary for success in college.

_____

_____

2. What are the attributes of a critical thinker?

_____

_____

3. What are the four steps of problem solving?

_____

_____

4. Name five strategies for becoming more creative.

_____

_____

5. Name five strategies for problem solving in math and science.

_____

_____

Conquering Fear of Failure

Keith Brofsky/Getty Images

In the Classroom

Gloria Ramone is a single mom who works part time and lives and attends school in the inner city. She is eager to complete her education, begin her career, and earn a higher salary. She is a medical records student who wants her classes to be practical and relevant. Her school requires a class in critical thinking, but she is resisting it because she sees no practical application to her job. Her attitude is affecting her attendance and participation.

1. Offer ideas to help Gloria see the importance of critical thinking in decision making.

_____

_____

2. Help her connect decisions in school with job decisions.

_____

_____

In the Workplace

Gloria is now an office assistant for a team of doctors. She is also taking evening classes, working toward a health care administration degree. She has received praise for her work but wants to eventually move up to office manager or work for a health care company. Gloria is very interested in the insurance industry and loves to solve problems. New issues arise every day, and she has decisions to make. She has lots of practice predicting results and using critical thinking to solve problems. Gloria enjoys most of her courses but dreads the classes in finance and statistics because she has math anxiety.

3. What strategies in this chapter could help Gloria overcome math anxiety?

_____

_____

4. What are some affirmations Gloria could use to help her develop a positive attitude about math?

_____

_____

Applying the ABC Method of Self-Management

In the Journal Entry, you were asked to describe a decision you made that cost you a lot of time, money, or stress. How would critical thinking and creative problem solving have helped you make better decisions? How would having a positive, open mindset help?

_____

_____

_____

Apply the ABC Method to a difficult situation you have encountered, such as a financial dilemma, rigorous course, or personal crisis. Write a script.

A = Acknowledge: Accept reality and pay attention to your emotions.

_____

_____

_____

B = Breathe: Take a deep breath to calm down and feel beloved.

_____

_____

_____

C = Choose: Knowing you have many options, choose the most appropriate for the situation and that will result in positive long-term consequences.

_____

_____

_____

Sample Script: Even though I'm feeling sad, embarrassed, and frustrated, I love and accept myself and focus on learning and growing. I practice deep breathing see myself calm, centered, and relaxed. I allow my feelings to pass while I focus on positive action. I choose to use critical thinking to work through problems and allow myself to be creative and open to new ideas. I talk with my advisor, professors, and people who can help me make sound decisions. I am confident that I can learn critical thinking skills, increase my creativity and learn to explore various options. I know that learning to be a critical and creative thinker will help me in my career and in all aspects of life.

Apply Blooms Taxonomy

Different situations call for different levels of thinking. Although many, if not all, of these skills are required in every course you take, jot down classes or situations where you might rely more on a particular thinking skill. For example, in a speech class, you may be asked to evaluate others' speeches.

Critical Thinking Skill	Task	Class or Situation
Remembering	To recite, recall, and recognize facts, key terms, or events.	
Understanding	To comprehend and explain in your own words.	
Applying	To apply and use in a practical situation.	
Analyzing	To see the whole and break ideas into parts or steps.	
Evaluating	To critique the usefulness, quality, truth, and source of this idea.	
Creating	To invent something new with this idea.	

Preparing for Critical Thinking

Brainstorm alternative approaches and solutions to the problems that arise in your day-to-day activities at school, on the job, or at home. Consider things such as the potential consequences of certain decisions, timing, and related costs.

ISSUE/PROBLEM

_____

_____

_____

_____

_____

SOLUTION 1: _____

Pros	Cons

SOLUTION 2: _____

Pros	Cons

SOLUTION 3: _____

Pros	Cons

(continued)

REVIEW AND APPLICATIONS | CHAPTER 11

BEST SOLUTION AND WHY:

_____

_____

_____

Review the process from a fresh, creative approach. How else could you see this? Brainstorm with a friend or study group and ask for innovative ideas.

_____

_____

_____

_____

You Can Solve the Problem: Sue's Decision

Every day, life brings problems and choices. The kinds of choices you make can make your life easier or harder. Often, you do not know which direction to take. Use these six steps to work through the following case study:

Step 1 Know what the problem really is. Is it a daily problem? Is it a once-in-a-lifetime problem?

Step 2 List what you know about the problem. List what you don't know. Ask questions. Get help and advice.

Step 3 Explore alternate choices.

Step 4 Think about the pros and cons for the other choices. Arrange them from best to worst choice.

Step 5 Pick the choice you feel good about.

Step 6 Study what happens after you have made your choice. Are you happy about the choice? Would you make it again?

Case Study: Sue

Sue has been diagnosed with cancer. Her doctor has told her that it is in only one place in her body. The doctor wants to operate. He thinks he will be able to remove all of it, but he wants Sue to undergo 4 months of chemotherapy, which will make her feel very sick. It will make her tired, but it may also help keep the cancer from coming back and spreading.

Sue is not sure what to do. She has two small children who are not in school. Sue's husband works days and cannot help care for the children during the day. The rest of Sue's family lives far away, and she cannot afford day care. She wonders, "How will I be able to care for my children if I'm sick?"

The doctor has told Sue that she must make her own choice. Will she undergo the chemotherapy? She will talk with her husband, and they will make a choice together.

What is Sue's problem? What are her choices? What would you decide? Apply the six steps to help Sue make a good decision by writing responses to the following questions and statements.

Step 1 The problem is

_____

_____

_____

_____

Step 2

a. You know these things about the problem:

_____

_____

_____

_____

(continued)

b. You don't know these things about the problem:

_____

_____

_____

_____

Step 3 The other choices are

_____

_____

_____

_____

Step 4 Rank the choices, best to worst.

_____

_____

_____

_____

Step 5 Pick a choice the family might feel good about and explain why.

_____

_____

_____

_____

Step 6 What might happen to Sue and her family?

_____

_____

_____

_____

Assessing and Demonstrating Your Critical Thinking Skills

1. **Looking back:** Review your worksheets to find activities that helped you learn to make decisions and solve problems creatively. Jot down examples. Also, look for examples of how you learned to apply critical thinking skills to math and science.

   _____

   _____

   _____

   _____

   _____

2. **Taking stock:** What are your strengths in decision making and critical thinking? Are you creative? What areas would you like to improve?

   _____

   _____

   _____

   _____

   _____

3. **Looking forward:** How would you demonstrate critical thinking and creative problem-solving skills to an employer?

   _____

   _____

   _____

   _____

   _____

4. **Documentation:** Document your critical thinking and creative problem-solving skills. Which instructor or employer would write a letter of recommendation? Indicate here which person you'll contact. Add this letter to your portfolio.

   _____

   _____

   _____

   _____

   _____

Add this page to your Career Development Portfolio.

REVIEW AND APPLICATIONS | CHAPTER 11

Create a Healthy Mind, Body, and Spirit

12

LEARNING OUTCOMES

In this chapter, you will learn to

12-1 Explain the connection among the mind, body, and spirit

12-2 Identify the best ways to manage the stress in your life

12-3 Identify strategies to manage potential addictions

12-4 Identify strategies for better emotional health

12-5 Identify ways to protect yourself from disease, unplanned pregnancy, and acquaintance rape

12-6 Identify habits to help you overcome health-related obstacles

SELF-MANAGEMENT

grandriver/Getty Images

I'm stressed out with doing so much homework and trying to juggle everything. I haven't been getting enough sleep, and I've been stress eating fast food and not exercising. What can I do to manage my stress and be healthier? I just don't seem to have any willpower so I give up.

Do you feel overwhelmed and stressed by too many demands? Do you lack energy from too little sleep or exercise or from inadequate nutrition? In this chapter, you will learn how to manage stress and create healthy habits to last a lifetime. You will see yourself healthy and in charge of your mental, physical, and spiritual life. A positive mindset will create success through effort and focus.

JOURNAL ENTRY In **Worksheet 12.1**, describe a time when you felt overwhelmed, your energy was low, and felt unhealthy and stressed. Apply the self-management method.

> **❝** He who has
> health has hope; and
> he who has hope has
> everything. **❞**
> **ARABIC PROVERB**

Creating balance, managing stress, increasing energy, and providing time for renewal are essential to becoming a peak performer. In this world of multitasking and instant gratification, we need to slow down, become mindful of our purpose, and focus on important priorities. In this chapter, we will present principles and guidelines to help you develop the most effective methods of maintaining your health while learning how to cope with daily demands. You'll learn how to stick to your plan and be healthier.

Redefining Health: Connecting the Mind, Body, and Spirit

Many people think of health as the absence of disease. However, optimal health—or **wellness**—means living life fully with purpose, meaning, and vitality. Your overall wellness is largely determined by your decisions about how you live your life and the measures you take to avoid illness. Although genetics, age, and accidents also influence your health and are beyond your control, you can optimize your health by understanding the connection between your mind, body, and spirit. The habits you develop now will affect not only how long you live, but also the quality of life you enjoy. Let's start with your attitude.

The Mind

A positive, open mindset that is focused on growth is the foundation for creating health and well-being. *The belief that you can cultivate essential qualities through effort and practice will help you stick to a program even when the going gets tough.* These beliefs create habits to help you manage your emotions, attitude, and coping skills. Instead of letting everything slide when you experience mid-winter blues or loneliness, you get up, go to class, and take care of your mind and body so that when you feel better emotionally, your life is intact. If you are depressed, however, you should go to the counseling center and talk with a professional counselor. Focus on gratitude and positive thoughts. You know the power of thoughts and create resiliency through meditation, time in nature, supportive relationships, exercise, and embracing challenges and effort.

The Body

Physical wellness requires eating healthy foods, exercising, getting plenty of sleep, recognizing the symptoms of disease, making responsible decisions about sex, avoiding harmful habits, improving your immune system, and taking steps to prevent illness and physical harm. Most of us know we should be exercising more and eating more fruits and vegetables; however, too often we have difficulty putting these tips into daily practice. *The key is creating a positive mindset that focuses on growth and creating healthy habits.*

The Spirit

Spiritual wellness is living your life with meaning and is the essence of wholeness. It requires thinking about and clarifying your values and questioning the purpose, beliefs, and principles that give your life meaning. *This means taking time for reflection, mindfulness, and inner work.* Spirituality may include your religious beliefs or a belief in a higher power, but it also encompasses your willingness to serve others; your sense of ethics and honesty; your relationship to people, nature, and animals; your definition of the purpose of life; the legacy you want to leave; and how you fit into this universe. In **Chapter 3**, we discussed Maslow's hierarchy of needs. At the highest level, self-actualized people achieve fulfillment, creativity, and greater spiritual growth. The body, mind, and spirit are interconnected. Research indicates that if you live with love, honesty, forgiveness, and meaning you are more likely to be healthy and happy. Students who enjoyed their lives and studies were more likely to have a sense of underlying purpose in life.

Understanding the connection among the mind, body, and spirit will help you develop skills for coping with the demands of school and work. Reports, deadlines, tests, performance reviews, conflicts, commuting, family responsibilities, and presentations are all part of life. These demands create a great deal of stress. Stress is not an external event but how you see and respond, and it affects all aspects of your mind, body, and spirit.

• Fighting the Flu

Each year, 36,000 people in the United States die from seasonal flu-related causes, making it important to understand how to protect yourself from contracting the flu. *Do you know what to do to decrease your risk of getting the flu?*

Martin Botvidsson/Getty Images

Awareness and Prevention

The first step in managing your health is awareness. Identify the negative ways you've coped with stress. You may not even realize you eat every time you watch television, drink several cans of diet soda while you study, or nibble while you fix dinner. You may start drinking alcohol or smoking when you're under stress instead of learning healthy coping skills. Awareness can also help you identify when you've made a number of decisions and your willpower is depleted. It's the end of a long day of classes and work, and you don't have the discipline to make healthy choices. Improving your health begins with observing your daily habits and replacing unproductive ones with beneficial choices. *That's the beauty of a positive mindset and habits.*

BETTER HABITS FOR STRESS PREVENTION

Habits create structure and through practice you simply follow the plan. It frees you up and takes away the stress of making more choices. Choose attitudes and behaviors that help you cope. The *trigger* is feeling depleted and overwhelmed with physical signs such as tension in your shoulders or the beginning of a tension headache. You have planned ahead for these stressful times and created a *routine* that includes taking a few minutes to stretch and *breathe deeply until you are calm. Reward* yourself for taking these "mini-vacations" by creating a routine that includes taking frequent breaks to eat a healthy snack, stretch, listen to music, go for a walk, or chat with a friend. Soon you will quickly tune in to the triggers for stress, immediately go through your routine to calm down, and relax. Now you have a lasting habit that rewards with a feeling of being more in control. The right mindset and habits provide discipline and keep you fresh and emotionally full.

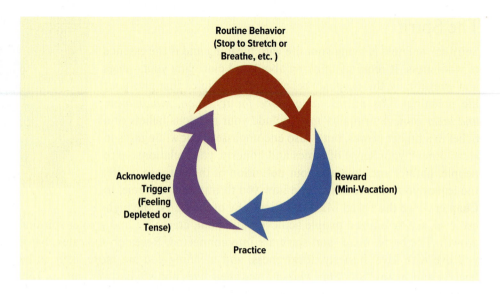

Trigger is feeling overwhelmed and depleted. *Routine* includes frequent breaks to be playful and chat with friends. *Reward* is socializing with friends, eating healthy snacks, exercising, and feeling in control and positive.

CANCER

It's important to observe how your body feels and if you experience discomfort or a change in your body. If you can identify symptoms and early warning signs of an illness, you can take action to protect yourself from diseases, such as cancer. One in three people will develop cancer in their lifetime. At **www.cancer.org**, the American Cancer Society provides guidelines for the early detection of specific cancers, such as skin cancer, which is diagnosed more than one million times each year. Signs and symptoms such as unexplained weight loss of 10 pounds or more, persistent fever, fatigue, pain, and skin changes can be caused by a range of conditions, including cancer, and should be taken seriously. **Figure 12.1** includes more specific signs and symptoms of cancer. While these are the most common, there are many other signs. See your doctor or the health center for advice.

DIABETES

Although more than 11 million people are living with cancer in the United States, an estimated 26 million people (almost nine percent of the population) have diabetes, making it one of the *fastest-growing health issues.* Close to 86 million American adults have prediabetes and 90 percent don't know it. Prediabetes means your blood glucose levels are higher than normal, but not high enough to be diagnosed

Figure **12.1**

Cancer Caution Signs

Although these are the most common specific signs of cancer, they could be symptoms of other health issues. *Do you routinely discuss any concerns with your physician?*

Flashon Studio/Shutterstock

See your doctor if you experience any of the following:

- Change in bowel habits or bladder function
- Sores that do not heal
- Unusual bleeding or discharge
- Thickening or lump in breast or other parts of the body
- Indigestion or trouble swallowing
- Recent change in a wart or mole
- Nagging cough or hoarseness

as diabetic. This condition can lead to heart disease, stroke, and type 2 diabetes. Several factors are involved (including genetics), but the rise in rates of obesity (more than 34 percent of U.S. adults over age 20 are considered obese) is thought to contribute to the increase in cases of diabetes. Obesity is a risk factor for many illnesses (including heart disease and cancer) and costs almost $150 billion in medical expenses each year. Eating a healthy diet with more fruits, veggies, and protein and less sugar and white carbs and exercising can help prevent this disease. To obtain the most current information about the National Diabetes Prevention Program, visit **www.cdc.gov/diabetes/prevention**.

Strategies for Good Health Management

1. **Eat healthy foods.** Eat a nutritious diet daily to control your weight and blood pressure and to reduce depression, anxiety, headaches, fatigue, and insomnia. Eating healthy small snacks throughout the day (protein, nuts, seeds, fruits, and veggies) also keeps glucose levels steady and helps with concentration and energy. The *Dietary Guidelines for Americans,* published jointly every five years by the Department of Health and Human Services and the U.S. Department of Agriculture, provides authoritative advice about how good dietary habits can promote health and reduce risk for major chronic diseases. The latest edition can be found at **www.health.gov/dietaryguidelines**. Additionally, the following general guidelines will help you make healthy choices in your diet:

   - *Eat a variety of foods.* Include fiber, lots of fruits and vegetables, milk, eggs, meats, poultry, fish, and olive oil in your diet. See **Peak Progress 12.1** for suggested descriptions of various balanced diets. Keep it simple. For example, eat a big salad every day, as well as some protein, vegetables, and several pieces of fruit. You should get your vitamins from a variety of food; however, if you are not eating as well as you should, some experts suggest taking vitamin and mineral supplements for optimal health. *Many people do not get enough vitamin D, especially in the winter months.*

   - *Increase your fiber.* Having a healthy digestive system helps reduce your risk of constipation, diverticulosis, hemorrhoids, high cholesterol, obesity, colon cancer, diabetes, and heart disease. Whole grains, beans, fruits, and vegetables are good sources of fiber.

   - *Reduce the amount of animal fat in your diet.* Too much animal fat can increase the level of cholesterol in your blood, which can affect your cardiovascular system, causing your body to get less oxygen.

   - *Broil or bake rather than fry.* Use olive oil or another monounsaturated fat.

   - *Cut down on salt.* Salt is an ingredient in many prepared foods. You may be surprised that white bread is the leading source of sodium in the average diet.

   - *Cut down on sugar.* Eating refined sugar creates a sudden drop in blood sugar, shakiness, and a need for more glucose. This can lead to type 2 diabetes, obesity, and other health problems. Cut down on fruit juice, soda, and sweet snacks.

   - *Forget diets.* Research indicates that diet soft drinks may actually hamper your efforts to control calories, confusing your body as to how many calories it has consumed. Many low-fat foods are loaded with sugar. Don't diet; just eat healthy, whole foods. *Eat mindfully and savor each bite* as you socialize and connect with friends and family. Drink water with your meal and stop when you're full. Exercise.

Peak Progress

Eating for Health and Energy

MEDITERRANEAN DIET

Researchers have studied the effects of diet for years and have tried to agree on the best diet for most people. In 1993, scientists and nutritionists from the United States and Europe met to look at the traditional Mediterranean diet, which may have prolonged life and prevented disease for centuries in Mediterranean countries. The experts released a model similar to that of the U.S. Department of Agriculture's (USDA's) original food guide pyramid. (See pyramid illustrations below.) Many of these suggestions have remained consistent and emphasize eating whole foods such as fruits, vegetables, whole grains, low-fat milk products, lean meats, beans, eggs, and nuts.

MY PLATE

The food guide pyramid developed by the USDA has continued to change over the years, and in 2011 it was replaced with a plate, helping consumers understand how their meals should be divided among the various food groups. Each "color" on the plate is tied to a specific food group (orange = grains, green = vegetables, etc.). To determine your needs and create a good eating plan, go to **www.choosemyplate.gov** and look for the SuperTracker application, which can help you plan, analyze, and track your diet and physical activity. You can also use **Worksheet 12.3** to get a snapshot of your eating habits.

DASH

Dietary Approaches to Stop Hypertension (DASH) is designed to combat high blood pressure and is widely recommended by physicians, the *Dietary Guidelines for Americans,* and the American Heart Association. The goal is to eliminate the need for medications by eating a diet high in potassium, magnesium, calcium, and fiber, and that is moderately high in protein and low in saturated fat and total fat. Although these can be found in fruits, vegetables, grains, and low-fat dairy, many consumers need help initially determining the best food sources and serving sizes. Go to **www.dashdiet.org** for more information.

Source: www.choosemyplate.gov

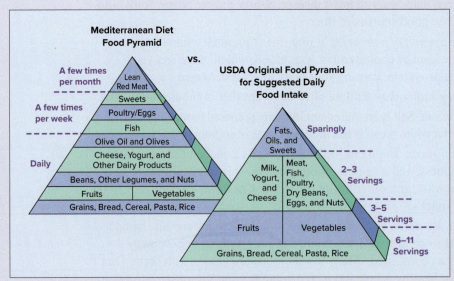

Sources: U.S. Department of Agriculture, U.S. Department of Health and Human Services.

- *Cut down or eliminate sodas.* Sodas and energy drinks can make you nervous, jittery, and irritable and affect your sleep if you drink them at night. Many people find them addictive. Coffee can enhance alertness and effectiveness and research has shown that drinking two or three cups is actually healthy for most people. Green tea is high in antioxidants. Get used to drinking plain water often and with your meals.

- *Moderation is key.* If you drink alcoholic beverages, do it in moderation: one or two drinks no more than three times a week. Too much alcohol increases the risk for certain cancers, cirrhosis of the liver, damage to the heart and brain, and stroke. Never drink and drive. The drinking habits you create can affect your entire life.

- *Drink water.* It's important to keep yourself hydrated, as about 60 percent of your body is made up of water. Fluid needs differ based on overall health, exercise levels, and so on, but a good rule of thumb is to drink as many ounces of water as about 30 percent of your body weight. For a 150-pound person, that means drinking about 45 ounces per day. Choose water as your mealtime beverage, and drink a glass between meals. Also hydrate before, during, and after exercise.

2. **Maintain a healthy weight.** People spend millions of dollars every year on diet programs, exercise equipment, and promises of a quick fix. Focus on being healthy and adding whole foods instead of fast foods. Building energy and health by nourishing and caring for the body takes a long-term commitment to good habits. The following general guidelines will help you maintain your ideal weight:

- *Exercise. To increase your energy, health, and stamina, build physical activity into your life.* If you have time and are in a safe area, park your car a little farther out in the parking lot and walk a few extra steps. Sign up for an exercise class or jog on a track. Explore fitness resources at your school or community.

- *Keep it simple.* Change one habit at a time. Instead of overwhelming yourself with a new meal plan and strict exercise regimen (on top of your other daily responsibilities) change one habit at a time. Make lunch instead of grabbing it on the way back from class. For example, have a salad every day and lean protein. Carry nuts and fruit with you instead of a candy bar.

- *Stop eating after 6:00 or 7:00 p.m.* Some people find that not eating after six at night is an effective way to stay healthy. Research has shown that giving your body a rest from eating for 10 hours or so helps it repair itself.

• Coffeehouse Blues

The caffeine in coffee can be pleasurable in moderate amounts, but, because it is addictive, there's a downside to drinking too much. *What are some other ways to increase your energy besides consuming caffeine?*

Caia Image/Glow Images

Personal Evaluation Notebook

Reviewing Your Health

Read the following and write your comments on the lines provided.

1. Do you maintain healthy fitness goals?

_____

_____

_____

2. Describe a few of your healthy eating habits.

_____

_____

_____

3. Describe a few of your unhealthy eating habits.

_____

_____

_____

4. Do you feel you have control over your eating? Explain.

_____

_____

_____

5. What can you do to make positive and lasting changes in your eating habits?

_____

_____

_____

Review your habits and reflect on simple ways to eat healthier. For example, "I'm going to fill up much of my plate with veggies, salad, and fruit. When I want a snack, I'm going to have a handful of nuts and seeds, an apple, and water."

- *Eat regularly.* Establish a pattern of three meals a day or five small meals. Have at least a light breakfast to stoke your metabolism. If you are really rushed, carry fruits, raw vegetables, or seeds and nuts with you. Eat a bigger lunch.
- *Create healthy habits.* Think about what triggers your urge to eat and when and why. *Eat consciously and only when you're hungry.* Eat to sustain your

body, not because you are depressed, lonely, bored, thirsty, or worried. Create a healthy routine. Sit down and eat in one or two locations, such as the dining room or at the kitchen table. Resist the urge to eat on the run, sample food while you are cooking, munch in bed, or eat sugary snacks throughout the day. Reward yourself by making dinner an occasion to connect with friends. Use critical thinking as you explore your eating patterns in **Personal Evaluation Notebook 12.1**. Check out these websites and apps: Productive, a habit tracker app, **zenhabits.net**, **habitlist.com**, and **tinyhabits.com**.

- *Get help.* If you are overly concerned with being thin or have a problem with eating too little (anorexia nervosa) or vomit as a way to control your weight (bulimia), get immediate help. Anorexia and bulimia are serious illnesses that require medical treatment. Go to the health center. Don't wait. (See **Peak Progress 12.2**.)

3. **Renew energy through rest.** Research has confirmed the relationship between sleep and learning and memory in adolescents. You need to feel rested to perform well. Sleep doesn't just strengthen learning, but it also helps with long-term memory. There is research behind the notion of "sleeping on it," so review information right before going to sleep.[1] The key is not to focus on the number of hours but, rather, whether you feel rested, alert, and energized. Most people need more sleep than they get and would be less irritable, happier, and more alert and creative with a little more sleep. If you wake up tired, try going to bed earlier for a night or two, and then establish a consistent bedtime. Also find time to relax each day. Use critical thinking in **Personal Evaluation Notebook 12.2** to assess your commitment to getting rest.

4. **Increase physical activity.** *Regular exercise reduces stress and strengthens every organ in the body.* It reduces heart disease risk, strengthens the immune system, stimulates the lymphatic system, and increases functional capacity. Exercise burns calories and stimulates the brain to release endorphins,

Peak Progress   12.2

Eating Disorders

Anorexia nervosa is an eating disorder which involves a distorted body image and eating very little to be thin.

Bulimia nervosa is another eating disorder; it involves binge eating and purging through forced vomiting or the use of laxatives. It can cause long-term dental damage. Both anorexia and bulimia can lead to organ damage and failure, chemical imbalances, bone loss, and even death. If you think you might have an eating disorders go to the health center immediately or see a doctor.

The National Association of Anorexia Nervosa and Associated Disorders estimates that approximately eight million people in the United States have anorexia nervosa, bulimia nervosa, and related eating disorders. Essentially, about three of every 100 people in this country eat in a way disordered enough to warrant treatment. Research suggests that about four of every 100 college-age women have bulimia nervosa.

If you are dealing with an eating disorder, or suspect a friend or a family member is struggling with a disorder, seek help immediately. To learn more, visit the National Eating Disorders Association website at **www.nationaleatingdisorders.org** or call (800) 931-2237.

Personal Evaluation Notebook   12.2

Getting Proper Rest

Read the following and write your comments on the lines provided.

1. Do you generally wake up in the morning feeling rested and eager to start the day or tired with little energy? _____

2. How many times do you hit the snooze button before getting out of bed?

   _____

3. What prevents you from getting enough rest?

   _____

   _____

4. Besides sleep, what activities can renew your body and spirit?

   _____

   _____

Reflect on how you can create positive habits for getting more sleep. For example, "I'm going to unplug from cell phones, iPad, and TV for at least an hour before bed and review flash cards or note cards right before I go to sleep."

---

natural chemicals that increase feelings of well-being. *It is also a key habit and affects many other areas of your life.* People who make a habit of exercising quit smoking, drink less, sleep better, and eat healthier. National physical activity guidelines recommend at least 150 minutes of moderate-intensity (30 minutes, 5 days) or 75 minutes of vigorous aerobic exercise (25 minutes, 3 days) per week. These two types of aerobic exercise can be combined to meet national goals. Exercising to build strength, muscular endurance, and flexibility is recommended two to three days per week for building healthy bones and further enhancing health benefits. The key is to accumulate the recommended minutes. Consider moderate activities (such as brisk walking), vigorous aerobic activities (swimming, dancing, jogging), vigorous sports and recreation (tennis, hiking), muscle fitness (resistance training), and flexibility exercises (yoga, stretching). Start slowly, build gradually, commit to smart personal goals, and be consistent. If you experience pain beyond normal soreness while exercising, stop and consult your physician. Assess your commitment to exercise in **Personal Evaluation Notebook 12.3**.

5. **Use technology.** There are many websites and apps that can help you reduce stress and increase your health: Headspace, Buddhify, Sleepio, Calm, 7 Minute Workout, Relax Melodies, Health (iOS), Zen Habits, and depressioncheck.

6. **Establish healthy relationships.** Research has shown that a strong social network is a strong predictor of health and well-being.[2] Sharing a good talk

Personal Evaluation Notebook 12.3

Committing to Exercise

Read the following and write your comments on the lines provided.

1. Describe your current commitment to physical activity.

   _____

   _____

   _____

2. What are your excuses for not exercising? What can you do to overcome these barriers?

   _____

   _____

   _____

3. Set your exercise goal.

   _____

   _____

   _____

Think about small ways you can create healthy habits. For example, walk to classes, bike with friends, take the stairs, or hike on weekends. Choose to exercise every day. You might go to the health center and ask a professional for more tips and to make certain you're healthy enough for a vigorous exercise program.

or wonderful evening with a friend is deeply satisfying. So is the sense of accomplishment after completing a team project. Indeed, other people can help us think through problems, develop self-confidence, conquer fears, develop courage, brainstorm ideas, overcome boredom and fatigue, and increase our joy and laughter. But sometimes we

- Get so busy at school and work that we ignore friends and family.
- Are shy and find it difficult to build friendships.
- Approach friendship as a competitive sport.

   It takes sensitivity and awareness to value others' needs. It also takes courage to overcome shyness. The key is to see the enormous value of friendships. Friends bring great joy and fellowship to life. Life's sorrows and setbacks are lessened when you have friends to support you through difficult times. (We'll further discuss building healthy relationships in **Chapter 13**.)

• Increasing Energy

Whether your physical activity routine includes power walking around your neighborhood or daily CrossFit workouts, establish a consistent pattern of exercise. *How can you fit in 150 minutes of moderate or 75 minutes of vigorous exercise per week?*

Andres Rodriguez/Alamy Stock Photo

Research has shown that anxiety and eating disorders often go together and show a surge in high school and college.[3] Melissa is determined not to succumb to the "freshman 10" and gain weight at school. In fact, she does the opposite and eats little all day before going out at night with her friends. She believes she looks good even though she's very thin. Her friends have also noticed that she has become anxious and stressed about grades, choosing a major, and other aspects of college.

- What negative psychological and physical patterns regarding food is Melissa displaying?
- How might her diet affect her success in school?
- What should Melissa do differently to meet her goal of a healthy weight? Use creative and critical thinking tools to help her.

Source: Frances E. Jensen, *The Teenage Brain: A Neuroscientist's Survival Guide to Raising Adolescents and Young Adults* (New York: Harper Collins, 2015).

THINK
CREATIVELY AND CRITICALLY

Manage Stress

College students face many demands: papers, tests, deadlines, studying, finances, relationships, and conflicts. Coping with stress means being able to manage difficult circumstances, solve problems, resolve conflicts, and juggle the daily demands of school, work, and home. Stress is the body's natural reaction to *external events* (e.g., taking an exam or giving a speech) and *internal events* (e.g., fear, worry, or unresolved anger). Stress is normal and, in fact, necessary for a vital life. *View challenging events as a chance to learn and grow* and channel stress instead of dealing with it in unproductive ways, such as:

- Denying, ignoring, or repressing feelings or problems.
- Lashing out at other people.
- Using alcohol, tobacco, or other drugs to reduce tension.
- Unhealthy or dangerous eating habits.
- Giving up and telling yourself you're a failure.

Life is a series of changes, and they require you to adapt and cope. The death of a close family member or friend, a serious illness or accident, divorce, break ups, financial problems, and loss of a job are very difficult. It is important to realize that your perception of and reaction to many difficult life events determine how they affect you. Even positive events can be stressful such as a wedding, a promotion, the birth of a baby, a new romantic relationship, and even vacations. *Choose a positive mindset that focuses on making the best of each situation and see it as a*

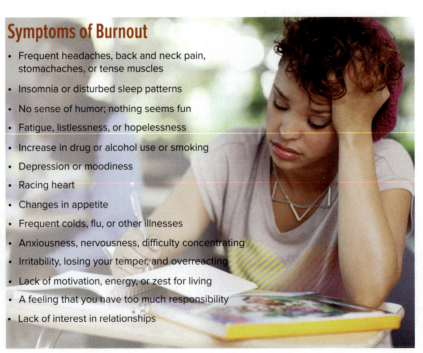

Symptoms of Burnout

- Frequent headaches, back and neck pain, stomachaches, or tense muscles
- Insomnia or disturbed sleep patterns
- No sense of humor; nothing seems fun
- Fatigue, listlessness, or hopelessness
- Increase in drug or alcohol use or smoking
- Depression or moodiness
- Racing heart
- Changes in appetite
- Frequent colds, flu, or other illnesses
- Anxiousness, nervousness, difficulty concentrating
- Irritability, losing your temper, and overreacting
- Lack of motivation, energy, or zest for living
- A feeling that you have too much responsibility
- Lack of interest in relationships

Paul Bradbury/age fotostock

chance to grow and learn. With supportive friends, time, perseverance, and sheer grit you can thrive and flourish.

You can choose to see stress as a challenge or something to avoid. You can adopt a positive, optimistic outlook; use resources; and re-channel energy in productive ways. You can learn to manage stress with coping strategies:

1. **Be mindful.** Become attuned to your body and emotions. The transition to college is major and can cause loneliness and physical symptoms of stress, such as frequent headaches or a depressed or irritable mood. Acknowledge your emotions and forge ahead. "I accept that I'm feeling overwhelmed or down today. I will go to class, exercise, chat with a friend, eat well, and do what I know makes me feel better. I will persist."

2. **Exercise regularly.** *Exercise is one of the best ways to reduce stress.* It helps you to relax your muscles, clears your thoughts, and promotes a sense of well-being. Most people have more energy when they exercise regularly. It can also distract you from ruminating on grievances, negative thoughts, and falling into unhealthy habits such as overeating.

3. **Dispute negative thoughts.** *A positive, open mindset helps you challenge self-defeating thoughts and replace them with realistic, hopeful thoughts that focus on growth and learning.*

4. **Rest and renew your mind, body, and spirit.** Everyone needs to rest, not only through sleep but also through deep relaxation. Too little of either causes irritability, depression, inability to concentrate, and memory loss. Yoga and pilates are great ways to unwind, stretch and tone the muscles, and focus energy through mindfulness. *Create a time for yourself when you are mindful—your mind is at rest and quiet.* Go for a walk, get a hobby, listen to music, create art, dance, sing, or get a massage. Visualization is another powerful technique for relaxing your body and reducing anxiety.

5. **Use breathing methods.** *Deep breathing reduces stress, energizes the body, and helps you find peace through mindfulness.* Many people breathe in short, shallow breaths, especially when under stress. Begin by sitting or standing up straight; breathe through your nose, fill your lungs completely, push out your abdomen, and exhale slowly and fully. Focus on a word, a sound, or your breathing, and give it your full attention. You can do a variation of this anytime during the day, even if you can't escape to a quiet spot. *Practice being fully in the present moment.* Research has shown that mindfulness has a powerful influence over your health, well-being, and happiness.[4] *Mindfulness really is key for reducing stress.*

6. **Develop hobbies, interests, and ideas.** Sports, crafts, reading, and collecting can add fun and meaning to your life. Many get satisfaction from developing an interest in a cause or need, such as protecting the environment, spending time with older adults, becoming an activist and fighting for change in politics, volunteering or supporting the local animal shelter, or working at a food bank. Mental exercise is also important—read, complete crossword puzzles, and play challenging board games. Attend lectures, take workshops and seminars, and brainstorm creative ideas or current subjects with well-read friends. Make friends with creative people who inspire and renew you.

7. **Create a support system.** The support and comfort of family and friends can help you clear your mind, make better decisions, reduce stress, increase your health, and create a sense of well-being. Express your feelings, fears, and problems to people you trust. A support group of people with similar

experiences and goals can give you a sense of security, personal fulfillment, and motivation.

8. **Take mini-vacations.** When you are waiting on hold or in line, pull out a novel and enjoy a few moments of reading or practice deep breathing, small stretches, or visualize the tension flowing out of your body. Get up and stretch periodically while you're studying. Mini-vacations can keep you relaxed, creative, and make you grateful for being alive.

9. **Rehearse a feared or stressful event.** When you mentally rehearse a stressful event beforehand, your fears become known and manageable. Prepare for likely events and write out a plan. For example, practice giving speeches or taking tests. This can also apply to work situations. Let's say you work in a coffee shop. You know you will have impatient and rude customers so you write out a script, practice staying calm and helpful, focus on solving the problem, resist taking the attack personally, and reward yourself with the wonderful satisfaction of knowing that you are in control of your emotions and actions.

10. **Try meditation.** Meditation is any method used to train the mind to be calm and achieve a state of consciousness that reduces stress and distractions. Some techniques focus on a mantra or saying and others encourage awareness of the breath by being aware moment by moment. Research has shown that people who regularly meditate have lower blood pressure and less stress.[5] Many people insist that they have achieved clarity, insights, and a sense of well-being and reduced their level of stress through meditation and mindfulness. A popular app is Headspace. Others are mood check-ins, Calm, Insight Timer, and GPS for the Soul.

11. **Create balance in your life.** Work hard and then have fun and play. Assess whether your activities are distractions or opportunities. Say "no" to requests that do not enrich your life (recall **Peak Progress 4.3**). Set time limits on work, demands from others, and study; reward yourself for finishing tasks by being playful and having fun.

12. **Develop a sense of humor.** *Nothing reduces stress like a hearty laugh or spontaneous fun.* Laughing produces endorphins, natural chemicals that strengthen the immune system and produce a sense of well-being. Laughter also increases oxygen flow to the brain and causes other positive physiological changes. Smile, laugh, and be grateful.

13. **Plan; don't worry.** A disorganized life is stressful. Write down what has to be done each day; don't rely on your memory. Take a few minutes the night before to pack your lunch and list the next day's priorities. Get up 20 minutes early so that you don't have to rush. Set aside time each day to plan, solve problems, and explore solutions. When your time is up, leave the problems until your next scheduled session.

14. **Be assertive.** Stand up for your rights, express your preferences, and acknowledge your feelings. Assertive communication helps you solve problems, rather than build resentment and anger, and increases your confidence and control over your life. Speak up, ask for what you want in a respectful way, and then let it go and move on. Don't hold on to resentments or grievances. Put your energy into creating a wonderful life.

15. **Keep a journal.** A journal can give you insight into what types of situations you find stressful and how you respond to them. Be honest with yourself and take stock of your successes and setbacks. Don't just record daily events, but

include reflection, mindfulness, and insights into your thoughts, feelings, and reactions. Jot down inspirational quotes and always include the positive events that happen every day. This becomes a gratitude journal to help you stay focused on the positive.

16. **Get professional help.** Grief after a loss or major transition is normal. Allow yourself time to grieve in order to experience and release your emotional pain. However, if your sadness, depression, or anger continues despite your best efforts, or if you are suicidal, get professional help. With a counselor's guidance, you can gain insight into your pattern of reacting to stress and modify your perception and behavior. (See **Peak Progress 12.3** on using the Adult Learning Cycle to create a more healthy balance.)

Unhealthy Addictions

Addiction is a disease that can be treated. Unfortunately, many people turn to alcohol, other drugs, cigarettes, vaping, and prescription pills to relieve stress. A big concern health professionals have about students smoking or drinking every day is that it delays developing coping skills, resulting in serious problems. Rather than risking your health and potential lifelong addictions, practice coping strategies, such as facing your problems head on, resolving conflicts through communication, and finding creative solutions. *Unhealthy behaviors will only escalate your problems. Research has shown that the same adolescent brain that learns so quickly because it is primed for learning is unfortunately also more prone to addictions.* Because their brains are still developing, teenagers and young adults get addicted to substances faster than adults and, once addicted, have much greater difficulty ridding themselves of the habit. *Often this addiction lasts their entire lives.*

Alcohol Abuse

Alcohol is a drug that can alter moods, become habit-forming, and cause changes in the body. It depresses the central nervous system, delaying reaction times and clouding personal judgment. Just one night of heavy drinking can impair your ability to think abstractly for up to 30 days.

There are more than 25 million people with an alcohol addiction in the United States and most began drinking in high school and college.

For most adults, a glass of wine or a beer at dinner is not a problem, but even a small amount of alcohol can cause slowed reactions and poor judgment. See **Figure 12.2** on how to "Party Safely."

Students often believe there's no problem if they drink just beer, but a six-pack of beer contains the same amount of alcohol as six drinks of hard liquor—or one beer is equivalent to one shot of hard liquor. **Binge drinking** means consuming five or more drinks in a row for men, or four or more drinks in a row for women, at least once in the previous two weeks. *Binge drinking can lead to serious problems,* including fights, injuries, academic problems, suspension, DUIs, blackouts, and even death. Learn to drink responsibly.

Alcoholism is a chronic disease that can be progressive and even fatal. A major life lesson is to think for yourself and be responsible for your choices and behavior.

Nicotine Addiction

Despite the risks, yet 46 million adults in the United States smoke cigarettes, e-cigarettes, and vape. Get the facts about nicotine addiction. Check out **www.cancer.org/healthy/stayawayfromtobacco/guidetoquittingsmoking/**.

Illegal Drug Use

The cost of drug abuse to American society is approximately $50 billion a year. Almost 80 percent of people in their mid-twenties have tried illegal drugs.

Marijuana is now a legal drug in many states. Get the facts on any drug you are taking!

Figure **12.2**

Party Safely: Tips for moderating alcohol while partying

Prescription and Over-the-Counter Medication Abuse

When used as directed, medications can be beneficial. However, roughly one in five people in the United States have used prescription drugs for nonmedical reasons. Likewise, over-the-counter (OTC) drugs are abused for the high or other effects they produce—but often with serious consequences, especially when taken in large doses or combined with other drugs. Medicines containing dextromethorphan (DXM), such as cold medications, are the most abused OTC drugs. Excessive doses can lead to hallucinations, seizures, brain damage, and death. As mentioned in **Chapter 9**, Adderall is often abused by students who think it gives them an edge while studying, helping them to focus. However, the potential side effects far outweigh any benefits.

Social Media Addictions

Addictive behavior comes in many forms, not just substance abuse. Just as an alcoholic feels happy when drinking, social media can be addicting too. Do you have to have your phone with you at all times? Do you have your phone next to you in bed?

THE COSTS OF SMOKING

- Cigarette smoking-related diseases cause about 443,600 deaths each year in the United States, killing more Americans than alcohol, car accidents, suicide, AIDS, homicide, and illegal drugs combined.
- Cigarette smoking is directly responsible for 87 percent of all lung cancer cases.
- The Environmental Protection Agency estimates that secondhand smoke causes about 3,400 lung cancer deaths and 46,000 heart disease deaths in nonsmokers each year.
- Nonsmokers married to smokers have a 30 percent greater risk for lung cancer than those married to nonsmokers.
- Secondhand smoke contains more than 4,000 chemicals: 200 are poisons and 63 cause cancer.
- Smoking costs the United States more than $190 billion each year in health care costs and lost productivity.
- On average, adults who smoke cigarettes die 14 years earlier than nonsmokers.

Digital Vision/Getty Images

• The Last Text

Many people find it hard to put down their phone, even when driving. However, 3,331 people were killed and almost 390,000 injured in 2011 due to distracted driving. Drivers who use handheld devices are four times more likely to get into crashes serious enough to injure themselves. *Do you text and drive? Do you agree with laws that prohibit use of digital devices while driving? What other distractions can cause accidents?*

https://www.edgarsnyder.com/car-accident/cause-of-accident/cell-phone/cell-phone-statistics.html

antoniodiaz/Shutterstock

Do you check your phone often even when you're with others? Do you spend hours on sites? Is social media keeping you from your goals? Do you check social media for news instead of listening to a variety of reputable news sources? *Addiction is an abnormal relationship with an object or event and involves repeatedly using a substance or performing a behavior.* Beginning as a pleasurable act or a means of escape, it progresses until it becomes a compulsive behavior that causes significant problems. Do you have a pattern of addiction? If you don't get this under control now, it will only get worse. *Reflect on what triggers an urge to get involved with unhealthy habits and replace the trigger and routine with healthy habits.* Reward yourself by being with friends who also have healthy habits and support you. Seek help through the health center, counseling center, or psychology department if you're addicted. Don't wait.

A person trying to overcome an addiction may experience anxiety, irritability, or moodiness. You may become withdrawn, depressed, or aggressive. You must take the initiative to get help.

Here are some additional steps to take to deal with an addiction:

- *Admit there is a problem.* The first step in solving a problem is to face it. Many people with addictions react to problems with denial. They may do well in school or hold down a job and, therefore, don't see a problem, even if others around them do see a problem. If you think you have lost control or are involved with someone who has, admit it and take charge of your life. Replace negative habits with positive ones.

- *Take responsibility for addiction and recovery.* You are responsible for your behavior. Several support groups and treatment programs are available for various addictions. Search the Internet for resources in your area, or contact the following:

  Alcoholism: Alcoholics Anonymous: **www.aa.org**

  Distracted driving: U.S. Department of Transportation website for Distracted Driving: **www.distraction.gov**

  Drug abuse: National Institute on Drug Abuse: **www.drugabuse.gov**

  Gambling: National Council on Problem Gambling: **www.ncpgambling.org**

  Sexual behavior: The Society for the Advancement of Sexual Health: **www.sash.net**

  Smoking: Centers for Disease Control and Prevention, Smoking and Tobacco Use: **www.cdc.gov/tobacco**

Codependency

Even if you do not abuse alcohol or other drugs, your life may be affected by someone who does. A common term used to describe non-addicted people whose lives are affected by an addict is **codependency**. Codependent people exhibit numerous self-defeating behaviors, such as low self-esteem; lack of strong, emotionally fulfilling relationships; lack of self-control; and over-controlling behavior. A codependent person may

- *Avoid facing the problem of addiction.* Denying, making excuses, justifying, rationalizing, blaming, controlling, and covering up are all games that a codependent person plays in an effort to cope with living with an addict.

- *Take responsibility for the addict's life.* This may include lying; taking over a job, an assignment, or a deadline; or somehow rescuing the addict.
- *Be obsessed with controlling the addict's behavior.* A codependent person may hide bottles; put on a happy face; hide feelings of anger; confuse love and pity; and feel that, if only they could help more, the addict would quit.

If you feel you have problems in your life as a result of growing up in an alcoholic family or may be codependent, get help. Organizations such as Adult Children of Alcoholics (ACA) address the issues of people who grew up in alcoholic homes. Call today.

Emotional Health

Everyone gets depressed occasionally as a result of difficult situations. However, sometimes stress and emotional problems interfere with your goals or ability to cope. If you are depressed without a real cause, it may be due to chemical imbalances in the brain. When this happens, it is then time to ask for help. Go to the health center or counseling department and talk with a professional.

Depression

Depression is an emotional state of sadness ranging from mild discouragement to utter hopelessness. Anxiety, like depression, is a frequent complaint of new college students. If you are experiencing depression or anxiety that interferes with normal functioning, ask for help from the counseling center or health center. Don't wait. There is help available.

Depression can occur as a response to the following situations:

- *Loss.* The death of a loved one, divorce, the breakup of a relationship, the loss of a job, involvement in a robbery or an assault, or any other major change, loss, disappointment, or violation can trigger depression.
- *Health changes.* Physical changes, such as a serious illness, an injury, childbirth, or menopause, can produce chemical changes that can cause depression.
- *An accident.* A car accident can be very traumatic, leading to feelings of being out of control and depression. Even if you were not seriously injured, feelings of hopelessness or guilt can result from an accident.
- *Unhealthy relationships.* Unresolved conflicts in relationships can cause depression. It is so easy to be negative, but healthy relationships need to be supportive and positive. Research suggests that stable relationships require that good interactions outnumber bad interactions by at least five to one.[6]
- *Loneliness.* Loneliness can seem like a physical illness—painful or as dark as if someone has thrown a heavy blanket over your life. *It is often felt by freshmen who have left home and haven't yet rebuilt a social network.* (We'll discuss loneliness in more detail in **Chapter 13**.) *Get involved* in school activities and in the community, get a part-time job, volunteer, and develop new relationships through clubs, spiritual groups, sports, theater, and political activities. A support system is a vital for well-being. When you connect and get involved, it does get better. So get going.
- *Peer pressure.* You may feel pressured to get involved in alcohol, other drugs, smoking, or sex. When you have doubts, stop and think about the consequences. Ask why you are allowing others to define your values

WARNING SIGNS OF DEPRESSION

- Sleep disturbance (sleeping too much or too little, constantly waking up)
- Increase in or loss of appetite
- Overuse of alcohol or prescription and/or nonprescription drugs
- Withdrawal from family and friends, leading to feelings of isolation
- Avoidance of teachers, classmates, and co-workers and lack of attendance
- Recurring feelings of anxiety
- Anger and irritability for no apparent reason
- Loss of interest in formerly pleasurable activities
- A feeling that simple activities are too much trouble
- A feeling that other people have much more than you have

paolo81/Getty Images

and boundaries. When you do something you are uncomfortable with, you may experience depression or sadness as if you have lost a sense of who you really are.

- *Daily demands.* You may feel overwhelmed by too many demands, such as deadlines or the pressure to choose a major. Nontraditional, or reentry, students often must juggle school, work, family, and care of their home. Set priorities, ask for help, and try to eliminate or reduce unimportant or routine tasks. Delegate whenever possible.

Depression can be triggered by many events. Some of these relate to certain stages in life. For example, adolescents are just beginning to realize who they are and are trying to cope with the responsibilities of freedom and adulthood. Someone facing middle age may regret the loss of youth or unrealized career goals or may miss children who are leaving home. For an elderly person, the loss of physical strength, illness, the death of friends, and growing dependency may prompt depression. Research has shown that adolescent depression is more likely to be chronic.[7] When depression causes persistent sadness and continues beyond a month, severe depression may be present. Check out **https://www.cdc.gov/violenceprevention/suicide/riskprotectivefactors.html**.

Suicide

More than 4,000 people in the United States between the ages of 16 and 25 die from suicide each year, making it the third leading cause of death for young people. Suicidal thoughts occur when a feeling of hopelessness sets in and problems seem unbearable. Suicidal people think the pain will never end, but it will get better. If you or someone you know exhibits warning signs, suffers from depression, or seems suicidal, take these steps:

1. **Remain calm.** People do care. Repeat the true saying that suicide is a permanent solution to a temporary problem. This too shall pass. Help is available.
2. **Take this seriously.** Don't ignore the situation.

WARNING SIGNS OF SUICIDE

- Excessive alcohol or other drug use
- Significant changes in emotions (hyperactivity, withdrawal, mood swings)
- Significant changes in weight or in sleeping, eating, or studying patterns
- Feelings of hopelessness or helplessness
- Little time spent with or a lack of close, supportive friends
- Nonsupportive family ties
- Rare participation in group activities
- Recent loss or traumatic or stressful events
- Suicidal statements
- A close friend or family member who committed suicide
- Attempted suicide in the past
- Participation in dangerous activities
- A plan for committing suicide or for giving away possessions

KatarzynaBialasiewicz/Getty Images

3. **Talk.** Share your thoughts and feelings and encourage the other person to talk.

4. **Listen attentively.** Listen without moralizing or judging. Acknowledge feelings.

5. **Get professional help.** Counseling can help and is confidential. Call a crisis hot line, health center, school or community counseling center, or mental health department for a list of agencies that can help. If helping a friend, get the name of a counselor for the person to call, or make the call and offer to drive to the appointment.

6. **Get a promise.** Promise yourself and others that you will talk with a professional when depressed and helpless. Reaching out shows strength, not weakness.

7. **Remove guns.** Get rid of drugs, pills, and razors. Don't make it easy to inflict harm.

8. **Be with others.** Get support if you are depressed. Don't be alone.

9. **Follow up.** Stay in touch with friends and your counselor. Follow up if you are helping a person or if you are getting professional help, taking medication, coping well with life, and so on.

10. **Get informed.** There are resources to help if you or someone is suicidal. This can be very stressful. Try these sources: American Foundation for Suicide Prevention at **www.afsp.org** and **https://afsp.org/about-suicide/ risk-factors-and-warning-signs/**.

Protecting Your Body

Reliable information about sex can help you handle the many physical and emotional changes you will experience in life. Although sex is a basic human drive and natural part of life, there are dangers, including sexually transmitted infections, and unplanned pregnancies. Your level of sexual activity is a personal choice and can change with knowledge, understanding, and awareness. Having been sexually active at one time does not rule out a choice to be celibate now. No one should pressure you into sexual intercourse. If you decide to be sexually active, you need to make responsible decisions and protect yourself.

Sexually Transmitted Infections (STIs)

Sexually transmitted infections, or STIs, are spread through sexual contact (including genital, vaginal, anal, and oral contact) with an infected partner who may appear healthy and symptom-free. See **Figure 12.3** for a list of STIs and their symptoms, treatments, and risks. *STIs infect significant numbers of young adults.* Even if treated early, STIs are a major health risk and can damage the reproductive organs and cause infertility or cancer.

Human papillomavirus (HPV) is the most common STI. Approximately 79 million Americans are currently infected with HPV, and 14 million people become newly infected each year. Anyone participating in vaginal, anal, or oral sex can contract HPV. HPV is so common that nearly all sexually active people get it at some point in their lives, with 90 percent of infections clearing up on their own. There are more than 40 types of HPV that can infect both men and women, leading to genital warts and cancer people ages 11 to 26 to prevent HPV prior to becoming sexually active. Cervarix is another vaccine to protect against the types of HPV that cause most cervical cancers.

Acquired immune deficiency syndrome (AIDS) weakens the immune system and leads to an inability to fight infection. HIV can be transmitted through sexual contact, by sharing nonsterile intravenous needles or blood transfusions. It can also be passed on genetically while a fetus is in utero. There are many options for treatment.

HIV cannot be transmitted by saliva or casual contact, such as sharing utensils or shaking hands. Therapies using a combination of drugs have succeeded in controlling the progression of the disease. Although there is currently no cure for AIDS, there is help. Go to the student health center or local health department for testing. The Public Health Service has a toll-free AIDS hotline (800-342-AIDS), and local and state hotlines are available.

To avoid contracting any STI, follow these guidelines:

- Know your partner. It takes time and awareness to develop a healthy relationship.
- Ask a prospective partner about their health. Don't assume anything based on looks, class, or behavior.
- No matter what the other person's health status is, explain that you always use safety precautions. (Avoid unnecessary or unknown risks with sexual partners by always using a condom.)
- Latex condoms and dental dams can help protect against most sexually transmitted diseases. However, abstinence is the only totally effective method of preventing the spread of STIs, as well as pregnancy.

Birth Control

If your relationship is intimate enough for sex, it should be open enough to discuss birth control and pregnancy if birth control fails. Both partners need to stop and ask, "How would an unwanted pregnancy change my life? What choices would I make?"

Sexually Transmitted Infection	What Are the Common Symptoms?	What Is the Treatment?	What Are the Risks?
AIDS/HIV	No symptoms for years; some carriers can be HIV+; you may develop mild infections or chronic signs and symptoms such as fever, rash, headache, sore throat, etc. https://www.mayoclinic.org/diseases-conditions/hiv-aids/symptoms-causes/syc-20373524	No known cure; medical treatments can slow the disease	Weakening of the immune system; life-threatening infections
Chlamydia	Known as the "silent" disease because most infected people have no symptoms; others may experience discharge from genitals or a burning sensation when urinating	Antibiotics	More susceptible to developing pelvic inflammatory disease and infertility, and to having premature babies; can infect baby's eyes and respiratory tract during delivery
Genital herpes	Ulcers (sores) or blisters around the genitals	No cure; antiviral medications can shorten and prevent outbreaks	Highly contagious; become more susceptible to HIV infection; can also be spread via oral sex
Genital warts	The virus (human papillomavirus, or HPV) lives in the skin or mucous membranes and usually causes no symptoms; some will get visible genital warts	No cure, although the infection usually goes away on its own; cancer-related types of HPV are more likely to persist	Higher risk of cervical cancer
Gonorrhea	Symptoms include a painful or burning sensation when urinating; men may have a white, yellow, or green discharge from the penis or painful or swollen testicles; women may have an increased vaginal discharge or vaginal bleeding between periods; however, most women have no symptoms	Antibiotics	More susceptible to pelvic inflammatory disease, infertility, and HIV
Syphilis	Early symptoms include one or multiple sores; later symptoms vary from a rash to fever, hair loss, sore throat, and fatigue	Antibiotics	Untreated, can lead to damage of internal organs, paralysis, blindness, and death
Trichomoniasis	Men may experience temporary irritation inside the penis, mild discharge, or slight burning after urination or ejaculation; women may have a yellow-green vaginal discharge with a strong odor	Prescription drugs	More susceptible to contracting HIV; giving birth to premature or underweight babies

Source: Centers for Disease Control and Prevention, Division of Sexually Transmitted Diseases, www.cdc.gov/std.

Figure **12.3**

STIs: Symptoms, Treatments, and Risks

Because STIs are a serious health risk, it is important to separate fact from myth when considering your options for protection. *In what ways can knowing the facts about STIs protect you?*

Many contraceptives are available, but only abstinence is 100 percent foolproof. Current contraceptives include birth control pills, condoms, diaphragms, sponges, spermicidal foams, cervical caps, intrauterine devices (IUDs), and long-term implants. Douching and withdrawal do not prevent pregnancy and should not be used for birth control. Discuss birth control methods with your partner and with a qualified health professional.

Consent

Katie, a sophomore living off-campus, is on her third date with Jeff, who is in her English class. They have been having a great time together, and Jeff is attentive and loving. In fact, Katie has told friends that he puts her on a pedestal. After a movie, they are sitting on her living room couch, drinking wine, talking, and sharing hugs and kisses. Jeff's kissing becomes more aggressive, and Katie pushes his hands away and tells him she feels uncomfortable. She explains that she wants to take the relationship slowly, and is not ready for sex. Jeff respects her decision. He understands that Katie has not given consent to take their relationship further.

It is important that both partners recognize consent. If you do not want to have sex, express your wishes clearly and without apology.

Here are a few suggestions:

1. **Make your expectations clear.** *Send clear messages and make certain that your body language, tone of voice, and word choices match your feelings.* In a direct, forceful, serious tone, let others know when consent is not given. If you don't want to get physically intimate, don't allow anyone to talk you into it. Be aware of your limits and feelings, and communicate them assertively. Say, "No," loudly and clearly.

2. **Meet in public places.** Until you know someone well, arrange to meet where others will be around. Double-date whenever possible or go out with a group of friends. *Agree with friends that you will not leave a party alone or with someone you do not know well.*

3. **Trust your intuition.** Be aware of your surroundings, and trust your instincts. *If the situation doesn't feel right, leave.* If you feel ill, get help immediately. If you plan to go to a movie, to a party, or for a walk, ask a friend to go with you. If you're on a date, tell others when you expect to be back, take your cell phone, and leave your date's name. If something doesn't feel right, contact your roommate or a friend or take a cab home.

4. **Take your time.** *Take time to know a person before you spend time alone.* Don't take chances because someone looks nice or knows someone you know. Don't invite anyone to your home unless you know this person well. Otherwise, make certain a roommate or friends are around. Relationships that start slowly are built on friendship and are healthier and safer. Be cautious and smart.

5. **Recognize that alcohol and other drugs can be dangerous.** They can inhibit resistance, increase aggression, and impair decision-making skills. If you are intoxicated, you may not be able to protect yourself or notice the signals that should warn you of danger. Never leave your drink unattended, and do not accept drinks from a common container.

6. **Learn to read the danger signals of an unhealthy relationship.** Be concerned if you are dating someone who

- Pressures you sexually
- Refers to people as sex objects
- Drinks heavily or uses drugs and pressures you to drink or take drugs
- Doesn't respect your wants, needs, or opinions
- Is possessive or jealous
- Wants to make decisions for you—tells you whom you may be friends with or what clothes to wear
- Has a temper and acts rashly
- Is physically abusive
- Is verbally and emotionally abusive through insults, belittling comments, or "sulking" behavior
- Becomes angry when you say, "No"

7. **Be safe and vigilant.** Make wise choices, use common sense, and do everything possible to protect yourself. Don't go jogging alone or in isolated areas, lock your doors and windows, and don't pick up hitchhikers. Know your campus and community well, and stay out of dark, secluded areas. If you are taking a night class, find the safest place to park your car. Use a campus escort, or arrange to walk to your car with a friend or group from your class. Contact the local recreation center or police to learn if a self-defense course is available and ways you can protect yourself.

8. **Get professional help.** Men as well as women can become victims of physical, sexual, and mental abuse. Speak up and challenge demeaning and cruel jokes and attitudes by learning more about consent. Check the counseling center for support.

Overcoming Obstacles with Better Habits

On your journey to creating optimal health, you will run into obstacles. *A positive mindset focuses on growth, learning, and effort. It builds resiliency through grit and perseverance.* Create habits that flow from these powerful beliefs. With effort, you can create lasting change.

Willpower isn't just a skill that you learn. It's really more like a muscle, and if you increase willpower in one area, it often spills over to other parts of your life. Some habits are called *keystone habits* because they affect other areas of your life. Exercise is a keystone habit. For example, participants who worked out at the gym or consistently jogged drank less alcohol, smoked less or quit, drank less caffeine, and ate less junk food. People who took a money management program where they set goals and became more disciplined with saving not only improved their finances, but also exercised more, ate healthier, watched less television, and also drank less. The same results occurred when students were enrolled in an academic improvement program that focused on creating positive study habits. What happens is that you change the way you think and that changes your behavior.

If you identify the trigger and rewards, you can change the behavior and rewards. Let's say that you've had a few nights of binge drinking and you realize how destructive this is to your body and how awful you feel the next day. You've realized that the *trigger* for drinking is the burst of stimulation to your evening, a way to become more social and less inhibited. You create a *routine* that allows you

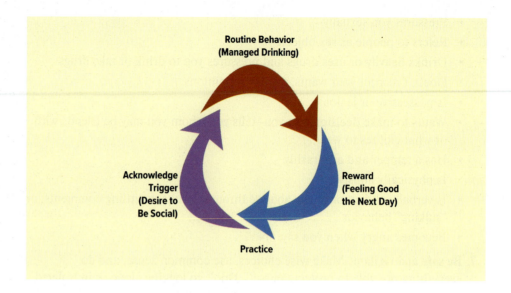

Routine Behavior
(Managed Drinking)

Acknowledge
Trigger
(Desire to
Be Social)

Reward
(Feeling Good
the Next Day)

Practice

to drink one drink an hour, twice a week, and no more than three drinks in one day. Evenings that you don't drink, you are the designated driver and with a clear mind you see the effects of too much alcohol on others. This observation strengthens your routine. Your *reward* is staying sober and in control and feeling good the next day. This routine satisfies your craving for socializing, having a good time with friends, and, most of all, the wonderful feeling that you are learning to drink in moderation. You take pride in your self-control and discipline.

Let's look at what is involved in creating a habit and apply it to the **Self-Management** feature at the opening of the chapter. The young woman, Lisa, is overwhelmed with starting college, meeting new people, feeling homesick, and missing old friends. She started smoking in high school when she hung out with her artist friends and smoking and socializing were soon linked together, but not only do her new roommates not smoke, but they find it disgusting. In fact, the culture at this college is focused on health, outdoor sports, and exercise so

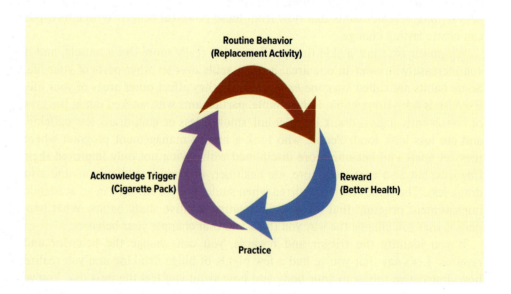

Routine Behavior
(Replacement Activity)

Acknowledge Trigger
(Cigarette Pack)

Reward
(Better Health)

Practice

few students or faculty smoke. Lisa decides to focus on one thing to help her adjust to college and help her feel more in control and less overwhelmed. She decides that when the craving for nicotine hits, she would create a new *routine* and go for a walk or jog with one of her roommates. She threw away her pack of Lucky Strike Lights, which was a *trigger*. She replaced the old trigger with a new trigger—running shoes. Now being outdoors, walking with friends, and socializing were linked. The *reward* she gets is the accomplishment of quitting smoking, feeling healthier, and socializing. Soon she joined the Outdoors Activity Club. This one habit shifted her thinking in many ways. She began to create a study routine with several students and started exercising more and eating healthier. She made a lot of new friends and adjusted quickly. Within weeks, she felt like she belonged at this college and her life was in control. Despite the stresses of college, Lisa no longer felt overwhelmed.

TAKING CHARGE

Summary

In this chapter, I learned to

- **Connect my mind, body, and spirit.** I envision my mind, body, and spirit as a whole system and realize that everything is connected. I observe my thoughts, how my body feels, my level of stress, my negative habits, what I eat and drink, and changes or discomfort in my body. I create a positive, growth mindset that builds resiliency.

- **Eat a variety of healthy foods in moderation.** I increase my consumption of fresh fruits and vegetables; include good fiber sources; limit animal fat; avoid fried foods; cut down on salt, sugar, "diet" foods, and caffeine; and take a multivitamin supplement every day. This helps me maintain healthy eating habits, increases my self-esteem, and gives me energy.

- **Exercise regularly.** I combine moderate and vigorous intensity aerobic exercise each week. I also choose activities two to three days per week that build strength, muscular endurance, and flexibility. I balance rest and relaxation with active sports, such as bicycling, dancing, or swimming. Being active helps my body become stronger, gives me energy, and increases my sense of well-being.

- **Develop healthy relationships.** Spending time with friends who are supportive and share my interests is a great source of satisfaction, and it adds to my energy and enjoyment of life. Friendships bring great joy and fellowship.

- **Reduce stress.** I have developed strategies for reducing stress, including exercising, doing deep breathing, disputing negative thoughts and beliefs, developing a sense of humor, rehearsing feared events, and creating balance in my life.

- **Use critical thinking to avoid drugs.** Alcohol is a toxin. Heavy drinking can damage the brain, increase the risk of heart disease, depress the immune system, and cause liver failure. Alcohol and other drugs can cause memory loss and impair reasoning.

- **Get help for addictions.** I recognize the signs of addiction to food, gambling, and alcohol and other drugs and know when to seek help. I know that campus and community resources can help me or someone I know who has a drinking or other drug problem.

- **Observe my emotional health.** Although I know life has its ups and downs, I am aware of times when I don't bounce back after a disappointment or loss. Some warning signs of depression are changes in sleep patterns and appetite, drug use, and feelings of anxiety, anger, isolation, and disinterest. Severe depression and suicidal tendencies occur when feelings are extreme.

- **Protect my body.** I protect myself from illness, sexually transmitted infections, unwanted pregnancies, and rape. I am knowledgeable, aware, and proactive. I visit the health center, use safety precautions, and learn self-defense techniques.

Performance Strategies

Following are the top 10 tips for achieving a healthy lifestyle:

- Be aware of your body, your emotions, your unhealthy habits, and unexpected changes.
- Focus on healthy eating and a balanced diet.
- Exercise regularly.
- Get enough rest and renewal time.
- Develop supportive and healthy relationships.
- Develop coping strategies for managing stress.
- Avoid addictive substances, such as cigarettes, alcohol, and other drugs.
- Get help immediately for depression and mental distress.
- Protect yourself from sexually transmitted infections and unwanted pregnancy.

Tech for Success

- **Health on the Web.** More sites on the Internet are devoted to health than any other topic. However, how do you know which sites provide accurate information? Start with government, professional organization, and nonprofit sites. Many of these offer questions to ask or red flags to look for when consulting with physicians or purchasing products on the Internet.

- **Assess yourself.** You will find a vast array of free personal assessment tools on the Internet. You can explore everything from ideal body weight to your risk of developing a certain cancer. Use assessments to help you identify patterns and behaviors you want to change. As with all information on the Internet, check the source or research behind the assessment tool.

- **Just what is in that burger? The website of almost every fast-food chain provides the caloric breakdown of its most popular items.** Before your next trip to your favorite restaurant, look up the calories and fat content of your usual order. Is it what you expected, or even higher? Does this information affect your selections?

- **Music to my ears.** You may enjoy listening through headphones or earbuds, but follow the 60/60 rule to preserve your hearing: no more than 60 percent volume for no more than 60 minutes at a stretch.

Endnotes

[1] Robert Stickgold, "Sleep-Dependent Memory Consolidation," *Nature* 437, no. 7063 (Oct. 27, 2005), pp 1272–78.

[2] Frances E. Jensen, *The Teenage Brain: A Neuroscientist's Survival Guide to Raising Adolescents and Young Adults* (New York: HarperCollins, 2015).

[3] Julianne Holt-Lunstad, Timothy B. Smith, and J. Bradley Layton, "Social Relationships and Mortality Risk: A Meta-Analytic Review," *PLoS Medicine* 7, no. 7 (July 27, 2010), http://journals.plos.org/plosmedicine/article?id=10.1371%2Fjournal.pmed.1000316, accessed April 3, 2016.

[4] Julianne Holt-Lunstad, Timothy B. Smith, and J. Bradley Layton, "Social Relationships and Mortality Risk: A Meta-Analytic Review," *PLoS Medicine* 7, no. 7 (July 27, 2010), http://journals.plos.org/plosmedicine/article?id=10.1371%2Fjournal.pmed.1000316, accessed April 3, 2016.

[5] Jon Kabat-Zinn, "Mindfulness-Based Interventions in Context: Past, Present, and Future," *Clinical Psychology: Science and Practice* 10, no. 2 (2003), pp 144–56.

[6] John Gottman, *Why Marriages Succeed or Fail: And How You Can Make Yours Last* (New York: Simon and Schuster, 1995).

[7] Jensen, *The Teenage Brain.*

Study Team Notes

Career *in* Focus

Tony Ferraro
FIREFIGHTER

Related Majors: Fire Science, Public Administration

Preventing Stress and Fatigue at Work

Tony Ferraro has been a member of his city's fire department for 25 years. Three years ago, he was promoted to captain. He and the other firefighters at his station respond to fire alarms using various techniques to put out fires. They also respond to medical emergencies by providing emergency medical assistance until an ambulance arrives. When not out on calls, Tony and his crew maintain their equipment, participate in drills and advanced firefighting classes, and keep physically fit.

Tony works two or three 24-hour shifts a week, during which time he lives and eats at the fire station. Because firefighting involves considerable risks for injury or even death, the job is stressful and demanding. Being alert, physically fit, calm, and clear-headed is critical for making sound decisions. To stay healthy mentally and physically, Tony studies a form of karate that helps him not only stay in shape but also remain calm and focused. In addition, he drinks no more than one to two cups of coffee a day and has given up smoking.

As captain of his fire station, Tony has initiated better eating habits in the kitchen by posting a food guide and talking to the other firefighters about reducing fat and salt in their diet. In addition, he observes the firefighters for signs of stress and makes suggestions when needed, such as taking time off or getting more rest. The company's health insurance policy includes coverage for counseling. Once after a particularly stressful period, Tony invited a stress counselor to speak and offer services at the station.

CRITICAL THINKING Why do firefighters need to work toward goals for physical, emotional, and mental health?

Peak Performer Profile

Mark Herzlich Jr.

When Sandon Mark Herzlich Jr. found out he had Ewing's Sarcoma, a rare form of cancer, he went home and sulked for two hours. After those two hours were over, Herzlich realized, "This [cancer] has got to be something I overcome. Once I made that decision, I was ready."

Herzlich, a linebacker with the Boston College Eagles football team, had already beaten the odds in his sports career. As a college freshman, he received Freshman All-American team honorable mention from the *College Football News.* In his junior season, Herzlich was named a First-team All-American, the ACC Defensive Player of the Year, and a finalist for the Lott Trophy. He was ranked as the 45th best prospect for the 2009 NFL Draft before announcing his decision to return to Boston College the following season to finish his degree.

After his diagnosis in May 2008, Herzlich returned to school, and to the field, to provide others help during his illness. He ran with the team at the beginning of games and served as a right-hand man for the team coach. His behind-the-scenes work was even more valuable. He spent his time providing orientation to incoming freshmen, counseling kids with cancer, and raising about $200,000 through "Uplifting Athletes," an agency that raises awareness of rare diseases.

Herzlich has said of his volunteer activities, "I like this being part of me. It's something that's exciting, in that I get to be able to help other people." He was, however, also excited for his return as a player for the Boston College Eagles, after his cancer-free diagnosis in October of 2009. Now a professional football player, he takes care of himself by not taking any risks that could hurt his recovering body, and routinely checks for any lingering effects of the cancer and its treatment. In all areas, Herzlich defines a peak performer: in mind, body, and spirit.

PERFORMANCE THINKING How did Herzlich's refusal to "sulk" put him onto a path toward self-determination and success over cancer? How do his actions personify those characteristics of a peak performer? If you have anything troubling you in your life, how can you use Herzlich's example to help better your own situation?

CHECK IT OUT At **https://www.ranker.com/list/athletes-who-are-disabled/people-in-sports**, you can read about the 18 most famous athletes with disabilities. Do you recognize any of the names? What else might these athletes have overcome? Think not only of bodily limitations but the limitations of other people's perceptions, attitudes, and other regulating guidelines.

Starting Today

At least one strategy I learned in this chapter that I plan to try right away is

_____

_____

_____

What changes must I make in order for this strategy to be most effective?

_____

_____

_____

Review Questions

Based on what you have learned in this chapter, write your answers to the following questions:

1. What are five strategies for good health management?

_____

_____

2. What are some of the benefits of aerobic exercise?

_____

_____

3. Why is it important to manage your stress?

_____

_____

4. Cite two statistics or facts about alcohol.

_____

_____

5. List four symptoms of depression.

_____

_____

Increasing Your Energy Level

In the Classroom

Danny Mendez, a business major in marketing, works part time at a sporting goods store, is president of his fraternity, and is on the soccer team. This demanding schedule is manageable because Danny's energy is high. However, around midterm he feels overwhelmed with stress. He needs to find ways to increase his energy, maintain his good health, and manage his stress.

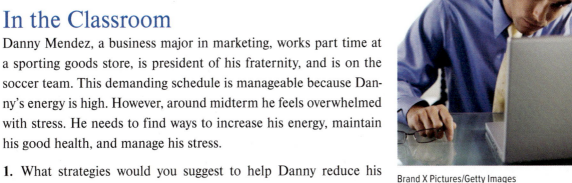

Brand X Pictures/Getty Images

1. What strategies would you suggest to help Danny reduce his stress?

_____

_____

2. What could you suggest to Danny to increase his energy level?

_____

_____

In the Workplace

Danny is now a marketing manager for a large advertising agency. He often travels to meet with current and prospective clients. When Danny returns, he finds work piled on his desk—advertising campaign issues, personnel problems, and production delays. Danny's energy has always been high, but lately he eats too much fast food, has started smoking again, and rarely exercises anymore. He keeps saying he'll get back on track when he has time.

3. What habits should Danny adopt to reduce his stress and fatigue?

_____

_____

4. What strategies in this chapter can help him increase his energy?

_____

_____

Applying the ABC Method of Self-Management

In the **Journal Entry**, you were asked to describe a time when you had low energy, felt unhealthy and stressed. How would having a positive, open attitude help you?

_____

_____

_____

Apply the ABC Method to work through the scenario and achieve a positive outcome.

A = Acknowledge: Accept reality and pay attention to your emotions.

_____

_____

_____

B = Breathe: Take a deep breath to calm down and feel beloved.

_____

_____

_____

C = Choose: Knowing you have many options, choose the most appropriate for the situation and that will result in positive long-term consequences.

_____

_____

_____

Sample Script: Even though I'm feeling exhausted, frustrated, and stressed, I love and accept myself and want to learn and grow. I breathe deeply and see myself as healthy and calm. I resist giving up and resorting to stress eating. Instead, I choose to create healthy habits and invest time in exercising, eating well, and getting enough sleep. I use the power of habit to create triggers that help me exercise such as putting out my jogging shoes and making it easy to go for a morning run. I practice meditation and mindfulness to help me tolerate anxious feelings and allow them to pass. I focus on creating healthy physical and mental habits that will help me in my career and in all aspects of my life. My intention is to create healthy habits for a lifetime of joy, meaning, and well-being.

Stress Performance Test

Read the following list of situations. Then think back over the last few months. Have you experienced these situations? If so, put a check mark in the column that best indicates how you coped with the experience.

	Overwhelmed (3)	Moderately Stressed (2)	Handled Effectively (1)	Did Not Experience/Not Applicable (0)
1. No time for goals	_____	_____	_____	_____
2. Lack of money	_____	_____	_____	_____
3. Uncomfortable living and study areas	_____	_____	_____	_____
4. Long working hours	_____	_____	_____	_____
5. Boring, uninteresting job	_____	_____	_____	_____
6. Conflict with roommate, family, and so on	_____	_____	_____	_____
7. Conflict with instructors	_____	_____	_____	_____
8. Too many responsibilities	_____	_____	_____	_____
9. Deadline pressures	_____	_____	_____	_____
10. Boring classes	_____	_____	_____	_____
11. Too many changes in life	_____	_____	_____	_____
12. Lack of motivation	_____	_____	_____	_____
13. Difficulty finding housing	_____	_____	_____	_____
14. Little emotional support from family	_____	_____	_____	_____
15. Poor grades	_____	_____	_____	_____
16. Parents/partners have set standards and expectations that are too high	_____	_____	_____	_____

	Overwhelmed (3)	Moderately Stressed (2)	Handled Effectively (1)	Did Not Experience/ Not Applicable (0)
17. Unclear on goals	_____	_____	_____	_____
18. Too many interruptions	_____	_____	_____	_____
19. Health problems	_____	_____	_____	_____
20. Dependency on alcohol, other drugs	_____	_____	_____	_____
21. Too much socializing	_____	_____	_____	_____
22. Lack of career/life goals	_____	_____	_____	_____
23. Speaking/test-taking anxiety	_____	_____	_____	_____
24. Lack of relationships, friends	_____	_____	_____	_____
25. Lack of self-esteem	_____	_____	_____	_____
Subtotals	_____	_____	_____	_____

Add your 1s, 2s, and 3s to give yourself a total score:

Totals   _____ + _____ + _____ = _____

Total score

SCORES

25–36   Peak performer (you have learned how to function effectively under stress)

37–48   Persistent coper (you handle stress in most situations but have some difficulty coping and feel overwhelmed sometimes)

49–60   Stress walker (you often feel overwhelmed and exhausted, which affects your performance)

60+   Burnout potential (you need help coping; stress is taking a toll on your health and emotions, and you risk burning out)

If you score more than 39 points, make an appointment to talk with a professional who can give you strategies to cope with stress.

I Am What I Eat

This exercise aims to make you aware of your food choices. Starting on Monday, record *everything* you consume for one week, including water. Exact measurements aren't necessary. "Other" includes additional snacks, a water break, and so on. (For a complete diet analysis, create a profile at **www.choosemyplate.gov** or another online program designed to track and analyze your food intake and physical activity.)

Meal	Monday	Tuesday	Wednesday	Thursday	Friday	Saturday	Sunday
Breakfast							
Snack							
Lunch							
Snack							
Dinner							
Other							

1. Which type of liquid did you drink most often (water, coffee, milk, juice, etc.)? _____

2. How many soft drinks did you consume each day? (Use 12 ounces—the size of a soft drink can—as one drink, and divide by the number of days to get an average.) Are they usually diet or nondiet drinks? _____

   _____

3. How many drinks were caffeinated? _____

   _____

4. About how many times per day (or week) do you consume the following?

   • whole grains _____   • foods high in sugar _____
   • red meat _____   • fried foods _____
   • green, leafy vegetables _____   • alcohol _____

5. Do you tend to eat fewer but bigger meals each day or many smaller meals? Or another pattern? _____

   _____

6. How many meals were bought at a restaurant, including via a drive thru or convenience store? _____

_____

7. Of those meals, how many would you consider healthy choices? Did you consciously make a healthier selection versus something else you would have normally ordered? _____

_____

8. Compare your eating and drinking habits on the weekend with the rest of the week. Are there obvious differences? If yes, explain. _____

_____

9. Based on your food choices this week, what changes should you make to improve your diet? How easy or difficult will it be to make healthier choices? _____

_____

You don't need to obsess with your diet, just become aware and conscious of what you're eating and strive to eat unrefined, whole foods that focus on fruit, a variety of vegetables, and lean protein.

Inventory of Interests

Developing outside interests can help reduce stress in your life. Interests are activities that you enjoy and pique your curiosity. Besides reducing stress, they may help you determine your life's work and career path. For example, an interest in the outdoors may lead to a major in natural resources, then to a career as a park ranger. A passion for working with cars may lead to a certificate in auto mechanics and thus to your own auto repair shop.

Fill in the following inventory to help you determine a career that coincides with activities you enjoy. Review this later to see if your interests change.

1. My interests are

_____

_____

_____

_____

2. Answer the following questions:

a. What websites, blogs, and news sources do I like to visit and read?

_____

_____

_____

_____

b. What kinds of books and magazines do I like to read?

_____

_____

_____

_____

c. When I have free time, what do I like to do? (Check the areas that interest you.)

Reading	_____	Working with people	_____
Writing	_____	Working with computers	_____
Sports	_____	Building or remodeling	_____
Outdoor activities	_____	Creating artwork	_____
Traveling	_____	Public speaking	_____

Other Activities

_____

_____

_____

Build Supportive and Diverse Relationships

LEARNING OUTCOMES

In this chapter, you will learn to

13-1 Identify strategies for communicating and building rapport

13-2 Identify strategies for overcoming communication obstacles

13-3 Identify methods of building healthy relationships

13-4 Explain the importance and benefits of diversity

SELF-MANAGEMENT

I work at a coffee shop part time. I'm prompt, am good at my work, and love the people I work with. However, some customers are really rude and I've lost my temper more than once and I feel angry, hurt, and scared. I need a way to deal effectively with rude and screaming customers.

PeopleImages/Getty Images

College offers many new experiences and exposes you to a wide variety of people from different cultures and with different backgrounds, opinions, and interests. If you have an open, growth mindset, you will embrace the challenge of meeting new people and learning to get along with roommates and professors. Part-time jobs expose you to many new situations and expectations. Difficult people can be frustrating, but these new situations provide you an opportunity to grow and become a better communicator at school, work, and in social and group settings. In this chapter, you will learn how to create healthy relationships, solve conflicts, work effectively in a team, become more assertive, handle criticism, and build rapport with a diverse group of people.

JOURNAL ENTRY In **Worksheet 13.1**, describe a difficult or confrontational situation in which you lost your temper or had trouble communicating your needs and ideas in an assertive, direct, and calm manner. How would a positive attitude help?

N o one exists in a vacuum. You can learn to read efficiently, write fluid prose, score high on tests, or memorize anything you want, but success will elude you if you cannot communicate and build rapport with different people. People spend nearly 70 percent of their waking hours communicating and interacting with others. SCANS lists interpersonal relationships, communication, an understanding of diversity, and team skills as essential for job success. Let's look at ways to understand and relate to people, solve conflicts, and be an effective team member.

The Importance of Effective Communication and Rapport

Communication is giving and receiving ideas, feelings, and information. Note the word *receiving.* Some people are good at speaking but are not effective listeners. Poor listening is one of the biggest barriers to effective communication. Miscommunication wastes billions of dollars in business and damages relationships.

What do you really want when you communicate with someone else? Do you want people to listen to you, understand your feelings, and relate to your message? Building **rapport** is the ability to find common ground with another person based on respect, empathy, and trust. Finding **common ground** is the basis of mutual interests and core values.

Some people have a knack for building rapport and making others feel comfortable and accepted. They are sensitive to nonverbal cues and the responses they elicit from other people. They have developed empathy and make people feel valued. They are comfortable with themselves and with people from different cultures and backgrounds. They can put their egos aside and focus on the other person with genuine interest and appreciation. *With effort and a positive mindset, you can learn to build rapport and appreciate and celebrate differences.* People will want to be near you because you make them feel good about themselves, treat them as important, and create a comfortable climate.

Strategies for Building Communication and Rapport

1. **Create a positive mindset.** If your intention is to build understanding and acceptance, it will be reflected in your tone and body language. If you are judgmental, however, this message will come through, regardless of your words. *A positive, open mindset is open to growth and willing to learn to see relationships as an opportunity to validate and enhance each other's potential and goals.* The growth message is, "How can I help?"

2. **Be an attentive listener.** In Chapter 6, we explored how to be an effective listener by using strategies such as the following:

   - *Listen; don't talk.* Don't change the subject unless the speaker is finished. Be patient and don't interrupt. Listen for feelings, undertones, and meanings in what people are saying. Observe nonverbal cues: posture, tone of voice, eye contact, body movements, and facial expressions.

- *Put the speaker at ease.* Create a supportive, open climate by being warm and friendly, showing interest, and smiling.
- *Withhold criticism.* Criticizing puts people on the defensive and blocks communication. Arguing almost never changes someone's mind, and it may widen the communication gap.
- *Paraphrase.* Restating in your own words what the speaker has said shows you are interested in the other person's point. Then ask for feedback: "Did I understand you correctly? Are you asking for help with your paper? I think you're right to move on."
- *Know when you cannot listen.* If you know you do not have time to pay close attention to the speaker, say so. For example, if you have a lot of studying to do and your roommate wants to talk about a date, you may want to say respectfully, "I'd like to know more about your date, but I have to read this chapter. Can we talk about it when I'm done or let's have dinner together? I want to hear everything." *You also may want to delay discussions when you are angry, tired, hungry, or stressed.* Just make sure to respond in a respectful tone of voice. Listen for cues. If someone you love really needs to talk, do your best to listen attentively for at least 10 or 15 minutes and then make plans to get together. "Let's talk more over dinner."

3. **Pay attention to body language.** Look at the speaker and appear attentive, interested, and alert. In contrast, crossing your arms, frowning, leaning back in your chair, avoiding eye contact, sighing, and shaking your head say, "I don't like you and I don't want to listen." When your eyes wander, you appear uninterested or bored. Instead, create an attentive, supportive climate: Look at the other person, relax and uncross your arms, and lean slightly toward the person. Some experts say that 70 percent of what is communicated is done through nonverbal communication, or body language.[1] If you intend to build rapport, your words must match your body language.

4. **Be respectful.** Many organizations are training employees in the importance of business etiquette—respect for and consideration of the feelings and needs of others. *Civility, manners, and respect are the basis of all healthy relationships.* People need consideration and appreciation, whether in the classroom, on the job, or at home. It is especially important to be open-minded and respectful and accepting of different cultures, gender, and life experiences. When you listen and show civility, you will learn the value of diversity and learn to see the world through different viewpoints. See **Peak Progress 13.1** on applying these principles to communicating online.

5. **Use warmth and humor.** Avoid sarcasm and jokes at the expense of another person's feelings, but don't take yourself too seriously or take things personally. Humor puts people at ease and can dissipate tension. Wit, kindness, and a sincere smile create warmth and understanding and can open the door to building rapport. Celebrate diversity by showing your interest, curiosity, and respect. Learn to laugh at the irony of life instead of being

Socially Acceptable Technology

The use of technology has replaced face-to-face communication for many people. Not only has a short e-mail or text become more convenient than a phone call or a stroll down the hallway, but many social networking sites, such as Facebook and Twitter, provide the tremendous opportunity to communicate instantly with designated groups.

As popular and convenient as these communication sites have become, they also have their pitfalls. Because you are looking at a screen, it's easy to forget you are interacting with human beings. Misunderstandings can occur because there are no nonverbal cues and voice inflections. *Talk directly when possible* and follow a few guidelines:

- *Be respectful to others.* Technology has been used to belittle, threaten, and harass others, which is known as **cyberbullying** or cyberstalking. *Do not vent your frustrations and anger or torment others.* Don't allow yourself to be a victim of cyber attacks; tell the campus police and contact the site owner. Unplug often.

- *Do not provide personal information.* Not only could your identity be compromised financially, but it also could be used by a predator to rob or physically harm you. If you are selling products on sites such as eBay or craigslist, never meet the buyer or seller alone. Don't give out too much personal information or post photos that may embarrass you later. Ask yourself how a future employer would react to them.

- *Do not send inappropriate material.* Although **sexting** is a consensual act between willing participants, it's something you should only do with someone you trust. If one of the participants is a minor, it's a crime that can lead to criminal prosecution. If a minor sends nude photographs of themselves, it is child pornography. Sending someone unsolicited sexual messages or pictures is harassment.

- *If you think you shouldn't send it, don't.* Remember that virtual material can be available forever. If you think someone could take an e-mail or a posting the wrong way, it's better to take the time to reword it, have a trusted friend read it first, let it sit overnight, or not send it at all. When in doubt, talk in person.

defensive or angry. A sunny disposition is one of the most engaging qualities that draws you to others. Take less offense and learn to laugh.

6. **Relate to a person's personality style.** In Chapter 1, we learned that people have different styles of relating. You need not label people, but cues can be a guide that indicate preference. For example, if your boss is an extrovert and likes to talk, be a good listener and ask about research interests, family, or recent vacations. Cues may indicate a creative personality, so you'll want to explore ideas, be flexible, look at the big picture, present imaginative work, and provide visual stimuli. It all comes down to learning to work well with diverse people, showing respect, and being flexible.

7. **Relate to a person's learning or working style.** Integrate all learning styles. Enhance your visual presentation by turning in an attractive paper that is neat and uses illustrations whenever appropriate. Maintain eye contact and return visual clues, such as nods, smiles, and other reassurances. Don't label people as extroverts or introverts; or visual, auditory, or kinesthetic learners, but to be sensitive to cues and look for strengths. For example, "My lab partner is logical, thorough, likes details and facts, and likes working alone. Recognizing these cues will help me to present information logically and precisely when working with him. My goal is to enhance our relationship."

8. **Be a team player.** To be effective, value diverse perspectives and learn to work with a variety of people. You can have fun and also contribute fairly to your team. You build team rapport not by being charming and a good conversationalist, but by being clear on expectations, deadlines, commitment, and follow-through and respecting differences. Review meeting dates, deadlines, and work assignments. The foundation of teamwork is effective communication, responsibility, and respecting different styles.

Assertive Communication

Assertive communication is expressing yourself in a direct and civil manner. You may not always feel you have the right to speak up for what you need, particularly in new situations where you see yourself as powerless and dependent. However, only you can take responsibility for clarifying your expectations, expressing your needs, and making your own decisions. You might tend to act passively in some situations, aggressively in others, and assertively in still others. In most situations, however, strive to communicate in an assertive and respectful manner.

- *Some people are so passive that they* rarely express feelings, opinions, and desires. It is fine to be shy or want to avoid conflict, but it is also important to be able to express your needs and give your opinions in a calm way.
- *Aggressive* people are often sarcastic, critical, and controlling. They want to win at any cost and sometimes blame others for making them angry. They may resort to insults and criticisms, which breaks down communication and harms relationships.
- *Passive-aggressive* people appear passive but act aggressively. For example, a passive-aggressive roommate will leave nasty notes rather than confront you directly.
- *Assertive* people state their views and needs directly; are respectful, use confident body language; speak in a clear, strong voice; and take responsibility for their actions.

Practice developing assertive responses in **Personal Evaluation Notebook 13.1**.

Communicating with Instructors and Advisors

Develop professional relationships with your instructors and advisors, just as you would with your supervisor at work. Try a few of these tips to increase rapport:

1. **Clarify expectations.** Make certain you understand the objectives and expectations of your instructors. Most instructors will give you extra help and feedback if you take the initiative. For instance, before a paper is due, hand in a draft and say, "I want to make sure I'm covering the important points in this paper. Am I on the right track? What reference sources would you like me to use? What can I add to make this an A paper?"

2. **Clarify concerns.** If you don't understand or you disagree with a grade on a test or paper, ask for an appointment with the instructor. Approach the situation with a supportive attitude: "I like this course and want to do well in it. I don't know why I got a C on this paper because I thought I had met the objectives. Could you show me what points you think should be changed? Could I make these corrections for a higher grade?" Show respect and appreciation for your

Personal Evaluation Notebook

Assertive Communication Role-Playing

Read the following situations. Then develop an assertive response for each one.

1. **Situation:** You receive a B on your test, and you think you deserve an A. What would you say to your instructor?

   Assertive response: _____

2. **Situation:** A friend asks you to read their term paper. She tells you it is the best paper she has ever written. However, you find several glaring errors.

   Assertive response: _____

3. **Situation:** Your roommate asks to borrow your new car. You don't want to lend it.

   Assertive response: _____

4. **Situation:** An acquaintance makes sexual advances. You are not interested.

   Assertive response: _____

5. **Situation:** You go to a party and your date pressures you to drink.

   Assertive response: _____

6. **Situation:** Your roommate's friend has moved in and doesn't pay rent.

   Assertive response: _____

7. **Situation:** Your sibling borrowed your favorite sweater and stained it.

   Assertive response: _____

8. **Situation:** A friend lights up a cigarette, and you are allergic to smoke.

   Assertive response: _____

9. **Situation:** You want your roommate or spouse to help you keep the apartment clean.

   Assertive response: _____

10. **Situation:** Your mother wants you to come home for the weekend, but you have to study for a major test.

    Assertive response: _____

(Discuss effective ways to improve communication in a small group.)

ASSERTIVENESS TIPS:

State the problem in clear terms.
Be clear on your position and what you want: "I cannot study with the music so loud."

Express your feelings.
Use "I" messages instead of "You" messages: "I feel frustrated when the music is too loud, because I have to study for a test."

Make your request.
"Please turn the music down; especially after 10 o'clock."

Use assertive body language.
Stay calm, use direct eye contact, square your shoulders, and speak in a clear, low tone.

State the consequences.
Always start with the positive: "If you will turn down the volume on your music, I can study better and our relationship will be more positive." If you don't get the results you want, try saying, "I'm going to have to go to our landlord to discuss this problem."

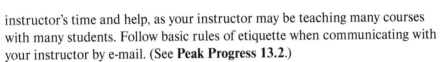

Helder Almeida/Shutterstock

instructor's time and help, as your instructor may be teaching many courses with many students. Follow basic rules of etiquette when communicating with your instructor by e-mail. (See **Peak Progress 13.2**.)

3. **Adapt to your instructor's teaching style.** Approach each class with a positive attitude, and don't expect that all instructors will teach according to your learning style. Being flexible and open will also help you adapt and work well with co-workers and supervisors. (See "Adjust Your Learning Style to Your Instructor's Teaching Style," in Chapter 1, for specific tips.)

4. **Be open to learning.** Create a positive, open mind that is open to growth. Be supportive of the instructor and focus on curiosity and learning. If you are a returning student, you may find that the instructor is younger than you are and may lack life experiences. Value the training, education, and knowledge the instructor brings to class. The same rule applies to the workplace. No one likes to be friends with or work with a person who has a know-it-all, judging, negative, or fixed attitude.

5. **Take responsibility for your own learning.** You are responsible for your own learning and career success. You may be tempted to skip classes, but you will miss valuable class discussions, question-and-answer sessions, explanations, reviews of concepts, expectations about tests, contact with students, and structure to help you stay focused. If you feel overwhelmed in a class, don't have the required skills, or need extra help with writing, speaking, computers, or math, get help and talk with your advisor. For example, suppose you need to take a chemistry class, but you haven't had a class in the subject for a couple of years and barely passed. You might want to audit

Peak Progress

E-Mail Etiquette with Instructors

Although you may have established a friendly, personable relationship with your instructor or advisor, you should always treat them with the respect due to any employer or evaluator of your performance or behavior. Because technology has allowed us to communicate more quickly, we often forget to practice the basic rules of communication etiquette. When e-mailing your instructor for help, clarification, or advice, keep in mind the following:

1. **Use proper spelling, grammar, and punctuation.** Although you may be used to text messaging in lowercase letters, proper e-mail etiquette calls for writing the e-mail just as you would a letter or paper. Start each sentence with a capital letter and end each sentence with punctuation (period, question mark, etc.). It's also common e-mail knowledge that you should not write in all capital letters, which designates "shouting" or intense urgency. Always use spell-check before sending, and read it through at least once more.

2. **Avoid using slang, abbreviations, or "emojis."** You wouldn't say "OMW (for "on my way") in a letter to a potential employer or include emojis. Those are fine in messages to friends, but not to instructors or employers.

3. **Use proper greetings.** You wouldn't start a letter to your instructor with "Hey, Jim." "Dear Dr. Smith" is appropriate; "Hello, Dr. Smith" is also acceptable.

4. **Make it clear who you are.** Because instructors interact with many people daily, they can't decipher who you are by your email account (**bhappy16@gmail.com**). Quickly make it clear who you are ("I'm Beatrice Jones in your English 305 course"). Put your full name (and phone number, if necessary) at the end of your e-mail.

5. **Be smart about your e-mail address.** Although you may think **hot2trot@gmail.com** gets attention, it won't garner much respect (and possibly even a response) from an instructor or a future employer. Plus, with the myriad of spam messages and computer viruses, your instructor may even be hesitant to open your e-mail.

6. **Be concise and to the point.** Remember that your instructor has many people to respond to during the day: students, other faculty members, and administrators (not to mention people involved in their research work, professional memberships, and consulting obligations). In your message subject line, clearly state the overall point: "Question about today's discussion on learning styles." In one or two paragraphs, briefly ask your question or make your point. Include just the essential details. If you feel your point may be lost, either put your question at the very beginning or highlight it in bold or another color.

7. **Respectfully include a "due date," if necessary.** Never say to an instructor, "I must hear from you by. . . ." However, your issue may be time-sensitive for a reason, such as a registration deadline. If you need a response by a certain time, indicate that politely: "It would be great to have your response by this Friday, as I have to turn in my forms by that afternoon." If you haven't received a response, send a follow-up: "Just checking to make sure you received my e-mail." When something is urgent, e-mail may not be the appropriate mode of communication. Call the instructor, drop by his or her office, catch him or her in class, or schedule an appointment. Do not let e-mail be an excuse for not getting an important answer.

8. **Leave in the message thread.** If there has been a string of e-mails to this point, it's always better to leave them in if you can, in case the recipient needs to refresh his or her memory about the issue.

9. **Do not use graphics.** Unless necessary, do not be creative with the typeface, graphics, or backgrounds in your e-mails. They only make the e-mail harder to read and increase the file size.

10. **Always say, "Thank you."** Get in the habit of ending e-mails with a *thank you, thanks,* or *I appreciate your help.* People will respond to you faster and more often if their efforts are acknowledged and appreciated.

it first, take it pass/fail if possible, take it at a community college in the summer, or get tutoring from day one. Focus on learning and growth.

6. **Take an interest in your professors.** Connection is key. Visit them during office hours to discuss your grades and future coursework. Ask about your professor's degrees, colleges attended, work experience, and what projects they are working on for professional growth. A large part of building rapport is showing genuine interest, appreciation, and respect. Focus on learning and doing well and when it comes time for you to ask for a letter of recommendation, the professor will know who you are and be supportive.

7. **Network.** Building your professional network begins in college. Form professional relationships with other students, your advisor, a few key professors, club advisors, staff, and community professionals. Exchange e-mails and ask people on campus (who know you well) if you may use them as a reference or if they would be willing to write a letter of recommendation for graduate school, an internship, or your first job.

• **Connecting with Your Instructor**

Develop a rapport with your instructor by taking the initiative to ask for feedback and help when you need it and in plenty of time to put the advice into action. *Are you working on assignments or papers right now that you should be consulting with your instructor about?*

Conflict

Conflicts can occur between family members, co-workers, neighbors, roommates, friends, teammates, and instructors and students. Some common causes are misperceptions and prejudices; miscommunication; repetitive negative behavior; and differing expectations, opinions, beliefs, and values. Be calm and bring problems to the surface so you can find creative solutions to conflicts. Use your observation and critical thinking skills to complete **Personal Evaluation Notebooks 13.2** and **13.3** about conflict resolution.

The common responses to conflict are to avoid it, compromise, accommodate others, or cooperate with others. Following are a few suggestions that focus on cooperation as a means of resolving conflict.

1. **Define the conflict.** Focus on the problem, not the other person: "The conflict is that Joe is doing most of the talking in my study group and I want to move on and solve the problem so that the group can be more productive and everyone is engaged."

2. **Convert "You" statements into "I" statements.** Making "I" statements instead of "You" statements communicates information without pointing the finger at the other person and putting them on the defensive. Instead of saying, "You talk too much," say, "I feel angry when one person does all the talking because we need to hear the opinions of other people before we can make an informed decision." Use a three-part formula:

   "I FEEL (emotions) _____ WHEN (behavior) _____ BECAUSE (reason) _____."

3. **Attentively listen to the other person's concerns and criticism.** Don't interrupt or start your defense. Really concentrate on the other person's perceptions, feelings, and expectations. Give physical cues that you are listening. Listen to what is said, how it is said, and when it is said. Listen also for what is not being said. Ask for clarification, avoid jumping to assumptions, and don't hurry the speaker.

Personal Evaluation Notebook 13.2

Observing Conflict

Read the following questions and write your answers on the lines provided.

1. Observe how others handle conflict, compliments, and criticism. What ineffective behaviors do you notice?

   _____

   _____

2. What behaviors do you use under stress that you would like to change?

   _____

   _____

3. What do you intend to do the next time you are in a conflict with someone?

   _____

   _____

If there is a mediation class on campus or in the community, take it. Resolving conflict is such an important skill and will serve you well in college and in your career.

4. **Develop empathy.** Empathy is the ability to share another's emotions, thoughts, or feelings in order to understand the person better. By taking the role of the other, you can develop the ability to see and feel the situation through his or her eyes. Sympathy is feeling compassion for a person, which can border on pity or condescension. An empathetic attitude says, "I am here with you." Empathy allows for the distance needed to maintain objectivity so that the problem can be solved.

5. **Stay calm.** Control your emotions and don't lose your temper. Acknowledge feelings: "I see you are upset, and I really want to know what your concerns are. Please talk more slowly." Listen to the message without overreacting or becoming defensive.

6. **Focus on the problem.** Don't use detours, be defensive, or attack the person. "You think I'm messy. Look at your room. You're a real pig." Instead, focus on the problem: "If I do the dishes the same evening I cook, will you feel more comfortable?" Trust that you can both speak your minds calmly and without damaging your relationship.

7. **Ask for specific details and clarification.** The key is to understand the issue at hand: "Can you describe a specific incident when you think I was rude?"

Personal Evaluation Notebook

Conflict Resolution

Describe a conflict you have not yet resolved. Think of resolution techniques that would be helpful. Respond to the following statements.

1. Describe the problem.

_____

_____

2. Express your feelings.

_____

_____

3. State what you want.

_____

_____

4. Predict the consequences.

_____

_____

Look around your campus or community for examples of conflicts and apply these real-life situations to this process. Notice if opposing sides treat each other with respect and are able to compromise and settle disagreements. If your campus has a student mediation group, check it out.

8. Create solutions. You might say, "I can see that this is a problem. What can I do to solve it? What procedures or options can we explore? Can we find common ground?"

9. Apologize. If you think the situation warrants it, apologize: "I'm sorry. I didn't hear your concerns. I was wrong not to be more respectful of your viewpoint." It defuses anger and builds trust and respect.

10. Forgive. There are times when a conflict just can't be resolved, even though you have been hurt by the words or actions of someone else. Rather than holding onto that anger and resentment, let go of those feelings and forgive the other person for being human and simply move on. Forgiveness does not mean you discount the situation or absolve the other person from responsibility, but you accept that the circumstances cannot be changed and decide to focus on the positive aspects in your life. You move on. Think of a time when you were forgiven by someone you offended or hurt. How did you feel?

Constructive Feedback

Part of effective communication is being open to feedback in order to grow and learn. Start with the attitude that the critic has good intentions and is offering constructive feedback meant to be supportive and useful for improvement. Criticism is negative and often harsh; it doesn't offer options and can create defensiveness and tension.

GIVING CONSTRUCTIVE FEEDBACK

Your feedback will be asked for more often if you give it in a nurturing way.

1. **Establish a supportive climate.** People need to feel safe when receiving feedback or criticism. Choose a convenient time and a private place to talk. If possible, sit next to the person instead of behind a barrier, such as a desk. Be warm and open.

2. **Ask permission to offer feedback.** Don't blindside someone with your feedback. First ask if he or she would like to hear your feedback. "Do you want to talk about the test?"

3. **Focus on the behavior, not the person.** Define one specific behavior instead of several issues at once. "Do you think you studied enough? You go to a lot of parties."

4. **Stay calm.** Look at the person, keep your voice low and calm, be positive, and avoid threats. Be brief and to the point. "I understand you're upset, let's explore options."

5. **Be balanced.** Let the other person know you like him or her and appreciate the person's good qualities or behaviors. Avoid words such as *always* and *never*.

6. **Explain.** Detail the behavior and why a change is in order. Offer to help. "You said you want to get better grades, but you spent the weekend at parties. Let's study together."

RECEIVING CRITICISM OR FEEDBACK

Learn to accept and grow from feedback even if it feels like criticism. Choose to see it as necessary for growth and learning for school and job success. Here are some tips:

1. **Listen with an open mind.** No one is perfect so relax and listen attentively when your instructor, boss, co-worker, roommate, spouse, or classmate makes suggestions or offers feedback. Listen to details, ask questions, and say that you'll take this feedback into consideration. Take time to reflect if you've heard similar criticism before?

2. **Pay attention to nonverbal cues.** If the person is aloof, sarcastic, or angry, ask if you did something to offend the person. "You've been very quiet today. Did I offend you?"

3. **Ask for clarification.** Clarify the criticism—for example, "Professor Walker, you gave me a C on this paper. Could you explain what points you consider to be inadequate?"

4. **Ask for suggestions.** If the criticism is constructive, ask for suggestions—for example, "How can I improve this paper?" Summarize the discussion and

clarify the next steps. Know what you need to do to correct the situation. Don't make excuses for your behavior. If the criticism is true, change your behavior.

5. **Explain your viewpoint.** If the criticism feels unfair, discuss it openly. Don't let resentments smolder and build. Practice saying, "Thank you for your viewpoint and your courage in telling me what is bothering you. However, I don't think the criticism is fair." Criticism reflects how another person views your behavior at a certain time. It is not necessarily reality but an interpretation. Relax and put it in perspective.

Dealing with Shyness

Shyness is common, especially when people are adjusting to new situations and meeting new people. There are many advantages to being a quiet introvert, enjoying your own company, and having a few close friends. However, if shyness keeps you from speaking up in class, getting to know your instructors, giving presentations, or making new friends, it is interfering with your success. *A positive, open mindset will help you focus on growth and courage as you speak up, ask questions, and make new friends.* You can stretch yourself, build rapport, and be an effective conversationalist by following these strategies:

1. **Create a positive mindset.** Instead of a negative fixed mindset that says, "I can't change," use positive affirmations, "I'm confident, people like me, and I like people. I'm making new friends. I am accepted and appreciated. *I can grow and enhance my qualities with effort and grit."*

2. **Use direct eye contact if possible.** Looking at people reinforces your confidence and shows connection and warmth.

3. **Ask questions and show genuine interest.** *Ask open-ended questions, show genuine interest, and give others a chance to talk.* For example, instead of asking Jennifer if she is finished with an assigned term paper (yes/no), ask her how she is progressing with the paper (open-ended question) and how she feels about it. See **Peak Progress 13.3** for tips on making small talk and initiating conversations.

4. **Listen to other points of view.** Even if you don't agree with other people's points of view, listen and respond tactfully, thoughtfully, and with interest. You have something to contribute, and exchanging different views is a great way to learn and grow.

5. **Use humor.** Most people like to laugh. Poking good-natured fun at yourself lightens the conversation, as does a funny joke or story. Just be sensitive and appropriate.

6. **Focus on the benefits.** Making friends helps you develop your sense of community and belonging. It can ease the loneliness many students feel and help you grow and learn.

7. **Take action.** Join clubs and activities. Volunteer in an organization that sponsors service learning. Join study groups or ask one of your classmates to study with you. Get a part-time job or get involved in community organizations. Try out for a play or choir—really stretch yourself. Reach out to others and make friends with a broad range of people.

> **Minds are like parachutes. They only function when they are open.**
>
> **SIR JAMES DEWAR**
> *Chemist and physicist*

Whether you are meeting students in class, a business client, a first date, or the patient next to you in the doctor's office, the art of small talk can help you get to know people better and overcome awkward situations.

- *Ask questions to get the conversation rolling.* Most people love to talk about themselves. Greet others with a smile and greeting. "How's your day going?" If appropriate, encourage openness with the phrase, "Tell me more."
- *Mention current events.* Bring up recent happenings in the news, sports, your community, or weather. Avoid political discussions unless you agree.
- *Talk about television shows, movies, books, or other current events.* Share your interests to see what you might have in common or can learn from each other.
- *Mention places in the community.* Ask if the person has had a chance to see the new stadium or a jazz club that just opened. What restaurant would the person recommend to someone visiting from out of town?
- *Listen and pay attention.* Show interest, ask questions, and be alert and present.

- *Use your body language.* Keep your arms uncrossed, relax, and be comfortable.
- *Be positive and friendly.* Smile, use appropriate humor that is warm and friendly.
- *Use the person's name.* If this isn't your first meeting, using the person's name makes him or her feel more important. Follow up on your last conversation: "How did your son's team do in that soccer tournament?" or "Were you happy with your grade on the economics paper?" People are impressed when you remember something about them.
- *Stay on common ground.* If you are stuck trying to come up with something to say, talk about whatever you know you have in common, such as a class.
- *If all else fails, use the weather.* It may be a cliché, but initiate a conversation by talking about the surroundings: "Can you believe this hot spell we're having?" "I'm sure the baseball team is feeling the heat. Do you ever go to their games?" "I've had to use the inside track for walking lately. How are you coping?"

Overcome Obstacles to Effective Communication

Communication is the lifeblood of personal relationships and the foundation of effective teams. Learning to work effectively with your study team, advisor, professors, roommates, co-workers, and supervisors is essential for success at school, at work, and in personal relationships. A landmark study in 2010 involving more than 300,000 participants found that relationships and having a strong social network was a stronger predictor of survival than exercise, hypertension, alcohol use, and even smoking. Social relationships are key to mental and physical health.[2] It is well worth investing time and energy in forming strong social networks at school, at work, and in your personal life and in looking at the barriers that keep you from communicating more effectively. *Start with a positive, open mindset that is focused on growth, learning, and mutual support.*

A major barrier to effective communication is the assumption that the other person knows what you mean. It is easy to think that what you say is what your listener hears, but communication is a complex system, with so many barriers to overcome that it is a wonder anyone ever really communicates. These barriers include distractions;

the need to be right; and cultural, religious, social, and gender differences. However, the biggest barrier to effective communication is poor listening skills. *Listening is one of the most important skills for school and job success and for healthy relationships.* Instead of a passive activity, effective listening must be viewed as an active, focused, and whole-body process. *Attentive or mindful listening is the conscious effort not only to hear words, but to understand meaning.*

Attentive Listening

Communication can be difficult under perfect conditions; add stress, distractions, conflict, and deadlines and attentive listening can be a challenge. You may start the day feeling positive and able to cope with difficult people and situations. However, when you go through a day of classes and work, you deplete your willpower and it is easy to become stressed and to react instead of attentively listening and responding calmly. *A positive mindset and habits can create growth, discipline, and resiliency.* This can help you in your daily life at college, whether it's dealing with a difficult professor, roommate, or financial aid situation, and continue into your career. Many businesses are aware of the importance of communication and listening and require customer service employees to be trained in how to deal with angry and rude customers. Learning to be respectful, thoughtful, and an attentive listener to colleagues at work can spill over to better communication at home.

Unlike creating a habit for exercising, eating better, drinking less, and quitting smoking (things we know we should do anyway), planning a positive habit for improving your relationships requires insight, sensitivity, and empathy. You're not just dealing with jogging shoes and setting goals. You need a positive mindset that focuses on growth and being present as you deal with a real person with feelings and needs. Positive relationships can enrich your life and are worth investing time and effort. *Start with gratitude.* Thank your advisor for valuable information and guidance, your professor for a great lecture, or a friend for support. Be attentive as you listen to their response. In quiet reflection, ask yourself, "*What does it cost to be kinder?* Am I willing to invest effort in healthy relationships? Am I willing to grow, change, and make this effort a daily habit?"

When you listen attentively, you don't allow your chattering mind, noise, judgments, or cell phone to distract you. You don't allow your thoughts—like what you're going to say—to get in the way. *The key to effective relationships is attentive listening.* Try these tips:

- **Pause.** Before you respond, take a deep breath and be quiet. Listen. Practice mindfulness and meditate even for just a few minutes every day. This can help quiet the chattering mind and allow you to be calm and focused so you can really listen.

- **Listen for understanding.** See the idea from another viewpoint instead of your own opinion or beliefs. Ask questions and show genuine interest in understanding.

- **Model behavior of attentive listening.** Show that you're listening by leaning slightly forward, being alert, using eye contact, nodding your head and saying "uh huh," and paraphrasing to indicate your understand.

- **Be aware of triggers.** *What* words or situations trigger reactions in you? *Who* do you shut down and not listen to or scold or criticize? *When* are you most defensive or unwilling to listen? *Where* do you shut down, work or home? *Why* do you treat certain people with disrespect by not listening attentively?

Creating Better Communication Habits

Create better communication habits to help you grow. Let's say you receive a low grade on a paper. Your first instinct is probably to go up to the instructor and defend yourself. The *trigger* is a situation in which you want someone to listen, and therefore you will need to listen back as well. Rather than going straight up to the professor, visit the professor during their very next office hour or make an appointment. Think about what you want to say, but also what the instructor may want to say. Therefore, your new *routine* is active listening. Your *reward* is a better relationship with your instructor and perhaps a better grade in the future. This can be applied to any situation. When you catch yourself wanting to be heard or feeling defensive, remember that you will need to listen as well.

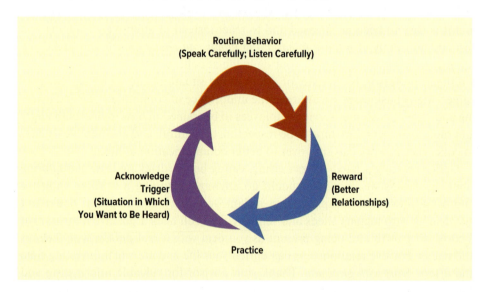

Routine Behavior
(Speak Carefully; Listen Carefully)

Acknowledge Trigger
(Situation in Which You Want to Be Heard)

Reward
(Better Relationships)

Practice

Look for patterns that seem to occur in your relationships as you complete **Personal Evaluation Notebook 13.4**.

Build Healthy Relationships

Relationships are vital for your mental and physical health, sense of well-being, and pure enjoyment of life. Problems in relationships can consume time and energy, and affect your self-esteem. Because feeling good about yourself is one key to all-around success, it is important to assess how you handle relationships with partners, friends, and family.

Romantic Relationships

Success in life can be even more meaningful when you are part of a loving, supportive relationship. However, too often we define ourselves by success in romantic endeavors rather than understanding what we gain emotionally by a rewarding relationship. Following are tips for building healthy relationships.

1. **Progress slowly.** Take time to get to know the other person and how they feel and react to situations. Relationships that move too fast or are based on intense and instant sexuality often end quickly. Solid relationships need time to develop through the stages of companionship and friendship.

2. **Have realistic expectations.** Some people think a good romantic relationship will magically improve their lives, even if they make no effort to change their

Personal Evaluation Notebook 13.4

Patterns in Relationships

Look for patterns in your relationships. Recall situations that occur again and again. For example, you may have the same problem communicating with instructors or advisors or conflicts with several roommates, co-workers, or supervisors. Once you see the patterns and consequences of your interactions, you can begin to think and act differently. When you take responsibility for changing your inner world of beliefs and thoughts, your outer world will also change. You will create more empathy and understanding. Write about what seems to be a recurring theme or pattern in your relationships. As the poet Maya Angelou said, *"I've learned that people will forget what you said, forget what you did, but people will never forget how you made them feel."*

_____

_____

_____

_____

_____

_____

_____

_____

_____

_____

_____

thinking or behavior. A relationship can't solve life's problems; only you can solve your problems. Focus on fulfilling your own needs and becoming the person you want to be, rather than dedicating all your time to finding a romantic partner.

3. **Be honest.** Don't reveal your entire past to a casual acquaintance or first date. At the appropriate time, however, you need to be honest about your feelings, basic values, and major life experiences. For example, if you have alcohol or drug problems or have been married before, the other person should know that as your relationship progresses.

4. **Be supportive and respectful.** A healthy relationship is mutually supportive of the growth and well-being of each partner and is based on respect for the other person's feelings and rights. An unhealthy relationship is not. No one owns another person, nor does anyone have a right to harm another physically or emotionally. An unhealthy relationship is possessive and controlling and lacks trust.

• **Equal Parts**

A healthy relationship is based on honesty, trust, and mutual support. *Why do some partners have a difficult time ending an unhealthy relationship?*

Darren Greenwood/Design Pics

5. **Know that change can occur.** Emotionally healthy people know that not all relationships will develop into romantic and intimate commitments. *Knowing how to end or let go of a relationship is as important as knowing how to form healthy relationships.* It is acceptable and normal to say no to an acquaintance who asks you out or to decide you don't want a romantic relationship or friendship to continue after a few dates. No one should date, have sex, or stay in a relationship out of guilt, fear, or obligation. It is harder to terminate a relationship if it progressed too fast or if the expectations for the relationship differ. Talk about your expectations and realize that your worth does not depend on someone's wanting or not wanting to date you.

6. **Keep the lines of communication open.** Trouble occurs in relationships when you think you know how the other person feels or would react to a situation. For example, you may assume that a relationship is intimate, but the other person may regard it as casual.

Communication in a healthy relationship is open enough to discuss even sensitive topics, such as birth control, sexually transmitted diseases, and unplanned pregnancy. Take a moment to reflect on your relationships in **Personal Evaluation Notebook 13.5**.

Relationships with the People You Live With

If you share your living space with a roommate, partner, or family member, it's important to create an open environment for communicating needs, problems, and solutions. The following suggestions will help you create rapport and improve communication with your roommates and family members.

1. **Clarify expectations of a roommate.** List the factors you feel are important for a roommate on your housing application or in an ad. If you don't want a smoker or pets, say so. Sometimes it is best not to live with a good friend—rooming together has ruined more than one friendship. Plus, getting to know new people with different backgrounds and experiences is a great opportunity.

2. **Discuss expectations when first meeting your roommate.** Define what neatness means to you. Discuss how both of you feel about overnight guests, drinking, drugs, choice and volume of music, housework, food sharing, quiet times, and so on. Consider developing a "roommate contract," which specifies certain expectations and responsibilities (including financial ones, if need be).

3. **Clarify concerns and agree to communicate.** Don't mope or whine about a grievance or leave nasty notes. Communicate honestly and kindly. It's important to understand each other's views and expectations and try to work out conflicts. If your roommate likes to have the dishes done after each meal, try to comply rather than prove that he or she is a neat freak. If you like to have friends over but your roommate goes to bed early or is studying, entertain in the early evenings, be quiet, or go out in the late evenings.

4. **Treat your roommate and family members with respect and civility.** Don't give orders or make demands. Calmly listen to each other's needs. Think about your tone of voice, body language, and choice of words. Sometimes we treat family, friends, and roommates with less respect than strangers. Be kind, supportive, and respectful.

Personal Evaluation Notebook 13.5

Healthy Relationships

Read the following statements and questions, and respond to them on the lines provided.

1. List the factors you believe are essential for a healthy relationship.

   _____

   _____

2. What do you believe contributes to unhealthy relationships?

   _____

   _____

3. Who are your friends?

   _____

   _____

4. Describe some of your other relationships, such as with instructors.

   _____

   _____

5. List the ways that your relationships support you and your goals.

   _____

   _____

6. List the ways that unhealthy relationships may undermine you and your goals.

   _____

   _____

   _____

5. **Don't borrow unless necessary.** A lot of problems result over borrowing money, clothes, jewelry, cars, and so on. The best advice is not to borrow. However, if you must borrow, ask permission first and return the item in good shape or replace it if you lose or damage it. Fill the tank of a borrowed car with gas, for instance. Immediately pay back all money you borrow.

6. **Keep your agreements.** Make a list of chores, agree on tasks, and do your share. When you say you will do something, do it. When you agree on a time, be punctual. Try to be flexible, however, so that annoyances don't build.

7. **Accept others' beliefs.** Don't try to change anyone's beliefs. Listen openly and, when necessary, agree that your viewpoints are different.

Research has shown that supportive and healthy relationships are the best predictors of longevity, well-being, and happiness throughout the entire lifespan. The craving for belonging, acceptance, and friendship enhances all areas of life.[3]

Maxine is at the breaking point. She has walked into the kitchen to make breakfast, only to find that her roommate, Jamie, must have had the late-night munchies again, as evidenced by the dirty pans on the stove, grated cheese on the floor, and a half-eaten taco abandoned on the coffee table. Use creativity and critical thinking to help Maxine deal with her frustration and anger.

- If you were Maxine, would you leave a note, text, or discuss the situation later?
- Develop some "I" statements that Maxine can use to discuss the situation with her roommate.
- How would assertive communication help instead of passive, aggressive, or passive/aggressive?

THINK
CREATIVELY AND CRITICALLY

8. **Respect others' privacy.** Don't enter each other's bedroom or private space without asking. Don't pry, read personal mail, or eavesdrop on conversations. Be cautious about posting photos of your roommate on social media sites. Ask permission first or be certain your roommate approves of the photo.

9. **Get to know each other.** Set aside time for occasional shared activities. Cook a meal, take a walk, or go to a movie. You don't need to be your roommate's best friend, but you should feel comfortable sharing a room or an apartment. Appreciate all your relationships and try not to focus on little faults or inconveniences.

Appreciate Diversity

Colleges and workplaces reflect the changing **diversity** in our society—in gender, race, age, ethnicity, sexual orientation, physical ability, learning styles, abilities, social and economic background, and religion. We tend to surround ourselves with people who are similar to us and to see the world in a certain way. However, college is an excellent place to grow, learn, and get to know, understand, and value other cultures and people with different life experiences, talents, and political and social views. Expand your horizons and cultivate a wide variety of friends and acquaintances who see the world differently. Communication breaks down walls, corrects false beliefs, and enriches your life. Build common ground.

As a contributing member of society and the workforce, it is essential that you use critical thinking to assess your assumptions, judgments, and views about people who are different from you. Cultural sensitivity is the foundation for building common ground. (See **Figure 13.1**.)

Communication Strategies for Celebrating Diversity

Here are some strategies you can use for developing effective communication with diverse groups of people. (See **Peak Progress 13.4** on how to apply the Adult Learning Cycle.)

1. **Create a positive mindset.** *Be willing to grow and learn to build rapport.* If you have a negative attitude to a group or person, examine your prejudices. (See **Figure 13.2**.) Unfortunately, **discrimination**—treating someone differently based on a characteristic—still occurs and varies by society. **Sexism** (a belief or an attitude that one sex is inferior or less valuable), **homophobia** (an irrational fear of the LGBT community, and **racial profiling** (using racial or ethnic characteristics in determining whether a person is considered likely to commit a particular type of crime or an illegal act) are just a few examples of what we personally experience and impose on others daily.

Culturally Biased	Culturally in Denial	Culturally Aware	Culturally Sensitive and Respectful	Culturally Responsible and Active
Believes different groups have positive and negative characteristics as a whole	Believes there is no problem; everyone should be the same	Tries to understand and increase awareness; is aware that experiences differ for people based on their culture	Respects people from diverse cultural and social backgrounds; seeks out contact with people from diverse backgrounds; encourages people to value and respect their cultural identity	Acts on commitment to eliminate oppression; seeks to include full participation of diverse cultural groups in decision making

Figure 13.1
Cultural Understanding

Different categories of cultural understanding are seen in our society. *In what column do you believe you fit and why?*

Peak Progress 13.4

Applying the Adult Learning Cycle to Become a Better Communicator

1. **FEEL and LISTEN.** *Why do I want to learn this?* Effective communication is the most important skill I can acquire, practice, and perfect. By being more assertive, I avoid resentment and thoughts that I'm being taken advantage of. I can succinctly express my views, wants, and impressions, as well as my innovative ideas and decisions. I'll listen to my thoughts and feelings and allow them to work for me.

2. **OBSERVE and VISUALIZE.** *How does this work?* I observe people who are assertive and confident when expressing themselves and their views. What techniques or mannerisms do they use when communicating? I'll also observe people who are passive or aggressive and learn from their mistakes. How do others respond? I'll try using new strategies for dealing with fear, resentment, and anger. What situations, times, and people trigger passive or aggressive responses.

3. **THINK and WRITE.** *What does this mean?* I'll use critical thinking to explore what works for me. When do I feel more confident and comfortable interacting with others? Do I believe I'm presenting my ideas so that others understand my point of view? Am I more respectful of others' opinions and feelings? I'll avoid using negative self-talk and focus on a positive attitude and outlook.

I will write out a response for imagined situations and practice it aloud.

4. **DO and PRACTICE.** *What can I do with this?* I will practice being more assertive. I will make a commitment to be direct, kind, and respectful. Each day, I'll work on one area. For example, when my roommate plays music too loudly, I'll express my needs assertively and respectfully.

5. **TEACH and PRACTICE AGAIN.** *Whom can I share this with?* I'll ask others if they have ever felt misunderstood and what they changed to express themselves better. I'll share my experiences and the strategies that have worked for me. I'll volunteer to help others in my study group.

Use the VARK system of integrating learning styles to help you think through and apply the Adult Learning Cycle. *Visualize* yourself becoming more assertive. *Observe* people who you admire for their direct, above-board, and assertive communication. *Listen* to how they respond. *Write out* a plan for dealing with imagined unpleasant communication situations and *read* how you will respond. *Now do it. Practice* your script again and again. Stay calm and focused. Be respectful; keep your voice even and low. Demonstrate to others how to communicate in a kind and assertive style.

Figure **13.2**

Understanding the Meaning

Attitudes are thoughts and feelings. *Behaviors* are what we do—how we act out our thoughts and feelings. If we work on eliminating stereotypes and prejudices, we can affect the outcome: discrimination. *Have you ever felt prejudice? How have you dealt with that feeling?*

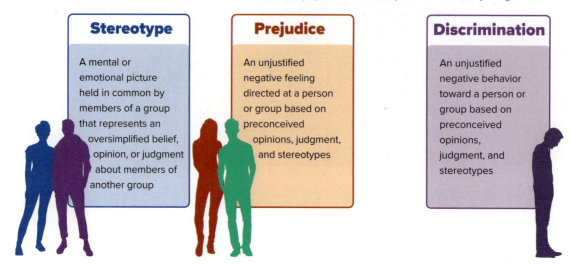

Stereotype	**Prejudice**	**Discrimination**
A mental or emotional picture held in common by members of a group that represents an oversimplified belief, opinion, or judgment about members of another group	An unjustified negative feeling directed at a person or group based on preconceived opinions, judgment, and stereotypes	An unjustified negative behavior toward a person or group based on preconceived opinions, judgment, and stereotypes

2. **See the value in diversity.** We are a rich nation because of different races, cultures, backgrounds, and viewpoints. Understanding others helps to break through barriers and appreciate diversity. Sharing different viewpoints teaches you new and interesting ways of seeing situations and approaching problems. Classrooms and workplaces are enriched by diversity. *The key*

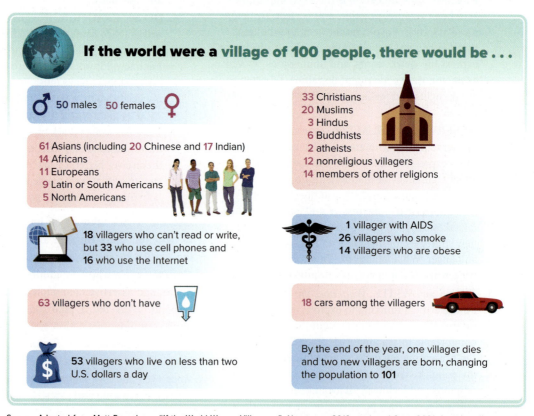

If the world were a village of 100 people, there would be . . .

♂ 50 males   50 females ♀

61 Asians (including 20 Chinese and 17 Indian)
14 Africans
11 Europeans
9 Latin or South Americans
5 North Americans

18 villagers who can't read or write, but 33 who use cell phones and 16 who use the Internet

63 villagers who don't have 💧

53 villagers who live on less than two U.S. dollars a day

33 Christians
20 Muslims
3 Hindus
6 Buddhists
2 atheists
12 nonreligious villagers
14 members of other religions

1 villager with AIDS
26 villagers who smoke
14 villagers who are obese

18 cars among the villagers

By the end of the year, one villager dies and two new villagers are born, changing the population to **101**

Source: Adapted from Matt Rosenberg, "If the World Were a Village. . ." *About.com,* 2019; retrieved Sept. 2021, from http://geography.about.com/od/obtainpopulationdata/a/worldvillage.htm.

Personal Evaluation Notebook 13.6

Appreciating Diversity

A. Read the following, and write your comments on the lines provided.
   1. Is your attitude toward people who differ from you in gender, race, sexual orientation, or culture one of acceptance or exclusion?

   _____

   2. Have you ever attended a political event for a party other than the one you support? If so, do you seek to understand different viewpoints?

   _____

   3. Would you speak up if someone's gender, cultural, racial, sexual, or ethnic background were discussed in a stereotypical manner? How?

   _____

   4. Do you consider yourself to be sensitive and respectful? Why or why not?

   _____

   5. How do you show a sensitive, respectful attitude even when someone sees the world differently? For example, can you have a civil discussion about abortion or gay marriage with someone who has an opposite view?

   _____

B. Look at the excuses some students use for not meeting different people. Write strategies for overcoming these excuses.

   1. **Excuse:** I'm afraid of rejection or of getting into an argument.

      Strategy: _____

   2. **Excuse:** I feel more comfortable within my own group.

      Strategy: _____

   3. **Excuse:** You can't change people's minds or beliefs, so what is the point?

      Strategy: _____

   4. **Excuse:** I might say something embarrassing or feel uncomfortable.

      Strategy: _____

   5. **Excuse:** People who are different from me wouldn't want me in their group.

      Strategy: _____

to creativity is to be open to new ideas and viewpoints. Complete **Personal Evaluation Notebook 13.6** to determine your attitudes.

3. **See and treat people as individuals.** Look beyond preconceived notions and see people as individuals, not members of a particular group. See **Personal Evaluation Notebook 13.7** to determine your uniqueness.

Personal Evaluation Notebook

What Do You Want to Be Called?

Ingram Publishing

White, Black, Hispanic, Asian, Native American, Pacific Islander. At some point in your life, you've probably had to check off your race or ethnicity on a form. But what if none of those categories truly reflects your personal identity or accommodates those of us (the majority) who have come from multiple backgrounds? Some people of Central and South American origin prefer to be called Hispanic; others prefer Latino. Many prefer to use their specific place of origin—Guatemalan, Mexican, Puerto Rican, Cuban, and so on. In the same way, some descendants of the indigenous of the United States prefer specific tribal names, such as Sioux, Navajo, Apache, or simply Native American.

In general, most people agree that all people have a right to be called what they want to be called and not have a group name imposed on them by someone else. How would you "label" yourself or do you resist labels?

_____

_____

Source: James W. Fraser, Teach: A Question of Teaching (New York: McGraw-Hill, 2011).

---

66 Feelings of worth can flourish only in an atmosphere where individual differences are appreciated, mistakes are tolerated, communication is open, and rules are flexible. 99

VIRGINIA SATIR, AUTHOR

4. **Treat people with respect and consideration.** You can be respectful even if someone's behavior is unacceptable or you don't agree with him or her.

5. **Focus on similarities.** As humans, we all experience similar emotions, fears, and needs for appreciation and respect. Don't let differences dominate your interactions. However, don't act as if people are all alike and share the same experiences. Values and experiences differ based on a person's culture, religion, background, and experiences.

6. **Get involved.** Take a cultural diversity course or workshop at college or in the community. Visit with people from other religions. Go to lectures, read, and look for opportunities to become acquainted with other cultures.

7. **Take risks.** Don't avoid contact with other cultures because you fear making a mistake, saying the wrong thing, or inadvertently offending someone. Cultivate friendships with people of different cultures, races, and viewpoints. Share your own culture's foods and customs with others. Knowledge of other cultures can help you appreciate your roots.

8. **Apologize when you make a mistake.** Mistakes happen, even with the best intentions. Occasionally, strong feelings or misunderstandings result from past experiences with racism or sexism. Thus, don't take it personally if

someone does not respond as positively as you had hoped. Sometimes bridging the gap requires extra effort. Apologize, seek to understand, and move on.

9. **Speak out.** It is not enough to be aware that values and experiences differ from culture to culture; you must act on this knowledge. Speak out whenever you hear or see discrimination in school or at work. This takes courage, but you can do it.

10. **Encourage representation.** Encourage active participation by members of diverse cultural and social groups in clubs, student and local government, college meetings, community groups, and decision-making teams. Don't hold a self-righteous attitude that says, "I belong to the right political party, religion, or social cause." Open your mind and explore different views with a sincere willingness to learn.

11. **Study abroad.** If you have the resources, look into a national or an international exchange program. A semester abroad is a tremendous learning experience. You can also get to know students on your campus from other countries or states. Attend events sponsored by the exchange programs. Check out internships in different locations.

Diversity in the Workplace

As the workplace has become more diverse, it has become a more inclusive environment. **Inclusion** is a sense of belonging—feeling respected and valued for who you are. You feel you have support and commitment from others, so that you can do your best work. Attitudes and behavior from top management can set this tone for the whole company. Many top managers approach this by asking themselves, "How can I instruct others to celebrate differences in race, gender, religion, and sexual orientation?" *"How can I set an example, create a climate of respect, and encourage people to value differences?"*

As a result of our cultural explosion, many organizations offer diversity awareness training to help employees relate comfortably to each other and appreciate diversity. These programs give employees a chance to develop and strengthen critical thinking skills and reduce stereotypical thinking and prejudice. Firm guidelines clearly communicate the consequences of discrimination, which is illegal and can be grounds for court action.

Organizations are obligated to ensure that all employees know what behaviors are illegal and inappropriate, the consequences for such behavior, and to create a safe atmosphere for complaints. *Diverse relationships offer an opportunity for growth, learning, and mutual support.* Consider your study or work teams as you complete **Peak Progress 13.5**.

Sexual Harassment at School and Work

Sexual harassment is behavior that is unwelcome, unwanted, and degrading. It can be destructive to the mental, emotional, and physical well-being of the person being harassed. It is also costly to the school and work climate. Employee turnover, loss of productivity, expensive lawsuits, and a negative work environment are just some of the consequences. Think about your attitudes, beliefs, and behaviors. Err on the side of discretion and avoid being too chummy or touchy, disclosing too many details about your personal life, or making jokes that may be inappropriate.

Evaluate the effectiveness of a work team, a study team, or any other team using the following list of skills. Score each item from 1 to 10 (10 = most effective).

Team Function

- Commitment to tasks
- Oral communication skills
- Listening skills
- Writing skills
- Conflict-resolution skills
- Decision-making skills
- Creative problem solving
- Openness to brainstorming and new ideas
- Team spirit and cohesiveness
- Encouragement of critical thinking
- Interest in quality decisions
- Professionalism
- Team integrity and concern for ethics
- Punctuality in starting and ending meetings

When a score is totaled, the team can discuss answers to these questions:

1. How can this team be more effective?

   _____

   _____

   _____

   _____

2. What can individual members do to strengthen the team?

   _____

   _____

   _____

   _____

Organizations are responsible for establishing guidelines and employing someone to talk to if you have a complaint or concern. Organizations with more than 25 employees are legally required to have written procedures concerning sexual harassment.

If you feel uncomfortable in a situation or are being sexually harassed, you should

1. **Speak up.** Identify the unwanted behavior, and clearly insist that it stop immediately.

2. **Document the harassment.** Keep a log of incidents, including the dates, behavior, and witnesses. Keep copies of any inappropriate e-mails or other correspondence.

3. **Document your performance.** The harasser may be someone who evaluates your work and may retaliate by giving you poor marks. Keep copies of performance evaluations, papers, exams, and correspondence that support the quality of your work.

4. **Read the organization's sexual harassment policy.** All reports of harassment will be followed up on. Know the procedures and who will be involved in the investigation.

5. **Contact the appropriate authorities.** At school, this may be the affirmative action or student affairs office, dean of students, or ombudsman. At work, consult with the human resources department.

6. **Mention the harassment to others.** Chances are, others have experienced harassment from the same person and will join your grievance.

7. **Do not make excuses for the harasser.** It is the harasser's behavior that is unwarranted, not your reactions to it.

Everyone's goal should always be to create a supportive, respectful, and productive environment—one that makes all colleagues feel comfortable and valued.

TAKING CHARGE

Summary

In this chapter, I learned to

- **Create a positive mindset.** I'm willing to put effort into building rapport and growing and learning. I clarify my intention, am an attentive listener, restate the speaker's point, and am respectful and considerate. I use humor when appropriate and want to learn about different people. I look for the best in others and appreciate their strengths. Relationships are an opportunity for mutual support.

- **Be assertive.** I express myself in a direct, above-board, and respectful manner. I can express feelings and opinions calmly, confidently, and authentically without offending others. I do not use sarcasm or criticism to express myself.

- **Communicate with instructors and advisors.** I meet with my instructors often to clarify expectations, get help with homework, consult on drafts of papers or speeches, discuss ways to prepare for tests, get advice about project requirements, and discuss grades or assignments. I attend every class, adapt to my instructor's teaching style, and am positive and open to learning. I take an interest in my instructor's research or area of expertise. Because I have built rapport with my instructor, I feel comfortable asking for a letter of reference.

- **Accept feedback and criticism.** I know that, to grow and learn, I must be open to feedback. I do not take offense when criticism is offered in the spirit of helpfulness. I listen, stay calm, and ask for clarification and suggestions. If I make mistakes, I apologize and try to make amends.

- **Overcome shyness.** When shyness interferes with making friends, speaking in front of groups, working with others, or getting to know my instructors, I must learn to be more confident and outgoing. I use visualization and affirmations to dispute negative self-talk. I use direct eye contact, am warm and friendly, ask questions, and listen. I relax, am able to laugh at myself, and use humor when it is appropriate.

- **Clarify miscommunications.** I do not assume I know what the other person thinks or says. I clear up misunderstandings by asking for clarification and paraphrasing what I think I've heard. I focus on listening and seek to understand, rather than to be right. I use "I" statements, apologize for my mistakes, and forgive others.

- **Develop healthy relationships.** I value friendships and take time to get to know others. My relationships are built on honesty, trust, respect, and open communication. I support others' goals and values, and I expect them to respect and support mine. I talk about expectations with friends, both casual and romantic.

- **Communicate with roommates and family.** To improve communication, I clarify and discuss expectations concerning guests, neatness, noise, borrowing, bills, privacy, and other issues that could cause problems. We agree to respect each other's beliefs, views, and private space.

- **Appreciate diversity.** I value diversity and seek to build rapport by sharing different backgrounds, experiences, values, interests, and viewpoints, I can learn new and interesting ways of seeing situations and solving problems. I look for ways to become acquainted with other cultures and opportunities to work with a variety of people.

- **Recognize sexual harassment.** Sexual harassment is behavior that is unwelcome, unwanted, degrading, and detrimental to school and work.

Performance Strategies

Following are the top 10 tips for building supportive, diverse relationships:

- Find common ground.
- Attentively listen to understand.
- Use body language and eye contact.
- Use warmth and humor.
- Communicate in an assertive, clear, calm, and direct yet kind manner.
- Solve conflicts through cooperation.
- Learn to receive and give constructive criticism.
- Make time to develop diverse, supportive, and healthy relationships.
- Clarify relationship expectations.
- Seek interactions with people from various backgrounds.

Tech for Success

- **Happy virtual birthday.** People love being remembered on their birthdays. If you don't have the time to drop a card in the mail, send an e-card instead. Many free e-card sites and apps are available, and many subscription-based sites offer reminder features.

- **Are you oversharing?** Most of us have taken a "selfie" (photo you take of yourself to post to a social media site) now and then. But how much personal information and opinions do you share online? Are you a culprit—or victim—of posting every event that happens in your day, down to what you ate for lunch? Although you might think your escapades are interesting, your acquaintances may not want to join you on every adventure and read every rambling thought you have. Use a personal journal to record your thoughts.

Endnotes

[1] Albert Mehrabian, *Nonverbal Communication* (New Jersey: Aldine Transaction, 2009).

[2] Julianne Holt-Lunstad, Timothy B. Smith, and J. Bradley Layton, "Social Relationships and Mortality Risk: A Meta-analytic Review." *PLoS Medicine* 7, no. 7 (July 27, 2010), http://journals.plos.org/plosmedicine/article?id=10.1371%2Fjournal.pmed.1000316 (accessed April 3, 2016).

[3] Daniel J. Siegel, *Brainstorm: The Power and Purpose of the Teenage Brain* (New York: Penguin Random House, 2015).

Study Team Notes

Career *in* Focus

Hero Images/Getty Images

Kathy Brown
MARINE BIOLOGIST

Related Major: Biological Science

Team Building at Work

Kathy Brown is a marine biologist who manages teams researching saltwater organisms outside Monterey, California. Currently, she is head of a project to gain more knowledge on the navigation techniques of gray whales during migration.

Although Kathy is a top-rate biologist and researcher with a Ph.D., she can accomplish her project goals only by building teams of researchers who work together effectively. To do this, she carefully considers the personalities and leadership styles of each researcher while forming teams. Kathy provides preproject training in communication skills, group decision making, diversity, and conflict resolution. She lets teams brainstorm ideas and come up with solutions for studying wild animals in a controlled experiment. Kathy also has teams rate their effectiveness in several key functions, including creative problem solving and team spirit.

Finally, the teams are sent to sea to set up labs and conduct research from ocean vessels. Kathy travels from vessel to vessel to encourage teamwork, check research procedures, and help solve problems. She ensures that each team knows how to reach her at all times, day and night.

Because teamwork is so important to the overall results, Kathy will not rehire anyone who cannot work as a part of a team. She knows that even the most-educated and skillful researchers will fail if they cannot work effectively and cooperatively with a variety of people.

CRITICAL THINKING Why do you think team building is an important part of a science research project?

Peak Performer Profile

Christy Haubegger

At first glance, the glossy magazine looks like many others on the newsstands. The cover offers a snapshot of the current issue: a profile of a famous celebrity, beauty and fashion tips, and a self-help article to improve the inner being. The big, bold letters across the top, however, spell the difference. This is *Latina,* the first bilingual magazine targeted at Hispanic American women and the inspiration of founder Christy Haubegger. More than 2 million bilingual, bicultural women are avid readers of this popular magazine.

Born in Houston, Texas, in 1968, Haubegger has described herself as a "chubby Mexican-American baby adopted by parents who were tall, thin, and blond." As a teenager during the mega-media 1980s, she was especially sensitive to the lack of Hispanic role models in women's magazines. It was a void waiting to be filled. At the age of 20, Haubegger received a bachelor's degree in philosophy from the University of Texas.

At 23, she earned her law degree from Stanford, where she joined the editorial staff of the *Law Review,* rising to the position of senior editor: "My experience as senior editor gave me a start in the worlds of journalism and publishing."

Haubegger also took a course in marketing. In that class, she had to write a business plan for a favorite enterprise. *Latina* magazine was born. As one of the best-known publications for Hispanic American women, *Latina* covers issues such as health, politics, family, and finance, as well as beauty and entertainment.

Named as one of *Advertising Age*'s "Women to Watch" and *Newsweek*'s "Women of the New Century," Haubegger was tapped by President Obama, along with 27 other distinguished Americans, for the President's Commission on White House Fellowships. Her work through *Latina* and other ventures has definitely given Hispanic women a voice and reminds them that they are part of the American Dream.

PERFORMANCE THINKING If you were assessing the characteristics that make Christy Haubegger a successful entrepreneur, which would you say are the most important?

CHECK IT OUT Go to **www.latina.com** to see the numerous online features the magazine offers of interest to the U.S. Latin community.

Starting Today

At least one strategy I learned in this chapter that I plan to try right away is

_____

_____

_____

What changes must I make in order for this strategy to be most effective?

_____

_____

_____

Review Questions

Based on what you have learned in this chapter, write your answers to the following questions:

1. Describe five strategies for building rapport.

_____

_____

2. How do assertive people communicate?

_____

_____

3. Describe three ways to handle conflict.

_____

_____

4. Name a barrier to effective communication and how to overcome it.

_____

_____

5. List three strategies for creating rapport and improving communication with people you live with.

_____

_____

Successful Teamwork

In the Classroom

Brian Chase is an electronics student who works part time in an electronics firm. He likes working with his hands and enjoys his technical classes. However, one marketing class is difficult for him. The instructor has formed permanent class teams with weekly case studies to present to the class and a final team project to complete. Brian dislikes relying on others for a final grade and gets frustrated trying to keep the team members focused on their tasks. Some people are late for meetings, others don't do their share of the work, and two team members have a personality conflict.

1. What suggestions do you have for Brian to help him work more effectively with others?

   _____

   _____

2. What strategies in the chapter would increase Brian's listening and team-building skills?

   _____

   _____

In the Workplace

Brian is now a manager of service technicians for a large security company that provides security equipment and alarm systems for banks, hotels, and industrial firms. His department must work closely with salespeople, systems design specialists, clerical staff, and maintenance personnel. Brian is having trouble convincing his technicians that they are part of the team. Sometimes they don't listen to the advice of the salespeople, clerical staff, or each other, which results in miscommunication and frustration.

3. How might Brian build rapport within and among various departments?

   _____

   _____

4. What strategies in this chapter could help create a solid team?

   _____

   _____

Applying the ABC Method of Self-Management

In the **Journal Entry**, you were asked to describe a difficult or confrontational situation in which you lost your temper or felt uncomfortable communicating your needs and ideas assertively, directly, and calmly. How would a positive, open attitude have helped you?

_____

_____

_____

Apply the ABC Method to explore how you can achieve a positive outcome. Write a script.

A = Acknowledge: Accept reality and pay attention to your emotions.

_____

_____

_____

B = Breathe: Take a deep breath to calm down and feel beloved.

_____

_____

_____

C = Choose: Knowing you have many options, choose the most appropriate for the situation and that will result in positive long-term consequences.

_____

_____

_____

Sample Script: Even though I'm feeling angry and embarrassed that I lost my temper, I love and accept myself and want to learn and grow. I take a deep breath and feel calm, centered and patient. I focus on being in the present moment as I calmly state my needs. I focus on breathing, listening, allowing the other person time to express their needs and frustration. I will not allow another person to control my emotions or behavior. I will talk with my supervisor for guidance, observe how other employees react in positive and negative ways. I will also check out mediation resources and workshops. I intend to learn ways to control my emotions, communicate in a direct, calm, and effective manner regardless of the other person's behavior. I see myself as calm, centered, and positive. Learning effective communication skills, especially with difficult people, is a skill that will help me in my career and in all aspects of my life.

Study Team Relationships

List some strategies for helping your study team be more organized and effective.

1. Before the Meeting

_____

_____

_____

_____

2. During the Meeting

_____

_____

_____

_____

3. After the Meeting

_____

_____

_____

_____

4. Think of effective ways to deal with the following list of challenges.

Challenges	Solutions
Latecomers or no-shows	_____
Passive members	_____
Negative attitudes	_____
Low energy	_____
Arguments	_____
Lack of preparation	_____
Socializing	_____
Members who dominate	_____

Appreciating Diversity

Assess your appreciation for diversity and check Yes or No for each of the following comments.

	Yes	No
1. I am committed to increasing my awareness of and sensitivity to diversity.	_____	_____
2. I ask questions and don't assume that I know about various groups.	_____	_____
3. I use critical thinking to question my assumptions and examine my views.	_____	_____
4. I strive to be sensitive to and respectful of differences in people.	_____	_____
5. I listen carefully and seek to understand people with different views and perspectives.	_____	_____
6. I realize I have biases, but I work to overcome prejudices and stereotypes.	_____	_____
7. I do not use offensive language.	_____	_____
8. I apologize if I unintentionally offend someone. I do not argue or make excuses.	_____	_____
9. I celebrate differences and see diversity as positive.	_____	_____
10. I speak up if I hear others speaking with prejudice.	_____	_____
11. I try to read about other cultures and customs.	_____	_____
12. I do not tell offensive jokes.	_____	_____
13. I encourage members of diverse cultural and social groups to participate in clubs and decision-making groups.	_____	_____

As you review your responses, think of areas where you can improve. List at least one of those areas and possible strategies you could use:

_____

_____

Are You Assertive, Aggressive, or Passive?

Next to each statement, write the number that best describes how you usually feel when relating to other people.

3 = mostly true   2 = sometimes true   1 = rarely true

_____ **1.** I often feel resentful because people use me.

_____ **2.** If someone is rude, I have a right to be rude, too.

_____ **3.** I am a confident, interesting person.

_____ **4.** I am shy and don't like speaking in public.

_____ **5.** I use sarcasm if I need to make my point with another person.

_____ **6.** I can ask for a higher grade if I feel I deserve it.

_____ **7.** People interrupt me often, but I prefer not to bring their attention to it.

_____ **8.** I can talk louder than other people and can get them to back down.

_____ **9.** I feel competent with my skills and accomplishments without bragging.

_____ **10.** People take advantage of my good nature and willingness to help.

_____ **11.** I go along with people so that they will like me or will give me what I want.

_____ **12.** I ask for help when I need it and give honest compliments easily.

_____ **13.** I can't say no when someone wants to borrow something.

_____ **14.** I like to win arguments and control the conversation.

_____ **15.** It is easy for me to express my true feelings directly.

_____ **16.** I don't like to express anger, so I often keep it inside or make a joke.

_____ **17.** People often get angry with me when I give them feedback.

_____ **18.** I respect other people's rights and can stand up for myself.

_____ **19.** I speak in a soft, quiet voice and don't look people in the eyes.

_____ **20.** I speak in a loud voice, make my point forcefully, and can stare someone in the eye.

_____ **21.** I speak clearly and concisely and use direct eye contact.

Scoring

Total your answers to questions 1, 4, 7, 10, 13, 16, 19 (passive): _____

Total your answers to questions 3, 6, 9, 12, 15, 18, 21 (assertive): _____

Total your answers to questions 2, 5, 8, 11, 14, 17, 20 (aggressive): _____

Your highest score indicates your prevalent pattern.

Are you more passive, assertive, or aggressive—or a combination?

Has your tendency toward one behavior helped or hurt you in situations?

What can you do to become more assertive and communicate effectively?

Assessing Your Relationship Skills

Skills in building diverse and healthy relationships are essential for success in school and throughout your career. Take stock of your relationship skills, and look ahead as you do the following exercises. Add this page to your Career Development Portfolio.

1. **Looking back:** Review your worksheets to find situations in which you learned to build rapport, listen, overcome shyness, resolve conflict, work with diversity, and be assertive. List the situations on the lines provided.

   _____

   _____

   _____

   _____

   _____

2. **Taking stock:** Describe your people skills. What are your strengths in building relationships? What areas do you want to improve?

   _____

   _____

   _____

   _____

   _____

3. **Looking forward:** Indicate how you would demonstrate to an employer that you can work well with a variety of people.

   _____

   _____

   _____

   _____

   _____

4. **Documentation:** Include documentation and examples of team and relationship skills. Ask an advisor, a friend, a supervisor, or an instructor to write a letter of support for you in this area. Keep this letter in your portfolio.

   _____

   _____

   _____

   _____

   _____

Explore Majors and Careers

14

LEARNING OUTCOMES

In this chapter, you will learn to

14-1 Explain the relationship between college success and job success

14-2 Explain how to build a career development portfolio

14-3 Demonstrate how a positive, open mindset creates success

14-4 Identify the steps for taking charge of your career development

SELF-MANAGEMENT

I'm not certain if the major I chose will lead to the job I want. One of my biggest fears is that I'll be stuck in a dead-end job and won't have an interesting career. What if I spent all this time and money and still can't get a good job? I feel as if I'm the only person who is indecisive. I'm not sure I believe in myself enough to make this big decision. What if I fail? I'm feeling anxious and frustrated.

sturti/Getty Images

Have you ever wondered if you're learning the skills and developing the qualities that will help you get and keep the job you want? Sometimes it's difficult to see the connection between college and the world of work. Have you ever taken a class and wondered how it relates to real life and if it will help you be more successful? How do you integrate all you are learning to make it meaningful and personal? In this chapter, you will learn steps for exploring college majors and careers. You will see that career planning is an exciting, lifelong process that starts with translating experiences and skills you are acquiring in school into a useful Career Development Portfolio.

JOURNAL ENTRY In **Worksheet 14.1**, describe feeling frustrated about choosing a major or career or feeling anxious that the information you're learning in classes will really benefit you in your career. How would having an open and positive mindset help you?

Early Roman philosopher Plotinus of Delphi (AD 205–270) recognized three main universal career concerns:

- Who am I?
- What shall I do?
- What shall become of me?

To these three questions, add the following: *Why* am I in college? *Where* should I focus my energy? *How* can I create a positive, open mindset and positive habits? *Will I be able to grow and learn? When* am I going to start making positive changes for college and career success? *Who* can help me meet my goals? Questions can give you a framework for self-assessment and help you understand who you are and what you want in life. In this rapidly changing world, you may have a chance to do many kinds of work. The average working American will have three to six careers and 12 to 15 jobs over a lifetime. Many of the career opportunities that will be available in 10 years don't even exist today. Thus, career planning is more than just picking a profession. It involves learning about yourself and what you want out of life. The gig economy is now the pattern for many young people. Many people work part-time jobs at night or on the weekend to supplement their income or for artistic expression.

In this chapter, we'll examine ways to choose a college major and explore careers, including step-by-step instructions on how to assemble a Career Development Portfolio. With a positive, open mindset, you'll relish change as a chance to grow.

Connecting School and Job Success

66 Tell me, what is it you plan to do with your one wild and precious life? 99

MARY OLIVER
poet

The path to career success began the day you started classes. The same mindset, habits, attitudes, and personal qualities required for school success are also key for job success. The same strategies—assessing yourself, knowing your learning style, thinking critically, creatively solving problems, effectively communicating, and establishing healthy relationships—apply to major and career exploration. Research has shown that too many students put their social life ahead of academics and these poor academic performers were more likely than other recent graduates to be unemployed, stuck in unskilled jobs, or fired or laid off in their first jobs. *With a positive growth mindset, you can choose to put effort and attention into academic classes instead of going the party route.*[1] There is no substitute for effort and time on task—in school and work. No one questions the importance of cooperative relationships at work, yet too few students get to know their professors and advisor. Treat college as an important job because it is. College is the time to reflect, explore and think about your values and purpose. What makes life meaningful?

Exploring and Choosing a Major

In our society, people are identified by their profession: "What do you do for a living?" In college, the question is "What is your major?" A college major helps give you structure, goals, and meaning. It provides fellowship with instructors and other students.

Some first-year students know that they want to be an engineer, a writer, a business owner, a nurse, or a computer programmer. Most, however, want to explore many majors. The reasons that some students find choosing a college major daunting include:

- Have many interests, so it is difficult to narrow them to one major
- Have not assessed their interests, values, or goals
- Have not explored the wide range of majors at their school
- Have difficulty making decisions
- Fear they will get stuck with a major they won't like
- Fear a major will lead to a career they dislike
- Are influenced by family expectations
- Are unsure of the job market
- Know they like a specific subject area but don't know what they can do with it

If you are unsure of your college major, you're not alone. On some campuses, "undeclared" is the most frequent major. The average student changes majors three times. Community colleges are experiencing a growth in students who want to change careers, study for a vocation, or learn new skills. Many students already have a four-year degree but now want to learn computer science, business, cooking, woodworking, real estate, nursing, firefighting, or fashion design. What you want to do at 18 may be very different from what you want to do at 40, 50, or 60. You may have studied what you love, but now you need additional skills to find a good-paying job. *You'll never regret earning a four-year degree that will help you advance professionally and enrich you personally.* The strategies for choosing a major are similar to those for choosing a career:

1. **Assess yourself.** People are happiest when they do work that is consistent with their values and interest. Return to Chapter 1 and review assessment tools. In Chapter 3, we reviewed Maslow's hierarchy of needs, which identifies what motivates people and creates meaning and purpose. Self-actualization is the process of fulfilling your potential and requires listening to your inner voice as well as exploring many majors. *With a positive, open mindset, you know that with effort you can learn and grow, develop new skills, cultivate qualities, improve abilities, and thrive on change.*

2. **The science and math path.** If you think you might want to major in science, start taking required classes. Some classes are difficult, but don't let that discourage you from getting help and mastering the basics. If you are good at math, science, and the liberal arts, consider staying in science and math and getting a minor in the arts. You can always switch, and your math and science classes will count for other majors. For example, Sal started in science but realized he loved dance. He earned a biology degree, got a teaching credential, and now teaches biology full time and dance part time. In the summers, he puts on musicals for the local theatre group. You can also get a master's later, but you'll have the necessary classes behind you for many majors.

3. **Meet with career counselors and advisors.** Counselors are trained to offer and interpret self-assessment tools and interest inventories. They can help you clarify values, talents, and skills; offer insight into your interests, personality type, and goals; and help you link majors with careers. Academic advisors can help you determine required classes for majors and which units transfer and apply.

4. **Talk with alumni.** Discuss possible majors with alumni in related fields. The alumni office can connect you with alumni in the community. Professionals know the variety of skills necessary for entry-level jobs in different occupations and can also tell you which classes they recommend. Rotary is a well-respected, international club made up of business professionals in all walks of life (they welcome young people).

5. **Explore through college classes.** Taking general education classes is a great way to experience various disciplines, get to know instructors and students, and still meet college requirements. You might want to take an extra class during the summer.

6. **Explore through the course listings.** Check out departments and courses to find a major you didn't know existed and research courses that would complement certain majors.

7. **Go to the academic department.** Go to the departments of majors you are interested in and gather more information about requirements, job outlook, and possible careers.

8. **Get an internship or volunteer.** Check with your professors and advisor in each department for internships. *Many students gain experience and have found full-time jobs after graduation through internships or volunteer work.* You want to build skills to make you more employable so focus on transferrable skills that will be relevant to your job success. Try co-ops, campus jobs, volunteer work, part-time jobs, and service learning activities for hands-on experience (see **Peak Progress 14.1**). Campus clubs, extracurricular activities, and international exchange programs can offer new experiences, leadership opportunities, and growth that expand your perspective. Check out Rotary Clubs, non-profits, and political organizations.

9. **Be creative with your major.** Your school may have an interdisciplinary major, a self-designed major, or a broad liberal arts major that allows you to take a wide range of courses in areas that interest you. Many employers look for liberal arts graduates who are skilled in writing, critical thinking, reasoning, and creative problem solving and can work well with diverse groups. Be proactive about exploring majors and careers.

10. **Be persistent.** Majors are launching pads. Make a decision, pick a major early on and stick with it. This enables you to line up internships that will expand your experience, skills, and help you grow. Students who change majors usually get behind and have to stay in college longer. If you are fairly close to earning a degree in a certain major, graduate and then go on. You can always go to a community college, graduate school, or professional school to invest further in your skills. For example, Bruce earned a forestry degree but realized during his junior year that he liked finance. So he wrapped up his forestry degree and went on to take training to be a certified financial planner. Over the years he took many more workshops and classes, but his first degree was all he needed to get started. *A college degree in any major is better than quitting because you are undecided. Be persistent! Focus on growing and learning.*

Consult with your advisor often. If you delay too long, you may discover that some of your courses won't count toward your selected major and other courses still need to be taken. You may also find that your GPA isn't high enough to get into a preferred program.

Finally, remind yourself that getting a college degree in any major will help launch your career. A college degree—plus a positive attitude, qualities, consistent

Service Learning

As we discussed in Chapter 5, service learning enables you to use what you are learning in the classroom to solve real-life problems. The service reinforces and strengthens the learning, and the learning reinforces and strengthens the service. You learn about democracy and citizenship while becoming an active contributing citizen.

Many colleges offer courses that provide service learning opportunities. These courses include structured time for you to reflect on your service and learning experiences through a mix of writing, reading, speaking, listening, and creating in groups and individual work. This fosters the development of personal qualities—empathy, personal values, beliefs, awareness, self-esteem, self-confidence, and social responsibility. Credit is awarded for learning, not for a required number of service hours.

Service learning has many benefits:

- It gives you opportunities to use newly acquired skills and knowledge in real-life situations.
- It fills a need for volunteer support in the community and uses that need as a foundation for participants to examine themselves, their society, and their future.
- It tracks progress toward learning objectives and goals.
- The service performed is valuable and significant for the community.
- You feel empowered by contributing to your community.

Service learning experiences can be personally rewarding and enriching and they are important points in a portfolio or résumé. As employers assess equally qualified job applicants, they look for experiences, skills, or qualities that make one candidate stand out. They also allow you to work with professionals who may become mentors, give you invaluable advice, provide job contacts, and may open doors for you in the future.

Source: Adapted from "What Is Service-Learning?" Corporation for National and Community Service, www.learnandserve.gov; Mark Cooper, Florida International University, "Four Things Faculty Want to Know About!"

effort, experience, skills, and positive habits—go a long way toward creating opportunities. *Stay the course.*

Values, Interests, Abilities, and Skills

Self-assessment is lifelong. Reflect on your values, interests, innate abilities, and already acquired skills to help you decide which career direction you want to take and thus which major course of study you should pursue. Relish growth and change as you learn.

VALUES

Values are the importance you attach to various factors in your life. They are formed in early childhood and are influenced by parents, teachers, the environment, and your culture. They can change and be enhanced with experience, insight, reflection, and a desire to fulfill your full potential. You will be much happier if your career reflects your values. Complete **Personal Evaluation Notebook 14.1** to determine your personal values.

INTERESTS

Interests are the activities and subjects that cause you to feel comfortable, enthusiastic, or passionate. Psychologist John L. Holland explored interests and their relation to college major and career choice. His theory suggests that career choice often reflects personality type and that most people fit into one of six occupational

> **❝** Mostly I just followed my inner feelings and passions . . . and kept going to where it got warmer and warmer, until it finally got hot. . . . Everybody has talent. It's just a matter of moving around until you've discovered what it is. **❞**
>
> **GEORGE LUCAS**
> *Director and creator of Star Wars*

WORDS TO SUCCEED

Personal Evaluation Notebook 14.1

Your Values

Your values influence what will satisfy you in a career. By each value, rank them as

1 = Not that important 2 = Somewhat important 3 = Most important

Overall Values	**Rank**
Security	_____
Helping others	_____
Recognition	_____
Collaborating with others	_____
Religious or spiritual beliefs	_____
Adventure	_____
Variety	_____
Serving community/national/international concerns	_____
Artistic/creative expression	_____
Personal growth and learning	_____
Focusing on family	_____
Others	_____

Specific Factors You Value in a Career	**Rank**
High salary	_____
Great deal of freedom/autonomy	_____
Flexible working hours	_____
Opportunities for advancement	_____
Good vacation/benefits	_____
Supportive co-workers	_____
Working with others	_____
Working alone	_____
Telecommuting/working at home	_____
Working outdoors	_____
Social environment	_____
Job status	_____
Clean and comfortable working environment	_____
Others	_____

Take note of the factors you rated "3," as these values are most important to you.

personality types, which are largely determined by their interests. Revisit Chapter 1 and compare with Holland's types. See if you fall into one or two of the categories:

- *Realistic.* Realistic people have athletic or mechanical ability and prefer to work with objects, machines, tools, machines, plants, animals, or to be outdoors. They like to work with their hands. Possible careers include big data engineering, data analyst, big data analysis, web designing, architect, optician, surveyor, laboratory technician, wildlife biologist, park ranger. automotive mechanic, zoologist, engineer, chef, and bus or truck driver.
- *Investigative.* Investigative people like to observe, learn, investigate, analyze, evaluate, or solve problems. They enjoy academic and scientific challenges. Possible careers include researchers, computer programmer, pilot, mathematics or science teacher, surgical technician, doctor, economist, and chemist.
- *Artistic.* Artistic people have creative, innovative, or intuitive abilities and like to work in unstructured situations. Possible careers include actor, commercial artist, public relations representative, editor, decorator, fashion designer, and photojournalist.
- *Social.* Social people like to work with people—to inform, enlighten, help, train, develop, or cure. They have strong verbal and written skills. Possible careers include social worker, minister, psychologist, parole officer, teacher, and rehabilitation therapist.
- *Enterprising.* Enterprising people enjoy leading—influencing, persuading, performing, or managing to meet organizational goals or achieve economic gain. Possible careers include small business owner, communications consultant, stockbroker, sales representative, restaurant manager, and motivational speaker.
- *Conventional.* Conventional people like to work with data, have clerical or numerical abilities, are detail-oriented, and follow directions well. They like working with numbers and facts and enjoy bringing situations to closure. Possible careers include accountant, court reporter, credit manager, military officer, and title examiner.

ABILITIES

Abilities are innate talents or gifts that can be enhanced through effort and practice. Determine your natural ability to understand mathematics, play musical instruments, write or use words to persuade, dance, play sports, resolve conflict, or handle a crisis calmly.

SKILLS

Skills are capabilities you have learned and developed. They often have a more technical connotation than abilities. Some skills are job-specific, such as operating a bulldozer, conducting lab tests, or editing manuscripts. **Transferable skills** are those that can be used in a variety of careers, such as negotiating, analyzing data, preparing presentations, effectively managing people or resources, and using technology. *With effort and a positive growth mindset you can learn new skills, cultivate essential qualities, and continually learn.*

It's important to identify your skills to see how they can be developed throughout your career. What careers using these skills might you like to explore?

People	Data	Mechanical
Instructing	Analyzing	Handling
Supervising	Coordinating	Setting up
Negotiating	Comparing	Driving
Entertaining	Computing	Operating
Persuading	Compiling	Selecting

Exploring Careers

After assessing your personal values and what you are looking for in a career, you can determine what opportunities lie ahead. The strategies for choosing a major also apply to determining a career path. Investigate these resources:

- *Career center.* Career center personnel can give you information about career trends, opportunities, salaries, and job availability and connect you to alumni.

- *Library.* Your school or local library has many resources, such as the *Dictionary of Occupational Titles, The New Guide for Occupational Exploration,* and the classic *What Color Is Your Parachute?* by Richard Bowles.

- *Professional organizations.* Visit the websites of professional organizations in your field of interest and consider joining at a student discount. Find out what you would receive with a membership, such as access to journals and job listings. At the website or in journals, look for individuals who have received promotions or contributed to the field. See if any are local or provide contact information. Most professionals enjoy talking to young people who are entering their field and are happy to offer advice.

- *Your network.* Personal contacts are excellent ways to explore careers and find a job. In Chapter 5, you learned that networking provides access to people who can serve as mentors and connect you to opportunities. Create and cultivate personal and professional contacts. Talk with instructors, advisors, counselors, and other students. Collect business cards and e-mail addresses. (See **Worksheets 14.6** and **14.7** on potential questions to ask professionals and hiring managers.)

- *Government organizations.* Several organizations, such as the U.S. Department of Labor, track job statistics, predict future opportunities, and provide employment guidance. The *Occupational Outlook Handbook* (go to the Bureau of Labor Statistics website at **www.bls.gov/ooh**) lists the outlook for hundreds of types of jobs and provides employment guidance, such as job search and application methods, places to learn about job openings, and résumé and job interview tips. See **Peak Progress 14.2** on using the Adult Learning Cycle when exploring.

- *Websites and apps.* Check out the following: indeed, LinkedIn, glassdoor, Quick Resume, chrisguillebeau.com, jobhuntersbible.com, lifehacker.com, and calnewport.com/blog. Put energy and commitment into displaying your skills and illustrating your talents on LinkedIn.

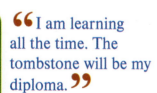

WORDS TO SUCCEED

66 I am learning all the time. The tombstone will be my diploma. 99

EARTHA KITT
Entertainer; passed away December 25, 2008

Build a Career Development Portfolio

A Career Development Portfolio is an online/digital or hard copy collection of documents that highlight your strengths, skills, and competencies. It includes grades, classes, certificates, letters of recommendation, awards, lists of activities, inventories you've taken, and samples of written work. A portfolio can help you connect what you have learned in school to your current or future work, and it

Peak Progress

Applying the Adult Learning Cycle to Exploring Majors and Careers

1. **FEEL and LISTEN.** *Why do I want to learn this?* I want to explore a number of majors so that I'm sure I'm using my talents and interests. I want to cast a wide net and not just drift into a major or career. I want to honor my feelings and temperament and not force myself into a major or career that wouldn't be right for me. I'll listen to my intuition and to others who are knowledgeable.

2. **OBSERVE and VISUALIZE.** *How does this work?* I will observe other people in various majors and careers and reflect on qualities that are necessary to succeed.

3. **THINK and WRITE.** *What does this mean?* I'll use critical thinking to explore majors and careers and write down priorities such as independence, high visibility, flexible hours, ability to work from home, and management opportunities. Which careers fit my personality and skills? Which skills am I willing to learn? What are positives and drawbacks of each career? Is my mindset focused on growth and resiliency? I'll write out my intentions, goals, and strengths and talk with people in certain careers.

4. **DO and PRACTICE.** *What can I do with this?* I'll jump in and get involved. I'll seek out acquaintances in the field, instructors, professional organizations, and introductory courses. If the career choice still looks promising, I'll identify ways I can gain experience or related skills required for the profession, such as joining a club or securing an internship. I'll contact the career center and do one thing each week that helps me to accomplish those tasks. I will get involved and engaged.

5. **TEACH and PRACTICE AGAIN.** *Whom can I share this with?* Relay your impressions and reservations to your family, friends, or fellow students who are also career searching. Some will ask you questions that will make you think about where you are in selecting a major and what your next steps should be. Share with others.

Use the VARK system of integrating learning styles to help you think through and apply the Adult Learning Cycle. *Visualize* yourself in several careers. What imagery seems natural? If you could create your perfect day or *fantasy* career, what would it look like? *Look* at pictures of people in different careers. *Observe* people at work. *Listen* to people describe their jobs. Ask questions. *Write* out a summary of your perfect day. What factors are important to you. *Read* it out loud. Talk with alumni from your university and interview people in various careers. *Do and apply;* look for internships, part-time jobs, or volunteer opportunities where you can actually try out jobs. If you conclude that you are still undecided, explore other career options and retry some or all of the steps. Practice visualization when you need help focusing. Eventually, you will find a career path that suits your personality and interests. Now get going.

---

demonstrates you have the necessary education, skills, competencies, and personal qualities to perform a job.

Even if you have little work experience, this documentation can give you an edge when applying for a job. For example, Janel convinced an employer to hire her based on her portfolio: She showed the manager samples of her work and the certificates she had earned. Miguel used his portfolio to receive a promotion based on documentation of his skills and experience. Include volunteer work and essential qualities you can demonstrate.

Your Career Development Portfolio helps you

- Plan and design your educational program and postgraduate learning
- Describe how your experiences have helped you grow professionally
- Document skills and accomplishments in and out of the classroom
- Link your skills and qualities with what an employer is looking for
- Identify areas you want to augment or improve
- Record and organize experiences for your résumé and job interviews
- Express talents creatively and artistically

- Justify college credit for prior learning and military, internship, or life experiences
- Document and demonstrate essential qualities such as honesty, responsibility, and grit

When Should You Start Your Portfolio?

Today. Start by putting assessments, journal entries, and worksheets at the end of each chapter, into your portfolio. Add papers, coursework, job experiences, internships, and examples of personal qualities to your portfolio. Include awards, examples of leadership, and letters of recommendation. *Give examples of how you have demonstrated a positive mindset that has helped you learn, grow, and bounce back.* By the time you graduate, you will have a portfolio that is distinctly personal and persuasive.

A sample planning guide appears in **Figure 14.1**. Modify to fit your needs.

How to Organize and Assemble Your Portfolio

You may be developing your portfolio as a general documented system of achievements and professional growth, as a graduation requirement for your major, or for a more specific reason, such as obtaining credit for prior learning experiences.

Determine the best way to show your portfolio to others. You may want to develop a digital and physical portfolio. Print copies on high-quality, durable paper and keep it safe.

Elements of Your Portfolio

If you need to submit your portfolio to your school for review or evaluation, follow established guidelines. The following sections describe elements for most portfolios.

TITLE, OR COVER, PAGE

Include a title page with the title of your document, your name, the name of the college, and the date. See **Figure 14.2** for an example. Make it unique with your own logo.

CONTENTS PAGE

On the contents page, list the sections of the portfolio. Make certain that the page numbers and titles are correct. See **Figure 14.2** for an example of a contents page.

INTRODUCTION

In the introduction, discuss the purpose of your portfolio and the goals you are trying to achieve with its development. See **Figure 14.3** for an example of an introduction page.

LIST OF SIGNIFICANT LIFE EXPERIENCES

The next section of your portfolio is a year-by-year account or timeline of your significant life experiences. Resources to consult include family members, friends, photo albums, and journals. Include experiences that are important because you

- Found the experience enjoyable (or painful)
- Learned something new about yourself
- Achieved something you value
- Received recognition
- Expended considerable time, energy, or money

Freshman Year

- Begin your Career Development Portfolio.
- Explore and join clubs, and get involved on campus.
- Assess your interests, skills, values, goals, and personality.
- Go to the career center at your school, and explore majors and careers.
- Set goals for your first year.
- Explore college majors and minors.
- Explore the community.
- Network with professors and students. Get good grades.
- Keep a journal. Label the first section "Self-Assessment." Begin to write your autobiography.
- Label another section "Exploring Careers."

Sophomore Year

- Add to your Career Development Portfolio.
- Start a file about careers and majors.
- Choose a major.
- Review general education requirements.
- Continue to explore resources in the community.
- Build your network.
- Join clubs and take a leadership role.
- Read articles and books about your major area.
- Find a part-time job or volunteer your time.
- Start or update your résumé.
- Explore internships and co-op programs.
- Add a section to your journal called "Job Skills and Qualities."

Junior Year

- Update and expand your Career Development Portfolio.
- Gain more job experience.
- Write and submit a major contract, outline your program, and apply for graduation.
- Join student organizations and professional organizations, and add to your network.
- Develop relationships with faculty, administrators, and other students.
- Identify a mentor or someone you can model to achieve your goals.
- Start to read the journal of your profession.
- Obtain an internship, or gain additional job experience.
- Update your journal with job tips and articles about your field.
- Update your résumé.
- Visit the career center on campus for help with your résumé, internships, and job opportunities.

Senior Year

- Refine your Career Development Portfolio.
- Put your job search into high gear. Go to the career center for advice.
- Read recruitment materials. Schedule interviews with companies.
- Update and polish your résumé and print copies. Write cover letters.
- Actively network! Keep a list of contacts and their telephone numbers, e-mails, etc.
- Join professional organizations and attend conferences.
- Start sending out résumés and attending job fairs.
- Find a mentor to help you with your job search and career planning.
- Meet with an evaluator or advisor to review graduation requirements.
- Log interviews in your journal or notebook.

Figure **14.1**

Career Development Portfolio Planning Guide

This planning guide will help you review your skills and maintain your Career Development Portfolio as you move toward your career goal. *What other strategies can you use to prepare for your career?*

Figure 14.2

Career Development Portfolio Elements

The presentation of your Career Development Portfolio reflects your personality and makes a valuable first impression. *What elements could be modified to better reflect your field of study?*

<table>
<tr><th>Sample Title Page</th><th colspan="2">Sample Contents Page</th></tr>
<tr><td rowspan="13">

CAREER DEVELOPMENT PORTFOLIO

Kim Anderson
Louis College

April 30, 2017

</td><td colspan="2" align="center">**CONTENTS**</td></tr>
<tr><td>Introduction</td><td>1</td></tr>
<tr><td>List of Significant Life Experiences</td><td>2</td></tr>
<tr><td>Analysis of Accomplishments</td><td>3</td></tr>
<tr><td>Inventory of Skills and Competencies</td><td>5</td></tr>
<tr><td>Inventory of Personal Qualities</td><td>6</td></tr>
<tr><td>Documentation</td><td>7</td></tr>
<tr><td>Work Philosophy and Goals</td><td>9</td></tr>
<tr><td>Résumé</td><td>11</td></tr>
<tr><td>Samples of Work</td><td>13</td></tr>
<tr><td>Summary of Transcripts</td><td>17</td></tr>
<tr><td>Credentials, Certificates, Workshops</td><td>18</td></tr>
<tr><td>Experience</td><td>25</td></tr>
<tr><td>Bibliography</td><td>27</td></tr>
</table>

This section can also be written as an autobiography. It can include

- Graduation and formal education
- Jobs/promotions
- Marriage/divorce and other events in your family
- Special projects
- Volunteer work
- Training and workshops
- Self-study or reentry into college
- Extensive travel
- Hobbies and crafts
- Military service

Figure 14.3

Sample Introduction Page

The introduction highlights the goals of the portfolio. *How might this person use her portfolio during her job hunt?*

INTRODUCTION

My Career Development Portfolio reflects many hours of introspection and documentation. I recently made a career change and would like to pursue further opportunities in the marketing field. Thus, I plan to obtain my Bachelor's degree in Business Administration at Louis College. My career goal is to eventually become a store manager or a regional marketing director for a large retail department store.

ANALYSIS OF ACCOMPLISHMENTS

Identify, describe, and demonstrate what you learned and how you learned it. Include knowledge, skills, competencies, qualities, and values. Give examples and demonstrate these qualities and skills. Did these experiences

- Help you make decisions?
- Help you clarify values and set goals?
- Help you learn something new?
- Broaden your view of life?
- Expand your interactions and engagement with people from diverse backgrounds?
- Help you take responsibility?
- Increase your confidence and self-esteem?
- Result in self-understanding and believing in yourself?
- Help you create a positive, open mindset focused on growth?

> "You have to believe in yourself when no one else does. That's what makes you a winner."
>
> **VENUS WILLIAMS**
> *Olympic gold medalist and professional tennis champion*

WORDS TO SUCCEED

INVENTORY OF SKILLS AND COMPETENCIES

Use your completed Career Development Portfolio worksheets, inventories from the career center, and activities in this text to record your skills, transferable skills, and competencies. Use SCANS as a guide (see **Figure 14.4**) and **Personal Evaluation Notebook 14.2** for help with transferable skills.

As you take college courses, determine which skills you are learning in the classroom may translate to job skills. For example, long-term budgeting goals learned in a personal finance course can be helpful in managing project budgets on the job. Keep a list of these skills.

INVENTORY OF PERSONAL QUALITIES

SCANS lists important personal qualities for success in the workplace: responsibility, a positive attitude, dependability, self-esteem, sociability, integrity, and self-control. These qualities set you apart from others in the workplace. Use critical thinking to explore ways to demonstrate personal qualities in **Personal Evaluation Notebook 14.3**.

Basic Skills: reading, writing, listening, speaking, and math

Thinking Skills: critical thinking, creative problem solving, knowing how to learn, reasoning, and mental visualization

Personal Qualities: responsibility, positive attitude, dependability, self-esteem, sociability, integrity, and self-management

Interpersonal Skills: teaches others, team member, leadership, works well with diverse groups, and serves clients and customers

Information: acquires, evaluates, organizes, maintains, and uses technology

Systems: understands, monitors, corrects, designs, and improves systems

Resources: allocates time, money, material, people, and space

Technology: selects, applies, maintains, and troubleshoots

Figure **14.4**
SCANS Skills
Acquiring these skills and competencies will help you succeed throughout your career. *Which of these skills do you need to develop?*

Personal Evaluation Notebook 14.2

Transferable Skills

1. What transferable skills do you have?

   _____

   _____

2. What specific content skills do you have that indicate a specialized knowledge or ability, such as plumbing, computer programming, or cooking?

   _____

   _____

3. List your daily activities and determine the skills involved in each. Then consider what you like about the activities, such as the environment, interactions with others, or a certain emotional reaction—for example, "I like bike riding because I am outdoors with friends, and the exercise feels great."

Activity	Skills Involved	Factors
Bike riding	Balance, stamina, discipline	Being outdoors

DOCUMENTATION

For your Career Development Portfolio, document each of the SCANS skills, competencies, and personal qualities. Indicate how and when you learned each. Include letters of support and recommendation. These letters can be from your employer, co-workers, community members, and clients or customers expressing their appreciation.

WORK PHILOSOPHY AND GOALS

Effort, hard work, and the willingness to grow and learn are key to success. Your work philosophy is a statement about your mindset. Do you have grit and perseverance or do you give up easily? For example, "My immediate goal is to graduate with a certificate in fashion design. In 5 years, I intend to earn a college degree in business with an emphasis in marketing. I am a lifelong learner and have perseverance. Goals include:

- To hold a leadership role in fashion design
- To upgrade my skills and personal qualities constantly
- To belong to at least one professional organization"

Personal Evaluation Notebook 14.3

Inventory of Personal Qualities

Indicate how you have learned and demonstrated each of the SCANS qualities and how you would demonstrate them to an employer. Add other personal qualities.

1. Responsibility: _____
   _____
   _____

2. Positive attitude: _____
   _____
   _____

3. Dependability: _____
   _____
   _____

4. Self-esteem: _____
   _____
   _____

5. Sociability: _____
   _____
   _____

6. Integrity: _____
   _____
   _____

7. Self-control: _____
   _____
   _____

Expand on your short-term, medium-range, and long-term goals. Include a mission statement and career objectives (see Chapter 1 and **Figure 14.5**). Write your goals according to the roles you perform and what you hope to accomplish in life. Consider:

- Do I want to improve my skills and personal qualities?
- Do I want to change careers or jobs?

Figure 14.5

Sample Mission Statement

As discussed in Chapter 1, a mission statement reveals your aspirations, states your philosophy on work and life, and reflects your highest values. *What other types of information can your mission statement reveal?*

Mission Statement: Anna Marcos

My mission is to use my talent in fashion design to create beauty and art. As a women's clothing designer, I want to influence the future development of fashion for women of all ages. I seek opportunities to learn more about how fashion affects confidence and self-esteem and how that can be reflected in affordable clothing lines. I strive to enjoy healthy and supportive personal relationships, collaborative and creative teams at work, and community involvement that promotes empowerment and success for women of all socioeconomic classes.

Long-Term Goals

Career goals: I want to own my own fashion design company.
Educational goals: I want to teach and lead workshops.
Family goals: I want to be a supportive parent.
Community goals: I want to belong to different community organizations.
Financial goals: I want to earn enough money to live comfortably and provide my family with the basic needs and more.

Medium-Range Goals

Career goals: I want to be a manager of a fashion company.
Educational goals: I want to earn a college degree in business and marketing.

Short-Term Goals

Career goals: I want to obtain an entry-level job in fashion design.
Educational goals: I want to earn a certificate in fashion design.

- Do I want to become more competent in my present job or earn a promotion?
- Do I want to spend more time in one or more areas of my life?
- Do I want to learn a new hobby or explore areas of interest?
- Do I want to become more involved in community service?
- Do I want to improve my personal qualities?
- Do I want to improve my human relations skills?
- Do I want to spend more time with my family?

Return to Chapter 4 and review **Personal Evaluation Notebook 4.3**, "Looking Ahead: Your Goals." Reflect on what you wrote, and update it. Make it a habit to reflect on what you are learning in class and connect it to work and life. How are these experiences changing the way you see yourself, others, and the world? How are they changing your values, interests, and goals? Record these questions in your portfolio.

RÉSUMÉ

The purpose of a résumé is to show your strengths, accomplishments, and skills and their connections to an employer's needs. Your résumé is almost always the first contact an employer will have with you because most companies initially screen potential candidates through online applications. You want it to stand out, highlight your skills and competencies, look professional, and, ideally, fit on one page. Several online services can help you format your résumé, design it to fit the needs of specific professions, link it to hiring companies, and allow you to create your own home page. Also, résumé classes may be offered in the career center. See **Figure 14.6** for a sample résumé.

Keep an updated résumé in your portfolio to build on. Although your résumé's final format and content may depend on the preferences of your prospective employers or career field, you will most likely include the following components:

1. **Personal information.** Include your name, address, phone number, and e-mail address. If you have a temporary or school address, also include a permanent

CAITLYN J. JENSEN

1423 10th Street
Arlin, Minnesota 52561
(320) 555-2896
cjjensen@att.net

JOB OBJECTIVE: To obtain an entry-level position as a travel agent

WORK EXPERIENCE
University Travel Agency, Arlin, Minnesota
Tour Guide, August 2012–present
- Arrange tours to historic sites in a four-state area. Responsibilities include contacting rail and bus carriers, arranging for local guides at each site, making hotel and restaurant reservations, and providing historical information about points of interest.

- Develop tours for holidays and special events. Responsibilities include event planning, ticketing, and coordination of travel and event schedules.

- Specialized tour planning resulted in 24 percent increase in tour revenues over the preceding year.

Arlin Area Convention Center
Intern Tourist Coordinator, December 2008–June 2012
- Established initial contact with prospective speakers, coordinated schedules, and finalized all arrangements. Set up database of tours.

- Organized receptions for groups up to 250, including reserving meeting rooms, contacting caterers, finalizing menus, and preparing seating charts.

EDUCATION
Arlin Community College, Arlin, Minnesota
  Associate of Arts in Business, June 2013
  Magna Cum Laude graduate

Cross Pointe Career School, Arlin, Minnesota
  Certificate in Tourism, June 2011

HONORS AND AWARDS
Academic Dean's List
Recipient of Arlin Rotary Scholarship, 2011

COLLEGE AND COMMUNITY ACTIVITIES
Vice President, Tourist Club, 2012–2013
Co-chaired 2012 home-tour fund-raising event for Big Sisters

PROFESSIONAL MEMBERSHIP
Arlin Area Convention and Visitors Bureau

REFERENCES
Available upon request.

Figure **14.6**

Sample Résumé

An effective résumé should be clear, concise, and eye-catching to create the best possible first impression. *What is the most important element of your résumé?*

address. Don't include marital status, height, weight, health, interests, a picture, or hobbies unless they are relevant to the job. Keep your résumé simple.

2. **Job objective.** Include a job objective if you will accept only a specific job. You may be willing to accept various jobs in a company, especially if you're a new graduate with little experience. If you decide not to list a job objective, use your cover letter to relate your résumé to the specific job for which you are applying.

3. **Work experience.** List the title of your last job first, dates worked, and a brief description of your duties. Don't clutter your résumé with needless details or irrelevant jobs. You can elaborate on specific duties in your cover letter and in the interview.

4. **Educational background.** List your highest degree first, school attended, dates, and major field of study. Include educational experience that may be relevant to the job, such as certification, licensing, advanced training, intensive seminars, and summer study programs. Don't list individual classes on your résumé. Your cover letter can mention any classes that relate directly to the job you are applying for.

5. **Honors and awards.** List honors and awards that are related to the job or indicate excellence. In addition, you may want to list other qualifications related to the job, such as fluency in another language.

6. **College and community activities.** List activities that show leadership abilities and a willingness to contribute.

7. **Professional memberships and activities.** List professional memberships, speeches, or research projects connected with your profession.

8. **References.** Gather three to five references, including employment, academic, and character references. Ask instructors for a general letter before you leave their last class or soon after. (If you receive an actual letter versus an e-mail attachment, scan the letter and create a digital file to submit to future employers.) Fellow members of professional associations, club advisors, a coach, and students who have worked with you on projects can also provide good character references. See **Figure 14.7** for a sample request for a recommendation. Ask your supervisor for a letter before you leave a job. Be sure to ask your references for permission to use their names and contact information. Don't print your references on the bottom of your résumé. It's best to include "References available upon request" and list them on a separate sheet of paper. Provide that list only if asked to do so. You may not want your references to be called until you have an interview. Include letters of recommendation in your portfolio.

SAMPLES OF WORK

Think of how you can visually demonstrate your expertise in your field. Work samples can include articles, portions of a book, artwork, fashion sketches, drawings, photos of work, poetry, pictures, food demonstrations, brochures, job descriptions, and performance reviews. Include samples of flyers or digital samples of music or media projects on DVD.

SUMMARY OF TRANSCRIPTS

Include a copy of all transcripts of college work.

May 2, 2022

Eva Atkins
Chair of the Fashion Department
Green Briar Business Institute
100 North Bank Street
Glenwood, New Hampshire 03827

Dear Professor Atkins:

I was a student of yours last term in Fashion Design and earned an *A* in your class. I am currently assembling my Career Development Portfolio so I can apply for summer positions in the fashion business. Would you please write a letter of recommendation addressing the following skills and competencies?

- My positive attitude and enthusiasm
- My ability to work with diverse people in teams
- My computer and technical skills
- My skills in design and art

I have also included my résumé, which highlights my experience, my GPA, and selected classes. If it is convenient, I would like to stop by your office next week and pick up your signed letter of recommendation or please feel free to send a file to my e-mail address provided below. Your advice and counsel have meant so much to me over the last three years. You have served as an instructor, an advisor, and a mentor. Thank you again for all your help and support. Please call or e-mail me if you have questions.

Sincerely,
Susan Sanchos
Susan Sanchos
242 Cherry Lane
Glenwood, New Hampshire 03827
Home phone: (304) 555-8293
e-mail: susans@edu.glow.com

Figure 14.7

Request for a Letter of Recommendation

Instructors, advisors, coaches, and previous employers are ideal candidates to ask for a letter of recommendation. *Whom might you ask to write a letter of recommendation?*

CREDENTIALS, CERTIFICATES, AND WORKSHOPS

Include a copy of credentials and certificates. List workshops, seminars, training sessions, conferences, continuing education courses, and other examples of lifelong learning.

EXPERIENCE

Include internships, leadership experiences in clubs and sports, volunteer work, service to the community, and travel experiences related to your goals. You can also include awards, honors, and certificates of recognition.

BIBLIOGRAPHY

Include a bibliography of books you have read that pertain to your major, career goals, or occupation. Consider annotating those that you found most helpful and why.

PORTFOLIO COVER LETTER

If you are submitting your portfolio for review, include a cover letter that indicates the purpose of the submission (such as to prove previous experiences or college credit), a list of the documents enclosed, a brief review, and a request for a response (such as an interview or acceptance). See **Figure 14.8** for an example of a portfolio cover letter.

Figure 14.8

Portfolio Cover Letter

Because your portfolio showcases your variety of experiences, your cover letter should pinpoint the reason you are presenting it for review at this time. *What are some possible reasons for submitting your portfolio for review?*

737 Grandview Avenue
Euclid, Ohio 43322

October 2, 2022

Dr. Kathryn Keys
Director of Assessment of Prior Learning
Louis College
333 West Street
Columbus, Ohio 43082

Dear Dr. Keys:

I am submitting my portfolio for credit for prior learning. I am applying for credit for the following courses:

Marketing 201	Retail Marketing
Management 180	Introduction to Management
Business Writing 100	Introduction to Business Writing

I completed my portfolio while taking the course Special Topics 350. My experiences are detailed in the portfolio and I believe they qualify me for six units of college credit. I look forward to meeting you to discuss this further. I will call your office next week to arrange an appointment. If you have questions, please contact me at (202) 555-5556 or kanderson@att.net.

Sincerely,
Kim Anderson
Kim Anderson

Overcome the Barriers to Portfolio Development

The biggest barrier to portfolio development is procrastination. It takes time to gather samples. The idea of a portfolio may sound good, but you also think of these excuses:

- It's a lot of work and I don't have the time.
- I wouldn't know where to start.
- I'll do it when I'm ready for a job.
- I don't have enough work samples.

A Career Development Portfolio is an ongoing process. If you are resisting or procrastinating, work with a partner or study group. Together you can organize supplies, brainstorm ideas, review each other's philosophies and goals, and assemble the contents.

Plan the Job Hunt

Many resources are available when you begin your job search: career center counselors, instructors, mentors, and alumni. Numerous Internet sites match employers with future employees. Most major employers list their job openings on their websites. Review job descriptions posted by potential employers to see what types of jobs they often have available and what types of qualifications they are looking for. This can also help you determine if you need to redesign or enhance your portfolio to fulfill certain requirements.

Technology will help you with your job search. For example, LinkedIn's main app helps students fill out profiles and join a professional social network. A new

LinkedIn app asks three questions: Which school do you attend, what's your major, and when are you graduating? The answers generate career path suggestions based on the LinkedIn network of school alumni who also earned the same degree. The app will then recommend companies that might fit your background and major. The app even suggests other career paths that the student may not have considered. It will also call up articles about how to interview, how to negotiate a salary, and career tips for job success.

Whether you are a two-year, four-year, or transfer student, you will want to put your job search to work during your first year by talking with professors, advisors, and career center professionals and getting your career portfolio started. At the start of your senior year, you need to kick your search into high gear by talking often with career center staff, deepening your professional contacts, securing an internship, finalizing a résumé, and practicing interviewing and applying for jobs. Check out: jobhuntersbible.com.

Submitting a Cover Letter

A cover letter is a written introduction; it should state what job you are applying for and what you can contribute and how you can benefit the company. Find out to whom you should address your cover letter. Call the personnel office to determine the correct name and title. Express enthusiasm and highlight how your education, skills, and experience relate to the job.

Submit your cover letter along with your résumé and, if applicable, parts of your portfolio. (Because most job applications or letters of inquiry are submitted via company websites, follow their guidelines regarding submission of your application, résumé, or sample materials.) Follow up with a phone call in a week or two to verify that your résumé was received. Ask if additional information is needed and when a decision will be made.

As you develop your portfolio, include good examples of helpful cover letters. See **Figure 14.9** for a sample cover letter.

Interviewing

The résumé and cover letter open the door, but the job interview is when you can clearly articulate why you are the best person for the job. Be aware of the importance of verbal and nonverbal communication skills. Here are some interview strategies:

1. **Be punctual.** A good first impression is important and can be lasting. If you arrive late, you have already said a great deal about yourself. Be sure you know the interview's time and location. Allow time for traffic and parking.

2. **Be professional.** Know the interviewer's name and title, including the pronunciation of the interviewer's name. Don't sit down until the interviewer does. Never call anyone by their first name unless you are asked to.

3. **Dress appropriately for the job.** In most situations, wear clean, pressed, conservative business clothes in a neutral color. Your nails and hair should be clean, trimmed, and neat. Keep makeup light and wear little jewelry unless

• **The Hand Shake**

In most cultures, a hand shake at the beginning and end of an interview is considered a sign of respect, enthusiasm, and confidence. Some people are not comfortable shaking hands because of shyness or hygiene concerns. However, career counselors say to initiate a firm hand shake (discreetly wiping sweaty palms beforehand if necessary). *Do you routinely shake hands with instructors or other acquaintances?*

Chris Ryan/age fotostock

Figure 14.9

Sample Cover letter

A good cover letter captures the employer's attention (in a positive way) and shows how your qualifications connect to what is being sought for the position. *Whom might you ask to review your cover letter before you send it?*

July 1, 2022

Dr. Sonia Murphy
North Clinic Health Care
2331 Terrace Street
Chicago, Illinois 69691

Dear Dr. Murphy:

Mr. David Leeland, Director of Internships for Bakers College, informed me of your advertisement for a medical assistant. I am interested in being considered for the position.

Your medical office has an excellent reputation, especially regarding health care for women. I have taken several courses in women's health and volunteer at the hospital in a women's health support group. I believe I can make a significant contribution to your office.

My work experiences and internship have provided valuable hands-on experience. I set up a new computer program for payroll in my internship position. In addition to excellent office skills, I also have clinical experience and people skills. I speak Spanish and have used it often in my volunteer work in hospitals.

I have paid for most of my college education through scholarships and work-study. My grades are excellent, and I have been on the dean's list in my medical and health classes. I have also completed advanced computer and office procedures classes.

I will call you on Tuesday, July 18, to make sure you received this letter and to find out when you might be able to arrange an interview. Thank you for your consideration.

Sincerely,

Julia Andrews

Julia Andrews
242 Cherry Lane
Chicago, Illinois 69692
Home phone: (304) 555-5593
e-mail: juliaa@edu.BakersC.com

you're in a fashion job. Leave extra clothing in an outside office, and simply carry a pen, a pad of paper, small purse, and a small folder with extra copies of your résumé and references.

4. **Learn about the company.** The Internet makes researching employers easy, as most companies have a website, even if just for informational purposes. Be prepared and show that you know about the company. What product(s) does it make? What is the competition? Refer to the company when you give examples.

5. **Learn about the position.** Before you interview, request a job description from the personnel office. What kind of employee—and with what skills—is the company looking for? You will likely be asked why you are interested in the job. Be prepared to answer.

6. **Relate your experience to the job.** Use every question as an opportunity to show how your skills relate to the job. Use examples from school, previous jobs, internships, volunteer work, leadership in clubs, and experiences growing up to indicate that you have the personal qualities, aptitudes, and skills needed at the new job.

7. **Be honest.** Although it is important to be confident and stress your strengths, honesty is equally important. Someone will verify your background, so do not exaggerate your accomplishments, grade point average, or experience.

8. **Focus on how you can benefit the company.** Don't ask about benefits, salary, or vacations until you are offered the job. During a first interview, try to show how you can contribute to the organization. Don't appear too eager to move up through the company or suggest you are more interested in gaining experience than in contributing.

9. **Be poised and relaxed.** Avoid nervous habits, such as tapping your pencil, playing with your hair, or covering your mouth with your hand. Watch language such as *you know, ah,* and *stuff like that.* Don't smoke, chew gum, or fidget.

10. **Be attentive.** Being poised and giving your full attention to the hiring manager is important. Speak with confidence, interest, and sincerity.

11. **Turn off electronic devices.** Even if the interviewer needs to take a call during your interview, never answer your phone or read or respond to a text during your interview. Your focus should be on establishing a rapport with your interviewer.

12. **Practice interviewing.** Consider recording a mock interview. Most colleges offer this service through the career center or media department. Rehearse questions and be prepared to answer directly.

13. **Anticipate question types.** Expect open-ended questions, such as "What are your strengths and weaknesses?" "Tell me about your best work experience," and "How do you handle stress?" Decide in advance what information is pertinent and reveals your strengths—for example, "I learned to get along with a diverse group of people when I worked for the park service." Check out https://www.csuchico.edu/careers/students-and-alumni/job-search-tools/sample-questions.shtml and SimplyHired.

14. **Close the interview on a positive note.** Thank the interviewer for their time, shake hands, and say you are looking forward to hearing from them.

15. **Send a thank-you note.** A follow-up thank-you note is especially important. Surprisingly, few job seekers actually send one. A thank-you note shows gratitude, and most employers think a person who appreciates an

Marketing "Me"

Practice for an interview by completing the following:

- My traits that help me be successful are

- I'm experienced in

- I'm knowledgeable about

- I'm capable of operating the following

- I can contribute to this company because

Eric Audras/Getty Images

Figure **14.10**

Sample Follow-Up Letter

A follow-up letter is another opportunity to set yourself apart from other job candidates. *What should you include in your follow-up letter?*

May 29, 2022

Mr. Henry Sanders
The Mountain View Store
10 Rock Lane
Alpine, Montana 79442

Dear Mr. Sanders:

Thank you for taking the time yesterday to meet with me concerning the position of sales representative. I enjoyed meeting you and your employees, learning more about your growing company, and touring your facilities. I was especially impressed with your new line of outdoor wear. It is easy to see why you lead the industry in sales.

I am even more excited about joining your sales team now that I have visited with you. I have the education, training, enthusiasm, and personal qualities necessary to succeed in business. I am confident I would fit in with your staff and make a real contribution to the sales team.

Thank you again for the interview and an enjoyable morning.

Sincerely,

John A. Bennett

John A. Bennett
124 East Buttermilk Lane
LaCrosse, Wisconsin 54601
Home phone: (608) 555-4958
e-mail: johnb@shast.edu

---

opportunity will appreciate the job. It reminds the interviewer about you and gives you a chance to reiterate your interest in the position and company and to add anything you forgot to mention previously. Send thank-you notes to every person involved in the interview: the hiring manager, administrative assistant, human resources personnel, and others who were especially helpful. E-mail is the easiest and quickest way to send a thank-you note, but a card will help you stand out. Either way, make sure your note stands out either by specifically mentioning a topic you discussed or by providing further research you have done since the conversation. See **Figure 14.10** for a sample follow-up letter.

16. **Determine what's next.** Although you may be eager for a response, do not bombard the employer with e-mails and phone calls. Ask the human resources manager or hiring manager how the company notifies candidates about the hiring process. Some organizations send a letter or e-mail that declines further interest, or others have so many interviews that, unfortunately, they do not call unless you are a selected candidate. The interview process can be lengthy. Explore many potential opportunities.

• **If You Post It, It Will Come . . . Back to Haunt You**
Sites such as Instagram, Twitter, and LinkedIn are often reviewed by companies as they check the background of job candidates. What may seem as a harmless, humorous video on YouTube today may be the reason you are turned down for a job tomorrow. *Have you posted anything online that you would not want a potential employer to see?*

pixelfit/Getty Images

Take Charge of Your Career

Few jobs are guaranteed. At some time in your career, you may find yourself suddenly out of work and needing new skills, personal qualities, or experiences. When jobs are eliminated, the remaining employees must take on more work, along with responsibility for managing their work progress. Salary increases and advancement are based on performance and production, rather than seniority. *So keep learning and growing.*

Follow these steps to keep you marketable:

1. **Be resilient.** You need to be flexible and able to bounce back in order to succeed. Learn resiliency when faced with a difficult course or go to Plan B when you don't get your first choice for an internship. Create a positive mindset that focuses on growth and learning. Demonstrate that you are persistent, willing to work hard, and persevere.

2. **Get a mentor.** Professional contacts are extremely important and none so key as someone in your profession who will guide and support you and give you valuable feedback. Be willing to ask for help. A mentor can be your sounding board or someone to whom you can go to ask questions about the office culture, unwritten rules, and ways to be successful. Keep boundaries clear. Do not become romantically involved with anyone you work closely with and never with someone to whom you report or whom you supervise. You can also be a mentor. Check out mentoring programs on campus and local community organizations such as Big Sister/Big Brother Clubs.

3. **Conduct your performance review.** Don't wait for your annual review to assess how you are achieving your goals. Review the process before your review and map your performance and productivity. Continually ask yourself, "How have I added value to the company? What have I done to contribute? How have I demonstrated that I'm a team player?" Document the goals you've achieved, dates, and accomplishments.

4. **Keep your portfolio and résumé up to date.** Add examples of successful assignments and team projects that you can use to demonstrate your skills and performance to your current or a potential employer. Update with new personal information, education, and responsibilities. Be prepared for when opportunities arise.

5. **Watch job trends.** Technology has affected and will continue to shape future job opportunities. How will it affect the field you are pursuing? Will you need more training? Is it opening up new kinds of jobs? Watch related fields where growth is predicted. For example, government actions and the focus on clean energy and global environmental issues are expected to fuel the creation of "green" jobs (also known as green-collar jobs) in various industries. According to the Clean Edge research firm, by 2019, the global biofuels market, wind power, and solar energy will have expanded and may hit more than $100 billion in revenues in each area. Other trends in employment will result from demographic changes, such as growth in the elderly and very young populations. (In 2007, the United States experienced the greatest baby boom to date.) Read the business section of the newspaper or the local business journal to see what trends and opportunities your community is experiencing.

6. **Look over the horizon.** As the global economy grows and companies expand overseas, you may find exciting opportunities in other countries. If relocation is an option for you, consider what additional skills would be useful, such as the ability to speak and write in other languages and knowledge of other customs and cultures.

> **"Don't go around saying the world owes you a living. The world owes you nothing. It was here first."**
>
> MARK TWAIN
> *Author*

Research has shown that the brains of adolescents and young adults have a great deal of creative exploration, conceptual thinking, and abstract reasoning. They love new ideas, innovation, imagining, and perceiving the world in creative ways. As we get older, we can feel stuck or in a rut and have trouble using creative thinking.[2]

After 10 years on the job, Christina just got laid off from her IT position because her company decided to outsource the work overseas. She wouldn't say she "loved" the job, but it paid the bills and gave her flexible hours, which was important to her as a single mom of two young boys. Her sister, an instructor at a local university, is pushing her to go back to school at night to get an advanced degree, even though Christina just finished repaying her student loans. Using creativity and critical thinking, help Christina with her decision.

- What pros and cons should she consider when making this decision?
- If she enrolls in school, should she get an advanced degree or pursue other careers she is interested in?
- How can she find out if her skills would transfer to other types of jobs?

THINK
CREATIVELY AND CRITICALLY

7. **Further your education.** See if your employer offers additional training in job skills or related topics, such as conflict resolution, diversity, team building, communication, or motivation. Does your employer provide tuition reimbursement if you take academic courses online or from a local college? Must the courses be directly tied to the job or advanced certification? Determine which degrees or certifications would make you a more knowledgeable professional and more valuable to an employer. See if related workshops or seminars are available locally or online. An employee who learns new skills, cross-trains in various positions, and has excellent human relations skills will be sought after and promoted. Complete **Personal Evaluation Notebook 14.4** to assess how your skills have improved during just the past few months. Check out the following: calnewport.com/blog, lifehacker.com, brainpickings.org, www.about.com, www.mindtools.com, and alltop.com.

8. **Be a lifelong learner.** Besides furthering your formal education, be a person who values learning and is well-read and educated. Read a variety of books, papers, professional journals, and magazines. Keep up with popular culture in addition to knowing history.

9. **Keep networking.** Get to know professors and ask for recommendations. Networking can help you land your first job, but you'll also attain many subsequent jobs based on whom you know. As people change employers, they build substantial contacts at related companies. Your colleague who is leaving today for a higher position at another company may hire you away tomorrow. Get involved in professional organizations, and join online business sites that link you with other professionals in your field.

10. **Be your own "career coach."** The most important person you report to is the one you see in the mirror. Only you know what type of work keeps you motivated and makes you passionate about contributing day after day. This is *your* career and *your* life—only you can make the best of it by learning to endure the challenging times, overcome setbacks, gain valuable knowledge, and be a better person from the experience. What Hsi-Tang Chih Tsang, renowned Zen master, said 1,200 years ago is still true: *"Although gold dust is precious, when it gets in your eyes it obstructs your vision."* If you focus on your values, positive personal qualities, and mission in life, you will attain whatever you deem precious—and you will become a true peak performer.

Your belief that you can change and grow creates a passion for learning, grit, and perseverance. These beliefs help you bounce back from set backs. Studying with a group also creates learning and recall; jogging or working out with someone enhances your success with an exercise program due to mutual support and encouragement. Engage!

Personal Evaluation Notebook   14.4

Assessment Is Lifelong

Read the following skills. Then rate your skill level on a scale of 1 to 5 (1 being poor and 5 being excellent). Refer back to **Personal Evaluation Notebook 1.3** in Chapter 1, and compare it with your answers here. Have you improved your skills and competencies?

	Excellent	Satisfactory		Poor
Skills	5	4	3	2	1

1. Reading _____
2. Writing _____
3. Speaking _____
4. Mathematics _____
5. Listening and note taking _____
6. Critical thinking and reasoning _____
7. Creative problem solving _____
8. Positive visualization _____
9. Knowing how you learn _____
10. Honesty and integrity _____
11. Positive attitude and motivation _____
12. Responsibility _____
13. Flexibility/ability to adapt to change _____
14. Self-management and emotional control _____
15. Self-esteem and confidence _____
16. Time management _____
17. Money management _____
18. Management and leadership of people _____
19. Interpersonal and communication skills _____
20. Ability to work well with cultural diversity _____
21. Organization and evaluation of information _____
22. Understanding technology _____
23. Commitment and effort _____

Assess your results. What are your strongest skills? What skills need the most improvement?

Do you have a better understanding of how you learned these skills and competencies?
Do you know how to document and demonstrate them?

Following are six broad skill areas that can be transferred to many situations or jobs:

- Communication skills
- Human relations skills
- Organization, management, and leadership skills
- Technical and mechanical skills
- Innovation and creativity skills
- Research and planning skills

How would each of these skill areas relate to your major or career choice?
What other skill areas might your major or career choice include?

TAKING CHARGE

Summary

In this chapter, I learned to

- **Explore potential majors and career paths.** To determine my major course of study, I consult with available resources, such as a career counselor, family, and friends; explore the college catalog; visit academic departments; and participate in classes, workshops, internships, and service learning opportunities.

- **Assess my values, interests, abilities, and skills.** Knowing my values helps me identify what I will value in a future career. I have certain interests that may lead me in one occupational direction. I have qualities, skills, and transferable skills that apply to many different fields. I can demonstrate a positive, open mindset that embraces growth.

- **See the value of Career Development Portfolios.** My portfolio helps me assess, highlight, and demonstrate my strengths, skills, and competencies. Starting my portfolio early helps me get organized and update, edit, and add to it throughout college.

- **Organize essential elements.** Assembling my portfolio helps me collect and organize work samples, information, lists, examples, transcripts, credentials, certificates, workshop experiences, and documentation of personal qualities.

- **List significant life experiences and accomplishments.** I include such experiences as formal education, special classes and projects, volunteer work and service learning, jobs, travel, hobbies, military service, special recognition, and accomplishments and events that helped me learn new skills or something about myself or others. I list books I have read that pertain to my major and helped me develop a certain philosophy.

- **Document skills and competencies.** I connect essential skills to school and work, and I look for transferable skills. I document critical thinking, interpersonal, technology, financial, and basic skills related to school and job success and samples of my work.

- **Create an effective résumé.** My résumé is an essential document that helps me highlight my education, work experience, awards, professional memberships, and activities.

- **Write a cover letter, and prepare for an interview.** My cover letter succinctly communicates my interest in and qualifications for a specific job. I prepare for an interview by researching the company, understanding the job requirements, and practicing responses to anticipated questions. I am on time for the interview, well groomed, and dressed appropriately. I focus on how I can contribute to the company, using personal examples and positive body language. I end the interview on a positive note, ask about follow up, and thank the hiring manager immediately in a letter.

- **Take charge of my career.** I realize that job opportunities are constantly changing, and I must be proactive by continually assessing my performance and abilities, keeping my portfolio and résumé up to date, and watching job trends for new opportunities and ways to improve my skills. I continue to cultivate personal contacts that benefit me personally and professionally, and I know only I can determine what's important to me in a career and life. I take the time to learn more about career opportunities, and I observe workplace trends, especially needs for additional education and training.

Performance Strategies

Following are the top 10 tips for planning a career:

- Determine what you value in life and a career. What gives your life meaning?
- Know how to connect essential skills and competencies to school and work.
- Assemble your portfolio, and frequently review, assess, and update it.
- Document skills, competencies, and personal qualities in your portfolio.
- Include essential elements in your portfolio; résumé, transcripts, and accomplishments.
- Value, document, and demonstrate service learning and volunteer work on campus and in the community.
- Use your portfolio to reflect on your work philosophy and life mission, as well as to set goals and priorities.
- Prepare for the job-hunting and interview process early.
- Be prepared for changes in job opportunities and expectations.
- Take personal responsibility for directing your career.

Tech for Success

- **Your résumé online.** Most potential employers prefer to receive your résumé and supporting documents by e-mail or online either via the company's website or an employment service. Programs and services are available to help you develop your portfolio online. Some include virtual space for storing digital files, such as graphic images, videos, and PowerPoint presentations. Your school may use its preferred source for developing a portfolio, so consult your advisor as you get started.

- **Job search websites.** Job search sites, such as **monster. com,** allow you to upload your résumé or create one using their format, which then feeds into their search engine. When you start your job hunt, it's worth investigating these and more specialized sites that cater to the field you are pursuing. Also, check out any professional organizations in the field, as they may also provide job listings online.

Endnotes

[1] Richard Arum and Josipa Roksa, *Aspiring Adults Adrift: Tentative Transitions of College Graduates* (Chicago: University of Chicago Press, 2014).

[2] Daniel J. Siegel, *Brainstorm: The Power and Purpose of the Teenage Brain* (New York: Penguin Random House, 2015).

Study Team Notes

Career *in* Focus

Doug Menuez/Getty Images

Steven Price
SOCIAL STUDIES TEACHER/LEGISLATOR

Related Majors: Education, Social Studies, Political Science

Career Planning Is Lifelong

Steven Price taught social studies at a high school. With an avid interest in politics, Steven soon developed a strong curriculum for teaching government and current affairs. He was well known in the district for his innovative classes in which students researched and debated local issues and then voted on them.

Throughout the years, Steven remained active in a local political party. Each year, he could be counted on to help hand out flyers and canvass neighborhoods before the September primaries and November elections. One year, a party member suggested that Steven run for state legislator.

Steven took the offer seriously. After 21 years of teaching, he felt ready for a change. He had enjoyed being in the classroom, especially when his students shared his passion for politics. However, he felt that, as a state legislator, he could more directly bring about changes in his community. He took a leave of absence from his teaching job. He filed the appropriate papers and worked hard with a campaign manager to get his name out to the voters in his district. Because Steven had maintained a Career Development Portfolio over the years, the manager was able to use the collected information to promote Steven.

Using his years of experience teaching government and current affairs, Steven felt rejuvenated and excited as he worked on his political campaign. His lifelong commitment to politics paid off when he won the election! He was glad he had taken the risk. The career change was a positive move for both Steven and his community.

CRITICAL THINKING What might have happened to Steven if he had not taken the risks of moving to a different career?

Peak Performer Profile

Ursula Burns

As you contemplate any future career, it's important to consider what you value, what you enjoy doing, and how those important factors should play a role in your decisions. Ursula Burns, CEO of Xerox and the first African-American woman to be named CEO of a *Fortune* 500 company, exemplifies someone who worked through that process to determine what career area to pursue.

Burns grew up on the Lower East Side of Manhattan in a low-income housing project where crime and poverty were rampant. Burns claims that, when she was a child, her mother's constant hard work and attitude kept her unaware of her family's poverty. Her mother, Olga, ran an at-home day care, took in ironing, and raised three children alone. As Burns says, "She gave us courage. She gave us will and love. I can still hear her telling me that where you are is not who you are."

This advice followed Burns throughout her long career. From a young age, she excelled in mathematics. When it came time for college, she went to the library to research top-paying jobs for people with math or science degrees. Acknowledging her strengths and interests, Burns ultimately decided to pursue a degree in mechanical engineering instead of other degrees her teachers thought she should consider. She attended the Polytechnic Institute of New York and earned her graduate degree from Columbia University.

Burns quickly worked her way up the corporate ladder, beginning as an engineering intern for Xerox in 1980. Her work ethic and straightforward approach to business earned her respect in the company. In 2009, she was named CEO of the $17 billion corporation. *Forbes* magazine ranked her the 14th most powerful woman in the world, and she was named among *Bloomberg Businessweek*'s Top 20 Inspirational Leaders, placing her amid the likes of Bill Gates and former president Bill Clinton. She was chosen by President Barack Obama to help direct the national STEM program, which focuses on providing equal science, technology, engineering, and mathematics education to all students. Ultimately, Burns will not only make a tremendous impact on the performance of a multibillion-dollar company but also help shape the nation's curriculum and global leadership position in the fields of science and technology.

PERFORMANCE THINKING Which values and interests are important to you? How are they reflected in the job or career you are studying for? Do your strengths and personal qualities coincide with the skills and abilities needed for success in this career? Are there alternate career areas you should also explore? How does Ursula Burns's mother's advice, "Where you are is not who you are," apply to your life?

CHECK IT OUT Read *Bloomberg Businessweek*'s list of qualities possessed by inspirational leaders (**http://www.bloomberg. com/news/articles/2007-10-10/the-seven-secrets-of-inspiring-leadersbusinessweek-business-news-stock-market-and-financial- advice**). Keep track of your score as indicated in the directions. Are you acting as an inspirational leader? In what ways could you become more of a leader in your classes or school organizations?

Starting Today

At least one strategy I learned in this chapter that I plan to try right away is

_____

_____

_____

What changes must I make in order for this strategy to be most effective?

_____

_____

_____

Review Questions

Based on what you have learned in this chapter, write your answers to the following questions:

1. Why is it important to determine your values during career planning?

_____

_____

2. Define *transferable skill* and give an example.

_____

_____

3. What is a purpose of a Career Development Portfolio?

_____

_____

4. Name at least four elements that should be included in a portfolio.

_____

_____

5. What information should be included in a résumé?

_____

_____

Exploring Careers

In the Classroom

Maria Lewis likes making presentations, enjoys working with children, and is a crusader for equality and the environment. She also values family, home, and community. Making a lot of money is less important to her than making a difference and enjoying what she does. Now that her children are grown, she wants to complete a college degree. However, she is hesitant because she has been out of school for many years.

McGraw-Hill Education

1. How would you help Maria with her decision?

_____

_____

2. What careers would you have Maria explore?

_____

_____

In the Workplace

Maria completed a degree in childhood development. She has been a caregiver at a children's day care center for two years. She enjoys her job but feels it is time for a change. If she wants to advance in her field, she has to travel and go into management. She wants more time off to spend with her family, write, and become more involved in community action groups. Maria would like to stay in a related field. She likes working with children but also enjoys giving presentations and workshops and writing. She has thought about consulting, writing, or starting her own small business.

3. What strategies in this chapter would help Maria with her career change?

_____

_____

4. What one habit would you recommend to Maria to help her plan her career?

_____

_____

Applying the ABC Method of Self-Management

In the **Journal Entry**, you were asked to describe a time when you were anxious about choosing a major or career or wondering if the information you're learning will benefit you in your career. Explain how a positive mindset helped you?

_____

Use the ABC Method to help you with clarity. Write a script.

A = Acknowledge: Accept reality and pay attention to your emotions.

_____

_____

_____

B = Breathe: Take a deep breath to calm down and feel beloved.

_____

_____

_____

C = Choose: Knowing you have many options, choose the most appropriate for the situation and that will result in positive long-term consequences.

_____

_____

_____

Sample Script: Even though I'm embarrassed that I'm so indecisive and feeling fearful and sad, I love and accept myself. I breathe deeply, calm down, and allow these feelings to pass. I remind myself that many people have trouble choosing a major or career and that most people have many jobs and careers over a lifetime. I resist the urge to just choose any major or drop out of college because I'm not certain what I want to do. I choose to be kind and patient with myself and explore all options. I'll go to the Career Center and talk with my advisor about options. I'll explore my strengths, values, goals, and interests. I'll practice mindfulness and mediation to calm down and be present in the moment. I'm grateful to have the opportunity to be in college. A college degree is a huge advantage in any career. I will also explore getting a basic liberal arts degree and explore learning specific skills and training at a community college. I know that I can always specialize my education with additional training or a master's degree or credential. So, I choose to relax, explore, and use critical thinking and creativity to discover who I am, what I love to do, my strengths and interests. Learning about different careers and being open-minded will help me in my future.

_____

_____

See yourself creating a portfolio that helps you organize the information you're learning and relate it to job success. See yourself with a confident, positive, open mindset that is focused on growth and learning. See yourself focused with a vision and purpose and working in a job you love. You will put in effort and perseverance to succeed.

You Can Solve the Problem: Majors

Every day, life brings problems and choices. The kinds of choices you make can make your life easier or harder. Often, you do not know which direction to take. Use these six steps to work through the following case study:

Step 1   Know what the problem really is. Is it a daily problem? Is it a once-in-a-lifetime problem?

Step 2   List what you know about the problem. List what you don't know. Ask questions. Get help and advice.

Step 3   Explore alternate choices.

Step 4   Think about the pros and cons for the other choices. Arrange them from best to worst choice.

Step 5   Pick the choice you feel good about.

Step 6   Study what happens after you have made your choice. Are you happy about the choice? Would you make it again?

CASE STUDY: SUE'S MAJOR

Sue has to choose a major before she enters her sophomore year. This is causing her stress and anxiety. She excels in math, science, and the arts. In addition, she has many interests and abilities. Her parents want her to go into engineering, but her dance professor thinks she should major in theatre and dance. She also loves philosophy and music.

Sue is not sure what to do. She has been to the career center and talked with her academic advisor. Because she has interests and skills in several areas, there is no one clear path to take.

What is Sue's problem? What are her choices? What would you decide if you were in her shoes? Apply the six steps to help Sue make a good decision by writing responses to the following questions and statements.

Step 1 The problem is

_____

_____

_____

_____

Step 2
   a. You know these things about the problem:

_____

_____

_____

_____

(continued)

b. You don't know these things about the problem:

_____

_____

_____

_____

Step 3 The other choices are

_____

_____

_____

_____

Step 4 Rank the choices, best to worst.

_____

_____

_____

_____

Step 5 Pick a choice that Sue and her parents might feel good about and explain why.

_____

_____

_____

_____

Step 6 What are likely consequences for Sue if she makes this choice?

_____

_____

_____

_____

You Can Solve the Problem: Careers

Every day, life brings problems and choices. The kinds of choices you make can make your life easier or harder. Often, you do not know which direction to take. Use these six steps to work through the following case study:

Step 1 Know what the problem really is. Is it a daily problem? Is it a once-in-a-lifetime problem?

Step 2 List what you know about the problem. List what you don't know. Ask questions. Get help and advice.

Step 3 Explore alternate choices.

Step 4 Think about the pros and cons for the other choices. Arrange them from best to worst choice.

Step 5 Pick the choice you feel good about.

Step 6 Study what happens after you have made your choice. Are you happy about the choice? Would you make it again?

CASE STUDY: SUE'S CAREER

Sue has been an engineer for over 25 years and has been very successful. Throughout this time, she has kept up her interest in the arts and has been an active volunteer. She has danced in local productions every year, sung and acted in local opera and theatre groups, volunteered at her daughter's school teaching dance to young girls, and helped out with plays.

The theatre and art teacher at the high school recently told Sue that she would be retiring in a few years and suggested that Sue consider preparing for the job. Sue took this suggestion seriously. She felt ready for a change. Her children are older and she and her husband would like to travel more. They are frugal, spend wisely, and are financially secure, but still saving for retirement. They are also helping their two daughters with college.

Sue would need to return to school and obtain a teaching credential and take additional classes. Could they live on one income for a short time? Sue is not sure what to do. She has a wonderful career that pays very well and she enjoys it. She is accomplished and competent. Several of her friends and colleagues have told her she'd be crazy to quit at her peak earning. However, when Sue is teaching dance, acting, singing, and helping to direct plays, she feels alive and passionate.

What is Sue's problem? What are her choices? What would you decide if you were in her shoes? Apply the six steps to help Sue make a good decision by writing responses to the following questions and statements.

Step 1 The problem is

_____

_____

_____

_____

(continued)

Step 2

a. You know these things about the problem:

_____

_____

_____

_____

b. You don't know these things about the problem:

_____

_____

_____

_____

Step 3   The other choices are

_____

_____

_____

_____

Step 4   Rank the choices, best to worst.

_____

_____

_____

_____

Step 5   Pick a choice Sue might feel good about and explain why.

_____

_____

_____

_____

Step 6   What might happen to Sue?

_____

_____

_____

_____

Checklist for Choosing a Major

Use the Adult Learning Cycle to explore majors and career opportunities.

FEEL AND LISTEN

- What are the most important criteria for my future career, such as independence, high visibility, flexible hours, ability to work from home, and management opportunities?
- What is my personality type and/or temperament?
- Do the careers that fit my personality offer these features?
- What skills do I already have that would be useful or necessary?

OBSERVE AND VISUALIZE

- Do I know anyone currently working in this field whom I could interview or talk to?
- Which instructors at my school would be most knowledgeable about the field? Who are the most approachable and available to advise me?
- What are the major professional organizations in this field? Have I explored their websites for additional information? Can I join these organizations as a student? Would it be worth the investment?
- Which courses should I be enrolled in now or next semester that will further introduce me to this area?
- I've visited the career center at my school and have talked with my advisor and/or a career counselor about:

THINK AND WRITE

- What positives am I hearing?
- What drawbacks am I hearing?
- What education and skills will be necessary for me to pursue this major and career?
- Are there related professions that seem appealing?

DO AND PRACTICE

- I've constructed a time line for gaining experience in this area that includes tasks such as
  1. Securing an internship; to be secured by
  2. Joining a student club; to be involved by
  3. Participating in related volunteer activities; to be accomplished by
  4. Getting a related part-time job; to be hired by
  5. Other:

TEACH AND PRACTICE AGAIN

- I have relayed my impressions to my family and/or friends. Some of their questions/responses are
- I have talked with fellow students about their major and career search. Some tips I have learned from them are
- The most important resources I have found that I would recommend to others are

As of now, the major/career I would like to continue exploring is

_____

_____

REVIEW AND APPLICATIONS | CHAPTER 14

Preparing Your Résumé

To prepare for writing your résumé, start thinking about the information you will include. On the following lines, summarize your skills and qualifications, and match them to the requirements of the job you are seeking. Use proactive words and verbs. Here are some examples:

- *Organized* a group of after-school tutors for math and accounting courses
- *Wrote* and *published* articles for the school newspaper
- *Participated* in a student academic advisory board
- *Developed* a new accounting system
- *Managed* the petty cash accounts for the PTA
- *Created* PowerPoint presentations for a charity benefit

You should not be discouraged if you have only a few action phrases to write at this time. Add to your list as you continue your studies and become an active participant in school activities and with your courses of study.

SKILLS AND QUALIFICATIONS

1. _____

2. _____

3. _____

4. _____

5. _____

6. _____

7. _____

8. _____

9. _____

10. _____

Informational Interview: What's the Job Like?

List the types of jobs you think you would like. Then list people you know in those types of jobs. Ask family, friends, neighbors, or instructors, or contact the alumni office or local Rotary or chamber of commerce to see if they can arrange an interview. The purpose of each interview is to find out about the person's career and what the job is really like. You will also be establishing a contact for the future. Remember to send a thank-you note after each interview.

Following is a list of potential questions to ask.

Person interviewed _____ Date _____

Job title _____ Contact e-mail _____

1. Why did you choose your career? _____

_____

_____

2. What do you do on a typical day? _____

_____

_____

3. What do you like best about your job? _____

_____

_____

4. What do you like least? _____

_____

_____

5. What classes, internships, jobs, certifications, or experiences do you wish you had explored when you were in college? _____

_____

_____

6. If you had to do it again, would you choose the same job? If not, what would you do differently? _____

_____

_____

7. What advice can you give me for planning my career? _____

_____

_____

Informational Interview: Who Are You Looking For?

Make a list of the types of jobs you think you would like. Then list local companies that may hire for those kinds of positions. Check out their websites to see what types of positions are available and job descriptions, so that you understand their general responsibilities and qualifications. Find out who the hiring managers are (or if they have a human resources department). Contact this person to request an informational interview. Following is a list of potential questions to ask. Remember to send a thank-you note after each interview.

Person interviewed _____   Date _____

Job title _____   Contact e-mail _____

1. What specific skills and education do you want in a candidate for this position?

   _____

   _____

2. What two or three traits or qualities are very important in this position?

   _____

   _____

3. What are the difficult aspects of this position?

   _____

   _____

4. Are there areas of professional development in this position?

   _____

   _____

5. What is generally the beginning salary for this position?

   _____

   _____

6. What could I be doing right now that would make me more marketable for your company?

   _____

   _____

Exploring Careers

Go to the library or career center and find careers you've never heard of or are interested in exploring. Do the following exercises. Then add this page to your Career Development Portfolio.

1. Use the Internet to explore at least one career. List the career and skills, education, and abilities needed to be successful.

   _____

   _____

   _____

2. What is the long-term outlook for this career? Is it a growing field? How does technology impact it?

   _____

   _____

   _____

3. List your skills and interests. Then list the careers that match these skills and interests. Create names for careers if they are unusual.

Skills/Interests	**Possible Careers**
_____	_____
_____	_____
_____	_____

4. Review your list of skills and interests. What stands out? Do you like working with people or accomplishing tasks? Think of as many jobs as you can that relate to your skills and interests. Your skills and interests are valuable clues about your future career.

   _____

   _____

   _____

5. Describe an ideal career that involves the skills you most enjoy using. Include the location of this ideal career and the kinds of co-workers, customers, and employees you would encounter.

   _____

   _____

   _____

Glossary

A

abilities Innate talents or gifts that can be enhanced through study and practice.

acronym A word formed from the first letter of a series of other words.

acrostic A made-up sentence in which the first letter of each word stands for something.

affirmation Positive self-talk or an internal thought that counters self-defeating thought patterns with positive, hopeful, or realistic thoughts.

assertive communication Expressing oneself in a direct and civil manner.

attentive listening A decision to be fully focused with the intent of understanding the speaker.

B

binge drinking Excessive consumption of alcohol within a short duration of time.

blogging Writing personal reflections and commentary on a website, often in a journal format, and including hyperlinks to other sources.

body smart People who have physical and kinesthetic intelligence; have the ability to understand and control their bodies; and have tactical sensitivity, like movement, and handle objects skillfully.

C

cheating Using or providing unauthorized help.

chunking Breaking up long lists of information or numbers to make them easier to remember.

civility Interacting with others with respect, kindness, and good manners.

codependency A psychological condition or a relationship in which a person is controlled or manipulated by another who is affected by an addictive condition.

common ground A basis of mutual interest or similarities of core values.

communication Giving and receiving ideas, feelings, and information.

comprehension Understanding main ideas and details.

computer literacy The ability to use electronic tools including computers, digital devices, and social media to conduct your searches.

critical thinking A logical, rational, systematic thought process that is necessary to understand, analyze, and evaluate information in order to solve a problem or situation.

cultural literacy Being aware and having fundamental knowledge about what has gone on in the past and what is going on now in the world.

cyberbullying When technology is used as a means to belittle, threaten, and harass others.

D

decision making Determining or selecting the best or most effective answer or solution.

decoding The process of breaking words into individual sounds.

deductive reasoning Drawing conclusions based on going from the general to the specific.

discrimination Treating someone differently based on a characteristic.

diversity Differences in gender, race, age, ethnicity, sexual orientation, physical ability, learning styles and learning abilities, social and economic background, and religion.

E

emotional intelligence The ability to understand and manage oneself and relate effectively to others.

empathy Understanding and having compassion for others.

ethics The principles of conduct that govern a group or society.

external locus of control The belief that success or failure is due to outside influences, such as fate, luck, or other people.

extrovert A person who is outgoing, social, optimistic, and often uncomfortable with being alone.

F

fair use The legal and ethical use of a direct quote from the Internet or another source, including a book, in something you claim as your own work.

feeler A person who is sensitive to the concerns and feelings of others, values harmony, and dislikes creating conflict.

formal outline A traditional outline that uses Roman numerals and capital letters to highlight main points.

G

grit A combination of passion, perseverance, and hardiness (a combination of commitment and control).

H

habits The behaviors and activities you perform unconsciously as a result of frequent repetition. They can be actively cultivated and changed if you put your mind to it.

hardiness A personal characteristic that combines commitment, control, and challenge, giving one the courage and motivation to turn rough patches into opportunities for personal growth.

homophobia An irrational fear of gays and lesbians.

I

important priorities Essential tasks or activities that support a person's goals and that can be scheduled with some flexibility.

Inclusion A sense of belonging—feeling respected and valued for who you are.

inductive reasoning Generalizing from specific concepts to broad principles.

inference Passing from one statement, judgment, or datum considered as true to another whose truth is based on that of the former.

informal outline A free form of outline that uses dashes and indenting to highlight main points.

interests Activities and subjects that cause you to feel comfortable, excited, enthusiastic, or passionate.

internal locus of control The belief that control over life is due to behavior choices or character.

interpreting Developing ideas and summarizing the material.

introvert A person who tends to like time alone, solitude, and reflection and prefers the world of ideas and thoughts.

intuitive People who are more comfortable with theories, abstraction, imagination, and speculation.

J

judgers People who prefer orderly, planned, and structured learning and working environments.

K

key habit Habits that impact multiple aspects of your life: exercising, sleeping better, eating better.

L

logic smart People who have logical/mathematical intelligence; like numbers, puzzles, and logic; and have the ability to reason, solve problems, create hypotheses, and think in terms of cause and effect.

M

maturity The ability to control impulses, to think beyond the moment, and to consider how words and actions affect others.

media literacy The ability to use critical thinking when you read books or magazines, use the Internet, watch television or films, listen to the radio, listen to or read advertisements, or interact with any type of media.

memorization The transfer of information from short-term memory into long-term memory.

mentor A role model who takes a special interest in another's goals and personal and professional development.

mind map A visual, holistic form of note taking that starts with the main idea placed in the center of a page and branches out with subtopics through associations and patterns.

mindfulness The state of being totally in the moment and part of the process.

mission statement A written statement focusing on desired values, philosophies, and principles.

mnemonic A memory trick.

motivation An inner drive that moves a person to action.

multitasking Performing many tasks, jobs, or responsibilities simultaneously.

music smart People who have rhythm and melody intelligence; the ability to appreciate, perceive, and produce rhythms.

N

networking Exchanging information or services for the purpose of enriching individuals, groups, or institutions.

note taking A method of creating order and arranging thoughts and materials to help a person retain information.

O

ongoing activities Necessary "maintenance" tasks that should be managed carefully so that they don't take up too much time.

outdoor smart People who have environmental intelligence and are good at measuring, charting, and observing animals and plants.

P

paraphrase To restate another's ideas in your own words.

people smart People who have interpersonal intelligence; like to talk and work with people, join groups, and solve problems as part of a team; and have the ability to work with and understand people, as well as to perceive and be responsive to the moods, intentions, and desires of other people.

perceiver A person who prefers flexibility and spontaneity and likes to allow life to unfold.

picture smart People who have spatial intelligence; like to draw, sketch, and visualize information; and have the ability to perceive in three-dimensional space and re-create various aspects of the visual world.

plagiarism To steal and pass off the ideas or words of another as one's own.

problem solving Creating or identifying potential answers or solutions to a question or problem.

procrastination Deliberately putting off tasks.

R

racial profiling Using racial or ethnic characteristics to determine whether a person is likely to commit a particular type of crime or illegal act.

rapport The ability to find common ground with another person based on respect, empathy, and trust.

recall To call back or summon back to awareness. The more often you recall information, the stronger your memory becomes.

reflect To think about something in a purposeful way with the intention of creating new meaning.

resilient Able to recover from or adjust easily to misfortune or change.

retention The process of storing information.

reward The reason you perform the routine behavior or habit.

routine behavior The behavior (or habit) you usually perform when you see the trigger.

S

self-assessment Recognition of the need to learn new tasks and subjects, relate more effectively with others, set goals, manage time and stress, and create a balanced and productive life.

self-esteem How you feel about yourself; sense of self-worth.

self-management A positive, open attitude is focused on growth and learning.

self-smart People who have intrapersonal and inner intelligance and the ability to be contemplative, self-disciplined, and introspective.

sensors People who learn best from their senses and feel comfortable with facts and concrete data.

sexism A belief or an attitude that one gender is inferior or less valuable.

sexting Exchanging sexually explicit material, often via cell phone.

skills Capabilities that have been learned and developed.

T

thinker A person who likes to analyze problems using facts and rational logic.

transferable skills Skills that can be used in a variety of careers.

trigger Anything that consciously or unconsciously sets a habit into motion. Example: running shoes at the door remind you to go for a run.

trivial activities Nonessential activities that are completely discretionary and do not directly support a person's goals.

U

urgent priorities Tasks or activities that support a person's goals and must be accomplished by a specified date or time to avoid negative consequences.

V

values Worth or importance you attach to various factors in your life.

visualization The use of imagery to see goals clearly and envision engaging successfully in new, positive behavior.

W

wellness To live life fully with purpose, meaning, and vitality.

word smart People who have verbal/linguistic intelligence; like to read, talk, and write about information; and have the ability to argue, persuade, entertain, and teach with words.

Bibliography

INTRODUCTION

Secretary's Commission on Achieving Necessary Skills, U.S. Department of Labor. "What Work Requires of Schools: A SCANS Report for America." 2006.

CHAPTER 1: BE A LIFELONG LEARNER

Armstrong, Thomas. *In Their Own Way: Discovering and Encouraging Your Child's Multiple Intelligences.* New York: Tarcher/Putnam, 2000.

Bach-y-Rita, Paul. *Brain Mechanisms and Sensory Substitution.* New York: Academic Press, 1972.

Buzan, Tony. *Use Both Sides of Your Brain.* New York: Dutton, 1991.

Dusek, J. A., H. H. Out, A. L. Wohlhueter, M. Bhasin, L. F. Zerbini, M. G. Joseph, H. Benson, and T. A. Libermann. "Genomic Counter-Stress Changes Induced by the Relaxation Response." *PLoS ONE* 3, no. 7 (2008), p. e2576.

Ellis, Albert, and Robert A. Harper. *A Guide to Rational Living.* New York: Prentice-Hall, 1961.

Galvan, A. "Neural Plasticity of Development and Learning." *Human Brain Mapping* 31, no. 6 (June 2010).

Gardner, Howard. *Frames of Mind: The Theory of Multiple Intelligences.* New York: Basic Books, 1993.

Hoffman, Donald D. *Visual Intelligence.* New York: Norton & Co. 1998.

Kolb, David A. *Experiential Learning: Experience as the Source of Learning and Development.* Englewoods Cliffs, NJ: Prentice-Hall, 1984.

Springer, S., and G. Deutsch. *Left Brain, Right Brain: Perspectives from Cognitive Science.* 5th ed. New York: W. H. Freeman & Co., 1998.

William, Linda V. *Teaching for the Two-Sided Mind: A Guide to Right Brain/Left Brain Education.* New York: Simon & Schuster, 1983.

CHAPTER 2: BUILD PEAK HABITS

Amen, Daniel G. *Change Your Brain, Change Your Life.* New York: Three Rivers Press, 1998.

Andrews, Mark A. W. "Why Do We Use Facial Expressions to Convey Emotions?" *Scientific American,* November 1, 2010.

Duhigg, Charles. *The Power of Habit: Why We Do What We Do in Life and Business.* New York: Random House, 2012.

Ferrett, Sharon K. *Positive Attitudes at Work.* Burr Ridge, IL: Irwin, 1994.

Goldsmith, Marshall. *Triggers: Creating Behavior That Lasts.* New York: Crown Business, 2015.

Graybiel, Ann M. "MIT Researcher Sheds Light on Why Habits Are Hard to Make and Break," *MIT News* (October 20, 1999), http://news.mit.edu/1999/habits (accessed March 1, 2016).

Kolb, B., and I. Q. Whishaw. "Brain Plasticity and Behavior." *Annual Review of Psychology* 49 (1998), pp. 43–64.

Lyubomirsky, S., L. King, and E. Diener. "The Benefits of Frequent Positive Affect: Does Happiness Lead to Success?" *Psychological Bulletin* 131 (2005), pp. 803–55.

Nielsen, Jared A., Brandon A. Zielinski, Michael A. Ferguson, Janet E. Lainhart, and Jeffrey S. Anderson. "An Evaluation of the Left-Brain vs. Right-Brain Hypothesis with Resting State Functional Connectivity Magnetic Resonance Imaging." *PLoS One* 8, no. 8 (August 14, 2013), http://journals.plos.org/plosone/article?id=10.1371/journal.pone.0071275 (accessed April 17, 2016).

Seligman, Martin E. P. *Authentic Happiness: Using the New Positive Psychology to Realize Your Potential for Lasting Fulfillment.* New York: Simon and Schuster, 2002.

Siegel, Daniel J. *Brainstorm: The Power and Purpose of the Teenage Brain.* New York: Penguin Random House, 2015.

CHAPTER 3: EXPAND YOUR EMOTIONAL INTELLIGENCE

Beckman, M. "Crime, Culpability, and the Adolescent Brain." *Science* 305, no. 5684 (July 30, 2004).

Davidson, R. J. "Well-Being and Affective Style: Neural Substrates and Biobehavioural Correlates." *Philosophical Transactions of the Royal Society* 359, no. 1449 (September 29, 2004), pp. 1395–411.

Dusek, J. A., H. H. Out, A. L. Wohlhueter, M. Bhasin, L. F. Zerbini, M. G. Joseph, H. Benson, and T. A. Libermann. "Genomic Counter-Stress Changes Induced by the Relaxation Response." *PLoS One* 3, no. 7 (2008), p. e2576.

Goleman, D. *Emotional Intelligence: Why It Can Matter More Than IQ.* New York: Bantam, 1995.

James, W. *The Principles of Psychology,* vol. 1. New York: Henry Holt, 1890.

Maslow, Abraham H. *The Farther Reaches of Human Nature,* New York: Viking Compass, 1972.

Niedenthal, P. "Embodying Emotions." *Science* 316 (2007), p. 1002.

CHAPTER 4: MANAGE YOUR TIME

Bawden, D., and L. Robinson. "The Dark Side of Information: Overload, Anxiety and Other Paradoxes and Pathologies." *Journal of Information Science* 35, no. 2 (April 2009).

Bureau of Labor Statistics, U.S. Department of Labor. "Education Pays." January 2013.

Carr, N. *The Shallows: What the Internet Is Doing to Our Brains.* New York: W.W. Norton, 2010.

Koch, Richard. *The 80/20 Principle: The Secret to Success by Achieving More with Less,* New York: Random House, 1998.

Lakein, Alan. *How to Get Control of Your Time and Your Life.* New York: New American Library, 1973; reissued 1996.

Mosher, D. "High Wired: Does Addictive Internet Use Restructure the Brain?" *Scientific American,* June 17, 2011.

Rosen, C. "The Myth of Multitasking." *New Atlantis,* Spring 2008.

CHAPTER 5: MAXIMIZE YOUR RESOURCES

The College Board. "Annual Survey of Colleges." 2012.

Duhigg, Charles. *The Power of Habit: Why We Do What We Do in Life and Business.* New York: Random House, 2012.

Levitin, Daniel J. *This is Your Brain on Music: The Science of a Human Obsession,* New York: Penguin Books, 2007.

McCullough, M. E., S. D. Kilpatrick, R. A. Emmons, and D. B. Larson. "Is Gratitude a Moral Affect?" *Psychological Bulletin* 127 (2001), pp. 249–66.

Pecina, S., K. S. Smith, and K. C. Berridge. "Hedonic Hot Spots in the Brain." *The Neuroscientist* 12 (2006), pp. 500–511.

Siegel, Daniel J. *Brainstorm: The Power and Purpose of the Teenage Brain.* New York: Penguin Random House, 2015.

CHAPTER 6: LISTEN AND TAKE EFFECTIVE NOTES

Berridge, K. C., and T. E. Robinson. "What Is the Role of Dopamine in Reward: Hedonic Impact, Reward Learning, or Incentive Salience?" *Brain Research Reviews* 28 (1998), pp. 309–69.

Brazeau, G. "Handouts in the Classroom: Is Note Taking a Lost Skill?" *American Journal of Pharmaceutical Education* 70, no. 2 (April 15, 2006).

Duhigg, Charles. *The Power of Habit: Why We Do What We Do in Life and Business.* New York: Random House, 2012.

Elbow, P. *A Community of Writers.* New York: McGraw-Hill, 2001.

Hoffman, Donald D. *Visual Intelligence.* New York: Norton & Co., 1998.

Medina, John. *Brain Rules.* Seattle: Pear Press, 2008.

Siegel, Daniel J. *Brainstorm: The Power and Purpose of the Teenage Brain.* New York: Penguin Random House, 2015.

CHAPTER 7: ACTIVELY READ

National Endowment for the Arts. "To Read or Not to Read: A Question of National Consequence." March 2013.

Nielsen, J. "How Users Read on the Web." Nielsen Norman Group (October 1, 1997), http://www.nngroup.com/articles/how-users-read-on-the-web/ (accessed February 29, 2015).

Siegel, Daniel J. *Brainstorm: The Power and Purpose of the Teenage Brain.* New York: Penguin Random House, 2015.

Taylor, Jill Bolte. *My Stroke of Insight: A Brain Scientist's Personal Journey.* New York: Viking Penguin, 2008.

Van Blerkom, M. S., and D. L. Van Blerkom. "Self-Monitoring Strategies Used by Developmental and Non-Developmental College Students." *Journal of College Reading and Learning* 34, no. 2 (2004), pp. 45–61.

Wood, Brittany, Mark S. Rea, Barbara Plitick, and Mariana G. Figueiro. "Light Level and Duration of Exposure Determine the Impact of Self-Luminous Tablets on Melatonin Suppression." *Applied Ergonomics* 44, no. 2 (March 2013), pp. 237–40.

CHAPTER 8: IMPROVE YOUR MEMORY SKILLS

Allstate/Sperling's Best Places. "'Allstate America's Teen Driving Hotspots' Study." Executive Summary. May 2008.

Bavelier, D., and H. Neville. "Neuroplasticity, Developmental." In *Encyclopedia of the Human Brain,* vol. e, ed. V. S. Ramachandran. Amsterdam: Academic Press, 2002, p. 561.

Beckman, M. "Crime, Culpability, and the Adolescent Brain." *Science* 305, no. 5684 (July 30, 2004).

Brant, A. M., et al. "The Nature and Nurture of High IQ: An Extended Sensitive Period of Intellectual Development." *Psychological Science* 24, no. 8 (August 2013), pp. 1487–95.

Gluck, Mark A., Eduardo Mercado, and Catherine E. Myers. *Learning and Memory: From Brain to Behavior.* New York: Worth Publishers, 2007.

Kandel, E. R. "The Molecular Biology of Memory Storage: A Dialog between Genes and Synapses." In *Nobel Lectures in Physiology or Medicine 1996–2000,* ed. Hans Jornvall. Singapore: World Scientific Publishing Co., 2003, p. 402.

McDermott, Terry. *101 Theory Drive: A Neuroscientist's Quest for Memory.* New York: Pantheon Books, 2010.

Naveh-Benjamin, M., A. Kilb, and T. Fisher. "Concurrent Task Effects on Memory Encoding and Retrieval: Further Support for Asymmetry." *Memory & Cognition* 34, no. 1 (January 2006), pp. 90–101.

Scott-Taylor, T. "The Implications of Neurological Models of Memory for Learning and Teaching." *Investigations in University Teaching and Learning* 6, no. 1 (Autumn 2010).

Siegel, D. J. "Memory: An Overview." *Journal of the American Academy of Child and Adolescent Psychiatry* 40, no. 9 (2001).

CHAPTER 9: EXCEL AT TAKING TESTS

Baumeister, Roy F. *Willpower: Rediscovering the Greatest Human Strength.* New York: Penguin Press, 2011.

Casey, B., N. Tottenham, et al. "Transitional and Translational Studies of Risk for Anxiety." *Depression and Anxiety* 28, no. 1 (January 2011), pp. 18–28.

Csikszentmihalyi, M. *Flow: The Psychology of Optimal Experience.* New York: HarperCollins, 1990.

Nolting, Paul D. *Math Study Skills Workbook.* Boston: Cengage Learning, 2012.

Ramirez, F., and S. Beilock. "Writing about Testing Worries Boosts Exam Performance in the Classroom." *Science* 331 (January 14, 2011).

CHAPTER 10: EXPRESS YOURSELF IN WRITING AND SPEECH

Dusek, J. A., H. H. Out, A. L. Wohlhueter, M. Bhasin, L. F. Zerbini, M. G. Joseph. H. Benson, and T. A. Libermann. "Genomic Counter-Stress Changes Induced by the Relaxation Response." *PLoS One* 3, no. 7 (2008), p. e2576.

Dwyer, Karen K., and Marlina M. Davidson. "Is Public Speaking Really More Feared Than Death?" *Communication Research Reports,* April–June 2012.

Flaherty, A. "Writing Like Crazy: A Word on the Brain." *The Chronicle of Higher Education* 50 (2003).

Rico, G. *Writing the Natural Way.* New York: Penguin, 2000.

Siegel, Daniel J. *Brainstorm: The Power and Purpose of the Teenage Brain.* New York: Penguin Random House, 2015.

CHAPTER 11: BECOME A CRITICAL THINKER AND CREATIVE PROBLEM SOLVER

Achor, Shawn. *The Happiness Advantage.* New York: Crown Business, 2010.

Cameron, Julia. *The Vein of Gold: A Journey to Your Creative Heart.* New York: Putnam, 1997.

Catmull, Ed. *Creativity, Inc.: Overcoming the Unseen Forces That Stand in the Way of True Inspiration.* New York: Random House, 2014.

Eagleman, David. *Incognito: The Secret Life of the Brain.* New York: Pantheon Books, 2011.

Gelb, M. J. *Discover Your Genius: How to Think Like History's Ten Most Revolutionary Minds.* New York: HarperCollins, 2002.

Gilbert, Elizabeth. *Big Magic: Creative Living Beyond Fear.* New York: Penguin, 2015.

Jensen, Frances E. *The Teenage Brain: A Neuroscientist's Survival Guide to Raising Adolescents and Young Adults.* New York: HarperCollins, 2015.

Kahneman, Daniel. *Thinking, Fast and Slow.* New York: Farrar, Straus and Giroux, 2011.

Katie, B. *Loving What Is: Four Questions That Can Change Your Life.* New York: Harmony Books, 2002.

Kaufman, Scott B., and Carolyn Gregoire. *Wired to Create.* New York: Penguin Publishing, 2015.

Kondo, Marie. *The Life-Changing Magic of Tidying Up: The Japanese Art of Decluttering and Organizing.* Berkeley, CA: Ten Speed Press, 2015.

Kotter, John P., and Lorne A. Whitehead. *Buy-In: Saving Your Good Idea from Getting Shot Down.* Boston: Harvard Press, 2010.

Michalko, Michael. *Thinkertoys: A Handbook of Creative-Thinking Techniques.* Berkeley, CA: Ten Speed Press, 2006.

Pink, Daniel H. *A Whole New Mind: Why Right Brainers Will Rule the Future.* New York: Penguin Publishing, 2006.

Shingles, Richard. "A Guide to Bloom's Taxonomy." *The Innovative Instructor Blog* (January 30, 2015), http://ii.library.jhu.edu/2015/01/30/a-guide-to-blooms-taxonomy/.

Siegel, Daniel J. *Brainstorm: The Power and Purpose of the Teenage Brain.* New York: Penguin Random House, 2015.

von Oech, Roger. *A Kick in The Seat of the Pants: Using Your Explorer, Artist, Judge, & Warrior to Be More Creative.* New York: Harper and Row, 1986.

CHAPTER 12: CREATE A HEALTHY MIND, BODY, AND SPIRIT

American Foundation for Suicide Prevention. "Risk Factors for Suicide." 2010. https://afsp.org/?s=risk+factors+for+suicide (accessed April 14, 2016).

Centers for Disease Control and Prevention. "Health Habits of Adults Aged 18–29." *Report on Nation's Health,* February 18, 2009.

Gottman, John. *Why Marriages Succeed or Fail: And How You Can Make Yours Last.* New York: Simon and Schuster, 1995.

Holt-Lunstad, Julianne, Timothy B. Smith, and J. Bradley Layton. "Social Relationships and Mortality Risk: A Meta-Analytic Review." *PLoS Medicine* 7, no. 7 (July 27, 2010). http://journals.plos.org/plosmedicine/article?id=10.1371%2Fjournal.pmed.1000316 (accessed April 3, 2016).

Jensen, Frances E. *The Teenage Brain: A Neuroscientist's Survival Guide to Raising Adolescents and Young Adults.* New York: HarperCollins, 2015.

Kabat-Zinn, Jon. "Mindfulness-Based Interventions in Context: Past, Present, and Future." *Clinical Psychology: Science and Practice* 10, no. 2 (2003), pp. 144–56.

Kessler, David A. *Capture: Unraveling The Mystery of Mental Suffering.* New York: HarperCollins, 2016.

McQueeny, T., B. Schweinsburg, and S. Tapert. "Altered White Matter Integrity in Adolescent Binge Drinkers." *Alcoholism: Clinical and Experimental Research* 33, no. 7 (July 2009).

Nielsen, Jared A., Brandon A. Zielinski, Michael A. Ferguson, Janet E. Lainhart, and Jeffrey S. Anderson. "An Evaluation of the Left-Brain vs. Right-Brain Hypothesis with Resting State Functional Connectivity Magnetic Resonance Imaging." *PLoS One* 8, no. 8 (August 14, 2013), http://journals.plos.org/plosone/article?id=10.1371/journal.pone.0071275 (accessed April 17, 2016).

Seligman, M. E. P. "Learned Helplessness." *Annual Review of Medicine* 23 (1972), pp. 407–12.

Stickgold, Robert. "Sleep-Dependent Memory Consolidation." *Nature* 437, no. 7063 (Oct. 27, 2005), pp. 1272–78.

U.S. Food and Drug Administration. "Revised Dietary Guidelines to Help Americans Live Healthier Lives." 2012.

Weiser, M., S. Zarka, N. Werbeloff, E. Kravitz, and G. Lubin. "Cognitive Test Scores in Male Adolescent Cigarette Smokers Compared to Non-Smokers: A Population-Based Study." *Addiction* 105, no. 2 (February 2010), pp. 358–63.

CHAPTER 13: BUILD SUPPORTIVE AND DIVERSE RELATIONSHIPS

Gottman, J. *Why Marriages Succeed or Fail: And How You Can Make Yours Last.* New York: Simon and Schuster, 1995.

Holt-Lunstad, Julianne, Timothy B. Smith, and J. Bradley Layton. "Social Relationships and Mortality Risk: A Meta-Analytic Review." *PLoS Medicine* 7, no. 7 (July 27, 2010), http://journals.plos.org/plosmedicine/article?id=10.1371%2Fjournal.pmed.1000316 (accessed April 3, 2016).

Mehrabian, Albert. *Nonverbal Communication.* New Jersey: Aldine Transaction, 2009.

Neff, K. D. *Self-Compassion: Handbook of Individual Differences in Social Behavior.* New York: Guilford Press, 2009.

Rosenberg, Matt. "If the World Were a Village. . ." *About Education,* August 5, 2007. http://geography.about.com/od/obtainpopulationdata/a/worldvillage.htm.

Siegel, Daniel J. *Brainstorm: The Power and Purpose of the Teenage Brain.* New York: Penguin Random House, 2015.

Stein, D. J., and K. G. Thomas. "Psychobiology of Mindfulness." *CNS Spectrum* 13 (2008), pp. 752–56.

CHAPTER 14: EXPLORE MAJORS AND CAREERS

Arum, Richard, and Josipa Roksa. *Aspiring Adults Adrift: Tentative Transitions of College Graduates.* Chicago: University of Chicago Press, 2014.

Bolles, R. N. *What Color Is Your Parachute?* Berkeley, CA: Ten Speed Press, 2007.

Doidge, Norman. *The Brain That Changes Itself: Stories of Personal Triumph from the Frontiers of Brain Science.* New York: Penguin Books, 2007.

Ferrett, Sharon K. *Getting and Keeping the Job You Want: A Practical Job Search Handbook,* 2nd ed. Burr Ridge, IL: Irwin, 2000.

Levine, M. *Ready or Nor, Here Life Comes.* New York: Simon & Schuster, 2005.

Rowh, M. "Choosing a Major." *Career World* 31, no. 5 (2003), p. 21.

Selingo, Jeffrey J. *There Is Life after College: What Parents and Students Should Know About Navigating School to Prepare for the Jobs of Tomorrow.* New York: HarperCollins, 2016.

Selingo, Jeffrey J. "Will You Spring, Stroll or Stumble into a Career?" *New York Times,* April 5, 2015, http://www.nytimes.com/2016/04/10/education/edlife/will-you-sprint-stroll-or-stumble-into-a-career.html?smid=nytcore-iphone-share&smprod=nytcore-iphone&_r=0 (assessed April 12, 2016).

Siegel, Daniel J. *Brainstorm: The Power and Purpose of the Teenage Brain.* New York: Penguin Random House, 2015.

Van Blerkom, M. S., and D. L. Van Blerkom. "Self-Monitoring Strategies Used by Developmental and Non-Developmental College Students." *Journal of College Reading and Learning* 34, no. 2 (2004), pp. 45–61.

Features Guide

Index

Practice, 322
Predictions
    in active listening, 179–180
    in the Five-Part Reading System, 210
Pregnancy, 398
Prejudices, 436, 438
Preliminary reading, 305
Preparation, in Five-Part Reading System, 209
Prescription drugs, 393, 396, 399
Previewing
    in Five-Part Reading System, 209–210
    in note taking, 185
Price, Steven, 484
Priorities
    setting of, 109–113
    to-do-lists, 114, 138
Privacy, 436
Problem solving, **338.** *See also* Creative problem solving
Procrastination, **120**–122
Professional organizations, 462
Program resources, 148–151, 156
Project board, 115, 117
Projection, 348
Psychologists, 198
Psychology, active reading and, 215
Psychology Types (Jung), 21
Public interest groups, 213
Public speaking. *See* Speaking skills and process
Publishers, 447
Punctuality, 475
Purpose
    in active reading, 212
    in writing, 305
Puzzles, used for problem solving, 349–350

Q

Questions
    attentive listening, 179–180
    Five-Part Reading System, 210
    interview, 477
    problem solving, 343, 345–346
    SQ3R Reading System, 210, 212
    test preparation, 273
    types of, 345
Quick Resume, 462
Quiet time, 123
Quotations, 307

R

Racial profiling, **436**
Rapport, **418**–421
Reaction, control of, 88–89
Reader/writer learners, 16, 18
Reader's Guide to Periodical Literature, 306, 319
Reading. *See* Active reading
Reading systems, 209–214
Realistic people, 461
Reasoning, 346–347
Recall, **250**
Recitation
    memory strategy, 255
    SQ3R Reading System, 212
Records office, 148
Recreational centers, 151
Reentry students, 155–156

Reference materials, 305, 319
References, 472
Reflection
    active reading and, 218
    journal writing, 8, 20, 35, 351, 391
    self-management tool, **7,** 9
    test anxiety, 288–289
Reframing, 84
Registration office, 148
Rehearsal, 286, 322, 390
Reinforcement contract, 99
Relationships
    diversity in, 436–443
    establishing healthy, 387–388
    patterns in, 433
    people you live with, 434–436
    romantic, 432–434
    sexual harassment, 441–443
    signs of unhealthy, 400
    support system, 91, 122, 389
Relax Melodies, 386
Relaxation, 352, 389
Remembering, in Bloom's Taxonomy, 338–339
Repetition, as memory strategy, 255
Representation, 441
Research process. *See also* Writing skills and process
    checklists, 308, 317
    citing sources, 312, 314–315
    credibility of sources, 320, 321
    information literacy, 318–320
    library research, 149, 166, 318–319, 462
    note taking (*See* Note taking)
    online research, 152, 157, 319–321
    outlines (*See* Outlines)
Resilience, 9, 50, 89–**90,** 479
Resource maximization, 143–176
    community resources, 156, 174
    commuter students, 154–155
    family responsibilities, 124–127, 133
    financial resources, 157–164
    online learning, 125–126, 189, 276, 280
    online sources, 151–152, 156–157
    people resources, 145–148, 156
    program resources, 148–151, 156
    returning students, 155–156
    students with disabilities, 153–154, 168, 193, 226
    technology, 152
    you as a resource, 164–165
Respect
    communication, 419
    listening and, 77, 179
    in relationships, 434, 436
Responsibility
    examples of, 75
    as good quality, 50
    juggling of, 124–127, 133
    for learning, 423, 425
    locus of control, 75
    as obstacle to change, 56
    peak performers and, 74
    personal, 75–76
Rest, 385–386, 389
Restaurant owners, 366
Résumé, 470–472, 479, 483, 494
Retention of information, 191–192, **208,** 247, 251
Returning students, 155–156
Review process
    in active reading, 210, 212
    note taking and (*See* Note taking)

Your School's Resources

Check your school's website, look through the catalog, or go to student services to determine which resources are available, especially those that are of particular interest to you and your needs. In the Notes section, include information such as location, office hours, fees, and so on. *These services are for you, so use them!*

Resource	Notes	Contact/phone/e-mail
Activities/Clubs Office		
Adult and Re-entry Center		
Advising Center		
Alumni Office		
Art Gallery/Museum		
Bookstore		
Career Center/Employment Services		
Chaplain/Religious Services		
Child Care Center		
Cinema/Theater		
Computer Lab(s)		
Continuing Education		
Disability Center (learning or physical disabilities)		
Distance Learning		
Financial Aid		
Health Clinic		
Honors Program		
Housing Center		
Information Center		
Intramural Sports		
Language Lab		
Learning Center		
Library Services		

(continued)

Resource	Notes	Contact/phone/e-mail
Lost and Found		
Math Lab		
Multicultural Center		
Off-Campus Housing and Services		
Ombudsman/Conflict Resolution		
Performing Arts Center		
Photography Lab		
Police/Campus Security		
Post Office/Delivery Services		
Printing/Copying Center		
Registration Office		
School Newspaper		
Student Government Office		
Study Abroad/Exchange		
Testing Center		
Tutorial Services		
Volunteer Services		
Wellness and Recreation Center/ Gymnasium		
Work-Study Center		
Writing Lab		
Other:		
Other:		
Other:		